CHURCHILL

Strategy and History

Tuvia Ben-Moshe

LYNNE RIENNER PUBLISHERS

HARVESTER WHEATSHEAF

DA
566.9
C5
B38
1992

Published in the United States of America in 1992 by
Lynne Rienner Publishers, Inc.
1800 30th Street, Boulder, Colorado 80301

and in the United Kingdom in 1992 by
Harvester Wheatsheaf
66 Wood Lane End, Hemel Hempstead
Hertfordshire HP2 4HP
A division of
Simon & Schuster International Group

© 1992 by Lynne Rienner Publishers, Inc. All rights reserved

Library of Congress Cataloging-in-Publication Data
Ben-Moshe, Tuvia.
　Churchill, strategy and history / by Tuvia Ben-Moshe.
　Includes bibliographical references and index.
　ISBN 1-55587-142-9
　1. Churchill, Winston, Sir, 1874–1965—Military leadership.
2. Great Britain—History, Military—20th century. 3. Strategic
forces—Great Britain—History. I. Title.
DA566.9.C5B38 1991
941.084'092—dc20   90-26495
                                                      CIP

British Cataloguing in Publication Data
Ben-Moshe, Tuvia
　Churchill: strategy and history.
　I. Title
　941.082092

　ISBN 0-7450-1179-9

Printed and bound in the United States of America

The paper used in this publication meets the requirements
of the American National Standard for Permanence of
Paper for Printed Library Materials Z39.48.

Contents

List of Maps	vi
Acknowledgments	vii
Introduction	1
1 From Isolation to "Continental Commitment," 1900–1914	7
2 From the Baltic to Gallipoli, 1914–1915	29
3 "How Are We to Win the War?" 1916–1918	71
4 History and the "Continental Commitment," 1919–1939	83
5 The Genesis of the "Mediterranean Strategy," 1940–1941	121
6 The Formation of Anglo-American Strategy, 1941–1942	167
7 The "Mediterranean Strategy" at Its Height, 1942–1943	197
8 "First Catch Your Hare": The Political Dimension of Strategy	225
9 "This Battle Has Been Forced Upon Us": Overlord, 1943–1944	245
10 Grand Strategy: The Soviet Menace and the End of the War, 1943–1945	277
11 Conclusions: Churchill in War and Peace	317
Appendix: List of Operation Code Names	335
Notes	337
Bibliography	381
Index	387
About the Book and the Author	397

Maps

Europe in 1914	28
Europe and the Mediterranean in 1939	122
The Central and Eastern Mediterranean and The Aegean Islands	139

Acknowledgments

I owe the Leonard Davies Institute for International Relations of The Hebrew University in Jerusalem, and the Friends of the Hebrew University in Britain, a debt of gratitude for their financial assistance.

I also would like to acknowledge with thanks those authors and publishers for quotations I have used from works of which they hold the copyright. I am particularly grateful to Houghton Mifflin, Heinemann, and the staff of the Public Record Office, London.

I am grateful to all those at Lynne Rienner Publishers who helped in the preparation of the book.

Special thanks are due to Professor Dan Horowitz, to Professor Norman Rose for his valuable advice, to Professor Stuart Cohen for his competent translation and comments, and to the late Meir Verete, a distinguished scholar, whose memory I keep with affection.

Finally, I am also lucky to have two friends, Dr. Menachem Hofnung and Mr. Avner Halperin, whose friendhip has supported me during many arduous days. Other intimates, to whom I am enormously indebted, have preferred to keep their anonymity: to C.S.F., J.A., H.H., and H.R.

Tuvia Ben-Moshe
Haifa University
Summer 1991

Introduction

> In all battles two things are usually required of the Commander-in-Chief: to make a good plan for his army and, secondly, to keep a strong reserve. . . . To make a plan, through reconnaisance of the country where the battle is to be fought is needed. . . . But in order to make his plan, the General must not only reconnoitre the battle-ground, he must also study the achievements of the great Captains of the past.

These lines are not taken from the works of Marshal de Saxe or Clausewitz, but from a short essay written by Churchill that he entitled "Painting as a Pastime." In that piece, Churchill praised painting as a source of pleasure and a hobby, and depicted the artist as a general who directs battles on his canvas.[1] Indeed, he employed terms, similes, and metaphors taken from warfare to describe almost every field of human activity. Thus, for instance, he likened the scientific community to an army that advances farther than any other: "The most remote and perilous point which is occupied by the furthest advance patrol becomes immediately occupied by the whole strength of the army."[2] This literary style impressed some of Churchill's audiences, but annoyed others.[3]

Almost all of Churchill's writings were concerned with wars and their consequences. Even his *History of the English Speaking Peoples*, the most general of his books, is devoted almost entirely to consecutive analyses of wars, international relations, statesmanship, and the depiction of battles. Social, economic, and scientific matters, as well as developments in political thought and philosophy, are virtually ignored.[4] Altogether, Churchill had little interest in the modern and revolutionary intellectual trends of the nineteenth and twentieth centuries, be they Marxist or Freudian. In response to the suggestion that he read Margaret Mead's *Coming of Age in Samoa*, a book that caused a stir in both academic and nonacademic circles when first published in 1929, Churchill remarked: "I cannot undertake to mix myself up in the troubles of Samoa. I have quite enough of my own to look after in Epping."[5] His short association with the great masters of Russian literature ended after an invitation to write an article on Tolstoy's *Anna Karenina:* "I have read 'Anna Karenina' and am not much attracted by these thin-skinned, self-disturbing Russian boobs," was his dismissive comment.[6] As to English literature, his taste was conservative. The historian J. H. Plumb defined it as a mixture of "the Bible, Shakespeare, Milton, Dickens and a little Trollope, topped off with Rudyard Kipling." To this list must be added R. L. Stevenson's *Treasure Island,* which he read dozens of times. Churchill painted, and for an amateur was a good artist; but he had no great interest in art.[7] He was interested in technology, and especially in its military implications; but he possessed only the most rudimentary knowledge of the various natural sciences.

Above all, Churchill almost instinctively avoided deep enquiry and reflection on the essence of the human nature and spirit. *The Anatomy of Courage,* the distinctive work written by Churchill's personal physician on a subject that might have been expected to interest a man of his own experience, he dismissed as "all this psychological nonesense."[8] Churchill was an extreme extrovert, who sought in action and in incessant contact with the outside world a refuge from all thought and meditation about his own inner self. That was why he showed little interest in or understanding of the inner motivation of others.[9] This was true of both his attitude toward his contemporaries and friends and his analyses of the activities of the heroes of history.

Churchill's enthusiasm for warlike activity is renowned. In his youth he pursued wars all over the globe with what amounted to desperation; by the time he was first elected to Parliament at the age of twenty-eight, he had already been involved in wars on three continents. Men who worked at his side were amazed by the satisfaction and pleasure that he evinced during the two world wars. Even when he became seriously ill during World War II, "events," in his own words, 'continued to offer irresistable distraction.'[10] To the astonishment of Robert Menzies, prime minister of Australia, he responded: "Why do people regard a period like this as 'years lost out of our lives' when beyond question it is the most interesting period of them? Why do we regard history as of the past and forget we are making it?[11]

Churchill maintained that "the story of the human race is war." He believed wars to be a central feature of human history, and that periods of peace were no more than brief lulls in the incessant torrent of wars. He rejected the tendencies in historical research that regarded great battles as expressions of deep and continuous historical trends, mere froth on the waves of history. Great battles, Churchill insisted, constitute the most crucial and decisive events in "secular history."[12] He was also dismissive of a pious approach that altogether opposed resort to arms. Wars, he maintained, could provide solutions to complicated international problems whose complexity defied rulers and diplomacy.[13] As he remarked to his personal secretary John Colville in 1940: "People talked a lot of nonesense when they said nothing was ever settled by war. Nothing in history was ever settled *except* by wars."[14] Nevertheless, Churchill—a nonbeliever in a deity—rejected a deterministic explanation for the outbreak of war. "A war postponed may be a war prevented. The combinations of states vary as years pass. . . . Time and peace solve many problems and men's thoughts move on to new spheres."[15] He was sensitive to the fact that the limitations, mistakes, and misunderstandings of decision makers constitute an entirely random range of factors, totally devoid of prior intention or planning, and that they too could bring about wars. Indeed, he specified them as having been an important cause of the outbreak of World War I. "There is always more error than design in human affairs," he said.[16]

Nevertheless, Churchill's attitude toward war was ambivalent. Those who described him as a warmonger did not fathom the depths of his feelings. He was repelled by war at the very same time that he was attracted to it. Observing German military maneuvers in 1909, he wrote to his wife: "Much as war attracts me & fascinates my mind with its tremendous situations—I feel more deeply every year—& can measure the feeling here in the midst of arms—what vile & wicked folly & barbarism it all is."[17] However, notwithstanding these sentiments, Churchill did admit that his life's greatest ambition had always been "to command great victorious armies in battle."[18] Even when he attained senior office in the British government, he "declared that a political career was nothing to him in comparison with military glory."[19] That is what makes so surprising his decision to interrupt his successful military career in full flood, and embark on a life in politics. Churchill himself never provided a satisfactory answer to that issue. He claimed that economic necessity dictated his decision.[20] True, the family fortunes were at a low ebb, principally because of the spendthrift habits of his mother, Lady Randolph. Even so, Churchill himself was not penurious—unlike Napoleon, a figure whom Churchill much admired, and who at his age and rank had indeed walked the streets of Paris hungry. There was really no financial reason for Churchill to abandon the opportunity to realize his life's ambition. A. Storr has suggested that Churchill found it difficult to adapt to the life of discipline and boredom so characteristic of the peacetime Victorian army.[21] To this observation must be added his weakness for the indulgences of life, which are in part denied to men on active military service.

These are reasonable explanations, but not decisive ones. The principal cause has to be sought in Churchill's ambition and exceptional lust for power and influence, rooted (it has been suggested) in the structure of his depressive and extrovert personality and in the absence of parental love during his childhood.[22] His ambition to attain power and influence did indeed equal his ambition for military renown. He was too impatient to suffer extremely slow advancement through the ranks of the British Army and to await the outbreak of a war that might never occur. Political life promised greater rewards and speedier progress. Unawares, Churchill in fact revealed his own motives when placing responsibility for the inadequate quality of the British high command on the fact that a military career did not attract men of talent, since "most of the rewards of British public life went to the politicians."[23]

The young Churchill did not hide the enormity of his ambitions. Colonel (as he then was) Ian Hamilton attempted to dampen at least the most extreme of those ambitions, warning his twenty-four-year-old friend that "it would be satisfactory to achieve the combination of Marlborough, Napier,[24] and Pitt, but in the existing specialized era, such dreams are of the idlest texture."[25] Churchill, however, was undeterred by Hamilton's skepticism. He managed to realize that dream almost in its entirety. Like the elder Pitt, he was a premier and statesman who presided over the management of a world war; like Marlborough, he was a military strategist—even though he did not command an army in the field; and finally, like Napier, he was a military historian who wrote works on two world wars and on the life and campaigns of the Duke of Marlborough.

But to what extent did Churchill also achieve a conceptual and operational synthesis between military strategy and policy in peace and war? What were his qualities of strategic decision taking? How was he influenced by history when he crystallized his strategic concepts, and what was the weight of this factor relative to others that contributed to their formulation? What were the consequences of his strategic notions, positions, and decisions on the course of the two world wars and their outcomes? And finally, what is the degree of historical reliability and credibility to be given to his two books on both world wars?

These are the central questions that this study will attempt to analyze. It concentrates on Churchill as a strategist, but posits military strategy and policy as two dimensions of the same reality. Most of the time, the book focuses on the area in which the highest level of military strategy fuses with the political dimension. Churchill's political thinking is analyzed in a way that does not permit its differentiation from his strategic-military conceptions. Where appropriate, however, an examination has also been made of the influences of tactical and operational considerations on the highest level of military strategy and the process whereby they fuse with the political dimension.

It was almost by accident that I embarked on the path to the subject of this book. My initial intention was to investigate the influence of history and its understanding on decision makers. Churchill seemed to me an ideally suitable figure to start with, as the first of several case studies. I devoted years to the study of strategy and military history. When I began to peruse the documents, my opinions on the strategic issues of World War II were already formed. To a marked degree, they conformed to the British perspectives and positions during the war. I was convinced by the versions propounded by Churchill, official British history, and other authors. In addition, I thought that little could be added to the substantial research already in existence about the higher strategy of the war. Today, when I observe matters in retrospect, I feel that my attitude at that time was in part influenced by the fact that most of the literature on military history that I read in my youth consisted of translated works by British authors that largely dealt with the British side of the wars to which Britain was a party. (Then there existed no alternatives, except for Hebrew translations of Russian literature on the war—mostly propagandist in nature. My father's service in the British Army during World War II also exacerbated my tendency.)

I first read Churchill's *The Second World War*, in Hebrew translation, when I was thirteen or fourteen years old. However, while my attention was concentrated on the search for the "history" in Churchill's strategic thought during World War II, I was surprised to discover that my opinions on the management of British strategy did not accord with the documents that I was reading for the first time. I immediately grasped that, before searching for the influence of history on the formation of Churchill's outlook, it was more important to know what the true course of history had been—a task that, as I have said, I thought was superfluous. It was thus that the subject changed and became larger, although I have still preserved some aspects of the initial subject in the body of the present study.

Despite the plethora of writings on Churchill, no study has hitherto examined him as a strategist from a panoramic perspective. Rather, attention has been concentrated on different aspects and periods of his strategic activity during his career. As a result, this giant figure has been broken into several pieces; and since no appropriate note has been taken of the links between the several parts, the price has been the absence of an overall picture of the personality. True, the partial nature of the analyses of Churchill's strategic activity has not prevented their authors from drawing general conclusions about his qualities as a strategist, but some of these seem to be rash. On the other hand, the various existing biographies assimilate Churchill's image as a strategist into the other political and personal subjects with which they treat, so that this particular subject does not receive the attention and examination it deserves.

Basic to this present study is the recognition that, if Churchill's strategic thought and decisions during World War II are to be properly understood and analyzed, a thorough inquiry must be conducted about the development of his thinking during the period that stretches from the time he took his first political steps at the turn of the century until the outbreak of war in 1939. Particularly important is a study of his strategic plans and his behavior as a decision taker in World War I. Quite apart from its intrinsic value for the purposes of creating the wide perspective and appropriate prism for the examination of Churchill's behavior during World War II, such a study is also important because it offers an opportunity for comparison. Generally similar, the two world wars can be compared; however, they were also significantly different. Therefore, by adopting a comparative perspective, it is possible to sift out the particular and random circumstances of each war and individual strategic moves, and to discern the broad lines and persistent characteristics of Churchill's strategic thinking and decision-taking behavior. It is by that means, together with others, that the present study aims at its highest purpose: a definitive estimate of Churchill as a strategist as well as a historian.

1

From Isolation to "Continental Commitment," 1900-1914

For centuries, the basic strategic and political dilemma confronting British statesmen has been the character of their nation's involvement on the European continent in times of war and peace. At root, this dilemma was the consequence of Britain's geopolitical situation: an island-state, separated from the continent by a narrow strip of water.

In different periods, British decision makers could choose between three basic political and strategic choices. One was isolation, which demanded a degree of naval supremacy capable of secluding Britain from European upheavals. The second choice was a derivative of the fundamental recognition of the need for political and military intervention on the continent and the maintenance of a European balance of power. Its implementation would be achieved by reaching agreement with possible allies in both peace and war. In war, strategy would be based upon Britain's economic and logistic support for its allies, and the employment of its naval strength against the enemy's fleet and overseas possessions, as well as the imposition of a naval blockade on its homeland. This "maritime school" advocated amphibious attacks on the European littoral, in conjunction with the armies of Britain's continental allies.

The third option shared the perspectives of the second. Where it differed, however, was in its conception of wartime strategy. The latter, it was maintained, should be based on both naval supremacy and on the dispatch of a large British army (large, that is, by the standards of the British population and of the period), which could fight alongside Britain's continental allies. This strategy was variously defined as either the "continental school" or the "continental commitment." The latter designation seems more appropriate since it conveys a hint of the ambivalent feelings that British statesmen, especially in this century, have harbored about a military alliance and the dispatch of a large British army to the European mainland.

The boundaries between these three alternatives were never clear in practice, not even in the minds of the decision makers. Admittedly, for much of the course of British history the crucial dilemmas and debates were concentrated on the choice between a naval-peripheral strategy and deep military involvement on the continent. At times, however, support for the maritime school merely masked a more fundamental thrust toward isolation and dissociation from Britain's position as the upholder of the European balance of power. The apex of this particular dilemma was reached during the twentieth century, and the examination of Churchill's attitude toward the subject will constitute the backbone of this entire study.

■

Churchill was self-taught. By his own admission, until he was twenty-two he knew very little about history, philosophy, and economics.[1] He gained his education as a young subaltern in India, where he spent his spare time—albeit not systematically—reading works dealing with these topics and with the art of writing. Matters were not very different when it came to his military education. At Sandhurst, the British Army's officer academy, the knowledge he acquired covered only the very lowest level of tactics.[2] A review of the books he read during that period of auto-didactic endeavor indicates that he did become versed in Roman and English history, principally learned from the works of Macaulay and Gibbon, but knew less about philosophy and economics (i.e., Adam Smith). He read almost nothing concerned with theoretical works of high politics and strategy. There is no evidence that he studied Clausewitz or Jomini, the greatest military thinkers of the age, although he did read Mahan's *The Influence of Sea Power Upon History*.[3] His own early books, which describe the campaigns in which he participated, contain very few references to the higher aspects of strategy and politics; especially sparse are considerations of Britain's European policies.[4]

The absence of a systematic education in high strategy was common among the British officer class, especially in its lower echelons. It did not, however, prevent Churchill from forming fixed opinions. His preference for the naval-peripheral school became evident even while he was a junior officer in India. He then objected strongly to intervention on the Continent and to Lord Lansdowne's attempts to expand the British Army. Any growth in the army, he wrote to his mother from India in 1896, would impose an unnecessary burden on the British economy. British security ought to be based on a strong navy capable of ensuring "command of the sea." Security needs would be met by a small army designed for employment in imperial defense.[5] This is a surprising position, coming as it did from an Army officer who still had high hopes of a military career.

The shift from the Army to the world of politics did not change Churchill's views, but only strengthened them. Once elected to Parliament, he launched repeated attacks on the then Secretary of State for War, St. John Broderick, and these continued throughout the early years of the century. The issue between them was Broderick's attempts to initiate reforms in the Army, which—in accordance with models adopted on the Continent—he planned to expand to a strength of three corps. Of course, Churchill was not an impartial critic of that design: among his motives was the strong desire to make an impression and to continue to represent the views of his father, Lord Randolph. Nevertheless, his attacks on Broderick basically stemmed from a sincere belief in his own strategic opinions.

As early as his maiden speech to the House of Commons, Churchill criticized the intention to expand the regular army and increase its budget at the expense of the navy upon which, he insisted, depended Britain's defense and imperial power. He claimed that the planned creation of the three corps, which were essentially designed to constitute an expeditionary force, might lead Britain to intervene in a European war. "The honour and security of the British Empire," he proclaimed, "do not depend, and can never depend, on the British Army."[6]

Influenced by the continuing Anglo-Boer War in South Africa, Broderick argued that Britain was presently a military nation perforce, and that it had to transform the chance of current circumstances into a permanent fact of life. An evidently agitated Churchill responded with an article in the *Daily Mail* in 1901:

> The course of our history, the geography of these islands, the character of their people, show that the Empire which it is our duty to maintain is essentially commercial and marine. No empire in human records has owed less to military strength. The greatest battles we have ever won were in point of numbers fought mainly by foreigners. The finest commanders we have produced led aliens to victory in greater measure than their own countrymen.

Basing himself on Macaulay, Churchill claimed that the absence of a standing army had contributed to the development of Britain's political life and economic prosperity; he also contended that the Empire's might and wealth was the consequence of the command of international commerce and markets. British naval superiority had made possible the flourishing of overseas commerce. This was because it had both isolated Britain from the European continent and enabled a handful of soldiers to conquer distant territories. Only unsurpassed naval strength could safeguard the world trade vital to Britain's survival. There was no need for a large regular army to defend the British Isles or to make war on European powers. Quite apart from defense, the Navy also supplies the necessary offensive capability.[7]

Churchill maintained that Britain had to conduct a foreign policy that would preclude its involvement in struggles on the European mainland. It had to exploit the natural advantages that allowed dispensing with the need for large land forces, while other powers were constrained to maintain both fleets and large armies. This was the initial advantage that had facilitated the growth of the British Empire. There was no need, he claimed, to imitate foreign continental strategic doctrines.[8] In an emergency, the powerful fleet would grant sufficient time for the formation of a large militia that would render Britain absolutely secure. He emphasized that the European wars of the future would not be like those of the past; they would be wars of nations. The rival states would mobilize their entire economic and human resources and the bitter struggle could last for years. Under those circumstances, the three corps could make only a negligible contribution and would prove incapable of influencing the opening stages of war when it broke out. Britain would in any case have to await the training of a mass army.[9]

In the light of the experience of the Boer War, Churchill judged a militia army to be not very much less competent than a standing army. His readiness to base Britain's strength on land in an emergency on such a force stemmed from his assessment that citizens could be rapidly trained for military activity and that modern weapons increased the power of the defense.[10] He believed that modern warfare would demand individual initiative and intelligence, and would lessen the need for the extensive exercises demanded of standing armies in the past. Moreover, he believed that the experience of history demonstrated that a volunteer force, although ineffective when fighting on foreign soil, constituted the most expedient means of defending the homeland.[11]

In 1901, Churchill was one of the few MPs to vote against the army reforms. His position and fears were exaggerated, since Broderick and the British government had no intention of promoting either continental involvement or the establishment of a large standing army. On the contrary, the dominant doctrine of the age was in fact that propounded by the isolationist school, which advocated reliance on naval strength. The Army General Staff (infra, the General Staff), which was to become the principal advocate of a British "continental commitment" prior to World War I, did not begin to consider the dispatch of a British army to the mainland until ca. 1905–1906.[12] The gathering storm clouds of the German threat were barely visible on the horizon and many, Churchill included, were still unaware of their ominous nature. The purpose of the reforms was to train an efficient army for Britain's defense and for service overseas, but not on the European continent.

In 1904 Churchill transferred his allegiance from the Conservative to the Liberal party. One of his primary reasons for crossing the floor of the House of Commons was his opposition to the implementation of the policy of tariff impositions in defense of British trade. He proferred his candidacy for a parliamentary seat in Manchester, the home of the school of "free trade" founded by Cobden and Bright. In his address to the local branch of the Liberal party he recalled his consistent opposition to militarism, to monopolies, and to the rise in army expenditures, as well as his efforts to stifle the plan to raise three corps. He added that the time had also come for reductions in naval expenditures. He believed that such cuts would act as a restraint on Britain's foreign and colonial policies.[13] Like Cobden, Churchill maintained that "free trade"—the unrestricted commercial association between peoples—would lower the barriers of international estrangement and facilitate the development of mutual interests that would strengthen the forces working against war and ultimately lead to its elimination among civilized nations. He claimed that the protracted period of European peace, which had lasted for forty years, owed more to the expansion of international trade than to the endeavors of rulers and diplomats.[14]

Cobden had opposed war because he regarded military expenditure as a shameful waste, which undermined the processes of national economic and social development. He believed that peoples were by nature peace loving; responsibility for the outbreaks of wars lay with the governments and the narrow aristocratic castes that supported them. Cobden advocated something akin to political laissez-faire—the less government intervention, the greater the chance for world peace. He and Bright had rejected the concept of the European balance of power and of British intervention in its support. In splendid isolation, both had opposed the Crimean War.[15]

There is no doubt that Churchill was attached, at times almost mystically so, to the principle of "free trade" in the strict economic sense. However, as will be seen, he soon divested himself—without many withdrawal pains — of the political dimensions that had also been so central for Bright and Cobden.

In his famous work, *The Influence of Sea Power upon History*, Alfred Thayer Mahan had also emphasized the importance of commerce in the shaping of relations among peoples and the determination of their destinies. He believed that history lent itself to the deduction of permanent strategic principles. Consequently, he maintained that the conclusions that he had drawn from a study of the influence of sea power in the past would also remain true in the future.[16] Mahan had begun his book when he suddenly grasped that Rome's victory over Carthage had principally been the result of its command of the Mediterranean.[17] Inspired by this insight, he had turned his attention to an analysis of the reasons for the growth of the British Empire, and there discovered the analogy he sought. Mahan reached the conclusion that "command of the sea" and, thereby, of world commerce, constituted the key to imperial growth. Transport by sea was more efficacious than by land; thus maritime trade was the best means of amassing economic power. The relative standing of an individual nation was the consequence of its ability to ensure its own unrestricted maritime commerce and to deny that freedom to other states. It followed that the sea had become the principal theater for competition and collision between nations who strove for economic power.

Sea power, both naval and commercial, made possible the seizure of territories, resources, and raw materials that are the foundations of imperial prosperity and growth. Moreover, once those assets were attained, it was maritime strength that preserved the vital link between the homeland and its overseas possessions. Britain enjoyed the basic geographic benefits that gave it a relative advantage in the establishment of naval mastery and its total exploitation. Britain's European rivals labored under the burden of having to maintain large armies and suffered from the devastation that continental wars wreaked on their territories. Simultaneously, moreover, they had been constrained to maintain navies against the rising maritime strength of England, which had no need of large armies. Britain's sea power had been the cause of the growth of the British Empire at the expense of Spain, Portugal, and France, which had declined as world powers.[18] But Mahan's strategic analysis was monodimensional; he paid almost no attention to the campaigns on the Continent and to the nature of British military intervention in those wars. Virtually ignored, too, were the interactions between such campaigns and naval warfare.

Mahan's book constituted a superlative polemic for the "maritime school" in British strategic thought; it also exerted a profound influence on Kaiser Wilhelm II of Germany, on Theodore Roosevelt, and on another Roosevelt, Franklin Delano (who committed Mahan to memory)—and ultimately on the rulers of Japan, the rising naval power. Churchill read Mahan while still in India, and in his last days was to attribute to the book a deep influence on the course of twentieth-century history. Mahan, he said, had "dwelt upon the immense advantages which Britain had reaped through sea power, and how her greatness had been founded entirely, or almost entirely, upon it."[19] There can be no doubt of the close similarity between Churchill's strategic positions at this stage and Mahan's conclusions.

Those positions, together with other factors, imbued Churchill with a degree of complacency. He was slow to discern Germany's naval challenge to Britain and threat to Europe. Even at the end of 1908, by which time Anglo-German naval rivalry had already gained momentum, he opposed the views of those who considered war between Britain and Germany inevitable, castigating them as "alarmists" and denying the existence of a real conflict of worldwide interests between the two nations. He recalled that in the recent past very similar allegations had been made about the possibility of war with Russia and France; but these had been refuted by the conclusion of agreements that had improved Britain's relations with both countries. He repeated that sea power would safeguard Britain, "free us from the curse of Continental militarism," and obviate the need for alignment with another great power. In 1908–1909 he was one of the few persons not affected by the "naval scare" then rife in Britain. Churchill and Lloyd George, who were currently advocating social reforms in Britain, opposed the grandiose naval construction schemes that had the support of most ministers, the press, and a somewhat hysterical public. Churchill maintained that the Tories were unnecessarily inciting public alarm, which could only exacerbate Anglo-German relations.[20]

At this point we can pause to summarize Churchill's positions prior to their surprising transformation. His public utterances showed an affinity with those of the radical and pacifist wing of the British political system. After the conclusion of the Boer War, he had put himself against the rising tide of nationalism in British society. In 1906, when serving as Under-Secretary of State for the Colonies to Lord Elgin, he had been one of the proponents of full and immediate autonomy for the Boers in South Africa, a position he maintained notwithstanding the virulent—but ineffective—opposition of the Conservatives, led by Balfour, Milner, and Lansdowne, and of the Foreign Office. He had always believed that, once complete victory had been attained, the victors had to act with magnanimity toward the vanquished.[21] His strategic position was somewhere between "isolationism" and the "maritime school": he believed that sea power would suffice to isolate Britain from Europe and ensure the interests of the Empire. These were views very different from those held by the War Office and the General Staff, who for some years had been working toward the intensification of military and political contacts with France—a tendency that had at the same time begun to take slow root in the Foreign Office headed by Sir Edward Grey.

The first shifts in Churchill's strategic position began to appear in 1910. His visit to Germany in 1909 convinced him that that country faced deep social and economic problems, which would compel its leadership to choose between two political alternatives. One was that of external adventurism, the other—and opposite—a restrained foreign policy.[22] A few months later Churchill supported the army reforms proposed by Haldane, the Secretary for War, one of whose primary objectives was reorganizing the regular army into an expeditionary force to be dispatched to France in the event of an outbreak of war with Germany. As early as 1909 the Committee of Imperial Defence (CID) had reached the conclusion—never, in fact, confirmed by the Cabinet—that the moment war broke out with Germany it would be imperative to send five divisions to fight alongside the French.[23]

Churchill denied that he had changed the views that had earlier led him to oppose Broderick's reforms (which had never been implemented). At the same time, however, he commended Haldane's intention to expand the regular army and base it on a divisional framework, which, contrary to the corps structure designed by Broderick, would facilitate its dispatch overseas. He maintained that this regular army, together with the militia units (the Territorial Army) earmarked for the defense of Britain itself, would provide a good nucleus for the massive and swift expansion of the army once war broke out. But he did insist that the army could not be sent overseas until Britain had attained naval supremacy by either a decisive battle or by the imposition of a blockade on enemy anchorages.[24] Precisely what he meant by the term "overseas" he never clarified. But his statements of the time indicate that he still viewed these forces through the prism of direct imperial defense and did not intend them to be employed on the European mainland. Nevertheless, and despite his refusal to admit the fact, he already stood on the bank of the Rubicon.

It was the Agadir crisis of 1911 that most severely shook Churchill, who was then Home Secretary, and caused a transformation in his opinions. His reaction was virtually instinctive; he rediscovered the importance of the principle of the balance of power. He appealed to Lloyd George, the Chancellor of the Exchequer, to adopt a firm stand against Germany, explaining that

> It is not for Morocco, nor indeed for Belgium, that I would take part in this terrible business. One cause alone could justify our participation—to prevent France from being trampled down and looted by the Prussian junkers—a disaster

ruinous to the world, and swiftly fatal to our country.[25]

Churchill pressed Lloyd George and Grey to conclude an immediate alliance with France should negotiations during the Agadir crisis break down, to promote military coordination with Belgium, and—lastly—to establish a triple alliance between Britain, France, and Russia. Most important of all, and contrary to the Admiralty's position, he was strongly supportive of the General Staff's opinion that all the regular army divisions should immediately be dispatched to France. The crystallization of this point of view was in no small measure influenced by the personal briefing on the military situation in Europe that he received from General Henry Wilson, the Director of Military Operations.[26] Churchill even advocated imposition of partial conscription in the event of a declaration of war,[27] a notion the British public of the time regarded as almost sacrilegious, even though it did have the support of such powerful advocates as Lord Roberts, the military historian S. Wilkinson, and Colonel Repington, the military correspondent of *The Times*, all of whom sought to introduce peacetime conscription too.[28] Roberts was of the opinion that Britain would not enjoy the temporal leeway to establish an army that could intervene on the Continent in decisive force and at the decisive moment.[29] Churchill, on the other hand, did believe that Britain's naval supremacy would provide the time to establish a large land force after the outbreak of war.[30] Eventually, compulsory conscription would be imposed, but not until the middle of World War I (1916), and then only with considerable difficulty.

Once the Agadir crisis had passed, most senior Ministers thought it still possible to adopt an isolationist policy toward Europe. Many leading politicians were suspicious and skeptical of the concept of the European balance of power and of Britain's role in its maintenance. Such suspicions were voiced not only by the radical wing of the Liberal party and by the Labour party; they were also expressed by outright imperialists who believed that superior naval strength would enable Britain to avoid intervention on the Continent. Most statesmen took no clear stand on the issue, and despite their support for France during the crisis were wary of entering into any definite political and military commitment on France's behalf until the outbreak of war. During the crisis itself, there existed sufficient common ground between the supporters and opponents of continental intervention for them to form a solid front. Both feared a direct German threat to explicit British interests in the eastern Atlantic and at the Straits of Gibraltar; both were also troubled by the possibility that the French and Germans might ally at Britain's expense. On the other hand, the General Staff and War Office persistently, at least from 1909 on, pressed for a military and political commitment to France and for the dispatch of a British army to the Continent on the outbreak of war.[31]

From this stage onward, Churchill sided with the General Staff. It is principally his practical understanding of political and strategic realities that explains his rapid shift from attacks on the tendency to expand the Army and

Navy, from opposition to a British continental involvement, and from isolationism based on British naval superiority, to a strategy of political and military support for France. Within the latter context, he now preferred sending a British army to the Continent to military aid based mainly, as the Admiralty advocated, on sea power alone. This was no passing caprice, but a fundamental and lasting transformation in his strategic thinking. Churchill's own claim that he had not changed his positions since he was twenty-five years old[32] is not true of his strategic conceptions, although it is correct as far as his political and social outlooks are concerned.[33] The very sharpness of Churchill's turnabout may be indicative of some lack of confidence in the strategic position he had previously held.

The Agadir crisis unmasked the absence of an agreed war plan among the military and naval arms, as well as basic indecisiveness at the political level with regard to British action in the event of a European war. It transpired that the Admiralty had no clear plan worked out in detail. Arthur Wilson, the First Sea Lord, opposed General Henry Wilson's desire for the immediate dispatch of the British regular army to France. Britain's strategic contribution, the former maintained, ought to be based on sea power within whose framework the country's small army would be employed in amphibious operations. He suggested a series of naval attacks and minor amphibious assaults on the northwestern seaboard of Germany, a "close blockade," and, finally, the landing of forces on Germany's Baltic coastline. The "Baltic scheme" was at this stage more of an idea than a realistic plan. Admiral John Fisher, Wilson's distinguished predecessor, had previously toyed with the idea. During the Agadir crisis, however, Churchill—together with Haldane and Grey—came out in strong support of the army's position. He doubted very much whether Wilson's ideas could be implemented or be of any value.[34] (Nevertheless, when war did break out, he energetically worked for the acceptance of similar plans—albeit without changing his basic strategic conception).

Haldane and other senior Cabinet ministers were dismayed at the Admiralty's lack of war plans in general, let alone specific operational directives, as well as the absence of coordination with the General Staff. Haldane and such civilian military experts as Wilkinson and Colonel Repington maintained that in order to repair these deficiencies the Admiralty—like the Army—had to set up a general staff. But Wilson, like Fisher before him, opposed the establishment of a naval staff. One reason was their fear that a body of that nature might have an adverse effect on their authority as First Lords; another was their conviction that the very nature of naval warfare obviated the Admiralty's need for a framework whose operation would resemble that of an army general staff. After the Agadir crisis, Haldane pressed Asquith, the Prime Minister, to initiate the establishment of a naval staff with the objective of promoting strategic coordination with the Army. The issue was complicated by the fact that R. McKenna, the First Lord of the Admiralty, supported the stand taken by Admiral Wilson. Asquith's solution was to replace McKenna with Churchill. McKenna believed that the reasons for his dismissal centered on the strategic dilemma. After all, during the Agadir crisis he had sided with the Admiralty and had opposed a British commitment to France, fearing that it might encourage the latter to initiate war against Germany. But, as already noted, Asquith and the Cabinet had in fact taken no decisions regarding France at the political and strategic levels. Nor had they made a choice between the opposing positions of the Army and the Navy with regard to the nature of Britain's military intervention should the country become involved in Franco-German hostilities. All such decisions were indeed postponed until the outbreak of war. Asquith wished merely to improve the Admiralty's efficiency, although Haldane of course did harbor more far-reaching ambitions.[35]

During the course of the Agadir crisis Churchill composed one of the most important memoranda of his life, which he entitled "Military Aspects of the Continental Problem."[36] Central to the document was the claim that: "France will not be able to end the war successfully by any action on the frontiers. She will not be strong enough to invade Germany. Her only chance is to conquer Germany in France."

Churchill believed that the German attack, which he presumed would be launched by way of Belgium, should be allowed to run its course. The French, with the assistance of a British expeditionary force, should not initiate a decisive counteroffensive until Germany's supply lines had been stretched and its northern flank weakened by the depth of its advance into France. He considered that deep penetration would bring about the erosion of Germany's numerical superiority, since it would force the German Army to disperse its forces in order to secure lines of supply and to invest dominant forts and towns, including Paris itself. He claimed that determined French resistance on the borders, or French offensives in the early stages of the war, would be totally useless. The French could not stem the massive German tide on the borders; and a premature offensive would enfeeble the French army and impair the chances of a decisive counterattack. Churchill did not even hesitate to predict a timetable. In his opinion,

> By the fortieth day Germany should be extended at full strain both internally and on her war fronts, and this strain will become daily more severe and ultimately overwhelming, unless it is relieved by decisive victories in France.

It followed that France had to avoid giving decisive battle until the fortieth day after the commencement of the German attack. Only thereafter would it prove possible to attain a numerical balance of forces, which in fact would become increasingly favorable to the Allies the longer the campaign lasted. The dispatch of a British military expeditionary force to France and the prior coordination of military plans with the French were vital, since they would provide the French army with the moral support it needed to stand firm during the initial difficult and dangerous stage of the fighting. By the fortieth day a British force of 290,000 men could be amassed; this would comprise the six divisions of the expeditionary force to be dispatched to France immediately on the outbreak of war and 100,000 more men drawn from troops of the Anglo-Indian army who would be sent to France later. This combined force would play a major role in the counteroffensive. Churchill proposed its deployment in the rear of the French left flank, to prevent it from being worn down before the great counterattack.[37]

This was without question a brilliant assessment of the initial stages of the war, especially the timing of the turn in the German offensive's fortunes. Churchill was immensely proud of the fact, and it increased his self-confidence in his own strategic understanding. When he redistributed his memorandum to his Cabinet colleagues after the opening phase of the war, his standing in that forum was also enhanced—a circumstance not without significance when the decision was taken to launch the Dardanelles offensive. Nevertheless, and contrary to the claims suggested by both Churchill and others,[38] his assessment was not dissimilar to that of the generals. Ever since 1905 the General Staff had been of the opinion that the German offensive would traverse Belgium. In 1906 that body had also appreciated that, if it were to be at all useful, the British expeditionary force would have to be sent to France rather than to Belgium. In 1909 the Committee of Imperial Defence had concluded that five divisions would have to be sent to France as soon as possible to intervene in the decisive land battle.[39] The more General Wilson's status had risen during the years preceding the war, the more these lines of thought had hardened in the General Staff. In effect Churchill's memorandum was itself based on precisely the same assessments.

Where Churchill's opinions did differ from those of the British General Staff—and even more from those of the French—was in the response that he advocated to the expected German maneuver. Imbued with the moral offensive doctrine encapsulated in *offensive à l'outrance*, the French believed that the answer to a German thrust through Belgium was a parallel French attack through the Saarland into Lorraine, embodied in the disastrous Plan 17.[40] The British General Staff viewed the problem principally from the perspective of the quantitative balance of forces. The six British divisions were meant to create a numerical parity with the main German onslaught of forty divisions, against which the French could deploy only thirty-seven to thirty-nine divisions of their own. In accordance with the French plan, the British forces were to be placed on the extreme left of the French line. Churchill, on the other hand, proposed lines of operation founded, first and foremost, on the power of flexible defense and based upon the law of "friction," which would blunt the momentum of the German advance. Correct, then, was Churchill's claim in *The World Crisis* that his memorandum was based on the assumption that the power of the defense over offense had immeasurably increased.[41] His second assumption was that the Germans would so stretch their lines of supply and become so tied up in logistic difficulties that they would loose their equilibrium, thus making possible the subsequent decisive counterattack. This assumption, too, was justified.

As early as 1901, Churchill had recognized that a large modern army was to a high degree dependent on regular supplies brought up by railways, and that the operational size of the army was determined by the capacity of transportation facilities in its rear.[42] (However, after the First World War he did not attribute great weight to the logistic factor; on the contrary, he maintained that the implementation of the Schlieffen Plan had failed because the German right flank had been weakened in disregard of its author's original orders, and because the Germans had shown a lack of willpower at the decisive stage.)[43]

This strategic analysis did have its deficiencies. For one thing, it rested upon French readiness to make a temporary sacrifice of a sizable populated area; for another, it called upon the British General Staff to forego—albeit, again, only temporarily—use of some of the French ports vital to the maintenance of communications with Britain. It seems that even had the French acknowledged the accuracy of Churchill's assumptions, they would have been incapable of implementing their consequent tenets. The moral support to be gained from the arrival of a British expeditionary force would not appropriately compensate for the damage done to the morale of the public and the troops by the abandonment of French soil to the Germans.

In light of the conclusions of Churchill's memorandum, his position does raise some questions. He knew of the French intention to launch a counterattack on the Saar into Lorraine as soon as the Germans began their offensive. His view that the French army had to adopt a strategy of flexible defense until the fortieth day after the German attack was not accepted. It is clear from the memorandum that the attainment of a turning point after the fortieth day was contingent upon the French army not being worn down by a premature counteroffensive, especially one launched simultaneously with the German attack.[44] The latter course was likely to bring about a French defeat—an eventuality that, from Churchill's viewpoint, would negate much of the *military* value in the transport of six British divisions to France. That being the case, it is strange that until the outbreak of war he persistently supported the dispatch to France of all the divisions available despite the French plan and despite their planned deployment in forward positions. Churchill's own prediction was that under those circumstances the expeditionary force would be swallowed up in the human mass traversing northeastern France and propelled hither and thither like a cork on the waves—which is in fact what happened and what critics had foretold. In this situation, it would have been militarily preferable to send all six divisions to Antwerp with the purpose of creating a threat to the German flank. An alternative was to work toward the peacetime expansion of the expeditionary force, so that (as Lord Roberts claimed) its influence would be the consequence of the weight of its mass. Churchill recommended neither course. Possibly, he did not push his own strategic evaluation to its logical end—this was not, as we shall see, an uncommon characteristic. But it seems that in this case Churchill, although sensitive to the deficiencies, supported the dispatch of an expeditionary force to France because of the supreme importance he attached to the political and moral effects of this move and to the grant of priority to the western theater in the first stage of the war.

Therein indeed lies a paradox. Churchill's estimates regarding time and place, whose accuracy aroused such amazement, were based on the assumption that his strategic concept would be adopted. In the event, however, those assessments proved to be accurate despite the fact that the French acted in direct contradiction to his basic thinking and recommendations. In the case of strategic predictions, as in every other sphere of life, a bit of luck does no harm.

■

Immediately after his appointment as First Lord of the Admiralty, Churchill attempted to set up a naval staff. Late in October 1911 he wrote another memorandum, which adds a further dimension to his previous paper and to the understanding of his strategic thinking. He claimed that the establishment of a body such as the naval staff was essential for the implementation of appropriate preparations for war. Good preparation demanded that the war of the future be analyzed from the following angles:

> firstly, of the probable dangers that may arise; secondly, of the best method of meeting them as taught by the principles to be deduced from the events of history; and thirdly, of the most efficient application of war material of the era. [45]

It was precisely the protracted period of peace that necessitated the establishment of a staff that could monitor the massive and incessant changes in military technology. In the past, the slow pace of technological development and the brevity of the intervals in the fleet's actions permitted a continual process of deduction and adaptation. Most naval officers had been given sound technological training; but very deficient was their understanding of those strategic principles that include naval warfare and its links with foreign policy. As if echoing Mahan, Churchill contended that the general principles of strategy had remained constant throughout history; to enhance his case he added that it was concurred with by all historians. Those principles, he asserted, could be learned from military history. "Only war itself, or the historical study of war," he claimed, "can teach what results or effects may be expected from any particular variety of war policy." The correct study of history, he went on, would have spared mistakes committed in the past. Naval officers had to receive instruction in the highest level of strategy at the Royal Naval College, where the curriculum would be based upon the study of the works of the naval historians Mahan, Corbett, and Colomb. It was thus that suitable cadres would be trained for service on the naval staff. The staff itself would be charged with the preparation and planning of operational and strategic plans for war under the direction of the First Sea Lord.[46]

A. Wilson, the First Sea Lord, was adamant in his opposition to this proposal,[47] and Churchill was not able to establish the naval staff until Wilson was dismissed. Even so, the spirit that the latter had represented lived on. The "materialistic school" remained the dominant ethos of the naval officer class. Jellicoe, whom Churchill appointed to command the Grand Fleet on Fisher's advice, first read Mahan in 1917. But even Churchill, as we shall see, displayed contradictions between the intellectual ideal he preached and the method of thought and deduction he himself practiced.

It was precisely in 1911 that Julian Corbett, who lectured at the Royal Naval College and until 1914 served as a kind of historical adviser to the Admiralty, published his most important book, *Some Principles of Maritime Strategy*, a theoretical and historical distillation of his previous researches.[48] This is a more sophisticated work than Mahan's, because Corbett aimed at the full understanding of military thought and strategy that had been developed in Europe, especially by Clausewitz, and their integration with naval strategy. He commenced his book with a correct observation, which many of his predecessors and successors tended to forget:

> It scarcely needs saying that it is almost impossible that a war can be decided by naval action alone. Unaided, naval pressure can only work by a process of exhaustion. Its effects must always be slow and so galling both to our commercial community and to neutrals, that the tendency is always to accept terms of peace that are far from conclusive. . . . The paramount concern, then, of maritime strategy is to determine the mutual relations of your army and navy in a plan of war.[49]

Corbett made a precise distinction between what he regarded as a continental strategy that aimed at "unlimited war," whose theoretical concepts had been developed by Clausewitz, and a specific and traditional British strategy. As crystallized during the course of Britain's historical experience, the latter was based upon "limited war." Corbett claimed that British attempts in the past to wage war in accordance with continental forms were "almost invariably accompanied by a popular repugnance, as though there were something in it antagonistic to the national instinct."[50]

> [The] British or maritime form is in fact the application of the limited method to the unlimited form, as ancillary to the larger operations of our allies—a method which has usually been open to us because the control of the sea has enabled us to select a theatre in effect truly limited.[51]

Corbett maintained that Britain's naval mastery had enabled it to create an *independent* land theater of its own, supplied by sea. Conversely, that mastery had also denied its antagonists freedom to concentrate in the same theater of war land forces superior to the limited forces available to Britain. The exemplar he had in mind was the Duke of Wellington's successful Peninsular Campaign. In that instance, he claimed, a limited strategy had attained an unlimited aim—the fall of Napoleon. Corbett emphasized, however, that this "British strategy," of limited war for the purpose of unlimited objectives, was feasible only where the theater selected for the offensive could be quarantined through naval superiority. Its prior condition, therefore, was the attainment of maritime mastery through the defeat of the enemy's fleet.[52] In an attempt to preserve the spirit of Clausewitz's teachings, Corbett stressed that the successes attained by way of the British "limited war" strategy should not lead to illusions: "Whatever the form of war, there is no likelihood of our ever going back to the old fallacy of attempting to decide wars by manoevres. All forms alike demand the use of battles."[53]

In any case, should the circumstances of war make it impossible for Britain to open its own limited and independent theater, Britain still possessed two inferior options: one was to dispatch its army to the continent, where it would fight alongside allies in accordance with the "continental form"; the other was to employ its army in amphibious operations with the purpose of diverting the enemy's forces and rendering assistance to its own continental allies. Such had been the strategy adopted during the Seven Years' War, which Corbett, somewhat contradicting his own earlier statements, regarded as an expression of the nature of British strategy in its most pure and successful form. Corbett maintained that previous diversionary amphibious operations, including such failures as the Walcheren expedition of 1809, had achieved their aim. They had brought about the dispersal of large enemy forces and had generated a considerable psychological effect. The worst course, Corbett believed, would be to send British troops to fight alongside the nation's allies and to make war in the continental style. "Intimate concerted action" of British and other forces had failed time and again. Even the first stage of the Peninsular War, when British forces had been employed alongside the Spanish army, had ended in failure.[54]

For all his cleverness Corbett's conception did not in sum differ very much from that of Mahan. During the course of this book, the reader will have an opportunity to gauge the extent to which the strategic interpretations of both men were valid and were considered so by Churchill in his own subsequent historical researches. What is already apparent, however, is the problematic nature of Corbett's assertion that Britain could attain unlimited objectives by employing limited means. Corbett was aware of the recent technological changes that made possible the rapid transfer of massive forces from one end of the Continent to the other; but he did not consider their implications sufficiently revolutionary to contradict his conclusions.[55]

Churchill read Corbett's *Some Principles of Maritime Strategy*.[56] Also, it was apparently by way of that book that—for the first and, perhaps, last time—he became acquainted with Clausewitzian notions of war and strategy. Surprisingly, none of Churchill's writings or speeches contains a single direct reference to Clausewitz's ideas. In any case, Churchill sent the Navy's officers to learn strategy and history from Corbett. But at the same time he himself advocated and promoted a strategic course that Corbett considered the very worst, one contrary to the "national instinct" and to the British historical experience—namely, sending a British army to fight alongside an allied army on the Continent, even should this involve its subordination to the latter's continental strategy.

Churchill's support for the "continental commitment" was the result of the fact that, in principle, he grasped the essence of the balance-of-power concept and of Britain's role in its maintenance. As much is shown by the fact that even in 1912 (and notwithstanding the fundamental change in his attitudes and his leading role in the naval race) he continued to deny the existence of a direct conflict of British and German interests.[57] He grasped that both political and operational circumstances rendered a deep British "continental commitment" the only method whereby Britain could prevent a French defeat and German hegemony over Europe.

The transformation in his strategic position was not the result of a study of the course and lessons of British military history as he then understood them. Rather, he reached his new position through a combination of sober and intuitive thought and an analysis of the European strategic and political situation of 1911. In effect, his conclusion negated his current understanding of the character of British military history. It is difficult to discern any supporting historical echoes or analogies in his memorandum of August 1911 in support of the "continental commitment." This is in marked contrast to the plethora of such justifications on the same subject both before 1911 and during the 1930s. What is more, Churchill remained steadfastly faithful to this view until the outbreak of the Second World War, despite the severe pressures that threatened to undermine it.

Admiral Fisher, who virtually served as Churchill's informal adviser between 1911 and 1914, had begun to exert such pressure as early as the end of 1911, when he advised Churchill that: "Fighting policy should be formed on Navy not on Army views. 100,000 soldiers embarked in Transports—and kept 'en l'air'—demobilize one million German soldiers from the Vosges frontier."[58]

Although he accepted many of Fisher's recommendations, Churchill did not heed this piece of strategic advice. Instead, he stuck to the Army's position. What is more, he did so despite pressure from the Admiralty, despite the natural tendency for a Minister to support the views of the department he represents, and despite his inclination to peripheral-amphibious operations.

During the course of 1912 Churchill worked toward the concentration of British naval power in the North Sea. Reacting to Germany's recent Supplementary Naval Law, and following lines of strategy previously laid down by Fisher, he decided to move the Mediterranean Fleet from its base at Malta to Gibraltar, so that it could support the Grand Fleet in the North Sea. No more than a few cruisers were to remain on station in Malta. To that end, Churchill was ready to weaken Britain's naval standing and imperial strength in the eastern and central Mediterranean. This was despite the fact that Austria-Hungary and Italy had also begun to construct capital ships similar to those of the Dreadnought class, and that both were allied to Germany within the framework of the Triple Alliance. Defending his plan, Churchill maintained that the majority of Britain's vessels had to be concentrated in preparation for the decisive battle with the German navy, which would take place in the North Sea. As he wrote to Haldane: "If we win the big battle in the decisive theatre, we can put everything else straight afterwards. If we lose it, there will not be any afterwards. London is the key of Egypt—don't lose it." [59] He saw no point in an increase of expenditure in order to construct a Mediterranean Fleet that would be larger than the combined fleets of Austria-Hungary and Italy, as well as preserving a 60 percent advantage over the German fleet.

Churchill's primary considerations were purely operational. As early as 1910, and hence long before taking office at the Admiralty, he had come out against the opinion that the Navy had to undergo considerable expansion in order to carry the heavy burden of widespread imperial commitments. Such a position, he maintained, would necessitate the establishment of naval bases everywhere, and was impracticable. "Command of the sea" is attained by a decisive battle or by a series of such engagements.[60] It would be a mistake to distinguish between command of one sea or another and command of the sea in general. "The command of the Mediterranean cannot be treated as if it were something isolated or wholly separated from the general command of the sea," he contended in characteristic Mahanian style.[61]

Churchill's plan angered every segment of the British political spectrum and generated intense argument in the Cabinet. In effect, the debate illuminated all the various attitudes and opinions in the country about the "continental commitment." Liberals and Radicals regarded it as a deliberate step in the direction of a military alliance with France, and were apprehensive that it would restrict Britain's freedom of action when the time came to choose between peace and war. That was the prevailing feeling in the Cabinet. On the other hand, imperialists such as Lord Roberts, Kitchener, and Lord Esher feared that it would jeopardize Egypt, reduce British prestige in the Orient, and have an adverse effect on British control over India.[62] In part, however, they too were worried about reliance on France and suspected that deep involvement on the Continent would endanger Britain's imperial orientation. The Foreign Office feared the loss of political influence over the Ottoman Empire, Italy, and Spain; the War Office feared for the future of its garrisons in Egypt, Malta, and Cyprus. It was thus that a curious alliance was forged between imperialists and Radicals, who supported the additional expansion of the Navy in order to preserve Britain's maritime supremacy in both the North and the Mediterranean seas.[63] The compromise eventually reached was that, in addition to preserving continuous and clear superiority in home waters, the Admiralty would also establish a Mediterranean fleet equal in strength to the most powerful Mediterranean power, barring France. Ultimately, that decision was not put into effect because the Admiralty lacked the necessary funds to do so.

This episode casts light on two important points in Churchill's long-term strategic thinking. The first concerns his attitude toward political and military coordination with France in peacetime: although he maintained that Britain had to throw the full weight of its military power behind France should war break out between her and Germany, he believed that Britain could and should also preserve its freedom of action. One year after Agadir he wrote to Grey that: "circumstances might arise which in my judgement would make it desirable and right for us to come to the aid of France with all our force by land and sea." But in the same breath he went on to express his anxiety "to safeguard . . . our freedom of choice if the occasion arises, and consequent power to influence French policy beforehand." Although the French had decided in June 1912 to transfer their naval forces from the Channel ports and to combine them with their Mediterranean fleet, Churchill still informed the French naval attaché that the recent naval moves had not created any form of British commitment to France.[64] He said, "Everyone who knows the facts must feel that we have the obligations of an alliance without its advantages and above all without its precise definitions."[65] But not even this appreciation caused Churchill to conclude that it would be preferable to enter into a peacetime alliance with France. As will be seen, however, he did change his views during the course of the following decades.

The second point to arise from the Mediterranean Fleet episode is Churchill's attitude toward the problem of imperial defense. Put another way, what it illuminates is his view on the question of the links between strategic-operational courses and the protection and promotion of Britain's imperial objectives. His attitude toward the future of the Empire had not changed since the beginning of the century: its preservation, although not its expansion, remained his primary concern. But he was not moved by that objective to adopt a strategic line that would be based on sheer defense of the Empire and the isolation of Britain from Europe. That was, indeed, the stand taken by Lord Esher, who in the same year wrote:

> Great Britain stands today at the parting of her imperial way. . . . Britain either is not or is one of the Great Powers of the world. Her position in this respect depends solely upon sea command, and sea command on the Mediterranean. . . . We should be mad to entangle ourselves in a continental strife on land. Our medium is the ocean way. . . . This Mediterranean question is the vital essence of our being.[66]

Churchill, on the other hand, reached the conclusion that Britain's imperial strength was closely tied up with the political situation on the European mainland and the maintenance of Britain's continental interests. Imperial defense begins inside, not outside, Europe. Were a European power to attain continental supremacy it could mobilize Europe's resources and then pose a threat more dangerous than any other to the Empire's existence. This had been the cornerstone of Churchill's strategic thinking ever since its transformation in 1911, and he was to deepen his understanding of its roots during the 1930s. It determined his readiness to make sacrifices and tactical retreats from imperial interests, some of which were extremely important, in order to attain a strategic decision against the central threat he saw emerging within Europe itself.

Churchill's critics frequently claim that he preferred strategic moves whose objective was the promotion of British imperial interests to those that could more efficiently have defeated Germany in the two world wars. That claim is false—imperial motives were not the dominant factor in the determination of his strategic preferences. The Mediterranean Fleet episode is the first of a series of examples which prove the case.

British naval strategy on the eve of World War I presupposed a decisive battle with the German fleet. The idea that such a battle would be fought during the very first stages of the war came to be regarded as axiomatic by Churchill and the Admiralty.[67] Fisher even went so far as to predict that Armageddon would occur as early as the first day of the war. Consequently, the Admiralty concentrated all its planning on that battle, while neglecting other possible elements, including amphibious warfare.[68] As much is evident from its failure to prepare detailed plans and appropriate vessels for amphibious operations, or to conduct joint amphibious exercises with the Army. That situation had several causes. Throughout its long naval history, the Admiralty had always regarded amphibious operations as a Cinderella; the experience accumulated in the past had been forgotten during the decades of peace and British maritime supremacy since Waterloo; and there never existed a very high spirit of cooperation and mutual esteem between Navy and Army officers.[69] But the principal factor was the absolute preference for a "continental strategy" over the "maritime school." That order of priorities was ensured by Churchill's presence on the Board of the Admiralty. The task of the Navy was to ensure the immediate passage of the entire British expeditionary force to France.[70]

It would be a mistake to attribute to Churchill sole responsibility for the decay of amphibious warfare on the eve of World War I. During their tenures in office as First Sea Lords, Fisher and Wilson had contemplated such operations; but they had taken no practical steps to promote their ideas (whose operational difficulties will be discussed in the following chapter). As will be clearly seen, Churchill himself was an outright supporter of amphibious warfare, even when subordinating the Navy's position to that of the Army.

The closer war drew, the more hardened became Churchill's opinion that it would be a lengthy business.[71] He hoped that once the German offensive in the west had been halted or smashed, it would be possible to commence amphibious operations in the peripheral European theaters. That would be done by using some of the numerous forces to be raised in Britain immediately after hostilities commenced. But Churchill was mistaken to think that it would prove possible to improvise and rapidly prepare Army and Navy forces for amphibious warfare on a large scale. As will be seen, this error was the result of his incomplete understanding of the problems involved in that type of operation.[72] But it also goes some way toward explaining why he failed to prepare the Navy for amphibious warfare. He might also have feared that moves to foster amphibious plans prior to the outbreak of war might weigh against a decision being taken to dispatch the Army to France on the fateful day.

Another dispute interwoven with the larger debate between the Army and the Admiralty (representing, respectively, the "continental" and "maritime" schools) focused on defending the British Isles against invasion. This was a subject with which the public too showed concern, and was debated intermittently between the beginning of the century and the very outbreak of World War I. The Admiralty was persistent in maintaining an opinion categorized as the "blue-water school," which argued that Britain's naval supremacy would suffice to foil any invasion attempt. The Army and its civilian representatives, however, put forward the contrary viewpoint, contending that naval power alone could not provide Britain with a defense against a sudden and massive amphibious assault. Advocates of this, the "bolt-from-the-blue school," insisted on the need to maintain a large armed force in Britain itself; some, such as Lord Roberts, even argued that compulsory conscription was required.[73]

The Admiralty's attitude stemmed from two concerns: one was for the integrity of its traditional status as the senior service and the dominant influence on the formulation of British strategy; the other was that cuts might be made in its budget for naval construction. It wished to stunt the growth in power of the "continental school" because a large British Army would possess the capability to send forces to fight on the Continent. But the Admiralty got tied up in a contradiction of its own making: on the one hand, it contended that naval power provided Britain with adequate defense; on the other, it maintained that the nation's offensive strategy had to be based on amphibious and peripheral operations on enemy coastlines. The inconsistency of these two contentions lay in the fact that precisely those operational factors supposedly preventing a German amphibious invasion of Britain would also work the other way around—precluding the possibility of British amphibious offensives.[74] The Germans, after all, enjoyed local naval superiority along their own littoral and in the Baltic, a large army, and an excellent railway network.

The attitude adopted by the Army was more consistent. Admittedly, its fear that the Germans intended to invade Britain was groundless; but when arguing against the practicability of amphibious operations or the idea of sending the expeditionary force to threaten the German flank in Belgium all by itself, the Army could justifiably point to the extent of the German forces, whose size was far greater than their British counterparts.

Churchill's own attitude was singular, and less self-contradictory. Ever since the danger of an invasion of Britain had first been mooted he had contended that the fleet could deny success to any such operation. This was a natural attitude for him to adopt at a time when he was still an ardent supporter of the "maritime school" and an opponent of the Army's expansion. True, Churchill did warn against absolute reliance on the Navy; the enemy, he cautioned, might be able to slip by and carry out minor amphibious operations, which, however, it would take no more than a militia force to repel. Indeed, as we have seen, prior to 1910 he opposed *both* the expansion of the regular army and any intent to reduce local militia units.[75] In 1907 he supported the establishment of a Territorial Army (i.e., militia) alongside a restricted regular army; he contended that the "Territorials," together with the Royal Navy, could foil a German invasion attempt and free the regular army for service overseas. But at this stage he thought that the Army should be sent overseas solely for imperial defense.[76]

In 1910 he contended that the land force in Britain had to be large enough to compel the Germans to dispatch a massive force of their own if they wished their invasion to succeed. But, because of its size, such a force would be detected and destroyed by the Navy. Conversely, the Germans would be deterred from sending over small landing parties, which, although they might be able to slip past the Royal Navy, would be overwhelmed by superior forces once they reached the British Isles.[77] Even after the Agadir crisis and the transformation of his attitude toward a continental commitment, his position on this subject did not change very much. Using the same logic, he continued to argue that the security attained by the combination of sea power and the Territorial Army would permit the immediate dispatch of the entire regular army to France. Thus, while the Admiralty's position was designed to make insubstantial the importance of the Army, Churchill adopted a similar position with the purpose of promoting the "continental" strategy held by the Army itself. The irony of the situation lies in the fact that, when war did break out, it was Kitchener—the army veteran and new Secretary of State for War—who was dissatisfied with Churchill's assurances that the fleet had altogether ensured Britain's defense against invasion and that the regular army's entire complement of six divisions could be shipped to France. Disregarding all the preparations of the General Staff, he decided to send only four divisions.[78]

This episode illustrates the basis of Churchill's strategic attitude. He strove to synthesize and harmonize the "continental" and "maritime" schools, which he regarded as complementary rather than as opposites. His analysis of the strategic position prior to 1914 and during the interwar period led him to conclude that a large British army had to be sent to France once war commenced. Moreover, this move had to precede the opening of other fronts relying upon British sea power, or the launching of offensive amphibious operations. Churchill reached that conclusion even though a maritime-peripheral strategy remained his own preferred inclination—and one to which he himself sometimes succumbed, especially when his strategic calculations went awry or when the course of the war took an unexpected or undesirable turn. The analysis of Churchillian strategy during the two world wars in effect constitutes an analysis of his attempts to attain a synthesis between "continental" and "peripheral" strategies. It is along those lines that the following chapter will assess his concept and his strength as a strategic decision taker during World War I.

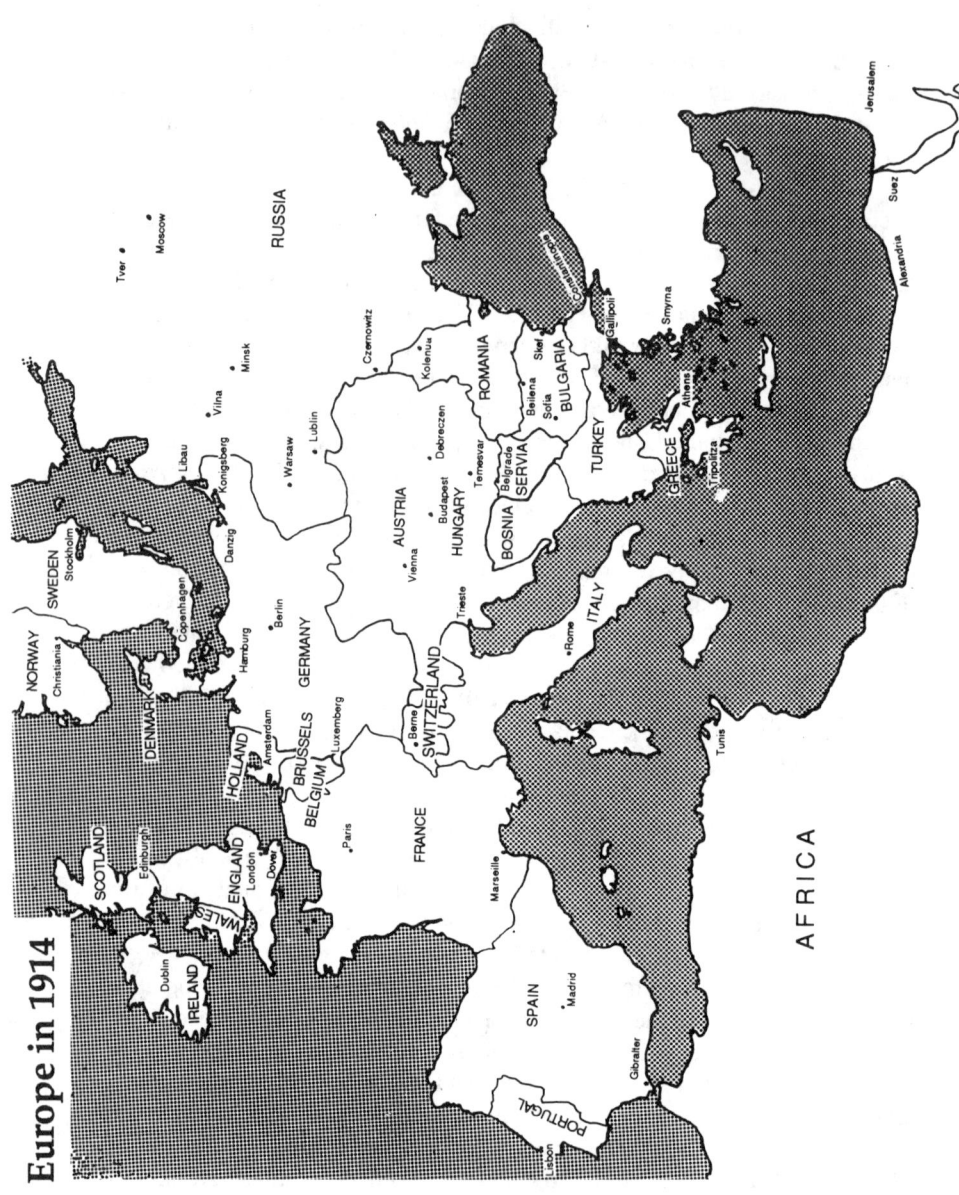

2

From the Baltic to Gallipoli, 1914-1915

Churchill played an important role in the tortuous Cabinet debates of July 1914 that preceded Britain's entry into World War I. What he then emphasized was the maintenance of Belgium's neutrality, any blow against which would compel Britain to uphold its guarantee to that country. In fact, however, the Belgian problem was not his primary consideration. His real concern in 1914, as had been the case during the 1911 Agadir crisis, was the European balance of power and his fear that Germany might defeat France. Convinced that the Germans would attack France by way of Belgium,[1] the purpose of his stand was to bring around those Ministers who did not share his fears over the fate of the European balance in general and of France in particular. Ultimately, it was the German invasion of Belgium that made up the minds of most of the Ministers who either opposed Britain's entry into the war or who had been undecided.

Once the decision to enter the war had been taken, Churchill—against not inconsiderable opposition—pressed for the immediate dispatch of the British Expeditionary Force (BEF) to France. He hoped that, if properly employed, it might play an important role in stemming the German offensive. He also appreciated its vital strategic function. The force would provide a nucleus for the large British armies to be subsequently raised, most of which would also be sent to France—which would thus become the main theater of the British Army.[2] The BEF was indeed shipped to France, albeit not in full, and played an important role in holding off the Germans at the Battle of the Marne.

In *The World Crisis*, where he discusses World War I, Churchill defined what he termed "the general principles" that formed his strategic conception throughout the war:

1. The Decisive theatre is the theatre where a vital decision may be obtained at any given time. The main theatre is that in which the main armies or fleets are stationed. This is not at all times the Decisive the-

atre.
2. If the fronts or centres of armies cannot be broken, their flanks should be turned. If these flanks rest on the seas, the manoeuvres to turn them must be amphibious and dependent on sea power.
3. The least-guarded strategic points should be selected for attack, not those most strongly guarded.
4. In any hostile combination, once it is certain that the strongest Power cannot be directly defeated itself, but cannot stand without the weakest, it is the weakest that should be attacked.
5. No offensive on land should be launched until an effective means—numbers, surprise, munitions, or mechanical devices—of carrying it through has been discovered.[3]

Churchill adopted some of these principles from the very outbreak of the war. Others he in effect developed during its course, or retrospectively advocated, thereby also justifying his positions. The theoretical validity of these principles can be questioned. Take, for instance, the third, in which Churchill proposes assaults on the enemy's "least-guarded" strategic points. By their nature, these are likely to be the least important points, since a sensible adversary will do its best to defend those whose downfall might lead to defeat. Thus, the principles ought to be assessed in the light of real events, rather than from a theoretical standpoint.

Churchill's distinction between the "main" and "decisive" theaters constitutes an original contribution to strategic thought. According to that definition, Churchill—correctly or not—at the beginning of the war considered the western front to constitute both categories. Throughout the conflict, he remained convinced that the "main theatre" was located in France. His consideration of flanking amphibious operations and the opening of new fronts on the European periphery might thus be thought to have served the purpose outlined in the second of his own principles. Once he had seen the impossibility of breaking through the German lines in France, his aim was to discover the "decisive theatre" elsewhere. In fact, that was not the case. From the very outbreak of war, and while still working toward a situation whereby France would become the main theater, Churchill also began to promote amphibious operational plans for the German coast and the opening of new fronts on the European periphery. Almost instinctively, he was aiming at the harmonization of the "maritime" and "continental" schools.

A bitter surprise foiled his attempt to achieve that strategic synthesis. The German fleet remained in its harbors and refused to come out for the decisive naval engagement upon which Churchill and the Admiralty had pinned their hopes. Churchill proclaimed that a naval victory constituted an essential prerequisite for the implementation of the plans against Germany that had been hatching since the beginning of the war.[4] When months had elapsed and the German strategy had become clear, he lost some of his equilibrium; the German fleet, he threatened, would be smoked out like mice from their holes. But with the German battleships resting at anchor in well-defended ports (adjacent to the entrance to the Kiel Canal leading to the Baltic), it proved impossible to force them to give battle.[5]

The naval historian, A. J. Marder, maintains that the Admiralty's shortsightedness was the consequence of its chiefs being ignorant of history. They possessed only a superficial view of British naval history, considering the decisive engagement—such as Trafalgar—to be the basic and ideal type of naval warfare. What they overlooked was that the principal features of past naval warfare had been blockades, the defense of trade routes, and raids on enemy commerce. Engagements between fleets had been rare, and even where fought had sometimes been inconclusive. One of the reasons for this distortion was the Admiralty's misconstruing of Mahan's emphasis on the importance of the great battle at sea.[6]

Churchill, it will be recalled, had noticed the Navy's ignorance of history and had attempted to rectify the situation. In a memorandum on the nature of "Command of the Sea," which he wrote about a year before the outbreak of the war, he warned that "this [naval] decision may be indefinitely delayed, and may perhaps never be obtained in the whole course of the war."[7] Even his phraseology echoed that of Corbett, whose *Some Principles of Maritime Strategy* had pointed out the difficulties Britain had previously experienced when attempting to force a decisive naval engagement on its adversaries.[8] Land powers possessed of inferior maritime strength preferred to adopt a defensive naval strategy; like France under Napoleon, they sought to evade a naval decision until they had reached one on the Continent.[9] Mahan too had noted that between the sixteenth and eighteenth centuries enemies with weak fleets had avoided giving the British fleet decisive battle.[10] Fisher, whom Churchill reinstated as First Sea Lord, discovered this historical truth (apparently via Corbett) in January 1915, when he informed Churchill that it had been commonplace. The French had acted thus during the Seven Years' War, and when they kept Nelson waiting for two years outside Toulon. Fisher believed that German apprehensions stemmed from their numerical inferiority and from the fear that a defeat would lay bare their northern coastline, especially in the Baltic, to Anglo-Russian attacks.[11] Churchill, however, based his strategy on a decisive engagement at the outbreak of war. He did so despite Mahan and Corbett, despite his own memorandum, despite his exhortations to learn from history, and notwithstanding the possibility of arriving at the correct conclusion by an estimate of the balance of forces on the eve of war and from an assessment based on the German viewpoint. His vision was clouded by his own wishful thinking and by his romantic yearning for the gigantic naval confrontation.

Even after the First World War, Churchill criticized the German fleet for not joining the Germany army, which had pinned its hopes on a swift and fateful decision at the onset of hostilities.[12] This was the first in a series of criticisms Churchill was wont to make against the wisdom of the strategic decisions taken by Britain's enemies during the two world wars, whenever they did not act as he thought fit. Even had the German fleet been "under the command of a Nelson" (as one British admiral put it[13]), it hardly stood a chance of defeating the numerically superior British Navy. However, as a "fleet in being" it did defend Germany's northern coast and transform the Baltic Sea into a German lake.[14] This was an important strategic contribution, which throughout the war frustrated the fulfillment of Churchill's offensive plans.

Immediately on the outbreak of war, and while still awaiting the decisive naval engagement, Churchill began to cast about for amphibious naval offensives against the enemy. Until the end of 1914, he thought mainly in terms of an attack into the Baltic.[15] This idea had been proposed by several persons, especially Admiral Fisher, several years before the war and had undergone various adaptations. But its basic notion remained the attainment of naval command of the Baltic, the opening of a convenient link to Russia, and—ultimately—the landing of forces (some of them Russian) on Germany's Baltic coast in Pomerania, thereby creating a threat north of Berlin. Churchill believed that this move would lead Denmark and Holland, both neutral, to join the war on the Entente's side.[16] As early as August 19, he asked Grand Duke Nicholas, the Russian Commander in Chief, to consent to the plan. The latter did indeed agree in principle; but the refusal of the German fleet to come out for a decisive naval engagement prevented Churchill and Fisher from making any progress toward the implementation of the grand "Baltic scheme."[17] Another of his proposals was for an amphibious landing in Schleswig-Holstein (either with the cooperation of the Danes or even in violation of their neutrality) with the object of blocking the Kiel Canal. Churchill thereby hoped to force the German fleet to give decisive battle. But its obvious difficulties prevented this idea from becoming operational.

It was another idea that crystallized into a plan that, in time, was expanded and to which were added objectives wider than those originally envisaged. As early as January 1913 Churchill had instructed the Admiralty to examine the possibility of capturing an island in the vicinity of the German littoral and other coasts in northern Europe and turning it into a naval and military base. The island of Borkum was found to be most suitable for this sort of operation.[18] Fisher himself had talked to Churchill about his own ideas for the conquest of Borkum as long ago as 1907. But while Fisher had gradually lost interest in the island, it had continued to exercise Churchill's mind.[19] One of the largest in the Frisian Islands, Borkum lies close to the Heligoland Bight and the estuaries of the Jade and the Elbe, the German fleet's main anchorages. Churchill intended to take Borkum by an amphibious assault and there to set up a permanent base for naval vessels and submarines that would operate under the very noses of the Germans and impose a sort of "close blockade" on their harbors in the Heligoland Bight.

Churchill began to examine the Borkum plan at the end of July, when the German navy's determination to evade a decisive engagement was not yet apparent. But he thereafter adapted it to the new situation. The Germans, he claimed, would not be able to abide a British base so close to their coast, and would therefore be forced to take their fleet out into action. The conquest of Borkum and the destruction of the German fleet in a naval engagement would serve as a springboard to Schleswig-Holstein or to a direct assault into the Baltic. The Admiralty experts were from the start skeptical about the feasibility of the plan. Jellicoe, who commanded the Grand Fleet, doubted that it would be possible to hold the island after its capture because it lay within German artillery range.[20] Fisher initially showed great interest in the move, principally because he became convinced that the conquest of Borkum would precipitate the great naval engagement. But his enthusiasm soon waned.

At the end of November 1914, apparently for the first and only time,[21] Fisher formulated a written version of his "Baltic scheme." In composing his memorandum he received assistance from Corbett, and his central argument focused on an analogy taken from the Seven Years' War. Fisher maintained that as early as the spring of 1915 the entire battle fleet should sail to the Baltic and that Russian forces should be landed in Pomerania with the purpose of threatening Berlin and cutting Germany's supply lines leading east. His memorandum also advocated a massive mine-laying program, designed to confine the German ships to their harbors and thus neutralize their navy, which might otherwise be able to inflict a counterblow in the North Sea and thereby cut communications with the British fleet in the Baltic Sea. Fisher concluded with an appeal that Britain adopt an offensive naval strategy and be prepared to run high risks.[22]

Churchill's attitude toward the "Baltic scheme" was comparatively prosaic, and he made no use of historical analogies. However, he did fully support Fisher. "The Baltic is the only theatre in which naval action can appreciably shorten the war," he wrote. Nevertheless, he maintained that Fisher's plan had to be preceded by the capture of Borkum or the blocking of the Kiel Canal. The mass mining program was no substitute.[23] Therein lay the fine distinction between their outlooks. Both men were enthusiastic about the "Baltic scheme," but Churchill insisted on the need for a prior blow against the German navy by the capture of Borkum. Fisher thought that his plan could be implemented without an intermediate stage or a decisive engagement. Comparatively, then, Churchill was more cautious and more realistic.

It is almost universally agreed that the "Baltic scheme" was a risky plan, and that without the prior destruction of the German navy it stood almost no chance of success. Employing various means, the enemy could easily have cut off the British fleet in the Baltic from its home bases. Moreover, even had the German navy been first destroyed, it is highly doubtful whether the plan would have succeeded. The Baltic Sea was to be a German lake during World War II too, even though the Germans did not then possess a large surface fleet. In 1914 Fisher and Churchill had still not fully grasped that the landing of massive forces against opposition confronts logistic and operational difficulties that modern technological developments had further augmented. The Germans were operating on interior lines and enjoyed the benefits of a sophisticated railway network that enabled them to concentrate forces in greater strength and at greater speed than their adversaries. The Baltic coast lies close to the industrial complex around Berlin, while the British logistic base would have been some 1,000 kilometers to the rear. Manpower apart, there was little the Russians could have contributed. For these and other reasons, the "Baltic scheme" was sternly opposed both inside and outside the Navy.[24] Fisher's own behavior is something of an enigma. He refused to discuss his plan and work out its details with the Army or Navy staffs.[25] However, with the exception of events in France, until January 1915 Churchill's attentions were principally focused on the examination and promotion of naval operations against the northern coastline of Europe and Germany.

Churchill's involvement in the Antwerp affair reveals unchanging traits in his character and in his nature as a strategist and decision taker. When the Germans attacked Belgium, the Belgian army and government withdrew to Antwerp, and by September 28 the Germans had laid siege to this ancient fortress town. At the beginning of October, London learned that the Belgian government intended to evacuate Antwerp on October 3. Were Antwerp to fall, the principal Channel ports would have been threatened and communications between Britain and France endangered. In France itself the Germans had been halted at the Marne, and the campaign there had now reached the stage of "the race to the sea," with each side attempting to outflank the other from the north. The British position was particularly sensitive, since the Germans threatened to cut off the Expeditionary Force from the British Isles. Kitchener, Grey, and Churchill decided that every effort had to be made to encourage the Belgians to continue their resistance, so that the Germans might be held up and Field Marshal Sir John French would be able to reinforce the defense around the Channel ports. On October 3 Churchill (apparently at his own initiative, albeit with Kitchener's support[26]) crossed over to Antwerp to examine the situation and promote that objective. He was so enthusiastic about his new task that on October 5 he informed Asquith he was ready to resign his Admiralty post and accept a senior military appointment that would give him "full powers of a commander of a detached force in the field."[27] There were very few British forces in Antwerp. Churchill's proposition was scoffed at in the Cabinet and rejected by Asquith.[28] Kitchener, however, was ready to commission him with the rank of Lieutenant-General. In order to reinforce Antwerp, Churchill dispatched all of the Navy's ground units. A plan was worked out whereby Field Marshal French would advance toward Antwerp, attain command of the coastal strip, and link up with the port. This move failed, and on October 10 Antwerp fell with heavy losses.

The Antwerp episode generated anger against Churchill among the British public and within the Admiralty. Notwithstanding Kitchener's considerable share in the events leading up to the fiasco, principal responsibility was attributed to Churchill.[29] This was the last in a series of minor failures for which he was blamed, for the most part unjustly. In his defense, he claimed that by holding out for a few extra days Antwerp had delayed the German advance, and had enabled French to draw up his forces on lines easier to defend against the German attack toward Ypres and the Channel ports. Otherwise Dunkirk would have fallen.[30] Postwar research neither confirms nor contradicts Churchill's claim. However, his original objective had been for Antwerp to hold out until relieved by Allied forces. It is hard to imagine that he would have been prepared to relinquish the Admiralty for the sake of an assured failure—even if it had been able to delay somewhat the German advance.

Nevertheless, the basic strategic concept that had brought Churchill to Antwerp was sound. On the basis of his strategic assessment of future developments on the Continent, Churchill had as early as the Agadir crisis maintained the need to develop a northern threat to the flank of the German armies that would advance into France through southern Belgium. He had then emphasized the importance of Antwerp and its reinforcement by British troops.[31] When war broke out, he even suggested that Russian forces be transferred to Ostend for that purpose; early in September he had also suggested sending British forces to Antwerp (an idea Kitchener rejected at that stage).[32]

Churchill had not intended a real attack on the German flank (for which there were insufficient troops) but the use of limited forces to create a psychological threat and thereby undermine Germany's offensive plans. His support for the dispatch of the entire BEF to fight alongside the French army in France did not contradict his hope that a threat could also be created in the north. Rather, it constituted a miniature version of his strategic conception which attempted to integrate the "continental" and "maritime" schools. It is ironic that the German failure on the Marne was indeed in large part due to a loss of nerve; however, the threat from the north was minor and not buttressed by British intervention until *after* the Marne failure. By the time Churchill traveled to Antwerp, the Germans' offensive had been halted. They were now in a position to divert considerable forces to conquering the besieged city and dominating the coastal strip. They also now possessed ample time to do so. It follows that the original strategic logic behind the move, together with the chance to retain Antwerp, had effectively dissipated before Churchill reached the city. The move could now only win Field Marshal French breathing space for the organization of his lines and the defense of the Channel ports. Churchill's behavior, together with the supreme importance he attributed to Antwerp's defense and his optimism, indicates that he had failed to grasp the fundamental change in the city's strategic value after the turning point at the Marne. Sheer inertia led him to attempt the implementation of a plan whose expectations were now irrelevant. This symptom was to recur.

It was no momentary caprice that prompted the former lieutenant of Hussars to propose that he resign his post as First Lord of the Admiralty and receive an independent field commission, with two officers of the rank of

Major-General under him. By his own admission, Churchill considered that Antwerp offered a heaven-sent opportunity "to command great victorious armies in battle."[33] Like Napoleon, he wanted to transform Antwerp into his Toulon. So strong was this ambition that it dulled his senses; he was incapable of appreciating that—even had he received the command he sought—his chances of success were slim. This ambition for direct command exerted a profound influence on his functioning as First Lord and, subsequently, as Prime Minister. Deep involvement in the strategic, operational, and technical dimensions of the conduct of land and sea war vicariously quenched his thirst for field command. But the price was friction—sometimes severe—with his military advisors and even the loss of a balanced perspective between the military and political planes. This, too, was to be a recurring trait.

Churchill's attention was drawn to Turkey at the very outbreak of the war, when the German battle cruiser *Goeben* and its escort, the light cruiser *Breslau*, managed to slip away from the British ships shadowing them and reach Constantinople. Their incorporation into Turkey's navy profoundly affected the latter's entry into the war two-and-a-half months later. Churchill was outraged by the heavy sense of failure and by the public outcry against the Admiralty's handling of the incident. In mid-August he suggested that a flotilla of torpedo boats be sent through the Dardanelles in order to sink the *Goeben*; but Kitchener, Grey, and Asquith opposed any move that might have precipitated Turkey's entry into the war on Germany's side and endanger Britain's control over the Muslim portions of the Empire.[34] Churchill's rage cooled, and he ordered the local naval commander to avoid all hostile moves against Turkey.[35]

At the end of August, while still engrossed in his plans for operations in the Baltic and on the coast of northern Europe, Churchill received a dispatch from the British naval attaché in Constantinople, Admiral Limpus, who was considered an authority on Turkey and had intimate knowledge of the Dardanelles. Limpus remarked on the fluid political situation at Constantinople and the economic difficulties there. He also reported that foreign diplomats in the city were of the opinion that Turkey would lose its independence were it to join the war on one side or the other. Limpus himself hoped that Turkey would remain neutral; but he nevertheless reviewed Britain's possible military options against it should that not be the case. He suggested that the Greeks attack the land strip between Smyrna and the Dardanelles and seize the fortifications in the southern section of the Straits; Britain would send torpedo boats through the Dardanelles to the Sea of Marmora with the object of isolating the Gallipoli garrison from Constantinople and, ultimately, of cutting communications between Constantinople and the south. He also advocated inciting rebellions throughout the Ottoman Empire. If these operations could be "methodically undertaken and persistently carried out, [they] would succeed, and would annihilate the remaining power of Turkey."[36] On the very next day, however, Major Cunliffe-Owen (the British military attaché to Turkey) maintained that naval action alone would not force the Dardanelles. Land forces would also have to be employed to command the Straits and ensure lasting results.³⁷

At about the same time, Churchill raised the idea of forming a Balkan federation against Germany, based on Rumania, Bulgaria, Greece, and Serbia. He was aware of the disputes and age-old hatreds between the peoples of these states, but thought that they might be enticed and united by slices of Austria-Hungary. Responding to this proposal, Grey said that words alone would not influence the Balkan states to take action.³⁸ At the end of August, the Greeks made the British an offer of military assistance against Turkey. This impelled Churchill, with Kitchener's agreement, to ask the Army General Staff to examine the possibility that the Greek army might conquer the Gallipoli peninsula; with its help, a British naval force could enter the Sea of Marmora by way of the Dardanelles.³⁹ (There existed no common land frontier between Turkey and Greece. Bulgaria, which lay between them, was still neutral.) Major-General Callwell, Director of Military Operations, replied to Churchill that an amphibious assault on the Gallipoli peninsula would be very difficult. He pointed out that this subject had been examined in 1906 by the Committee of Imperial Defence and the General Staff. It had been concluded that an assault of that nature was not possible. Since that time, the defensive system on the Gallipoli peninsula had been strengthened and its garrison reinforced. Callwell did not retract that opinion when Churchill and other officers in the Admirality tried to question it.⁴⁰

Unwilling to add Turkey to their enemies, the Russians were at this stage in any case opposed to Anglo-Greek operations against the Turks. For the same reason, and because of the situation in France, Grey doubted the utility of action in the Mediterranean area prior to a turn of the tide in the west.⁴¹ In response, Churchill told Grey that—if employed in conjunction with sea power—50,000 men would suffice to remove the Turkish threat, and to that end he suggested transferring Russian forces from Vladivostok.⁴² However, the Greek proposal was not serious, and the subject of an attack on the Dardanelles, was shelved. During the following month-and-a-half Churchill turned his attention to events in France, to naval conflicts, to awaiting the decisive sea engagement, to the defense of Antwerp, and to the various plans for operations on the northern coast of Europe.

On October 31, after the *Goeben's* bombardment of Odessa, the British ultimatum to Turkey expired; an Anglo-French declaration of war followed on November 5. Characteristically, Churchill made haste. As early as November 1, he had ordered Vice-Admiral Carden, the commander of the naval force in the eastern Mediterranean, to bombard the forts at the entrance to the Dardanelles, an operation carried out on November 3.⁴³ Retrospectively, the bombardment was widely considered to have been a serious error; it stimulated the Turks to improve the defense of the Straits.⁴⁴ In both his evidence to the Royal Commission that investigated the Dardanelles campaign (the Commission of Inquiry into the Operations at the Dardanelles; hereafter, the Dardanelles Commission) and in *The World Crisis*, Churchill claimed that the bombardment had been intended to obtain technical information about the coastal batteries of the Dardanelles. But the Admiralty in fact already possessed detailed intelligence, thanks principally to the industry of Admiral Limpus. Moreover, Limpus and Admiral Slade had already warned that an action of that sort would be useless.[45] It seems that Churchill's principal purpose—if such it can be called—was to satisfy his wish for immediate retaliation against Turkey. "It is a good thing to give a prompt blow," he wrote to Fisher.[46] Had he at this stage seriously considered a large-scale operation against the Dardanelles, he would have given the bombardment further thought.

Only at the end of November did Churchill again raise the idea of forcing the Dardanelles. When discussion turned to the defense of Egypt at the very first meeting of the War Council, he declared "that the ideal method of defending Egypt was by an attack on the Gallipoli Peninsula. This, if successful, would give us control of the Dardanelles, and we could dictate terms at Constantinople." But he acknowledged that such an operation would require extensive troops, which, as Kitchener made plain at this and other forums, were not currently available. Churchill's tone was that of a man who raises an idea he knows cannot be carried out. Fisher showed interest in the possibility of a Greek attack on the Gallipoli peninsula. Grey replied that the chances were slim; Greece and Rumania would not work with Britain and France until assured that Bulgaria would remain neutral.[47]

At the War Council's next meeting, held six days later, Churchill raised his plan to seize Borkum. Fisher, although unenthusiastic, supported Churchill because of the importance he attached to implementing an offensive strategy. Kitchener poured cold water on the idea, remarking that he did not have the required troops. He claimed that the Borkum plan would necessitate the diversion of forces from France, a move made impossible by the need to pin down as many German troops as possible in the west to relieve pressure on the Russians.[48] On December 5 Balfour was under the impression that Churchill was enthusiastic about the conquest of the islands of Borkum and Sylt; but on the same day Asquith considered him to be enthused by the idea of an attack on the Dardanelles.[49] Churchill wanted an offensive operation against either the northern or the southern coast of Europe; and at this juncture clearly preferred the former. On December 2, he wrote a detailed memorandum on the method of attacking Borkum[50] and—it will be recalled—at the end of the month wrote to Fisher that the Baltic was the only theater in which the war might be shortened.

During December, by which time the stalemate in the west and the new character of the war had become apparent, strategic alternatives began to be studied in London. The question was where, and in what quantities, to send some of the new armies that Kitchener would have raised by the spring of 1915. Fisher, as we have seen, advocated the "Baltic scheme"; but Hankey and Lloyd George had southeastern Europe in mind. Hankey, the Secretary to the War Council, composed a highly influential memorandum at the end of December. This analyzed the nature of the stalemate in the west and the technical means whereby it might be broken, and then suggested an alternative method based on British sea power. Hankey claimed that when in the past Britain had been incapable of acting directly against a continental foe, it had operated against its overseas possessions and territories. The intention had been to use these assets at the peace table, as counterweights to the enemy's continental victories. Hankey maintained that Britain had to strike at Turkey, Germany's ally, and at Germany's colonies. A demonstration of Anglo-French readiness to send forces to the Balkans, he claimed, would help assuage the doubts of the states of that region and resolve their conflicts of interest. He suggested devoting three corps to a campaign against Turkey and pointed out the enormous benefits that would accrue to the Allies once the Dardanelles and Constantinople had fallen: the restoration of communications with Russia and a drop in the price of grain. However, the memorandum was vague about the nature and objectives of the military moves. Precisely where the Anglo-French expeditionary force was meant to operate was not specified.

Hankey's plan was clearly inspired by the "maritime school's" interpretation of past British strategy. His objective was to acquire assets that could be used as bargaining counters during peace talks. He assumed that the Germans would agree to negotiations once they had been worn down by the blockade, even though he appreciated that the process was likely to be protracted.[51] It did not occur to him that Germany would not rush to trade the rich industrial regions of Belgium and northeastern France for its worthless colonies and the restoration of its influence in Turkey and the Balkans. Even less did he foresee that opposition to negotiations with Germany would emanate from within Britain and his own government.

Three days later Lloyd George presented the War Council with a memorandum of his own. Like Hankey, he considered it unlikely that the German lines in the west could be pierced. Now that Germany was in command of rich areas of Europe, he also questioned the utility of economic pressure. He further maintained that the plans to attack in the Baltic and along Germany's northern coast were hazardous. He proposed two operations whose objective was the defeat of Germany "by the process of knocking out the props under her": one against Austria-Hungary, the other against Turkey. His own preference was for the dispatch of a large portion of Kitchener's new army, some 600,000 men, to Salonika or the Dalmatian coast. Once they had been shown that Britain and France were prepared to send so large a force and to open a front in southeastern Europe, the Serbs, Rumanians, and Greeks—despite everything—would cooperate with the move. Either Austria-Hungary would succumb to the combined pressure from Russia and the Balkans, or the Germans would have to send considerable forces to its defense. In the latter case, the Germans would have to thin out their lines elsewhere, thus enabling the Allies to exploit their own numerical superiority on other fronts. Lloyd George's second proposed operation, to be launched together with the Balkan campaign, was an amphibious assault on the Syrian coast. This would cut Turkey's supply lines to Egypt and thereby avert a threat to that region. It would also deal a mortal blow to Turkey's imperial possessions.[52] Although Lloyd George and Hankey had never previously discussed their plans, their ideas were remarkably similar.[53]

Lloyd George's memorandum contained most of the basic arguments put forward by the "eastern school," whose general lines of disagreement with the "western school" had by the end of 1914 already become apparent. At this stage, Churchill was far from being an "easterner." He accepted Hankey's and Lloyd George's prediction that the west would be deadlocked; but he still hoped to break the stalemate by operations in the northern European theater. At the end of December, and concurrently with the memoranda tabled by Hankey and Lloyd George, Churchill presented Asquith and the War Council with his plan to conquer Borkum as a first step to command of the Baltic and the landing of troops in Pomerania.[54] However, on the very same day, he informed Asquith that he had spoken to Hankey, with whose plan he "substantially" concurred. He added, "I wanted Gallipoli attacked on the Turkish declaration of war."[55] This was a surprising statement, considering that the subject of Gallipoli had not hitherto concerned him very much and that Hankey's memorandum does not refer to a direct assault on the peninsula. In his memoirs, Hankey claimed that he had thought that the Dardanelles would be opened only after Turkey had been defeated by a combined attack of the Balkan states and the Entente forces sent to the region.[56]

On January 1, while these matters were still under discussion, Grand Duke Nicholas asked for British help. The Turks had attacked in the Caucasus and his German front was under severe pressure. His request was for a diversionary operation to draw Turkish forces away from the Caucasus.[57] On the following day, Kitchener informed Churchill that no troops were available; perhaps a demonstration by a naval operation at the Dardanelles might impede the transfer of Turkish troops to the Caucasus from the west.[58] On January 3, Fisher presented Churchill with a plan that in effect constituted an adaptation of what Fisher termed "Hankey's plan" for a combined assault on Turkey. The Greeks would attack the Gallipoli peninsula; old British battleships would force the Dardanelles; the Bulgarians would launch an offensive against Constantinople, and the Serbs, Rumanians, and Russians would go against Austria-Hungary; and 75,000 British soldiers, some of whom would be drawn from French's command in France, would land at Besika Bay on Turkey's Asiatic shore near the entrance to the Dardanelles.[59] This was sheer fantasy. At the current stage of the war, neither Bulgaria nor Greece was prepared for military cooperation with the Entente powers. The Greeks would not have let their archenemies conquer Constantinople; French would not have agreed to the transfer of forces from France to the East. Thus matters had effectively reached an impasse. Without an impressive Anglo-French success against the Turks, the Balkan states would not have moved toward alignment with the Entente; on the other hand, it was their assistance the Entente powers needed—especially on land—if they were to ensure their own success against Turkey.

It was in order to break that impasse that Churchill seized on Fisher's plan to force the Dardanelles with old and surplus battleships. True, Fisher had specified the need for the military conquest of the Gallipoli peninsula concurrently with the attempt to force a naval passage; but since troops were not available, Churchill hoped that the operation might be accomplished by warships alone. With Fisher's assent, he sent a telegram to Vice-Admiral Carden, whose squadron lay off the Straits, asking him to examine the possibility of forcing the Dardanelles with ships only. "Importance of results would justify severe loss," he added.[60] Nevertheless, at this juncture it was Fisher who was most enthusiastic about the idea of an attack on Turkey. Churchill still stood by his Borkum plan. "Germany is the foe, and it is bad war to seek cheaper victories and easier antagonists," he wrote to Fisher on the following day.[61]

Carden's response imparted impetus to the idea. It would be impossible to force the Dardanelles at one blow, he replied; but a slow and gradual thrust with numerous vessels might succeed.[62] The next day, Churchill informed Carden that "high authorities" agreed with his assessment and requested a detailed plan.[63] Fisher was not one of those "high authorities." Churchill later claimed that he had received the verbal assent of Vice-Admiral Oliver, Chief of the Admiralty War Staff, and of Admiral Jackson, an expert on naval gunnery.[64] But the latter's memorandum—written on the same day, although not read by Churchill until after his reply to Carden had been dispatched—took no definite stand one way or the other. Instead, it drew attention to the several hazards. Like Carden, Jackson maintained that success would only be gained by a slow and methodical penetration; he also pointed out that, once the naval force had entered the Sea of Marmora, it would confront the difficulties caused by its expected losses, ammunition shortages and the absence of a secure line of supply.[65] The first strains in the relationship between Churchill and his naval advisers were becoming apparent.

However, even at this stage Churchill was far from being committed to the Dardanelles plan. On January 7 the War Council held another in its series of frequent discussions on the forthcoming strategic moves. Lloyd George maintained that the new armies being raised in Britain had to be sent elsewhere than France. Initially, Churchill tried to win adherents for the Zeebrugge plan, whose objective was the occupation of the Belgian coast by French's army combined with an amphibious assault. That plan was dismissed by Kitchener on the grounds that it was not presently possible. Churchill—who was himself not particularly enthusiastic about Zeebrugge—immediately raised his beloved plan to seize Borkum, which he described at some length. This the War Council did approve in principle, but its implementation was made conditional on a detailed examination of its feasibility.[66]

Therein lay the problem. As formulated during the course of January, expert Admiralty opinion on the Borkum plan was severely critical.[67] Its disappearance from the agenda was one of the circumstances that paved the way to the Dardanelles. On the next day, January 8, the War Council again convened.

Lloyd George pressed for the adoption of his Balkan strategy; but Kitchener ruled out Lloyd George's plans to land at Ragusa (Dubrovnik) on the Adriatic coast, or at Salonika. It would be impossible to do so until Greece had joined the Allies. More to the point, the deployment of a large body of troops in the Balkans presented logistic problems: the roads were few and in poor condition; only one railway track connected Salonika and Serbia, and that was vulnerable to sabotage and capable of supplying, at the most, 200,000 men. Similarly, Kitchener dismissed the plans for assaults on Germany's northern coast. He concluded by saying that the Dardanelles seemed to him to be the most suitable objective for combined attack by land and sea forces. Should it succeed, the assault would renew the link with Russia. It would "settle the Near Eastern question," and draw Greece—and perhaps Bulgaria and Rumania—to the side of the Entente. Hankey added that it would also enable use of the Danube as an artery of communications and supply for an advance into Austria-Hungary. Kitchener also raised the possibility of attacking Turkey on the Syrian coast at Alexandretta. Nevertheless, his basic strategic position was that absolute priority be given to the west. He wanted to send most of the forces to France, and pointed out that some of the operations mentioned above could be carried out only after a German offensive in the west would be repelled.

Churchill did not refer to the Dardanelles plan at all. On the contrary, he still tried to push his plans for the northern periphery. He suggested that Holland be pressured and induced to enter the war; that a naval base be established on the Dutch coast; and then to attack Germany in the direction of Essen. The advantages to be gained by that move, if accomplished, would exceed any to be obtained in the Mediterranean. Grey explained that the principal obstacle lay in Holland's fear that its entry into the war would precipitate its conquest by Germany. The Dutch would do nothing until they sensed that the Allies could defend them against a German invasion. That was the dominant fear of all the small neutral countries of the Balkans and of northern Europe who were sitting on the fence. Although fully aware of that truth, Churchill tended to ignore it during both world wars. The War Council adjourned with the views of Kitchener and French, the "westerners," firmly in the ascendant.[68]

After this debate Churchill still continued to prefer the northern flank. He made it clear that he would not be prepared to examine possible options on Europe's southern flank until finally convinced that the Borkum and Baltic plans could not be carried out.[69]

January 11 saw the arrival of Carden's detailed plan to force the Dardanelles by naval action alone. Subsequently, this was to be severely criticized for being too general in nature.[70] At this stage, however, its deficiencies were not great enough to prevent Fisher from proposing that the *Queen Elizabeth*, the most powerful battleship in the world, be sent to the Dardanelles, where it might complete its gunnery practice against the coastal forts before joining the Grand Fleet.[71] It was now that Churchill renewed his interest in an attack on Turkey and that matters began to move apace. When he raised

Carden's plan for discussion at the Admiralty's War Staff, he was apparently supported (albeit in a lukewarm fashion) by the naval experts.[72] Fisher was optimistic. Admittedly, on the same day of the War Staff meeting, Fisher did say that Constantinople could be reached swiftly and easily were the Greeks to make a land attack on the Gallipoli peninsula *concurrently* (author's emphasis) with the British naval assault on the Dardanelles.[73] But there are solid grounds for maintaining that, at this juncture, Fisher did not rule out the possibility that naval force alone might succeed. For Churchill, that was enough. On January 13, after an extended discussion in the War Council about possible operations on the western front, Churchill put forward the idea of a naval action to force the Dardanelles. In his own words:

> The Admiralty were studying the question, and believed that a plan could be made for systematically reducing all the forts within a few weeks. Once the forts were reduced the minefields could be cleared, and the Fleet would proceed up to Constantinople and destroy the "Goeben."

The response of the civilian members of the War Council was highly favorable. Fisher and Wilson said nothing. Kitchener, who (as we have seen) had previously shown considerable interest in the plan to attack the Dardanelles but had rejected its implementation for lack of troops, now found that Churchill was proposing a solution that required no ground forces. Accordingly, he considered the attack worth a try, adding that "we could leave off the bombardment if it did not prove effective." Similar claims, to the effect that the attempt to force the Dardanelles could always be halted, had previously enabled Churchill to obtain the Admiralty officers' reserved support.

All members of the War Council, French included, basically agreed that complete success in the west was not feasible; could the stalemate itself not be broken, alternative theaters of operations had to be sought. The Council decided that, were the western front still deadlocked in the spring of 1915, British forces would be dispatched elsewhere. Furthermore, "the Admiralty should also prepare for a naval expedition in February to bombard and take the Gallipoli peninsula, with Constantinople as its objective."[74]

This discussion raises several questions. Churchill did not explain how the Gallipoli peninsula was to be "taken" without the use of land forces, what the ships would do off Constantinople once the *Goeben* had been sunk, nor what the ultimate objectives were. He did not inform the War Council of the basic problem pointed out to him by Admiral Jackson: namely, the question of ensuring the fleet's supply lines once it had entered the Sea of Marmora. Unless troops took possession of both shores of the Straits, the fleet in the Marmora would soon have to reverse its course because of lack of ammunition. None of the members of the War Council either questioned or examined Churchill. True, at their previous meeting, Kitchener had already outlined the general aims of an operation in the Gallipoli region: to renew the link with Russia, to force Turkey out of the war, and to enlist the Balkan states. But he had then been referring to a combined operation. No one asked how the same objectives might now be attained by naval action alone. The development of the plan, and of the attendant queries and doubts, followed the decision on its implementation rather than the other way around.

It is at this juncture that certain interim conclusions can be drawn. In the draft of *The World Crisis* Churchill wrote:

> Up till the end of the year my mind turned on the whole to intervening on the Northern rather than on the Southern flank . . . even while the Dardanelles was on I always regarded it as long as I was in power only as an interim operation, and all the plans for the Borkum-Baltic project were going forward.[75]

Churchill deleted this passage from the final version of his book, where he underplayed the importance he had attached to projects on the northern periphery and projected the Dardanelles plan as the center of his strategic thinking during the war. That is one reason why historians have claimed that "from the first month of the war...Churchill had his eye on the Dardanelles."[76] Our own survey hitherto suggests, however, that the Dardanelles plan was only one of several Churchill had been considering since the outbreak of war; moreover, he regarded it as secondary to the "Borkum-Baltic" scheme. Neither was the Dardanelles idea itself the original product of Churchill's own mind. Rather, it was a patchwork, consisting of elements of ideas and plans that had been previously examined and that several persons had proposed ever since the beginning of the war. It was not because of the stalemate in the west that Churchill advocated his projects for operations on the northern and southern flanks of Europe; he had from the outset considered them complementary to the campaign on the western front. The contribution of the stalemate was that it enabled him to obtain the assent of his colleagues in London to actions on the European periphery. Churchill did not adopt the Dardanelles project until made to realize that no land forces could be spared for action on either the northern coast or in southern Europe, that there was to be no decisive naval engagement, and that neither the Admiralty nor the War Council would support operations in the north. Only then did he seize upon a plan that could be rapidly carried out and for which widespread support could be obtained with comparative ease. Ever impatient, he sought to send the Navy into offensive action as soon as possible. As far as he was concerned, the Dardanelles plan constituted the best available rather than the best possible. However, once the opportunity had presented itself and the basic decision had been taken, he obstinantly clung to the plan.

Referring in *The World Crisis* to the origins, development, and validity of the idea to force a naval passage through the Dardanelles, Churchill wrote:

> It will be seen that the genesis of this plan and its elaboration were purely naval and professional in their character. It was Admiral Carden and his staff gunnery officers who proposed the gradual method of piecemeal reduction by long-range bombardment. It was Sir H. Jackson and the Admiralty staff who embraced this

idea and studied and approved its details . . . I did not and I could not make the plan. But when it had been made by the naval authorities, and fashioned and endorsed by high technical authorities and approved by the First Sea Lord, I seized upon it and set it on the path of action, and thereafter espoused it with all my resources. When others weakened or changed their opinion without adducing new reasons, I held them strongly to their previous decisions.[77]

That passage can be regarded as a summary of Churchill's defense; it mixes truths with falsehoods. Far from being accurate is his depiction of the plan as one the Admiralty alone spontaneously forged and developed. Churchill's romantic imagination had harbored a similar idea while he was still a young cavalry officer in India, where he had written *Savrola*, a novel whose protagonist he cast in the image of his own character and ambitions. Subsequently, Churchill himself portrayed the novel's tone: "We had plenty of fighting and politics, interspersed with such philosophizings as I was capable of, all leading up to the grand finale of an ironclad fleet forcing a sort of Dardanelles to quell the rebellious capital."[78]

It is difficult to assess the degree to which Churchill's mind was working subconsciously when in real life he proposed a similar possibility. Certainly, the idea of sending battleships into the very heart of the enemy's lines remained in the back of his mind. In 1911 he had ruled that "it should be remembered that it is no longer possible to force the Dardanelles, and nobody would expose a fleet to such peril."[79] However, an entry in Captain Richmond's diary of October 1914 reveals that Churchill wanted to send old battleships up the Elbe River ("but for what purpose except to be sunk I did not understand").[80] The following January, when Fisher proposed that old British battleships should force the Dardanelles in *combination* with an attack by Greek forces on the Gallipoli peninsula, Churchill pounced on the first part of the plan. (This did not contradict the view he had held in 1911; he had then been referring to ships of the line, whereas the present plan was based on the use of old battleships, some of which were in any case destined to be scrapped.)

It is highly doubtful whether Fisher and his Admiralty colleagues, especially Carden, would have initiated the idea of forcing the Dardanelles by naval action alone. Fisher had made a close study of the subject when a senior officer in the Mediterranean, and had reached the conclusion that it would be impossible to force the Straits. Had Churchill not turned to Carden, the idea would probably never have gotten off the ground and reached the stages of planning and execution. Thus Churchill's claim that the genesis of the plan lay in the professional circles of the Admiralty is inaccurate. Some historians have suggested that Churchill worded his inquiry to Carden in a way designed to elicit a favorable response;[81] but the importance of this point must not be exaggerated. Whatever the phrasing, Carden could have responded in the light of his own intentions and assessments. It was Carden's idea to launch a slow and methodical assault (one which surprised Fisher), and there the Admiralty's professional contribution to the plan commenced. Nevertheless, Churchill exaggerates when saying that the Admiralty staff "embraced" and "endorsed" the plan, terms that convey a sense of enthusiasm. The Dardanelles Commission repeatedly investigated the attitudes of Churchill's naval advisers. So too, subsequently, have historians. Almost all agree that their predisposition was ambivalent. From the start, Sir Henry Jackson and Sir Arthur Wilson doubted the practicability of the plan. Oliver, the Chief of the Admiralty War Staff, did consider Carden's plan feasible, and was a consistent supporter. Uncertainty surrounds the attitude of Fisher, the most important figure, without whose assent no operational orders could have been issued. Fisher believed only in a combined operation; but between January 11 and 13 apparently became convinced that naval action could succeed by itself. Had that not been the case, he would not have ordered the dispatch of the *Queen Elizabeth*.

Common to all of Churchill's advisers was their reluctance to come out definitely for or against Carden's plan. In general, they assumed that a retreat could be effected the moment advance proved impossible. [82] That sufficed for the First Lord to present the project to the War Council as the Admiralty's plan.

■

With that background in mind we can return to the march of events. Once the decision to implement the Gallipoli plan had been taken on January 13, Asquith became enthusiastic;[83] but Fisher began to lose faith in it. His opposition was based on two claims, which he repeated throughout the episode. One was his fear that British power in the North Sea would be weakened by the transfer of naval forces to the Mediterranean. The second was that, at Gallipoli itself, large land forces had to be employed as well as the Navy.[84] On January 25, Fisher presented Churchill with a memorandum in which he made explicit his opposition to an assault at the Dardanelles, emphasizing the problem of British superiority in the North Sea.[85] Churchill's immediate reply dismissed this charge; in fact, the British advantage had increased since the beginning of the war. Churchill refused to distribute Fisher's memorandum to the members of the War Council, although he did agree to pass it on to Prime Minister Asquith.[86] In reply, Fisher stressed that he had no objections to actions at Zeebrugge or the Dardanelles provided that use at the same time be made of massive ground forces, which would ensure that the gains would be permanent.[87] Because of this disagreement, Fisher refused to attend the War Council on January 28, although he did succumb to Churchill's pressure that they both meet with Asquith before the meeting. After that discussion, Asquith felt that he had managed to persuade Fisher to withdraw his opposition to the assault on the Dardanelles.[88] Reluctantly, Fisher attended what was to be an extremely important meeting of the War Council, and one that accurately reflected the play of forces at work behind this strategic move.

As soon as the meeting began, Churchill raised the subject of the Dardanelles and in effect asked for the plan to be endorsed once again. He pointed out that preparations were nearing completion and that the attack could begin in February. Fisher objected, saying that he had understood that the topic would not be brought up in that day's meeting and that "the Prime Minister was well aware of his own views in regard to it." Asquith responded that in view of the steps already taken, the subject could not be postponed. Fisher stood up and threatened to leave the meeting; he was not persuaded to return to his place until after a short conversation with Kitchener, who had immediately risen from his own chair. During the discussion that followed this incident all of the participants expressed their support for the plan, of which they had high hopes. In the words of Kitchener, the dominant personality, the naval assault was "vitally important"; were it to succeed, the plan would produce gains equivalent to those of a great and victorious campaign. Its advantage, he added, was that the attempted attack could always be halted should progress prove impossible. (Subsequently, Kitchener was to be one of the first to forget that advantage.) Balfour and Grey, the civilian members of the council, were lavish in their enthusiasm for the benefits the success of the plan might bring. Once Churchill had received renewed backing to go ahead with the plan, he summarized the first meeting of the day by saying that it was still "the ultimate object of the Navy...to obtain access to the Baltic."[89]

The War Council devoted its second meeting of January 28 to a discussion of its earlier decision to send British forces to other theaters should the spring bring stalemate in the west. With Kitchener's concurrence (at least in principle), the General Staff proposed that in that case troops should be sent to the Balkans. Hovering over the debate was the shadow of an expected attack on Serbia in the spring. Lloyd George pressed for forces to be sent to the Balkans and to Serbia at once. Kitchener expressed his basic agreement with the idea, but ruled that no forces could presently be sent to the Balkans: for one thing, none were available; for another, he expected a German offensive in the west within the month. He did add, however, that half a million soldiers could ultimately be sent to Serbia.[90] No decision was taken on the subject. But it is a fair assumption that Kitchener, together with the General Staff and the politicians, was clearly inclined to send a large army to some part of the Balkans as soon as the position in France had been clarified and once the troops in Britain had completed their training in the spring. However, it did not occur to either Churchill or any one else to suggest that the naval assault on the Dardanelles be deferred until some of those forces could be used in conjunction with the fleet.

That evening, Fisher and Churchill met in private. The First Sea Lord was again persuaded to attack the Dardanelles, provided that he retained the right to halt the operation. Thereafter, the War Council authorized the Admiralty to proceed as planned.

In *The World Crisis*, Churchill did not conceal "the great and continuous pressure which I put upon the old Admiral."[91] The draft of the book (in a passage omitted from the final version) admits that to have been his "greatest mistake": although Fisher did give his consent to the naval operation, his lack of enthusiasm had an adverse effect on the spirit and persistence with which it was carried out.[92] Against Churchill it has been claimed that he deliberately concealed from the War Council the opinions of his naval advisers. But it is difficult to understand how he could have done so, even if that had been his deliberate intention. Fisher sent his memorandum straight to Asquith, and had written it with the assistance of Hankey himself. Churchill did attempt to ensure that his disagreements with Fisher would not be decided by the War Council, but he did not conceal their existence. Unwilling to have the issue settled by a number of Ministers for whose strategic wisdom he had no respect, he referred it to Asquith.

Because he did not think it appropriate to disagree with his own Minister in front of others, Fisher himself chose to remain silent. Nevertheless, most members of the War Council were aware of his views.[93] That being so, it is surprising that none bothered to ask Fisher to lay out his reservations, especially since—even at this early stage of the war—Churchill was already being accused of several failures and of unnecessary interference in the operational aspects of the Admiralty's work. To judge by the correspondence and diaries of British politicians, current estimates of his abilities were mixed. Although regarded as a brilliant and multitalented personality, he was also considered to be a man who possessed an unrestrained ambition for power, who was unbalanced and adventurous, and whose sense of judgment was flawed. The explanation is likely to be simple. Most of the senior politicians on the War Council were themselves attracted to the plan. It promised substantial gains at little cost. Many were in any case in favor of action in the Balkans.[94] Churchill exercised his not inconsiderable powers of persuasion on persons who were ready to be persuaded.

With the exception of Kitchener (a former senior Army officer), the war was at this stage firmly under civilian direction: the few military members of the War Council hardly opened their mouths; Kitchener neutralized the General Staff, and concentrated most power in his own hands; Churchill was decidedly in charge at the Admiralty; it was with Kitchener that Ministers discussed strategic ideas. The civilian branch of government did not have the benefit of adequate military intelligence and assessments, and made no particular effort to obtain them. To complicate matters even further, Kitchener was enigmatic and kept his thoughts to himself. He pronounced positions that he rarely substantiated. Thus, even by the standards of a democracy, an unnatural imbalance was created between statesmen and soldiers.[95] Depending on one's viewpoint, Churchill can be said to have benefited from this situation or to have been its victim.

No one began to have second thoughts until after the decision to implement the naval assault had already been taken. During the month of February the subject of discussion was the dispatch of ground forces to operate in conjunction with the fleet. On February 10 Hankey wrote to Balfour that—Churchill apart—the entire Admiralty considered that without land forces a naval attack could not succeed.[96] Sir Henry Jackson maintained that an assault by naval bombardment alone would not be "a sound military operation" unless complemented by an army that could ensure the fleet's supply route.⁹⁷ Asquith was also convinced of the need for land forces. On February 16 the War Council again convened for a meeting whose discussion was not recorded. It was decided that the Twenty-Ninth Division, the only regular division Kitchener had left, and one considered to be excellent, would be sent to the Island of Lemnos (close to the Dardanelles) in order to cooperate with the fleet.⁹⁸ Since the naval attack was to commence on February 18, the division could not arrive in time (in fact the attack was launched on February 19). But Kitchener assured Churchill: "You get through! I will find the men."⁹⁹ It was still assumed that troops would consolidate and garrison positions on the peninsula after the straits had been forced by the fleet. Once again, nobody thought to postpone the naval action. Churchill, however, did begin to press strongly for the dispatch of additional forces to the region. He maintained that a force of at least about 50,000 men had to be held in local readiness (at Lemnos or in Egypt). Its purpose would be to reap the fruits of the naval breakthrough and "either to seize the Gallipoli peninsula when it has been evacuated, or to occupy C'nople if a revolution takes place."¹⁰⁰

At the War Council meeting of February 19, Kitchener announced that, because of the recent Russian defeat in eastern Prussia and his fears of an expected German attack in the west, he had decided to postpone the dispatch of the Twenty-Ninth Division to the Near East. For the purpose of the Dardanelles attack, however, he was meanwhile prepared to send to Lemnos the New Zealand and Australian (ANZAC) troops presently stationed in Egypt, a total of some 39,000 men. Churchill protested, claiming that a local force of 50,000 was the minimum required to ensure the success of the enterprise. "We should never forgive ourselves," he warned, "if this promising operation failed owing to insufficient military support at the critical moment." His new tone differed from the one he had adopted when advocating an exclusively naval operation, and his position is unclear. In effect, 50,000 men were already situated in the region: 40,000 ANZAC troops and 10,000 men of the Naval Division. Churchill maintained that these forces did not meet the required standards: the ANZAC troops had not yet completed their training and needed to be stiffened by a force of the very highest quality, such as the Twenty-Ninth Division. What he did not explain was why they had to be stiffened. As put to Kitchener, his earlier claim was that these troops would be used to take Gallipoli and Constantinople *after* the peninsula had been evacuated and *after* the outbreak of revolt in Constantinople. In other words, they would not be required to undertake any real fighting. The Twenty-Ninth Division remained in Britain, and it was decided to send two ANZAC divisions from Egypt to Lemnos.¹⁰¹

A few days later, Lloyd George wrote a memorandum pinning great hopes on the operation at the Dardanelles but emphasizing that, should it fail, the result would be catastrophe in the Balkans. To avert that danger, considerable forces had to be prepared for dispatch to the region, as well as to Greece and

Serbia. Fisher agreed.[102] The following day, Churchill distributed a memorandum of his own that doubled to 100,000 the size of the force required for action against Constantinople and the Turkish army in Thrace *after* (my emphasis) the Dardanelles had been forced by the fleet.[103]

Together with the subject of the Twenty-Ninth Division, dispatch of forces to the Near East was again raised at the War Council on February 24. Kitchener found it hard to understand Churchill's present desire for 100,000 men in the region. In his opinion, the Turkish garrison on Gallipoli would be afraid of being cut off and therefore withdraw as soon as the Navy had forced the Dardanelles. So would the Sultan, the Constantinople garrison, and the Turkish army in Thrace, which, to avert being stranded on the other side of the Bosphorus, would cross into Asiatic Turkey. Together with Lloyd George, Kitchener asked Churchill whether he wanted a ground attack on Gallipoli if the fleet failed to break through. Churchill replied that the force was meant to operate off Constantinople or, in order to support British diplomacy in the area, in conjunction with the Balkan states. He explained that he had no intention of employing the forces on Gallipoli. "He could, however, conceive a case where the Navy had almost succeeded, but where a military force would just make the difference between failure and success." Kitchener remained unconvinced. If really necessary, he was prepared to dispatch the Twenty-Ninth Division; but added that if it became apparent that the Navy could not break through by itself, the Army would have to come to his aid since "the effect of a defeat in the Orient would be very serious." Moreover, withdrawal was impossible; Britain was committed by the wide publicity given to the attack on the Dardanelles, which had begun on February 19. Grey buttressed that argument by saying that "failure would be morally equivalent to a great defeat on land."[104]

Kitchener had forgotten one of the principal factors that had led him to endorse the naval attack on the Dardanelles: the possibility of an uncomplicated withdrawal. By determining that Britain could not afford a defeat in the Orient (an opinion no one questioned) Lloyd George, Kitchener, and Grey had precluded a new examination of the strategic situation when the naval breakthrough failed. They had thus sown the seeds of the great campaign on Gallipoli.

Debate continued at the War Council meeting of February 26. Churchill described Carden's progress; on learning that an army was to be sent to the region, he remarked, the Admiral had requested permission to land forces on the tip of the Gallipoli peninsula (which meant that Carden had begun to lose his confidence in the ability to force the Dardanelles by ships alone). The Admiralty (i.e., Churchill) had replied that the plan was based entirely on a naval breakthrough and that an army was being sent only in order to reap the fruits of success. He again asked Kitchener to send the Twenty-Ninth Division immediately, saying that the objective of the large-scale forces he requested was "to occupy Constantinople and to compel a surrender of all Turkish forces remaining in Europe after the fleet had obtained command of the Sea of

Marmora."[105] (In a letter written to Asquith, Lloyd George, and Balfour on the previous day, Churchill had argued otherwise: a force of 115,000 men could be amassed by March 21, which, should the naval attack have by then failed, would assault the Gallipoli peninsula; should the breakthrough succeed, it would be employed against Constantinople. For some reason, he did not inform Kitchener and the War Council of the first objective.)[106] Kitchener refused, on the grounds that he could not presently send there the only reserve he possessed for posting to France in the event of a German offensive. He feared that the Germans could rapidly transfer troops from east to west after a Russian defeat.

He also found it difficult to understand why Churchill was insisting on the Twenty-Ninth Division. "From his knowledge of Constantinople and the East," Kitchener said, he felt convinced "that the whole situation in Constantinople would change the moment the fleet had secured a passage through the Dardanelles." Under those circumstances, he considered that the forces already concentrated in the Near East would suffice. Churchill dismissed Kitchener's fears. He believed that one division in the west would not make much difference, but could be decisive in the eastern Mediterranean. Besides, the Germans could not rapidly transfer forces to the west. "If a disaster occurred in Turkey owing to insufficiency of troops," he announced, "he must disclaim all responsibility."[107] (Consistent with this announcement, on February 27 Churchill committed to "the record"—and to history—his view that without the Twenty-Ninth Division the forces allotted to operation in Turkey would not be enough, even if the Navy did enter the Marmora.)[108] This was a strange statement, considering that it had been Churchill who had convinced the War Council that an exclusively naval action would lead to great events at Turkey's expense. The fate of the Twenty-Ninth Division was not settled at this meeting.

Throughout this time, Carden was proceeding very slowly; due to poor weather, days passed without any action. Nevertheless, the success of the attacks on the outer forts generated satisfaction. The War Council again met on March 3, when discussion concentrated on what would happen at Constantinople once the ships had forced the Dardanelles and on Turkey's fate after its collapse. Kitchener announced that he would take a decision about the Twenty-Ninth Division on March 10. Fisher and Grey argued that the process of the breakthrough in the Dardanelles had to be accelerated. Grey's reason was his fear of a further Russian defeat; Fisher's fear was that Austrian submarines might reach the area. Churchill maintained that it would be wrong to send to the Balkans more forces than were required to encourage the states of the region to form an anti-German front. "He was still of opinion that our proper line of strategy was an advance in the north through Holland and the Baltic. . . . The operation in the East should be regarded merely as an interlude."[109]

At the beginning of March, General Birdwood (whom Kitchener had sent to examine the situation in the Dardanelles) estimated that the Navy would not manage to force the Straits without army support. He raised the possibility of landing at Cape Helles, on the southern tip of the Gallipoli peninsula.[110]

Kitchener replied that there was no intention of the Army assaulting the peninsula as long as the Navy believed that it could break through by itself. But he added that, were this to prove impossible, a large-scale military operation would be mounted.[111] Kitchener had good reasons for thus replying to Birdwood. On the same day Churchill had written to him that, although 40,000 British soldiers (not including the Twenty-Ninth Division, whose fate had not yet been settled) would be ready for action on March 20 against "Turkish soil," "I wish to make it clear that the naval operations in the Dardanelles cannot be delayed for troop movements, as we must get into the Marmora as soon as possible in the normal course."

He earmarked these troops for action off Constantinople after the naval breakthrough.[112] But on the same day Fisher wrote to Churchill: "The more I consider the Dardanelles—the less I like it."[113]

It was at about this time that Greece suggested sending forces to attack Gallipoli. The Russians forthwith vetoed the proposal, fearing that the Greeks would later demand their share in Constantinople. In *The World Crisis* Churchill emphasized this episode; his object was to demonstrate both the immediate favorable reaction in the Balkans to the British move at the Dardanelles and the opportunities that had been squandered. But, as had previously been the case, the Greek offer was not serious; it had been made in the context of the struggle between the pro-British and pro-German factions in the Greek government. Greece retracted its offer because of opposition by its own king and general staff, not because of the Russian veto.[114] While still busy with moves in southeastern Europe, Churchill wrote to Admiral Jellicoe that he hoped the attack on Borkum would be carried out in mid-May, to be followed by a breakthrough into the Baltic.[115]

On March 10 the War Council devoted most of its attention to the distribution of spoils after Turkey's fall. At the same meeting Kitchener announced that he was sending the Twenty-Ninth Division east. Churchill said that the Admiralty still believed that the Navy could force the Dardanelles by itself.[116] The Twenty-Ninth Division, then, began to move about three weeks late. Carden, at all events, on the same day sent a discouraging telegram. The operations hitherto attempted, he claimed, showed that the ships' guns could not silence the forts; most of the damage to the outer forts had been caused by demolition parties landed on the coast.[117] Sir Henry Jackson immediately reached the necessary conclusion, and wrote to Oliver that ground forces had to be employed to conquer the Gallipoli peninsula. He repeated his claim that a naval breakthrough alone would result in heavy losses, without ensuring the supply lines of the ships that would force a passage to the Marmora.[118]

Unaffected by these events, Churchill began to lose his patience. With the assent of Fisher and Oliver he sent off a telegram to Carden pressing him to act decisively, even at the cost of heavy losses. Two days later he repeated that request.[119] Carden's reply was affirmative, but added that operations had immediately to be commenced on the Gallipoli peninsula with the object of securing lines of supply once the fleet had penetrated to the Marmora.[120] On the following day, Fisher again asked Churchill either to abandon the naval assault or to commence military operations against the peninsula at once. He suggested that the War Council be immediately convened to decide the matter.[121] Churchill responded that he had no wish to involve the War Council: "It is after all only asking a lot of ignorant people to meddle in our business." He concluded by saying that he would settle the matter with Kitchener.[122]

A further attempt to penetrate the Straits failed on the night of March 13–14. Thereafter Carden, together with De Robeck, his second-in-command, and Keyes, his chief of staff, decided to attempt a breakthrough with a large force on March 18. This was not a tactical change, namely a shift from a slow assault in several stages to a single thrust, but an expansion of the penetrating force and an escalation in the intensity of the attack. Carden's health broke down the next day, and he was replaced by De Robeck. The attack of March 18 failed: of the sixteen battleships participating in the assault, three were sunk and three others disabled for several weeks. Casualties, especially among the British, were not very high; the naval losses were caused by mines, not by the coastal batteries. But not until after the war did De Robeck discover the precise reasons for the damage to his ships.

Men on the spot and in London were not initially discouraged by the failure. Notwithstanding the blow to his confidence, De Robeck intended to renew the naval attack within a few days. But that was not the view of General Hamilton, whom Kitchener had sent to command the army to be employed in the region. The Navy, he wrote to Kitchener, could not force the Straits by itself; large-scale military operations would have to be carried out on the Gallipoli peninsula[123] But Hamilton faced severe and unexpected logistic difficulties. The troops and equipment sent to Lemnos and Alexandria had been loaded aboard indiscriminately. Units had become separated from their equipment. Under those circumstances, they could not be disembarked on a hostile coast. In the absence of suitable loading and off-loading facilities on Lemnos, Hamilton decided to return those units already on the island to Alexandria, so that they could reorganize. Meanwhile the Twenty-Ninth Division, without which the assault would not be launched, was due to reach Alexandria on April 2. But it too had been loaded aboard in the same muddled fashion. This meant that the amphibious attack would only be possible around the middle of April, and not immediately after the failure of the naval attack. The Turks had ample time to rush reinforcements to the area.

Two causes brought about this failure. The first and most important was that it was not made plain to the persons concerned at the War Office and the Admiralty that the forces would be disembarked in the face of enemy resistance. As we have seen, it was thought that they would be employed after a naval breakthrough and against a defeated and retreating Turkish army. That was why they were loaded in the conventional manner convenient for troop transport. The second cause lay in the deficiencies of the person responsible at the Admiralty.[124]

The War Council met again on March 19. Without argument, it endorsed Churchill's request that De Robeck be permitted to make another attempt at forcing the Dardanelles should he think it fit. Fisher maintained that he had previously anticipated the loss of at least twelve battleships before the fleet could reach the Marmora. Kitchener announced Hamilton's decision to reorganize his force at Alexandria, but made no mention of the General's pessimistic assessment of the chances of another naval attempt. Ironically, it was at this moment of crisis that most of the discussion at the War Council was devoted to the distribution of Turkey's Asiatic possessions.[125] In any case, on March 20 the Admiralty sent additional old battleships to replace those damaged.

Meanwhile, De Robeck began to have second thoughts about a further attempt at a naval breakthrough. On March 23 he informed Hamilton of his conclusion that the Straits could not be forced without a large ground operation. Hamilton had already received a telegram from Kitchener implying that he should not hesitate to attack Gallipoli if necessary, and did not need much persuading. It was at this moment that the decision for a military campaign on Gallipoli was really taken. De Robeck set out his own considerations in a message that he sent to the Admiralty on the same day. He emphasized that, unless the Army took the Gallipoli peninsula, his supply lines would be endangered after the fleet had entered the Marmora. He also pointed out that naval bombardment was incapable of silencing most of the batteries stationed around the Straits.[126] De Robeck was further concerned by other factors. Hamilton estimated that the Army would be ready to act on April 14; between March 19 and 25 the weather was stormy. Together with Keyes, who was longing to renew the naval breakthrough, De Robeck reached the conclusion that the mine-sweeping force had to be reorganized, but it would not be ready before April 4. His only Dreadnought capable of taking on the *Goeben* had been damaged and the *Queen Elizabeth* could not be risked in the Straits. De Robeck had to await a replacement from Britain. This meant that there was a very short interval between the day on which the naval assault could be resumed and that on which the Army could attack. Accordingly, the Admiral decided to force the Straits in conjunction with the land campaign.[127]

Churchill disagreed with the admiral's decision. On the same day, March 23, he drafted a message attempting to persuade De Robeck not to await the land attack in mid-April but once more to attempt a naval breakthrough by himself. He pointed out the danger of the arrival of German and Austrian submarines, and of the heavy losses (5,000 men) the Army was expected to sustain. He also laid out the glorious possibilities that would open up after the ships had broken through, all at the cost of a few old vessels.[128] With one exception, none of the Admiralty's War Staff supported this message, which was never sent, and Fisher had threatened to resign if it were. Their opinion was that the decision should be left to De Robeck and Hamilton. Churchill did have fellow spirits in Kitchener, Balfour, and Asquith, who thought that a second breakthrough should be immediately attempted,[129] but he could not force his will on the Admiralty. Hamilton and De Robeck were determined to employ the Army first.[130]

In a final effort, and notwithstanding Fisher's objections, Churchill sent De Robeck a telegram whose wording was similar to those he had used on March 23; but he did not mention that the Admiralty staff had already decided against another attempt to break through.[131] To Fisher, he wrote that De Robeck should not fear for his supply lines after the passage of the fleet. Like Kitchener, Churchill thought that the entry of British ships into the Marmora would threaten the supply lines of the Turkish garrison on Gallipoli, and therefore force its withdrawal. De Robeck's reply was negative, and repeated his arguments.[132] With great reluctance, Churchill informed the Admiral that he had been persuaded of the vital nature of a combined operation by the reasons De Robeck had specified in his last dispatch.[133] The truth is that he never agreed with De Robeck's decision. He was forced into submission by the lack of support from Fisher and the Admiralty and by the absolute conviction shown by Hamilton and De Robeck.[134]

Despite the drama being acted out at the Dardanelles and in London, Churchill found the time to write a lengthy memorandum, whose composition must have been protracted, in which he worked out his plan for an attack on Borkum, leading to the penetration of the Baltic.[135]

Fisher had begun to loathe the entire notion of the Dardanelles operation. During the interim period prior to the amphibious landing, he tried to press Churchill to reexamine this strategic move. To that end, he proposed that the War Council be convened. What he mainly feared was the weakening of the British fleet in the North Sea and the news that Germany might invade Holland. But he also doubted Hamilton's ability to mount the amphibious assault successfully. Fisher suggested the examination of such other possibilities as a landing at Alexandretta, on the Syrian coast, instead of at the Dardanelles.[136]

Churchill dismissed Fisher's arguments. As before, he maintained that the balance of forces in the North Sea gave no cause for alarm; the matter should not be discussed at the War Council but clarified with Kitchener.[137] Kitchener was decidedly in favor of carrying out the amphibious assault; Asquith agreed with both of them.[138] On the other hand, Hankey and Balfour began to waver. At an informal meeting of the War Council attended by the Prime Minister, Kitchener, Churchill, and Hankey, the latter expressed doubts whether a landing on the enemy coast was at all possible. (The Turks now had 70,000 soldiers on the Gallipoli peninsula and the advantage of surprise had long since been forfeited). Hankey feared that a failure might undermine Britain's entire Balkan position. Robertson, Chief of Staff of the BEF in France, had similar doubts. Balfour, who was doubtless aware of Hankey's misgivings, pointed out to Churchill that he had previously supported the assault on the Dardanelles when it had involved only a naval action; but the land operation seemed to him to be too dangerous. As an interim measure he suggested an attack on Syria instead of at the Dardanelles, while awaiting the cooperation of the Balkan states. Churchill's response to Hankey was that "he anticipated no difficulty in effecting a landing." To Balfour he replied that the Army people were of the opinion that they could make a successful landing, and that it was because of their influence that the Admiralty had deferred a renewed attempt to force the Straits until after a military operation had been undertaken.[139] The latter part of this statement was inaccurate; but Churchill was not the only optimist. It must not be forgotten that this was to have been the first British amphibious assault carried out under modern conditions of warfare.

Hankey was not moved by Churchill's placatory tone, and on April 12 presented Asquith with a memorandum that again pointed out the dangers inherent in the amphibious assault. In his opinion, the attack was something of a gamble, based on the supposition of the inferior fighting spirit of the Turks.[140] This memorandum did not shake Asquith out of his usual apathy or persuade him to convene the War Council before the landing was mounted. The shift from an exclusively naval action to a large-scale army operation was effected almost automatically. This was made possible because Kitchener, with the assent of the others, had long since ruled that reasons of imperial prestige precluded the possibility of any withdrawal from the operation, even were the naval action to fail. The operational decision was taken by the men on the spot, Hamilton and De Robeck. Churchill's contribution was to prevent a reexamination of the entire strategic move after the failure of March 18.

Hamilton's forces landed on April 25; after suffering heavy casualties, they managed to hang on to the fringes of the Gallipoli peninsula. Early in May, the situation on the peninsula was deadlocked. In view of the Army's difficulties, De Robeck began to think of renewing the naval attack. But his enquiry as to the Admiralty's views noted the many hazards, and in effect dictated the terms of the reply,[141] especially since news had been received of the arrival of German submarines in the eastern Mediterranean. De Robeck's enquiry renewed the confrontation between Churchill and Fisher. The latter bluntly opposed a naval assault, but added nothing new to his arguments. Churchill attempted to give De Robeck authority to attack should he think it fit to do so. Fisher insisted that the right of command and of veto be exclusively his own—a right that naturally befitted his status as First Sea Lord, but which he had to fight for. Asquith intervened on Fisher's side.[142] Churchill maintained that it was not his intention altogether to force the Dardanelles; all he intended was that the Navy destroy the coastal forts and sweep the mines at the southern entrance to the Straits in order to improve the effectiveness of its support to the land forces.[143] Fisher suspected that this would merely be the first step toward an attempt at a full breakthrough. Their tug-of-war lasted several days; on May 13 Fisher won. In a joint telegram, Churchill and Fisher informed De Robeck that the time for an independent naval move had passed. He had to wait until the Army had completed its mission.[144]

At the War Council meeting of May 14 the mood was grim. Its members indulged in mutual accusations, with all employing inaccurate arguments. Churchill fired the first shot in Kitchener's direction: "If we had known three months ago that an army of from 80,000 to 100,000 men would now be available for an attack on the Dardanelles, the naval attack would never have been undertaken."

Kitchener replied that he had agreed to the operation because he had been convinced by Churchill that the Navy could force the Straits by itself; on that basis, he had believed that the political advantages justified the risk. He also maintained that he had understood that, should the Navy fail, the Army would have to be used—a strange argument considering that his initial enthusiasm for the proposal to launch a naval attack had been generated by the fact that ground forces would not have to be employed and by the possibility, in the event of failure, of effecting an immediate and uncomplicated withdrawal. With the same degree of accuracy, Fisher claimed that "he had been no party to the Dardanelles operations."

Nevertheless, Kitchener (pessimistically) and Churchill (optimistically) agreed that the forces in the Dardanelles had to be reinforced and that the land campaign should be pursued with full force. Kitchener, the former Sirdar of the Egyptian army, feared that a retreat would create serious repercussions in the Empire, and especially in Egypt.[145]

Fisher appreciated that an expansion of the campaign in the Dardanelles meant the diversion of additional naval forces to that theater, whose very name brought on a paroxysm of rage. Only one last straw was required to break him, and it was Churchill who insensitively cast it on Fisher's back. On the evening of May 14, the delicate subject of the scope of naval reinforcements to the Dardanelles was settled between Fisher and Churchill, to the former's satisfaction. But the next morning Fisher came across papers in which Churchill requested additional reinforcements, far larger than those they had agreed upon only a few hours earlier. That was too much for Fisher, who tendered his resignation. This event brought about the collapse of Asquith's government, which was at that time, in any case, at the center of a public storm over the shortage of artillery shells. The result was the formation of a coalition government and Churchill's resignation.

From the moment Churchill ceased to be First Lord of the Admiralty, he no longer possessed operational responsibility for the continuation of the Gallipoli campaign. There exists no direct link between him and the military operations, moves, and failures that happened after his resignation. Many people were troubled by the degree of his responsibility and share in the initiation of the Gallipoli campaign and its failure. The more the subject is studied, the more the new analyst finds confusing the conflicting commentaries of his predecessors. An answer will be given to this problem; but it has to be remembered that, from the viewpoint of this book, it is important to study the Gallipoli episode in depth to be also able to analyze characteristics of Churchill's strategic thinking and decision-taking method and so understand his management of World War

II. For various reasons, characteristic Churchillian traces are more pronounced in this episode than in other instances.

It is in *The World Crisis* that Churchill sets out his defense of his actions during this episode and his positions during the war. There he argues that one of the main reasons for the failure lay in the fact that the British government was drawn into this operation; its decisions were taken in installments and forces were consequently dispatched piecemeal instead of in accordance with a general, ratified plan. This method of decision making prevented a simultaneous and combined operation by the Army and Navy, which all agreed, both at the time and in retrospect, would have been preferable to any other course and would certainly have ensured the campaign's success.[146]

Churchill placed principal responsibility for that situation on Kitchener's broad shoulders: the latter had difficulty in deciding between west and east; he was lacking in broad strategic vision and carried along by events; his hesitations and frequent changes of mind meant that decisions were neither prompt nor consistent, and prevented the launching of a combined operation for which suitable forces were ready as early as the beginning of January 1915.[147] Naturally, when absolving himself of blame for the failure, Churchill also concentrated on Kitchener's delay in sending the Twenty-Ninth Division.

In his evidence before the Dardanelles Commission,[148] and in *The World Crisis*, Churchill claimed that the Twenty-Ninth Division would have arrived in time—had it been dispatched without delay and had its supplies and transport been loaded in a manner befitting its immediate disembarkation for combat. It thus could have joined the other forces already at Alexandria and Lemnos the moment that the naval assault reached its peak on March 18. At that stage, only one Turkish division was on the peninsula: "But without the Twenty-Ninth Division, the army could do nothing. This was the vital *Key* decision [Churchill's emphasis], whose movements and arrival governed everything."[149] Because of the delay, the land attack was postponed by a month, during which the Turks strengthened their forces and the element of surprise was entirely dissipated. Thus was lost the opportunity to effect a combined operation with that asset.

The Commission, too, was strongly critical of the Twenty-Ninth Division's delay. Marder, the distinguished naval historian, also considers that had Kitchener acted energetically at the end of February, it would have been possible to mount an amphibious operation that could almost certainly have led to the capture of the peninsula.[150]

Kitchener's part in the episode is dubious; but Churchill's is also amazing. As we have seen, from mid-February Churchill did press Kitchener to send forces to the region. But he claimed that their objective would be to hold Gallipoli after its evacuation by the Turks and to take Constantinople should revolt break out there. On the evidence available, Kitchener was not told that the forces were meant to take part in a combined operation concurrently with the Navy or in a separate amphibious assault designed to oust the Turks from the peninsula. That is why Kitchener repeatedly (and seemingly incomprehensibly) asked Churchill why he demanded such large forces and the Twenty-Ninth Division; had the Navy succeeded, the forces already massed in the eastern Mediterranean could have carried out their task. Each of Churchill's responses repeated the announcement that the Navy could force the Dardanelles by itself. However, even while claiming that troops were to be employed only in order to secure the Navy's gains, he simultaneously threatened to disclaim all responsibility if the Twenty-Ninth Division was not sent to the Near East in time.[151]

The inconsistency between Churchill's threats and behavior, on the one hand, and the objects that—so he claimed—he had in mind for the forces, on the other, occasions astonishment. The logical explanation is that, by the second half of February, Churchill had lost his confidence in the Navy's ability to force the Straits by itself, but found it difficult to admit as much and retract the assurances to the War Council that had put into motion the creaky apparatus of strategic decision taking. Instead, he sought to insure himself against the possibility that the Navy would fail to force the Straits by concentrating in the area Army forces, which, in that event, could immediately take the peninsula. Churchill feared that, once the decision on an exclusively naval action had been taken on his initiative, he would have lost face by demanding a combined operation. Moreover, there was also a risk that the entire campaign would have been canceled. He hoped to resolve this dilemma by making sure that the Twenty-Ninth Division and other forces reached Lemnos before or during the principal naval attack.

Churchill's declining confidence in the success of the naval attack did not lead him to conclude that he had to work toward a combined operation in the full sense of completely synchronizing the Army's and Navy's moves. Instead, what he envisaged was that each would operate on its own. The Navy would attempt to break through by itself—should it succeed, well and good; if not, the Army would immediately move in. *After* the War Council's decision to let the Navy force the Straits by itself, he reached the conclusion that—*as far as he was concerned*—the best solution was a stage-by-stage operation. One reason was that, notwithstanding the decline in his own confidence, he still believed that the naval attack might succeed. Another was that this was the way to extricate himself from the personal complication in which he had become entangled by his assurance to the War Council that the Navy could force a passage to Constantinople by itself.

Only thus is it possible to explain Churchill's failure to work toward a simultaneous and combined operation, even when he could have done so on his own authority and without any dependence on Kitchener. The opportunity existed after the decision of February 16 to dispatch the Twenty-Ninth Division, taken two days before the naval assault on the Dardanelles was to begin. It would have been a simple matter, and one that would have very much pleased Fisher, for Churchill to have ordered Carden to postpone the opening of the naval assault until the Twenty-Ninth Division had arrived in early March. That moment had passed by February 19; Carden had already launched his attack and Kitchener had changed his mind about the Twenty-Ninth Division. A second opportunity existed after Kitchener had again released the Twenty-Ninth Division on March 10. Early that month, even before Kitchener did so, Churchill had told him that he could not await the arrival of the forces. Moreover, when Kitchener did eventually release the Twenty-Ninth Division, Churchill increased his pressure on Carden to bring his assault to a swift conclusion instead of waiting a little longer in order to synchronize the division's arrival with the main naval attack.[152] It is therefore no wonder that Kitchener replied to Birdwood that, as long as the Admiralty considered the Navy capable of breaking through alone, there was no need to attack the peninsula—nor that he should have informed Hamilton that the Army's operation was only secondary.

It is this situation that refutes Churchill's claim to the War Council on May 14 that he would not have launched the naval attack had he known three months ago (i.e., in mid-February) that large land forces would now (in May) be located in the Dardanelles area. On the other hand, had Churchill been certain early in January, before the decision on naval action was taken, that massive ground forces would be available the following spring, he might possibly have refrained from proposing the exclusively naval assault.

Another exercise of Churchill's wishful thinking about the Twenty-Ninth Division relates to an internal circumstance: if only the force had been transported in time and its equipment loaded in a manner that would have enabled it to go on the offensive immediately. Admittedly, the fault was in part technical; but here too one of its principal causes was Churchill's assurances to Kitchener that land forces were intended only to perform policing and holding operations. There was no sufficient reason for Kitchener to verify that the logistic system would rest on a planned amphibious assault against enemy resistance. The same is true for the persons directly responsible. Obviously, the only reason they might have done so was in order to plan for the worst possible case. It is difficult to know why Kitchener did not take this course. Churchill, however, refrained from explicit mention of just such a "worst case"; otherwise he would have undermined the credibility of his claim that the Navy could break through alone. He thus fell into a trap of his own making, from which the men on the spot had to extricate themselves unaided.

In *The World Crisis*, Churchill rejects the Commission's conclusion that he should have awaited the creation of a suitable Anglo-French expeditionary force and have mounted an amphibious operation without attempting a naval breakthrough. In his own words:

> Nothing less than the ocular demonstration and practical proof of the strategic meaning of the Dardanelles, and the effects of attacking it on every Balkan and Mediterranean Power, would have lighted up men's minds sufficiently to make a large abstraction of troops from the main theatre a possibility. I do not believe

that anything less than those tremendous hopes, reinforced as they were by dire necessity, would have enabled Lord Kitchener to wrest an army from France and Flanders.[153]

To enhance his case, he claims that the expectation of unfavorable developments in the Balkans and the east prevented a delay in the naval breakthrough.

This is not an accurate representation. If he is referring to the forces required for the success of the combined operation (while the peninsula was still held by scant Turkish forces), these were promised to him during February, before the naval assault had reached its height or even commenced. Most were already concentrated in the fighting area. And as we have seen, Churchill deliberately refrained from putting off the naval assault. There was no need for an "ocular demonstration" to convince Kitchener. More important is the fact that, as early as January 13, the War Council had determined that a large proportion of the new British armies would be sent to another theater were there to be a stalemate in the west. On January 28 Kitchener himself made it clear that he supported the General Staff's intention to send forces to the Balkans. The implication is clear: the prevailing feeling in the War Council was that an army greater than that considered necessary for success at Gallipoli had to be dispatched to the eastern Mediterranean. The only problem was one of timing; as usual, Churchill was in a hurry.

The self-made contradictions in which Churchill entrapped himself during the period of decision making are also apparent in the vociferous defense he recorded in *The World Crisis*. He attacked Kitchener for not sending the Twenty-Ninth Division early enough, accusing him of thereby preventing a combined operation that would have succeeded; at the same, he claimed that there was no time to await the arrival of troops; finally, he criticized De Robeck for preferring to wait for a land attack instead of making a second attempt to break through.[154] With considerable success, Churchill thus tried to have both ends of a stick which (to extend the metaphor) had been broken asunder.

Churchill's words in the above quotation, together with the stratagems in which he indulged to have forces sent to the east—after the decision had been taken in principle for an exclusively naval action—convey the impression of a deliberate and predetermined plan. He initially proposed the naval breakthrough to tempt the War Council into accepting a strategic move against Turkey; he thereafter worked toward filling in the missing stage, that of raising troops for a combined operation. This method of procedure is not inconsistent with his behavior on other occasions. This charge has been commonly adduced by Churchill's critics with respect to this episode. But even one of the most recent critics, R. Prior (who considers this to be the most reasonable explanation for Churchill's behavior) admits that the documents now available do not allow the case to be proved.[155]

The reason the documents do not prove the case is simple: Churchill did not deliberately set out to mislead the War Council. It will be remembered that, on receiving Carden's affirmative reply to his request that the Admiral examine the possibility of a naval passage, Churchill did not rush to present the War Council with the plan; instead, he still attempted to promote his northern European schemes. Churchill did not become mesmerized by the Dardanelles until after Carden's detailed plans had arrived on January 11 and the chances of northern operations had very much receded. There are good reasons to assume that at this stage he wholeheartedly believed that an exclusively naval operation could indeed attain the strategic objectives of which he spoke. His own doubts did not arise until *after* the decision in principle of January 13, when they were stimulated by second thoughts on his part and by the pressure exerted by Fisher and Jackson. Thus he then began to work for the dispatch of land forces to the vicinity of the Dardanelles, so that they might act as a guarantee and security should the Navy fail. What in retrospect appears to have been a cunning plan was, in sum, the result of insufficient consideration, haste, overenthusiasm and, ultimately, *a change of mind*. That, too, is the explanation for his inconsistent behavior and the apparent contradictions in his claims during and after the episode. In part, such contradictions were caused by Churchill's wish to cover up for moves and arguments that he had previously put forward with insufficient thought.

Another cause Churchill cited for his failure to await the arrival of troops was the sensitive situation in the Balkans and on the eastern front. It will be remembered that the principal stimulant for initiating the move to launch a *naval* assault on the Dardanelles was the pressure on Russia in the Caucasus and the grand duke's appeal for help. This cause had effectively dissipated within a few days; early in January, the Russians defeated the Turks. True, the Grand Duke did not bother to report the change in the Caucasus situation and to cancel his appeal that the Turks be diverted; but London was aware of the true state of affairs.[156] Thus the main reason for the urgency of the operation had passed by the time that Churchill first raised the plan for a naval action at the War Council on January 13. Nevertheless, in both his evidence to the Dardanelles Commission and in *The World Crisis*, Churchill still explained the need for immediate action (i.e., without awaiting a combined operation) by reference to the need to relieve the pressure on Russia in the Caucasus.[157] This contradicted the opinion he adduced in *The Eastern Front*, to the effect that the failure of the Turkish assault in the Caucasus was predictable, due to local weather and topographical conditions as well as the natural advantages enjoyed by the defense.[158] (Justifying the continuation of the campaign after the failure of March 18, the Dardanelles Commission also emphasized the need to relieve pressure on the Russians in the Caucasus. But even Churchill admitted that the Russian position was by that stage already sound.)[159]

The lack of clarity about developments in the Caucasus was symptomatic, and illuminates one of the basic problems underlying the offensive against Turkey. Churchill himself indicated as much in *The Eastern Front*. At that stage of the war, he claims, British decision takers knew little of events on the eastern front ("the full significance of Tannenberg was only gradually understood"); throughout the conflict, the mechanisms at their disposal for the gathering and evaluation of intelligence was altogether primitive.[160] The War Council decided on this serious strategic move when in possession of very little information about events in the east, at Constantinople, and in the Balkans. This deficiency was even more deleterious than is usually the case since the success of the move was predicated on the nature of the response expected from the Turkish population and government in Constantinople when the ships reached the capital, whereas "conventional" strategic plans are based on the defeat of the enemy's military forces. In proferring sociopolitical analyses and in assessing the information they received from the region, members of the War Council seem merely to have indulged their prejudices about "the Orient."

When developments in the Caucasus did not justify haste in the commencement of the naval action, there remained the Balkan problem as a reason for such urgency. It was feared that British inactivity in the Balkans would further undermine the status of the Entente powers in this region, as well as in Italy. Thus seen, Churchill's sense of urgency is indeed justified. It has to be noted, however, that at issue was in effect a delay of just a few weeks; all that was required was to postpone the beginning of the naval attack until the arrival of the Twenty-Ninth Division and the other forces. There existed two alternatives: one was not to wait, and to launch only a naval attack whose chances of failure were not slight; the other was to mount a combined operation, which stood a greater chance of success even though the short delay did involve some risks. A military victory would, in any case, have repaired the losses (if any) incurred in the Balkans by the delay. Not even the British failure of March 18 distanced Italy from the Entente powers, whom she joined on April 26, while Bulgaria joined the Central Powers only in October 1915. Without noticing the fact, Churchill himself said which alternative he would have chosen. In May, when he and Kitchener were hurling accusations at each other, he claimed that—had he known at the beginning of the year that such large ground forces would be located in the region in the spring—he would never have initiated the naval assault.

The conclusion of this analysis is that the failure to mount a combined operation was very largely due to Churchill's entanglement in the concept of the stage-by-stage offensive, together with his unjustified haste. Kitchener made his own contribution. Admittedly, the latter's behavior is now more understandable, since it is clear why he felt no urgency to dispatch the Twenty-Ninth Division to the Near East. On the other hand, his failure to send it at all is incomprehensible. It is difficult to believe that this single division could have tipped the scales if the Germans launched a new offensive in the west, in which dozens of enemy divisions would have taken part.

Churchill based his defense on other arguments: no one suggested withdrawing from the campaign once the great naval attack of March 18 had failed; opponents of the action could have made their voices heard even prior to that circumstance, when it became apparent that Carden had made little progress since commencing his operation on February 19; no one suggested attacking Alexandretta instead of Gallipoli when the former could have been taken with ease; Asquith did not even find it appropriate to convene the War Council. "No formal decision to make a land attack was even noted in the records of the Cabinet on the War Council.... The silent plunge into this vast military adventure must be regarded as an extraordinary episode."[161] Similarly, neither the War Office nor the General Staff undertook proper staff work before deciding to land on the peninsula. Churchill claimed that his wish to renew the naval assault immediately after the failure of March 18 also stemmed from his appreciation of the considerable risks involved in the amphibious landing.[162]

These claims constitute a mélange of truths and falsehoods, and of self-delusions. To begin with the former: as the previous analysis has shown, the roots of the decision to expand the Dardanelles campaign into a land campaign lay with Kitchener and his fear of the loss of Britain's prestige in the east; the operational decision was taken by the commanders on the spot, Hamilton and De Robeck. But there is no foundation for the charge that no one attempted to reconsider the very continuation of the campaign. First, there is no basis for the argument that opponents of the operation could have acted before March 18, when apprised of Carden's slow progress; in fact, since the naval passage was originally projected as a slow operation, no one needed to consider the attempt to have reached its conclusion. Prior to March 18 the Navy incurred no losses. Even before March 18—and more strongly thereafter—Fisher did propose canceling the naval assault or, alternatively, mounting only a combined operation; he also asked Churchill to raise the entire matter anew before the War Council, a suggestion Churchill rejected.[163] Moreover, Fisher and Balfour did propose an alternative attack on Alexandretta, while Hankey was fearful of, and warned about, the consequences of the landing itself. It was Churchill who rejected Fisher's requests and took care to ensure that matters would not be clarified at the War Council but with Kitchener and Asquith in a smaller forum. Similarly, he foresaw no difficulty in effecting the landing itself.[164]

Churchill devoted an entire chapter in *The World Crisis* to proving that, had the naval breakthrough been renewed immediately after the failure of March 18, it would have succeeded and attained all the strategic objectives to which he aspired.[165] This is not the place to discuss the technical and tactical problems that have to be understood if this argument is to be proved or disproved. Expert opinion is divided, and will remain so. Logically, the fact of failure places the onus of proof on those who maintain that this move could have been successful. But this is a difficult task. In his first analysis of the episode, Arthur Marder, for instance, estimated that a further attempt at a naval breakthrough undertaken within a fortnight of the failure of March 18 might have succeeded, provided that it had the assistance of the land forces already located in the region and that the mine-sweeping force had been reorganized. But the supposition that revolution would break out in Constantinople and the

Turks' collapse was, in his opinion, "little more than a matter of faith."[166] Some years later, Marder changed his opinion and attempted to prove Churchill's case, arguing that had the fleet renewed its attempt it could have forced the Dardanelles and by itself eliminated Turkey from the war.[167] He calculates that the chances of success would have been at least even had the Dardanelles breakthrough been carried out between April 4 and mid-April, but not before April 4. The chances of the move off Constantinople succeeding were similarly fifty-fifty.[168] For some reason, Marder made no aggregate of these figures for the entire operation; this is a necessary calculation since forcing the Dardanelles without Constantinople falling would have been meaningless. When the sums are made, the chances of success turn out to have been 25 percent, or one success for every four attempts. By all accounts, these are high odds that in fact destroy the case that he and Churchill attempted to construct. (In *The World Crisis* Churchill concentrated on attempting to prove that an immediate second breakthrough would have been successful; he was shaky in his treatment of the problem of how the ships would force Turkey to surrender once they had reached the shores of Constantinople.)

Of course, against the slim chances of success must be weighed the price of failure. In this case, the losses anticipated amounted to a few old battleships and their crews. To Churchill and others this seemed a small price to pay for the enticing gains. In his speech of resignation from the government in 1915 Churchill described the attempt to force the Straits as "a legitimate war gamble," an expression that incensed members of Parliament and the public.[169] Their anger was generated by misunderstanding (Churchill was thought to have been referring to the entire Gallipoli campaign rather than to the naval action alone) as well as by some degree of ignorance. In war, decision takers operate in a particularly large ambience of uncertainty, and every strategic move is something of a gamble.

Even if strategic decision taking does involve risks, these can be hazarded only after meticulous assessment and calculation. The question is whether De Robeck and Hamilton, considering the information they possessed (and even that which is retrospectively available), were mistaken in deciding to postpone the second naval attempt and await the land operation. In attempting to fault De Robeck's decision, Marder—without noticing the fact—in effect provides it with a justification. If (as his own calculations lead one to suggest) the naval action's chances were slim between April 4 and the middle of that month—and nonexistent before April 4, why should De Robeck have made a renewed attempt and not waited for the land attack, which was *supposed* to have been launched in mid-April (although, in effect, was not done so until the end of the month). Most of the people involved, including Hamilton and Kitchener, estimated that the ground attack would succeed without undue problems. Indeed, no one doubts that another attempted breakthrough would have stood a far greater chance had the Gallipoli peninsula been first conquered, in whole or in part. De Robeck had to wait for just ten more days. He had no reason to dispute

Army opinion that the land attack stood a good chance; but he did have solid grounds for believing that another naval action would fail. Not until the end of the war did he learn why his ships had been sunk during the attack of March 18; it later transpired that the reason lay in the string of mines placed parallel to the shore rather than across the Straits. Thus analyzed, the decision not to renew the attack but to await the amphibious operation seems eminently reasonable.

In summarizing the strategic move at the Dardanelles and Churchill's responsibility for its failure, analysts must beware two hazards. One is that, by its very nature, the present study subjects Churchill's own actions, advantages, and weaknesses to minute examination; less attention is paid to others who played an important role in the episode. Conversely, the second hazard can lead to the opposite result: in estimating Churchill's part in this episode, one is likely to be favorably biased by his gigantic image, fashioned in the wake of World War II.

Shortly after the end of the Gallipoli campaign, Churchill claimed that "history will vindicate the conception, and the errors in execution will on the whole leave me clear."[170] He never retracted that claim. Well, it seems that "history" is today somewhat confused. Marder entangled himself in the thickets of the episode. Alan Moorehead and Robert Rhodes James, who analyzed the Gallipoli campaign anew during the 1950s and 1960s, reached contradictory conclusions. Moorehead—an ardent supporter of the strategic concept underlying the Dardanelles campaign—claims that the strategic move has been justified by both historical perspective and the trend of historical research.[171] Rhodes James, on the other hand, maintains that the strategic concept was from the first misguided and that operational factors doomed the plan to failure. "Very recently," he adds, "opinion has been hardening against the whole operation and against Churchill's part in its initiation."[172] More accurate is B. E. Schmitt who, in his up-to-date work on World War I, says that the predominant historical view hitherto is that the strategic idea was brilliant but its execution was a failure.[173] Virtually the same opinion was voiced by Brigadier-General C. F. Aspinall-Oglander in his official history of the campaign, written sixty years ago.[174]

For various reasons, Churchill has been singularly identified with the strategic idea that led to the Gallipoli campaign.[175] But the genesis of the idea, in its widest sense, did not lie with Churchill but in a complex of ideas proposed by several men. He preferred to attack Borkum and to break through into the Baltic, but was compelled to make do with a move against Turkey. What gave rise to the impression that Churchill was the sole author of the idea was his stubbornness in translating it into reality; his own reconstruction in *The World Crisis* (where he attributes minor importance to his simultaneous northern European plans and assumes full responsibility for the strategic idea behind the move); the fact that the very men who were associated with the inception of the idea disassociated themselves from it after the campaign's failure; and

Churchill's enforced resignation because of that failure.

Of itself, the idea was indeed enchanting and imaginative. But the very breadth of its strategic vision instilled greater hopes than it in fact warranted. The Dardanelles could have been forced had a *combined* operation been mounted at the *beginning* of the attack[176] (either an amphibious assault on the peninsula concurrent with a naval rush at the Straits, or an amphibious assault on the peninsula that would have paved the way to a naval action thereafter). The chances of eliminating Turkey from the war and renewing the connection with Russia were good, provided that the land forces concentrated in the region would have been sufficient both to conquer the Gallipoli peninsula and to launch a combined land and sea attack on Constantinople. Doubtful, on the other hand, was the second phase of the plan, involving the establishment of a Balkan front that would reap the benefits of the first phase. Churchill claimed that a conjunction between the Balkan states and the forces of the Entente "must have involved the downfall of Austria and Turkey and the speedy, victorious termination of the war."[177] This was a fatal mirage from which he unfortunately found it difficult to escape. There were considerable difficulties in establishing a Balkan front, both because of the deep internal rifts among the Balkan states themselves and because of Russia's position.[178] The latter was disinterested in a Balkan League, among other reasons because its existence would have made it difficult for her to obtain Constantinople; by the same token, the Bulgarians and Greeks were very much opposed to Russian command of Constantinople. It will be recalled that the Russians refused to cooperate with the Greeks even when cut off from the outer world and after suffering a series of defeats. Their resistance would have increased even further had the fall of Constantinople to the British freed their country from its stranglehold.

Notwithstanding these difficulties, the elimination of Turkey from the war might have rallied most of the Balkan states to the side of the Entente, at least temporarily. But that would not have solved the basic problem entailed in the military weakness of a Balkan front. Churchill made much of the numbers of soldiers who would join the Entente camp; but he ignored the fact that the troops in question constituted peasant armies, entirely bereft of an organizational infrastructure and modern military equipment. These states had no industrial base; their armies could have made a military contribution only with the massive logistic support of Britain and France, who would have had to supply them with everything from bootlaces to artillery. The region itself possessed primitive transport arteries and a minuscule number of ports capable of handling a reasonable amount of shipping. Even had the connection with Russia been renewed in 1915, Britain and France did not then possess sufficient equipment and ammunition for their ally; even less could they have provided such supplies to Balkan armies.[179]

It is true that the Austro-Hungarian army was inferior to the German; but, if stiffened by the Germans, it could have hit the Balkan states hard. The Germans enjoyed the advantage of interior lines and, at moments of crisis, could have immediately intervened to foil any threat (just as they did in Rumania and Italy) before Britain and France had managed to amass in the region sizable forces with an adequate logistic base. It follows that there is no foundation for Churchill's claim that the addition of the Balkan states would have brought the war to a speedy conclusion.

Churchill's desire to establish a Balkan front could hardly have been motivated by imperial considerations in this region. The reason is simple: the moment that Britain agreed to Russia's acquisition of Constantinople after the war—the prevention of which had long been the focus of Britain's imperial interest in the Balkans—it ceased to possess any concern of an imperial nature in the region. In effect, had Britain's diplomatic and strategic course in the Balkans succeeded, it would have been Russia who, with British assent, would have become the dominant regional power (an eventuality that further decreased the chances of uniting the Balkan states in a military front). Besides, with the exception of limited influence in Greece, Britain possessed no sway in the Balkans in 1914. Churchill's interest in the region was primarily of a strategic and military nature. His own preference was for the northern theater and he attached supreme importance to the "main theatre" in the west—and in neither did Britain possess a direct *imperial* interest. It follows that imperial considerations exerted no direct influence on the formulation of his military strategy during the war.

Although the idea of establishing a Balkan front was thus built on shaky foundations, success in the first phase would have sufficed to justify the move. Turkey's elimination from the war and the reestablishment of the connection with Russia would have strengthened the latter's powers of military resistance and have slowed down, at least, the process leading to the outbreak of internal Russian crisis. The Anglo-Turkish struggle in Mesopotamia and Palestine would have been averted. Britain and France would certainly have benefited substantially from those circumstances; but they would not have decided the war, nor even perhaps have shortened its duration very much.

The harshest critics of the Gallipoli campaign have overlooked the fact that the strategic consequences of its failure were slight. This was despite the fact of the failure itself and of the heavy losses incurred (themselves small in proportion to those suffered during an average western offensive) as well as the decline in the Entente powers' status in the Balkans. The Gallipoli campaign had no adverse effect on their defensive capability in the west; on the other hand, neither did it prevent the exploitation of strategic opportunities in other theaters—for the simple reason that no such opportunities arose either on the western front or the northern shores of Europe.

Thus, there is some partial truth to Churchill's claim that history would vindicate the concept to whose creation he was a party. But what of his responsibility for the failure in execution? It cannot be denied that the commanders in the field did commit errors of judgment and of execution throughout the land and naval campaigns. But the roots of the operational failure lay in London's process of decision making and method of planning. The principal reason for the failure of the commanders on the spot lay in the absence of a decision to mount a combined offensive at the start. For all the heroism of Britain's and Australia's youth, senior commanders in the field were unable to extricate themselves from the quagmire into which their masters had led them. Yet that is in effect what Churchill demanded of them when severely criticizing them (Hamilton, his friend, apart) in *The World Crisis*. But since he, together with Kitchener, bore principal responsibility for the fact that a combined offensive had not been mounted, he was the last person entitled to make such criticisms. His responsibility for the failure at Gallipoli is greatest at precisely the operational level, where he (like some of his critics) considered himself to be blameless.

Churchill's most important lesson from the Gallipoli episode was that "my one fatal mistake was trying to achieve a great enterprise without having the plenary authority which could so easily have carried it to success."[180] Given his character, that comes as no surprise. However, since in this case clear defects are apparent in Churchill's method of decision taking, it remains to be seen whether the same defects recurred when he did possess supreme authority during World War II. If not, then it may be deduced that the defects apparent during the Gallipoli episode were the result of external pressures at work within the decision-making system of the times and of the particular strategic circumstances of the case. But if they do recur in circumstances that bear comparison with those of Gallipoli, then it may be concluded that one is dealing with a personal syndrome and not a question of the distribution of authority.

3

"How Are We to Win the War?"
1916-1918

Once he had been forced to resign as First Lord of the Admiralty, Churchill was gradually removed from the focus of power and influence in the Cabinet, and was no longer a party to the strategic management of the war. That remained his situation even after his return to the government as Minister of Munitions in June 1917; but it did not prevent him from continuing to express firm—albeit not always clear or coherent—opinions on the conduct of war strategy.

Churchill's strategy rested on two foundations. The first, as we have already seen, was his ambition to achieve a synthesis between the "continental" and "maritime-peripheral" schools. The second was his opposition to a compromise peace and his insistence on the necessity for Germany's decisive defeat.

Churchill had begun to think in terms of total war before anyone else in Britain. Early in the 1930s he wrote: "I have always urged fighting wars and other contentions with might and main till overwhelming victory, and then offering the hand of friendship to the vanquished."[1] During the Boer War he had called for "victory at any price" and had supported Kitchener's extreme measures against the Boer civilian population.[2] Even then he had emphasized that the nature of modern warfare demands the total exploitation of a nation's human and material resources to bring about the enemy's defeat.[3] Similarly, from the very outbreak of the war he had obstinately opposed every attempt to bring it to a conclusion by reaching a compromise peace with Germany. In general, this opinion was shared by the British political leadership, but there were moments when the possibility of a compromise peace was seriously discussed—especially after the United States had entered the conflict and Russia had effectively left it at the end of 1917. Until the middle of 1916 Lloyd George had himself considered reaching a negotiated peace;[4] when apprised of the fact, Churchill was prepared to "part company" with him "for ever."[5] He maintained that: "Not to win decisively is to have all this misery over again after an uneasy truce and to fight it over again, probably under less favourable circumstances and, perhaps, alone."[6]

Churchill regarded the war as an ideological struggle that brooked no compromise. Whereas in the past monarchies had fought over successions or economic and commercial interests, "this war," he stated, "has become a conflict between Christian civilization and scientific barbarism, between nations where peoples own Governments, and nations where the Governments own peoples. ... The struggle is between right and wrong...."[7] He emphasized that a contest of that type demanded a clear-cut solution, because the victor had to possess the capability to impose his will on the vanquished.[8] Considering that the roots of German aggression and military might lay in what he termed "Prussian Militarism," Churchill aimed to uproot that evil by bringing about a social change within Germany itself. In his opinion, that would be accomplished when the Germans had themselves been brought to their senses by decisive military defeat and when the Allies had thereby also attained absolute power.[9] (Even during World War II, he continued to maintain this one-dimensional view, which attributed the German problem to "Prussian Militarism.")

The ambition to achieve total victory over Germany reflected the very nature of Churchill's personality; another contributory influence, however, was that of radical liberalism. Precisely the same Radicals whose opinions Churchill had shared before 1910, and who had opposed Britain's entry into the war, had changed their tune once the conflict had broken out. They then transmuted the war into an ideological crusade aimed at the defeat of German militarism, the universal dissemination of democracy, and the establishment of a new world order. They hoped to do away with the old diplomacy and the balance-of-power system, to both of which they attributed a large share of the blame for the outbreak of the war. They thereby aspired to give meaning to a conflict they had not wished for. As H. G. Wells put it, this was to be "the war to end war."[10] Churchill's own path had been convoluted. When supporting Britain's entry into the war on behalf of the principle of the maintenance of the balance of power, he had discarded most of his earlier radical opinions; but he did nevertheless proclaim extreme war aims—some of them idealistic—which were akin to those posited by the Radicals. On the other hand, he was skeptical about their intention to establish a new world order and their negation of the balance-of--power principle. However, as would be seen, although he became a "realist," he could never entirely free himself of an idealistic attitude toward international relations.

Ultimately, of course, Churchill's opposition to a compromise peace was also rooted in military considerations. He estimated that the Allies had only to show stamina for Germany to succumb to its inferiority in human and economic resources. It was on that basis that he rejected the public proposals put forward by Lord Lansdowne, the former Foreign Secretary, the last of which (in July 1918) called for an end to the war and peace negotiations with Germany.[11]

However, once the aim of war becomes the total defeat of the enemy then even the strategy and means employed in its pursuit become unlimited. Both logic and practice dictate a direct correlation between the objectives of war and the strategy employed in war. From the perspective of war aims there existed no difference between Churchill and Haig, Robertson and the other advocates of the "western school." The latter also aimed at the total defeat of Germany and its army. Churchill took issue with some of their operational and strategic proposals, but the intensity of that disagreement was less than is conventionally thought. When at the end of 1914 Hankey and Lloyd George proposed to break the stalemate in the west by means of a Balkan "eastern" strategy, their aim was the attainment of territorial and political gains that could be used as a basis for negotiations toward a compromise peace with Germany. Churchill, however, supported the Balkan strategy without at all concurring with that line of thinking. To his mind, the strategic move against Turkey and in the Balkans was only meant to promote the total defeat of Germany.

After his resignation from the Admiralty in May 1915, Churchill pressed for the concentration of effort at Gallipoli until a decision had been reached. He opposed any retreat, including the successful withdrawal from Gallipoli effected at the end of 1915. In October he suggested that the strategic line to be pursued in 1916 should consist of absolute abstention from offensives in the west and the continuation of the Gallipoli offensive.[12] His hope of salvaging his personal prestige seems to have influenced his strategic judgment. It was at this point that the inner balance that had characterized his strategic thinking prior to the war and its first stage began to become unhinged; its equilibrium was not restored until the very end of the conflict.

His words when he finally resigned from the government in November 1915 were almost prophetic (although their content was also voiced by others). "Old wars were decided by their episodes rather than by their tendencies. In this war the tendencies are far more important than the episodes. Without winning any sensational victories, we may win the war." The Entente powers' command of the sea, their numerical superiority, and "the rapid and enormous destruction of the German military manhood" would result in the collapse of Germany's infrastructure, even if its lines were not themselves breached.[13]

From about this point on, Churchill began to base his strategy on a war of attrition against Germany. In effect, his dispute with the decision makers in London focused on the manner whereby that aim might most effectively be attained. For most of the war, Churchill was a consistent opponent of the large-scale offensives initiated in the west by the French, and by Kitchener, Robertson, and Haig. This was not because he did not recognize the importance of the western theater, which he always considered the main one—and at some stages of the war also the decisive one. Rather, his opposition reflected his opinion that such attacks were premature. In August 1916 he wrote a convincing memorandum that contradicted the conventional assessment, demonstrating that British losses in the recent offensives had greatly exceeded those suffered by the Germans.[14] He maintained that those inopportune attacks had resulted in the attrition of the Anglo-French forces and had retarded the agglomeration of the strength necessary for a decisive blow in the west.[15] Another serious influence on his view was his inherent humanism and his horror at what he considered to be futile slaughter—especially when his personal prestige was not at stake. Therein lay the crux of the dispute between Churchill and the British generals. Haig and Robertson contended that, even if such offensives would not lead to an immediate decision on the battlefield, they would draw so much German blood that they would eventually result in the "complete overthrow" of the enemy.[16]

Even while preferring the adoption of a defensive strategic posture in the west until the time came for the decisive blow in that theater, Churchill still hoped to revive the strategic maneuver and flanking attack. Addressing Parliament early in 1917, he stated that

> the vital part of the problem of man-power is the frugality of its use....
> Machines save life, machine power is a substitute for man-power, brains will save blood, manoeuvre is a great diluting agent to slaughter, and can be made to reduce the quantity of slaughter required to effect any particular object. Generally it is not considered in the simple use of force but in the adroit augmentation and application of force. A great manoeuvre of war, the kind of manoeuvre for which the great generals of the past were rendered famous, bears the same relation to the ordinary application of force as the pully or lever in its ordinary application to power. Past commanders won fame by novel and unexpected methods. In the first two years of this war there were great possibilities of manoeuvres both geographical and mechanical, and there are still great possibilities.[17]

Churchill regarded the maneuver in a multidimensional light. Maneuver began on the battlefield itself, on the enemy's flank and in his rear; it also found expression in military technology, in timing, in the psychological dimension, and in diplomatic moves. The success of one side in drawing a state into its camp is equivalent to a great victory in battle.[18] But he did not consider the maneuver, in its various forms, as a substitute for the decisive battle or for the carnage of war. He was fully aware that a mixture of those elements was vital if the decision were to be attained. His own ideal was clear: "Battles are won by slaughter and manoeuvre. The greater the General, the more he contributes in manoeuvre, the less he demands in slaughter."[19] However, he found it difficult to propose reasonable solutions, both with regard to the methods of attrition and slaughter and with regard to the way in which the grand maneuver might once again be introduced into the war.

From the very beginning of the war it had become apparent to Churchill and others that the effect of a blockade would be extremely slow. For operational reasons, the blockade was imposed at considerable distance from the German coastline, a circumstance that impaired its effectiveness. Germany's command of the Baltic Sea enabled it to transport vital raw materials from Sweden, while Holland's neutrality acted as a kind of air vent, supplying Germany with access to international trade. Furthermore, Germany was able to obtain most of the resources it still lacked from the territories that it had conquered in the east (an area which, by the end of 1915, encompassed Serbia, most of Galicia, Poland and Lithuania, and portions of White Russia and Latvia; at the end of 1916, it also mastered Rumania). Churchill himself thought that Germany's preferred strategy ought to have been aimed at the defeat of Russia and the economic consolidation of eastern conquests, while maintaining a defensive posture in the west. In his opinion, Falkenhayn should have pursued that course in 1916 rather than attacking Verdun.[20] Although the Germans did not adopt that strategy, they came close. Verdun apart, between the failure of the Schlieffen Plan and the March offensive of 1918 they refrained from attacks in the west. However partial, their eastern conquests were large enough to grant them considerable staying power. Hence, if the Allies were to hasten Germany's defeat, they had no choice but to kill as many Germans as possible. Most of Britain's senior statesmen and soldiers had reached that conclusion as early as the summer of 1915.[21] Churchill, it will be recalled, had also noted that need.[22] But how could that aim be accomplished if the Germans adopted a defensive posture in the west and if, as Churchill maintained, the Entente powers were themselves to refrain from offensives on that front? To an extent, he did appreciate the weakness of his own position. He maintained that it did not imply that France and Britain were to be idle in the west; rather, they could thin out their lines to entice the Germans to attack and then trap them in an enormous salient.[23] But that was an anemic proposal, which quite underestimated the Germans' tactical shrewdness. Falkenhayn warned against precisely that danger as early as the beginning of 1915,[24] and it is extremely doubtful that the French would have been prepared to yield ground—even temporarily.

Similarly vague was Churchill's response to the question as to how the grand maneuver was to be renewed. In *The World Crisis* he admitted that after 1915 the political and strategic possibilities for maneuver on the enemy's periphery had seriously declined.[25] At the beginning of 1917 he stated that the Allies had missed the opportunity for action in the Balkans; effective results in that region depended on the deployment of massive forces, whose transportation and provision were beyond available shipping capacity.[26]

Unfortunately, in 1917 the shipping problem had not only curtailed the possibility of creating new fronts on the European periphery; for Britain, it had also become a matter of survival. The German adoption of "unrestricted" submarine warfare at the beginning of 1917 raised shipping losses to an unacceptable level. Had the sinkings continued at the same rate, Britain would have been unable to maintain supplies to its civilian economy and to the large army in France.[27] The Germans were close to forcing Britain out of the war, and would have managed to do so had it not been for the last-minute introduction of the convoy system, which reduced shipping losses abruptly.

Prior to the war, Churchill had agreed with the Admiralty's view that submarines did not represent a real threat to the British merchant marine. He had opposed the adoption of a defensive approach—such as convoy escorts—to attacks on the shipping lanes by commerce raiders; the latter, he thought, could be neutralized by "a policy of vigorous offence" against their bases.[28] As long as the German threat to shipping seemed to have been successfully contained, he continued to consider that the conditions of modern technology had reduced the power of the maritime raider.[29] But in 1917, with the rate of sinkings climbing monthly, Churchill became as embarrassed as were the Admiralty experts. Unlike most of them, however, he did have an answer. The root of the problem, he claimed, lay in the Navy's search for defensive solutions at a time when it should have been adopting offensive measures aimed at pinning the enemy down.[30] In April, Lloyd George and the Admiralty did eventually decide on the convoy system, although its introduction was delayed until the end of July. However, by the beginning of that month Churchill had returned to the government, and he again proposed the Borkum plan as a solution to the submarine problem. Indeed, that scheme had by now become his pet panacea for all of Britain's strategic woes.

Churchill's memorandum on this subject was one of the longest he ever wrote. The basic idea contained nothing that was new; he merely adapted it to the novel conditions of the war. He contended that the time had come to impose on Germany the "close blockade" that had been neglected prior to the outbreak of war. By seizing Borkum and turning it into a naval base of its own, Britain would be able to blockade the Heligoland Bight. The naval confrontation would compel the German submarine force to concentrate its attentions on this zone and thereby considerably reduce pressure on the Atlantic. The German fleet would be forced to leave its anchorages and give battle. The capture of Borkum would also serve other purposes: it would create a diversion on the northern flank, to be exploited once the great offensive was launched in the west after the arrival of the Americans in France; it would hasten Holland's entry into the war; and it would lead to the conquest of Schleswig-Holstein and to British command of the Baltic. The main portion of the memorandum was devoted to a punctilious examination of the problems involved in taking and holding the island, and to their solutions.[31]

Of all his proposals, the clearest and most well known were those that concerned the construction of artificial and towed harbors and of tank-carrying landing craft. But not even brilliant technical ideas could buttress a strategic plan that the Admiralty experts pronounced impracticable when they examined it anew at the end of 1917. As Admiral Keyes (who had been an enthusiastic supporter of the Dardanelles plan) wrote to Churchill that the "Borkum plan simply wasn't *War* under modern conditions."[32]

Some difference of opinion exists as to whether the introduction of the convoy system was forced on the Navy by the politicians (meaning Lloyd George), or whether the Admiralty reached a similar conclusion on its own account once the United States had entered the war. Most scholars take the former view and even Marder (who favors the Navy's version of the episode) considers that it was their characteristic ignorance of history that prevented senior officers at the Admiralty from having a broad grasp of the issue. An awareness of history would have helped them to appreciate that the convoy system was feasible and enabled them to introduce it at an earlier stage.[33] After all, it had proven its effectiveness for centuries, and had been particularly successful during the Napoleonic Wars. Mahan, too, had been absolutely clear on the subject; the lesson of the wars of the past, he pronounced, was that it was better to adopt a convoy system against maritime raiders than to seek them out. (On the other hand, it must be noted that Corbett had later questioned the effectiveness of convoys in modern conditions, noting that they were unwieldy and expensive.)[34]

Churchill had no doubt that it was the political echelon that had saved Britain from defeat.[35] The "astonishing [fact] that the politicians were right and the Admiralty authorities were wrong" he took as a "guidance for the future."[36] The episode reinforced the conclusion he had already reached after Gallipoli: "The experts were frequently wrong. The politicians were frequently right."[37] But this was a case in which Churchill was one of the erring politicians. Notwithstanding his exhortations to learn from history, he too had failed to consider the convoy system an effective means of solving the problem. This was not the last time that his characteristic leanings toward the offensive were to undermine his strategic judgment.

The hopes Churchill placed in the Borkum plan were not restricted to solving the submarine crisis. He also aimed thereby to reintroduce the element of grand maneuver into the war. In that same month of July he also proposed an attack on Alexandretta[38] and supported an offensive against Turkey from the direction of Egypt. But shortly thereafter, at the end of 1917, he opposed the reinforcement of the eastern theater, since he feared that the western theater—where he expected the Germans to launch a massive attack in 1918[39]—might thereby be weakened too much. Unlike Lloyd George, who enthusiastically revived the campaign against Turkey and strengthened the Salonika front, Churchill was far from being an "easterner." The worsening situation in Russia, together with the entry of the United States into the war in April 1917, excited his interest in the western front, of which he now had new hopes. In October he asserted that the quickest way to achieve a decisive victory over Germany was to smash its army on the western front. In his own words:

> It would be a thousand pities to discard this direct and obvious method of victory in favour of weaker, more roundabout, protracted and far less decisive strategy, unless we are convinced that we have not the power to conquer on the Western Front.[40]

He advised that the Allies await the arrival of the Americans; amass sufficient superiority in the west; and then, in 1918, launch a massive offensive based on tanks.[41] In March and June 1918, while the great German offensive was in full swing, Churchill demanded that detailed preparations be drawn up for a decisive attack in the west in 1919, to be based on the massive employment of tanks, planes, and gas.[42] His ideas bore a marked resemblance to the well-known 1919 Plan, which fortunately did not have to be carried out. He was critical of the utility of the developing campaign against Turkey in the Near East. The forces transferred from the western front to Allenby's command did bring triumphs, but those had no effect on the fateful campaign being fought in the west in 1918. As Churchill later recalled: "Enough was sent East to be a dangerous dispersion, and never at one time enough to compel a prompt conclusion . . . the clash of the Western and Eastern schools produced incoherence and half-measures."[43] Translated into Churchill's own terminology, the east had ceased to be "the decisive theatre"; in the 1917-1918 period the west had once again become both the "main" and "decisive" theater.

These comments again highlight the internal problematics of the strategy Churchill preached since the beginning of 1916. On the one hand, there existed no "decisive theatre" other than the "main theatre"; neither was it possible to open up other fronts on the enemy's littoral. On the other hand, an offensive in the west had to await the attainment of decisive quantitative superiority. How then was Germany to be defeated if it did not itself attack in the west? Russia was slowly collapsing and Germany was adding the resources of the east to the French industrial assets that it already possessed. In that situation, and with that kind of strategy, the war could have lasted far longer than it did. Other than mass attacks in the west, the British and French leadership could conceive of no option that might exacerbate the attrition of Germany and delay its capacity to launch a major offensive against Russia.

In *The World Crisis* Churchill argued that Germany's collapse was not brought about by the major offensives in the west of 1916 and 1917; rather, the German army was worn down by the failure of Ludendorff's major offensive of March 1918. The Germans sustained some 700,000 casualties in that offensive, while during the same period they mobilized no more than 150,000 new conscripts. The attrition of German manpower caused by the March offensive, Churchill claimed, had converged with the apex of the blockade and the aggregation of psychological strain, thus producing a murderous combination. Had Ludendorff not attacked in the west, Germany would have been able to stand firm throughout 1918.[44]

Churchill was correct to point out that British and French losses during the course of their western offensives were larger than those inflicted on the Germans.[45] His error lay in his treating the 1918 German offensive as an isolated move; in fact, its far-reaching results bore a direct relation to the accumulated losses that Germany had previously suffered. Churchill simply refused to admit the extent to which Germany's manpower had already been worn down. To have done so would have contradicted his own opposition to the large-scale attacks in the west. No mathematical expertise is required to conclude that it was the severe erosion in the annual quotas of conscripts between 1915 and 1917 that prevented Germany making up the enormous manpower deficiencies created by the failure of the offensive in 1918.

There is no way of evading the fact that, notwithstanding the operational folly of their implementation, the great Allied offensives in the west did make a vital contribution to Germany's collapse. After the war, Churchill himself privately admitted as much to H. A. L. Fisher, whom he informed "that economic causes were very subsidiary in determining German defeat, but that if the English and French had ceased attacking, Germany, though strong, could not have won."[46]

Churchill wanted to have the best of all worlds: he wished to avoid the extremely costly direct offensives in the west; but at the same time he called for a strategy of attrition (which also involved killing as many Germans as possible) and for the sort of grand maneuver that had not been feasible since 1916. The circumstances of World War I made it impossible to satisfy these demands. The sole logical answer to his approach was a compromise peace, to be reached even from a position of some allied inferiority. But the fact that Churchill was not prepared to settle for anything less than total victory over Germany made it impossible to realize that option. It is a mistake to attribute the offensives in the west to the politicians' loss of control over the military or to their having been mesmerized by the Generals' assurance that such attacks would win the war. Absolutely fundamental to the military's position was the fact that the politicians, for their own varied reasons, opposed any compromise peace. (Lloyd George changed his position the moment he assumed power.) Once they adopted that stand, the politicians immediately deprived themselves of a central pivot of leverage in their tussle with the military over the shaping of strategy. Churchill somewhat contradicted himself when arguing that Germany ought to have adopted a defensive strategy in the west in 1918, thereby creating conditions that would have enabled its forcing the Allies to negotiate on terms favorable to Germany,[47] while he and many others were opposed to any compromise peace.

Churchill's explanations for Germany's defeat amount to a maladroit attempt to combine an objective military interpretation of the war with a justification for his own strategic views during its course. He claimed that the Germans brought disaster on themselves by committing three major strategic blunders. The first was their decision to invade France by way of Belgium, which led to Britain's entry into the war. The second was their decision to embark on unrestricted submarine warfare at the beginning of 1917, which dragged the United States into the conflict. The third was their decision to launch an offensive in the west in 1918.[48] To these three blunders, which he itemized in that order, he often added another in both *The World Crisis* and one of his other books: instead of attacking Verdun (in the west) in 1916, the Germans should then have moved eastward in order to defeat Russia, take over its economic resources, and threaten the British Empire from the north.[49] He maintained that the mistake of the German military leadership lay in its failure to take the economic dimension into account in its military considerations and plans.

Few observers are likely to quibble with Churchill's catalog of Germany's strategic blunders. Of themselves, however, they do not explain why the German collapse occurred in 1918 and not very much later. Churchill himself insisted that, despite the arrival of the Americans, Germany could have imposed peace negotiations on terms favorable to itself had it only refrained from launching offensives in the west; moreover, and as has already been pointed out, the influence of the failure of Ludendorff's attack in 1918 can only be explained by reference to the previous Anglo-French offensives on the western front. Indirectly, Churchill's explanation reveals the weaknesses in his own strategic thinking and, for all their lack of humanity, the strengths of the opinions held by Haig and Robertson. In the main, albeit unwittingly, his strategy was based on the assumption that the Germans would commit serious mistakes at the very highest level of strategic formulation. Bearing in mind what in fact transpired during both world wars, it could in retrospect be argued that this was not an unrealistic line to take. But the German weakness could not have been known at the time of World War I. Besides, and as a general rule, strategy cannot consist almost entirely of awaiting the antagonist's errors; on the contrary, its formulators must assume that their enemy will act with the utmost strategic wisdom. But had the latter been the case, Churchill would have found himself in a state of severe contradiction. By his own admission, he considered that the Germans' best strategic policy was to remain on the defensive in the west and strike out in the east. However, had the Allies adopted Churchill's advice to refrain from attacks in the west until they had amassed decisive superiority, they would then have encouraged the German high command to adopt an "eastern strategy" and also have played into that strategy's hands.

Churchill gave the following account of the immediate causes for the German collapse: "Yet it was only indirectly from the tremendous collisions in the West that the final blow to German resisting power came."

It was precisely the much-disputed Balkan theater that

> was destined to produce the culminating decision. The strength of . . . a chain, however ponderous, is that of its weakest link. The Bulgarian link was about to snap, and with it the remaining cohesion of the whole hostile coalition. This event was not, however, induced by local circumstances. It resulted from the consternation which followed the defeat of the German armies in France. . . . The reactions were reciprocal: the German defeats undermined Bulgarian resistance, and the Bulgarian surrender pulled out the linchpin of the German combination.[50]

This account attaches far too much weight to the influence of Bulgaria's exit from the war on Germany's final collapse. Churchill wrote as he did in order to substantiate his own overall strategy, to justify his search for a harmonious synthesis between the "main theatre" and fronts on the European periphery and, above all, in defense of the Balkan concept that he had held during the early stages of the war. In effect, the fronts did not exert a reciprocal and bilateral effect on each other. Once Russia had left the war, only the German attack in the west allowed Bulgaria's withdrawal from the war to have an impact on its course. Germany had sufficient forces at its disposal to deal with any problem in the east. For three years, the Franco-British force on the Salonika front had sat idle and helpless. The Bulgarians only dropped their resistance when the few German troops that had stiffened their lines were transferred to the west to fill the gaps there. Germany's fate was sealed by the failure of its western offensive, by the cumulative influence of the blockade, by the Allied counteroffensive on August 8 (the German army's "black day"), by Ludendorff's nervous collapse, by the beginnings of social and political dissolution at the front and in the rear, and above all by the continuous influx of massive American forces. The period from August to November 1918, during which Bulgaria withdrew from the war, was only a "dragging anti-climax."[51] Churchill did grasp that the decision was attained in the west. Nevertheless, he was hypnotized by his own words and began to believe that there had indeed existed a causal and real link between Bulgaria's withdrawal from the war and Germany's collapse. This illusion he carried over into World War II.

Throughout the war, Churchill sought to attain and apply a strategic synthesis of the "continental" and "peripheral-maritime" schools. The strategic conceptions he held prior to the war and until the second half of 1915 were basically sound, principally because he recognized the vital nature and priority of the westernEuropean theater. He got into difficulties and failed when he attempted to apply the peripheral dimension of his conception. Between late in 1915 and the end of the war, his strategic thinking was vitiated by its own inner contradictions. Hitherto, his main problems had concerned the nature and feasibility of moves on the European periphery; during the latter period of the war, however, they stemmed from the very nature of the strategic conception itself. Nevertheless, this problematic aspect of his strategy made itself felt only when the issue concerned was the method of bringing about Germany's defeat — Churchill knew how not to lose the war, but not how to win it.

The broad tenor of the spirit conveyed in Churchill's *The World Crisis* is that, had his strategic plans been fully accepted and properly carried out, the war would have been shorter and less costly to the Allies.[52] That conviction has been strengthened by others: R. Blake observed that Churchill's powerful personal and political position during World War II was in part due to the fact that he enjoyed "far greater prestige as a military expert, based on the subsequent vindication of his strategical views in World War I." Liddell Hart similarly recorded that during World War I, Churchill's "[strategic] vision excelled that of most of his contemporaries."[53] The conclusion suggested by the past two chapters of the present study, however, is different: had the strategy that Churchill advocated after the end of 1915 indeed been fully implemented, then Germany would not have been defeated in 1918. Perhaps the war would not have been terminated by a decisive Allied victory, as Churchill wished, but would have ended in a compromise peace.

4

History and the "Continental Commitment," 1919-1939

The Strategist as Economist—the Economist as Strategist

Britain's strategic position after the war was worse than it had been during the period prior to 1914. Imperial responsibilities increased considerably after 1919, while the means of sustaining them declined in both absolute and relative terms.[1] Moreover, the development of air power and the growth of a school of thought, in both Britain and elsewhere, that regarded it as a self-contained means of attaining a strategic decision, seemed to have fatally undermined the invulnerability of the British Isles and the sense of security instilled by the Royal Navy. These two circumstances served to underscore the basic lesson of the war: that the security of Britain could not be divorced from that of western Europe.[2] Moreover, and as Churchill fully appreciated, the course of the war had shown just how fine the European balance of power was.[3] Germany had stood virtually alone against a triple alliance of the other continental powers. To repulse Germany, the latter had been required to make supreme efforts; in order to defeat Germany they had needed the additional weight of the United States. The implication was that the sharp asymmetry in the balance of power (potential though it may have been as long as Germany remained disarmed) did not leave Britain many policy choices—it had lost much of its freedom of maneuver.

Although these facts and conclusions reinforced the positions maintained by the "continental school" in British strategic thought, the debate on the nation's future involvement in the continent became even more fierce between the two world wars. The powerful sentimental reaction of the British public and its leadership to the awful bloodshed on the western front "unfortunately. . . tended afterwards to distort the debate about the correctness or otherwise of the strategic principles on which the campaigns of the war had been planned." Correctly or not, these sentiments were strengthened by supporters of the "eastern school" and "tended to obscure how much and for how long Britain's security had been intimately related to the security of western Europe."[4] Few were prepared to draw the ultimate conclusions. There was indeed a latent recognition that Britain's security depended on that of western Europe. But it was extremely difficult to deduce therefrom that the security of western Europe required the involvement of large British land forces on the Continent.[5]

Another circumstance preventing a clear view of Britain's strategic problems during this period was the powerful influence exerted on decision makers by public opinion. True, such influence had also been apparent prior to 1914 but the ruling elite, which was still aristocratic in nature, had then been far less sensitive to its force. The postwar period, however, witnessed the emergence of a large electorate imbued with a class consciousness, which preferred social reforms to financial outlays on armaments. Moreover, this electorate brought to power politicians and governments acutely sensitive to its feelings and which regarded public opinion "as the final court of jurisdiction."[6] To this must be added the fact that the political and strategic positions adopted by the politicians were in most cases also influenced by their own harsh experiences during the war. Thus it was that a process of feedback was created between the political elite and its pacifist electorate. So much was this so that it confused the boundaries between leaders and their followings.[7]

■

Churchill played an important part in the formulation of defense policy during the 1920s. He was Secretary of State for War and Air when, in 1919, the "ten years' rule" was laid down as the guideline for the scope and character of British armament. In broad outline, the rule provided that the various defense estimates should be framed on the assumption "that the British Empire will not be engaged in any great war during the next ten years, and that no expeditionary force is required for this purpose."[8] This rule was successively renewed in 1925, 1926, and 1927; in 1928, when Churchill was Chancellor of the Exchequer, the government adopted his recommendation that it be considered permanent "until, on the initiative of the Foreign Office or one of the fighting services or otherwise, it is decided to alter it."[9] Not until March 1932 was the rule rescinded by Ramsay MacDonald's Government.

Nobody now questions the fact that the adoption of the "ten years' rule" had a deleterious effect on Britain's defense position during the 1930s. Some historians have claimed that Churchill was the person responsible for its initiation.[10] In fact, it was proposed by Austen Chamberlain, then Chancellor of the Exchequer, and Sir Maurice Hankey, Secretary to the Cabinet and to the Committee of Imperial Defence,[11] Churchill did no more than enthusiastically follow their lead and "refine" the rule. It enjoyed the support of a large number of Ministers in various governments, and the Chiefs of Staff did not themselves oppose its initiation.[12]

As had previously been the case, Churchill's name was associated with the rule and its contingent policy because of the zeal he invested in Britain's disarmament during the 1920s. As Secretary of State for War and Air he supported massive reductions in the Army and its budget, and when appointed Chancellor of the Exchequer in 1924 he wielded the ax in cuts with unflagging energy. His economic thinking was conservative, and a balanced budget his ambition. As at the beginning of the century, he still believed that Britain's advantage over other European powers lay in its ability to prosper during peacetime without the need to incur the expenses involved in maintaining a large army. (However, it must be noted that most of the cuts during his tenure in office were directed against future plans for naval construction, since there was nothing further to reduce in the Army's budget.)

In 1921 the lapse of the Anglo-Japanese alliance forged in 1902, and the deepening rivalry between the United States and Japan, brought British decision makers to a new crossroad. The genesis of a U.S.-Japanese naval race, together with the fact that certain circles in the United States were challenging the Royal Navy's hegemony, threatened to drag Britain into the maelstrom of a new naval race that, as her leaders appreciated, the country did not possess the economic strength to sustain.

Churchill's first, almost reflexive, reaction was that Britain had to retain its standing as the world's leading naval power. "I am sure," he wrote to Balfour, "that we shall be judged all over the world in peacetime on the numbers of Capital ships available."[13] But within a few months his ardor had cooled. Once he had studied all sides of the problem, he became a convinced supporter of the Dominion position that Britain had to prefer the United States to Japan. His arguments did not differ very much from those that prompted the British government to sign the Washington Treaty in 1922 although—as usual—the geostrategic perspective was central to his thinking.

Churchill determined that the potential threat in the Far East lay in Japan rather than in the United States. It would be "meaningless" to conclude an alliance with the former for the purpose of ensuring the safety of Australia and New Zealand; the arrangement would in effect rest upon Japan's goodwill. The correct course was to deter Japan. Britain had therefore to strengthen its ties of friendship with the United States, since the combination of British and U.S. naval power would leave Japan helpless. Conversely, an alliance between Japan and Britain would impell the United States to build a fleet larger than their combined navies. The resultant Anglo-American naval race would prove dangerous from both military and economic points of view.[14]

While Churchill regarded the Washington Naval Treaty as a British success,[15] it has been described by the historian C. Barnett as one of the greatest catastrophes in British history.[16] He is not alone in attempting to draw a direct line stretching from the Washington Treaty to the policy pursued by the British government at the end of the 1930s. The agreement unquestionably constituted a turning point in Britain's imperial history. The establishment of a numerical ratio of 5:5:3 between the capital ships possessed by Britain, the United States, and Japan endowed the latter with naval superiority in the western Pacific and created a situation of Anglo-American naval parity. Moreover, this was at a time when Britain's defense responsibilities were dispersed over all the seven seas and were far more extensive than those of either Japan or the United States. But in fact British statesmen of the times could never have reached an agreement that could have simultaneously attained the disarmament agreement vital for the British economy, preserved good relations with Japan, ensured American friendship, and also prevented Japanese naval superiority in the Far East. As P. Kennedy has put it, Britain's greatest error was that it "was unlucky." There was little likelihood that it would have to cope with the sort of contemporaneous and triple threat in each of its principal naval theaters, which in fact occurred at the end of the 1930s.[17]

In effect, Britain's choice meant that the defense of the Far East, as well as the task of halting future Japanese expansion and ultimately defending Australia and New Zealand, would also fall on the U.S. shoulders—even without a clear commitment on the part of the United States. Even inadvertently, the latter would have to defend British interests in the Far East when safeguarding its own. Churchill, with his markedly idiosyncratic view of Anglo-American relations, came close to this conclusion as early as 1924, at a time when it was barely perceived by others. As much can be indirectly ascertained from his refusal to construct a naval base at Singapore.[18]

Economic circumstances, as well as the limitations imposed by the Washington Treaty, prevented Britain from maintaining a standing fleet in the Far East powerful enough to contend with Japan. The Admiralty's plan was that, in the event of an Anglo-Japanese war, the majority of the fleet would be dispatched to the enlarged and fortified anchorage at Singapore. Parsimony apart, Churchill had two other reasons for opposing that idea. One was his conviction that there was not "the slightest chance" of a war with Japan "in our lifetime." The second was that logistic difficulties would preclude a Japanese invasion of Australia. Japan would not be able to operate large land forces at the end of a maritime line of supply 5,000 miles long. Even if the United States did not enter the war, the Japanese invasion would be repelled by Australian and British imperial forces. (To extend further Churchill's line of reasoning: any attempt on the part of Japan to overcome her logistic difficulties by adopting the course of "island hopping" would certainly encounter U.S. resistance.) Should Britain and Japan come into conflict over China, the transfer of the majority of the fleet to the Far East to take part in what would necessarily be a protracted war would place Britain at the mercy of a hostile European power.[19] Thus, he remained faithful to his basic position regarding the nature of the strategic link between Europe and imperial defense.

Churchill's assessment was justified by the events of World War II. Even when the construction of the naval base at Singapore was completed, the German and Italian threat prevented the dispatch to the Far East of a naval force powerful enough to repulse the Japanese fleet. During the Abyssinian (Ethiopian) crisis, when Britain enjoyed marked naval supremacy in European waters and the German fleet was still in its infancy, the Lords of the Admiralty were unwilling to confront Italy and its navy, notwithstanding the latter's obvious numerical and strategic inferiority. What they feared was a *future* threat in the Far East.[20] They were even less likely to have sent the majority of the fleet to the Far East after the emergence of a German threat in the waters of northern Europe.

It is difficult to estimate the damage caused by the "ten years' rule." All three services were affected. The RAF was far from completing the establishment of the fifty-two squadrons projected by a program decided upon as early as the beginning of the 1920s. The Army was hit hardest of all. But it is difficult to gauge the extent to which the damage thus caused exceeded that which would in any case have occurred. Any island nation that had no immediate enemies, but which labored under the burden of economic difficulties, would have seriously reduced its military expenditures—even without the magic formula of the rule. Nevertheless, it did very much help the Exchequer to persist in its policy of cuts throughout the 1920s and 1930s. The Chiefs of Staff could not confirm that war would not break out within the next ten years and, at the same time, oppose the program of reductions. Still less were they able to obtain the resources required for long-term armament programs.

The persistent pronouncement that another ten years of peace could be expected did clearly generate in high military and political circles an atmosphere of mental torpor and overconfidence. But the greatest danger of the rule lay in its assumptions: that Britain's decision makers of the future would be able to identify any potential threat in good time and that the transformation from a process of disarmament to one of rearmament would be swift. It is true, as Churchill claims, that the decision to rescind the rule came at just the right moment, in 1932, and left sufficient time for rearmament, provided that it was pursued energetically.[21] In fact, however, three more years were to elapse before Britain commenced substantive rearmament.[22] Besides, the policies to which the rule gave rise brought about the atrophy of frameworks for military development and production, and thus in any case impeded a process of speedy rearmament.[23] It was unrealistic to suppose that a future government, especially if it be one led by the Labour party or even the Liberals, would be capable of swiftly changing course and of instituting an unpopular policy of rearmament.[24] Churchill was himself not insensitive to that danger.[25] Fortunately, the greater danger—that the threat would not be identified in time—was avoided. But that stroke of luck cannot be attributed to the vigilance and exceptional clearsightedness of Britain's leaders. Had the dictators exercised more restraint and discretion when undertaking their own policies of rearmament and aggression, it might have taken Britain longer to reassess the situation and rescind the "ten years' rule."

In 1919, when still Secretary of State for War and Air, Churchill maintained that in the past nations had declined after winning wars because they had mismanaged their economies. He assured the House of Commons that he would greatly reduce the size of the Army.[26] However, in his *Marlborough: His Life and Times*, written in the mid-1930s, he lamented that England's recurrent mistake had been in demobilizing too hastily; in so doing, it had forfeited the fruits of victories. That had been the case, Churchill wrote, after the peace treaties signed at Ryswick (1697), Utrecht (1714), and Paris (1763); the pattern had recurred after the Napoleonic Wars and after the Great War. In each instance, the disbandment of the Army, and sometimes the reduction of the Navy, had prevented the timely exercise of England's weight in Europe and had thereby facilitated the rise of the vanquished.[27] Unfortunately, that lesson was learned too late.

Maintaining the European Balance of Power: Demise of a Principle

During the immediate postwar period, Anglo-French relations were at a decidedly low ebb. Indeed, the entire question of a military alliance with France was now affected by deep emotions. Francophobia was rife among the British public, a reaction to the massive losses on French soil and to the claim that France had dragged Britain into a war which George Milne, subsequently the Chief of the Imperial General Staff (CIGS), termed "abnormal."[28]

Churchill's approach was less sentimental, even though it had undergone transformations since the end of the war. He aimed to reestablish the correct equilibrium of the European balance of power. Like Lloyd George, Keynes, Smuts, and other worthy Britons, he was interested in setting Germany back on its feet so that it could serve as a buffer against the Bolshevik danger and contribute to the rehabilitation of both the European and British economies. He was far more concerned than his Cabinet colleagues about the Bolshevik threat. He feared that a harsh attitude on the part of France, together with the full implementation of the anti-German clauses of the Treaty of Versailles, might lead to German-Soviet cooperation. (Hereafter in this book the correct term "Soviet Union" will be employed interchangeably with the less accurate "Russia." The reason is that Churchill himself continued to use the older term. As will be seen, there was more to this usage than mere semantics or force of habit.) In August 1920, when the Red Army achieved its farthest advance and was close to the Vistula, he proposed the establishment of a triple alliance between France, Britain, and Germany to halt Soviet expansion in Europe. The implication of that alliance, Churchill acknowledged, would be a profound revision of Versailles and Germany's acceptance in full partnership in the future leadership of Europe. Should France and Germany refuse to enter into that sort of arrangement, Britain's second-best strategy would be a policy of isolation—founded on strong naval and air power. Britain might even have to come to a convenient arrangement of its own with Bolshevik Russia. Far worse was the course adopted by the government, which made no choice whatsoever and thus fell between both stools.[29]

The obstacle to the "appeasement" of Germany—to use Churchill's own term—was France, whose aggressive attitude toward Germany was aggravated by its own military superiority. Churchill was not slow to appreciate that the policy of the French was rooted in the fact that they were "obsessed with fear for the future" when Germany's menacing military power might be revived.[30] He believed that the only way to allay those fears and bring France and Germany closer together was to conclude an Anglo-French alliance or to offer a British guarantee to defend France. Indeed an open alliance would be made conditional on France's willingness for rapprochement with Germany. That remained his position between the signing of the Versailles Treaty and the fall of the Lloyd George government in 1922. His basic aims were identical with those of his Cabinet partners—the appeasement of Germany and the restoration of the European balance of power; where he differed was in his chosen path to those objectives. Their attitude at times verged on antagonism toward France and they shuddered at the thought of an alliance with it; but Churchill attempted to achieve the same aims by outright intervention on the Continent.[31]

Two years later, in 1924, Baldwin appointed Churchill his Chancellor of the Exchequer and Austen Chamberlain his Foreign Secretary. It was a time when Franco-German relations were still under the cloud brought on by the Ruhr crisis and its residue. Like his predecessors, Chamberlain aimed at the establishment of a stable European peace by moderate changes in the Treaty of Versailles and by the encouragement of a Franco-German rapprochement. His own inclinations were decidedly francophile, and when he suggested the formation of a firm Anglo-French alliance to the British Cabinet, his thinking was very much in line with that propounded by Churchill three years earlier. He hoped that an alliance with France would dispel the latter's chronic fears of Germany, and thus bring about a Franco-German rapprochement and the reconstitution of the Concert of Europe. But the idea was strongly opposed by the Cabinet and by all sections of the political public.

Even Churchill was one of the fiercest opponents of that alliance. Seemingly, this was a complete *volte-face*. He even found himself in disagreement with the Chiefs of Staff and the Army General Staff. The latter were skeptical about the contribution the League of Nations could make to the security of Britain and France. On the other hand, they were absolutely in favor of a French alliance. In the words used by the Army General Staff:

> For us it is only incidentally a question of French security, essentially it is a matter of British security. . . . The true strategic frontier of Great Britain is the Rhine; her security depends entirely upon the present frontiers of France, Belgium and Holland being maintained and remaining in friendly hands. . . . Any line of policy which permitted Germany (with or without allies) first to swallow up France and then to deal with Great Britain would be fatal strategically.[32]

The General Staff favored a "continental commitment." They explained that the moment such an alliance with France came into operation, all of Britain's land, sea, and air forces would have to participate in the campaign. Britain would not be able to limit its intervention to one service or the other. They added, correctly, that "the question at issue is clearly not well understood by the majority of the British public."³³ (Little did they imagine that their successors in the 1930s would also find it difficult to understand.)

The reason for the change in Churchill's attitude is not to be sought in the "ulterior motives" against Chamberlain suspected by Sir Eyre Crowe, the Permanent Under-Secretary of the Foreign Office. Neither is it correct to say that he abandoned the principle of the balance of power and thereby, in Barnett's phrase, "turned his back on the course of English history."³⁴ His aims had not altered one bit; but he had changed his tactical approach. His new attitude was the result of his clever, perhaps too clever, calculation of the European balance of power. He rejected the claim that Britain could not suffer German control of France's Channel ports. "We dwelt . . . for centuries when these same Channel ports were in the possession of the greatest European military Power, and when that Power—France—was almost increasingly hostile to us." Provided that Britain assured itself of naval and air superiority, there was no reason why it could not stand alone for an unlimited period, as had been the case during the Napoleonic Wars. "It should never be admitted in this argument that England cannot, if the worst comes to the worst, stand alone. I decline to accept as an axiom that our fate is involved in that of France."³⁵ He believed that Britain still possessed the room for maneuver which enabled it to demand that France pay a suitable price. To his colleagues on the Committee of Imperial Defence he explained that the change in his attitude had been occasioned by Raymond Poincaré's aggressive attitude toward Germany. "France, with us, would feel strong enough to keep the antagonism alive, and after all, that is what is going to shatter the peace of the world."³⁶ He feared that a continuation of the age-old Franco-German dispute would lead to the outbreak of "another Armageddon, victory which would compass our ruin." It was his assessment that the present situation, in which France was strong and Germany disarmed, had created the breathing space which permitted that dispute to be settled once and for all. Churchill was convinced that Germany would never accept its new eastern frontiers. Hence, a true Franco-German peace was dependent not only on the withdrawal of Allied forces from German territories in the west, but also on the revision of Germany's eastern borders.³⁷ "If," he claimed, "an [Anglo-French] union meant security in peace and victory in war the case would be justified." But not even combined Anglo-French strength was equivalent to Germany's potential power; the latter could only be equalled by a combination of France and Britain with either Russia or the United States. An Anglo-French alliance would not deter Germany from attacking in the east; it would only impose upon Britain the burden of a harsh dilemma.

Chamberlain feared that a dangerous worsening of Franco-German relations was already imminent; but Churchill saw no immediate danger. He concluded that there was no reason to make haste and conclude an alliance with France at the present time; Britain should wait another few years. Germany might initiate a process of rearmament, as a result of which France's fears would increase and its dependence on Britain become greater. Britain should undertake a permanent and irrevocable commitment to France only after obtaining the concessions, particularly with regard to the eastern frontiers, that would serve as the basis for a true Franco-German peace.[38]

The readiness of Gustav Stresemann, Germany's Foreign Minister, to join an agreement whereby his country recognized its western frontiers as laid down at Versailles enabled the British Cabinet to agree to guarantee these borders against any aggressor. That provided the basis for the well-known Locarno Treaty of October 1925. Churchill even tried to prevent the grant of an explicit two-way guarantee to France and to Germany.[39] (For reasons that he kept to himself, in the relevant passages of his *The Second World War* Churchill makes no mention of his opposition to the proposed alliance with France and his ambivalent attitude toward the Locarno Treaty.)[40] His proposal was rejected; however, Locarno was sufficiently vague about the implementation of the British and Italian guarantee. The British believed that they had retained their freedom of decision for future involvement on the Continent and that they had in effect even reduced their commitment to any such involvement.[41]

From a military point of view, nothing was done to give the treaty any teeth by establishing an expeditionary force to deploy on the European mainland. On the contrary, by 1926 the Army had been so reduced in size that the Chiefs of Staff were then forced to state that its primary objective was imperial defense. The trend toward giving priority to imperial defense over the continental commitment was thereafter accentuated and reached a peak in 1930. Moreover, since Britain had guaranteed to maintain the Franco-German frontier against any aggressor, it refrained from military coordination with France.[42] Most important of all, Stresemann refused to recognize Germany's eastern frontiers and France refused to exert pressure on her own eastern allies. The central problem referred to by Churchill—the eastern frontiers—thus remained. "Locarno," in the words of the historian A. J. P. Taylor, "gave to Europe a period of peace and hope."[43] The hope was that Germany's eastern frontiers would be settled at the next stage. However, the problem of Danzig and the Polish Corridor became the immediate cause and excuse for the outbreak of World War II.

While Churchill's diagnosis was sound, his prognosis was less so. True, the degree of additional security the French attained as a result of the British guarantee, which was not conditional on a solution of the eastern frontiers, may not have encouraged them to solve that problem. Moreover, and as Churchill had feared, after Locarno Britain did lose its power of influence over France. But he was quite wrong to assume that the decline of French power in the face of an increase in German strength would enable Britain to impose a solution to the German problem. British influence over France was powerful during the 1930s. But Germany's destinies were then guided by persons whose appetites would not have been sated even by the complete revision of its eastern frontiers. In any case, such revisions were of doubtful value, since they were the result of Anglo-French weakness rather than strength.

Churchill objected to the talks on disarmament held during the late 1920s and early 1930s. To his mind, since France had no intention of attacking Germany, the maintenance of France's level of armaments constituted the cornerstone for the construction of a stable balance of power. On the other hand, the disarmament of France at a time when Germany's eastern frontiers were still not settled might encourage the Germans to go to war. A weak French army would not leave Britain with many choices, and would force it to send an army to western Europe.[44] During the course of 1930 and 1931, by which time he no longer held ministerial office (and was not to do so until 1939), Churchill warned of Britain's military weakness. Those warnings were not generated by his fear of the German threat, or any other; on several occasions he reiterated his confidence that no European war could be expected for many years. What he feared was that the decline in Britain's power was causing it to lose its diplomatic maneuverability and influence even over its friends.[45] Since Churchill saw no prospect of war in the foreseeable future, he did not propose the abrogation of the "ten years' rule"—notwithstanding the military weakness about which he cautioned. But without rescinding the rule, it would have been difficult to trigger Britain's rearmament.

As early as 1928 Hankey tried to persuade the Chiefs of Staff of the need to define Germany as a "probable enemy." But they did not accept his view.[46] The government decided to reaffirm the "ten years' rule" in 1931. It did so despite the growing sense of alarm caused by the world economic crisis; despite the news of concealed rearmament in Germany and that country's domestic political crisis; despite the difficulties encountered in the disarmament talks; and notwithstanding the fact that several foreign governments had increased their military budgets.[47]

The only danger about which Churchill warned at this stage, and even then only mildly, was that posed by the Soviet Union. He feared that once it had completed its industrialization programs, Russia's outstanding organizational abilities would enable it to threaten the whole of Europe. The Soviet Union could only be repulsed by an alliance between the other nations of Europe and the United States.[48] But his antagonism toward communism did not prevent him from perceiving the threat that national socialism posed to Europe. He told Prince Bismarck, one of the officials at the German embassy in London, that he "was convinced that Hitler or his followers would seize the first available opportunity to resort to armed force." However, in the same breath he expressed his understanding of Germany's position with regard to her eastern borders.[49]

Blatant Japanese aggression in Manchuria at the end of 1931 did not disturb Churchill's peace of mind. At the time, he hardly referred to this problem. Possibly, he was distracted by his various other concerns (his involvement in an automobile accident in the United States confined him to his bed; subsequently, his research for his book on Marlborough took him to Germany). But it seems that his silence was also the result of the fact that he did have some understanding of Japanese motives.[50] Moreover, he thought that Japan would turn northward in order to prevent Soviet aggression in Asia, and not against the territories held by the old European powers and the United States in the south. Not even in 1940-1941 did he retreat from that assessment.

By contrast, the British Chiefs of Staff were alarmed by events in the Far East in 1931. The *Annual Review,* which they composed at the beginning of 1932, pointed out the weaknesses of imperial defense, especially in the Far East. They maintained that Britain might be drawn into a war there and therefore advocated the abrogation of the "ten years' rule," which they accused of having exerted a destructive influence on Britain's armed forces and military industry. They also proposed that the defense of the Far East be accorded priority in the rearmament process. Conspicuous is the absence of any real treatment of the future German threat. Imperial defense still came first on the list. In March 1932 the Committee of Imperial Defence accepted without demur both the assessments tabled by the Chiefs of Staff and their proposals. However, with the exception of the abrogation of the "ten years' rule," nothing was in effect done for the next eighteen months. This "almost unbelievable tardiness," to quote the official historian, stemmed from two principal causes: one was the severe economic situation in Britain; the other, the hopes Cabinet ministers harbored for the success of the Geneva talks on disarmament which opened in February 1932.[51]

In his own history of the Second World War, Churchill claimed that "I gave my first formal warning of approaching war" during the course of a speech he delivered in Parliament on May 13, 1932.[52] That was not an accurate recollection. The speech, in which he criticized the disarmament policy, contained arguments very similar to those he had employed in his earlier addresses, and in particular that of June 1931. The threat which he singled out for attention was that posed by Soviet Russia, not Germany.[53] Not until six months later did he clearly state that Germany was a danger to Europe. He did not believe in the sincerity of Germany's demand for parity in arms with France, and feared the further weakness of a German democracy in which members of the armed forces stood at the apex of power. Should Germany arm itself before its eastern frontiers had been rearranged, it would naturally aim to change them by force. He therefore suggested that the victorious powers take immediate action to solve the problem of those frontiers, while they still enjoyed military superiority. He called upon the government to make certain that Britain's military strength would be sufficient to ensure that the country would not be drawn into a war unwillingly. Britain should go to war only on the basis of a decision taken "by the heart and conscience of the nation."[54] Even after Hitler had gained power in March 1933, and although Churchill already depicted his regime as a military dictatorship, he claimed that the anomaly of the Polish Corridor had to be redressed.[55]

In March 1933 Churchill again attacked the intention to reduce France's military strength within the framework of the disarmament talks. On this occasion he resorted to the argument that most threatened the British public and politicians—any reduction in the French army while German rearmament proceeded apace would increase the likelihood and necessity of British intervention in a European war.[56] In October, Hitler walked out of both the League of Nations and the Geneva disarmament conference. This was a clear omen of things to come, and from that moment onward Churchill began to show an interest in the League. During the 1920s he had been extremely skeptical of the moral and practical foundations upon which the organization was based.[57] But once Germany had left the League, he began to regard it as an instrument with whose help the Concert of Europe might be revived and its members' stands against Germany be coordinated. In other words, the League might both prevent German rearmament and also repair the wrongs done to it at Versailles.[58] When the German problem became more acute, and the Abyssinia crisis confronted the League with its greatest test, Churchill announced—albeit not in public—"that his main interest in the League was a defence against Germany."[59]

There is a certain irony in this situation. Between the end of 1929 and 1935 Churchill invested what many people considered obsessive energy in a struggle against the government's trend toward introduction of reforms in India's administration; nevertheless, during the course of 1932 he began to sense the danger of approaching war because of events in Europe. The Chiefs of Staff and the British government, on the other hand, began to sense similar dangers because of events in the Far East. Thus, the argument that ensued between the two sides during the 1930s was not a result of Churchill's cautioning against the danger of war which others refused to recognize. From 1933, the political and strategic diagnosis by the politicians as well as the Chiefs was similar to Churchill's. Debate focused on the prognosis and on the correct solution to the problem.

During the same month in which Germany left the League, the Chiefs of Staff submitted their *Annual Review*, repeating their earlier warnings of the dangers threatening in the Far East. On this occasion, however, note was also taken of the dark shadow that Germany would cast over Europe in a few years' time because of the commencement of its armament program. Consequently, in November 1933 a subcommittee of the Committee of Imperial Defence was formed. Designated the "Defence Requirements Committee" (DRC), this body was supposed to examine the problems involved in Britain's defense and submit a plan for their solution. The proposals the DRC tabled in February 1934 took "Germany as the ultimate potential enemy against whom our 'long-range' defence policy has to be directed." Since Britain could not wage war in Europe and in the Far East at the same time, it had to aim at a rapprochement with Japan. The Committee's interest focused on the repair of the most serious deficiencies in the military system during the next five years, which it took to be the minimum period that Germany would require to complete its rearmament.

During that time, the Royal Air Force was supposed to augment its strength to fifty-two squadrons, some of which would be employed in the defense of Britain and of British bases in the Far East, while others would be posted to the Continent together with an expeditionary force. The latter would itself consist of a regular force of four infantry divisions, one cavalry division, and one armored brigade, which could be stationed in the Low Countries within a month. Explaining the proposal to dispatch this force to the Low Countries, the DRC stated:

> Their integrity is vital to us in order that we may obtain that depth in our defence of London which is so badly needed, and of which our geographical position will otherwise deprive us. If the Low Countries were in the hands of a hostile Power, not only would the frequency and intensity of air attacks on London be increased, but the whole of the industrial areas of the Midlands and North of England would be brought within the area of penetration of hostile air attacks.[60]

As Hankey had foreseen, the DRC's proposal to establish an expeditionary force met with immediate resistance in the Cabinet. Neville Chamberlain, Chancellor of the Exchequer, led the opposition to a continental commitment. Several reasons were adduced for such a position, but the most basic—and deepest—was the dread of a repetition of the horrors of a land campaign, such as had been experienced during the Great War. As Chamberlain told his colleagues: "Our experience in the last war indicated that we ought to put our major resources into our Navy and our Air Force . . . the Army must be maintained, so that it can be used in other parts of the world."[61]

Quite apart from thus proposing the alternative of an updated version of the "Maritime school," it was not difficult to attack the Committee's position with regards to the expeditionary force. No explanation was given as to how so small a force, with the help of Belgium's fortifications and army, might repel a German offensive. Because of differences of opinion among the Chiefs of Staff themselves, the Committee did not recommend the establishment of a reserve that could be sent in an orderly fashion to back up the expeditionary force. For logistic and operational reasons, as Chamberlain was quick to point out, Anglo-Belgian military cooperation would be useless without a French army and the use of French territory. On the other hand, the British government and Chiefs of Staff, although cognizant of the importance of Britain's strategic interests in the Low Countries, were not prepared to tie themselves down by an Anglo-Belgian military alliance. Still less were they prepared to conclude such an arrangement with France.[62] This position accelerated Belgium's move toward neutrality in 1936.

Confronted with the Cabinet's inquiries, the Chiefs of Staff explained that the expeditionary force would not only help remove the threat of German air attack from the Low Countries. It would also have an important moral effect, since its dispatch would demonstrate Britain's determination to employ its full military might.[63] Among themselves, however, the Chiefs were beset by disputes and uncertainty. As the senior officer of the Army, the CIGS, Field Marshal Sir Archibald Montgomery-Massingberd supported the establishment of an expeditionary force; however, he wanted to preserve its independence, not to commit it to the French and the Belgians. Marshal of the Royal Air Force Sir Edward Ellington, the Chief of Air Staff, doubted whether an expeditionary force was at all necessary. In any event, he was sure that none of the aircraft to comprise his projected fifty-two squadrons could be spared for dispatch to the Continent.[64] Furthermore, Admiral Sir Ernle Chatfield, the First Sea Lord, attributed as much importance to the Far Eastern theater as to the European.[65]

The Chiefs of Staff, then, did not themselves agree on a concerted strategic concept. In an approach born of bureaucratic caution and interservice rivalry, they demanded that each of the services be expanded—and even then only to a moderate degree. It was the civilian members of the DRC—Vansittart, the Permanent Under-Secretary of the Foreign Office, and Sir Warren Fisher, Permanent Under-Secretary to the Treasury—who pressed for the speedy acceleration of armament and had a clear view of the priorities.[66] Although particularly fearful of the air threat, Vansittart maintained that a large British expeditionary force had to operate alongside the French. He did not take it for granted that France would support Britain and protect its European interests.[67] But Hankey, the Committee's chairman, wavered throughout the 1930s between a "Continental strategy" and an imperial orientation. As the decade approached its end, his mind's pendulum swung increasingly toward the "maritime school."

Under those circumstances, Chamberlain and his Cabinet colleagues had no difficulty in determining strategic priorities by themselves. The RAF would be expanded beyond the fifty-two squadrons recommended to a strength of eighty squadrons. On the other hand, the sum that the DRC suggested be spent on the expansion of the Army was cut by half. Quite apart from opposing the very notion of a British army fighting on the Continent, members of the Cabinet feared that the public would misinterpret the Army's expansion as a decision to send it to Europe.[68]

In November 1935, at the height of the Ethiopian crisis and after Hitler had declared his renunciation of the armaments restrictions imposed on Germany at Versailles, the DRC submitted a second report to the Cabinet. As before, the Committee stressed the importance of the Low Countries to British security, in view of the German air threat. By 1939, the RAF was supposed to possess 1,736 first-line aircraft, including nearly 1,000 bombers. The Army would contain an expeditionary force of five divisions that could be deployed on the Continent within a fortnight, and would be backed up by a reserve of twelve divisions by which it could be reinforced over a period of eight months. The Navy would be expanded so that it might simultaneously deter the Japanese in the Far East and wage war against Germany. The Committee also recommended the preparation of an industrial base which could be speedily converted to full war production after the outbreak of hostilities. As Professor Howard puts it: "These proposals constituted the first serious programme to enable the British Armed Forces to take part in a major war against their most probable adversaries."⁶⁹ The members of the DRC emphasized the need to adopt a long-term policy that would ensure French military support should Britain become engaged in a war with either both Italy and Japan or both Germany and Japan.⁷⁰ But they made no reference to the simple idea of concluding a military alliance with France.

At the beginning of 1936 the Cabinet voted to accept in principle the DRC's recommendations with respect to the RAF and the Navy; but those which concerned the Army it found more difficult to swallow. True, there was no direct dispute about the need for an expeditionary force; but the establishment of a large supporting reserve did meet with stiff opposition, especially from Chamberlain. The reasons stated were economic and the priority which had to be accorded to the expansion of the Air Force in order to counter the considerable dread of strategic bombing. However, there was the latent fear that Britain might become involved in land warfare in Europe. Ministers argued that the public would not agree to such an expansion of the Army, and the official historian has recorded his impression that they "were not yet ready to accept the full implications of sending an Expeditionary Force, once again, to Europe."⁷¹ Nobody then expected the next war to be short; and it was clear that there was no real point in dispatching an expeditionary force into a protracted campaign without a sizable reserve. The Chiefs of Staff and the War Office made this point during the course of 1936, but to no avail.⁷²

The Cabinet's attitude was unaffected by either the worsening international situation or by the exacerbation of the German military threat. On the contrary, the trend toward isolationism was accentuated when Chamberlain was appointed Prime Minister in 1937. The end of that year saw the acceptance of a formula of "limited liability," in accordance with which the establishment of a small expeditionary force was given low priority. The Army's principal task was to defend the Empire and to protect Britain's air defenses. Accordingly, the expansion of the RAF and air defense were to be given highest priority. In the main, Britain would assist its potential allies in time of war in the air and at sea. Leslie Hore-Belisha, the Secretary of State for War, did plan the creation of an expeditionary force consisting of three divisions, but his preference was to dispatch it to an "Eastern theatre."⁷³ Thus the policy of "limited liability," or in effect no liability whatsoever, was merely a new version of the "maritime school." In the strategic circumstances prevailing on the eve of World War II it effectively amounted to isolationism.

Why—at precisely the moment of greatest international tension in Europe—did the Cabinet, with the not inconsiderable concurrence of its military advisers, reject the notion of creating a large army and undertaking a "continental commitment"?

Between 1935 and 1937 the Chiefs of Staff were increasingly impressed with the RAF's assessments of Germany's probable moves on the outbreak of

European war. The latter would prefer to take Britain out of the war by launching a massive air strike against the very heart of the country rather than to attack France on land first. The concept of an aerial "knockout blow" struck a responsive chord among the politicians, most of whom were in any case terrified (some almost obsessively so) by the thought of strategic bombing against British cities.[74] Financial constraints gave rise to the preference for investing large sums in air defense rather than in an expeditionary force and in the Army in general.[75] But economic factors do not adequately explain the government's position. After all, the "continental" strategy was also disqualified as a future strategy in time of war, when purely budgetary considerations would necessarily decline in importance.

And what had become of the arguments put forward by the Chiefs of Staff and the DRC: that an expeditionary force had to be dispatched to Belgium to prevent the establishment of German air bases in the Low Countries, and that it was politically and morally important to deploy that force alongside the Belgians and the French?

Two prominent historians, Howard and Bond, admit that they do not possess a clear answer. Professor Howard makes a stab at providing one by pointing out the changes which occurred when the first radar stations were installed in 1937 and when the RAF began to be equipped with long-range bombers capable of reaching German targets from within Britain itself. The appearance of a defensive solution to German air attack and the development of an air offensive capability from within Britain itself, he suggests, minimized Belgium's importance.[76]

This explanation is unsatisfactory. In 1937 and 1938 no one could have been sure that the air defense system would operate effectively. Moreover, even if it were to do so, it would not be ready for another few years. What if war broke out in the meantime? (At the end of 1938, during the Munich crisis, the Chiefs of Staff stated that Britain was defenseless against air bombardment.)[77] The same was true of the bombers. The RAF still did not possess a bomber that had either the range or effective bomb-load capacity to carry out effective strikes against Berlin or the industrial centers of eastern Germany. In 1934, the Air Staff had calculated that the weight of bombs the Germans could drop on England would double in quantity were their aircraft to operate from Belgium or Holland.[78] Geographical distances had not changed by the years 1937–1938. It would have been virtually foolish to have based Britain's grand strategy in 1938 on the operational capacities of the radar system and on the RAF's interception and bombing capability—and British military men of the time can hardly be described as fools.

Different circumstances explain the disregard of the importance previously attached to the moral and political effect of an expeditionary force. The fact is that the united front that the Chiefs of Staff presented to the Cabinet when advocating the dispatch of the Army to Belgium's defense concealed a protracted dispute among them about the need for a "continental commitment" and an expeditionary force, and about the order of interservice priorities.[79] In other words, they no longer shared the views held by their predecessors in the 1920s that "the true strategic frontier of Great Britian is the Rhine." Although the danger from the air constituted the principal argument in favor of an expeditionary force to Belgium, members of the Air Staff seriously doubted its necessity. As early as 1934, some of them had contended that: "our strategy should be based on a determination not to become involved in a Continental land campaign[s] like the last."[80] But even the senior echelons in the Army could find no way of furthering their case, since they shared the determination of their colleagues among the Chiefs of Staff not to commit Britain militarily to any nation on the Continent in peacetime.[81] This position directly and adversely affected the future of the Army, but not that of the other services. Conversely, the persistent opposition by the Chiefs of Staff to a military alliance with France enabled the Prime Minister (to whom news of their internal disagreements was leaked[82]) to question the very utility of an expeditionary force to the Continent.

But the major reason for the ultimate erosion of the notion of a "continental commitment" by the years 1937-1938 was the fact that the Chiefs of Staff did not analyze Britain's security problems from a perspective centered, first and foremost, on maintaining the European balance of power. When justifying the creation of an expeditionary force, they concentrated—time and again throughout the 1930s—on the need to avert the German air threat from the Low Countries. Their arguments were based on operational factors related to the frustration of one clearly defined threat; but they did not concern themselves with the cardinal question of the state of the military balance in Europe once Germany was completely rearmed. It was through the narrow lens of the direct defense of the British Isles against an air and naval threat that the need for military intervention on the Continent was perceived. That is why any improvement in the state of air defense sufficed to encourage them (goaded by the politicians) to take the small step in the direction of "limited liability." It is no wonder, then, that the Chiefs of Staff supported Chamberlain's policy at Munich. Their primary concerns were the sheer defense of Britain itself and of its Empire; less important, in their eyes, was the disappearance of the strong Czechoslovak army as a factor of importance in the European balance of power. However, as Professor Howard asks: "If that balance were to be overthrown, for how long would Home Defence be possible? And if Home Defence was not possible, what would then happen to the Empire?"[83]

Since military men adopted a negative attitude toward the need to maintain the European balance of power, it is not surprising to find that the politicians also abandoned that principle. Many of those who attained positions of executive power during the 1930s shared an ideological opposition to the balance-of-power principle and the measures required for its implementation. In its place they adopted a moral and legalistic approach to international relations. Instead of being merely a handmaid, diplomacy was transmuted into a substitute for military power and for strategic steps. The policy of appeasement was not born of notions based on the British strategic weaknesses to which the Chiefs of Staff referred on the eve of Munich. Rather, it was the product of a world view that had torn asunder the link between foreign policy and military strategy, and their order of priorities. Therefore, as the official historian puts it: "There is no evidence to suggest that Mr. Chamberlain and his colleagues would have changed that policy, had the country's military preparations been more advanced."[84] Also, no wonder that—before and during the Munich crisis—the British Cabinet made no attempt to compare Britain's strategic chances in a European war in 1938 with those that would exist at a later date.

Marlborough and the European Balance of Power

There were those who furnished intellectual underpinnings for the political and strategic positions taken during the 1930s by British decision makers. The most prominent was the military theorist and historian B. H. Liddell Hart. In his *The British Way in Warfare*, published in 1932, Liddell Hart attacked Britain's servitude during the last war to "continental fashions" formulated by Clausewitz and Foch. The country, he claimed, had thereby forsaken its traditional strategy, which had been "based on experience and proved by three centuries of success." Ever since the sixteenth century, England had acquired power by "steer[ing] clear of the delusive attraction of Continental victories" and by its wise employment of naval strategy. During the last war, Britain should never have created a large army and sent it to France. Instead, it should have supported allies by economic means and used its naval power to effect a link with Russia through the Dardanelles and to establish a Balkan-Danubian front. Even had the military struggle ended in stalemate, "fidelity to our tradition instead of to Clausewitz would have led us to negotiate for peace." By using "our usual bargaining counters" in the negotiations, Britain would have emerged strengthened from the war.[85] The weaknesses of this strategy have already been noted—without the presence of a large British army on French soil, France and Russia could not for long have withstood Germany's awesome military might. A Franco-Russian defeat would have led to Britain's downfall, or, at the very least, to the drastic decline of its status as a power.

Liddell Hart merely repeated Mahan and the historical commentary favored by supporters of the "maritime school." But in the second half of the 1930s he occupied a more influential position as Defense Correspondent of *The Times*, the newspaper that consistently supported the policy of "appeasement." March 1937 saw the publication of his *Europe in Arms*, in which he argued that Britain would have to adopt its traditional strategy in a future war; he opposed the dispatch of a British army to the Continent and even a small force for the defense of Belgium.[86] Chamberlain was one of the first to read that book; in a letter that he wrote to Liddell Hart in March 1937 congratulating him on its appearance, he expressed his conviction that "we shall never again send to the Continent an Army on the scale of that which we put into the field in the Great War." In October he recommended the book to the new Secretary of State for War, Hore-Belisha.[87] The latter had already been impressed with Liddell Hart and now appointed him his unofficial military adviser. During the critical years of 1937 and 1938 Liddell Hart became, in the words of his biographer, "the real strategic brain behind the War Minister."[88]

Liddell Hart's influence cannot be exaggerated. His writings and the advice that he gave Hore-Belisha only strengthened the ingrained concepts held by the political and military elite and constituted a clear echo of current public opinion.[89] Even after Hitler violated the Munich agreement and invaded Prague in March 1939—a move which revolutionized both public and official opinion—he continued to oppose the "continental commitment." His *The Defence of Britain*, which appeared in July 1939, argued for an isolationist strategy based entirely on air and naval power.[90] Like Mahan, Liddell Hart believed in the need to learn history's lessons, and that such a study provided the basis for the development and verification of military theory. But he was flexible in his use of history and historical facts in order to prove his opinions. The theory of "the indirect approach," which he then developed, was in effect based on the avoidance of direct confrontation at the strategic level with the main mass of the enemy; his approach naturally lent itself to the "maritime school" in British military history.[91]

Churchill read or perused Liddell Hart's book, *The British Way in Warfare*,[92] but had different opinions regarding the historical nature of British strategy. In 1929 he began writing his biography of John Churchill, the Duke of Marlborough, one of his own ancestors and one of the greatest soldiers in history. He did not complete the book until 1938, and Marlborough's life and times occupied his mind throughout the stormy years of the 1930s. To a large extent, the struggles waged by England during Marlborough's lifetime became the prism through which he observed Britain's political and military problems during the 1930s. To a lesser extent, he analyzed the wars waged by William III (1689-1702), Queen Anne, and Marlborough with reference to the dilemmas posed by his own times and by the Great War.

Churchill maintained that Louis XIV of France, like Napoleon and Kaiser Wilhelm II of Germany after him, had aimed to establish hegemony over Europe. If France had convulsed Europe in the past, it was Germany who did so now.[93] Without English intervention, Europe would have been unable to resist the ambitions of France, the most powerful of states. Unfortunately, England had been slow to realize the need to construct a European alliance against France. Admittedly, the triple alliance concluded in 1667 between the English, Dutch, and Swedes had deterred France from attempting to occupy territories that are now part of Belgium. But after the Treaty of Aix-la-Chapelle of 1668, William III had been unable to put together a political alliance against France. He was prevented from doing so by the English political elite's reluctance to get involved on the Continent, by the disbanding of the English army, and by his own decline in power. Encouraged by England's weakness, and by the absence of any substantial adversaries other than the Hapsburg Empire, Louis had attempted to gain complete control over the Spanish succession following the death of the childless Charles II.[94]

Churchill wrote that the strategic situation during the War of the Spanish Succession (1701-1714)—which he also designated a world war—was very similar to that of the Great War. Two allied nations, France and Spain, one powerful and the other weak, had-like Germany and Austria-Hungary after them—operated on internal lines and had enjoyed the advantages of initiative and the choice of the main theater. They were confronted by a coaltion of states—of which England was the linchpin—operating on external lines and possessing command of the North Sea, the English Channel, and subsequently of the Mediterranean.[95] In both cases, of course, England's decision makers had faced the same dilemma: what was to be the nature of England's military contribution? Conceptual differences reflected party divisions. The Tories preferred a strategy based on naval power and on peripheral actions against Spanish and French overseas possessions. "[The] Whigs, on the contrary, dwelt upon the theory familiar to us as the doctrine of the 'Decisive theatre,' and sought, with the largest army that could be maintained, to bring the war to an end by thrust at the heart of France."[96] The Whigs were "logical, precise, resolute, the wholehearted exponents of the great war on land and of England rising to the directing summit of the world."[97] Marlborough's great march to the Danube and his victory at Blenheim, which saved the coalition against France and terminated Louis' ambition to attain hegemony over Europe, constituted "the greatest violation of Tory [war] principles which could be conceived."[98]

Throughout his book, Churchill praises Marlborough's ambition to defeat the French in a decisive battle and seize Paris. He attacks the useless concepts advocated by the Tories and by the Dutch, who wished to wage a bloodless war and preserve their armies. In advocating the necessity of defeating the enemy by destroying his army, the Duke—so Churchill claimed—had been ahead of his time and had anticipated Frederick the Great and Napoleon.[99] Churchill tried to demonstrate that Marlborough had a broad grasp of the political and military components of the art of war. He had been required to maneuver between Tories and Whigs, who frequently alternated in office; to obtain the support of the supreme political authority and of those influential at court; to ensure the continuation of England's continental struggle when London's resolve weakened and to sustain its leading status in the conduct of the war; to secure operational cooperation with allies on the Continent; and only when he had accomplished all of this could he turn to the "easier" part—the defeat of the French on the battlefield.[100] Genius alone enabled Marlborough to surmount these difficulties. But these constraints prevented him from winning the war in reasonable time. It turned into a protracted war of attrition in which, although France was stopped and weakened, Dutch strength was also worn down.[101]

Because of Tory pressure, considerable land forces were sent to the Spanish theater. This was in spite of opposition by Marlborough, who considered it a dangerous diversion that would weaken allied strength in the main and decisive theater of the Low Countries (which was, according to Churchill, precisely what did happen).[102] Churchill rejected the "maritime school" as an alternative to a continental strategy, but did not object to naval-peripheral actions that might hasten the success of the land campaign. He emphasized that Marlborough had regarded land and naval warfare "as branches of the same trade."[103] England's command of the Mediterranean, which was "a potent factor underlying all the military operations," was attained by the pressure exerted by Marlborough, who wished to employ naval power on France's southern flank too.[104]

Churchill did not conceal his enthusiasm for two of Marlborough's grand plans, which combined land campaigns with naval action. The first, formulated in 1707, required Marlborough to exert pressure on the French in Flanders. At the same time, Prince Eugene of Savoy was to advance with his Austrian forces along France's southern coast and take the important and fortified port of Toulon, with the object of making it a base for an advance northward. Eugene was promised close naval support throughout the length of his march and in the conquest of Toulon. Because of the distance separating Marlborough's front from that held by Prince Eugene, the French would not be able to exploit the advantage conferred by internal lines. The conquest of Toulon would turn into

> the root of an immense rodent growth in the bowels of France, leading to a fatal collapse either on the northern or the southern front or perhaps both. Here was the way to achieve the full purpose of the Allies and finish the war.[105]

Marlborough's plan failed because Prince Eugene, who was a "land animal" by nature, was dilatory in his march on Toulon and because the French rushed reinforcements to the port from Spain rather than from Flanders.

After his victory at Oudenarde in 1708, the Duke drafted a plan whose purpose was to outflank the massive French fortifications in Flanders by way of the sea and to win the war by an assault on Paris. The idea was to land the army of 100,000 men commanded by Marlborough and Eugene on the French coast, establish a base at Abbeville and, during the advance on Paris, to keep it supplied by way of sea from Holland and England. Fearing the risks involved, Eugene opposed this plan; but Churchill considered its rejection to have been a serious error. It was feasible, and had it been carried out the French would have been forced to withdraw their forces from Flanders to Paris in order to defend their capital.[106] He added:

> Thus in our time we have seen the minds of men and all resources absorbed by the great offensives on the western Front, . . . while the dangerous prudence of conventional opinion prevented unexpected and so-called eccentric alternatives.[107]

Maurice Ashley, the historian who assisted Churchill with his researches on Marlborough, notes his determination "from the outset to make out the best case for his hero."[108] The depths of his identification with his subject is indeed apparent on every page; to a large extent he ascribed to the Duke traits of character and thought which were his own.[109] Wittingly or otherwise, Churchill also emphasized those elements in Marlborough's strategic conceptions that were akin to those he held. He compared the strategic situation on the eve of Marlborough's Danubian campaign to that existing at the end of 1914 when Turkey entered the war. By joining France and Spain, the Kingdom of Bavaria had cut Dutch and English communications with their Austrian ally; in the same way, Turkey's entry into the war on the side of the Central Powers cut the link between Russia and its western allies. In both cases, wrote Churchill, the dilemma was the same: to strike at the strategic center of gravity or to try to repair communications with a vital partner. "If they so resolved," the allies of 1914 would have been able to "strike down Turkey with ease and swiftness by a naval or amphibious operation." But Marlborough was forced to mount a long and dangerous march into the heart of Europe.[110] Churchill's belief is clear: the Dardanelles operation and his plans for offensives against the northern coast of Europe were foiled by precisely the same sort of unimaginative people who had prevented Marlborough from implementing his plans against Toulon and Abbeville and fighting a decisive battle after often maneuvering his adversaries into inferior positions. Churchill himself had thus been prevented from repeating "the march to the Danube" by a "march on Constantinople." It was the fate of both men to be constrained by human mediocrity. To say this is not to suggest that Churchill's positions during World War I were inspired by Marlborough's example. He did not hit upon this strategic analogy until he had begun his research, and when he did so the discovery was as unexpected as it was pleasurable. Hitherto, he had known of Marlborough's life and times in only the most general terms, and his knowledge was largely culled from Macaulay's *History of England*.[111]

Churchill attacked the British decision, taken against Marlborough's advice, to abandon its allies. The Treaty of Utrecht could not prevent the revival of France, with whom Britain was involved in war on four further occasions over the next 100 years. Had he enjoyed freedom of action, Marlborough could have defeated France and spared his country those trials. Nevertheless, the Duke's achievements were outstanding. His "continental policy," wrote Churchill, had laid the foundations for the British Empire, for British control in the "new world" and in Asia, and for Britain's greatness. His victories had changed the European balance of power: France was repulsed and weakened; Holland had ceased to be a naval and commercial adversary; Britain had gained command of the Mediterranean, and, despite the war, its economy flourished.[112]

This conclusion may have surprised Churchill himself. Influenced by Mahan and others, he had at the beginning of the century believed that the British Empire had been founded on naval power and on avoidance of involvement in land campaigns on the Continent. After 1911 he was forced to conclude that Britain had no option other than to dispatch armies to Europe. As a result of his historical research, however, he now concluded that the Empire had been primarily based on Britain's continental victories as well as on its naval strength. Thus was completed the revolution in his thinking that had begun in 1911.

Although the biography of Marlborough provides a key to an understanding of Churchill's interpretation of a major war in Britain's military history, his approach in that work is essentially horizontal. For examples of his longitudinal analysis of the historical process one has to turn to his next work, *A History of the English Speaking Peoples*, whose draft was completed before the outbreak of war in 1939 and was published without any substantial change during the mid-1950s. It is there that Churchill weaves a broad and rough thread linking his interpretation of British strategy during the War of Spanish Succession with that pursued during the Seven Years' War and the Revolutionary and Napoleonic wars.

Churchill depicted Chatham, the elder Pitt, as a strategic and political genius. He had overcome his own early delusions and had grasped that Britain could not defeat France in the Seven Years' War only by employing its naval arm against French commerce and possessions, however successful those operations may have been. Overcoming stubborn domestic opposition, Chatham had concluded an alliance with Prussia. But his fall had led to the return to power of the advocates of the "maritime school," to the abandonment of Prussia (which was left alone to face a European coalition and declined to the point of collapse), and to the 1763 Peace of Paris. Like Chatham, Churchill believed that the Peace of Paris had provided only an intermission before the next round of fighting, and that Britain should have continued the war until France and Spain had been utterly defeated.[113] (Churchill did not explain how that aim might have been accomplished, unless what he meant was that a large British army should have been sent to the Continent.) But he evinced no enthusiasm for the sort of war that Mahan, Corbett, and Liddell Hart considered to be British strategy's purest and most succesful expression.

Despite the lack of clarity that characterizes Churchill's strategic analysis of the Revolutionary and Napoleonic wars, a similar pattern of thought can be discerned. He considered Britain's initial strategy to have been mistaken, because the younger Pitt had believed in his country's ability to adopt a policy of isolation during the early stages of the French Revolution. Even when Britain had been forced into war against France by the direct threat posed to her interests in the Low Countries, Britain had erred in preferring to wage the conflict in "the old tradition of the eighteenth century"—by a naval war against France's commerce and overseas possessions. The new regime in Paris could have been brought down had Britain sent to the Continent a small but effective army, which would have acted in concert with the other monarchist European forces attacking France across the Rhine.[114] As it was, until Wellington's successes in the Iberian Peninsula in the years 1809–1810, the British had made a meager—and wasteful—contribution to the land war in Europe. Their amphibious assaults on the enemy's coast exerted no influence on the great land campaigns—contrary to the conclusion reached by Corbett thirty years earlier.[115] What he applauded was the Whig government's unsuccessful attempt to establish a grand army by means of conscription in the years 1806–1807.[116]

It is not clear what Churchill considered to be the precise reasons for Napoleon's fall, or the relative importance of the factors involved. He thinks that the struggle in the Iberian Peninsula weakened Napoleon by exhausting his forces and pinning them down; on the other hand, he maintains that from a strategic point of view, Napoleon could have relinquished Spain. That Churchill attributed the fall of France principally to the protracted struggle with the European armies may be deduced from his description of Bonaparte's failure in Russia in 1812, of the Prussian uprising, and of France's defeats in the great battles that took place after 1812. Whichever the case, Churchill—unlike Mahan—does not maintain that British naval power was the decisive cause of the French emperor's demise.[117]

These last two books suggest that, to Churchill's mind, Britain had no choice but to maintain the European balance of power; it could be done only by military involvement on the European mainland. Naval power did immunize Britain to invasion; but it could not either defeat a European enemy who sought to attain continental hegemony or prevent one such from mastering the Continent. The strength of sea power lay in its correct integration with a "continental" strategy.

Churchill may of course have observed British military history through the lens of his current strategic conception; but his approach does have the support of modern historical opinion since World War II. Correlli Barnett argues that it was Britain's massive intervention on the European mainland that determined its status as a European and world power. Britain could not escape such intervention once a struggle developed for European hegemony; indeed, 500 years of British history showed that naval power was sterile where struggles of that sort were concerned.[118] He considers Marlborough's victories in the War of the Spanish Succession to have been the direct cause of Britain's rise to status as the world's greatest naval power and to economic dominance.[119] Although more cautious, Paul Kennedy reaches the same conclusion: in his opinion, since the foundations of France's economic and military might lay on land, the reason for its exhaustion was "not the naval blockade but the cost of the military campaigns." Britain's recipe for success lay in its ability to husband its own naval and economic strength which was integrated with the maintenance of the balance of power on the Continent. True, dispatching a large land army to the Continent was more costly in men and treasure; but it had proven to be a far more effective means of maintaining the European balance.[120]

In a brilliant article Professor Michael Howard has added further weight to these arguments. Dismissing the historical interpretations tendered by Mahan,

Corbett, and (especially) Liddell Hart, he maintains that:

> First, a commitment of support to a Continental ally in the nearest available theatre, on the largest scale, that contemporary resources could afford, so far from being alien to traditional British strategy, was absolutely central to it. The flexibility provided by sea power certainly made possible other activities as well: colonial conquest, trade war, help to Allies in Central Europe, minor amphibious operations; but these were ancillary to the great decisions by land, and they continued to be so throughout the two world wars. Secondly, when we did have recourse to a purely maritime strategy, it was always as a result, not of free choice or of atavistic wisdom, but of *force majeure*. It was a strategy of necessity rather than of choice, of survival rather than of victory. It enabled us to escape from the shipwrecks which overtook our less fortunately-based Continental neighbours; it gave us a breathing space in which to try to attract other allies; it enabled us to run away . . . but it never enabled us to win." [121]

■

It now remains to examine the manner whereby Churchill's historical interpretation blended with his strategic opinions until the end of the 1930s.

It will be recalled that, throughout the 1930s, the military had advanced one principal argument in favor of sending a British army to the Continent: the need to defend Belgium in order to forestall a German air threat from Belgian territory. Churchill's point of departure was contrary, and quite free of the confusion and weakness stemming from that attitude. To his mind, the defense of specific British strategic interests on the Continent had to be secondary to the maintenance of the European balance of power; with the latter preserved, the former would in any case be ensured. Throughout the tangled events of the 1930s Churchill employed the concept of the balance of power, and of Britain's role in its maintenance, as an anchor in stormy waters and history "as a guide in present difficulties."[122] He informed the historian G. M. Trevelyan in 1935, when the latter was writing his biography of Sir Edward Grey:

> If England had not resisted German militarism, in my view the German hegemony of Europe would have been established and our island would have had to face a united Continental army. It is the same old story from the days of Marlborough and Napoleon . . . [Grey's] life's justification depends on whether England ought to have done in 1914 what she did against Philip II of Spain, against Louis XIV and against Napoleon. I have no doubt what the answer should be.[123]

Midway through 1935, Churchill wrote to Lord Rothermere:

> If [Hitler's] proposal means that we should come to an understanding with Germany to dominate Europe I think this would be contrary to the whole of our history. We have on all occasions been the friend of the second strongest power in Europe and have never yielded ourselves to the strongest power. . . . Only by taking this path and effort have we preserved ourselves and our liberties, and

reached our present position. I see no reason myself to change from this traditional view.[124]

About a year later he added: "I know of nothing in military, political, economic or scientific fact which makes me feel that we might not, or cannot, march along the same road." It was indeed tempting to think of joining the greatest power striving to attain hegemony in Europe; but once that one had attained its goal it would be Britain's turn to be destroyed.[125]

As we have seen, during the crisis of July 1914 Churchill adopted an uncompromising stand on the preservation of Belgium's sovereignty; he did so, not because he attached very much importance to that issue itself, but because he thus hoped to convince those of his colleagues who were otherwise hesitant to enter the war.[126] He employed the same tactic during the 1930s when attempting to influence those who refused to accept the logic in maintaining the European balance of power. Like the Chiefs of Staff, he pointed out the importance of Belgium in view of the German air threat. But unlike them, he made it clear that Britain could not defend Belgium without French support, and that the defense of the Low Countries was tied up with that of France. That was what made vital an alliance with France, which would also work to obviate the possibility of the latter foregoing the defense of the Low Countries and entrenching itself behind an extended Maginot Line, which would follow the Franco-Belgian border.[127] In other words, Britain's weakness in the air did not leave any choice—it had to establish commitments to France and other continental states.[128]

As early as 1935 Churchill began to think of the establishment of a "grand alliance" against Germany and called for the conclusion of an unequivocal and open military alliance with France. He remained steadfast in that attitude until the outbreak of World War II. Churchill maintained that before 1914 the Anglo-French Entente had burdened Britain with the responsibilities of an alliance without giving it the advantages that would have accrued had such an alliance been forged. The fuzziness in Britain's attitude toward France and to the issue of involvement in a future war had not deterred Germany; conversely, the lack of an alliance had limited Britain's ability to influence France. Addressing the House of Commons, he claimed that "my dislike of vague and indefinite commitments was ingrained in me by the experience through which I passed in the years before the war and at the moment of its outbreak."[129] Unconsciously, he thus admitted his mistake in advocating a policy of vagueness with regard to France before the war.

Churchill argued that the best way to deter Germany was to encircle it completely, using the League of Nations as an organizational cover for the establishment of a continental coalition against it. He emphasized that the Soviet Union had to be included in any such coalition, which was why he welcomed its entry into the League in 1934.[130] Although he did doubt Russia's strength, he recognized the vital nature of its military and logistic support to the political flank that would encircle Germany from the east. In Churchill's presence, Prime Minister Baldwin admitted that "It should not break my heart" were Hitler to move eastward;[131] but Churchill opposed giving Germany a free hand in southern and eastern Europe. He feared that Hitler would strike against the west in even greater force after establishing his mastery over eastern Europe and Soviet Russia. Indeed, once the German army had reached its full strength, Britain and France would require Soviet Russia's numerical contribution.[132]

There was something ironic in Churchill's call to include the Soviet Union in an anti-German coalition at such an early stage. Communism's outright opponent was capable of detaching himself from his ideological stand and of acknowledging the Soviet Union's enormous contribution to the European balance of power. But his colleagues in the Conservative party, and especially Chamberlain, proved incapable of overcoming their abhorrence of bolshevism and their latent hope that Germany and the Soviet Union would go to war against each other. Their sentiments contributed substantially to the failure to establish a triple alliance of Britain, France, and the Soviet Union on the eve of World War II.

Churchill's calls to establish a "grand alliance" and a military alliance with France increased the more that the European situation worsened and Germany's strength mounted.[133] But while Churchill considered a grand alliance to be an effective means of stopping Hitler, Chamberlain and his Cabinet colleagues considered that any such arrangement would only incite Hitler's anger and frustrate their intentions of coming to a diplomatic arrangement with him.[134] Such an arrangement Chamberlain found in the Munich agreement, of which Churchill was so critical.

During the Czechoslovak crisis, the British government was influenced by the Chiefs of Staff's warnings that Britain was vulnerable to German bombers. As we have already seen, much of the energy expended in the debate on the German threat and on rearmament was devoted to a discussion of the impending threat from the air.[135] Churchill was prominent among those who placed this matter on the public agenda. Most of his speeches, especially between 1934 and 1937, concentrated on that subject and on a comparison of his own estimates of relative Anglo-German air strength with those provided by official sources. True, he was not one of the pioneers of the idea that air power possessed the ability to bring about a strategic decision independently. That was a view that had simultaneously grown up in the RAF and other air forces during the 1920s. Similarly, neither was he the first to conceive of the notion of mutual air deterrence, nor to think that Germany would attempt to deliver a "knockout" air blow against Britain at the opening stage of the war. But his argumentative ability did deepen even further the dread the British public and its leadership already had of bombing. As he himself admitted: "No doubt I painted the picture even darker than it was. The emphasis which I had put upon the two years' lag which afflicted us may well be judged inconsistent with my desire to come to grips with Hitler in October 1938."[136] Unwittingly, Churchill thus strengthened the trend of the policy pursued by the Cabinet and its unwillingness to enter into a military confrontation with Hitler in 1938. Nevertheless, the air problem—although the most persistent constraint influencing the formulation of British foreign policy during the 1930s—was not the only or the most decisive reason for the policy of appeasement.[137] Excessive warnings about the air danger had another important countereffect. They helped the opponents of a "continental commitment" and the conclusion of a military alliance with France to gain the upper hand in the years 1935-1938. This was because the call to give absolute priority to air defense served as an effective argument against the establishment of an expeditionary force and the forging of a military link with any state on the Continent.[138]

Fears of a German attack on Holland and the suspicion that, without British military support, France might abandon the Low Countries and even suffer a moral collapse, generated a change in the attitude of the Chiefs of Staff and the Cabinet at the beginning of February 1939. The Cabinet was then persuaded to initiate staff talks with the French and to agree that Britain give France a military commitment, albeit a limited one.[139] Churchill sensed the change in the Government's mood and called upon Chamberlain to deter Germany by clearly declaring Britain's intention to dispatch a large army to Europe should war break out.[140]

Hitler's entry into Prague, together with the consequent transformation in British public opinion, impelled Chamberlain to announce in March 1939 that Britain was giving a military guarantee to Poland, and later to Rumania and Greece too. Like Hitler, Churchill was also surprised by this move. He welcomed the step but, mindful of Britain's military inability to fulfill its assurances to Poland, asked whether the Cabinet had consulted the General Staff.[141] (In fact, the guarantee had been given against the advice of the Chiefs of Staff.) [142] In an attempt to invest the move with a degree of strategic sense, he called for the immediate establishment of a military alliance with the Soviet Union. The last war, he claimed, had emphasized how vital it was to have an eastern front such as could only be based on Russia. "Without any effective Eastern front, there can be no satisfactory defence of our interests in the West and without Russia there can be no effective Eastern front." Deprived of the backing of Soviet resources, the small states of eastern Europe could not survive. Sentiments, he argued, must be distinguished from interests—and Soviet interests constituted the basis for cooperation with the West.[143] Churchill maintained that the British government should have made its guarantee to Poland conditional on Poland's agreement to the entry of Soviet forces into its own territory and on Soviet assurances that those troops would be withdrawn as soon as the war was over.[144]

The suspicions that Poland (and, to a lesser extent, the other states of eastern Europe) harbored against the Soviet Union constituted an inherent stumbling block to the establishment of an eastern front centered around Russia. Hence its formation would have been a difficult task even had Chamberlain and

Halifax been enthusiastic about the idea. But by giving an almost unconditional guarantee to Poland, the British government had tied its hands before entering into talks with the Soviets. In so doing, it had also deprived itself of the option of choosing between Russia and Poland in the event of the failure of negotiations for the establishment of a grand eastern front. From a strategic point of view, the choice was plain—after March 1939 the Chiefs of Staff also pointed out to the Cabinet that an eastern front would be worthless without Soviet military and logistic backing. Moreover, an agreement with Russia would not have precluded the addition of other east European states. On the other hand, the guarantee to Poland enlarged the Soviet Union's room for maneuver and opened the way to its rapprochement with Germany. The Soviets could now be sure that a German attack on Poland would immediately lead to war between Germany and the powers of western Europe. The danger that Hitler could complete the conquest of Poland and then push on into Russia while Britain and France stood by, had virtually disappeared.[145] In practice, senior members of the Cabinet, with the assistance of the Foreign Office, continued to oppose an alliance with Soviet Russia even after they commenced talks with it in the summer of 1939.[146] In giving British guarantees to the states of eastern Europe while ignoring the vital importance of the Soviet Union, Chamberlain—to quote the official British historian—"made nonsense of his own policy, certainly at the military level, by willing the end but not the means."[147] Even earlier, his policy had lacked military logic. Unlike Chamberlain and his colleagues, Churchill had then managed to grasp the connection between policy and military power and had been able to unmask the weakness of that link in the government's policy.

■

Thus far in the present portion of our study, we have analyzed the conflicting historical interpretations of Britain's military strategy and have compared Churchill's positions with those of British decision makers during the 1930s. With that information to hand, we are now in a position more accurately to assess the degree of historical influence exerted on the crystallization of his strategic and political conceptions during that period.

At one level, the solution to this question seems simple. Churchill himself claimed to have deduced his positions during that decade from the lessons of British history. However, during the early years of the century he had argued that his opposition to military involvement on the Continent was a continuation of the British strategic tradition. He adduced no rationalization from the past in 1911, when he began to support the continental commitment. On the contrary, the new approach he adopted contradicted what he *then* understood to be the lessons of British history. The clear logical conclusion is that, by applying the same methods of reasoning he had employed when analyzing the comparable international situation in 1911, Churchill could have reached precisely the same conclusions during the 1930s. He could have done so without reference to the historical research he carried out between the two world wars. But it would be wrong to exaggerate the force of this conclusion by arguing that it entirely detracts from the importance of the historical lessons Churchill did distill from his studies. For one thing, they considerably broadened his general knowledge of military history. More important, they also made him particularly aware of Britain's everlasting need to send armies to the Continent; only thus might it implement the principle of the maintenance of the European balance of power. Finally, the act of writing his biography of Marlborough, a task that occupied him throughout the 1930s, strengthened his belief in the justice of his own arguments. It thus helped him in his almost single-handed public campaign.

Churchill had the advantage of being able to analyze the German problem with relative equanimity, because (as was noted at the outset of this study) he regarded war as a natural phenomenon of international relations. Although his historical studies were not responsible for that viewpoint, they did reinforce it. As he wrote in his *Life of Marlborough*: "Battles are the principal milestones in secular history."[148] Churchill did not consider Britain's involvement in the last war to have been a mistake. In this he was at odds with most of his contemporaries among the British political elite who, reflecting current public opinion, felt that experience to have been too traumatic to bear repetition. It is true that he did paint a dark picture of the face of future war,[149] but he continued to be fascinated by war. There is a whiff of the epic in the style that infuses his descriptions of Marlborough's battles. The realistic positions he adopted during the 1930s, together with his romantic attraction to war (which he never concealed), unjustifiably generated the impression that he was a war monger.[150] Churchill held no illusions about the necessity for war in certain international situations. But Chamberlain, in the name of a peace-seeking ideology, strove to cooperate with regimes which looked upon war as a vital foundation for the existence of their societies.

Operational Issues and Plans for War

Immediately after the end of World War I, Churchill argued that it would be wrong to think of the next war in terms of the last;[151] but in 1942 he admitted to Lord Moran that he had "certainly entered this war with a mentality born in the last war."[152] If his concepts and strategic plans on the eve of World War II are to be understood, attention must be focused on his attitudes toward several of the central tactical issues by which he and others were troubled. These will be discussed here in the order of the importance and the amount of time that he gave to them between the two world wars. First was the future of battleships under threat from the air; second, the menace that submarines posed to surface vessels, and its neutralization; third, the future of mechanization and the tank in future warfare. The bottom line of the analysis presented here is that Churchill erred in his assessments of each of these issues. His opinions, which were widely shared, were disproved by the course of World War II.

Battleships' survival in modern war gravely worried Churchill and constituted a problem of first-rate importance. If aircraft could sink battleships, then a land power would be able to neutralize Britain's naval strength relatively cheaply; the Royal Navy might find itself with a surfeit of useless battleships on its hands. A special committee set up early in the 1920s to discuss the issue concluded that battleships would continue to constitute the backbone of the fleet.[153] Throughout the period, Churchill's own views accorded with that opinion, but he was inwardly unsure of its validity.[154] At the beginning of 1936 he argued that battleships still had a future, but that they had to be immunized to air attack by various technical means. At the same time, he frequently requested further study of the topic before the construction of additional battleships was undertaken.[155] At the end of 1936, his fears were allayed when another commission on the subject reiterated the Admiralty's optimistic conclusions.[156] Churchill was convinced by the unequivocal assessments of the Navy experts with whom he was in contact, including Admiral of the Fleet Lord Chatfield.[157] Thereafter his confidence in the future of battleships hardened; as was the case with other Admiralty experts, it remained solid until painfully shaken during the course of World War II.[158] It follows that he did not regard aircraft and aircraft carriers as decisive weapon-systems in future naval warfare.

A similar fate awaited Churchill's assessments of the submarine menace. At the beginning of the 1930s he evinced concern about the prospective restrictions that agreements on arms control might impose on cruisers and destroyers. He feared that these would leave Britain with an insufficient number of vessels with which to defend its trade routes.[159] The Admiralty experts assuaged his fears. They placed their faith in sonar (ASDIC), whose development was completed during the 1930s, and explained that the effectiveness of this instrument for submarine detection obviated the Navy's need for a large quantity of antisubmarine vessels.[160] The Admiralty was extremely nonchalant about the prospective results of antisubmarine warfare in the next war; some of its senior officers even opposed the reintroduction of the convoy system. Because of the defensive nature of convoys, Churchill was not unsympathetic to this view—notwithstanding his opinion that the operation of convoys had been one of the fundamental lessons of the last war.[161] He was enthusiastic about ASDIC, and his confidence that submarines had lost their potency increased the nearer that World War II drew.[162]

On these two issues, then, Churchill agreed with expert Admiralty opinion—which was soon proved wrong. He was misled by professionals; but that does not suffice to explain his own errors. Admittedly, both subjects involved technical matters in which Churchill retroactively claimed to have no expertise (in other instances, he endeavored to become deeply involved in similar details— not without success). But his readiness to accept expert opinion, despite certain doubts of his own, nevertheless occasions surprise. After all, his own experience during the last war—and particularly, so he claimed, in the 1917 debates over the convoy system—had taught him that in most cases the politicians were right and the military experts wrong.[163] Moreover, even during the 1930s it was his natural inclination to be suspicious of military experts.[164] What tipped the scales in favor of his acceptance of the opinions proferred by the experts was that he found their conclusions congenial. Like others, Churchill had a romantic yearning for battleships and their big guns. During the course of the 1930s he composed long memoranda that compared the technical characteristics of battleships in the possession of various navies. But there was a more important reason for his acceptance of the naval experts' opinions. His own strategic plans for the next war were based on sea power, and specifically on the battleship's freedom of movement in narrow waters. His hopes of realizing those plans were complemented by the Admiralty experts' judgment that air power would not substantively curb naval operations.

A larger question hovered over the uncertainty about the operational future of the Navy: the status of a nation, whose might was based on maritime power and trade and whose possessions were widely dispersed, when confronted by rising land powers. What gave rise to this question was not only the nature of technological change on land, at sea, and in the air. It was also brought about by the different natures of the economic and industrial infrastructures at the disposal of Britain and its potential rivals. As early as 1904 Halford Mackinder, one of the founders of geopolitics, had announced the end of the "Columbian Epoch" of the last four hundred years, during which states whose power rested on the sea had attained world supremacy. Mackinder argued that world history is the story of the constant struggle between land nations and those located on the continental peripheries. He employed the term "geographical pivot of history" (later, "heartland") to describe the core of the Euroasian landmass, comprising Russia's European territories and part of its Asiatic lands as far as the waters of the Arctic Ocean. Thanks to the inherent advantages of sea power maritime states had, during the Columbian epoch, managed to withstand the pressure emanating from within the Continent and to attain world influence, of which Britain had acquired a substantial share. Modern transportation and technological change, however, would work to the advantage of those states whose power was land based. The "heartland" contains a plenitude of the human and mineral resources needed for modern industrialization and economic autarky; it is also invulnerable to attack from the sea. Whoever commanded that area would be able to dominate the three continents of Europe, Asia, and Africa (the "world island") and ultimately to attain world hegemony.

The expected decline of Britain troubled Mackinder; and, although his theory was hypothecated on the existence of permanent geographic foundations and resources, he believed that the maritime states could delay or even arrest their decline. In order to do so, they had to form a grand alliance among themselves against the land nations. (In 1919 he advocated that Britain and the United States enter into an alliance that additional maritime states would join.)

The idea that recent developments would lead to Britain's decline was also shared by such other British students of geopolitics as J. Fairgrieve and Vaughan Cornish, whose books appeared during and immediately after World War I and whose theses were based on arguments not dissimilar to Mackinder's. It is true that prior to World War II, Mackinder's theory was neither well known nor influential in Britain. But he was an MP between 1912 and 1922 and established close connections with such leading politicians as Leo Amery, Alfred Milner, Joseph Chamberlain, and Lord Rosebury. In 1919 he was appointed the southern-Russian representative of Lord Curzon, the Foreign Secretary. In response to Mackinder's gloomy conclusions, Leo Amery, who was an old friend of Churchill's, even attempted to develop a geopolitical theory of his own.[165]

There is little likelihood that Churchill had not heard of Mackinder; but nowhere in his writings and speeches is there any reference to the man and his ideas. Nor, for that matter, do they contain any real discussion of the effect that recent changes during the twentieth century might have on Britain's future as a world power. This is surprising: for one thing, themes unquestionably geopolitical in character did permeate the very foundations of Churchill's military and political thinking; for another, there is the evidence provided by the conclusions of his historical studies and by the problems that British naval power had faced in the last war. In the latter there were more than hints suggesting that there was something wrong in Mahan's thesis—even as an interpretation of the past (and Mackinder maintained that Mahan was right only where the past was concerned). A partial explanation for Churchill's failure to confront this issue may lie in his inclination (one shared by many other pragmatic Britons) to avoid all-embracing and semideterministic theories of the type that Mackinder propounded; to this must be added (as we shall see below) his deliberate avoidance of the analysis of long-term developments beyond the range of the immediate future. Whichever the case, Churchill did not reach the conclusion that what he understood to have been Britain's past strategic formula for success was no longer relevant.

In Germany, unlike Britain, Mackinder's theory did strike a responsive chord. It impressed the German General Karl Haushofer, who translated it into a German geopolitical concept at whose core was the notion of *lebensraum* in the east. During the 1930s, Haushofer lectured at the German War College (the Kriegsakademie) where he was professor of geopolitics. Earlier, he had taught Rudolf Hess, through whom he met Hitler at a time when the latter was crystallizing his own thoughts in *Mein Kampf*. Hitler was also influenced by these ideas; in his political philosophy, *lebensraum* and the conquest of European Russia became supreme aims, partly because the "heartland" territory was geographically congruent with another of his supreme objectives: the destruction of what he termed "judeo-bolshevism."[166] Not only does Mackinder's theory deepen our understanding of some of the subjects with which Churchill wrestled; it was also to reappear in the forthcoming war in another guise.

Finally, Churchill was also mistaken in his assessments of the future of armored forces. He admitted as much when describing the failure of the campaign in France in 1940. "Not having had access to official information for so many years," he wrote, "I did not comprehend the violence of the revolution effected since the last war by the incursion of a mass of fast-moving heavy armour." [167] It is true that immediately after World War I, when Secretary of State for War, he did attach importance to the role which would be played in a future war by mechanization in both armored and nonarmored forces.[168] But thereafter, as he informed Lord Moran, he had ceased to follow the development of the tank and its place on the battlefield of the future[169] and paid only scant attention to this subject during the 1920s and 1930s. He did occasionally demand that the British Army be entirely mechanized; but in 1938 he wrote that, because of the development of powerful antitank devices, he forsaw no future for the tank.[170] He had only loose contact with J. C. Fuller and Liddell Hart, the principal theorists of modern tank warfare in Britain; and during the course of World War II Churchill's relations with both men became antagonistic.[171] Besides, most advocates of armored warfare opposed the continental commitment, while officers with a conservative cast of mind supported it.[172] This too distanced Churchill from the former.

It comes as no surprise to learn that as soon as Churchill had what turned out to be an incorrect assessment of the future of armored warfare, he reiterated his conviction that the defense possessed a considerable advantage over the offense. As he later admitted: "I also rested under the impression of the superior power of the defensive provided it were actively conducted. I had neither the responsibility nor the continuous information to make a new measurement."[173] On the eve of World War II he predicted the same sort of deadlock at the fronts as had characterized World War I.[174] His mistake was not particularly exceptional. Liddell Hart, who did believe in the power of mechanized warfare, maintained that the period since the last war had witnessed an increase in the defense's advantage over the offense.[175] Churchill was incorrect in attributing his own misunderstanding to his lack of access to classified information. He was similarly at fault in air and naval matters, about which he possessed an abundance of such information.

Churchill's strategic plans for war were thus based on shaky assumptions. He assumed that the French, possessing both the Maginot Line and the advantage of the defense, would be able to halt a German attack; he overestimated the strength of their army—notwithstanding the skepticism of Sir Edmund Ironside (the CIGS), Fuller, and others.[176] Consequently, he maintained that France would be able to afford Britain the breathing space necessary for the establishment of a large army and its dispatch to the Continent. Another reason for his confidence in France lay in the fact that the French strategic conception, which was based on defense, complemented Churchill's own plans on the eve of World War I. It will be recalled that he had then maintained that France had to prefer a flexible defense. In part this had to be based on a line of fortifications along its border with Germany; in the main, however, it had to rest on the concentration of a large mobile reserve, whose object was to strike decisively at the enemy once it had become weakened by its own advance.[177] He now thought that the French were adopting a strategic plan which fundamentally accorded with his own. He was "dumbfounded" when, during the course of the campaign in France, he discovered that they had not established a strategic reserve.[178]

Assuming that Britain would possess sufficient time to establish a large army after war broke out, Churchill maintained that the government had meanwhile to undertake the economic and military preparations to enable it to raise dozens of divisions in a short space of time. That was why throughout the 1930s he called upon the government to set up a ministry that would be responsible for the speedy adaptation of British industry to total war and the establishment of a large army.[179] In 1938, at the height of the government's policy of isolation, he wrote to Hore-Belisha that he had to build an infrastructure suitable for organizing twenty divisions as soon as war broke out.[180] Churchill maintained that one of the reasons Britain had to send a large army to France was to enable influencing its partner and to map out the strategic moves of the war.[181] During the course of 1939 he began to become confident that an effective answer to enemy bombers had been found and that the civilian population would be able to withstand air attacks. He estimated that the war would be protracted, and that allied strategy had to be based on the attrition of Germany's manpower and economy. It was from these perspectives that, during the course of 1939, he wove his offensive plans for the first stages of the war. All shared the objective of tightening the economic and military ring around Germany.

Churchill maintained that should Italy enter the war, Britain had to attack it first. The initial objective had to be the attainment of naval command in the Mediterranean; that would cut off the Italian armies in North Africa and Abyssinia and bring about their destruction. The danger to Egypt and the Suez Canal would thereby disappear. He opposed the idea, which had begun to gain ground in the Admiralty, that Britain should abandon command of the central Mediterranean and retreat to its two extremities. He estimated that it would take the Royal Navy only a few weeks to defeat the Italian navy. The Italians would be forced into a decisive naval engagement by the threat the Royal Navy would pose to its supply lines to North Africa. Churchill argued that a swift decision had to be attained in the Mediterranean even at the cost of temporarily weakening the defense of the Far East and the Dominions—and this despite the fact that the latter had been promised the dispatch of large naval forces to the Far East in the event of war with Japan. In selecting this order of strategic priorities, Churchill remained faithful to the positions he had held during the debate on the naval base at Singapore. Nevertheless, his preference also stemmed from the fact that he still believed that Japan would refrain from attacking Britain and the United States in the Far East. He thought that the Japanese had little chance of taking Singapore, and that once the Italian fleet had been annihilated large forces could be sent to the Far East.

Simultaneous with the struggle against Italy, Britain had to begin to establish a Balkan front that would include Turkey. An Anglo-Turkish alliance would also increase the chances of an alliance between Turkey, Britain, and the Soviet Union. This was because of the coincidence of Turkey's and Russia's regional interests. Both wished to prevent Germany from penetrating Rumania and the estuary of the Danube, and from gaining mastery of the Black Sea. Churchill thought that once he had conquered Poland, Hitler would turn toward the Black Sea.[182]

Once Britain had gained command of the Mediterranean and removed the Italian threat to North Africa—and should Japan not attack in the Far East—the next step had to be in the direction of the Baltic. Churchill planned sending a battleship task force to the Baltic that would remove Germany's command of those waters, create a threat to its northern coastline, and cut its important commercial link with the Scandinavian states. The force itself would use a permanent Soviet naval base. As early as 1936 he outlined this plan to Hankey, who considered it utterly unrealistic.[183]

To put matters another way: as had been the case in the previous war, Churchill considered France to be the war's future center of gravity, and it was there that Britain's main army had to be located. In tandem, Germany and its allies would be attacked along Europe's two maritime flanks. He attached particular importance to his plans for action on the European periphery. One reason was his assessment of their direct military utility; a second was his conviction that their implementation, together with Hitler's own moves, would impel the Soviets in the direction of the "grand alliance" and thus complete the last link in the chain of Germany's encirclement. His perception of the first moves was clear, but he did not look any further. He left the choice of the subsequent steps to Germany's defeat until after the results of the opening moves had been ascertained.

There is nothing coincidental about this similarity in Churchill's projects for the two world wars. He continued to think in terms of the strategic conceptions that he had held during the previous war, and aimed at the fulfillment of designs which had then not been implemented or which had failed. As will be shown, his plans reflect a degree of mental rigidity; but even a mind less trammeled than was Churchill's by past experience would have been hard put to think of entirely innovative strategic methods whereby the Allies might defeat Germany. Since the last war, the geopolitical division of Europe had hardly altered. The confrontation was between virtually the same alignments of powers, each confronted with strategic problems similar to those they had faced in World War I. The most significant difference, and it was one that worked to the disadvantage of the Allies, lay in the neutrality of the Soviet Union. And it was Churchill who was sensitive to the importance of that situation and who attempted to repair it.

Neither were there many innovations in the British Chiefs of Staff's plans on the eve of World War II. Basic to their planning was the assumption that, in a protracted war against Germany and Italy, the Allies would enjoy the advantages bestowed by British naval power and by the imperial resources commanded by the United Kingdom and by France. It followed that, as early as the first stages of the conflict, Germany would attempt to reach a decision either by attacking Britain from the air—the Chiefs of Staff rejected the possibility of a German sea-borne invasion—or by invading France by way (so it was generally believed) of the Low Countries. They maintained that the Allies had to adopt a defensive posture during the first stages of the war and to await a formidable increase in British military strength. The Chiefs of Staff placed their faith in the Maginot Line, maintaining that its strong fortifications would compensate for the numerical inferiority of the Allied armies during the first stages.[184] They concurred with their French colleagues in that, after the opening stages of the conflict (during which their own forces would be organized and the German attack, if it took place, be repulsed), it was Italy that had to be defeated. Only thereafter would they embark on the third stage of the fighting, whose objective was the defeat of Germany.[185] Apart from placing considerable optimism in the results of economic attrition, they too had no clear idea as to how this last aim was to be attained. Moreover, the British Chiefs of Staff underrated the Soviet Union's military strength. Only after much time had elapsed did they, together with their French colleagues, reach the conclusion that only Soviet Russia could ensure the durability of an eastern front.[186]

There were only two important points on which Churchill's basic strategic concept differed from that of the Chiefs of Staff. One concerned Britain's order of priorities in a simultaneous war against Italy and Japan. The official view held by the Admiralty and the government was that the Far Eastern theater would be preferred to the Mediterranean and that the main portion of the fleet be dispatched to Singapore. It is true that doubts about the wisdom of that decision were voiced in Admiralty circles during the course of 1939; but Lord Chatfield, now Minister for the Coordination of Defence, remained steadfast in its support. Together with the other senior decision makers in London, the Admiralty entered World War II in some confusion about its order of strategic priorities, and with the earlier decision still in force.[187]

But it was the "Baltic scheme" which provided the most striking difference between Churchill's plans and those of the Chiefs of Staff. Leaving aside for the moment its operational difficulties, this was a very attractive plan. Churchill was correct to hope that it would encourage a military alliance between Soviet Russia and the West. Although he was apparently unaware of the fact, Russia's demand that a large Anglo-French naval force be sent to the Baltic did indeed recur in each of the various proposals for strategic cooperation submitted during the course of the military talks between the Soviet, British, and French delegations in the summer of 1939.[188] Moreover, Allied command of the Baltic would have had a most detrimental effect on Germany's war economy and considerably increased the effectiveness of the naval and economic blockade that the Chiefs of Staff proposed. Germany then imported 66 percent of the iron ore required for its steel production, and while half of that amount came from Lorraine in France, the remainder came from Sweden.[189] By preventing its supply from Sweden, as well as from France, Germany could have been hit hard. It is still a matter for debate among economic experts whether, as Churchill claimed, the effect would have been "immediately decisive" and whether, as Marder maintains, Germany was "vitally dependent" on the Swedish source.[190] (Needless to say, the situation changed once Germany had conquered Lorraine and established a land link with Spain, where iron ore is abundant.) But whichever the case, the plan was not given any serious consideration prior to the outbreak of war. The "Baltic scheme" was politely rejected by Chatfield [191] and opposed from the very start by Sir Dudley Pound, the First Sea Lord, who when war was declared had no clear offensive plans of his own.

The operations Churchill wished to mount were conditional on the immunity of warships to air attack and on their ability to operate freely in waters infested with enemy submarines. What strengthened his confidence that they could do so was the fact that Germany possessed no large surface fleet of its own. But the Germans were in complete command of the air over the Baltic and its approaches. Moreover, the Italians enjoyed air superiority over the central Mediterranean, as well as over the passages between its east and west basins and between the Italian mainland and North Africa. The implications of these circumstances soon became apparent. Like the Gallipoli plan, the strategic vision inherent in the "Baltic scheme" was doomed to founder on shoals of the operational level.

Whereas on the eve of World War I Churchill's thinking had been fresh and sharp, his assessments were now partly mistaken and characterized by conservatism. Nevertheless, when compared with the predictions of most military men in Britain and France, his is not an outstanding failure. It does not overshadow his great achievement during the 1930s, which consisted of his correct assessment of the existing and emerging political and strategic situation and his persistent advocacy of the correct way to repel the German threat. A. J. P. Taylor has argued that it will never be possible to resolve the debate over whether World War II might have been prevented by further concessions or by the adoption of a firmer stand. Perhaps either method might have succeeded had it been consistently adopted, but "the mixture of the two, practised by the British government, was the most likely to fail."[192] Admittedly, the first method would have prevented the outbreak of war in September 1939, but it is doubtful whether it could have prevented a European war at a later date. The second method—which was advocated by Churchill—would either have prevented war or ensured that when it did occur the Allies would have been in a far more favorable strategic position.

With the approach of the end of the 1930s, the validity of Churchill's concept at the political and strategic level was vindicated. But during the fateful years he had lacked all authority and did not attain supreme command until war came. During the Second World War, however, his assessments of the operational reality of modern warfare were faulty. Unfortunately, during wartime the operational level is just as important as is the strategic.

5

The Genesis of the "Mediterranean Strategy," 1940-1941

On the outbreak of war, Churchill was again appointed First Lord of the Admiralty, a position which gave him the authority to instigate action in accordance with the peripheral and naval dimensions of his plans. Despite his energetic pressure on behalf of operations on Europe's flanks, he retained the delicate balance between the "continental" and "maritime" strategies that had characterized his strategic concepts ever since 1911. Anticipating a German attack in the west, Churchill sought the early dispatch to France of as many ground forces as possible—including those that had not yet completed training. His aim was to station there an army of 1,000,000 men. But the CIGS, Sir Edmund Ironside, opposed the hasty and massive dispatch of forces which were for the most part still in the initial stages of formation.[1] During the German invasion of Poland, Churchill advised that the French attack Germany from the west, with British air support.[2] Nothing came of this idea, because the French were hesitant and the British military chiefs and the Cabinet were reluctant to be the first to initiate aerial bombardments.

Churchill justifiably suspected that under Chamberlain's direction the War Cabinet would avoid an expansion of Britain's military involvement on the Continent and accord priority to the expansion of the Navy and Air Force.[3] In September 1939 he emphasized to the Prime Minister the importance of maintaining a balance between the services in the construction of British military power, reminding him of the fact that the priority given to naval expansion in 1917–1918 had not lived up to expectations. Churchill maintained that Britain had to build up an army of fifty-five divisions, but added that some preference ought to be given to the Air Force, which "I sometimes think . . . may be the ultimate path by which victory will be gained."[4] But at the same time he elsewhere argued that air power would not substantially change the face of war.[5]

On the eve of the war Churchill's plans had assumed that, during the opening stages of the conflict, Allied offensive efforts would concentrate on the Mediterranean and Italy. But Italy had not yet entered the war, and Churchill's pressure for the establishment of a Balkan front was stiffly opposed by Ironside

Europe and the Mediterranean in 1939

and Halifax, the Foreign Secretary; the response of the Balkan states themselves was negative. Consequently, he was constrained to forego his initial preference for action on the southern periphery and to focus his attention on the northern theater. This reversed the situation which had applied during the previous war, when Churchill had turned to the southern flank of Europe and the Dardanelles only after he had found it impossible to fulfill his projects in the north.

Churchill aspired to implement plan "Catherine" (named after the Empress Catherine the Great of Russia), which involved rushing battleships into the Baltic and was in fact nothing but a new version of that old chestnut, the "Baltic scheme." The nomenclature symbolized the proposed objective to be attained: the Soviet Union and the Scandinavian states were to be brought into the war against Germany while, at the same time, the latter was to be denied the important raw materials it imported from Scandinavia. Pound, the First Sea Lord, objected to Catherine on the grounds that it was too risky, especially in view of the new hazard from the air. The Admiralty's opposition led Churchill to promote a less ambitious and less dangerous plan, whose objective was to impede the conveyance of iron ore from Sweden to Germany, transported by way of Norway during the winter, when the Baltic freezes over. Because of the diplomatic complications involved in the attendant violation of Swedish and Norwegian neutrality, the War Cabinet's handling of this plan was dilatory in the extreme. Churchill, however, persisted. Indeed, in an attempt to promote his idea he even supported the notion that Anglo-French forces be sent to assist Finland in its war with Soviet Russia. Although he did not initiate that proposal, which had the support of senior Cabinet Ministers and the French leadership, he hoped that by supporting it he would find it easier to get the Cabinet to approve an attack by way of Norway. But in thus attempting to maneuver between these various constraints, Churchill's strategic objectives became curiously contradictory. Assistance to Finland might have dragged France and Britain into war with Russia at the very time that the establishment of a western alliance with the Soviets against Germany was still Churchill's primary aim.

This contradiction can be traced back to Churchill's primary lesson from the failure of the Gallipoli campaign. His own conclusion, it will be recalled, was that he had erred when attempting to carry through a complex and combined operation at a time when he did not wield supreme authority. That lesson did not deter him from enthusiastically initiating the Norwegian campaign, even though forced to operate under similar restraints. He had no authority to bring the Army into action and had to cope with difficulties from his Cabinet colleagues before the campaign and during its conduct.[6] This circumstance explains why an analysis of the battle for Norway and of Churchill's responsibility for its failure can contribute nothing further to an understanding of his qualities as a strategist and decisionmaker than has already been learned from our study of his involvement in the Gallipoli campaign. A second reason for bypassing the Norway fiasco is that its strategic consequences were not far reaching. Once France had fallen and Germany was in command of Europe's Atlantic seaboard, Britain's geostrategic position was so precarious that German control over Norway made matters only marginally worse. It was the German bases on France's western coast that presented the main threat to the vital sea-lanes of the Atlantic Ocean. Furthermore, Britain's failure in Norway had no real influence on the Allied inability to repel the German attack on western Europe in the spring of 1940.

With his appointment as Prime Minister on May 10, 1940, Churchill had at last attained what he had always sought—supreme authority and power. But even before he had adjusted himself to his new position, he was confronted with a shocking and unexpected blow: the swift collapse of France. This entirely upset all of his strategic assessments and plans. Indeed, as far as his formulation of future strategy was concerned, the fall of France resulted in the loss of a conceptual balance that Churchill did not regain until the war was well advanced. Quite apart from shattering his earlier operational assessments of a future war, that event also destroyed what had ever since 1911 been the cornerstone of his strategic thinking vis-à-vis Germany: the vital nature of British and French land power in western Europe. Churchill found it harder to come to terms with this blow than did those politicians and soldiers who had, in any case, regarded the military continental connection with France as a liability rather than an asset. Immediately after the fall of France, Churchill blamed its collapse on Britain's failure to dispatch to the Continent a large army on a scale similar to that sent overseas at the parallel stage of the previous war.[7] To this he added, in his dinner-table talk at the end of a day's labors, the internal rot that had seeped into French society and the efficiency with which the Germans had devised their strategy and handled their army's operations.[8] Beyond that, however, he invested little thought in the reasons for France's defeat. Indeed, he neither initiated a debate on the question nor wrote anything about it.

■

Before discussing the development of British strategy during the summer of 1940, an analysis must be made of the nature of Churchill's power and authority within Britain's framework of decision making. Churchill himself faithfully depicted the situation when recalling: "It is true that I received a measure of loyal support in the direction of the war from Parliament and my Cabinet colleagues which may well be unprecedented, and that there were very few large issues upon which I was overruled."[9] Not even in the darkest days after Gallipoli did Churchill apparently hope to wield the degree of power which he commanded during the course of World War II. The decision-making apparatus that he set up was small, and cut to his own cloth. As well as being Prime Minister he was also Minister of Defence, in which capacity he was in direct contact with the Chiefs of Staff Committee; moreover, he also chaired the Defence Committee, whose members included the Chiefs of Staff and senior Ministers. Both of these two bodies were subordinated to the War Cabinet itself. Within a short space of time, both the Defence Committee (the number of whose meetings drastically decreased after 1941) and the War Cabinet were virtually deprived of all real authority. The process of decision making was vested in Churchill and the Chiefs of Staff who formulated the complexion of British strategy in a series of direct dialogues among themselves. What Churchill called the "large issues" were first thrashed out by the Prime Minister and Chiefs of Staff and only then brought for formal approval to the War Cabinet, whose meetings were thus transformed into something akin to briefing sessions. Although Churchill welcomed that development, it cannot be regarded as one he forced upon his Ministers; the latter preferred to leave the burden of strategic decision making to the Prime Minister and his military advisers. Diplomatic matters (which encompassed a sphere of great importance, since many diplomatic subjects were intimately bound up with questions of grand strategy) were entrusted to Anthony Eden, whose relationship with Churchill was intimate as well as complex. Thus it was that the framework of decision making constituted a triangle with Churchill at its apex. It was he who directed and managed British "grand strategy" by means of an intimate dialogue, oral as well as written, with the Chiefs of Staff on the one hand and Eden on the other.

■

From the moment that France fell, Churchill's hopes were pinned on the United States. Bringing the United States into the war became a supreme strategic objective. It had been President Roosevelt who on the outbreak of war had approached Chamberlain, Halifax, and Churchill; but on the British side the only person to show an interest in institutionalizing such personal contact was Churchill, who had always attached importance to U.S. involvement in Europe and to Anglo-American cooperation. Thus was initiated the famous epistolary link between the "Former Naval Person" and Roosevelt. As long as Churchill was First Lord, his correspondence with the president was restricted to naval matters, but even then Roosevelt evinced a degree of cooperation that exceeded the bounds permitted to the head of a neutral state,[10] and which made Churchill optimistic about the chances of the United States' entry into the war. Once aware of the trend of the campaign in France, he told his son Randolph that in order to attain victory, "I shall drag the United States in."[11] True, he had no real grounds for informing the French that the United States' entry was imminent (a declaration made with the object of encouraging them to continue their own military resistance).[12] But despite the skepticism of some of his Ministers and advisers and the repeated disappointment to his own accumulated expectations, Churchill remained confident that the United States would enter the war.

■

In the middle of August 1940, at the height of the Battle of Britain, Churchill decided to send about half of Britain's scant armored forces to the Middle East. This was a bold decision in which Churchill took considerable pride, and that reflected his confidence that any German attempt to invade Britain would be bound to fail. There are several—and contradictory—versions of the manner whereby that decision was arrived at. Colville, who was then Churchill's Private Secretary, claims that the Prime Minister instigated the movement of forces to the Middle East despite opposition from the Chiefs of Staff.[13] That is also the position of Fergusson, who cites the papers of Major-General John Kennedy, the Director of Military Operations. Liddell Hart's *History of the Second World War* follows them.[14] But entirely opposite is the picture painted in his *Memoirs* by General (later Lord) Hastings Ismay, who was at the time Head of the Office of the Minister of Defence and Churchill's representative at the Chiefs of Staff Committee. He claims that the idea was proposed by Sir John Dill, who had succeeded Ironside as CIGS, whereafter it was enthusiastically welcomed by Eden, then Secretary for War, and by Churchill.[15] Churchill's own account of this particular decision is nebulous. Butler, the official historian, maintains that it was arrived at jointly by the Prime Minister and the War Office, but without the participation of the War Cabinet,[16] which is also the view of Churchill's official biographer.[17] This Rashomon-like tale illustrates the necessity for sticking as closely as possible to the written documentation and for treating with caution the memoirs and testimonies of persons who were either close to the small circle of decision makers or part of it. Especially is this so since Churchill was (as he put it) himself "a strong believer in transacting official business by *The Written Word* [emphasis in the original]."[18] He insisted that communications made during the course of decisionmaking be either in writing or placed on record.

In any case Churchill's stated positions before and after the decision leave little room for doubt. The threat of an impending Italian attack on Egypt helped him to gain the consent of the Chiefs of Staff, and his initial directives to General Sir Archibald Wavell, Commander-in-Chief, Middle East, advocated a defensive posture.[19] But not even in this hour of distress was Churchill deterred from giving thought to the future offensive phase. During the course of non-commital ruminations with his colleagues in August 1940, he floated several offensive ideas for 1941: to conquer Oslo; to seize the Contentin-Cherbourg peninsula; to launch a massive raid on the Ruhr basin by way of the Low Countries with a force of 100,000 men; and to invade Italy.[20] From a practical point of view, Churchill began to indicate that the Middle East clearly constituted the fulcrum of his offensive plans. One of his first actions was to scotch the Admiralty's inclination to abandon the central Mediterranean and Malta; and as early as the beginning of August he decided that, were there to be no invasion of Britain by October, large British reinforcements would be dispatched to the Middle East.[21] Early in September, he wrote a memorandum in which he laid down priorities in the production of munitions for the services. He estimated that the utility of a blockade had been greatly reduced by Germany's domination of vast resources in Europe. Consequently, preference was to be given to the Air Force rather than to the Navy and Army, because air superiority and "bombers alone provide the means of victory." Nevertheless, Churchill did not retract his opinion that the Army had to be expanded to fifty-five divisions, and stated that "the only major theatre of war which can be forseen in 1940/41 is the Middle East." The sole limitations on the size of the forces to be sent to that region were those imposed by the availability of naval transport and local support facilities.[22]

On the very next day, September 4, the Chiefs of Staff submitted a memorandum dealing with "future strategy." Their thinking had hardly changed since the outbreak of war. They argued that Germany's economic situation had not been affected, despite the great extent of its European conquests. Unlike Churchill, they did not consider that Germany was less vulnerable to blockade, and estimated that its reserves of oil (a subject on which they laid particular stress) would become seriously depleted after June 1941. Thus, British strategy had to be based on the attrition of Germany, an end to be attained principally by attacks from the air. Once Germany had been worn down it would be possible to go on the offensive on all fronts in the spring of 1942. They emphasized that it was not their objective to build up a powerful Army that could invade the Continent and defeat the German army. The Army would enter Europe only when given the opportunity to do so after Germany had been severely weakened by strategic bombing, by blockade, by internal subversion, and by the organization of uprisings all over Europe. They noted the importance of eliminating Italy from the war: its collapse would remove the threat to the Middle East, permit Britain to strengthen its defenses in the Far East, and tighten the blockade on Germany. The main points of this memorandum were communicated to a U.S. military delegation that visited London late in August.[23] Churchill's response, delivered some five weeks later, was lukewarm. True, he did accept in principle the ideas put forward in the memorandum, but he questioned the very utility of long-range strategic planning at a time when the realities of the war were changing day by day. On those grounds, he maintained that there was no point in asking the War Cabinet to endorse the Chiefs' memorandum.[24]

Churchill continued to ponder the planning of a British Middle Eastern offensive while the Battle of Britain was still being fought.[25] At the end of October, by which time the height of the battle was past, he convened a well-attended meeting of the Defence Committee with the purpose of setting out his own strategic ideas. In his own words:

> The question might be asked "How are we to win the war?" This question was frequently posed in the years 1914–1918, but not even those at the centre of things could have possibly given a reply as late as August of the last year of the war.

This was no mere rhetorical flourish. Churchill reverted to the same words in several of the speeches that he delivered until the end of 1941. Their purpose was not only to boost morale; they also reflected his feeling that sharp and unexpected turns of events are an inherent characteristic of war and one that therefore negates the value of long-term strategic plans. Furthermore, his speech also constituted a latent admission (absent from *The World Crisis*) that during World War I he had possessed no clear idea of the way to defeat Germany.

For the present, Churchill continued, Britain had to exert pressure on Germany and Italy by means of blockade and unrestricted air-bombing: "In 1942 we shall be in a position to carry out large scale attacks overseas." The danger of an invasion of the United Kingdom had greatly receded; there was proof that Germany had for the time being abandoned that idea. The United States would help Britain to overcome its deficiencies in munitions. Sufficient forces would have to be kept in reserve for home defense, but "subject to that proviso it was intended to send reinforcements overseas to the maximum extent within the limits of shipping." Of the fifty-five British divisions whose establishment would be complete by the end of 1941, "25 to 30 divisions would be in the Middle East, which we would hope to reinforce at a rate of one division per month, or faster if shipping was available." The British commanders in the region were confident of their strength. Referring to developments in the Balkans (Italy had invaded Greece just three days previously), Churchill reiterated the need to send as many forces to the Middle East as shipping would allow. As to Germany, it would in 1941 be able to operate simultaneously in Spain and against Turkey and Russia, and also to provide Italy with logistic support. But "the Germans would inevitably turn their eyes to the Caspian and the prize of the Baku Oil fields. In that event, Russia would have to fight, as without oil for her agriculture, her people would starve."[26]

Churchill's statement did have long-term implications. Although he possessed no agreed and approved strategic master plan, nor even any confidence in a particular method of defeating Germany, he had decided that half of Britain's future army would be dispatched to the Middle East. (In fact, the proportion was somewhat larger, since the troops to be sent overseas were combat divisions, while those to be left in Britain were of an inferior quality and in part composed of antiaircraft units.) This meant that the crux of Britain's land effort was to be shifted from the Atlantic-European front to the Middle East.

Both the politicians[27] and the military supported the initiation of a British offensive against Italy. Churchill's controversies with his military advisers centered only on the pace and scope of the transfer of British forces to the Middle East and on the spheres of offensive operations within the region. At the meeting held at the end of October, Dill did voice some faint objections to the Prime Minister's decision that as many forces would be sent as shipping and the local logistic absorptive capacity would allow. Together with Kennedy, his Director of Military Operations, Dill feared that since there was sufficient shipping to transport the majority of the British Army, Britain's home defenses might thereby be weakened. The size of the forces that had always to be stationed in the British Isles was never specified. At this stage of the war (1940–1941) the

Army chiefs and Churchill were engaged in a sort of tug-of-war. The former wanted to build up and conserve the Army's strength in preparation for a major action in the future. Churchill, however, already wished to employ it on offensive operations that were not to their taste.[28]

A cluster of interconnected causes motivated Churchill to shift the axis of British strategy on land to the Mediterranean region. Contrary to accepted opinion, imperial interests in the region were not the primary influences on his thinking. It was indeed his ambition to retain the Empire; but ever since 1911 he had refrained from subordinating British strategy to this consideration whenever he thought it conflicted with moves that *to his mind* constituted the most efficient means of resisting Germany and bringing about its defeat. It is easy to confuse the strategic importance he attached to the region with Britain's imperial interests there. The two did not always coincide. It will be recalled that in 1912—despite the hue and cry raised by British imperialist circles—Churchill increased the Royal Navy's strength in the North Sea at the expense of its reduction in the Mediterranean. At the beginning of World War I his own preference had been for action on the northern coast of Europe; only because he had no other choice did he turn to the eastern Mediterranean. For military reasons, he had also wanted to establish a Balkan front. Immediately after the war, he had been less than enthusiastic about the addition of further Middle Eastern possessions to the Empire.[29] His studies on Marlborough had reinforced his feeling that both the eastern and western basins of the Mediterranean constitute areas of considerable strategic influence on the course of any war on the Continent. "We must retain that command of the Mediterranean which Marlborough, my illustrious ancestor, first established," he told Harold Nicolson in 1936.[30] When, before World War II, Churchill determined that Britain had to concentrate its efforts on the defeat of Italy, even at the price of temporarily weakening the Far East's defenses, he knew that he was running the risk of jeopardizing imperial interests in Asia and Australia. Clearly, he did not accord priority to the Middle East because he considered that theater to be of greater imperial importance than the other. Justifiably or not, his preference was above all determined by strategic considerations.

Of course, the force of circumstances also came into play. At this stage, North Africa was the only theater in which Britain could move from the defensive to the offensive against an enemy whom it might overcome. Nevertheless, Britain's ability to seize the initiative in this area was not a consequence of the fact that its troops were in any case stationed there; rather, the forces had been rushed to the Middle East in accordance with a policy initiated in August 1940 and confirmed that October. Thus a British offensive in the Mediterranean basin was not necessitated by natural strategic selection. A comparatively small force would have been able to defend Egypt as well as guard over the overland route to India and the Iranian oil fields. Already at the beginning of November, it was estimated that the local British forces enjoyed a certain advantage over the Italian army in Libya, despite their numerical inferiority.[31] Britain could have chosen to adopt a defensive posture in the region and to build up its military power while awaiting the entry of allies into the war.[32]

Clearly, Churchill was incapable of acquiescing in that strategic policy. It is also doubtful whether the Chiefs of Staff and political circles would have agreed with it. Which objectives, then, were to be attained by the twenty-five to thirty divisions that Churchill planned to send to the Mediterranean region? That only a few of their number would be needed to defeat the Italian forces in North Africa was an assumption which was speedily verified; the Prime Minister's denigration of Italy's military abilities knew no bounds.[33] He contemplated conquering Sicily once the Italians had been booted out of Africa. However, there is no evidence that at this stage either he or the Chiefs of Staff sought to invade the Italian mainland. What they aspired to was Italy's elimination from the war, an object which did not require so large a number of divisions since it was to be accomplished by defeating Italian forces in Africa, by attaining command of the Mediterranean, and by launching strategic strikes from the air. On the other hand, a military front comprising the Balkan states and stiffened by British troops could have provided a large sphere of operations for the lion's share of those divisions.

The above comments bring to the fore the question of future Anglo-American strategic cooperation. At the beginning of August the Americans raised the subject of the future of the British fleet in the event of Britain's defeat. Churchill asked Lord Lothian, the British ambassador in Washington, to make it plain to President Roosevelt that Britain would reserve its freedom of strategic action. But he added:

> Of course, if the United States entered the war and became an ally, we should conduct, the war with them in common, and make of our own initiative and in agreement with them whatever were the best dispositions at any period in the struggle for the final effectual defeat of the enemy.[34]

That approach might be considered logical, provided that it constituted a diplomatic tactic rather than the basis for military strategy. But there is no evidence that Churchill gave serious thought to the effect of current British strategy on the nature of Anglo-American military cooperation when the United States would enter the war. As we have seen, the center of gravity of Britain's land operations was supposed to be shifted to the Mediterranean. Yet, it was the Atlantic, the British Isles, and western Europe that constituted the natural logistic axis and center of gravity for Anglo-American cooperation in the future.

Churchill was not entirely oblivious to this interaction. Early in January 1941, on the very day that a British military delegation departed for talks in Washington, he informed the members of the Defence Committee that the recent successes in North Africa had justified the decision to dispatch massive reinforcements to the Middle East. He explained that the problem of shipping would be the principal restraint on operations overseas. Although Roosevelt was contemplating giving Britain considerable military assistance, "We did not, at present, need U.S. troops, in fact, it would be a mistake to use shipping to transport them."[35] Churchill's disregard of the operational implications of the United States' entry into the war stands in marked contrast to his confidence that it would indeed become involved sooner or later. Especially is this so in view of the fact that the indications pointing to the United States' impending military intervention were particularly encouraging in October 1940—at the very time that Churchill discussed with the Defence Committee his long-term intentions for the Middle East.[36] Churchill hoped that the turning point would be reached after the U.S. presidential elections to be held at the end of 1940.

What emerges from our discussion hitherto is that not since the fall of France (itself an event of revolutionary proportions from the strategic viewpoint) had Churchill conducted a fundamental and long-term analysis of Britain's strategic alternatives. Virtually mechanically, he had fallen back on whatever was left—and practicable—of the plans he had considered on the eve of war. The failure in Norway had removed the northern theater from the agenda; likewise, with Britain's expulsion from western Europe, Churchill's hopes of dispatching a large army to the Continent had vanished. All that remained, then, was the Mediterranean and the Balkans. Nevertheless, the decision to attack the Italians in Africa was not erroneous. By employing comparatively small land forces and exercising its massive naval strength, Britain could indeed have cut off Italy's foothold in that area. A swift conquest of northern Africa would also have prevented the German penetration of that continent and opened the Mediterranean shipping routes. Considerable savings could thereby have been effected in the shipping capacity wasted by the diversion to the Cape routes of transports destined for the Middle and Far East. Neither would future Anglo-American cooperation have been adversely affected. On the contrary, Britain's shipping capacity across the Atlantic would also have been augmented.

But to direct the war in the Mediterranean basin and extract from it maximum benefit at limited cost demanded clear judgment and expert craftsmanship. Even the small-scale offensive against the Italians, who enjoyed the advantage of internal lines, imposed severe logistic and organizational strains on Britain's military apparatus. Its offensive strategy in the Middle East could easily have lost its balance. Inauspicious omens were apparent even before the British campaign in North Africa began, when the Prime Minister's instructions were to rush as many forces to the region as shipping capacity would allow and to aim at the establishment of a Middle Eastern army of twenty-five to thirty divisions.

■

Discussion of the dispatch of an army to Greece dragged on from December 1940 until March 1941. One reason for analyzing the process whereby this decision was reached is the effects of the failure in Greece on the subsequent progress of the war. But to that must be added the unique circumstances surrounding the decision itself. Churchill was then at the very height of his power and prestige, which meant that he was able to initiate a military campaign and ensure that it was conducted as he wished by all the segments of government concerned. Also augmenting his freedom of action was the fact that Britain was then fighting alone; when devising its strategy Britain was not therefore constrained to take into account the pressures exerted by a powerful ally, such as the United States. There was, as yet, no sign of the dissonance and lack of clarity characteristic of the formulation of a joint strategy among allies. To this must be added the fact that the decision was not taken under exceptional pressures of time; considering that a war was on, the period with which we are here concerned was, if anything, comparatively calm: the danger of an invasion of Britain had for the moment receded; a Japanese onslaught in the Far East was not yet in sight; and the end of 1940 saw the removal by a lightning blow of the Italian threat to Egypt. But there was another side to the coin. At the same time that the various compellants to action were thus reduced, Churchill—as we shall see—was for the first time faced with the dilemma of having to choose between two strategic alternatives. Paradoxically, during the hectic days of May and June 1940, as well as during the ensuing Battle of Britain, he had not been forced to decide between evenly matched options. The pressure of events and the nature of their development had so effectively narrowed Britain's room for maneuver that Churchill and his colleagues were confronted with a "natural" strategic selection that left little room for hesitation. Such had been the case with the withdrawal of British forces from France and the decision to continue the struggle against Germany, about which there was never any real question. The Battle of Britain itself had been conducted by the military; Churchill's most important decision was to strengthen the forces in Egypt at the expense of those in Britain. An analysis of the decision to send an army to Greece thus provides an opportunity to examine Churchill's qualities as a strategist and as a decision maker in a particularly "pure" form, without the encumbrance of any background noise. Particularly is this so since he was himself of the opinion that it is precisely the small events that sometimes determine the course of wars. "It is these which should be studied and pondered over, for in them is revealed the profound significance of human choice and the sublime responsibility of men."[37]

Mention has already been made of Churchill's belief that in World War I an opportunity had been missed to form a grand Balkan front which "must have involved the downfall of Austria and Turkey and the speedy, victorious termination of the war."[38] He also maintained that Germany's ultimate collapse was the result of the combined effect of Bulgaria's exit from the conflict, of the advance along the "Salonika front," and of the failure of the great German offensive of 1918.[39] Between the two world wars, Churchill was wont to designate Greece, Yugoslavia, and Turkey as "powers"; indeed, under the leadership of Kemal Ataturk, one of the heroes of the Gallipoli campaign, he considered the Turks a "formidable power."[40] As for the Bulgarians, they were a strong and warlike race.⁴¹ In April 1939, after the Italian invasion of Albania, Churchill feared that German-Italian pressure on the Balkan states would force them "to make the best terms possible with Berlin and Rome." Having committed itself to defend Poland, Britain should also conclude with the Balkan states an alliance "which once effected might spell salvation."⁴² (On April 13 Britain and France did indeed extent guarantees for the defense of Greece and Rumania, should those states be threatened and their governments decide to fight.)

In mid-September 1939, Churchill proposed that the War Cabinet promote the formation of a Balkan front based on Turkey, Greece, and Yugoslavia, and including Bulgaria; its purpose would be to defend Rumania, which he considered to be the next country on Hitler's list. This proposal was opposed by Halifax, the Foreign Secretary, and by Ironside, the CIGS, both of whom maintained that the establishment of such a front would provoke Hitler to invade the Balkans and reap easy victories. Ironside reminded the Cabinet of Rumania's fate during the previous war when it had joined the Entente powers; the Balkan states, he maintained, should only enter the war when they could be given sufficient assistance. A somewhat annoyed Churchill responded that Germany would not gain easy victories over Yugoslavia and Turkey.⁴³ A few days later he presented the Cabinet with a memorandum in which he reiterated his view that Britain had to establish a Balkan front and thereby advance cooperation with the Russians in order to block Hitler in the east; ultimately, it was from that direction that offensives on Germany could be launched.⁴⁴

As long as Chamberlain was Prime Minister, the idea was shelved; but Churchill did not abandon it. The Balkan front was intimately bound up with the "Mediterranean strategy" that he began to put into effect in the summer of 1940. In August, Churchill ordered four bomber squadrons to be sent to the Middle East, there to be held in readiness for stationing in Greece should the latter enter the war.⁴⁵ On October 27, one day before the Italians opened their attack on Greece, he wrote to Roosevelt that there was a chance that British operations in the Middle East would soon spread to Greece and Turkey.⁴⁶ In the middle of October Eden, Secretary for War, was sent to the Middle East in order to spur the British high command in the region. On his arrival in Cairo, he discovered that General Sir Archibald Wavell, Commander-in-Chief, Middle East, was planning to attack the Italians in North Africa. At the beginning of November, Churchill began to press Eden to send as many forces as possible to Greece, stressing the country's importance, and in order to show Turkey and the world that Britain stood by her commitments.⁴⁷ Although he too desired the formation of a Balkan front, Eden agreed with Wavell that no assistance could be given to Greece unless the defense of Egypt was first ensured. Most of the resources then available in the Middle East were required for the planned offensive against the Italians.⁴⁸ Both men feared splitting the army between two fronts, even though on November 4 it was agreed to send air units to Greece. At the beginning of November, the British intelligence community estimated that Germany intended to attack Turkey by way of Bulgaria, and that the Italian attack on Greece was intended to draw from Egypt British forces which would be destroyed during the course of the German attack.[49] But the Prime Minister continued to exhort Eden and Dill to rush reinforcements to Greece and Crete.[50]

In his own book, *The Second World War*, Churchill claimed that the pressure he exerted on Eden and Dill came from a misunderstanding; in order to maintain secrecy, the latter had not informed London of the planned attack.[51] This explanation causes some surprise since information about Wavell's intended offensive can be gleaned even from those of Eden's dispatches to Churchill that were widely circulated. Moreover, on November 3 Eden wrote Churchill a letter in which, using a cipher known only to themselves, he explicitly outlined Wavell's plan and the dangers involved in dispatching a force to Greece at that time.[52] Churchill did not notify the War Cabinet and Chiefs of Staff of this report—on the contrary, at the Cabinet meeting held on the following day he continued to press for deeper British involvement in Greece. Nevertheless, on November 5 the Chiefs of Staff submitted their own appreciation that Hitler and Mussolini might possibly be trying to divert British forces from North Africa to the Balkans and that it would, in any case, not be possible to repel a German attack on Greece; hence their preference for not sending troops there and for restricting assistance to air and technical units.[53] It was not until Eden had returned to London on November 8 and had begun to exert his own influence that Churchill was persuaded to give priority to Wavell's offensive.

In a daring strike launched from aircraft carriers against the port of Taranto on November 13, half of the Italian battle fleet was either destroyed or effectively disabled. This victory gave Britain temporary naval command of the eastern and western Mediterranean—although not of the entire sea. The Italians, and subsequently the Germans, still controlled the central Mediterranean and its strategic nexus, the link between Italy and North Africa and between its eastern and western basins. It was they who possessed the advantages conferred by a combination of regional air superiority, internal lines, and command of the shores adjacent to the naval passages. The great sea battle had not generated the strategic shift that Churchill had envisioned on the eve of the war; it had merely improved Britain's naval position in the Mediterranean.

Success at Taranto, together with the fact that the Greeks had repulsed the Italian attack, convinced Churchill that for the time being attention had to be concentrated on Wavell's offensive. But before that got under way, the Prime Minister was careful to inform Wavell that he had to expect the center of gravity to shift from North Africa to the Balkans and be prepared to send troops to Turkey.[54] He began to press him to advance his attack on the Italians "before the Germans could come to their assistance" since "it is unlikely that Germany will leave her flagging ally unsupported indefinitely."[55] Mindful of the unsuccessful influence political interference had exerted on operations during World War I, Dill, the CIGS, tried to moderate Churchill's pressure on Wavell.[56]

At this stage, Wavell's own strategic assessment was clear. On November

17 he wrote that the Germans would not be able to remain inactive in the face of Italy's failure in Greece. It was to be expected that air assistance would soon be sent to Italy. For the time being, Germany apparently did not want to invade Yugoslavia or push Bulgaria into the war, but might perhaps be forced to do so. In any event, "as in the last war, Germany is on interior lines and can move more quickly to attack Greece or Turkey than we can to support them." Concurrently, the Chiefs of Staff laid down as a guideline their assessment that Britain's northern flank in the Mediterranean would not be endangered even should Greece fall to the Germans, provided that Britain controlled Crete and that Turkey remained neutral. It followed that Turkey was more important than Greece.[57] That appraisal remained steadfast throughout the Balkan crisis.

On "the other side of the hill," Hitler regarded Balkan developments with concern. The conquest of Yugoslavia and Greece had never been part of his political program. However, September and October 1940 saw the crystallization of a "peripheral strategy" whose object was to undermine Britain's position in the Middle East. It was within that framework that Hitler planned the dispatch of ground forces to North Africa and the conquest of Greece, principally in order to establish air bases on its territory.[58] Consideration of this "peripheral strategy" was short-lived. By the middle of November, after Molotov's visit to Berlin, Hitler had finally decided to invade the Soviet Union in the spring of 1941. The defeat of Britain thus became a secondary objective and he abandoned his offensive aims in the Middle East. His perspective on the Balkans had become solely defensive. True, the Italian defeat in Greece did threaten to upset his plans for an attack on the Soviet Union; Hitler wanted to be certain that his southern flank was secure and that Britain would not acquire a Balkan foothold. (He knew, for instance, that British squadrons had been sent to Greece.)[59] That explains why he gave orders to draw up plans for an attack on Greece by way of Rumania and Bulgaria, and also accounts for the intensity of his diplomatic efforts at the end of November and during the course of December to end the war between Greece and Italy. Aware of these efforts, the British made similarly energetic attempts to ensure that they failed. Their immediate object was to ensure that Italian forces would be pinned down on the Albanian front and thus unable to reinforce the Italian army in North Africa. They feared that General Ioannis Metaxas, the President of the Greek Council, might be inclined to accept a settlement with Italy and Germany, and that Greece would thereby become a neutral state.[60]

On November 18 the Greeks launched a counterattack that eventually drove the Italians back into Albania; on December 9 the "Wavell offensive" opened in North Africa, under the operational command of General Sir Richard O'Connor. The latter smashed the Italians, and on December 16 crossed the Egyptian-Libyan frontier and began his swift rout of the enemy forces retreating into Cyrenaica.

The Germans continued their efforts to bring about a Greek-Italian peace. But General Metaxas, who had no confidence in Hitler and was subject to

British pressure, rejected the German offers. The victories in Albania had made him optimistic about Greece's ability to defend itself single-handedly. Thus, he was careful to ensure that British involvement remained limited, although on December 23 he did agree to accept substantial British credits.[61] Confronted with the failure of his diplomatic efforts and the collapse of his ally in North Africa, Hitler rushed sizable reinforcements to Rumania at the end of December and the beginning of January. It must be borne in mind, however, that these troop movements were also integral to his preparations for an attack on the Soviet Union.

Meeting with the members of the Defence Committee and his military advisers at the beginning of January 1941, Churchill asserted that, in view of the developing German threat to Greece, the dispatch of forces to Greece and the prevention of a Greek-Italian peace was to be preferred to the completion of the conquest of Libya.[62] On January 8 he convened the Defence Committee, and opened the meeting by announcing the gist of the accumulated intelligence reports. These indicated that the Germans, whose forces were concentrated in Rumania, would on or around January 20 attack Greece by way of Bulgaria, and with the latter's consent. The German offensive force would comprise two armored divisions and 200 dive bombers. Since most of the Greek forces were concentrated on the Albanian border, their own position would be hopeless.

> The Russian attitude was unknown. A German advance was against her interests, as there was no doubt that the Germans' ultimate objective would be the oil of Baku. Russia would be much encouraged by Turkish resistance to Germany, and this in turn would depend upon the manner in which we could support the Greeks.

The assistance Britain could extend to Greece might not suffice, but there was no other way to show the world that Britain would do whatever possible to save her. Hence the continuation of the Libyan offensive was a matter of secondary importance. Possible objections by his military advisers, who made no comment whatsoever throughout the meeting, were countered by the Prime Minister's declaration that "from a political point of view it was imperative to help the Greeks against the Germans." Eden, who had been appointed Foreign Secretary the previous December, enthusiastically endorsed that opinion. It was decided that every effort had to be made to send forces to Greece, and that a military appreciation on the subject would be presented within forty-eight hours.[63] It arrived on the next day. In addition to repeating the various arguments advanced by Churchill, the Chiefs of Staff also reiterated the contention that political considerations made it imperative that Britain do all in its power to assist Greece. They did not voice an opinion as to whether this political consideration outweighed in importance the military factor. But this was a question immediately implicit in their military assessment. They remarked that they had always maintained it would take twenty divisions to throw back a German advance via Bulgaria and Yugoslavia. Should the Germans launch an attack on

Greece by January 20, their progress would be swift and British losses slight (since most of the British troops would still not have landed in Greece). However, should the latter manage to reach the scene of action in time "we feel that we could, at least, impose considerable delay on the German advance."[64]

Even should optimal conditions apply, the military assessment was thus pessimistic. But it is clear from the Chiefs' statement that the campaign would certainly be doomed to failure if the Germans attacked by January 20. Nevertheless, the Chiefs did not rule out sending ground forces to Greece to confront the German offensive they thought would be launched by that date. Their evaluation was in fact illogical. Although Dill had from the first objected to the Army's transfer to Greece,[65] he apparently considered that he would only incur Churchill's anger by expressing his objections in writing, and gain nothing. His attitude astonished Kennedy, who was similarly opposed to the move, and advised Dill to raise his objections, even if only for the record.[66] But Dill remained silent at the meeting of the Defence Committee held that evening, when it was decided that Wavell was to halt his advance after the conquest of Tobruk and accord top priority to military assistance to Greece. He was also to travel to Athens and confer with General Metaxas about the scope of British support.[67] Wavell was told that successful military assistance would have a decisive effect on Turkey's attitude and would also influence that of the United States and the Soviet Union. But Wavell was not impressed. On the following day, January 10, he sent a cable to London in which he argued that the German threat to the Balkans might be a bluff, designed to check Britain's advance in Libya. "Nothing we can do from here is likely to be in time to stop German advance if really intended, it will lead to most dangerous dispersion of force and is playing the enemy's game."[68] Churchill's response was forceful. He demanded that Wavell comply with decisions taken in London "for which we bear full responsibility." Moreover, he said, "Destruction of Greece will eclipse victories you have gained in Libya."[69]

When Wavell arrived in Athens, Metaxas turned down his offer of help, pointing out that the limited assistance the British could offer would be of no use. Insufficient to defend Salonika and Greece, it would only incite the Germans to attack. Greek (and Turkish) estimates of Hitler's Balkan intentions were similar to those held by Wavell and his staff in Cairo, and gave rise to fears that Britain was attempting to drag Greece into a war with Germany. For their part, the British, although prepared to send ground forces to the Greeks, were unwilling to supply them with military equipment alone—because they still feared that the Greeks aspired to conclude peace with Italy.[70] On January 16 the Defence Committee convened to discuss the Greek rejection of Britain's offer. Although absent from the meeting, Churchill did submit some guidelines in which he noted that the Greeks had to be left to decide what was in their own best interests. The meeting also pondered Germany's Balkan intentions, eventually concurring with the intelligence assessments reached in London that the Germans shortly intended to attack Greece by way of Bulgaria. Dill pointed out that if the Germans were to be checked at Salonika—which, as will shall see, was one of the strategic keys to the Balkans—forces had to be sent there immediately; and even so the chances of success were slim. Were the Greeks not to agree now, they could not be given effective assistance later on.[71] On January 18 Wavell wrote a memorandum to Dill on the value of British involvement in Greece. He considered that the forces Britain could dispatch would not prevent the German conquest of Salonika. Meanwhile, the advance into Libya would be halted and the Italians given a chance to recover. British air inferiority in the Middle East is "a most serious factor"; should further squadrons be sent to Greece "we shall be weak everywhere." Wavell advised that Britain come to terms with the Greek rejection of its offer and refrain from giving assurances that would include a promise of ground forces.[72]

Notwithstanding the Greek attitude, Churchill did not despair of establishing a Balkan front. He opened the meeting of the Defence Committee on January 20 by castigating the defensive attitude adopted by the Chiefs of Staff. Their proposals that Britain proceed to the conquest of all of Cyrenaica, to establishing a base at Benghazi, and to the conquest of key islands in the Dodecanese, he said, aroused his "considerable concern, since it seemed to lead to the minimum of aggressive action." He made it plain that "he was anxious to give the war a more active scope in the Mediterranean." Even with the benefit of hindsight, it is difficult to sympathize with Churchill's complaints. Just three months earlier, Britain had been confronted with the threat of invasion, its Army had been in the throes of recovery after its defeat in France, and the Italians had been poised to invade Egypt. It had been hoped that Wavell's offensive would remove the latter danger, but no one had envisioned the extent of the success achieved by O'Connor, whose forces were now swooping down on Tobruk—and about half of Italy's battleships had been entirely disabled. Simultaneously, Wavell had launched an offensive from Sudan and Kenya, designed to eliminate the Italian presence at the Horn of Africa. On January 20 the British Army in the Middle East was enjoying the momentum of a wide-scale offensive, all the more suprising in view of the limited size of Wavell's forces and the severity of his logistic problems.

Churchill went on to say that he did not agree with General Metaxas's claim that Germany's objectives in the Balkans were defensive. Britain could not force itself on Greece; but since the latter had rejected offers of help, it could not have any cause for complaint against Britain. Almost nothing could be done to prevent Greece from being overrun by Germany. But Benghazi had to be taken by only a small force and turned into Egypt's defensive flank; the main body of the army had to be concentrated in the Nile Delta as a strategic reserve and held in readiness for dispatch to Greece, Turkey, or elsewhere. Churchill also asked his military advisers to examine the possibility of taking Sardinia. Chief of the Air Staff Charles Portal responded that the conquest (and retention) of Sardinia would be made difficult by the enemy's local air superiority; it would be preferable to take Tripoli and thus entirely clear North Africa

of enemy troops; additional operations could then be mounted in the Middle East. Eden argued that Turkey constituted the key to the Middle East situation. Dill, as usual, said nothing. Churchill did not even react to Portal's proposal. The Committee accepted the Prime Minister's suggestion and on the following day he ordered Wavell to halt once he had reached Benghazi, to fortify the town, and to build up in the Nile Delta a strategic reserve of some four divisions that would go to Greece and to Turkey when the need to do so should arise.[73]

At the same meeting, discussion also turned to the possible objects of Germany's troop concentrations in the Balkans. Two explanations were proferred (apparently by Churchill himself). One was that Germany was in fact intending to invade Britain, and that its concentrations in the Balkans were designed to divert British forces and pin them down in the Middle East. But considering the difficulties confronting a German invasion attempt, the Committee members were generally agreed that this explanation was doubtful. An alternative suggestion was that Hitler was planning an attack on the Ukraine and the Caucasus—i.e., on Russia—with the object of preparing the economic infrastructure for a later onslaught on Britain and that the expected attack on Greece was part of that grand design.[74]

The minutes of the meeting provide no clue as to whether the Committee's members concurred with the latter explanation: its degree of similarity with Churchill's earlier assessments is, however, striking.[75] Nevertheless, it differed from the appreciations being submitted by the British intelligence community, and especially by British military intelligence (which had the greatest sway). Until the spring of 1941, the latter considered that Hitler did not intend to attack the Soviet Union and that the German troop concentrations in the East and the Balkans were primarily directed against Britain. They were locked into the conception that Hitler would not attack Russia until he had first defeated Britain. The deployment of German forces to Rumania was interpreted as a move prepatory to a breakthrough to the Middle East from the north. The explanation for the presence of the seventy German divisions identified in Poland was that they were designed to deter Soviet intervention and to act as a threat that would help Germany impose diplomatic conditions on Russia.[76] On the other hand, the predominant feeling at Wavell's headquarters in Cairo, at least until the end of February, was that Hitler did not intend to attack Greece; his object was to create a threat that would pin down British forces and thus ease Italy's position in North Africa and Albania.[77]

The official historian of Britain's intelligence does not attribute its failure to a lack of information or to German deception, but to a fundamental conception that did not give sufficient weight to the ideological and political factors guiding Germany's war aims.[78] In the winter of 1940–1941, the extent to which German ciphers were being decoded by the Ultra project was still limited. But even when the codes were systematically broken, the decrypts did not furnish direct information about strategic decisions taken by Hitler and the German high command; in the main, they only provided information about the movements of the Wehrmacht's units. Ultra did not prevent intelligence failures at the strategic level. (In all that follows, it must be remembered that the British strategic appraisals presented in this chapter and those that follow were also based on information received through Ultra.)

Churchill had a different opinion of Hitler's intentions. He was undoubtedly more sensitive to the ideological and political dimensions of Hitler's thinking and his specific aims in the east than was the British intelligence community, which was largely comprised of military men. More important still was the guidance provided by his conclusions about German strategy during World War I. Churchill, it will be recalled, maintained that once the Schlieffen plan had failed, the Germans should have adopted a defensive posture in the west and attacked in the east—defeating Russia, preventing the formation of a hostile Balkan coalition, and taking possession of the economic resources of the Ukraine and the Caucasus.[79] Now, in 1941, there existed no western front to prevent the Germans from turning eastward. At the end of June 1940 Churchill wrote to General Jan Smuts, the South African Prime Minister and a friend whose views he respected, that "if Hitler fails to beat us here, he will probably recoil eastward. Indeed, he may do this even without trying invasion."[80] On several occasions after October 1940 he described an invasion of the Ukraine and the Caucasus as an "ultimate" and "inevitable" German aim. He had good reasons for maintaining that Hitler would not repeat what he considered to have been Germany's great strategic error (he did not develop a disdain for "Corporal Hitler" until a later stage of the war). The march of events merely strengthened his confidence in the validity of the explanation he had raised before the war and was to stick to after its conclusion: Hitler, he maintained, was sequentially following a design prepared in advance.

Churchill, then, was not in thrall to the conception of the intelligence community, which maintained that Hitler would not attack Soviet Russia while the British Empire was still undefeated. But although his mind was more open, his assessments were impressionistic and not translated into practical action. Churchill did not insist on his own alternative "thesis" of an invasion of Russia. He remained wedded to the idea that Germany would attack Greece, since the chances that "Germany should at this stage, and before clearing the Balkan scene, open another major war with Russia seemed to me too good to be true."[81] Between mid-February and mid-March, the period when the decision to dispatch an army to Greece was finally made, British intelligence hardly concerned itself with Russo-German relations.[82]

On March 28 Churchill experienced what he termed "a lightening flash" of illumination, which revealed that Hitler intended to invade the Soviet Union in May 1941 and that the move would "certainly be his major purpose."[83] If this development is to be understood, later events must first be discussed. Thanks to Enigma decrypts of Luftwaffe messages, it became clear on March 26 that orders had been given to transfer three armored divisions and other important units from the Balkans to the Cracow region in Poland. This order was countermanded on March 27, when a pro-British coup d'état took place in Belgrade, Yugoslavia. Churchill's conclusion was that Hitler had ordered the transfer of his forces from the Balkans in preparation for an impending attack on Russia while he felt assured of Yugoslavian cooperation (Yugoslavia's Prince Paul had visited Berlin on March 18 and signed the Tripartite Pact), but that he had canceled the order when hearing of the coup. Using similar logic, the head of the German department in Air Intelligence also reached the same conclusion.[84] It was on this basis that Churchill sent Stalin his famous warning of April 3.[85] But that move had no effect whatsoever. Stalin was not the only person to remain unimpressed by the evidence; so too did most members of the British intelligence community who, as late as the end of May and the beginning of June, maintained that the defeat of Britain remained Hitler's primary objective.[86] (This incident provides a cameo example of why the revelation of the British decrypts early in the 1970s cannot effect a revolutionary change in the understanding of the conduct of the war at its highest strategic level. In his own description of the episode, Churchill merely substituted the fact of the Enigma decrypts with a reference to "an intelligence report from one of our most trusted sources." The same is true of other instances throughout the course of the war.)

Churchill's intuitive assessment that Hitler would turn eastward and eventually attack Russia helped him to reach an early understanding of the true import of the information that reached London. On the other hand, he did not transmute that assessment into a central element in the framework of strategic considerations respecting the utility of the establishment of a Balkan front, nor of the attendant dispatch of land forces to Greece. (He did not realize that the Germans intended to attack the Soviet Union in the spring until three weeks *after* it had finally been decided to send ground forces to Greece.) Had he done so, he would have been compelled to conclude that sending an army to Greece was not in Britain's strategic interest. After all, the British were fully cognizant of Hitler's efforts to patch together a Balkan peace and reach political settlements with the states of the region. During the first two weeks of February, even Military Intelligence fell back on the opinion that German troop concentrations in the Balkans were designed to bring the nations of the region to heel without resort to war.[87] From the British point of view, it was better to let Hitler reach a settlement with the Balkan countries than to divert him from his "ultimate" and "inevitable" objective—an attack on the Soviet Union. The formation of a Balkan front would only be justifiable once Hitler was embroiled in Russia; hence it had to await the opening of a land front against Germany in the east. To this must be added another consideration: Hitler, it was suspected, might still be attempting to entice British forces into a Balkan trap in order to leave himself free to invade Britain in the summer of 1941. True, that was deemed an unlikely possibility; but it did accord with the basic assumption held by British intelligence, and with the Chiefs of Staff's assessment that Germany—provided it did not attack the Soviet Union—had the capability to invade Britain and at the same time to mount offensives elsewhere in Europe.[88]

Even though he also possessed equally important operational arguments in its favor, Churchill himself did not reach this conclusion. He continued to think of the Soviet issue in terms of the positions he had held in 1938 and 1939. In spite of the radical strategic changes in Europe, which demanded a reassessment of the triangular link between Germany, Russia, and the Balkans, he still believed that the establishment of a Balkan front against Germany would create a common Anglo-Soviet denominator that, in turn, would force Russia's entry into the war. In that sense, he can be compared to a chess player who has given up hope of understanding the purpose of his opponent's moves and does not take them into account when continuing to form his own plans.

■

In mid-January news reached London and Cairo that German air units had arrived in the central Mediterranean.[89] This seemed to illustrate—and confirm—fears that the Germans could not permit their ally to endure incessant disasters in North Africa. Meanwhile, O'Connor continued his westward advance, taking Tobruk on January 22. He proceeded to move on Benghazi, the westernmost point of advance permitted to his forces. Tension relaxed after January 20, when the expected German attack on Greece did not materialize. At the beginning of February, British Military Intelligence stated that it had no proof that the Germans intended to advance beyond Bulgaria.[90] And late in January, Wavell informed the Chiefs of Staff of the possibility that, because of the German threat, the Greek-Italian war might soon come to an end, notwithstanding Greek declarations to the contrary.[91]

At the end of January, Churchill took pains to remind the Chiefs of Staff once again of the decision to halt Wavell's forces once Benghazi had been taken, and to concentrate in the Nile Delta a reserve intended for the Balkans.[92] He also addressed himself to President Ismet Inonu of Turkey, whom he tried to pursuade to join a Balkan league. Churchill offered to send ten bomber squadrons that, once on Turkish soil, would be capable of bombing German concentrations in Rumania and Bulgaria and threaten the Rumanian oil fields vital to Germany's needs. They would also be able to strike against the Baku oil fields, and thus prevent the Russians from helping Hitler.[93] Inonu turned the offer down.

Writing to Dill early in February, Leo Amery (Secretary of State for India, but not a member of the War Cabinet) argued that the conquest of Tripoli was preferable to the dispatch of an army to the Balkans. The Germans had to be prevented from establishing themselves at that port, since once they had done so it would prove extremely difficult to get them out. He maintained that command of the North African coast was a vital foundation for all future operations in the Balkans, Sardinia, or Sicily. There was no point in sending forces to Greece, since the Germans could not possibly be repelled. Dill fully supported these sentiments.[94] Amery also approached Churchill directly. He reiterated his remarks, emphazising the political aspect of the conquest of Tripoli. The fall of the city would convince General Weygand, who commanded Vichy forces in North Africa and who was in control of Tunis, to link up with the British. Subsequently, troops could be landed at Casablanca.[95]

O'Connor took Benghazi on February 6, and on the next day completed the battle of Beda-Fomm, in which he destroyed most of the Italian forces in retreat from Cyrenaica. Between him and Tripoli (where the Germans had not yet landed) there stood just one weakened Italian regiment, while the five Italian divisions stationed within the town itself were under strength and demoralized. O'Connor immediately grasped the nature of his opportunity. He proposed to Wavell that he be allowed to make a swift advance on Tripoli with a small force, to be supplied and assisted by units the Navy would land on the coastal road leading to the town.[96]

Meanwhile, on February 8, Anglo-Greek staff talks were renewed. M. Korysis, who succeeded General Metaxas after the latter's death on January 29, followed the policy laid down by his predecessor. He refused to accept British land forces before a German attack had actually commenced.[97]

On February 10, Wavell wrote to Dill that "Tripoli might yield to small force if despatched without delay." But he also added that the Balkan situation, together with the decisions on that matter taken in London, made him hesitant to act.[98] On the same day, the Defence Committee met to discuss the proposal for an advance on Tripoli submitted by O'Connor and Wavell. This was the first clear intimation of the dilemma—Tripoli vis-à-vis Athens.

On February 10 the Balkan situation continued to deteriorate. Military Intelligence estimated that the Germans had already concentrated some twenty-three divisions in Rumania. On March 12 they would be able to position themselves on the Greek-Bulgarian border with a force of six divisions, one of which was armored. Should they attack Greece on the same day, they would be in Salonika within a week. They could reach Athens with a force of ten divisions within the space of between three weeks and two months. Turkey would not come to Greece's assistance. In addition, there was a new wave of rumors about a Greek-Italian peace treaty.[99] It was with this information in hand that Churchill and his colleagues sat down to thrash out their dilemma. The meeting opened with a presentation of the arguments for and against a continuation of the advance on Tripoli.

The arguments in favor were that Tripoli could be taken by a small force; that the Italians would be thrown out of North Africa; a link would be effected with the Vichy French; and a counterattack thus be prevented. Conversely, "if we did not take Tripoli now, the Germans and Italians would be able to reinforce the place and establish strong air forces in the neighbourhood. It might be impossible to capture it later on." Against this was the argument that, in view of the uncertainty in the Balkans, it would be preferable not to disperse the forces concentrated in the delta with a view to their dispatch to southeastern Europe. It had already been decided that the Balkans had priority over further operations in Africa and that it would be a mistake to alter that decision. Even after Tripoli was taken it would be impossible to send convoys through the Mediterranean. Although the record is too vague to permit us to identify who presented which side of the case, the style of the latter comments strongly suggests that they were voiced by Churchill.[100] The minutes give no details of the ensuing debate, after which it was decided not to advance on Tripoli. The troops were to halt at Benghazi and further efforts were to be made to establish a Balkan front. The Chiefs of Staff pointed out that there was insufficient time to get forces to Salonika. The only possible chance of checking the Germans was to retreat to what was called the "lakes line." But in that case, the Greeks would have to relinquish two-thirds of their territory.

Eden responded that the only way to ensure Turkey's entry into the war was to give the Greeks effective assistance, without which there was no chance of setting up a Balkan front with Yugoslavia. The Greeks wanted to know the scale of forces Britain was prepared to send; once provided with that information they would be prepared to discuss a military plan. Churchill strongly supported Eden, stating that it would be a mistake to abandon Greece (although he added that even a neutral Turkey would accord with British objectives). He thought that, with the aid of British forces, the Greeks would be able to hold up the Germans long enough to induce Turkey and Yugoslavia to enter the war. It was agreed to send a high-level delegation to Athens in order to arrive at a political and military settlement with the Greeks.[101]

This decision expressed a preference for one course, which was still not realistic—after all, the Greeks and Turks had yet to agree to receive British ground forces—over another that was considered feasible but whose attainment depended on the speed of its execution. The soldiers were extremely resentful; Dill "felt so strongly about it that he was almost thinking of resigning."[102]

Basic to all military considerations was the fact that the logistic infrastructure available in the Balkans was still as poor as it had been during World War I. Were a Balkan front to be established, operational and logistic circumstances dictated that its crux would have to be located at Salonika, the large Greek port astride the principal railways to Turkey and Yugoslavia. The main Salonika-Skoplje-Belgrade line ran alongside the Vardar River; a branch line entered Greece farther south, via the Monastir valley, and while still within Greek territory turned eastward to link up with the main line shortly before Salonika. Thereafter, it proceeded to Istanbul. There did exist other means of providing the Turks with logistic support; but should Yugoslavia join the war against Germany and Italy, Salonika would constitute its sole link with the outside world. Indeed, without it Yugoslavia could not fight for longer than a few weeks. On land, Yugoslavia was surrounded by states that, directly or indirectly, were under German control. Moreover, Italian control of Albania, of the Adriatic, and of the latter's outlet to the Mediterranean, meant that Salonika was Yugoslavia's only means of access to the sea. The Chiefs of Staff several times pointed out that there existed no possibility of preempting the Germans and defending Salonika. Only if a defensive line were established much farther south might the Greeks perhaps be saved; but that would remove any possibility of keeping the Yugoslavs supplied. From this it followed that even if the latter could be tempted to join a Balkan front, they would immediately be smitten irrespective of the results of a campaign for Greece. On the other hand, a prior renunciation of Salonika would probably dissuade Yugoslavia and Turkey from coming into the war. Thus, at the very same time that Churchill and Eden were deciding to further their efforts to form a Balkan front (even at the cost of an advance on Tripoli), the current assessment of their military advisers was that there existed no operational possibility of maintaining it.

On February 11 it was decided that Eden and Dill should go to the Middle East and the Balkans. Dill saw no point in the journey and tried to persuade Churchill and his Ministers to send instead Major General Kennedy (who was strongly opposed to establishing a Balkan front). Dill informed members of the Defence Committee that Wavell would have difficulty in finding four divisions for transfer to Greece in the near future. Churchill rejected that assessment, saying that "we would have to intervene with at least 4 divisions, rising to 6 or 10 in the summer." Fearing, as he put it, that his prestige might suffer, Dill withdrew his request that Kennedy be sent in his place.[103] As he told his DMO: "The Prime Minister lost his temper with me. I could see the blood coming up his great neck and his eyes began to flash. He said: 'What you need out there is a Court Martial and a firing squad. Wavell has 300,000 men etc., etc.'"[104] The CIGS embarked on his journey convinced that the establishment of a Balkan front and the dispatch of British forces to Greece would be a serious error.[105] But he did not speak his mind until he was on the verge of departing for the Middle East.

Immediately thereafter Churchill composed two directives for Wavell and Eden. He told Wavell that he had to halt at Benghazi and concentrate his efforts on sending as much military assistance as possible to Greece. Greek operational plans were not known; he, Dill, and Eden had to discover what they were and to attain military coordination with the Greeks. Should it prove impossible to reach a good settlement with them, "then we must try to save as much from the wreck as possible"—the capture of Crete and other Greek islands, and a reconsideration of the advance on Tripoli. "But these will only be consolation prizes after the classic race has been lost."[106]

Churchill placed his directives to Eden in a sealed envelope, with the request that it be opened only after arrival at Gibraltar. The contents endowed Eden with wide and extraordinary powers. "His principal object will be the sending of speedy succour to Greece. For this purpose he will initiate any action he may think necessary." In short, "the Foreign Secretary will represent His Majesty's Government in all matters diplomatic and military . . . and not be deterred from acting upon his own authority if the urgency is too great to allow reference home."[107] Churchill knew that he was placing these wide powers at the disposal of an ambitious man who believed that a Balkan front should be established. Eden had orchestrated Britain's intensive diplomatic activity in the Balkans ever since his appointment to the Foreign Office the previous December. But Eden also had one flaw: he did not fully appreciate that diplomacy and policy had to have effective military and strategic backing. In the words of one of his biographers, "He blocked military resistance to a weak Germany in 1936 but favoured issuing reckless threats against her in 1939."[108] Alexander Cadogan, Permanent Under-Secretary at the Foreign Office, was quick to spot this failing, and confided to his diary his unsuccessful efforts to make the same point to Eden himself.[109] Kennedy did indicate to Eden that the Balkan front possessed no military basis, noting that the local armies were extremely weak and would in fact constitute a burden rather than an asset. Eden replied that such was the case in the military sense but not where the political front was concerned. Kennedy's response was that in wartime it is the military front that counts.[110]

In mid-February, while Dill and Eden were en route to Cairo, Kennedy wrote a memorandum expressing the feelings of the General Staff. He argued that Britain had to advance on Tripoli rather than transfer forces to Greece, and thereby forestall the establishment of a German base in North Africa. This opportunity might never recur. A link would be effected with Weygand and shipping in the central Mediterranean be made safe. Kennedy claimed that there were insufficient forces to be sent to Greece to confront twenty to twenty-five German divisions.[111] In a meeting with Churchill on the same day, Kennedy made the same points. To his surprise, he found the Prime Minister willing to listen. "Never again was I to find him so easy," he wrote. His own impression was that Churchill "seemed to be in considerable doubt as to the correct policy to follow" in regard to Greece, but that he still refused to acknowledge the importance of Tripoli.[112]

Three days later, Cadogan sent Churchill a letter that had received the prior blessing of senior officials in the Foreign Office. Cadogan argued that, since there was no chance of stopping the Germans in the Balkans, an advance on Tripoli and a linkup of forces with Weygand was preferable to a defeat there, a loss of prestige, and a negative effect on Turkey. He expected the Prime Minister to explode.[113] It is ironic that Foreign Office officials, who are conventionally supposed to attribute supreme importance to the diplomatic aspect of affairs, in this case opposed military assistance to Greece on the grounds that it would be ineffective. Churchill replied that Eden and Dill had been sent to clarify matters (a description that bore no relation to the task they had in fact been given). "If however Greece resolves to resist the German advance we shall have to help them with whatever troops we can get there in time." The alternative was a separate peace between Greece and Italy at German dictation, with the danger that German air bases would be established in Greece.[114] Churchill reduced his ability to withdraw should circumstances alter and he change his mind. Eden and Dill had also been sent in order to ensure that the Greeks would fight if invaded by Germany. That, indeed, was Eden's first demand when he met with them.[115] And, at the same time, British diplomacy in the Balkans continued to make unceasing efforts to prevent a peace between Greece and Italy.

On February 19 Eden and Dill arrived at Cairo, at which point Dill executed a *volte-face* and began to support the dispatch of British troops to Greece. Writing to his deputy on February 21, Dill said that his mind had been changed as a result of his talks with his military colleagues in Cairo, but Eden's version leads one to think that Dill's opinions had begun to alter even while he was still en route. Eden had plenty of time in which to persuade him and, on their arrival at Cairo, both men (apparently unaware of the text of the guidelines Churchill had sent to Wavell on February 11) were surprised to find that Wavell had also modified his own views and that he had commenced concentrating his troops in preparation for transfer to Greece.[116]

Although it is uncertain whether Dill had changed his mind before or after his arrival in Cairo, it is clear that he did so before he had discovered the nature of the Greeks' attitude and their operational plans. But the latter, besides being a logical prerequisite, had also been one of the prime purposes of his mission. Like Churchill and Eden, he and Wavell were now convinced that, were the Germans to be successfully fought in Greece, Turkey might be drawn into the war.[117] Disregarding the warnings of his intelligence officer as well as his own previous assessments, Wavell suddenly began to believe that Salonika could be defended, and minimized the chances that an Italian-German counterattack in North Africa might succeed. (Although Rommel had reached Tripoli on February 12, German ground troops had not yet done so.) He maintained that, should it transpire from the talks with the Greeks that there existed a good chance of establishing a stable front, troops would then have to be sent to Greece.[118] Dill, apparently influenced by Wavell and contrary to the opinion he had expressed in London, considered "that there is a fair military chance of successfully holding a line in Northern Greece if we act at once."[119]

In the meantime Churchill had begun to speak with two voices. One, weak and hesitant, pointed out the dangers involved in the dispatch of an army to Greece; the other, loud and decisive, was in favor of continuing the efforts to form a Balkan front. On February 20 he told the Cabinet that a peace treaty between Greece, Italy, and Germany would not necessarily constitute a disaster for Britain—quite the opposite of what he told Cadogan on the previous day—and that it would not be possible to send a sufficiently large force to Greece before the Germans attacked.[120] On the same day, he advised Eden (who was still in Cairo) not to enter into a commitment to Greece if he felt that to do so might lead to "another Norwegian fiasco." Churchill nevertheless added, "of course you know how valuable success would be."[121]

On February 22 Eden, Dill, and Wavell met with Korysis and General Papagos, the Greek Commander-in-Chief at the Tatoi Palace in Athens. At the very start of the talks Eden requested an assurance that the Greeks would resist a German attack. Once that had been given, discussion turned to military matters. Eden informed the Greeks that Britain could send out no more than

100,000 troops and five squadrons of aircraft in the immediate future. Korysis replied that this force would not be large enough to contend with the twenty-three German divisions and 500 aircraft amassed in Rumania. The presence of British troops might merely provoke the Germans to begin their offensive even earlier. The only chance of repelling the attack, he continued, lay in the immediate joining by Yugoslavia and Turkey in the campaign. Eden was forced to admit that he had no idea what the Turks and Yugoslavs might do.

When the military delegates met alone General Papagos said that there were two possible operational plans. Should Yugoslavia join the Allies, Salonika—its only outlet to the sea—could be defended, and indeed would have to be so. In that situation, the defense line would be drawn up on Greece's northern border with Bulgaria (the Nestos line). Should Yugoslavia not join in, it would be impossible to hold a line north of Salonika since the left flank would be open to attack from the direction of Yugoslavia and the Anglo-Greek forces might be trapped in Thrace. It would be essential to establish a line south of Salonika, beginning at the Aliakhmon estuary, passing northward to Mount Vermion and abutting the Yugoslav border (the Aliakhmon line). The British delegation agreed with Papagos's opinion. In discussion among themselves its members concluded that, in view of Yugoslavia's uncertain attitude, military logic dictated a withdawal to the Aliakhmon line.

Withdrawal to that line spelled the end of any hopes that a Balkan military front might be established. Without Salonika, Yugoslavia would not withstand a German onslaught, and neither would Turkey join a Balkan front. Dill and Wavell had journeyed to Athens with renewed hopes that Salonika could be defended. As soon as they had learned that there was little possibility of that, they ought to have reverted to their previous conclusion that it would be pointless to send troops to Greece at all. But having changed their minds once, they were incapable of doing so again. They could only pin their hopes on the Aliakhmon line, whose contours they did not even bother to reconnoiter.[122]

When the two sides held a concluding session at Tatoi on the same day, Wavell said that a withdrawal had to be effected to the Aliakhmon line. But under pressure from Eden it was decided to send a staff officer to Yugoslavia to explore its attitude. It was also agreed with the Greeks that "preparations should at once be made and put into execution to withdraw the Greek advance troops in Thrace and Macedonia to the line [i.e., the Aliakhmon line] which we should hold if the Yugoslavs did not come in."[123]

On February 24, after receipt of an optimistic report from Eden on the agreement reached at Tatoi, the War Cabinet met to decide on transferring troops to Greece. Also before the Cabinet was a report from Portal and Pound, in which they stressed that "the risks of failure are serious" and pointed out the disadvantageous consequences of the move should Yugoslavia or Turkey not participate. Nevertheless, they recommended going ahead. Churchill was certainly not dissuaded by this ambivalent assessment. He claimed that Eden advised the move despite being warned of the danger of "another Norwegian fiasco." He also noted the importance of the fact that Wavell and Dill had changed their attitude, and proclaimed himself in favor of sending ground forces to Greece because

> the results of which might be to bring Turkey and Yugoslavia in, and to force the Germans to bring more troops from Germany. The reaction of the United States would also be favourable. On the other hand, the difficulties of maintaining an army on land must not be overrated.

Cadogan doubted whether Yugoslavia would enter the war as well as its ability to stand up to Germany. Robert Menzies, the Australian Prime Minister, was similarly skeptical. Churchill replied that "the courage of the Serb race must not be forgotten. The Yugoslav Government was trembling, but the effect of our helping the Greeks might stiffen the resistance of the Balkan people." Should worst come to worst, most of the troops would be brought back to Egypt. Churchill requested, and received, the assent of every Cabinet Minister.[124] On the very same day, Churchill telegraphed to Eden: "While being under no illusions, we all send you the order, '"Full steam ahead.'"[125]

Eden traveled to Ankara with the object of persuading the Turks to join a Balkan front, but was unable to do so. On February 27 the Yugoslavs also rejected the suggestion. The next day Bulgaria signed the Tripartite Pact with Germany. The illusion of a Balkan front thus began to fade; but Eden continued to send London optimistic reports, which gave Cadogan and the members of the War Cabinet cause to wonder.[126] For his part Churchill continued to speak with two voices. On March 1 he exhorted Eden to concentrate his efforts on bringing Yugoslavia into the war. "I am absolutely ready to go in on a serious hazard if there is a reasonable chance of success, at any rate for a few months, and all preparations should go forward at fullest speed." But, if "you feel that there is not even a reasonable hope, you should still retain power to liberate Greeks from any bargain and at the same time liberate ourselves."[127] On the same day the Chiefs of Staff submitted a report that estimated that the maintenance of an expeditionary force in Greece would cost Britain the loss of about 1,000,000 tons of imports; and this at a time when shipping losses in the Atlantic were beginning to climb at an alarming rate.

On March 2 German forces in Rumania began to cross the Danube into Bulgaria, which joined the Axis powers. Eden and Dill returned to Athens, where they were surprised to learn that Papagos had not begun to withdraw his forces from the Nestos line to the Aliakhmon line. Eden claimed that this constituted a violation of the agreement reached at Tatoi, to which Papagos replied that it had been agreed to await the Yugoslav reply before finally deciding whether to withdraw to the Aliakhmon line. Meanwhile, only preparations were to have been undertaken. In any case, he had reached the conclusion that he possessed insufficient time to withdraw his forces from the north to the Aliakhmon. He feared that the Germans would interdict his forces as they were retreating to the line; he was also concerned about the reaction of Greece's

Macedonian population.[128] Even after the war was over, Eden and Wavell continued to maintain that their understanding of the agreement reached at Tatoi was different; Papagos was supposed to have made an immediate withdrawal. But, as cited above, the concluding paper of the talks speaks only of *the commencement of preparations* for withdrawal to the Aliakhmon. The written text, it seems, contradicts their version and supports that of Papagos.[129] Besides, neither did Eden's report to Churchill on the results of the Tatoi talks say that it had been decided on an immediate withdrawal to the Aliakhmon line.

What Eden had written was that "if we could be sure of Yugoslav moves it should be possible to hold a line farther north from the mouth of the Nestos to Beles, covering Salonika."[130] This hope does not square with an immediate Greek withdrawal to the Aliakhmon. Similarly, what was the point in Eden and Dill traveling to Ankara and in the dispatch of a special envoy to Belgrade (meanwhile replaced by a telegram) if Papagos was supposed to begin transferring his forces from Thrace and Macedonia? Had the Yugoslavs and Turks acceded to Britain's request, the defense of Salonika would have been vital—and that could only have been effected by staying on the Nestos line. In addition, it never occurred to General Heywood, who headed the British Military Mission in Athens, that he should have informed Eden and Dill or Wavell that Papagos had not begun to withdraw his forces from the Nestos.[131]

On the other hand, some indicators do support the British version. In the light of his previous dealings with Belgrade, Eden did not put much hope in Yugoslavia's entering the war. Subsequent to the Tatoi meeting he concentrated his efforts on Turkey. He did not tell Papagos that he had received a negative response from Yugoslavia on February 27 until his return to Athens on March 2. One can only assume that this was because he believed Papagos to be on his way to the Aliakhmon, as they had agreed. Eden fully appreciated the urgency of the matter. Papagos, however, although intellectually in favor of a withdrawal to the Aliakhmon, was emotionally torn by the prospect of abandoning Greek citizens and a considerable area of his homeland.

There thus seems to have been a misunderstanding between the British and the Greeks at Tatoi, whose roots lay in the lack of coordination between Eden and his own military advisers. Physical factors certainly played some part too. The members of the British delegation were worn out by the journey from Cairo. Dill had been sick even before he left London. The Tatoi document was drafted late at night after a day of exhausting discussions. But of even greater importance in the creation of a misunderstanding with the Greeks were two other circumstances. One was Eden's lack of skill and blind ambition to create a Balkan front. The other was the presence of two exhausted British generals who, on arrival in Athens, found that all the conditions that had recently caused them to change their minds about a Greek expedition no longer applied, but who nevertheless did not dare contemplate altering their opinions once again.

Not until March 5 did Eden report to London on what had transpired and on the new operational agreement that had been reached. Owing to the pressure of time, Papagos would keep his forces on the Nestos and transfer only three Greek divisions to the joint Anglo-Greek line on the Aliakhmon, which would be under British command. Although this disposition would disperse the Greek forces, Dill and Wavell "did not consider it by any means a hopeless proposition to check and hold" the Germans on the Aliakhmon and advised that Britain abide by the agreement with the Greeks.[132] Three days earlier, Wavell had informed London that he did not think that the German reinforcements recently landed in Tripoli constituted an immediate danger: no German attack on Benghazi could be launched before the end of the summer.[133]

London was astonished by the optimistic reports from Eden and Dill. At the meeting of the Defence Committee on the night of March 5, Churchill told its members that there was little chance of being prepared to meet the expected German onslaught in time. The Greeks had not fullfilled their undertaking to withdraw their forces to the Aliakhmon, while the transport of British forces to Greece would be slowed down by the Suez Canal being temporarily closed by German mines sown from the air. There was no sign that Yugoslavia and Turkey might join in. The Committee members assumed that there must be something unknown to London that might explain the positive attitude adopted by Eden and Dill.[134]

At the end of the meeting Churchill, with the assistance of Portal and Pound, wrote a letter to Eden that (in his own words) "certainly struck a different note."[135] The burden of his message was that

> we do not see any reasons for expecting success, except that, of course, we attach great weight to opinions of Dill and Wavell. We must liberate Greeks from feeling bound to reject a German ultimatum.... Loss of Greece and Balkans is by no means a major catastrophe for us, provided Turkey remains honest neutral.[136]

But by March 5 it was already too late. Nine British squadrons, together with their crews and accompanying antiaircraft defenses, were already stationed in Greece; so too was a forward army administrative unit; the first troop convoy had left Alexandria that very day.[137] On March 6 Field Marshal Smuts arrived in Cairo from South Africa, and gave the benefit of his advice. He itemized the well-known difficulties indicating that the Greek venture was hopeless. Nevertheless, "a provisional arrangement has been made and we have begun to carry it out. Therefore we cannot back out now."[138] Dill concurred with this view.[139] On that basis, Eden and Dill advised Churchill and the War Cabinet to go ahead as planned. Some Ministers were annoyed with Eden, because they thought he had tied Britain to Greece.[140] On the morning of March 7, before the War Cabinet convened, Churchill sent a telegram to Eden in which he requested a military appreciation justifying the move on grounds other than "noblesse oblige."[141] Eden's reply, which arrived after the Cabinet had already reached its decision, contained no new argument. In any case, Churchill's doubts had evaporated by the time he convened the Cabinet. He advised, "Go forward with a good heart" as planned. There existed a good chance of reaching the

Aliakhmon line in time and of checking the German advance, and there was still no cause to abandon hope that Yugoslavia might join the campaign. Even should the expeditionary force be compelled to withdraw from the Aliakhmon, it would do so over terrain that lent itself to defense. Britain's inferiority in the air, although undeniable, would not be any greater than it had been in several past instances. The members of the War Cabinet accepted Churchill's opinion without demur, although not (as Cadogan indicates) without mixed feelings. They were angry at having been dragged along in Eden's wake, but at the same time felt a "secret satisfaction" that a scapegoat was ready to hand.[142] Robert Menzies, the Australian Prime Minister, was the only person not to make a secret of his feelings. Although he did eventually support the Cabinet decision, he remarked that it was based on arguments that, as supplied by Eden and his military advisers, "told against, rather than in favour of, their advice."[143]

The rest of the story is known. Only 55,000 British troops managed to reach Greece, and the Allied forces remained strung out along both the Nestos and the Aliakhmon; on March 27 a pro-British coup took place in Belgrade; on April 6 the Germans unleashed an offensive on Yugoslavia and Greece. The German army advanced along two axes; one by way of Bulgaria and the other from Yugoslavia, following the line of the Vardar River (running south to the Nestos line) and the Monastir gap (cutting south to the Aliakhmon line). They thus circumvented both of the separate defensive lines in Greece. In the air, German superiority proved to be decisive. Greece was taken within less than a month. Most of the British troops were evacuated; but they left behind all their equipment and 10,000 of their comrades who were taken into captivity. Meanwhile, in North Africa, Rommel on April 2 opened a successful counterattack and began quickly to push the British eastward.

■

In *The Second World War* Churchill wrote: "I take full responsibility for the eventual decision, because I am sure I could have stopped it all if I had been convinced."[144] But he also emphasized that the final decision had been decisively influenced by the actions and advice of the men on the spot: Eden, Dill, and Wavell. A week after the decision was taken he wrote to Eden that "no one but you can combine and concert the momentous policy which you have *pressed* upon us."[145] A month later, in the wake of the disconcerting developments in North Africa and the Balkans, he maintained that the ultimate decision was taken on the basis of Wavell's appreciation (given on March 2) that no German counteroffensive in North Africa was to be expected in the near future. He cultivated that claim in his memoirs of the war;[146] nevertheless, his position was not altogether consistent. Defending his decision in Parliament shortly after the Greek failure, he said that he would have adopted the same course even had he known its results.[147] But some months later, he confided to his private secretary, John Colville, that the dispatch of an army to Greece had been his government's only mistake so far.[148] After the war, he vigorously defended his decision, claiming that its positive strategic implications outweighed the military defeat per se.

The historical verdict on this episode has tended to side with Churchill. In July 1942 the Prime Minister instigated an internal inquiry designed to disprove the rather weak accusation that he had bypassed his military advisers where Greece was concerned. This unique initiative itself indicates his extreme sensitivity to both the problem of his relations with his military advisers (which, in the light of the Gallipoli experience, was not new) and to the move itself. The superficial examination conducted by Churchill's Secretaries concluded that the accusation was groundless: the final decision had been taken on the basis of the favorable opinions submitted by Eden, Dill, and Wavell, and in light of the latter's mistaken assessment that the desert flank was well secured.[149] Less definitive are the conclusions of the official historian. Nothing more substantial than wishful thinking, he maintains, lay behind the idea of setting up a Balkan front; nevertheless, it is clear that all concerned, politicians and military alike, were convinced that a British army should be sent to Greece.[150] The military historian, M. van Creveld, reflects the consensus of opinion when he writes:

> Far removed from the scene of action, not receiving from his military advisers a purely military appreciation (neither, it must be added did he ask for one) the Prime Minister had little choice but to accept the conclusions of the men on the spot.[151]

Most of the accusations have been leveled at Eden and, to a lesser extent, Wavell and Dill.[152] Once attention is concentrated on Eden's actions after he had been sent to the Middle East, it does indeed become clear that every eager movement on his part served only to draw even tighter the net binding Britain to Greece. But it would be incorrect to analyze Eden's mission without reference to either the long period preceding it or to the complicated triangle of relations between the Foreign Secretary, the Prime Minister, and the soldiers. Notwithstanding his own pressure and the virtually limitless authority with which he had been endowed by Churchill, Eden could not have enforced his will and reached a military arrangement with the Greeks without the concurrence of Dill and Wavell. Once it had been decided to dispatch an army to Greece, Eden told Dill that, in the event of failure, he would be prepared to resign. Dill replied that he could see no reason to do so "since his action was based on military advice."[153] As had been the case on earlier occasions, the military was a critical—but also the weakest—link in the chain of decision making.

There is no doubt that Dill and Wavell would never have initiated the dispatch of a British army to Greece or the Balkans at this stage of the war. That was Churchill's idea. Persistent in his efforts to establish a foothold in the Balkans, he took care to keep Wavell on a leash tight enough to ensure that British forces could speedily be transferred to the region as soon as possible. It was this that lay behind the manner whereby he put Wavell in his place in mid-

January. Had the Greeks then accepted the British offer, retrospective analysts would have easily discerned that Churchill had forced his opinions on a reluctant CIGS (Dill), who was afraid to stand up for his views, and on the Commander-in-Chief in the Middle East (Wavell), who maintained that to make such a move was to fall into a German trap. Churchill, however, did not reconcile himself to the Greek rejection. He insisted on the establishment of a reserve force in the Nile Delta ready for transfer to the Balkans. He did so despite his own insistence that Britain had no moral obligation to Greece and despite restricting O'Connor's advance in North Africa. This signified that his attitude stemmed first and foremost from strategic motives; considerations of prestige or of moral commitment were decidedly secondary.

The crucial question is why Dill and Wavell altered their basic views around February 20. Dill's change of mind is particularly pertinent since he was Wavell's superior and experienced what appears to have been a sudden metamorphosis (either on the way to Cairo or in Cairo itself) even before he knew of the Greek operational plans. Except for the fact that the Balkan situation had deteriorated, no significant change had occurred in southeastern Europe or in North Africa during the journey. Neither, on his arrival in Cairo, did Dill discover any new fact of moment. When explaining his change of mind in his dispatches to London, he merely expressed his belief that a defense line in northern Greece could be held and that to do so would increase the likelihood of Turkey or Yugoslavia joining the campaign. It is possible that Wavell had convinced Dill that the Germans could be checked; but even if we assume that to be the case, it still does not explain why the CIGS should have supported the Balkan move and thereby contradicted his earlier opinion that the very idea of establishing a Balkan front at this stage of the war was strategically mistaken.

Dill caved in psychologically, and changed his mind. He did so in the face of pressure originating with Churchill and that was intensified by Eden during the protracted journey to the Middle East. Men who knew Dill were of the impression that he did not possess a forceful character. Hore-Belisha compared him unfavorably to his predecessor, Ironside (who had a strong character), regarding Dill as "more the staff officer—he has not the personality."[154] Cadogan's diary is replete with disparaging references to "ninny Dill";[155] and Lord Moran's keen eye discerned in him a man who "lacks . . . the he-man stuff."[156] All agree that Dill was easy to get on with and, in Colville's phrase, "the most charming of men."[157] That was a characteristic that would later stand him in very good stead when he became Britain's military representative to the United States, but one that is not usually associated with obstinacy. Churchill was very much the opposite. Particularly during this phase of the war, the Prime Minister showed himself bluntly impatient of disagreement, of ideas that contradicted his own, and of criticism from his subordinates.[158] His behavior toward Dill, especially, was customarily contemptuous, authoritarian, and hostile.[159] He considered Portal the strategist among the triumvirate of his service chiefs, and was fond of Pound, whom he favored. Dill, on the other hand, although deeply hurt by his Prime Minister, refrained from answering in kind. Consequently, it was he who was made lightning rod for Churchill's anger at the British military establishment.[160]

When Churchill's will clashed with Dill's, it was easy to predict whose would prevail. An additional factor transmuted that assumption into a certainty. Even when appointed CIGS in the summer of 1940, Dill was already exhausted. He continued to be physically frail throughout the entire period of discussion on the decision to assist Greece. Moreover, during the same time his wife was suffering a terminal illness. Before leaving for Cairo, Dill contracted a protracted chill that he did not manage to shake off. The journey to Cairo was by Eden's account trying, and Dill was very sick. On his return from the Middle East he was extremely weak.[161] Thus the CIGS set out for the Middle East with Churchill, in Dill's words, leading "the hunt";[162] his own powers of resistance were reduced by his own exhaustion and by the pressure Eden exerted during the course of the journey. To cap it all, on arrival in Cairo he was surprised to find that Wavell supported transferring ground troops to Greece. It was at this point that his opposition finally crumbled.

The state of Dill's mental plight can be deduced from his communication to Churchill shortly after the fall of Greece.

> I am sure that you, better than anyone else, must realise how difficult it is for a soldier to advise against a bold offensive plan. One lays oneself open to charges of defeatism, of inertia, or even of "cold feet." Human nature what it is, there is a natural tendency to acquiesce in an offensive plan of doubtful merit rather than to face such charges. It takes a lot of moral courage not to be afraid of being thought afraid.[163]

Even though Dill died before the end of the war, his thinking is easier to fathom than Wavell's, who took pains to conceal its true content. As soon as the Greek campaign was over, Wavell closed ranks with Churchill. During the mini-inquiry conducted during 1942, he accepted responsibility for the mistaken assessment of the timing of the German attack in North Africa, adding that he had "never questioned the decision to support Greece. . . . I am sure that our general strategy was correct in the circumstances."[164] Wavell had good reason for adopting that line during the course of the war, but his attempts to justify the move in Greece were sloppy. The documents leave no doubt that, at least during December and January, Wavell had opposed the dispatch of an army to Greece. Contrary to his subsequent recollections, the records of the time (which are the only ones that count) also show that he did believe O'Connor capable of taking Tripoli.[165] (After the war, O'Connor himself argued that Tripoli could have been taken had British efforts been directed toward that objective rather than turned toward Greece. Rommel was of a similar opinion.)[166] Like Dill, Wavell did not advance any new arguments that might account for his changing his mind. Indeed, he failed to convince himself entirely. His parting words to Dill were: "Jack, I hope, when this action is reviewed, you will be elected to sit on my court martial."[167] Wavell apparently altered his opinions after receipt of Churchill's letter of February 11. By the time Eden reached Cairo, his work had already been done.

Why did Dill and Wavell not take the opportunity of withdrawing from Britain's commitment to Greece, when the Prime Minister gave them the option to do so? The straightforward answer is that no such option in fact existed. When they traveled to Athens on February 22, Churchill's attitude had not fundamentally changed. True, his letter to Eden of February 20 did warn against "another Norwegian fiasco"; but the brunt of its message was that success should be attained. If we are to stick to the version of events recorded by Eden, Wavell, and Churchill, the British government was already irrevocably committed as early as February 24, when it ratified the Tatoi agreement on the assumption that Papagos would immediately withdraw his forces from the north. There is no way in which the British could have extricated themselves from an agreement once the other party was executing, or had already executed, so painful a move. Churchill's dispatch to Eden and Dill of March 1 was enigmatic and lent itself to various interpretations: while giving Eden authority to revoke the commitment to the Greek government should he feel it necessary to do so, Churchill also specified his own willingness to take high risks. On March 2 Eden and Dill discovered that the Greeks had not withdrawn their forces to the Aliakhmon line. Why did they not take this opportunity to withdraw from their undertakings? Both may have felt blameworthy for the misunderstanding with Papagos.

There was also Churchill's most recent letter, in which he expressed himself "absolutely ready to go in on a serious hazard if there is reasonable chance of success, at any rate for a few months, and all preparations should go ahead at fullest speed." Against that, there is Dill's description of his primary problem as how "to advise against a bold offensive plan" without "being thought afraid." In any case, the enterprise had already gathered momentum and could not now be canceled without considerable difficulty. Even though Eden did consider Papagos to have broken their agreement, it did not appear to him serious enough to warrant an immediate communication to London requesting advice. Eden apparently recalled the sentence in his own "letter of appointment" wherein Churchill charged him not to be "deterred from acting upon his own authority if the urgency is too great to allow reference home." Indeed, Eden was not deterred, and the report he sent on March 5 also contained the text of his new agreement with Papagos. By the time that Churchill subsequently wrote that it was preferable to withdraw from the arrangement with the Greeks, it was too late. He had reaped a whirlwind. Technically, Dill was correct when stating that "my complete defence will be to point to the dates of the telegrams."[168]

At this point in our investigation of Churchill's qualities as a decision maker in this episode, an attempt should be made to analyze him as a strategist before reaching any firm conclusions. In this context, the relevant question is what was Churchill's primary aim in sending a British army to Greece? During the course of the period itself, Churchill advanced a wide spectrum of interconnected reasons and objectives. One was to draw Turkey and Yugoslavia into the war in order to establish a Balkan front; another was to ensure that Turkey's attitude would be to Britain's advantage; a third was to advance the Soviet Union's entry into the war; a fourth was to prevent a Greek-Italian peace under German patronage; a fifth was Britain's moral commitment to Greece and the maintenance of British prestige in U.S. and other eyes; yet a sixth was to expand the offensive activities of the Army concentrated in the Middle East. The march of events at the beginning of March obscured matters even further. "Noblesse oblige" assumed bloated importance. For obvious reasons, Churchill emphasized this factor in his own memoirs—after all, there can hardly exist a better justification for a military failure—claiming that, even after the Tatoi agreement had been ratified by the Cabinet on February 24,"we had not committed ourselves to the Greek adventure . . . the preparations could be arrested by a single order."[169] But this version of events must be discounted. Had Papagos indeed been supposed to have begun withdrawing his forces from the Nestos to the Aliakhmon immediately after signing the Tatoi agreement (as Churchill, Eden, and the official British historian all maintain) there was no way "a single order" could have reversed his dispositions.

That the factor of prestige was decisive is a conclusion possible only if attention is concentrated on the first days of March and sight is lost of the wider panorama of circumstances that had for several previous months been building toward the Greek "adventure." Cruickshank maintains that it was generally agreed that the northern flank of the Middle East could be defended without Greece, provided that Turkey remained neutral and that Crete was well defended. It therefore follows that the principal motive that ultimately impelled Churchill and the Cabinet to undertake the move was Britain's moral commitment to Greece and the maintenance of prestige.[170] But an alternative conclusion can also be logically posited. If the northern flank could indeed be defended solely by Turkish neutrality and the fortification of Crete, then British land intervention in Greece has to be understood in offensive terms. That, it will be recalled, was precisely what Churchill advocated on January 20 when refusing to accept the Greek rejection and ordering the concentration of forces in the Nile Delta. Moreover, he took that action after declaring that Britain had no further moral obligation to Greece. Churchill was absolutely plain on this point—albeit not in his *The Second World War*. In 1948, at the time he was writing about the Greek episode in his book, Churchill once became slightly tipsy during the course of a dinner with Lord Boothby:

> They said that I was wrong to go to Greece in 1940 [sic]. But I did not do it simply to save the Greeks. Of course, honour and all that came in. But I wanted to form a Balkan Front. I wanted Yugoslavia, and I hoped for Turkey. That, with Greece, would have given us fifty divisions. A nut for the Germans to crack. Our intervention in Greece caused the revolution in Yugoslavia which drove out

THE GENESIS OF THE "MEDITERRANEAN STRATEGY," 1940–1941

Prince "Palsy"; and delayed the German invasion of Russia by six weeks. Vital weeks. So it was worth it.[171]

During wartime, Churchill regarded small states as pawns on the European chessboard. He believed that since Britain was also fighting for their independence, it could even violate their neutrality should the strategic need arise.[172] The maintenance of the British guarantee to Belgium was not the principal motive that had impelled him to support Britain's entry into the previous war. He wanted to attack Germany by way of neutral Holland and Denmark and drag them into war even against their own wishes.[173] At the beginning of World War II he initiated operations in Scandinavia, even at the cost of violating Norwegian and Swedish neutrality. Moreover, when working toward the entry of the Balkan states into the war, he was fully aware of the fate awaiting small states that decide to affiliate with one of the two contending sides in a great European war. His own work on Marlborough describes how the injured power reacts with the utmost ferocity, inflicting disaster upon them. Marlborough trampled on Bavaria and laid it waste after its decision to take France's side in 1704; the Duchy of Savoy had been conquered by the French once it had switched sides in 1703; that was also the fate that befell Rumania and Bulgaria during World War I.[174]

It is this perspective that prompts the conclusion that Churchill's primary objective was to establish a military front in the Balkans, an aim to which other secondary purposes and considerations were also appended. On the other hand, it would be wrong to dismiss the importance of moral considerations in the thinking of Dill and Wavell *after* the signing of the Tatoi agreement, since they had from the first doubted the efficacy of a military front in the Balkans.

A Balkan front would have been of little strategic value even if, by some miracle, Turkey and Yugoslavia would have coordinated their joining it. Any positive reason for its establishment had disappeared after June 1940. During the previous war, and at the commencement of World War II, Churchill had wanted the Balkans to constitute a supplementary front to the main front in France; but once France had fallen the Balkans would have been of strategic value only *after* the outbreak of war between Germany and the Soviet Union or the reestablishment of a land front in the west. From an operational point of view, all the arguments advanced against forming a Balkan front in World War I still applied. Indeed, in 1941 they were even more valid. The British were forced to keep this front supplied by a sea route that circumvented Africa while their enemies were fighting in their own backyard. (At the time the British did not even possess the light ammunition required by the Greeks, who were using weapons made in Germany and France.)[175]

The attempt to set up a doomed Balkan front was not Churchill's only strategic error. Still more serious was the manner in which he threw away a golden opportunity by choosing the Balkans over an advance on Tripoli. Not surprisingly, his own published work makes no mention of the Balkans-Tripoli dilemma that arose on February 10, nor of his decision in the matter.[176] Instead, *The Second World War* clouds the issue by placing disproportionate stress on what was in fact a less important factor: Wavell's failure to make a correct assessment of the timing and force of the German counterattack in North Africa. "The fact of the beating-in of the desert flank by Rommel," wrote Churchill, "had undermined and overthrown all the Greek projects on which we had embarked, with all their sullen dangers and glittering prizes in what was for us the supreme sphere of the Balkan War."[177] This is not a convincing argument.

Wavell did indeed make a serious mistake, but the basic strategic error lay in allowing the Germans to establish themselves in North Africa. Rommel's attack did not prevent Wavell from sending as many troops to Greece as he could until the beginning of the German attack in the Balkans on April 6. The British simply lost the race. Even had they won it, and the desert flank remained static, nothing would have changed. The Balkan campaign was lost even before it had begun, and the Germans would in any case have established themselves in the region of Tripoli. The silver lining in this cloud was that, once the German attack had opened, the collapse of the desert flank provided Wavell with an excuse to wriggle out of the despatch of further forces to Greece. Any reinforcements would have been wiped out and subjected to the same fate as the Australian units sent to Singapore, who were led straight from their ships into captivity. So mesmerized was Churchill by the mirage of a Balkan front that even on April 20, by which time the Aliakhmon line had been torn apart and Rommel had begun to smash British lines in Cyrenaica, he called for a desperate effort to make a stand at Thermopylae near Athens. If "the Tobruk position holds, we might even feel strong enough to reinforce from Egypt. I am most reluctant to see us quit, and if the troops were British only and the matter could be decided *on military grounds alone*, I would urge Wilson to fight if he thought it possible."[178]

Why, then, did Churchill persist until the bitter end in his efforts to set up a Balkan front? Logic dictated that the entire idea be abandoned: the formation of a Balkan front was beset by numerous dificulties; intelligence warned that the Germans undoubtedly possessed local superiority and an initial advantage in the race to advance troops to the front; there existed another strategic alternative; the "main theatre" in Europe had been destroyed; and Greece was not essential to the defense of the northern flank of the Middle East. The core of the answer, it seems, cannot be sought in a logical explanation. Churchill suffered from mental inertia. Wedded to ideas and plans that he had formulated before, he attempted to implement them even when new strategic circumstances rendered them irrelevant and impracticable. It will be recalled that this trait had first made itself apparent at the time of the Antwerp episode during World War I. In addition, he also pursued (or was pursued by) the ghosts of plans dating back to the previous war. Thus was created a baneful interaction between his attachment to earlier patterns of thought and plans, and his unbridled ambition to move to the offensive as soon as possible.[179]

THE GENESIS OF THE "MEDITERRANEAN STRATEGY," 1940-1.

As has already been pointed out, Churchill refused to acknowledge that decision to send a British army to Greece had been a major strategic error. As early as August 1941 he argued that the move in Greece had led to the coup in Yugoslavia and that both were responsible for the delay of the German attack on the Soviet Union, "and might after all prove to have been an advantage."[180] Once Hitler had been repulsed at the gates of Moscow in the winter of 1941-1942, Churchill—not surprisingly—became convinced of the validity of that assessment. In his book he argued that the British move in the Balkans justified itself more than had been expected. It forced Hitler to postpone the commencement of "Barbarossa" for five weeks. Although, by his own account, Britain had no knowledge of Hitler's impending attack on the Soviet Union, nevertheless

> if we had, we should have felt more confidence in the success of our [Balkan] policy. We should have seen that he risked falling between two stools, and might easily impair his supreme undertaking [Barbarossa] for the sake of a Balkan preliminary. This is what actually happened, but we could not know at the time.... No one can measure exactly what consequences this had before winter set in upon the fortunes of the German-Russian campaign. It is reasonable to believe that Moscow was saved thereby.[181]

This argument is entirely baseless. First, and as has already been pointed out, had the British indeed known earlier of Hitler's intention to invade the Soviet Union, they would have done better to avoid intervention in the Balkans so as not to divert him from that objective (unless Churchill aimed at a pro-Russian policy so altruistic that he was prepared to sacrifice British and Balkan lives in order to confound Hitler's plans.) Second, there was no connection between the Balkan campaign and the failure of the Barbarossa operation. Churchill's contention is the result of a causal, almost mechanistic, view of the ways in which a war unfolds. True, this is a conventionally accepted prism. Clausewitz himself argued that war has to be understood as the sum total of campaigns which affect each other and influence those that follow. Furthermore, he also maintained that the opening moves in war, even those limited in scope, have a decisive impact in determining the general face of war.[182] Churchill was of a similar opinion. As he wrote in *The World Crisis*:

> Much action and the play of forces even on a huge scale and with enormous material effects is often irrelevant and counts for little or nothing in the final result, but along the chain of commanding causation even the smallest events are vital, it is this which should be studied and pondered over, for in them is revealed the profound significance of human choice and the sublime responsibility of men.[183]

He argued that the small and obscure Battle of Gumbinnen, which preceded the Battle of Tannenberg, "set in motion several chains of causation violently and even decisively affecting the whole course of the Great War."[184] He was familiar with the notion of instigating a small-scale action, without a clear idea of what it might lead to but in the hope that it would generate significant changes in the course of the war. He believed in a strategy of "casting your bread upon the waters."[185] In the present case, he hoped—albeit without specifying the chain of causality—that the formation of a Balkan front would promote the Soviet Union's entry into the war. Were it possible to discern a causal connection between Britain's intervention in the Balkans, Germany's Balkan campaign, and its failure to reach Moscow, Churchill would indeed have had grounds for self-congratulation. But Churchill did not try to prove the connection; he simply emphasized the loss of five weeks in the original German timetable. This is not in itself a convincing argument; nevertheless, it has been assimilated into the historical commentary still conventional in the West. Not even the authors of the official British history, who accepted it with only minor changes, bothered to prove the existence of a direct causal link.[186] The version has not withstood the test of more rigorous research into the topic. The true causes for the postponement of Barbarossa were logistic difficulties and the Wehrmacht's lack of equipment, which were not connected to Germany's Balkan campaign. On the contrary, had they so wished, the Germans could have more quickly transferred the forces that had fought in the Balkans back to the southern starting lines assigned to them in Barbarossa. (In any case, those forces were minuscule in comparison to the massive armies that had been concentrated in the east and it was not the southern axis of advance that failed to attain its objectives). Neither did the coup in Yugoslavia impede the execution of Germany's plan to invade Greece; in effect, it enabled Germany to reach an even quicker military decision in the Balkans.[187]

Britain's move into the Balkans did have serious consequences, but these were of a quite different nature. Its failure in the Middle East in the spring of 1941 caused the British military machine, which was then undergoing a process of reconstruction and expansion, to lose its delicate balance. The Axis powers renewed the struggle in North Africa, and prolonged it for another two years. The British lost the initiative, and their commitments in this theater became very much deeper. As far as land campaigns were concerned, the British Empire's effort focused on the Mediterranean basin. True, the distribution of ground forces between the British Isles and the Mediterranean did ultimately approximate that laid down by Churchill in October 1940, but the conditions were entirely different from those he had then envisioned. Britain's entanglement in this theater dictated the complexion and timetable of Anglo-American strategy. Britain's center of gravity in the Mediterranean became a millstone around the neck of that strategy. On their own entry into the war, the Americans could not speedily shift it to the Atlantic and western Europe, which they considered to be the more natural theater. Paradoxically, it was precisely Britain's weakness in the Mediterranean which provided Churchill with a bargaining counter when he was formulating a joint strategy against Germany with the Americans. Had British forces taken Tripoli in 1941, the whole of North Africa would that year have fallen under Britain's direct or indirect control. Under those circumstances, it would have been easy to shift swiftly the Anglo-American effort to western Europe. In addition to all that, and as will be seen, Britain's military defeats in North Africa during the coming two years exerted a not inconsiderable influence on the crystallization of Churchill's strategic thinking (and of that of his military advisers) with regard to the supreme question—how Germany was to be defeated.

Hitler reaped considerable profits from Britain's Middle Eastern entanglement. For most of the time, he stationed no more than three divisions in North Africa; and it was with them that for two years he pinned down the British, and later U.S., war effort in a secondary theater that posed no direct threat to his own command over Europe and its industrial centers. A small military step, taken when he had no other choice and in order to save his Italian partners from defeat,[188] became one of his greatest strategic achievements—principally because of a grave error for which Churchill was responsible. In Rommel, whose reputation Churchill had good reasons to inflate, Hitler found the general who knew how to make the most of the golden opportunity that had come his way.

■

It is instructive to compare Churchill's involvement in the Gallipoli and Greek episodes. Such a comparison also makes it possible to substantiate—or disprove—Churchill's own primary conclusion from the Gallipoli campaign, which was that failure had resulted from the fact that he had not then possessed the full authority required to conduct a complex operation of that nature. One striking circumstance common to both episodes is the dissonance between the strategic-political plan and Britain's ability to execute it on the operational level. Churchill insisted on carrying out these two moves, notwithstanding the clear discrepancy between the tactical and operational capabilities at hand and the strategic goals they were supposed to achieve. This is especially so of the Balkan move in World War II, which lacked even the partial strategic justification for the Gallipoli campaign of World War I. In attempting to carry through his Balkan strategy, Churchill merely reinforced a conclusion that, before the war, he had himself drawn from Britain's military history: "All our misfortunes had arisen in the past from trying to do that for which we had not got the strength."[189]

In both cases, the positions adopted by the military veered between opposition and unwilling and unenthusiastic acquiescence. The initiative was Churchill's; the soldiers were drawn along in his wake. But whereas in the Gallipoli episode the tension between them broke into the open with Admiral Fisher's resignation, in the Greek case it was more latent. There were two reasons why in the latter instance controversy did not lead to open and direct confrontation. One was the presence of Dill and Wavell, whose personalities were so different from Fisher's; the other was that Churchill, benefiting from bitter experience, adopted a more subtle technique when exerting pressure on the military. He managed to orchestrate the decision-making process in a way that left him a sufficient margin of safety (both at the time and in history) where his personal and sole responsibility was concerned. Uncharacteristically, and in contrast to the lessons he had learned from Gallipoli, he invested Eden (and Dill) with the authority to make decisions on the spot—as though the telegraph had not yet been invented. He had acquired the ability to drag men, soldiers as well as civilians, against their will into an operation and then, with the help of their mistakes, to absolve himself of responsibility. His version of history blackened not only Kitchener and Fisher but the "men on the spot" too: in the case of Gallipoli it had been Carden, De Robeck, and the army commanders fighting on the peninsula; in that of Greece it was Dill, Wavell, and Eden, on the basis of whose advice from Athens and Cairo Churchill and the War Cabinet arrived at their decisions.

In both cases it was Churchill who initiated and promoted the first decisions and moves, who nurtured matters until they had reached the point of no return, and who then suddenly began to waver and hesitate. In the Dardanelles episode this occurred when he raised the questions of the deployment of the Twenty-Ninth Division and of ground support—after it had been decided to go ahead with the operation on the basis of his assurance that a naval action alone would suffice to attain the objective. In the Greek case, the same pattern emerged when he began to show signs of hesitation—after he had established the strategic reserve in the Nile Delta, checked O'Connor's advance, and sent Eden and Dill to the Middle East. The latter only became aware of Churchill's doubts once the die had in fact been cast.

Finally, despite the heavy losses incurred, the defeat at Gallipoli did not have a substantively deleterious effect on the military position of the Entente powers. Conversely, and despite the compataively light losses, the failure in Greece did have serious consequences for Britain's military standing and the development of future Anglo-American strategy.

This comparison indicates that the different scope of Churchill's authority in the two episodes is in fact of only marginal importance. Despite the several changes in the personalities concerned, as well as in the strategic and operational circumstances involved, Churchill revealed precisely the same personal failings as a decision maker and strategist. Since Churchill did not possess full authority in World War I, those failings render him and Kitchener jointly accountable for the disaster at Gallipoli. But since he did possess full command in World War II, it must be concluded that Churchill bears virtually sole responsibility for Britain's failure in the Middle East in the spring of 1941.

■

The crisis in the Middle East raised the question of the depth of Britain's commitment to defend the region. On April 27, Kennedy tried to convince Churchill that the fall of Egypt would not constitute a terminal point in the war and that Britain had clearly to specify the size of force and treasure it was prepared to invest in the retention of the Middle East. Kennedy himself maintained that, if necessary, the entire Middle East could be evacuated without impairing the successful continuation of the war, provided that that region did not absorb too many forces.[190] Churchill's reaction was one of uncontrollable rage. In the presence of senior officers, he accused Kennedy of defeatism and launched into a lengthy diatribe.[191] On the following day, he issued a directive ordering that every effort be made to strengthen Egypt's defenses.

> The loss of Egypt and the Middle East would be a disaster of the first magnitude to Great Britain, second only to successful invasion and final conquest.... The life and honour of Great Britain depends upon the successful defence of Egypt.[192]

The Chiefs of Staff did not go as far as Kennedy but, in response to Churchill's directive, they did "submit that it is an overstatement to say that the life ... of Great Britain depends upon the successful defence of Egypt." Britain was safe as long as there was no successful invasion of the United Kingdom and provided it won the "Battle of the Atlantic."[193] On April 29, they wrote a draft for the strategic assessment of the Middle East requested by President Roosevelt. After pointing out the region's importance, they stressed that "we must at all times bear in mind the fact that the war can only be won or lost in and around the United Kingdom."[194] Churchill contended that this document was not worth showing to Roosevelt. "It may be true that the war can only be *lost* [Churchill's emphasis] in and around the United Kingdom. It is not true it can only be won there. We are not told how it is to be won unless air bombing on a large scale is intended."[195]

Benefiting from the lessons he had learned during the Greek disaster, and prodded by Kennedy, Dill protested against the priority Churchill accorded to the defense of the Middle East. He maintained that "Egypt is not even second in order of priority, for it has been an accepted principle in our strategy that in the last resort the security of Singapore comes before that of Egypt." He believed that Germany's recent successes in Libya and the Balkans "have taught us once more their capacity for overcoming the most formidable difficulties." There was a real danger that the British Isles would be invaded; any reinforcement of the Middle East theater during the coming summer might impair the defense of the United Kingdom. Instead, Dill advised, Britain should limit itself in the coming months to maintaining the forces already stationed in the Mediterranean region.[196] Churchill was, by his own account, astonished to receive this document. The tone of his reply was angry, noting that the CIGS "would be prepared to face the loss of Egypt and the Nile Valley, together with the surrender or ruin of the army of half a million we have concentrated there, rather than lose Singapore." With a measure of validity, Churchill argued that—given the balance of forces at the opening of the campaign—Germany's Balkan success did not necessarily bear witness to the extraordinary fighting capacities of its army (this was before the battle for Crete had commenced).[197]

But he did not address the basic issue: the proportional division of British forces between the United Kingdom and the Middle East.

For the first time, Dill had challenged the Mediterranean strategy that Churchill had initiated in the summer of 1940. The Prime Minister aspired merely to persist along the lines which he had laid down at the end of October 1940 and with the order of priorities he had decided upon even before the outbreak of war: the defense of the British Isles and a swift decision in the Middle East—for which he was prepared to pay the price of temporarily weakening the Far East defense, even should Japan enter the war. Churchill's astonishment is understandable when it is remembered that Dill had hitherto not spoken plainly and that Churchill had grown accustomed to an almost monarchical degree of control over the conduct of the war. In any event, by the time Dill chose to act, it was already too late. After Greece, and especially after the fall of Crete, which was considered to be the bulwark of Britain's northern flank in the Mediterranean, the heavy wheel of momentum could no longer be halted and reversed. Britain's strength in the Middle East had to be reinforced in order to check and destroy the threats that shortly began to develop from both the north (with the German attack on the Soviet Union) and in Africa. Moreover, Dill suggested no real strategic alternative. True, Churchill did not himself know how the Mediterranean campaign might lead to the defeat of Germany. But the activist line he adopted gave him the advantage in any confrontation with the CIGS, whose position was apparently passive.

In an influential book entitled *The Mediterranean Strategy in the Second World War*, Professor M. Howard (one of the authors of the official British history of the war), argued that Britain's decision makers had no alternative "Mediterranean strategy" to the agreed Anglo-American strategy to invade western Europe (the question will be analyzed below). In order to substantiate his argument, Howard claims that the development of British, and later Allied, strategy after the fall of France was "a piecemeal affair, in which the military leaders had often simply to do what they could, where they could, with the forces which they had to hand." Britain's deepening commitment in the Mediterranean was not a response to imperial interests; rather it was the result of the play of prosaic circumstances and the inevitability of natural strategic selection.[198] In his words: "the Mediterranean strategy was in gestation between September and December 1942, at Casablanca it was born and legitimised" as a prelude to the "second front."[199] As a whole, this analysis is incorrect. Britain's "Mediterranean strategy" was launched in the summer of 1940; became bogged down in the spring of 1941; spun out of control; and eventually dragged along in its wake the combined Anglo-American strategy.

6

The Formation of Anglo-American Strategy, 1941-1942

In February and March 1941, while Churchill and his colleagues were still engrossed in the Balkan problem, Anglo-American staff talks took place in Washington. During the course of the discussions, which were initiated by the Americans, the British delegation defined Britain's strategy as one based on massive air attacks. These, they envisioned, would compel Germany to recall its troops and ultimately bring about the fall of the Nazi regime.[1] Based on the hypothetical assumption that the United States would be a party to the war, U.S. thinking acknowledged that Europe and the Atlantic would constitute the decisive theater, to which the United States would have to accord priority over the Far East. Even so, the Americans were already critical of the wisdom of a conception which advocated Germany's defeat solely by attrition and of Britain's deepening commitments in the Middle East.[2] In the final, nonbinding report (designated ABC-1) it was agreed that pressure on Germany had to be increased by diplomatic and economic measures as well as by strategic bombardment. The two sides also concurred on "the building up of the necessary forces for an eventual offensive against Germany,"[3] and on the immediate establishment of permanent military missions in London and Washington.

Early in March, Churchill wrote a directive which made it clear that it was out of the question to think of an invasion of the Continent against German opposition. This was because shipping capacity did not permit the transfer of large forces overseas; moreover, Britain had heavy military commitments in the Middle East. The British Army would not be able "to play a primary role in the defeat of the enemy. That task can only be done by the staying power of the Navy, and above all by the effect of Air predominance." The size and structure of the Army had to be commensurate with operations of a secondary order.[4] In a talk on the radio, broadcast a month earlier, he had said that he did not envision the need for large-scale U.S. armies, such as had been dispatched to Europe during the previous war.[5] Members of the Army General Staff strongly opposed Churchill's directive, arguing that it had been by means of their land forces that the Germans had attained their greatest successes.[6] Once again, however, they only pointed out the need for a large army for defensive purposes.[7] They did not state that such a force might be required in order to attain a decision on the Continent.

A "Review of Future Strategy" was presented by the Future Operations Section of the Joint Planning Staff (infra, Joint Planners) on June 14, 1941—the first general strategic assessment of its kind since the last such document ten months previously. Its authors declared the United States' entry into the war to be vital. But they added that, because of limitations on shipping resources, the United States would not be able to carry large forces to Europe. They also played down the Soviet Union's military weight. Their conclusion was that Germany's quantitative advantages, together with the fact that it was operating on internal lines, made it impossible to defeat it in the field. Germany could be worn down only by a strategy of attrition, i.e., blockade, massive air bombing, and—especially—internal subversion. Not until Germany had been severely weakened—a stage which they estimated would be reached in the autumn of 1942—would it be possible to deliver the final blow. Concurrent with large-scale uprisings, to be organized and coordinated from Britain, a British force of ten (mostly armored) divisions would then invade Europe with the purpose of liberating the Continent.[8]

This appraisal shared the fate of its predecessor; Churchill refused to endorse it, even though the Chiefs of Staff asked that he do so. In view of the speed with which changes occurred during wartime, he was skeptical of its utility and termed it academic and speculative.[9] Nevertheless in a review for members of the Defence Committee and senior officers, he did speak of the need to reinforce the Middle East to the maximum extent allowed by shipping; to broaden the scope of bombing on Germany; and "ultimately there were possibilities in landing large numbers of tanks to assist the conquered nations to rise against the Germans."[10]

On June 22 Germany fell upon the Soviet Union. One day before the attack began, Churchill told Colville that Russia would certainly be defeated, but that he intended to give it as much assistance as he could.[11] Fearful of an unfavorable reaction from right-wing Conservatives and even from Labour party ranks, Eden reminded Churchill that the Soviet regime was no better than the German; he suggested that future Anglo-Soviet contacts be restricted entirely to military matters. But Churchill dismissed that charge. Russia, he said, was now at war; many human beings were in distress; the Soviet regime and the Comintern had now to be forgotten.[12] On the very day of the invasion he offered the Soviet Union an alliance. Churchill's stance occasions no surprise. He had for some years been working toward the establishment of a grand alliance with the Soviets and, thanks to the German attack, that was now a realistic possibility (albeit one that had come about under conditions different from those which he envisioned). He was not prepared to let the chance slip because of ideological niceties. Churchill appreciated that Britain's military assistance would be marginal. His objective was to give the Soviets every incentive, even if it be only moral, to persevere in their resistance to the German invasion.

Would the Soviet Union be able to stand firm? Once operation Barbarossa had commenced, that was the great question confronting British intelligence and decision makers in London. Churchill's initial assessment was pessimistic. Like the intelligence community and Chiefs of Staff, he thought that Russia would soon collapse. That view was shared by members of the War Cabinet (other than Lord Beaverbrook, the Minister of Supply) and by Stafford Cripps, the Ambassador in Moscow.[13] A few days later, Churchill wrote to Smuts that it was difficult to estimate how long the Russians would be able to hold out. He still assumed that the main thrust of the German attack was toward the southeast, in the direction of the Caucasus,[14] even though the deployment of the German forces gave no indication that such was the case. At the beginning of August, and largely thanks to information received by Ultra, the Joint Intelligence Committee (JIC) concluded that Soviet resistance would persist for a considerable time. Consequently, the Germans would be unable to transfer forces of any substance to other theaters throughout 1941. In the light of that assessment, Churchill canceled the state of readiness required to meet a German invasion in 1941. As early as September, intelligence estimated that no German invasion of Britain was to be expected even in the spring of 1942.[15]

Soon after the commencement of the German offensive, Stalin began to clamor for the opening of a "second front." But Britain had very few operational means of aiding the Soviets; even its ability to send supplies to Russia was restricted. True, Churchill did order the Chiefs of Staff to examine plans for easing pressure on Russia by mounting a large-scale raid in northern France, involving 20,000 to 30,000 men. But the Chiefs maintained that no such operation was possible. Ultimately, Admiral Roger Keyes, Director of Combined Operations, could suggest nothing more than a raid involving only 300 men—a suggestion Churchill rejected on the grounds that the size of the proposed operation was disproportionate to the state of the war, and would simply arouse scorn. But he did acknowledge that a large-scale raid was out of the question.[16] At the same time, he ordered the Chiefs to consider a British landing in northern Norway, designed to establish a land and sea link with the Russians. However, the only realistic possibility left to the British was an offensive in North Africa—even though that too could not influence events on the Russian front. Quite independently of the Russian state of affairs, in mid-June Churchill in any case pressed Wavell to launch a premature counteroffensive (Battleaxe), which immediately turned into a resounding failure. Thereafter he began to exert pressure on Auchinleck, Wavell's replacement, to bring forward the date of his attack in Libya.[17] But Auchinleck refused to open his offensive before the autumn of 1941. Churchill recalled him to London, where he informed the general that it would be most unpleasant were the Russians to bear the main burden of the war while Britain did nothing at all. Eden added that should the Russians drive back the Germans without Britain having launched any offensive, the former would subsequently claim the credit for Germany's defeat.[18] But all was in vain: Auchinleck stuck to the timetable he had set for himself.

On July 24 a delegation of senior U.S. military officers, led by Harry Hopkins, visited London. Once again, the Americans criticized the weight given to the Middle East in British strategy. Maintaining that the "Battle of the Atlantic" would be the decisive engagement of the war, they maintained that it had to be given the highest priority. The weakness of their case lay in their argument that the Middle East could not be defended, and that no heavy commitments should therefore be entered into there. On the other hand, Hopkins—the only civilian among the group and President Roosevelt's close adviser—said that the President supported Britain's line, since the enemy had to be fought wherever he was to be found.[19] This discussion was still under way when Churchill sent Roosevelt a letter summarizing his thoughts on the future conduct of the war. His remarks were very much in the spirit of the document recently prepared by the Joint Planners: tighten the blockade, intensify internal subversion, and step up strategic bombing. "These measures may themselves produce an internal convulsion or collapse. But plans also ought to be made for coming to the aid of the conquered populations by landing armies of liberation when opportunity is ripe." To that end, he requested U.S. aid in the construction of naval craft suitable for the landing of forces on enemy coasts.[20]

Churchill brandished this letter, and another one along similar lines that he wrote to Roosevelt, in order to refute "the many accounts which are extant and multiplying of my supposed aversion from any kind of large-scale opposed-landing, such as took place in Normandy in 1944." He claimed that it was he who, even at that stage, was promoting the development of the amphibious equipment required for such large-scale operations. By his own account, as early as June 1940 he had taken off the shelf his old plan of July 1917 to take the island of Borkum, and maintained that some of the ideas contained in that scheme generated the construction of tank-landing craft and floating harbors.[21] There are two reasons why that evidence cannot be taken as proof that Churchill indeed intended to invade the Continent in the face of "large-scale oppos[ition]." One is that his thinking, together with that of the Chiefs of Staff, had hitherto been dominated by the idea that an assault on the Continent would be launched only when Germany was severely weakened and decayed from within. The second is that the accumulation of amphibious craft might signify various strategic ideas and objectives, of which a massive invasion of western Europe was only one. After all, the equipment concerned could also be employed for a landing on northern Norway, for seizing islands in the Aegean, for raids on enemy coasts, for the conquest of Sicily, or to bring supplies to the forces advancing along the coast of North Africa.

During the course of the Atlantic meeting between Churchill and Roosevelt in August 1941, the U.S. military participants were presented with the Joint Planners' document of the previous June. They questioned the utility of a strategy of attrition, of massive air bombardments, and of Britain's Mediterranean commitments. As Gwyer, the official British historian, puts it:

the Americans "were evidently disappointed at the lack of reference in the paper to any major land campaign in Europe beyond the operations in support of a general rising, which were proposed for the final phase."[22] The British responded that they could not abandon the Middle East and the Iranian oil fields because 600,000 men were already stationed in the region where an enormous infrastructure had been established; in the future it would provide a base from which to increase pressure on Italy. The Chiefs informed Churchill that they felt that they had managed to convince the Americans of the value of the "Mediterranean strategy." However, the latter had also cautioned against an overexpansion of Britain's efforts in the Middle East, lest it would exercise an adverse influence on other vital theaters. Also it might not have been possible to sustain that front.[23]

In August 1941 it was impossible to change course. The decision Churchill had made late in 1940 to rush to the Middle East as many forces as shipping could carry, and British entanglements in that region, had become Britain's most effective argument vis-à-vis the Americans in support of its strategy.

Churchill returned from the Atlantic meeting in high spirits. To members of the War Cabinet he quoted Roosevelt as saying "that he would wage war, but not declare it, and that he would become more and more provocative." This mood of optimism was confirmed by Halifax, the Ambassador in Washington, who reported that "the President and all the principal members of the Administration were anxious to come into the war and would be relieved if some incident . . . aided this event."[24]

At the end of August Churchill reached the conclusion that the Germans had tied themselves up in a protracted war in Russia; they could not reasonably expect to take the Caucasus during the course of the present year. Even should the Soviet Union collapse, no German attack on the Middle East from the north could be launched before the following spring.[25] Among the directives Churchill gave to Lord Beaverbrook, who was in September due to lead a British mission to Moscow (coinciding with a U.S. delegation), was an outline of his general strategic concept, with the request that it be passed on to Stalin. In the previous war too, he wrote, "we had no means of knowing when and how it would be decided; but we had to go on fighting everywhere that conditions allowed till the Nazi system breaks up as the Kaiser's system broke up last time." Germany would be worn down by propaganda, blockade, and massive air attacks on its cities. Notions that Britain might land twenty to thirty divisions on the western coast of Europe, or dispatch them to the Russian front, "have no foundation of reality on which to rest." The United States might soon enter the war in a full manner; should it do so, an attack on Germany might be possible in 1943.

> If German morale and unity were seriously weakened, and their hold upon the conquered European countries relaxed, it might be possible to land large numbers of armoured forces simultaneously on the shores of several of conquered countries, and raise wide spread revolts.[26]

At the beginning of October Churchill expressed doubts as to whether strategic bombing could decide the war. Even should Germany's cities suffer widespread damage, he wrote, that did not mean that its industry and the German army's control over Europe would be severely harmed. Losses inflicted on the bombers were high, while their bombing accuracy was low. He pointed out that, despite the conquest of the Low Countries and of France, the impact of German bombing raids on Britain was much less than had been anticipated. These remarks did not reflect an intention to alter the high priority given to air bombardment. But "if the United States enters the War" bombing "would have to be supplemented in 1943 by simultaneous attacks by armoured forces in many of the conquered countries which were ripe for revolt. . . . He is an unwise man who thinks there is any *certain* method of winning this war, or indeed any other war between equals in strength. The only plan is to persevere."[27]

On his return from Moscow, Beaverbrook began to press for a move that might ease the Russians' plight. He dismissed as baseless the argument that nothing could be done to help them. "We can, as soon as we decide to sacrifice long-term projects and a general view of the war which, though still cherished, became completely obsolete on the day on which Russia was attacked."[28] Beaverbrook maintained that an operation had to be immediately launched in Norway or in Libya (his own preference was for the northern theater). Churchill replied that he had pressed Auchinleck to bring forward his offensive. The same was true of the attack in Norway—which, however, his military advisers had convinced him would not be possible during the current year.[29] There is no reason to suspect Churchill's intentions; indeed his wish to invade Norway (ultimately formulated in operation Jupiter) verged on the obsessive. He also rejected Stalin's suggestion that British divisions be sent to the Caucasus. That, he thought, would be tantamount to sending coals to Newcastle: aside from the logistic difficulties, it would upset plans for the forthcoming British offensive in North Africa. (Beaverbrook, too, opposed the dispatch of forces to the Russian front.)[30]

Writing to Roosevelt at the end of October, Churchill expressed the hope that the success of Auchinleck's forthcoming offensive (Crusader) would enable troops to be landed in portions of North Africa under Vichy control.[31] The offensive itself opened on November 18, and heavy fighting continued throughout that month. The pace of the British advance accelerated in December. On December 7, the day Pearl Harbor was attacked, Rommel began to withdraw from Gazala; on December 8, when the United States and Britain declared war on Japan, Tobruk was relieved. Three days later Germany and Italy declared war on the United States.

It was thus in an optimistic frame of mind that on December 12 Churchill embarked on his sea voyage to coordinate strategy with the Americans. The U.S. military did not accord him an enthusiastic welcome. Preoccupied with the crisis in the Far East, they had not yet had the time for an in-depth discussion of their own on the general strategy of the war. While still en route to Washington, Churchill had been warned by Hopkins not to bring detailed plans to the meeting.[32] However, during the voyage, the Prime Minister and his Chiefs of Staff—jointly and separately—did formulate their positions on future Anglo-American strategy. On December 16 the latter presented Churchill with a Joint Planning Staff memorandum, "The Basis of Anglo-American Strategy." This determined that, since northwestern Africa was the natural region for U.S. operations, North Africa constituted the appropriate theater for immediate cooperation. Its total conquest was to be the springboard for eliminating Italy from the war. The Germans had failed in their attempt to defeat Russia. There now existed an important land front "from which to make a direct assault on the frontiers of Germany at the first sign of enemy disintegration." It followed that maximum Anglo-American support for the Soviet Union was an additonal and important component in the formula for softening Germany; the others were blockade, strategic bombing, and subversion. The move to the offensive would be accomplished by tightening the ring around Germany, by bringing Turkey into the war and knocking Italy out of it, and by the conquest of strategically important islands in the eastern Atlantic. At the final stage, once Germany had been severely weakened, simultaneous attacks would be launched: by the British from the west, by the Americans from the south, and by the Russians from the east. In view of the difficulties in the manufacture of landing craft and in shipping, they thought that no more than seventeen divisions could be brought into operation from Britain. Similar restrictions would also preclude the employment of massive U.S. forces at the final stage.[33] The Chiefs of Staff adopted this paper, which, with only minor changes, became their document designated "American-British Strategy" to be presented at the Washington conference.[34]

Churchill expressed his general agreement with the Chiefs' paper, but asked them to emphasize the element of a return to the Continent, because "he thought it important to put before the peoples of both the British Empire and the United States the mass invasion of the continent of Europe as the goal for 1943."[35] Meanwhile, as his ship was making its way westward, he committed to paper his own ideas on the future conduct of the war. His memorandum consisted of three parts: "The Atlantic Front," "The Pacific Front," and "The Campaign of 1943."[36] Since Churchill claimed that the western Allied war moves in 1942 and 1943 were carried out in " a very close correspondence" with the strategic line sketched in this document and that all the objectives were achieved in the order they were set forth, its detailed analysis is clearly vital. Another reason is his belief that the paper proves that "I always considered that a decisive assault upon the German-occupied countries on the largest possible scale was the only way in which the war could be won."[37]

In "The Atlantic Front" Churchill detailed his thoughts regarding 1942. He maintained that control of all North Africa was vital for the forthcoming stages. To that end he proposed a joint Anglo-American operation for the conquest of northwestern Africa (Gymnast), to be carried out with—or even without—Vichy's consent. Crusader's success hitherto gave Churchill reason to expect that Auchinleck would continue to inflict defeats on Rommel; the Allied forces advancing from east and west would meet up and North Africa would fall. He believed that the German threat from the north, by way of the Caucasus, had declined considerably and that steps had to be taken to bring Turkey into the war. He pinned great hopes on the strategic bombing of Germany. The damage inflicted on the Germans' industrial production, "combined with their Russian defeats, may produce important effects upon the will to fight of the German people, with consequential internal reactions upon the German Government." Hence the United States had to rush bombers to Britain, especially since their production in Britain itself had fallen behind schedule.[38]

In "The Pacific Front" Churchill wrote that the main Allied objective in this region had to be regaining command of the sea. This was to be accomplished by a massive construction program—especially of aircraft carriers because they could be built quicker and would be able "to cover the landing of troops in order to attack the enemy's new conquests." Even though policy in the Pacific was to be defensive, the Japanese should not be allowed to secure their conquests. Since the U.S. forces required in Europe in 1942 would not be large, he preferred that the United States initiate secondary operations in the Pacific; their objective would be to wear down the Japanese, whose resources were extremely limited. "What will harm us is for a vast United States Army of ten millions to be created which for at least two years while it was training would absorb all the available supplies and stand idle defending the American continent."[39]

In "The Campaign of 1943" the Prime Minister discussed the stages whereby Germany was to be defeated. He assumed a situation in which naval mastery of the Pacific had been attained, all of North Africa was in Allied hands, and Russia had stabilized its front against Germany. Moreover, "it might be that a footing would already have been established in Sicily and Italy, with reactions inside Italy which would be highly favourable." However,

> the war can only be ended through the defeat in Europe of the German armies, or through internal convulsions in Germany produced by the unfavourable course of the war, economic privations, and the Allied bombing offensive. . . . An internal collapse is always possible, but we must not count on this. Our plans must proceed upon the assumption that the resistance of the German Army and Air Force will continue at its present level.

That was why it was necessary to plan for the liberation of the occupied countries by means of simultaneous landings on their coasts

> strong enough to enable the conquered populations to revolt. By themselves they will never be able to revolt, owing to the ruthless counter-measures that will be employed, but if adequate and suitably equipped forces were landed in several of the following countries, namely, Norway, Denmark, Holland, Belgium, the

French Channel coasts and the French Atlantic coasts, as well as Italy and possibly the Balkans, the German garrisons would prove insufficient to cope with both the strength of the liberating forces and the fury of the revolting peoples.

Allied naval power would permit flexibility in the selection of the landing sites. The Germans would not be able to be strong everywhere. "In particular, they cannot move their armour about laterally from north to south or west to east [sic]." Should they retain most of their forces in the center, in Germany, they could only intervene after the massive landings had been effected. "It need not be assumed that great numbers of men are required. If the incursion of the armoured formations is successful, the uprising of the local populations, for whom weapons must be brought, will supply the corpus of the liberating offensive." The invading forces would number about forty armored divisions, some 600,000 men in all, half of them British. Once their move had succeeded, another 1,000,000 men would be landed with the object of wresting the occupied lands from Hitler's grasp.[40]

Pound, Dill, and Portal discerned what they termed "an important difference" between their plan and the Prime Minister's. (General Sir Alan Brooke, who had recently been appointed Dill's replacement as CIGS, remained in London.) According to Churchill's memorandum, liberating forces were to be landed on the Continent even while the German Army was at something like its present strength. But their attitude was that no invasion would be possible until after Germany's capacity for land and air resistance had been broken by massive air bombardments. Hence they maintained that priority had to be given to the expansion of the strategic bombing force. There was a danger that the expansion of the armies might impede the air effort. They advocated that Churchill place less emphasis on the idea of an invasion of Europe in 1943 and that, instead, he stress the need to intensify bombing attacks on Germany in 1943. In that year a land offensive would be possible against Italy, and in the Balkans too were Turkey to join the war. "The liberating operation" depended on the march of events; in any case, in their estimate, it might be feasible at the end of 1943 or—more likely—in 1944.[41]

In his response to the Chiefs, Churchill felt "bound to point out that in [their] notes there is no positive plan of any kind for reducing Germany to submission except air-bombing." Indeed, they made liberating landings dependent on the success of the air bombardments. Hitherto, however, these had been less successful than anticipated. If anything, the morale of Germany's population had risen. It could also disperse its industry and improve its air defense. Hence there was no guarantee that the raids would ever achieve their aims. Nevertheless Churchill maintained that he could find no substantial difference between the plans, only one of emphasis.[42] The Chiefs of Staff agreed that there were no real differences, although steps had to be taken to ensure that the building of forces designed to liberate Europe would not be accorded priority over the air offensive. (Churchill's marginal comment was that he could not see how the two things contradicted each other.)[43] Thus, within two days, the "important difference" between the Chiefs' plan and Churchill's had withered away. There is no recollection of its existence in the official British history or in Churchill's own memoirs.[44]

In effect the Prime Minister had retracted his directive that the European continent was to be invaded even while the German army was at its present strength. He did not have to withdraw very much to establish a position at which he had no substantial differences with his military advisers. Despite the assertion made at the beginning of his plan, it was in substance and implication similar to that of the army chiefs. As we shall see, Churchill left a logical and practical gap between the enunciation of his own premise and the operational plan that he outlined for Germany's defeat.

Of the several basic assumptions influencing the formulation of the Chiefs' and of Churchill's plans, one—which turned out to be false—was that shipping restrictions would render the transfer of large U.S. land forces to Europe impossible for several years to come. This assumption had already been incorporated into the document presented by the Joint Planners in June, and, in various guises, had turned up even earlier. The official British historian considers it responsible for the dismissal of the idea to launch a massive invasion of the Continent and beat the Wehrmacht with its 250 divisions.[45] But matters had not been at a standstill since June 1941. The Soviet Union and Germany had become locked in a titanic struggle, which unexpectedly persisted into December 1941. Should the Russians continue fighting, the number of Anglo-American divisions required to defeat the German army—which would be dispersed on two large fronts—would be considerably reduced (180 German divisions were now engaged on the Russian front). The Joint Planners June assessment was also based on the high rate of shipping losses in the Atlantic during the first half of that year. However, figures for the second half of 1941 (including December) showed a noticeable decline in losses at sea—in spite of the spread of the war to the Far East.[46]

Churchill would have needed no skill in advanced mathematics to calculate that there were grounds for questioning the assessments of both the Planners and of the Chiefs of Staff with respect to shipping limitations. In April 1940, 56,000 British troops had been stationed in the Middle East, in August 1940, some 80,000 men; a year later, in August 1941, their number had risen to 600,000 and a massive infrastructure had been set up in the region.[47] Equally instructive is the rate of reinforcement: in October 1940, Churchill had anticipated that 53,000 additional men would reach the Middle East within the following two months; in June 1941 he said that 30,000 to 40,000 men were being transferred to the region every month.[48] Thus, in the space of about one year, no less than 450,000 men were conveyed to the Middle East (if we reduce the number of local troops enlisted in the British Army in the Middle East), and the average rate of reinforcement was about 30,000 per month. These figures were attained despite the fact that most were transported in British ships alone, in the face of German submarines, and by the Cape-route— which is about four-and-a-half-times longer than the Atlantic route connecting Britain and the United States (London to Alexandria, by way of the Cape of Good Hope, 11,608 nautical miles; Liverpool to St. John, Newfoundland, 1,995 nautical miles; Liverpool to New York, 3,075 nautical miles). Thus it might have been possible to conclude that—at a similar rate, over a distance just one quarter of the Cape route, and with the aid of the United States' massive shipping capacity—large U.S. forces could have been speedily transferred to Britain. Churchill knew that the Americans had transported huge forces to Europe during the previous war. He mentioned that at the very same time he pointed out that they would not be required in the present conflict.[49] At the end of 1942, when he became temporarily involved in a dispute with his military advisers (to be discussed below), he queried their calculations and recalled that in 1918 the Americans had carried two million soldiers to France within the space of five months.[50]

In Washington, Churchill informed his hosts that there would be no need to transfer large U.S. forces to Europe. To the U.S. generals, who did not know what to make of Churchill's statement, Dill explained that "the general idea was that it would not be possible to undertake land operations on a large scale in Europe until the Germans showed signs of cracking."[51] Although the Americans had a different opinion, they for the present preferred not to air it—especially since they had not yet had the time to conduct a thorough examination of the logistic problem. Rear-Admiral T. K. Turner noted that, according to calculations made by the U.S. Navy, future shipping would permit the conveyance and maintenance overseas of forty-five U.S. divisions.[52] Unwittingly, the Admiral had put his finger on one of the main weaknesses of British strategic planning: it adhered too closely to present conditions and did not take into account the anticipated military inventory in the future. The ease with which the Chiefs of Staff and Churchill accepted this logistic limitation can be explained by the fact that it provided a neat justification for a strategic outlook to which they were in any case inclined.

Churchill's plan to land armored forces at several points along thousands of miles of the European coastline was based on the assumption that Germany would not be able to deal simultaneously with all the landings effected. Any large reserve force Germany might choose to concentrate in central Europe would not be able to react in time to the dispersed Allied landings. That assumption may have been correct; but within a few months it had been overturned. As will be seen, the claim that Germany would be able speedily to transfer large quantities of forces from the eastern front to rebuff an attempted invasion in the west was one that Churchill and the Chiefs of Staff persistently cited when expressing their fears of—and even opposition to—an Anglo-American invasion of France. In *The Second World War*, Churchill subsequently argued that one of Hitler's greatest mistakes during the war was his failure to establish a large strategic reserve in Germany, which he could move from one front to another.[53] But of the logistic and operational difficulties inherent in his own plan he made no mention. How did he think the forty armored divisions dispersed along Europe's coasts could be supplied? How would the masses participating in the uprisings be armed and supplied? Consistent with his own premise, he seems to have assumed that the offensive would be launched even when the German army was at its current strength. But, if that were the case, then it posed logistic and operational complications of a far higher order than did, under similar circumstances, the transfer of a U.S. army to Britain and an invasion of northern France. Of course, the logistic difficulties would decline considerably should the proposed dispersed landings be effected after the collapse of Germany's military organization. It is an indication that Churchill—despite his own premise—agreed with the Chiefs of Staff that no such move was to be undertaken before the Germans had indeed collapsed.

It was thus on this shaky foundation that Churchill built the last stage in his plan—armored landings carried out simultaneously with mass uprisings by the peoples of Europe. While the Chiefs' plan was conditional on a prior German collapse, Churchill's depended upon large-scale mass uprisings. (He did not assert that the landings should be put into operation even if no such uprisings took place.) Churchill's approach suffered from a logical flaw. The liberating forces, whose success depended upon the uprisings, would not be activated until it was known for sure that the subjugated peoples were indeed ready to rise. On the other hand, it was unreasonable to expect any insurrections to start until their leaders were certain that the armored forces had successfully landed in Europe. The Chiefs of Staff had called attention to this defect when the Joint Planners, had proposed a similar idea in June 1941.[54] However, the latter—unlike Churchill— had posited that the landings would take place *after* a German collapse, which would naturally provide encouragement to potential insurgents.

The genesis of the idea that Britain orchestrate a general revolt by the conquered peoples is not clear; nor is it possible to trace the manner whereby it was transformed into a foundation of Britain's strategic conceptions. Perhaps that notion came naturally to the leaders of a nation which, itself weak on land, stood alone against Hitler's armies that held complete control of Europe. Significantly, the Planners, notwithstanding certain doubts on the part of the Chiefs of Staff, developed at length the idea of a mass European revolt in their June 1941 memorandum.[55] But the romantic breadth and historical dimensions of the proposal are hardly commensurate with a professional military mode of thought; what it reflects, rather, is much of the Prime Minister's own nature. We do not know whether or not the Joint Planners derived the idea of a mass revolt from Churchill, but several references and analogies on his part can be discerned. He had, for instance, on several occasions referred to the story of the Spanish populace's uprising against foreign rule. In the draft to his *History of the English Speaking Peoples* he had described Peterborough's landing at Barcelona in 1706, during the War of Spanish Succession, a move he considered responsible for the local revolt and for the fact that the French were eventually forced to withdraw from Spain (although they did reconquer the country in 1707). During the Napoleonic Wars, Churchill wrote, spontaneous popular Spanish rebellions against French rule had led to the dispatch of the armies commanded by Sir John Moore and Sir Arthur Wellesley (later the Duke of Wellington) to fight in the successful war of the Iberian Peninsula. Defending the Norwegian fiasco in Parliament, he claimed that "Hitler's action in invading Scandinavia is as great a strategic and political error as that which was committed by Napoleon in 1807, when he invaded Spain." To retain his conquests, Hitler would have to divert numerous forces in order to deal with the opposition of the local population, which would enjoy Allied support.[56] When France was on the point of collapse, he attempted to persuade French leaders to undertake large-scale guerrilla warfare.

Quite apart from the faults already described, Churchill's plan contained a yet more fundamental defect. The United States' entry into the war, a development of revolutionary proportions, did not engender a revolutionary change in the Prime Minister's basic strategic conceptions (nor, for that matter, in those of his military advisers). This was despite the United States' enormous industrial and military potential, whose speedy realization during the previous war was a harbinger of things to come. The proposals contained in Churchill's plan held fast to strategic ideas he and his military advisers had conceived at a time when Britain had stood alone, and which were a consequence of that situation. Churchill's plan, like that submitted by the Chiefs, was based on the activity and inactivity of others—the Russians, the conquered peoples, and the Germans—but not on the doings of the Anglo-American armies. Long-term planning for victory in the war was not based on the advantages possessed by the strongest Allied power; instead, and as had previously been the case, it rested on the strengths—and, to a greater extent, on the weaknesses—of British military power. Lord Beaverbrook was correct to point out that Churchill and his military advisers had not changed their conceptions when the Soviet Union became a party to the war. But that omission could be understood on the grounds that, since geostrategic and operational circumstances in any case restricted British activity, no fundamental change in strategic conceptions was really necessary. Such, however, not the case when the United States entered the war.

Churchill sensed some of the weaknesses in the British approach. He was also aware that it troubled the Americans. As a politician, he was alive to the political implications of framing a joint Anglo-American strategy. As a strategist he had for years been emphasizing the importance of a fighting land front in western Europe. That was why the Chiefs of Staff called attention to "the important difference" between their plan and that submitted by the Prime Minister. But, in effect, his plan kept to the boundaries of the British conception. Within two days "the important difference" had disappeared. Having circumvented the subject, and after adding a further layer of complications and flaws in his own plan, Churchill returned to the point of departure—a prior German collapse. Thus his plan does not prove his contention that he had always supported a "large-scale opposed-landing" of Europe. On the contrary, the short-lived "important difference" between Churchill and his Chiefs of Staff soon became an "important difference" between the concepts held by Churchill and his military advisers, on the one hand, and the U.S. military, on the other.

When Churchill set out for Washington, his principal fear was that the Americans might prefer the Pacific front to the European. He discovered that, although influential forces within the United States were indeed pulling in that direction, Roosevelt and General George C. Marshall, the Chief of Staff of the U.S. Army, were adamant that first priority had to be accorded to the European theater. The U.S. Chiefs of Staff were impatient to conclude the talks. Apart from the pressing Pacific crisis, the view that the German army ought to be smashed by a massive onslaught on northwestern Europe was already crystallizing in the U.S. War Department. Hence they chose to avoid committing themselves too much until they had formulated their final plans.[57] Since the wording of the British chiefs' memorandum was especially vague about the final offensive stage against Germany, the Americans agreed to endorse it as a joint document.[58] Deleted, at their request, were the references to an Anglo-American offensive along the Mediterranean in 1942 and to "simultaneous landings in several of the occupied countries of North-Western Europe" in 1943—one of the key points in Churchill's plan. It was agreed that after Germany had been checked and worn down and North Africa conquered (by the British), there would be "a return to the Continent" in 1943 "across the Mediterranean, from Turkey into the Balkans, or by landings in Western Europe."[59] But, although the President showed interest in an Anglo-American landing in French North Africa (Gymnast), the opposition of the U.S. military chiefs prevented agreement on that operation.

Churchill returned to London in the belief that the Americans were enthusiastic about the idea of conquering northwestern Africa.[60] He awaited an opportune moment to raise it again. At the beginning of 1942, however, gloomy events were compelling him to concentrate his utmost attention on other matters. During the course of January, the Japanese completed their conquest of Malaya; on January 20 they invaded Burma; and Singapore fell on February 15. The situation in the Middle East was not very much better. Operation Crusader did not attain its original objectives. On January 21 Rommel launched a counterattack that pushed the British back to Gazala. By contrast, on December 10, the Russians had opened a winter offensive whose initial successes took London by surprise.

Meanwhile the British Joint Planning Staff continued to draw up plans for a landing in western Europe. The first, designated "Sledgehammer," was small in scope and conceived as an emergency measure designed to pin down German forces in the event of an anticipated Russian collapse. Alternatively, it could be implemented to exploit a sudden German collapse. The second plan was code-named Round-up, and differed from Sledgehammer only in its scope: provided that there were signs of an impending German collapse, a force of seventeen divisions would be landed in western Europe in 1943.⁶¹ In Washington, General Arnold of the U.S. Army Air Corps was, at this juncture, proposing the seizure of a bridgehead on the French coast in 1942 with the objective of involving the Germans in a massive campaign of air attrition over France. But the British military mission in the U.S. capital turned his suggestion down flat. One reason given was the belief that the shipping available did not allow such an operation; another was that the German army presently enjoyed a high state of morale.⁶² (Repeatedly, the latter argument was employed as another way of saying that no invasion was to be attempted as long as the German army was far from bending at the knees.)

At the end of February it became apparent that the Russians' winter offensive had been halted; this development caused the Joint Planners considerable concern.⁶³ They argued that the only way to provide the Russians with real assistance was to launch an offensive across the Channel. In their opinion, there was no call to take into account the implications that the implementation of Sledgehammer in 1942 might have on the possibility of launching Round-up in 1943. Should the Germans fail in Russia, Round-up could be launched even earlier; but should the Germans defeat the Russians, Round-up would in any case have to be postponed for an indefinite period. Unlike their representatives in Washington, they believed that there was sufficient time to concentrate the naval and air forces required to carry out Sledgehammer. Alan Brooke, the CIGS, rejected that argument, contending that Britain could not afford to lose six to eight divisions on a diversionary operation at the same time that it was about to dispatch four to five additional divisions to the Middle East. Britain's defense would be weakened to the point at which the Germans might successfully invade the United Kingdom.⁶⁴ Dudley Pound even suggested deferring the implementation of the offensive plans for 1943 agreed upon with the Americans. He maintained that the crux of the struggle now centered on oil and the Atlantic shipping lanes. Basing his argument on the assessment currently in vogue in the British intelligence, he insisted that Germany would lose the war unless it established control over additional oil reserves in 1942. For that reason, the war effort had to be concentrated in the area of southern Russia, Turkey, and the Middle East; the planned attack on North Africa, together with the return to the Continent in 1943, had both to be abandoned.⁶⁵

During the course of March, members of British intelligence concluded that in 1942 Germany would concentrate its war effort on the eastern front, in the region of southern Russia, with the object of reaching the Caucasian oilwells. Germany would neither attack in other regions nor reinforce its troops in North Africa. They estimated that Germany was prepared to take a calculated risk to attain a decisive victory in the present year, since its anticipated summer offensive would strain to the limit its economy, military industry, and oil reserves.⁶⁶

At the beginning of April 1942, the Americans completed their own plans, whose final version was designated the "Marshall Plan." The roots of this plan lie in the period prior to the United States' entry into the war.[67] As early as July 1941 Roosevelt had ordered the preparation of a blueprint that would serve the United States should it enter the war, and Major (as he then was) Albert Wedemeyer of the War Plans Division in the U.S. Army staff was selected to prepare it. Although not in favor of U.S. involvement in the war, Wedemeyer was a suitable choice. Ever since youth he had read widely in the fields of history, economics, and politics; he had also passed through the traditional course of training at U.S. war academies. But by his own account, he had acquired his true training as a strategist when a visiting student at the German Kriegsakademie between 1936 and 1938.[68]

Wedemeyer was especially influenced by Haushofer's lectures at that institution on Mackinder's geopolitical theory. He also studied the German version of Mackinder's concept, especially noting the fact that the Germans laid particular stress on the contribution of U.S. industrial capacity to their defeat in World War I.[69] Hence Wedemeyer reached the conclusion that Germany had to be prevented from controlling the Eurasian "heartland" and its resources. He opposed operations on the European periphery, which he regarded as a potential waste of military resources. He admitted that air and naval forces would make a substantial contribution to victory, but denied their ability to bring it about. Instead, he determined that the Allies must fight Germany by defeating its land forces and breaking its will to fight. The "Victory Program," in essence an organizational and economic proposal, was drafted on the basis of those assumptions. Wedemeyer and his aides calculated that the United States had to establish an army of 8.8 million men organized into 200 divisions, of which some 61 would be armored. This army would be ready for action in July 1943. They also estimated that projected U.S. shipping capacities would enable about three million troops to be transported and maintained overseas. Advantage would be taken of U.S. industrial capacity to produce a massive air force that would compensate for the lack of a sufficient quantitative advantage for the attacking forces on land. (Wedemeyer's calculations did not take into account the strength of the Red Army.)[70] In July 1943 the U.S. Army comprised ninty-one divisions and numbered over eight million men. The figures were not very much different when the war ended.[71]

When Eisenhower was appointed head of the Operations Division of the General Staff (which replaced the War Plans Division), he used "Victory Program" as a basis for his own planning. Fundamental to the latter was the concentration of Anglo-American land power in the United Kingdom and the defeat of the Wehrmacht in a land campaign that would follow the invasion of northern France. Marshall immediately adopted this idea. His own plan rested on the premise that western Europe constituted the most suitable theater for a joint Anglo-American offensive against Germany. Only Britain possessed the ports and facilities capable of speedily absorbing a large U.S. army. The Atlantic provided the shortest route between the United States and Britain. It was so vital that it would have to be defended even were some other war zone (such as the Mediterranean) to be selected as the center of gravity for Anglo-American operations. Hence, it was preferable to concentrate naval and transportation efforts on this route rather than to disperse energies on a number of routes. From an offensive point of view the shortest road to Germany crosses France, Belgium, and the Ruhr Valley, the heart of its war industry. Since this region lies close to the British Isles, more effective use could be made of the enormous air power that would be concentrated at existing British airfields.

Marshall stated that if a positive decision was taken at once, a large invasion force could be amassed in Britain, where a U.S. army of a million men, comprising thirty divisions, would be augmented by eighteen British divisions. This force would be ready to assault the French coast between Le Havre and Boulogne on April 1, 1943. The large margin of air superiority that the Allies enjoyed over northern France would deny the Germans the ability to reinforce their defenses in the west during and after the invasion. Marshall warned against dispersing the Anglo-American war effort, and stated that the only reason for dispatching forces elsewhere was to stabilize other fronts. (He feared not only a diversion of forces to the Middle East, but to the Pacific too.) He also submitted an "emergency" operation, whose aim was to seize a bridgehead on the French coast in 1942, and which was to be implemented were there signs of an impending Russian or German collapse.[72]

The inherent value of this plan lay in that, for the very first time, it put forward a proposal whose objective was a direct clash with the German army, at its present strength, and its defeat on the battlefield in accordance with a clear timetable. The plan was based on the advantages that the British and the Americans could give to each other. In contrast to the British approach, the plan was not dependent on evidence of acute weaknesses in the German military machine or its sudden collapse. It rested on actions which the Allies could themselves take and not on internal factors on the Continent over which they had little control.

On Marshall's advice, Roosevelt decided to send him to London at the head of a delegation that would also include Hopkins and Wedemeyer. The purpose of the trip was to secure Britain's immediate assent to the plan. While Marshall was still en route, Roosevelt informed Churchill that his heart and mind were in the plan (on the morning of the very day on which Marshall persuaded Roosevelt to support his plan, the President was still toying with ideas of employing U.S. troops in the Mediterranean);[73] and that if the war was to be won it was vital to carry the battle to the Continent itself and to provide the Russians with real assistance. Strategy in the Middle East had to be entirely defensive. Germany was incapable of launching a large offensive in that region as long as it was conducting a massive campaign in Russia.[74]

Aware that a U.S. plan was evolving, the British military mission in Washington had meanwhile compiled for review the draft of a parallel plan. Its authors stated that an invasion of Europe by way of northern France and the Low Countries was preferable to any other route of incursion. An assault on

Germany by way of Italy, the Iberian Peninsula, the Balkans, or Norway "would not threaten Germany directly and a comparatively small diversion of German land and air strength could hold our advance." Thus far their attitude accorded with that of the Americans. But the British mission then went on to say that no invasion would be possible if the Germans stationed a small number of armored divisions (with adequate air cover) behind the coastal fortifications of France. Portents of the success of the operation in 1943 would not appear unless the following conditions were satisfied: Germany had failed in its effort to defeat Russia, the strategic bombing raids had been successful, and damage had thereby been inflicted on German morale.[75] The Chiefs of Staff replied that this plan was remarkably similar to their own thinking (Churchill saw this correspondence).[76]

The British Chiefs of Staff met with Marshall on April 9. Their reaction to his plan was cool. Alan Brooke emphasized its many difficulties, as well as his concern for the state of the war in the Far and Middle East. He claimed that should the Germans decide to call a temporary halt in Russia and transfer the center of gravity to the Middle East, there would be insufficient forces there to repel them. This was a questionable argument, since Brooke and British intelligence were convinced that the Germans were concentrating their efforts for an offensive on the southern Russian front in the spring. Intelligence was also absolutely certain that the Germans did not intend to attack by way of Turkey.[77] Churchill and his military advisers were well aware that Germany's ability to reinforce the North African front was limited by the restricted capacity of the local harbors and the paucity of the roads under their control.[78] Brooke concluded by saying that the British did possess plans to invade the Continent in order to take advantage of a German defeat in Russia, but he questioned the wisdom of implementing the "Emergency operation" in the present year should Russia find itself in difficulties. Portal and Mountbatten reiterated that stand.[79]

Outwardly, at least, Churchill evinced more enthusiasm for Marshall's plan. Particularly was this so once he became aware that the Americans were extremely serious about their plan—a point emphasized several times by Hopkins, who felt that Churchill was treating the U.S. proposal too lightly.[80] One can only assume that the Prime Minister exercised his influence over his military advisers; for when they conferred on the following day (without any Americans being present) the Chiefs stated that "in the broadest terms General Marshall's proposal was in line with our strategy." However, they warned that if Britain accepted the plan "whole-heartedly," the Americans might invest all their efforts in its implementation and provide Britain with no assistance in other theaters. But without U.S. aid, it would be hard to prevent the Japanese and Germans from linking up. Britain had to make its agreement to the plan conditional on such assistance.[81] In a recommendation they submitted to the War Cabinet three days later, the Chiefs of Staff stated that they were in total agreement with Marshall's plan.[82]

The concluding meetings were held on April 14. In language laced with a tinge of enthusiasm, Churchill expressed his agreement with those details of the plan which concerned 1943. "The conception underlying it accorded with the classic principles of war—namely, concentration against the main enemy. One broad reservation must however be made—it was essential to carry on the defence of India and the Middle East." Alan Brooke supported the operation projected for 1943 but, in view of the danger of a junction of Japanese and German forces, again expressed reservations about the "Emergency" operation proposed for 1942. Marshall replied that he and President Roosevelt were very eager that U.S. forces participate in offensive operations in 1942; to that end the United States was prepared to suffer a high rate of casualties. He emphasized the need to avoid the diversion of troops to the Middle East and the Indian Ocean; attention had to be concentrated on the move in northwestern Europe.[83]

Marshall left London with a feeling that he had attained Britain's complete assent to his plan. Later, when the British rejected the "Emergency" operation and Churchill again mooted Gymnast, he felt that his partners had acted in bad faith. Wedemeyer had from the first doubted their sincerity, but Marshall and Hopkins were impressed by the British leaders' expressions of assent. Both the official British historian and General Ismay insist that the approval Churchill and the Chiefs of Staff expressed for the plan was sincere. However they do admit that the British should have made explicit their reservations and the limits of their understanding with the Americans.[84] The protocols of the discussions do not permit any definite judgment. In fact, the sincerity of the British side can only be assessed from the positions it adopted *after* assent to Marshall's plan had already been given.

There were two factors which made it easier for Churchill to accept the plan quickly. One was that its first stage, the transfer of U.S. forces to Britain and the establishment of the infrastructure required for an offensive in 1943 (Bolero), dovetailed with his own aim of ensuring the priority of the European theater over the Pacific. He feared that were Britain to oppose the plan the Americans might, after all, change their order of priorities.[85] (Thanks to reports received from the British military mission in Washington, he was aware of the struggle taking place within the U.S. military leadership; he also knew for a fact that considerable quantities of men and equipment had been sent to the Pacific during the previous four months.) The U.S. plan would provide Britain with a wider margin of security against a German invasion; in so doing it would give Britain the room for maneuver that might permit, at least during the implementation of Bolero, the dispatch of its own forces from the United Kingdom to other theaters. There does not, then, seem to have been anything accidental about the fact that Churchill and the Chiefs of Staff did not make much of their reservations. The Prime Minister preferred to establish an agreement in what the Chiefs designated "the broadest terms," because by standing firm he would have run the risk of a conflict with the Americans, which he was for the present anxious to avoid.

The second reason is that Churchill, as always, believed in the capriciousness of war. He hoped that changing circumstances would enable him to change the nature of Marshall's plan in accordance with his own wishes. Moreover, he had solid grounds for the assumption that during 1943 the war might in any case develop in a manner which accorded with the British conception. As we have seen, during the first half of 1942 British military intelligence became increasingly convinced that the Germans were concentrating all their efforts on preparations for a renewed attack on Russia, with the objective of finally defeating her and capturing the Caucasian oil fields. The Joint Intelligence Committee maintained that Hitler was in fact playing for the very highest stakes. The anticipated attack, they argued, would compel Germany to make the fullest use of its resources, and especially of its petroleum reserves.

Should this gamble fail, and the Germans realize that they could not avoid another winter campaign in Russia and had to face the threat of Anglo-American invasion in the west, "they may collapse with unexpected rapidity as they did in 1918." Since (from the Russians' point of view) the 1942 summer offensive would open under conditions far more favorable than had been the case the previous year, they stood a good chance of holding the Germans in check.[86] Churchill considered that estimate to be "very good."[87] Based on its findings he (like the Joint Planners[88]) might have assumed that if the anticipated German attack on Russia did not succeed, Germany would find itself in a state of collapse—or be close to it. The circumstances the British thought necessary for an invasion of the Continent would thus have materialized. However, should Hitler indeed manage to attain command of the Caucasus, the strategic situation on the Continent would have deteriorated so much that the idea of its invasion in 1943 would in any case have to be abandoned.

The degree of mutual Anglo-American understanding was not improved by the fact that code names for earlier British plans were transferred to the U.S. plan. Marshall's "Emergency" offensive for 1942 was entitled Sledgehammer, which (it will be recalled) was the code name for a similar British project. A new code, Bolero, was given to the entire logistic and administrative enterprise for the transfer of U.S. army to Britain and its preparation for the invasion projected for 1943, while the invasion of that year was entitled Round-up. The latter name, however, was taken from a British plan that, as we have seen, had been formulated during the winter of 1941–1942; based on a different concept, it had been conditional on a prior German collapse. In effect, it constituted an expanded version of Sledgehammer. Matters had become so entangled by the end of 1942 that Dill (the head of the British Military Mission in Washington) then asked London to clarify the meanings underlying the codenames "as the term 'Round-up' appears now to have various interpretations ranging from a full scale frontal attack against unbroken Germany to preparations to take advantage of a sudden crash in German military power."[89] The misunderstandings thus generated can be discerned well into 1943.[90] The confusion, however, was essentially one way. Churchill and his advisers knew what the Americans had in mind. But the Americans—although aware that the British were inclined to put their trust in a prior German collapse—were unable to pinpoint London's position at any given moment.

Early in May, shortly after Marshall's return to Washington, Churchill again reverted to his proposal for a landing in nothern Norway (code-named Jupiter) as an alternative to Sledgehammer in 1942. From the start, the Chiefs of Staff had been unenthusiastic about this idea. Alan Brooke remarked that he had never understood what Churchill hoped to gain by an invasion of Norway.[91] Of course, the operation did have immediate aims: a junction with the Russians in the far north, the provision of air cover for the convoys to Russia, and greater influence over Sweden and Finland. (However, the interruption of the flow of iron ore from Sweden to Germany had become of secondary importance once the Germans had got control of the Lorraine mines and established a land route to Spain, an important supplier of that resource.) True, Churchill did write that, after landing in northern Norway, "we could advance gradually southwards, unrolling the Nazi map of Europe from the top" (a phrase he was fond of repeating). In June, in a last effort to save Jupiter, he also proposed that operations in Norway might be expanded in the spring of 1943 as "a convenient prelude and accompaniment to Round-up."[92]

There were two main reasons why the Chiefs of Staff objected to Jupiter. One was the difficulty of effecting and sustaining a landing on a hostile shore when the enemy enjoyed local air superiority. Second, an operation on the scale of Jupiter—involving the needs of both the operation itself and the maintenance of the army in northern Norway—would impose heavy burdens on shipping and on the Royal Navy. (Pound maintained that the execution of Jupiter would require the use of all the escorts presently stationed in the western approaches to the British Isles.) They held that, for the same logistic reasons, Jupiter would have an adverse effect on the ability to implement Round-up in 1943.[93] These were weighty arguments, but they failed to move Churchill. A debate sprang up between the two sides on the operational aspects of Jupiter. But the central question—what the operation might contribute to Germany's defeat—was left in abeyance.

Churchill disagreed with the Chiefs' opinion that no landings were to be made on a hostile shore unless air superiority had been assured. Neither could he accept the corollary, that the range of fighter aircraft made a massive assault possible only on a small portion of the French coast, where the enemy had large ground forces in place. He supported his case by remarking that British forces had been landed on the Norwegian shore—and evacuated—despite the enemy's superiority in the air.[94] This was a strange response: local German air superiority had been the most decisive reason for Britain's defeat in Norway. Moreover Greece, Crete, and Malaya had repeatedly demonstrated the inability of an army to operate successfuly against an enemy who enjoyed total mastery of the air. Although Churchill realized that the operational rules of the game were changing, he found it difficult to adapt his strategic thinking to the new reality.

When in mid-June Churchill specified his thinking on the nature of Round-up in 1943, he really did no more than repeat the old outline of ideas that he had drawn at the end of 1941. At least six massive landings would be simultaneously launched in Denmark, Holland, the Pas-de-Calais, the Contentin peninsula, Brest, and at the Gironde estuary; Jupiter would be a diversion. He even advocated examining the possibility of landing troops on the northern coast of Spain, whence they would establish a base for an advance northward into France (Wellington's route). Those assaults that met with only light resistance would be developed and become the primary landings, with the others acting as diversions.[95] Quite apart from the enormous logistic difficulties posed by this plan, it also suffered from the defect that—with the exception of Pas-de-Calais and the Contentin peninsula—all the proposed landing sites were beyond the range of effective air cover. Even if at all feasible, the plan could not possibly be implemented until the German military machine disintegrated.

The reaction of senior commanders of the field forces in Britain was that the implementation of Churchill's plan would mean a dispersal of effort; simultaneous landings would have little effect unless carried out on a massive scale. But, if the latter was the case, they would divert resources from the principal landing (by which they of course meant, as Marshall's plan had determined, an assault on northern France).[96] Their reactions revealed either a lack of understanding or naivete. Churchill's plan was not designed to complement Marshall's, but to be its alternative.

However, Churchill and the Chiefs of Staff did agree that Sledgehammer was not to be implemented in 1942. Instead, Churchill pressed for the execution that year of Jupiter and for a landing in northwestern Africa (Gymnast). Alan Brooke, even though he rejected Jupiter out of hand and was not at first particularly excited about Gymnast either, eventually supported the latter as the lesser of two evils.

Early in June, the U.S. Navy scored a decisive victory over the Japanese fleet at Midway. Japanese expansion in the Pacific Ocean was thus brought to a halt, and the naval balance in that region tipped in the United States' favor. Nothing, however, had changed in the Middle East. Rommel severely bruised British armor at "Knightsbridge" and continued his advance eastward.

In the middle of June Dill reported to Churchill on affairs in Washington. Roosevelt and Marshall, it transpired, were at loggerheads. Because of the British attitude, the President's ardor for Sledgehammer had cooled; he was now expressing interest in Gymnast, primarily because he was determined to throw U.S. ground forces into battle on the European front during the current year. Marshall, on the other hand, adamantly exerted all his influence on behalf of Sledgehammer because he thought that, unless that plan was put into operation, the chances of effecting the planned invasion of France in 1943 would be very much reduced.[97] Now he waived his prior proviso that Sledgehammer be considered an emergency measure, which would become operational only in the event of the collapse of either Russia or Germany. Armed with this information, on June 17 Churchill again set out for Washington. His object was to deepen the divide between Roosevelt and Marshall, and to propose Gymnast as an alternative to Sledgehammer. Churchill knew that Roosevelt had been in favor of the idea of an Anglo-American invasion of northwestern Africa before becoming entranced by Marshall's plan in April; he now assumed that a mind that had been changed once could be altered again. Although Roosevelt wavered, Marshall proved obstinate enough to withstand Churchill's pressure. Gymnast was accorded a priority secondary only to operations in northern France and the Low Countries. Every effort, it was decided, would be made to implement Sledgehammer. Nevertheless Churchill did make some progress toward his objective. If it transpired that Sledgehammer could not be implemented, Gymnast would take its place. In part, that concession was the result of information from the North African front while Churchill was still in Washington. The fall of Tobruk on June 21 and Rommel's advance on Alamein had dealt heavy blows to British prestige, but those events also sustained the Prime Minister's argument that the situation in that theater had to be immediately retrieved. In the light of the British predicament, the Americans transported to the Middle East, in their own vessels, the first 300 Sherman tanks to roll off the production lines.

On June 28 the Germans opened their summer campaign in southern Russia. Nevertheless, Churchill and his Chiefs remained steadfast in their opposition to Sledgehammer. They did not undertake a reexamination of the operation after their return from Washington, even though it was a topic of continual review at the staff level by the Joint Planners. At the end of June, and with Churchill's ardent approval, the Chiefs determined that Sledgehammer would be implemented only in the event of a repetition of the sort of German collapse that had taken place in 1918.[98] There was no reference whatsoever to the other original proviso: assistance to the Russians if the latter proved to be on the verge of collapse. Indeed, the Chiefs of Staff decided that Round-up would itself become impracticable were the Russians to be close to collapse on September 15. Instead, Gymnast would have to be implemented before December 1942.[99]

Once he had made his own calculations, Marshall put his finger on the fundamental problem: the implementation of Gymnast in 1942 would render the execution of Round-up in 1943 logistically impossible. Accordingly, he pressed for the seizure of a bridgehead on the Cherbourg peninsula, to be maintained until the main invasion of France in 1943. He thus hoped to avoid the dispersion of forces, which he so much feared. In campaigning for Sledgehammer, Marshall was in fact fighting for the implementation of Round-up in 1943, in accordance with the plan to which the British had agreed.[100] By contrast, early in July Churchill and the Chiefs of Staff argued that it was precisely Sledgehammer which would have a serious adverse effect on the success of the massive invasion of France in the spring of 1943, especially from a logistic viewpoint.[101] But they were concerned less about the success of Round-up than ensuring that Sledgehammer would not be launched in 1942. As much became evident a few days later, when some of the Chiefs of Staff and their planners agreed with Marshall's assessment that an invasion of northwestern Africa would preclude the one of western Europe in 1943. The Chiefs particularly emphasized this point to Churchill.[102] In June, even before Churchill had set sail for Washington, Alan Brooke had noted the existence of a logistic correlation between Round-up and U.S. operations in the Middle East. Because of the shipping shortage, every U.S. division sent to the Middle East would mean a deduction of two-and-a-half to three divisions from the forces to be sent to Britain for Round-up.[103] Although that ratio would of course be reduced were U.S. forces to be employed in the western sector of North Africa, the trend remained clear. Nevertheless, despite that calculation, Brooke did not attempt to dissuade Churchill from pressing for Gymnast while in Washington. Neither did the last assessment induce him to disavow that plan. Needless to say, Churchill was even more intransigent.

It is clear that what primarily moved Churchill to reject Sledgehammer was neither logistic difficulties nor the shortage of landing craft, nor the fear that the chances of Round-up might be impaired. None of these considerations prevented him from meanwhile continuing to push for an invasion of northern Norway (Jupiter)—which from a logistic point of view was a more complex operation—and for Gymnast. Early in July, he even proposed the simultaneous execution of both projects in 1942 as an alternative to Sledgehammer.[104] Churchill refused to accept the assessments tabled by the Chiefs of Staff and by Marshall. Without substantiating his case, he maintained that the implementation of Gymnast would in no way cause the cancellation of the planned invasion of France in 1943.[105]

Meeting on July 7, the War Cabinet decided (on Churchill's recommendation) to cancel Sledgehammer altogether. The Americans, it was determined, would have to be persuaded to accept Gymnast instead.[106] Churchill continued to think in grand terms and to cut himself off from the difficulties posed by quotidian logistic minutiae. In mid-July he informed Roosevelt that Sledgehammer could not be carried out; instead, the Americans had to act in the western sector of North Africa and the British to cooperate with the Russians in northern Norway. Meanwhile, preparations for the implementation of Round-up in 1943 would proceed apace.[107] Marshall and Hopkins immediately departed for London to save Sledgehammer, which in fact meant saving the chances of an invasion of France in 1943. Marshall had lost faith in Churchill's declarations of support for Round-up in 1943. Mindful of that fact, Dill advised Churchill to convince Marshall of the sincerity of his intentions. He also went on to describe the state of affairs in Washington: Marshall maintained that Gymnast, quite apart from destroying the chances of launching Round-up, would also be of no help to the Russians. Nevertheless, he feared that the absence of any U.S. operation in the European theater in 1942 would create a preference for the Pacific theater, as was being demanded by U.S. Admiral King. Dill and his mission advised Churchill and the Chiefs that, in order to maintain good Anglo-American relations, they ought to be forthcoming in their negotiations with the Americans, even at the cost of courting the possible failure of Sledgehammer (whose opening stages, at least, they thought stood a good chance of success).[108]

Churchill did not adopt their recommendation. Dill's dispatch led him to conclude that, while Marshall had little room for maneuver (or threat), he himself held the best cards. Marshall would be forced to make do with Gymnast in order to preserve the priority of the European theater and thereby also comply with Roosevelt's wish that U.S. land forces engage the Germans during the course of the current year. What is more, Roosevelt would thereby be allowed to feel that he had done something to keep his promise to the Russians that a "second front" would be opened in 1942. Churchill's preparations for the arrival of the Americans were thorough, and he again tried to formulate his thoughts on the nature of Round-up. "We are ardently in favour" of this plan, he wrote; but then went on to ask whether the "second front" is "necessarily confined to an attack upon the western seaboard of France?"[109] He pointed out the enormous strength of the German war machine, which had been proven by the successes the three German divisions in action in North Africa had gained against "our greatly superior numbers and resources.[W]e have no excuse for underrating German military power in 1943 and 1944. . . . We have no right to count upon a collapse of German military power on the European Continent." Contradicting one of the premises upon which he had based his own plan at the end of 1941, he also went on to predict that the Germans could swiftly transfer fifty to sixty divisions from eastern to western Europe.[110]

Two days later, Churchill finalized his position. When conquered, North Africa could constitute the springboard for the attack on the European mainland.

> The flank attack [Gymnast] may become the main attack, and the main attack [Round-up] a holding operation in the early stages. Our second front will in fact comprise both the Atlantic and the Mediterranean coasts of Europe, and we can push either right-handed, left-handed or both-handed as our resources and circumstances permit.

The reference to a "right-handed" advance applied to Italy; only Sicily lay within effective cover range of fighter aircraft operating from the African coast. Moreover, Churchill had explicitly mentioned Italy and Sicily as operational objectives in the notes he compiled in preparation for the meeting with the U.S. delegation. He concluded by saying that "it is not wise to try now to look too far ahead." What had to be kept open were options "which allow of strategic manoeuvres according as events unfold." He directed the Chiefs of Staff to emphasize Britain's intention of opening a "second front" as soon as possible; but they were not to admit that Gymnast would preclude Round-up, even though it might temporarily affect Bolero.[111]

The ideas thus expressed were markedly different from those current in

U.S. circles, to whom they were deliberately not transmitted. Churchill deleted some of them from his memoirs. Ostensibly, they articulated a flexible strategic approach, but its flexibility stemmed from the fact that no sufficient account was taken of reality. If, as Churchill's military advisers concluded, logistic factors meant that Gymnast could only be implemented at Round-up's expense, how could both operations be carried out simultaneously or within only a brief interval? Even if Round-up would after all be launched in 1943 after Gymnast, the balance of forces that Churchill himself anticipated did not ensure success; Round-up could only be guaranteed if—again—the Germans had previously collapsed. As much is indicated by Churchill's own calculations. These showed that in June 1943 some thirty divisions would be stationed in the United Kingdom and fourteen in northwestern Africa.[112] These forces would not be enough to demolish a German army, which—especially in western Europe—was still intact and which (so he claimed) could be swiftly reinforced by the movement of a further fifty to sixty divisions from east to west.

In the event, there was no need for Churchill to instruct the Chiefs of Staff to conceal the fact that they agreed with their American colleagues about the reciprocal correlation between Gymnast and Round-up. The Prime Minister in any case possessed good bargaining assets. The strongest was that the British possessed the power of veto over Sledgehammer. This was because their troops would comprise most of the forces which that plan envisioned employing in the initial stages of the landing on the Contentin (Cherbourg) peninsula. Marshall, in effect, had no cards to play. He could only hope to convince Churchill and Brooke by persuasion and force of argument. But the latter, it transpired, were inadequate weapons and the discussions in London reached a deadlock. The ultimate decision was passed to Roosevelt who, in the face of the British refusal to implement Sledgehammer, came down in favor of Gymnast.

In their joint summation, the British and U.S. Chiefs of Staff concluded that

> it be understood that a commitment to this operation [Torch, the new code-name that replaced Gymnast] renders Round-up in all probability impracticable of successful execution in 1943 and therefore that we have definitely accepted a defensive encircling line of action for the Continental European theatre.

Torch would constitute the principal operation planned for 1943. Preparations for Round-up would continue, but an invasion would be possible only if there were signs of a clear decline in German strength.

Presenting this memorandum to the War Cabinet, the Prime Minister termed its content "most satisfactory." But he added that Torch would not necessarily be undertaken at the expense of Round-up in 1943. Although the invasion might be somewhat delayed, the Allies possessed sufficient forces to implement both operations. Alan Brooke protested, and quickly informed Ministers that the Chiefs of Staff entirely agreed with the Americans that Round-up could not be carried out in 1943 should Torch be launched as planned.¹¹³ Churchill did not bother to justify his refusal to accept this assessment. He now seemed to reject what he had previously accepted without question: the Chiefs of Staff's statement that shipping limitations precluded the transfer of large U.S. forces to Europe. Indeed, the implication of his stand was that shipping would suffice—within the space of less than a year—to reinforce the Middle East theater; to support the conquest of North Africa; and to transfer a large U.S. army to Britain preparatory to the invasion. It is highly unlikely that he had indeed become so optimistic about shipping capabilities. He probably assumed that an invasion of France in 1943 would be carried out after a German collapse, and that a large number of U.S. divisions would therefore not be required in the west. Tactical and political considerations also came into play. After all, if he were to accept Marshall's assessment that Gymnast would negate Round-up—and do so at the very time he was pressing for the former operation—how could he convince the Americans of the sincerity of his intention to carry out Round-up as planned? Furthermore, by adopting his present position he might also conciliate, for the time being, personalities who represented that section of the British public very desirous of opening the "second front" (such as Beaverbrook, who in February had resigned from the government and instigated a public campaign to that very end, and Sir Stafford Cripps, who had joined the Cabinet).¹¹⁴

In *The Second World War* Churchill did not set out the true importance of the dilemma: Gymnast at the expense of Round-up. On the contrary, his account intimates that only the Americans claimed that an invasion of northwestern Africa would preclude the invasion of France in 1943; he failed to mention that all of his own military advisers shared that opinion.¹¹⁵

But even before the British exercised their right of veto over Sledgehammer, strong forces of another sort had prevented Marshall from having his way. It will be recalled that Roosevelt's insistence on the participation of U.S. ground troops in the European theater in 1942 had narrowed the available choices to either Sledgehammer or Gymnast. The third alternative—progress with Bolero in 1942 prepatory to the main invasion in 1943—was ruled out because of Roosevelt's attitude and because Marshall feared an intensification within his own camp of the trend toward the Pacific. To this was added a secondary complication in the spring of 1942, when the President promised Molotov that a "second front" would be opened during the course of the current year (an undertaking which Churchill took great care not to give). By any gauge, an assault on Cherbourg under the circumstances expected at the end of 1942 was going to be difficult and hazardous. Marshall himself admitted as much when in London in July.¹¹⁶ Moreover, he departed from the objectives he had set for the "emergency" operation in his original plan. Sledgehammer had now become an entity in itself; in Marshall's mind it had become another kind of emergency operation, designed to preserve Round-up in 1943 and to counter the strong centrifugal pressures that threatened to scatter Anglo-American forces along the European periphery.

Developments in the Mediterranean theater also exerted a powerful pull on events. July 1942 was the least suitable of all times to try to persuade the British to concentrate their efforts on the northwestern region of Europe. Britain's standing in the Middle East had sunk to an unprecedented nadir. In that month Rommel reached Alamein, the furthest point to the east that Axis forces were ever to attain in North Africa. Cairo was in a state of some alarm and London in one of deep concern. Under such circumstances, it was impossible to persuade Churchill to run risks additional to those he already faced in Egypt and to commit British forces to an amphibious offensive on the French coasts that had hitherto been routed by a small number of German troops. The landing in northwestern Africa now seemed to be primarily a security measure; its object was to prevent the loss of British control over the Middle East, whose importance Roosevelt had stressed in the directives he issued to Marshall prior to the latter's departure for London.[117] Rommel would not be able to remain indifferent to the danger developing in his rear. It was vital, once and for all, to unravel the knot of Britain's complications in the Mediterranean. Thus Churchill was correct when he said that "strategic natural selection" had made Sledgehammer fall on its own and brought about its replacement by Gymnast.[118] But it must be remembered that the current situation in the Middle East was the product of a "natural selection" process whose genesis lay in Britain's failure in Greece.

It is highly doubtful whether Churchill and Alan Brooke had conducted a suitably thorough and unprejudiced examination of the possibility of implementing Sledgehammer. It will be recalled that in March, and hence even before Marshall had arrived with his plan, Alan Brooke had rejected a plan akin to Sledgehammer proposed by the Planners; instead, he had accorded absolute priority to the dispatch of additional divisions to the Middle East. His motives for doing so gained additional impetus in June and July. Immediately after Marshall's departure from London in April, Churchill continued to give his attention to operations that contradicted Sledgehammer. Lord Mountbatten, the Chief of Combined Operations, knew what he was writing when he—somewhat strangely—advised the War Cabinet that the implications and hazards associated with Sledgehammer should not be accepted "unless there is a firm intention of actually carrying out the operation."[119]

One researcher who has analyzed the fate of Sledgehammer concluded that the principal reason for Britain's refusal to carry out that plan lay in Churchill's lack of confidence that the British Army could match the Wehrmacht because of its failures in the years 1941–1942[120] (a claim that will be thoroughly examined below). Certainly it was one weighty factor. But the Sledgehammer episode does not, of itself, prove that it was the *principal* factor. This is because the local operational obstacles confronting the successful implementation of Sledgehammer, together with the pressing demands of other theaters of the war, were serious enough to deter even a political and military leadership confident in its army. What was needed to overcome the aversion to Sledgehammer was strong faith in the strategic concept behind the invasion of western Europe. There is no evidence that Britain's leaders possessed such faith. Their internal correspondence clearly reveals that Churchill attached only secondary importance to the fate of Round-up. Neither he nor Alan Brooke were in the least troubled by the statement that it would be precluded by Gymnast. Their preference was clear. Moreover, there exists no unambiguous indication that Churchill abandoned his own conception about the nature and form of the invasion of Europe. This differed from the American conception, which concentrated on northern France and was not conditional on a prior German collapse.

The U.S. agreement to a joint Anglo-American operation in northwestern Africa was a natural extension of, and victory for, the strategic line that Churchill had aimed for as early as 1941 (especially after the defeat in the Balkans) and that he had presented in his plans at the Washington meeting held at the end of that year.

7

The "Mediterranean Strategy" at Its Height, 1942-1943

Once operation Sledgehammer had been canceled and it had been decided to launch an invasion of northwestern Africa at the end of the year, Churchill and Alan Brooke arrived in Cairo on August 3 to deal with the military crisis in the Middle East. On August 12 Churchill met Stalin for the first time in Moscow, and spent the following three days filling him in on future Anglo-American strategy (see below).[1] On August 24 he returned to Britain. On August 19, while Churchill and Brooke were in Cairo on their way home, the raid on the port of Dieppe was launched—the largest such operation on the French coast prior to the landings of 1944. Heavy losses were incurred and the operation failed to attain its objective of seizing control of the port and town for the space of a few hours.

On hearing of the failure at Dieppe, Alan Brooke remarked that "it is a lesson to the people who are clamouring for the invasion of France." Churchill informed Lord Moran that, notwithstanding the losses, the operation had proven to be worthwhile since "we had learnt a lot."[2] He repeated that opinion after the war too. But Lord Beaverbrook, the advocate of a "second front," was incensed; he suspected that the Chiefs of Staff had sanctioned the raid in order to prove that an attack on western Europe would be hopeless.[3] It was Churchill who, by his own account, wanted "a large-scale operation . . . this summer," and who insisted that the Dieppe assault be carried out—even though on July 7 a decision to cancel the raid had been taken on operational grounds. Alan Brooke also supported that opinion.[4] Montgomery, who had helped to plan the original operation, opposed any attempt to implement it after July, especially since Dieppe remained its objective; but his advice was rejected.[5] The difference between the original and the new operation essentially boiled down to a change in the code name, from "Rutter" to "Jubilee." All this had transpired prior to the arrival in London of the U.S. delegation to discuss future strategy. The raid itself was launched after a decision had been taken to cancel Sledgehammer and while Churchill, Brooke, and even Montgomery were in the Middle East.

In *The Second World War*, Churchill claimed that he had himself joined his military advisers in reviewing the plans for the assault.[6] But the questions he asked four months later, when he began to investigate what had happened at Dieppe, indicate that he knew very little about the details of those plans. Indeed, he expressed his surprise at the planning. He thought an attempt to carry out a frontal assault on a fortified port to be a violation of the principles of warfare; instead, a landing should have been effected on the neighboring coasts and the town taken from the rear.[7] Ismay replied that Intelligence had underestimated the size of the German force defending Dieppe; moreover, it had been feared that flanking movements would require the tanks to operate too deeply within enemy-held territory.[8]

Both the Prime Minister and the official British history emphasize the importance of the contribution made by the experience gained during the Dieppe operation to the success of the massive invasion of western Europe.[9] But, if we are to judge from the reports to Washington, the lessons the British Chiefs of Staff derived from Dieppe were trite. The principal lesson was the need to train and integrate into one body the naval and ground forces intended for the amphibious assault. The Americans, notwithstanding the experience they had acquired in the Pacific, had to study the special conditions of the English Channel.[10] This amounted to a rehash of an old lesson. Even minds incapable of absorbing the results of the experience garnered at Gallipoli should have taken note of the U.S. practice of employing specially trained troops (the Marines) when carrying out amphibious assaults on defended enemy coasts in the Pacific. Churchill accepted his Chiefs' recommendation, with the reservation that it be limited to the troops who were to spearhead the attack, since not all the ground forces could be thus prepared. He argued that a drive to achieve perfection constituted a recipe for "paralysis."[11]

The report submitted by the Chiefs of Staff contains no mention of the arguments commonly adduced: that the operation demonstrated how difficult it was to seize a fortified port; that the very conquest of that objective would result in the harbor being totally inoperative during the first decisive days of the invasion; and that it would therefore be necessary to develop artificial harbors which would be hauled to the coast. The official British historian, although listing all these contentions, admits their absence from the Chiefs' report.[12] Neither does Churchill refer to them in that portion of *The Second World War* dealing with Dieppe. On the contrary, during the course of operation Torch, launched shortly after the Dieppe raid, the Anglo-American forces carried out yet another frontal assault—on the ports of Oran and Algiers (which similarly failed; the capture of those ports was ultimately due to the success of the large flanking landings on both sides of those cities). The Americans, who in the Pacific had avoided launching direct assaults on fortified ports, had objected to a frontal attack on Oran, considering it to be "a suicide mission."[13] In short, the lessons learned could have been arrived at by common sense. As was pointed out by Montgomery, one of the commanders of the Normandy invasion, the information required for the ultimate invasion would have been acquired even if the attack on Dieppe had never taken place.[14]

Butler, the official British historian, writes that the failure of the Dieppe raid illustrates what might have happened had Sledgehammer been carried out.[15] Operation Sledgehammer was certainly fraught with danger, but it is straining matters to arrive at conclusions as to its possible fate by referring to what happened at Dieppe. Unwittingly, Churchill himself put his finger on the primary difference between the two operations when examining plans for diversionary attacks on the French coast. One of these was operation Imperator, which for a time was even proposed as an alternative to Sledgehammer. Designed as a large-scale raid, Imperator envisioned landing an entire division on the French coast. This force would remain on the shoreline for two or three days, draw the Germans into a major air battle, and then retreat to England. Churchill considered Imperator doomed to failure, since it required troops both to land and withdraw from the enemy coast.[16] For large and regular forces, this was a far more complicated operation than a conventional amphibious assault. From that point of view, Sledgehammer was easier to implement. Churchill argued that the failure of Imperator would subsequently "be cited as another example of sentimental politics dominating the calm determination and common sense of professional advisers. . . . A whole set of inhibitions would grow up on our side prejudicial to effective action in 1943."[17] But if that was the case, why did he press for an operation like that at Dieppe, which—its scale apart (involving only about "one third" of the forces and time projected for Imperator)—was in all respects similar to the latter operation? The primary difficulty remained: the landing of forces on an enemy coastline and their withdrawal. Moreover, the Americans had already agreed to cancel Sledgehammer and it was known that amphibious experience would be obtained within the framework of operation Torch.

It is therefore difficult to arrive at a complete understanding of the considerations that favored the assault on Dieppe. If there did exist hidden motives, they were well concealed. At all events, Dieppe did certainly generate "inhibitions and prejudices" against a massive invasion of western Europe. Although, as will be seen, such sentiments had already begun to strike roots in the Middle East. Dieppe caused them to be even more deeply embedded. Even the U.S. planners were disheartened by the heavy losses the Canadians sustained at Dieppe. Only Marshall, as cool as ever, did not succumb to that atmosphere.[18]

The "lesson" from an operation such as was planned and executed at Dieppe is that anticipated failures will indeed materialize. That is precisely what gave grounds for hope. Mountbatten, who was responsible for combined operations, was encouraged by the results of the Dieppe raid. He pointed out to the Cabinet that two-thirds of the forces landed had been brought back to England.[19] Given the circumstances of the raid, that was a true amphibious feat which would not be demanded of the forces of the grand invasion.

While preparations for the Anglo-American invasion of North Africa and the British attack at El Alamein were being finalized, the British Joint Planners, together with the Chiefs of Staff and Churchill, began to discuss strategy for 1943 and beyond. No decisions were taken until the end of 1942, on the eve of the Anglo-American conference at Casablanca.

In mid-September, Churchill once again raised the idea of Jupiter, which he suggested should be implemented once the conquest of North Africa was complete. He argued that the Chiefs of Staff were exaggerating the difficulties of action in northern Norway. Should Torch be carried out as planned, the U.S. troops due to reach England within the framework of Bolero could be employed in Norway. At last taking cognizance of the problems imposed by logistics, he added that—should Jupiter be carried out in 1943—the invasion of France (Round-up) would be deferred until 1944.[20] When he composed this memorandum, Churchill still held fast to his earlier argument that, depite everything, the completion of Torch would make possible the implementation of Round-up in 1943. This implies that, for the sake of Jupiter, he was prepared to defer the invasion until 1944. But one week later he wrote to President Roosevelt that the invasion of North Africa would *wipe out* any chance of implementing Round-up in 1943. He proposed that, once the conquest of North Africa was complete, Norway be invaded—and not Sardinia, Sicily, or Italy.[21]

Meanwhile, the Joint Planners and Chiefs of Staff were about to finalize their ideas for future Anglo-American strategy. They reached that stage at precisely the time that they began to get a clearer picture of the Russian situation. They considered that the German threat to the Middle East from the north, which had again troubled them in the summer of 1942, was fast disappearing. As early as July, the Joint Intelligence Committee estimated that no German attack on Iran could begin before the spring of 1943. Alan Brooke considered that to be a somewhat optimistic assessment, but it was one Churchill was inclined to accept, especially after his own visit to Moscow. During the course of September, even Brooke reached the conclusion that Germany would not defeat Russia in 1942, and that another winter campaign was to be expected. The Chiefs became sure about that in their own minds in October and early November, when they were finally convinced that a stalemate existed on the eastern front.[22] Thus, British decision makers planned their next moves at a stage when they were in a position to confirm their assumption that the German attack of the summer of 1942 had not succeeded. Moreover, as previously pointed out, Intelligence estimated that the failure of Germany's attempt to attain a decision in the east in the current year, an attempt on which it had gambled all, was likely to bring about its collapse.

During the course of October, the Joint Planners determined that there were two alternative ways of defeating Germany. One was to invade western Europe and to defeat the German army before Germany's economic and military might had been broken. The other was to invade the Continent after the German army had been considerably weakened and Germany's industrial "machine" had been destroyed. They ruled that the second was the only possible course: an opposed invasion of the Continent would require extended preparations and the concentration of the invasion army in Britain. But that would itself rule out the possibility of a continuous offensive operation against Germany and, in turn, run the risk of causing Russia's defeat. Moreover, experience showed that it would be impossible to invade the Continent until the foundations of Germany's military strength had been undermined. The Joint Planners estimated that—even under the very best of circumstances—were a decision taken to devote Anglo-American efforts to building up forces in Britain in anticipation of the invasion, no assault could be launched before September 1943. Even then, it could only take place when German morale had been clearly seen to have collapsed.[23] Alan Brooke responded that he did not consider these to be two alternative courses, but two stages in an overall strategic plan. The first stage would concentrate on the weakening of Germany's military and economic might. During the coming eighteen months, the Anglo-American effort should be directed at increasing pressure on Germany. That meant providing all possible assistance to Russia, bringing Turkey into the war, carrying out bombing raids on Germany and Italy, and conquering either Sicily or Sardinia. The Continent would be invaded after this stage since "he was not in favour of venturing into the mainland of Europe until the Axis military power had been considerably weakened."[24] In fact there existed no difference between the course advocated by the planners and Alan Brooke's two stages.

At the end of the month Churchill wrote a memorandum that opened by declaring that its aim was to deny charges that the Prime Minister possessed no clear and general plan for the defeat of Germany. In fact, however, the document substantiates rather than refutes that accusation. Notwithstanding his message to Roosevelt of the previous month, Churchill repeated his claim that Torch would not cause the cancellation of Round-up in 1943, only its delay. The nature of the primary operation for 1943 would be determined by the results of the campaign at Alamein and the Anglo-American invasion of North Africa. If those were successful, the Mediterranean would be opened to shipping and an assault become possible against the soft underbelly of the Axis. Offensives could be launched against Sicily, southern Italy, Sardinia, the French Riviera, and (with Turkey's assistance) even the Balkans. In conclusion, the memorandum stated that there was no point in looking too far ahead; whatever happened, until the summer of 1943 the principal campaign would be waged in the Mediterranean.[25] Perhaps Churchill did indeed intend to commence operations in the latter theater during the spring and summer of 1943, after the conquest of North Africa. But, if so, he clearly did not assume that it would be possible simultaneously to concentrate in Britain a force sufficiently large for a grand invasion of western Europe in the autumn of 1943 against a German army which had not yet collapsed. That remains true even if he still thought that the implementation of Torch in that year would not necessitate the deferment of Round-up. Indeed, on the very same day, Churchill explained to Lord Cherwell

(F.A. Lindemann), his friend and scientific adviser, that Round-up would be carried out "provided the German demoralization is adequate."[26]

The British offensive at Alamein began on the night of October 24; after a series of stiff battles, a decision was attained on November 3. While that campaign was still under way, the Chiefs of Staff submitted their plans for future strategy. These were based on two fundamental principles. One was the security of the major shipping lanes, a condition required for future offensive operations. The second was that Russia was the only power capable of halting and defeating Germany, whose might on land neither Britain nor the United States could possibly challenge. Without adducing any specifics or sources, the Chiefs argued that the experience already earned was sufficient to demonstrate that no massive invasion of northern France would be possible unless Germany's military power had been weakened. Germany might be closer to collapse than external signs indicated. It had reached the limits of its manpower potential, its industrial productivity was in decline, it was suffering a severe shortage of oil, and—above all—it had lost control of the military campaign planned for 1942. Nevertheless, they added, an Anglo-American army had to be established in Britain since, even if German power was mortally weakened, the Wehrmacht would still be capable of offering resistance in western Europe. The Anglo-American force would enter the Continent "at the right psychological moment" or, to put matters another way, only "when there was a definite crack in German morale." That consideration, together with the fact that Germany's strategy was based on the sequential defeat of its enemies, meant that the primary gauge for the analysis of future Anglo-American operations had to be their contribution to continued Russian resistance to Germany. Germany must not be given breathing room to recoup its strength.

If Germany was to be weakened, bombing raids had to be stepped up during the course of 1943 and 1944 and reach a peak in the summer of 1944. In order to relieve pressure on the Russians, large amphibious operations would be carried out in those years: their objective would be to disperse and extend German forces from the east and tie them down in other regions of Europe. Once the conquest of North Africa was complete, over half of the British Army would be located overseas, for the large part in the Mediterranean. It was therefore preferable to select that region as the primary theater of Anglo-American operations and to turn it (and especially Italy) into a burden for Hitler. This could be accomplished by conquering Sardinia and Sicily and creating a threat to the southern littoral of Europe. The Chiefs of Staff did not recommend the invasion of Italy proper.[27]

Initially, Churchill's mind was fully occupied by the progress of the Alamein battles and the Allied landings in North Africa (carried out between November 7 and 9). Once those operations had been sucessfully completed, however, he turned his attention to the Chiefs' memorandum and immediately noted the weakness of the strategic line which they proposed. Their passive approach disappointed him; so did their statement that the Russian army was the only force capable of defeating the Wehrmacht. This meant, he wrote, that the Russians would have to bear the principal brunt of the ground fighting when Hitler attacked them for the third time, while the Anglo-American armies sat idle throughout 1943. The conquest of Sicily and Sardinia would not suffice. The Chiefs' plans implied that Germany would not be directly attacked in 1943, and perhaps not even in 1944; but it had been agreed with the Americans that Round-up would be implemented at the end of the summer of 1943 (this was a mistake as in July it had been decided to carry out Torch and in effect to abort Round-up), and he had himself promised as much to Stalin. "There is a prevailing inhibition against facing the Germans anywhere except on the other side of salt water," he complained. He added that it was hardly sensible to say that Round-up would not be carried out, even if circumstances in 1943 did prevent it being so, and at the same time to request the continued transfer of men and equipment from the United States to Britain (Bolero). He considered that the Chiefs of Staff were greatly overestimating the future influence of bombing raids, and wondered what they meant by saying that their object was to "stretch" the Germans. Do we, he ironically inquired, want the Germans to deepen their involvement in the Balkans and in Italy; or do we perhaps want to throw them out of those regions?[28] In any case, his suggestions as to how the Chiefs of Staff ought to alter their memorandum do not support the notion that he intended a massive invasion of France in the summer of 1943. On the contrary, his proposal was that the limited offensive in the Mediterranean advocated by the Chiefs be transformed into a grand offensive: an assault on the Italian mainland from the air as well as by land. Its objectives would be to eliminate Italy from the war, to bring Turkey in, and to test the possibility of cooperation with the Russians in the Balkans and of launching an invasion of southern France.[29]

Matters were aired at meetings Churchill held with his military advisers, some of them also attended by Smuts who was then in London. As an outside observer, Smuts found it difficult to detect any real difference between the Chiefs' positions and the suggestions Churchill had put to them in his memorandum of November 14. During the discussions themselves, Churchill reminded his audience of his promise to Stalin that Round-up, i.e., a "second front," would be launched in 1943. He noted that the Chiefs of Staff's plan might encourage the Americans to invest their resources in the Pacific, and expressed his sorrow that their memorandum was already in American hands. Alan Brooke replied that priority would first be given to setting up a strategic bombing force, and thereafter to the establishment in Britain of a large army whose object would be to enter the Continent when the suitable opportunity for doing so should arise: a premature attempt might prolong the war. Churchill was convinced, and decided that "it was clear that there were no fundamental differences of opinion between the Ministers and their military advisers." He asked them to redraft their memorandum in order to shift its emphasis—they were not to forget that the main points of the document would reach the Russians. It was also agreed that Churchill's own memorandum of November 14, which contains no reference to the implementation of Round-up in 1943, should be passed on to the Americans for review.[30]

Two days later Churchill again changed his mind. He could not, he wrote to the Chiefs of Staff, bear the thought that the Anglo-American military effort would be so limited in 1943; Torch was no substitute for Round-up. He asked the Chiefs to adduce conclusive proof that Round-up could not be implemented in 1943.[31]

The following day, November 19, the Chiefs of Staff received an announcement from Major General Hartle, Deputy Commander-in-Chief of the U.S. Army, European Theater of Operations. This stated that the Americans intended to slow down considerably the pace of their transfer of forces and equipment to Britain in the framework of Bolero. Hartle's announcement complemented earlier information received from the British military mission in Washington, to the effect that, once it had been decided to implement Torch and cancel Round-up, the Americans had begun to accord logistic priority to the Pacific theater.[32] Churchill consulted with the Chiefs and his senior ministers; he then wrote to President Roosevelt, expressing his fear that Bolero would be curtailed and that Round-up might possibly be impaired. He emphasized his support for Round-up and warned that any slowdown in Bolero might even prejudice the chances of carrying out the invasion in 1944.[33] Roosevelt replied that there was no intention of either withdrawing from the plan to invade western Europe or of impairing Bolero. But when Torch had been decided upon, it had been made clear that the operation would have an adverse effect on the concentration of forces in Britain in anticipation of Round-up.[34]

In *The Second World War* Churchill claimed that his message to Roosevelt "should incidentally, but I trust finally, dispose of the many American legends that I was inveterately hostile to the plan of a large-scale Channel crossing in 1943, and, still more, of the post-war Soviet assertions that I used the operation 'Torch' with the deliberate intention of preventing 'a second front in 1943.'"[35] But that was to tell only part of the story. Parallel with Hartle's announcement, Marshall (through Eisenhower and Mountbatten) had informed Churchill and the Chiefs of Staff that he

> would send no more American forces to the United Kingdom over and above the minimum needed for the defence of this island, until such time as the Combined Chiefs of Staff approved an offensive operation from the United Kingdom which did not depend upon a crack in German morale.[36]

In other words, the implementation of Bolero would depend upon a British recognition of the need to carry out the invasion of Europe against strong German resistance. Marshall hoped that by brandishing this threat he might change his partners' attitude; they were eager for U.S. equipment and troops to be transferred to Britain but were not enthusiastic about the Channel crossing, which was the purpose of such movements. The British had several reasons for their intense interest in Bolero. First, the continuation of its implementation at the planned pace ensured that the Americans would retain the priority of the European theater. And as has just been pointed out, Churchill feared that the limited offensive scope of the strategy suggested by his military advisers might encourage the Americans to divert reinforcements to the Pacific, notwithstanding the principle of "Europe first." Moreover, he had expressly told them that it was hardly wise to state that Round-up would not be carried out in 1943 while demanding that Bolero continue as planned.[37]

Second, the concentration of U.S. forces in the United Kingdom afforded British decision makers greater operational flexibility. Kennedy, the Director of Military Operations, wrote that the first stage of Marshall's plan had been "gladly accepted" because it fitted "all eventualities—a landing in Europe, the despatch of expeditions elsewhere, and, in the last resort, the defence of the United Kingdom in case things went wrong in Russia."[38] Churchill revealed his own thinking when describing his joy at the first Washington conference, at which the Americans agreed to his suggestion that they would send divisions to Northern Ireland.

> Every American division which crossed the Atlantic gave us freedom to send one of our matured British divisions out of the country to the Middle East or of course—and this was always in my mind—to North Africa. . . . Mr Stimson, the War Secretary, and his professional advisers also found this move to Ireland in harmony with their inclination to invade Europe at the earliest moment. Thus all went forward smoothly.[39]

The stationing of a U.S. army in the United Kingdom also freed additional British forces for dispatch overseas despite differences with Washington. Should that concentration be correctly apportioned, the forces gathered in the United Kingdom, U.S. as well as British, would still be of a strength to land on the Continent if the Germans were suddenly to collapse; but they would be too weak to mount an invasion against strong German resistance. In August, Lieutenant-General Nye, Alan Brooke's Vice-Chief of the General Staff, feared that a drastic cutback in Bolero—simultaneous with the transfer of additional British forces to the Mediterranean under Torch—would jeopardize the defense of the British Isles.[40] In November, by which time three U.S. divisions had been sent from Britain to North Africa, only two remained there. That situation continued until August 1943.[41] This was too small a force for the British to enjoy all the advantages of Bolero.

Finally, there was Churchill's belief that the best diversion "is a real attack which you subsequently decide not to carry through, the reserves for which are suddenly thrown into quite a different theatre."[42] That German forces were pinned down in western Europe by the presence of Anglo-American troops in the United Kingdom was an argument Churchill often repeated, especially in his communications with the Russians. There was undoubtedly some truth to that claim. But its validity would be impaired if the flow of U.S. forces to the

United Kingdom was decelerated at the same time that British and U.S. forces were being transferred to the Mediterranean. Such an eventuality would also reduce the possibility of camouflaging British strategic intentions in the Mediterranean.

Those considerations, combined with Marshall's threat, impelled Churchill to send Roosevelt ardent messages of support for Round-up. Even had Bolero proceeded as planned, there was little chance that Round-up could be carried out in 1943 against a German army that had not collapsed. Thus, even if at this stage Churchill did begin to have second thoughts about the nature of Round-up, he found himself sharing the Chiefs of Staff's concern about the fate of Bolero. The latter, after all, had already explicitly determined that Round-up ought to be implemented in *1944*, and only after a substantial dislocation of German power. Hence, and contrary to Churchill's claim, his message to Roosevelt does not prove that he supported a massive invasion of western Europe in 1943 while the German army was still intact.

On the day after he had dispatched his message to Roosevelt, Churchill estimated that strategic bombing and amphibious attacks on Italy would generate a revolution and internal collapse in that country, leading to the establishment of a government that would seek peace with the Allies. Nations defeated in war, he believed, take unexpected steps—as had Bulgaria in 1918. Should an Italian revolution indeed materialize, the Germans would prefer to withdraw to the Brenner Pass rather than conquer Italy and rule over a hostile population.[43] The assessment of German intentions in the event that Italy would leave the war, and the implications of that assessment for the formation of Anglo-American strategy, constituted an important and frequently recurring issue.

A meeting of the Defence Committee was held on November 29. Churchill agreed with the Chiefs of Staff that the British had to reject the American opinion that in 1943 attention should be concentrated on Round-up and not, once the conquest of North Africa was complete, on the continuation of additional operations in the Mediterranean. He approved their amended memorandum on future strategy, the change in which was largely cosmetic. The Chiefs of Staff continued to maintain that in the current year Anglo-American efforts should concentrate on the attrition of Germany and on operations in the Mediterranean designed to force Italy out of the war. At Churchill's request, the general tone of the reference to the future invasion of western Europe was now made more favorable. It is to be noted that, at this stage, the Chiefs believed that indirect pressure would do to bring about Italy's exit from the war. They did not want a land campaign on the Italian peninsula proper, because they feared it might give rise to complications and impose an unnecessary burden on the Allies.[44]

Churchill's opinions were as changeable as a weather vane. On the very same day, he wrote to the Chiefs of Staff that he found their attitude unacceptable, since it implied that no "second front" would be opened in 1943. In his opinion, once the conquest of Sardinia or Sicily had been completed in June

1943, Round-up could be implemented in August or September. He argued that Germany's defeats in the east had transformed the situation—the Germans would no longer be able to effect the speedy transfer of their forces from east to west.[45] In part, Churchill was influenced by the intelligence estimates that had been circulated at the end of 1942. Late in November, the German Sixth Army had been surrounded and cut off in the region of Stalingrad, and at the beginning of December the Joint Intelligence Committee presented a dismal picture of Germany's situation. The state of its oil reserves was "critical" and its manpower shortage severe. Morale was on the wane and several of the portents were similar to those that had preceded the German collapse in 1918. However (it was added), dread of the Gestapo might prevent a collapse. The committee estimated that Hitler would not sign a separate peace with either the Soviet Union or the western Allies. It was also true that there was little about which Hitler and Stalin could possibly agree. Nevertheless, Stalin might seek a separate peace were no Anglo-American activity on a large scale to take place in 1943. The committee emphasized the importance of not easing pressure on Germany. Should Italy collapse, Hitler would be unable to defend that country and the Balkans simultaneously. He would prefer to retreat to the Alps in order to retain the Balkans, to which he would attach greater importance. This was because of both that region's natural resources and that he might avert a threat to his lines of communication with the Russian front.[46]

On December 3, the issue was again thrashed out. Churchill repeated that in 1943 the Russians would again stand alone against the Wehrmacht, even though he had promised Stalin that a "second front" would be opened in that year. He argued that the strength of the German army in France had been overestimated—a simple numerical count of divisions was no real gauge; once the invasion was launched it would prove to be less awesome than feared. Alan Brooke and Portal reminded Churchill that in July, when the decision to launch Torch had been taken, it had been agreed with the Americans that the 1943 campaign would possess the character of "a defensive encircling" and that Round-up would not be executed. Churchill replied that he had never accepted that position, but had envisioned a large-scale offensive in 1943.[47] Brooke continued to claim that at none of the meetings he had attended during the Moscow visit had Churchill ever given any promise to Stalin about opening a "second front" in 1943. (In his memoirs, Brooke maintained that any such promise, if made, could only have been given during the final meeting with the Soviet dictator, held late at night and which Brooke himself did not attend. The truth is that the promise was given when Churchill first met Stalin at the Kremlin on August 12. It is recorded in the transcript, which also shows that Brooke was not present.[48] The CIGS himself was careful not to tie his country down by any such assurance.) Brooke explained to Churchill that the chances of entering the Continent and overcoming German resistance were not good, although U.S. forces had to be concentrated in the United Kingdom in order to exploit internal developments. Clement Attlee, the Deputy Prime Minister, supported the

Chiefs of Staff. When he wound up the meeting, Churchill remained unconvinced.[49]

Fundamental to the position adopted by the Chiefs of Staff was the assessment that it would be impossible to prepare for and implement Round-up in 1943, and at the same time augment the "Mediterranean strategy." They estimated that even if the Mediterranean campaign were to be frozen in 1943 and priority for that year accorded to Round-up, the invasion force concentrated in the British Isles would amount to about twenty-five divisions (according to later estimates, only between twenty-one and twenty-four divisions)—which would be insufficient to carry out the assault and far smaller than the forty-eight divisions laid down in Marshall's plan. Should the Mediterranean campaign be continued, Allied forces could be transferred home from that theater beginning in May 1943, and by September of the same year about twenty-one invasion divisions would be available (according to later estimates, only sixteen to eighteen divisions). In other words, in both cases the force concentrated in the British Isles would only be adequate if the Germans were to collapse or the Wehrmacht became drastically weakened. The Chiefs therefore thought it preferable to intensify the "Mediterranean strategy"; to do so would keep up the pressure on Germany and deny it the possibility of recovering at what seemed to the Chiefs a critical juncture.[50]

In order to buttress these logistic considerations, Alan Brooke repeated (at various forums) the argument that the Germans were capable of speedily transferring large forces from east to west; on the other hand, their poor lines of north-south communications would impede and slow down the flow of their reinforcements to Italy. This situation underlined the advantages of a strategy based on eliminating Italy from the war; it also opened up the possibility of entering the Balkans.[51] What is surprising about these calculations is the narrowness of the numerical difference between the two cases: while twenty-five divisions would be concentrated in Britain if priority were accorded to Round-up, twenty-one would be thus situated even if it were decided to begin their transfer from the Mediterranean only in May. Churchill himself questioned the validity of these calculations, reminding the Chiefs of Staff that in 1918 the Americans had transferred some two million troops to France within the space of five months.[52]

During the course of December the Americans clarified their position on future strategy. They maintained that no further operations should be undertaken in southern Europe after the conquest of North Africa. The Mediterranean would be opened to shipping under air cover supplied from the African coast. Efforts would be concentrated on transferring troops from North Africa and the United States to the United Kingdom in preparation for an assualt on western Europe in 1943. Marshall still thought that it would be impossible to implement Round-up in 1943. What he had in mind was a limited move on the lines of Sledgehammer, whose objective would be to establish a bridgehead on the Contentin (Cherbourg) peninsula as an overture to the main invasion in 1944.[53]

On December 15 Sir A. Clark-Kerr, Britain's ambassador in Moscow, met with the Chiefs of Staff in London. He informed them that Stalin was anticipating an Anglo-American invasion in 1943 involving, as he had been assured, a force of one million men. Portal replied that the Continent could not be entered until the Russians had defeated the Germans. Brooke explained that the invasion of France was ancillary to the Mediterranean campaign; its implementation was dependent on reasonable prospects of success. An invasion on the order that Stalin desired, a force of one million men, was "a physical impossibility." This was a surprising argument since Marshall's plan, to which Brooke had agreed in principle, did indeed call for one million U.S. troops to be in the United Kingdom by May 1943. Moreover, Churchill had recalled that fact during his visit to Moscow, when he had promised Stalin a "second front" in 1943.[54]

By this time, however, Churchill had several reasons for closing ranks with his military advisers. Among his considerations were the imminence of the Anglo-American meeting at Casablanca, the sluggishness of progress in North Africa, and the "threat" implied in the U.S. opposition to further operations in the Mediterranean. The Prime Minister now said that a "Mediterranean strategy" was to be preferred until the Americans could provide more optimistic logistic assessments about the possibility of implementing Round-up. He informed the Chiefs of Staff that the object of his request that they reevaluate the possibility of carrying out Round-up in 1943 had been "to ensure that both lines of strategy were fully explored." But the assault in the Mediterranean basin had to be on a larger scale. Sicily had to be conquered and a landing effected in southern Italy. The goals would be to force Italy out of the war, to prepare the base for an entry into the Balkans, and to ensure that Turkey joined the Allies.[55] Thus, the primary difference between Churchill's outlook and that of his Chiefs of Staff on the eve of the Casablanca conference boiled down to one issue: whereas the Prime Minister considered it necessary to invade the Italian peninsula, his advisers still believed that Italy could be eliminated from the war by indirect means.

Once he sensed that he had Churchill's final agreement to the Chiefs' position, Alan Brooke gave instructions to draft the documents on future strategy. His order was to be carried out in such a way as to ensure that cross-Channel operations would be placed third in order of importance—after the expansion of the assault in the Mediterranean and the enlargement of the Anglo-American strategic bombing force in the United Kingdom.[56] But at the end of December, Churchill sounded his last notes: he again asked his military advisers to investigate whether action would be possible simultaneously in both the Mediterranean and in western Europe.[57] Alan Brooke's nerves, which had never been very strong, were torn to shreds by the Prime Minister's vacillations; he turned Churchill down flat.[58] Churchill asked General Ismay to ensure that the memorandum of December 3, containing his argument that Round-up had to be implemented in August and September of 1943, would be restricted to the inner circle in Britain—and not even be passed on to the British military mission in Washington.[59] As always, Churchill took care to conceal from the Americans the existence of internal disputes between himself and his military advisers whilst ensuring that—through information received via his military mission in Washington—he himself enjoyed the advantages of his knowledge of parallel differences within the U.S. hierarchy. This was to be an important factor during the deliberations at Casablanca.

The Casablanca conference opened on January 14, 1943. Churchill and the Chiefs of Staff arrived more or less in agreement, but their U.S. colleagues were relatively unprepared. There existed no full coordination among the U.S. Chiefs of Staff themselves, or between them and President Roosevelt. Churchill was quick to exploit this opening. True, the position adopted by the U.S. military representatives was clear: once North Africa had been conquered, attention had to be concentrated on Bolero-Round-up and on a limited assault to establish a bridgehead on the French coast in 1943. But strategic circumstances prevented them from sticking to that position. The campaign in North Africa had become bogged down. As a last desperate measure, Hitler had rushed 100,000 men to Tunis; and during the course of December it became apparent that the conquest of the entire North African littoral would take longer than expected. These developments made Alan Brooke's and Churchill's work at Casablanca less difficult than they had anticipated.

When the Combined Chiefs of Staff conferred, Alan Brooke repeated all the arguments that had been raised in London in favor of a "Mediterranean strategy." Even should there be signs of a German collapse, he would still be pessimistic about the possibility of attacking in western Europe. This was because the conquest of Sicily or Sardinia would create a shortage of landing craft and crews, which it would be difficult to bring back in time. Marshall and King went to the root of their difference in outlook with their British colleagues: as articulated in Bolero-Round-up, the Americans possessed a clear plan that envisioned defeating Germany by a massive land campaign in Europe. Did the British possess a general, sequential plan, or was their outlook predicated solely on the exploitation of opportunities as they arose? Admittedly, it did seem logical to conquer Sicily once all of North Africa was in Allied hands, since that move would utilize the forces in any case located in that region. But how would it contribute to the defeat of Germany and what would be its sequel? In an attempt to refute Brooke's argument that the Germans could swiftly transfer large forces from east to west, Marshall again said that Anglo-American air superiority would preclude that possibility. He warned of the dangers inherent in dispersing resources on diversionary actions which departed from the main moves; they would act as a "suction pump." An expansion of amphibious operations in the Mediterranean would use up a considerable proportion of available landing craft; some would be put out of action and it would be difficult to transport the remainder to Britain in time.

Alan Brooke replied that it was Russia that would have to bear the main brunt of the fighting on land; the Anglo-American contribution would necessarily be slight until there were definite signs that Germany was weakening. Provided that German strength considerably declined, some form of action in northern France might be possible in the autumn of 1943. For those reasons, the Anglo-American effort had to concentrate on pinning down German forces to the Mediterranean region. At the same time, Brooke emphasized his opposition to a land assault on Italy proper, since it "might only immobilise a considerable force to no useful purpose." Portal sharpened the British view. He argued that no detailed plan for Germany's defeat could possibly be outlined. He pointed out the severe difficulties already confronting Germany, especially its chronic shortage of oil. Aerial bombardments would severely impair its industrial capability and the morale of its citizens. Moreover, "it seemed fairly certain that a point would be reached at which Germany would suddenly crack." Portal and Dill maintained that such an eventuality might reasonably be expected to occur in 1943. Alan Brooke argued "that the precarious internal situation of Germany might make it possible to achieve a final victory in the European theatre before the end of 1943." Reading the minutes, one can almost see the looks of disbelief on the faces of Marshall and King. Admiral King replied that he was very skeptical whether Germany would be beaten before 1944. It could only be defeated by a direct military operation; no reliance could be placed on a collapse of German morale. The United States and Britain could not afford a lengthy delay in the assault on Germany. Besides all else, failure to open a "second front" would anger the Russians. He suggested an attack on northern France even before 1944.[60]

Although Churchill entirely supported the position adopted by his military advisers, the categorical manner in which they had presented it to the Americans caused him some unease. He admitted to them that he adopted the attitude of a "residuary legatee" to the question of carrying out an operation such as Sledgehammer in 1943. Nevertheless, the British had to show greater readiness to implement it should suitable circumstances arise.[61] He believed that Britain's agreement to an operation of that sort might tempt the Americans to acquiesce in the conquest of Sicily, which was the next step he desired. It was in accordance with that approach that he avoided telling them that he wanted to invade Italy once the conquest of Sicily was complete.

Churchill was not called upon to employ all his powers of persuasion to win the Americans' agreement to expand the "Mediterranean strategy." Roosevelt kept a certain distance from his Chiefs of Staff. Marshall himself arrived at Casablanca convinced that Round-up could not be executed in 1943. He calculated that the choice lay between two options: one was an operation on the lines of Sledgehammer at the end of 1943, to be carried out subsequent to a sizable period of military inactivity on land after the conquest of North Africa had been completed; the other was the immediate continuation of Mediterranean operations. He was convinced that it was preferable to conquer Sicily, since the troops were in any case stationed in the region. The large savings in shipping thus effected would enable considerable naval efforts to be directed toward eliminating the German threat in the Atlantic. Moreover, once Sicily was taken, the Italians would be more likely to opt out of the war. Marshall stressed that the conquest of Sicily would preclude a limited landing in northern France during the current year. He noted that more forces would participate in the first assault wave on Sicily than were supposed to take part at a similar stage of the planned invasion of France.[62] (The number of landing craft employed during the first wave of the invasion of Sicily did indeed exceed that used on June 6, 1944, in Normandy. This demonstrates that there did exist in 1943 enough amphibious vessels for assaults on the scale originally envisioned by Round-up, but most were simply not in the correct theater.)[63]

The U.S. and British Chiefs of Staff agreed, then, on the following points: that victory in the Battle of the Atlantic was to constitute the primary objective in 1943; that Sicily was to be conquered in order to open the Mediterranean to shipping and step up pressure on Italy; and that bombing raids on Germany were to be intensified. Bolero would continue, but the Allies would enter the Continent only in the event of a German collapse or if the Germans transferred large numbers of forces from the west.[64]

The results of the Casablanca Conference constituted a victory for the British strategic line. [65] The Americans had been officially harnessed to the "Mediterranean strategy" that Churchill had initiated at the end of 1940; for the time being it was given priority over the invasion of western Europe. The Channel crossing had been deferred and no new target date, other than an innocuous reference to 1944, had been specified for that operation. Nevertheless, it would be incorrect to describe the conference as a decisive stage in the formation of Anglo-American strategy. The die had in fact been cast in 1942, *after* approval in principle had been given to Marshall's plan, when it had been decided to forego the implementation of Round-up and to carry out Torch in 1943 instead. The main impetus for that decision had been the momentum generated by the strategic tendencies created by the steps Churchill and his advisers had taken in 1940 and by the British failures of the spring of 1941.

■

As has been seen, at the end of 1942 Churchill was of two minds about the nature of strategy for 1943; he was particularly perturbed by the question of the invasion of France in that year. Although the Chiefs of Staff considered the issue to have been closed once the decision on Torch had been made in July 1942, a number of reasons combined to persuade Churchill to open it once again. First, there was the assurance which he had given to Stalin during his visit to Moscow in August 1942, to the effect that a "second front" would be opened in 1943. No less important was keeping his reputation for integrity in the eyes of the Americans, who had begun to suspect the intentions of the British after they had refused to implement Sledgehammer. Information from

Washington indicated that the Americans, quite apart from questioning the ability of the British Army itself, were indeed distrustful of the British direction of the war, which they suspected was designed to serve British interests. The same sources also reported the Americans' hope that the establishment of a large army would enable them to acquire full control over the conduct of the war, and even to impose a "pax americana" at Britain's expense when it was over.[66] Compared to the Prime Minister, the Chiefs of Staff were less sensitive to these considerations.

Second, at the end of 1942 Churchill received intelligence assessments, some of them already mentioned, which indicated the weakness of the Wehrmacht. General von Thoma, whom the British took captive after the Alamein campaign, reported that most of the 180 German divisions operating in the east were in effect only at brigade strength.[67] Furthermore, Ultra decrypts revealed that, with the commencement of operation Torch, the Germans had diverted eleven of the thirty-nine divisions they had stationed in the Low Countries and northern France to the conquest of southern France. (Nevertheless, the official historian of British intelligence believes that Churchill's assurance to Stalin constituted his main reason for requesting a reassessment of Round-up.)[68] To this must be added the fact that (despite some very tense moments) success had been secured at Alamein and that Torch had got under way. These developments inspired in Churchill some confidence (albeit not very much) in Britain's military ability—a confidence that, as will be seen, had been strongly undermined by the earlier failures in Greece, North Africa, and Malaya.

Third, Churchill almost invariably attributed supreme importance to the land struggle against Germany in western Europe. Considering that to be what he called "the main theatre," and on occasion "the decisive theatre," the accorded it a priority that outweighed all the other peripheral theaters in which he took some interest. But the fall of France had played havoc with his order of priorities. The fighting on the Mediterranean periphery, which he had at the outbreak of the war considered to be only complementary to the western European front, had become the main theater of ground operations. One reason was the march of events; another was his insufficiently considered determination to transfer there the *greater portion* of the British Army. More important, however, was the influence exerted by the failures in that region. As soon as there existed a glimmer of hope that the knot of entanglements in the Mediterranean basin was beginning to be unraveled at the end of 1942, it was only natural that Churchill should have turned his thoughts to the possibilities of future action in western Europe.

What upset Churchill's attempt to return to his old "continental" attitude was something deep, the full nature of which will be clarified below. He found it difficult to realign an order of priorities that had become reversed. In the past, he had considered the peripheral theaters in northern and southern Europe only supplementary to the "main theater" in the west. Now, however, it was solely on condition that operations in the Mediterranean theater would remain unaffected in the future that he was prepared to revive what Alan Brooke, in a phrase heavy with meaningful associations, termed the "Western Front conception."[69] During the course of his disputes with his military advisers, Churchill did not argue that an invasion, or even such a limited operation as Sledgehammer, had to be attempted at the expense of freezing operations in southern Europe. In other words, and even if we adopt the most flexible of all possible interpretations, he did not place a Channel crossing in 1943 at the very top of his list of priorities. Rather, and at the most, it held a position parallel to the expansion of the war in the Mediterranean in that year. But, as has been seen, such a strategic line was impossible in 1943. Furthermore, his attitude toward the nature of Round-up was in this period unclear. In October, it has already been noted, he wrote that Round-up would be carried out only after Germany had been sufficiently demoralized.[70] Thereafter, he never explicitly stated that he wanted to invade western Europe in order to defeat the Wehrmacht, even if German resistance would be significant. Kennedy, the Director of Military Operations, doubted whether the Prime Minister did indeed intend that the Continent had to be invaded while the German army was still intact. All Churchill wanted, he believed, was that his military advisers repeatedly check their data and conclusions in preparation for the meeting with the Americans.[71] It will be remembered that a bemused Dill had, at the end of December, asked London to clarify the intentions behind the code name Round-up.[72] At all events, in mid-December Churchill reverted to the position adopted by his military advisers; during the course of the Casablanca conference his attitude toward even such a limited operation as Sledgehammer was that of a "residuary legatee." It would therefore seem incorrect to claim, as does Professor Howard, the official British historian, that what he calls the "Autumn Debates" entirely invalidates the argument that throughout the war Churchill consistently accorded the Mediterranean strategy priority over any other strategic line.[73]

In *The Second World War* Churchill claimed that "no one could forsee at this time that Hitler would make his immense effort" and despatch to Tunis a force of 100,000 men (elsewhere the number he cites is 200,000) in order to check the Anglo-American invasion. That move delayed the conquest of all of North Africa from the end of 1942 to the beginning of May 1943. It was this delay, he writes, that was responsible for the fact that, as the Americans had forseen, Torch was ultimately carried out at the expense of Round-up in 1943. It was also thus that the invasion of western Europe, which Churchill claims he ardently desired in the summer of 1943, was delayed until 1944. But matters eventually turned out for the best. Hitler's decision to defend Tunis was a serious strategic mistake. The troops which he transferred to North Africa could have been employed to attack with greater strength in the east or to reinforce Germany's front against the planned invasion of the west in 1943. "I am sure now," Churchill wrote, "that even if Operation 'Torch' had ended as I hoped in

1942 ... the attempt to cross the Channel in 1943 would have led to a bloody defeat of the first magnitude. ... I became increasingly conscious of this during the whole of 1943."[74]

The first part of that argument is very shaky. The British Chiefs of Staff also maintained that, were Torch to be carried out, Round-up could not be implemented in 1943; that too was their position even before the delay in the conquest of North Africa had become apparent. Even if the Chiefs' calculations were grossly inaccurate, their forecast was bound to come true. One reason lay in the steps they took when (at the Prime Minister's urging) they decided on Torch instead of Sledgehammer. No less important were the steps (such as serious preparations for the invasion) that they did not take because of that decision. It will be recalled that Churchill had supported his case for canceling Sledgehammer and promoting Torch with the argument that the constantly changing face of war diminishes the importance of long-term calculations. But one who adopts that position cannot attempt to explain away his own failure by citing an unexpected move by his adversary. Besides, another unexpected development took place—the Germans did not collapse in 1943.

When the Casablanca conference ended, Churchill traveled to Turkey with the object of convincing that country's leaders to bring it into the war; but he failed.[75] After the conference, there was something of an intermission in joint strategic discussions. The commanders of the Anglo-American forces were occupied with the destruction of the Axis troops in North Africa and with preparations for the invasion of Sicily, which for the time being was the largest Anglo-American operation contemplated for 1943.

On January 10, 1943, the Russians launched their final assault on the German force trapped at Stalingrad. On January 18 the German siege of Leningrad was temporarily relieved. On January 31 the German Sixth Army at Stalingrad surrendered. On February 8 the Russians conquered Kursk and on February 16 they took Kharkov.

These victories influenced the intelligence estimate circulated in London in mid-February. The only surprising aspect of the document is that its conclusions undermined some of the arguments Alan Brooke and Churchill had deployed at Casablanca. The members of the Intelligence Committee thought that the Germans had lost the initiative in the campaign in the east and that they were now retreating in disarray. They doubted whether Germany could again reverse the tide. They maintained that the complement of the German garrisons in Europe was dangerously low. Most of the thirty-four divisions stationed throughout France and the Low Countries were inferior in quality. The Germans possessed no central reserve; they would find it difficult speedily to transfer sizable forces to France, especially in view of the pressure being exerted on them in the east. (One month previously, Alan Brooke and Churchill had cited Germany's ability to rush forces from the eastern front to the west as the danger to an invasion in 1943. But Russian pressure on the Germans had not then been any lighter.) The Intelligence Committee also took note of the emergence of groups hostile to the Nazi regime within Germany's armed forces and civilian population. The Chiefs of Staff endorsed the memorandum's conclusions, although they did add that they considered them to be somewhat optimistic.[76]

A few days after the appearance of this intelligence assessment, Churchill reminded Alan Brooke that it would be a mistake to evaluate the comparative strengths of competing armies simply by enumerating their respective divisions. He asked that henceforth, in addition to collating the numbers of divisions, comparisons also be made of the total number of troops, including the combatants in the respective units. He had before him a document discussing the numerical strength of the Wehrmacht; this showed that the functioning of each German division depleted Germany's available manpower by a sum total of 20,000 troops—a figure that included those service troops who did not actually constitute part of the division but who were directly or indirectly associated with it ("gross division" or "division slice"). In the British and U.S. armies, the numbers were 41,000 and 43,000, respectively.[77] Churchill, Lindemann, his scientific adviser, and Military Intelligence had some sharp exchanges at the end of 1942 and the beginning of 1943 about the actual size of a German division (i.e., the ratio between combatants and service personnel). This was consequent to the Prime Minister's continued criticism of the fact that the service "tail" of British units was too long. Analyses conducted after the war show the proportions to have been roughly as follows: a German division numbered about 11,000 troops out of a "division slice" of 19,000 men (58 percent); a British division about 15,500 out of 41,000 (38 percent); and a U.S. division some 15,500 out of 37,000 (42 percent). At the beginning of 1943 the complement of a German armored division was 167 armored vehicles, inclusive of tanks, while a U.S. division possessed 390 tanks, and other armored vehicles, and a British division 278 tanks and additional armored vehicles. In other words, the "on-paper" strength of a German armored division was only one-third of a British or U.S. division. In fact, the gap was even wider. In the period 1943–1944 German infantry and armored divisions were "thinned out" and thereby reduced to far below their nominal complement, while those of the western Allies were maintained at full strength and also had the benefit of a store of continuous replacements in equipment and personnel. British intelligence began to notice these facts at the end of 1942. Ultra provided a particularly clear picture of the location and strengths of German divisions. Ironically, no clear picture existed of the strength and deployment of the Russian divisions, both because Ultra provided no information and because the Russians were not eager to volunteer any.[78] The reader must bear these differences in mind when comparisons are later discussed. In his own work Churchill did not always follow the advice he had himself given to Alan Brooke. When he thought that the methodology would buttress his case, he on several occasions simply drew up a comparative count of division numbers.

In any case, the most recent intelligence estimates did not encourage

Churchill and the Chiefs of Staff to reconsider the quality of the decisions taken at Casablanca. On the contrary, two days after the appearance of the last estimate, Churchill asked his advisers to recheck—under conditions of strictest secrecy, an order probably intended to prevent a leak to the Americans—the possibility of carrying out Jupiter instead of Sledgehammer in 1943.[79] Early in March he argued that there was no point in expanding the special staff for the planning of the invasion of Europe, whose establishment had been decided upon at Casablanca. This was because there were hardly any U.S. forces in the British Isles, and none were due in the near future. Brooke agreed, and the appropriate orders were issued.[80]

Meanwhile, what the U.S. and British planners had already suspected during the Casablanca discussions now became clear to them: that the invasion of Sicily (Husky) would require the use of all existing landing craft, including those employed for training in Britain. Hence operation Sledgehammer, the capture of a bridgehead on the French coast—which had in any case not been decided upon at Casablanca—could not be carried out in 1943.[81]

At the beginning of April Churchill wrote to the Chiefs of Staff that he was not prepared to make do with the conquest of Sicily alone. Sicily constituted a springboard, not a self-contained objective. The next step had to be an assault on Italy proper. This was an extension of the line which he had maintained prior to Casablanca. Should the Germans prefer not to enter Italy, then it would collapse and the Allies would have to advance northward and meet the Germans at the Brenner Pass or on the French Riviera. Should the Germans elect to defend Italy with a force just large enough to prevent its collapse, the Allies would have to establish a hold on the heel and toe of the Italian peninsula, with the objective of reaching Naples and Rome. This move would also enable them to establish a foothold on the Dalmatian coast and thereby provide assistance to the Albanian and Yugoslav resistance. However, should the Germans choose to dispatch large numbers of troops to Italy, no invasion of the peninsula was to be attempted. Instead, efforts were to be made to capture the Dodecanese and to bring Turkey into the war.[82] The Chiefs of Staff responded that they had never thought that the conquest of Sicily would mark the culmination of operations in the Mediterranean during the current year. Their own estimate was that Italy would remain in the war and that, once Sicily was taken, the Germans would prefer to defend the peninsula with only limited forces. In that case the best course would be to establish a bridgehead in southern Italy and to advance northward.[83] This reply contradicted the information Alan Brooke had given his U.S. colleagues at Casablanca when, it will be recalled, he had argued that the British had no intention of invading Italy since such a move would only impose a heavy burden on the Allies. To judge from the position he and his colleagues adopted during the "Autumn Debates" with the Prime Minister, it can only be assumed that such had indeed been his true attitude during the Casablanca talks. Only subsequently did he change his mind.

On April 13 Churchill had a meeting with the Chiefs of Staff. He was somewhat surprised to learn that the conquest of Sicily would require so many landing craft that even those located in Britain would have to be sent to the Mediterranean. That, he said, had not been made clear during the Casablanca discussions; it meant that Sledgehammer would not be carried out in the current year. Alan Brooke reminded him that all had agreed at Casablanca that, in view of the shortage of landing craft, the implementation of Husky would preclude any cross-Channel operation of a scope above two brigades. Brooke added that the landing craft to be dispatched to the Mediterranean were not intended only for the conquest of Sicily; they would also be employed to exploit any consequent developments that might occur—in other words, an invasion of Italy. Any disappointment Churchill might have felt was well concealed, because he agreed that the conquest of Sicily and the exploitation of subsequent opportunities were to be preferred to implementing Sledgehammer in 1943.[84] His instructions were that, since Sledgehammer would not be put into operation during the current year, the tempo of Bolero was to be slowed down. Nevertheless he ruled that the latter operation was not to be brought to a complete halt; instead, the concentration of U.S. forces in Britain should continue. One reason was to prepare "for an overseas campaign in 1944"; another was to deceive the Germans and thereby pin them down in western Europe. At the same time he again asked that an examination be made of the possibility of carrying out Jupiter in January 1944.[85]

It was around this time that another intelligence estimate was circulated, dealing with German intentions during the current year and possible developments in Italy. The members of the Intelligence Committee considered that the Germans would in the spring open a limited assault in the region of Kursk-Kharkov on the Russian front. This move would be intended solely to improve their strategic position, since they were no longer capable of defeating Russia. Germany would assist Italy provided that it remained in the war, and it would be possible to defend it with a German force of no more than six divisions. Were Italy to collapse, the Germans would prefer to evacuate the country. Only thus might they retain the Balkans, to which they attached more importance, and replace the many Italian divisions that presently constituted a Balkan garrison. Alan Brooke concurred with that assessment, adding that in his opinion the Germans would also establish a strategic reserve.[86] Nevertheless, the Chiefs of Staff were wary of becoming infected with the whiff of overoptimism that permeated the estimates presented by the Joint Planners and Intelligence. Preparations had also to be made for an alternative possibility: that the landings on the toe of Italy might not bring about an Italian collapse and a consequent German withdrawal to the Brenner. In that case the development of a deeper military commitment on the Italian front was to be expected. But the dominant opinion was that expressed by Portal (alternatively, that which Churchill had articulated as early as the previous November): the collapse of Italy would force the Germans to withdraw at least to northern Italy. The reasons were that the Germans would not be able, simultaneously, to master the chaos that would ensue after the collapse, to fight the Allies, and replace the Italian divisions in the Balkans.[87]

A few days later Churchill wrote to Marshall. His "present personal view" respecting operations after the conquest of Sicily, he said, did not exceed the establishment of "lodgements" on the heel and toe of Italy, with the object of attaining command of the Adriatic and being in a position to supply the Serbs and Albanians.[88] This message was sent at the very same time that he and the Chiefs of Staff had already reached the conclusion that the best move was to advance northward across the waist of Italy and reach Rome, at least.

At the beginning of May Churchill and his military aides departed for the second Washington conference (Trident). His primary goal was to secure U.S. agreement with the notion that the Italian peninsula be the next objective once Sicily had been taken.[89]

On May 12, Axis forces in North Africa surrendered. During the course of April there was a drastic drop in the number of merchant ships sunk in the Atlantic. During May, which constituted the peak and turning point in the Battle of the Atlantic, some forty German submarines were sunk; at the end of the month, the submarine fleet withdrew from the Atlantic. In June the rate of Allied ships sunk fell to only 5 percent of the March figure—and the Atlantic campaign had been won. But the state of the deployment of Anglo-American ground forces was still far from being one that might gladden Marshall's heart. The forty-eight divisions he had hoped to station in the United Kingdom by May 1943 were still imaginary. Only two American divisions (some 59,000 men) were located in the British Isles; nine divisions (388,000 men) and some thirty-seven Combat Air Groups were situated in North Africa; about sixty-one divisions, most of which had completed their training, were still in the United States itself. At the same time, some thirteen U.S. divisions were in the Pacific.

Of the British forces, roughly 30 divisions, only 19 of which were combat divisions, in May were stationed in the British Isles, while some 29 divisions of the British Army (most of them combat divisions) were located in the Mediterranean region.[90] At about the same time (early June), of the 276 German divisions that could be considered combat units, about 180 were stationed on the Russian front—a figure that included 21 of the 25 armored divisions available to Germany. Roughly 33 divisions (as well as about another 10 that were not combatant) were located in western Europe; some 20 in Norway; about 5 to 6 in Italy; and some 10 in the Balkans. Germany's allies possessed about 22 additional divisions, most of which were stationed in Russia.[91]

The apportionment of Anglo-American forces between the Mediterranean and western European theaters was thus precisely the opposite of what it should have been. That being so, Marshall aimed to prevent the expansion of Mediterranean operations after the conquest of Sicily and to concentrate in the British Isles sufficient forces for a massive invasion of France in the spring of 1944. Time was pressing since preparations for the invasion of France were still in their infancy, even though a decision in principle on that move had been taken in April 1942. Marshall was determined to extract an explicit British commitment to a Channel crossing in the spring of 1944, for which he had the President's full backing. Churchill was confronted with a tough task. This time, the Americans were ready and united.

Churchill met with Roosevelt in Washington on May 11. On the following day, at a meeting attended by many participants, he laid out his position: the main aim for 1943 had to be to force Italy out of the war. He reminded his listeners that in 1918 "the defection of Bulgaria [had] brought the whole of the enemy structure crashing to the ground." Italy's collapse might mark the beginning of Germany's end. Once Sicily had been conquered, the huge Anglo-American armies in the Mediterranean could not be allowed to stand idle. Italy's elimination from the war would divert German forces from Russia in order to replace the Italian divisions in the Balkans; otherwise, Hitler would be compelled to withdraw from that region to the Danube. Such a move would seriously influence the prospects of Turkey joining the war. Landings had to be effected on Italy's toe and heel, whence contact could be established with the partisans active in the Balkans. Churchill emphasized Britain's commitment to an invasion of France in 1944—provided he was presented with a plan that stood a reasonable chance of success. Roosevelt, who had been well coached by Marshall, responded that the entry of large Anglo-American forces into Italy would create complications and play into the Germans' hands. The conquest of Italy might lead to the evacuation of the German forces presently stationed there and their dispatch to the Russian front. He argued that the best course was to make a Channel crossing; what had to be settled was a clear operational plan with an agreed target date.[92]

Without even bothering to conceal their mistrust of British intentions, the Americans wanted to settle matters with regard to an invasion of France in 1944. But Alan Brooke and his colleagues tried to extract a U.S. commitment to a ground operation against Italy. This deepened U.S. suspicions even further. The official British historian's comment on that situation is that it would have been better had the British Chiefs of Staff announced, from the very start, their attachment to an invasion of western Europe in 1944, which they could have "quite sincerely" been able to do.[93] More polished than his military advisers, Churchill did just that. The Americans did not accede to the British request for an invasion of Italy. In practice, however, they did give their general agreement to the continuation of joint operations in the Mediterranean. An understanding was reached whereby an examination of the next steps in that region would be undertaken once Sicily had been taken; the final decision would lie with General Eisenhower, the Supreme Commander of Allied forces in the Mediterranean. Various ideas were put forward. The Americans preferred to conquer Sardinia rather than enter Italy proper. Alan Brooke was prepared to act against Sardinia should it transpire that strong German forces were stationed in southern Italy. His object, as he put it, was to find the most suitable way of eliminating Italy from the war. Churchill did not agree with that position. He insisted on the need to attack the heel and toe of Italy and to step up assistance to the Balkan partisans.[94]

But while nothing had been agreed upon concerning Italy, matters had advanced with respect to the invasion of western Europe. The U.S. and British chiefs of staff decided on May 1, 1944, as a target date for the invasion. By then, twenty-nine Anglo-American assault divisions would be concentrated in the British Isles. Seven experienced divisions (three British and four American) would be transferred to the United Kingdom from the Mediterranean after early November 1943. Nine divisions of the invasion force would be employed during the first stage of the assault; the remaining twenty would tighten the Allied hold on the beachheads and advance inland. Once in France the invasion troops would be reinforced at the rate of three to five divisions per month, which would be transferred from the United States and elsewhere. Churchill expressed his pleasure at the fact that the invasion of France, an operation which he "had always been in favour of," had finally been agreed upon.[95] But he was far from satisfied with the results of the Washington meeting. As soon as it ended, at the end of May, he traveled to Algiers to meet with Eisenhower and his staff. His object was to persuade them to invade Italy. Churchill was, in his own words, determined to attain that goal[96] and he asked that Marshall join him so that a decision could be taken on the spot.

At Algiers Churchill waxed extremely emotional. To Marshall and Eisenhower he admitted how very passionate he was about the prospect of an invasion of Italy. He was, he said, even prepared to cut the British people's rations if to do so would ensure sufficient shipping to conduct the Italian campaign. On this occasion, he explicitly stated that he wanted to advance northward and take Rome.[97] He reiterated the need to provide assistance to the Balkan partisans once the Allies had established a hold on southern Italy. But he left the Americans in no doubt that he did not intend to send troops to the Balkans. Churchill again stressed that point when Eden—who had just arrived from London, without having had the opportunity to coordinate positions with his Prime Minister—raised the possibility that Allied forces might be sent to the Balkans in order to encourage Turkey to enter the war.[98] Not even in Algiers did Churchill convince Marshall and Eisenhower to give their immediate assent to the invasion of Italy as soon as Sicily had been taken; but he did manage to soften their opposition considerably. It was agreed that as early as possible after the landings on Sicily, Eisenhower would come to a decision and recommend to the Combined Chiefs of Staff whether to invade Italy or, alternatively, to conquer Sardinia and Corsica.

In the middle of June Churchill returned to London, where he waited impatiently for the assault on Sicily. He and the Chiefs of Staff continued to exert pressure on the Americans. But in June Eisenhower was still inclined to prefer an attack on Sardinia to one on the Italian peninsula.

On July 5, the Germans launched their massive attack at Kursk. On July 10, the Allies landed on the coast of Sicily. The initial stages of the latter operation seemed to go well; the resistance offered by the Italian garrisons on the island was feeble; Intelligence reported a decline in the morale of the Italian divisions stationed in the Balkans and there were signs of political instability in Italy itself (Mussolini was forced from power on July 25). This cluster of circumstances convinced Marshall and Eisenhower that the anticipated Italian collapse had to be exploited and accelerated by an invasion of the peninsula. The British forecast of developments on the Italian front appeared to be coming true. Even though he discerned signs that German resistance in Sicily was stiffening, on July 18 Eisenhower decided that southern Italy would be attacked as soon as the conquest of Sicily was complete. At the same time, however, the U.S. Chiefs of Staff laid down certain conditions: participation in the Italian campaign would be limited to those forces already stationed in the Mediterranean and there would be no going back on the May agreement on the invasion of France.[99] It was thus that the decision was taken to invade Italy—the "soft underbelly" of conquered Europe.

During and after the discussions in Washington, both the British Chiefs of Staff and Churchill had argued that Italy's exit from the war would result in the diversion of German troops from the Russian front and western Europe; by thus pinning them down in southern Europe, the Italian campaign would help to prepare the ground for the intended invasion of northern France. In the books that they published after the war, both Churchill and Brooke maintained that they had approached the Italian campaign as one of attrition and confinement, designed to serve the *main* move—the massive assault to be launched against western Europe. In Churchill's phrase, it "was the faithful and indispensable comrade and counterpart to the main cross-Channel operation."[100] Brooke claimed that such had been the foundation of "my strategy" in the war, which Marshall, however, had not fully comprehended.[101] That, too, is the explanation the official British history offers for the attitude which the British leadership adopted during the war.[102]

There are sound reasons for questioning the validity of those explanations. It may be wondered whether they do not constitute reconstructions of a strategic conception formulated after the *nature* of the Italian campaign and the *success* of the invasion of western Europe had both become apparent.

In January, the British Joint Planners pondered anticipated developments. Their conclusion was that somewhere between thirty-nine and forty-one German divisions could be expected to be stationed in the west in the spring of 1943. This number would not diminish even were the Germans to elect to renew their attacks in the east; neither would it be affected by whether or not they decided to defend Italy and the Mediterranean basin. Should Italy leave the war and the Germans prefer to withdraw to the Brenner Pass rather than defend the peninsula, the minuscule strategic reserve presently located in Germany would be doubled from seven to fifteen divisions. Nevertheless, the Joint Planners suggested further expanding the "Mediterranean strategy."[103] It will be recalled that at the end of April, when the fighting in North Africa was about to come to an end and the British decision to invade Italy was finally made, British intelligence and Joint Planners had estimated that the Germans would elect to evacuate Italy if it collapsed or left the war. Both Churchill and the Chiefs of Staff agreed that the Germans would most probably prefer to withdraw to northern Italy, or even to the Brenner, since that was the best of their options from a strategic point of view. Alan Brooke maintained that they would also establish a strategic reserve.[104]

Even late in September, some weeks after the invasion of Italy, British intelligence continued to forecast that the Germans would withdraw to a defensive line in northern Italy. Churchill had believed that such would be the course of events even before the Casablanca conference, at a time when his own Chiefs of Staff had objected to the very idea of an invasion of Italy itself. During the second Washington talks he had gone still further, saying that Hitler—once forced to choose between the defense of the Balkans or the diminution of his strength in the east—might also prefer to withdraw to the line of the Danube and the Sava. For his part, Brooke had dismissed Marshall's argument that aerial bombardments would of themselves do to take Italy out of the war. Italy, he said, had to be attacked on land; German opposition would not be stiff. But Marshall still had misgivings. Should the Germans decide to defend Italy, he retorted, their resistance would be very stubborn and the Allied advance would turn out to be a lengthy process.[105] Altogether, Churchill and Alan Brooke thus attempted to coax the Americans toward an invasion of Italy by the somewhat contradictory claim that the Italian campaign would be both easy and diversionary.

In *The Second World War*, Churchill wrote that Hitler's decision to defend every inch of Italy and to retain the Balkans was "a crowning error in strategy and war direction." Instead, he should have established a large strategic reserve that, by exploiting the advantage of interior lines, he could have moved about among the various war fronts.[106] (Altogether, Hitler had a nasty habit of committing enormous strategic blunders by not acting in accordance with Churchill's expectations. Churchill had used similar language to describe the German dictator's unexpected decision to dispatch sizable reinforcements to North Africa at the end of 1942.)[107] If Churchill's above arguments are correct, it is impossible to understand why he and Brooke invested so much effort in encouraging Hitler to establish a strategic reserve—something he had not hitherto done. But that is precisely what their own actions implied. After all, British assessments had themselves indicated that Italy would fall like a ripe fruit, but that Hitler's ability to establish a central reserve would increase. From the British viewpoint, it would be a very serious matter were the strategic reserve *in Germany* to be expanded by eight divisions (which was the figure anticipated by the Joint Planners). At Casablanca, Alan Brooke had tried to buttress his own case against a premature Channel crossing by convincing the Americans that the Germans could rush sizable forces from the *east* to the west; seven divisions, he said, could thus be simultaneously transferred within a fortnight.[108]

Even if Hitler were not to establish a strategic reserve, he could have eased the burdens inherent in defending southern Europe with large forces and made do with much smaller forces that would mount guard over the passes leading from that region into central Europe. To do so would certainly have facilitated his ability to maneuver his divisions between the eastern front and that to be opened in the west.

Prior to the commencement of the anticipated assault on Italy, Hitler had planned to defend his southern flank around Rome and to fight a rearguard action in the southern part of the peninsula. Contrary to British hopes, he had not intended to order a drastic withdrawal to the foothills of the Alps. Developments in the battle for southern Italy were one of the reasons that caused him to change his mind, and he gave orders for southern Italy to be stubbornly defended.[109] A decision by Hitler to withdraw to the north would have been a departure from his behavior throughout the war. He was temperamentally opposed to any withdrawal, even one designed to improve his army's strategic situation, and insisted that every inch of ground be fought for. That, indeed, was one of the main points of disagreement between the Fuehrer and his generals. What is more, that characteristic could not be unknown to those who had been trying to fathom his behavior over the Russian and North African fronts.

An analysis of Churchill's and Alan Brooke's own perspectives and assessments thus makes it difficult to understand how they could have expected to tie down and wear out large German forces in southern Europe by an attack on Italy—and thereby initiate what they claimed to be the preparatory move necessary for the planned assault on western Europe in 1944. Had their forecast indeed materialized, precisely the opposite would have occurred: Hitler's potential ability to frustrate an invasion in the west would have increased. Ironically enough, when Hitler decided to fight for every inch of Italy he endowed the British position with some measure of validity; *in 1944* a large German army was indeed tied down in that region. (What price was paid for that situation is a question that will be discussed below). The British had themselves considered such a development unlikely. But its ultimate occurrence was what enabled Churchill and Alan Brooke to paint a *retrospective* picture of a well-prepared design, comprising several phases, in accordance with which the Italian campaign was supposed to constitute a preliminary and vital stage in the successful invasion of western Europe. As we shall see, it was in fact Germany's stubborn fight for Italy that strengthened Churchill's opposition to carrying out the invasion of France in 1944.[110] That was indeed a strange reaction from someone whose plan had supposedly been vindicated by events.

8
"First Catch Your Hare": The Political Dimension of Strategy

The acid test of a strategist's quality and success lies in his ability to achieve a correct and creative synthesis between war's political dimension (alternatively, its ultimate political goals) and the conduct of military moves. This chapter will therefore focus on the nature of the convergence between Churchill's political conception and aims, on the one hand, and his military plans and operational actions during the course of World War II, on the other.

From the very outset of his prime ministry, Churchill refused to discuss and specify Britain's war aims in the War Cabinet or in Parliament. That was a position to which he held fast, notwithstanding pressures for its modification from various quarters. In May and August 1940 he declared Britain's objectives in the war to be "victory—victory at all costs" and the destruction of Hitler's Germany.[1] Attention, he maintained, had to be concentrated on the military conduct of the war, because the process of determining its aims might generate differences of opinion among the public and the British leadership. In April 1941 Churchill apparently did not even bother to read a long memorandum on Germany's postwar future written by the renowned economist John Maynard Keynes. "As you know," he replied to Eden, who had sent him the document, "I am very doubtful about the utility of attempts to plan the peace before we have won the war." He also questioned the feasibility of forecasting what state of affairs might prevail when the war would come to an end.[2]

Not until the later stages of the war did Churchill deviate from this basic line of thought. Nevertheless, he had hitherto not been averse to indulging in impressionistic and noncommital musings about the postwar world's character and political order. Even while First Lord of the Admiralty in Chamberlain's cabinet, he had suggested that, once peace was attained, efforts be made to establish a supranational body akin to the League of Nations, equipped with its own international court and air force.[3] During the course of a dinner conversation in August 1940, he told Colville, his private secretary, that after the war a body like the League of Nations had to be set up and that "there would be a United States of Europe, and this Island would be the link connecting this

Federation with the new world and able to hold the balance between the two." In response to Colville's inquiry whether he therefore aimed at the creation of a new form of the balance of power, Churchill—evidently discomforted—replied: "no, but at a 'balance of virtue.'"[4] He was only marginally more specific when, without overt enthusiasm, he addressed members of a Cabinet committee which discussed war aims at roughly the same time: what had to be set up was a Council of Europe, comprising federations of northern, central, and southern Europe together with the European powers; an international police force had also to be established. These were vague thoughts. The Prime Minister despised the committee and impeded its work.[5]

Stalin had different ideas about the way to conduct the war. In 1941, when Russia's position was at its most perilous, the Soviet dictator proposed that he and Churchill determine joint war aims and reach agreement on the nature of the peace and the postwar political structure. Churchill rejected the suggestion, saying that these were questions to be left to the peace conference that would be convened after the war.[6] But Stalin refused to let the matter lie. Principally, this was because his concern for European peace acted as a cover for his real aim which—even at this stage—was international recognition of the Soviet Union's borders as they were in June 1941, on the eve of the German invasion. He demanded that Britain officially recognize those borders when Eden visited Moscow in December 1941. In other words, he wanted acquiescence in Russia's 1940 annexation of the Baltic states, its possession of northern Bukovina and of Bessarabia (taken from Rumania), and in the new Russian-Finnish borders drawn at the end of the Winter War. Of course, Stalin also wanted Britain to recognize a new Soviet-Polish boundary; this was to follow the "line" suggested by Lloyd George and his Foreign Secretary, Lord Curzon, in 1920 which ran somewhat east of the positions reached by the Soviet Union at the end of 1939, when it had partitioned Poland with Germany in accordance with the Molotov-Ribbentrop pact. Stalin suggested that, after the war, Poland be shifted westward at Germany's expense, and that the latter's other victims also receive large slices of German territory. He further demanded the establishment of Soviet military bases in Rumania and Finland. Stalin was also interested in reaching an agreement with the British on Germany's future.

From Churchill's and Eden's point of view, the gravity of this situation lay in that Stalin had made the conclusion of any general Anglo-Soviet treaty of alliance conditional on Britain's recognition of Russia's Baltic annexations and its June 1941 boundaries with Rumania and Finland (although not the Curzon Line). True, there was a *quid pro quo*. To help the British digest his demands, Stalin intimated the Soviet Union's readiness to recognize Britain's influence in western Europe; after the war, British military bases would be established in Denmark and Norway; moreover, those parts of the agreement that affected Russia's borders would remain secret.[7] Even before arriving in Moscow, Eden had been in favor of going more than halfway to meet the Russians, but he was prevented from following his inclination to accede to Stalin's proposals because

Churchill and the War Cabinet had forbidden him to formulate an agreement respecting territorial arrangements.⁸ That was why no Anglo-Soviet alliance was concluded during Eden's Moscow visit. Nevertheless, the dilemma Stalin had posed for the British remained and could not be shelved. As we shall see, the manner whereby Churchill and Eden solved the problem of concluding an alliance in effect determined the course of British policy toward the Soviet Union until the war was almost at an end.

Although Churchill had declared his support for the Soviet Union when it was attacked, and despite wishing to assist it in its war against Germany, during the second half of 1941 the Prime Minister did not alter his basic position on the nature of the Soviet regime. As much is apparent from a minor episode that occurred at the end of 1941, which involved his son, Randolph. The latter, then serving in Cairo, had in the course of his duties written a pamphlet entitled "Political Aspects of the War" which was distributed among local British officers. This argued that nazism and communism had much in common and that the great democracies rejected both regimes in equal measure. Randolph added that a joint Anglo-Russian victory over Germany would not enlarge the scope of communist influence in Europe. On the contrary, it would distance even the Russian people from those communist doctrines that had brought them to the verge of catastrophe on the outbreak of war. Copies of the pamphlet fell into Italian hands, and its anticommunist statements provided grist for Germany's propoganda mill. Major-General F.H.N. Davidson, the Director of Military Intelligence, suggested that Churchill take action against the writer.⁹ But Churchill, who identified Randolph's authorship, replied that he fully agreed with the ideas set forth in the text; indeed, he thought they befitted every decent Englishman. Nevertheless, he did note that they were not consonant with current British sentiment toward Russia, and asked that steps be taken to ensure that he was himself in no way publicly associated with them.¹⁰

Initially, Churchill refused to accede to Russia's request that Britain declare war on Rumania, Finland, and Hungary; the first two states in that list, he argued, had been victims of Russian aggression. He only changed his mind when entreated to do so by Eden, who wanted to have something to give to Stalin when he arrived in Moscow.¹¹ Churchill's instinctive reaction was similarly negative when, on Eden's return from Moscow, the latter suggested accepting Stalin's demand that Britain recognize the annexation of the Baltic states. Any statement to that effect, the Prime Minister argued, would contradict the principles of the Atlantic Charter; like Roosevelt, Churchill thought that territorial questions had to be left to the peace conference after the war. Eden had argued that Britain had to recognize the annexation of those territories "irrespective of the wishes of their peoples," because Stalin regarded Britain's concurrence with Russia's 1941 boundaries to be "the acid test of our sincerity." The Foreign Secretary had added that, in any case, neither Britain nor the United States would be able to influence the situation prevailing in the Baltic region at the end of the war. Churchill, however, was not convinced. "No one can forsee how the balance of power will lie, or where the winning armies will stand. It seems probable, however, that the U.S. and British Empire, far from being exhausted, will be the most powerfully armed and economic bloc the world has ever seen, and that the Soviet Union will need our aid for reconstruction far more than we shall need theirs."[12]

Eden did not relent. During the course of January 1942 he worked hard to persuade the Prime Minister and the War Cabinet of the need to conclude an Anglo-Soviet alliance that would be based on Britain's almost complete acceptance of Stalin's demands. Especially important, in this context, is a memorandum he presented at the end of January. Not only did that document express opinions widespread in the Foreign Office; at root, it also articulated the position Britain was to adopt toward the Soviet Union until almost the very end of the war. The basis for Eden's memorandum was a simple argument derived from the principles associated with the concept of the balance of power: once the war had ended and Germany had been defeated, France would be too weak to counterpoise Russia's growing strength in Europe; neither would any other European nation be capable of fulfilling that role. Eden also argued that there existed no surety that Russia would not defeat Germany before the weight of Anglo-American power had made itself fully felt. (On his return from Moscow, he warned the War Cabinet that "it must be remembered that, if we won the war, Russian forces would probably penetrate into Germany and that at a later date she might well want more than her 1941 frontiers.")[13] Should that eventuality materialize, Russia might be tempted to establish Communist regimes in most of the states of Europe. Directly opposing the Prime Minister's position, Eden protested that "it would be unsafe to gamble on Russia emerging so exhausted from the war that she will be forced to collaborate with us without our having to make any concessions to her."

Why then, asked Eden, was Stalin making an Anglo-Soviet alliance conditional on Britain's recognition of his rights to territories he would in any case control should he defeat Germany? The Foreign Secretary's own answer was that Stalin was looking for an assurance that Britain was ready for and committed to postwar cooperation with Russia and that it would not join forces with the United States in order to impose an Anglo-American peace. That was why the recognition of the annexations was for him an acid test of British sincerity. Eden believed that Britain had to aim at the establishment of good relations with Russia; it could attain that goal by immediately accepting Stalin's demands. Moreover, the way to influence Russia's future course of action was to lay the groundwork for an understanding with it now. Stalin would thus be persuaded that by cooperating with the west during and after the war he might achieve advantages greater than those he could hope to obtain by taking unilateral action in postwar Europe. Moreover, a British policy of that sort would also prevent Soviet-German collaboration after the war and thus preclude Germany's revival as a European power.[14]

As January wore on the circle favoring Eden's attitude steadily widened.

Churchill too began to lean toward the Foreign Office's position. When the War Cabinet convened early in February to discuss the subject, Lord Beaverbrook stressed how important it was to accept the Russian demands at the present juncture; Britain might thus acquire Russian cooperation after the war. Sinclair, the leader of the Liberal party (who, although not a member of the War Cabinet, had been especially invited to this meeting), argued that in the event of an Allied victory the territories in question would in any case fall into Russian hands; in order to establish cordial relations with the Russians, it was therefore preferable to accept their demands now. Most ministers agreed. Eden explained that the present problem was to find a mode of acquiescing in the Russian demands which would be acceptable to the United States—which had strongly opposed recognition of Russia's territorial demands. The Prime Minister veered back and forth between his own original position and that suggested by Eden. He did not oppose the stand taken by the Foreign Office and most members of the War Cabinet. But he reverted to his claim that it was not at all clear what the situation at the end of the war would be; the correct course was to leave issues of that sort to the postwar peace conference. Nevertheless, he gave Eden authority to act in order to obtain the United States' agreement to Britain's readiness to accept Stalin's demands.[15]

Roosevelt refused to change his mind, and added that this was a matter on which he could reach independent agreement with Stalin. The British took that statement as a threat to their status. Churchill now moved very much closer to Eden's position. At the end of the month he informed the War Cabinet that U.S. negotiations with Russia would jeopardize Anglo-Soviet relations. Russia was interested in an agreement with Britain; "There was no doubt," he continued, "that Russia regarded this country [i.e., Britain] as of the greatest importance from the point of view of the post-war settlement of Europe, and wanted to work with us after the war." The other members of the Cabinet supported that line, and again emphasized the importance of an agreement with the Russians.[16]

At the beginning of March, Churchill asked Roosevelt to give him a free hand to conclude a treaty with the Soviet Union, even if it entailed bending the principles enunciated in the Atlantic Charter. He justified his request by saying that Russia needed encouragement if it was to withstand Germany's impending assault.[17] British pressures took on a pathetic air when Halifax, the Ambassador in Washington, told the Americans that their obstinancy might result in the establishment in Britain of a procommunist government headed by Sir Stafford Cripps. (At the time, Churchill's standing had suffered something of a setback because of the fall of Singapore and the defeats in Libya.) Despite British entreaties, however, Roosevelt and the State Department would not be moved; they even threatened a public denunciation of any Anglo-Soviet alliance concluded on the lines proposed.[18] At the end of March Churchill and Eden despaired of the possibility of gaining U.S. approval. The War Cabinet reached the conclusion that Britain's position would be prejudiced by a delay in the signature of the agreement with the Russians, whose political demands had to be met. After all, the Soviet Union was bearing the brunt of the fighting and receiving only meager military assistance from Britain. The Cabinet decided that the agreement had to be concluded and, moreover, to incorporate Stalin's territorial demands within its terms.[19]

Clearly, the subject to hand far exceeded the bounds of future Anglo-Soviet relations; in fact, it raised issues that affected the very nature of Britain's future status among the Great Powers in the postwar period. Eden and the senior officials in the Foreign Office hoped to carve out a special international position for Britain after the war by projecting it as both a European and an Atlantic power that could mediate between the Soviet Union and the United States. They thought that diplomacy would enable them to gain that position and thereby halt Britain's decline as a Great Power. Churchill, too, was a party to that aim. As we have seen, he was even at that stage hopeful of transforming Britain into a power that might serve as a link between the old world and the new.[20] But there had been no alteration in Eden's basic conception of the nature of international relations. We have earlier had occasion to remark on the dislocation in his thinking between the diplomatic and political dimensions of events, on the one hand, and their military dimension, on the other.[21] Precisely the same characteristic became apparent in his analysis of British policy toward the Soviet Union. Eden's diagnosis, and even his prognosis, did approximate reality. Indeed several of the predictions he made in 1942 were borne out by the march of events after 1945: Germany's defeat and France's enfeeblement did indeed deprive postwar Europe of its natural balance of power and thereby facilitated an increase in Russia's influence; what is more, Britain was clearly incapable of itself filling the vacuum thus created. Thus that development could have been foreseen as early as the beginning of 1942. But the course the Foreign Secretary chose to deal with the process that he himself expected to occur was hardly correct. His solution to the problem was diplomatic and, in effect, predicated on Soviet goodwill.

Eden appreciated that some price would have to be paid. Indeed he explicitly informed Halifax that, much as Britain appreciated Roosevelt's difficulties, "this country, as a European power for whom collaboration with a victorious U.S.S.R. after the war will be essential, cannot afford to neglect any opportunity of establishing intimate relations of confidence with Stalin." What made those "intimate relations" particularly important was the Foreign Office's suspicion, a suspicion that persisted throughout the war, that the United States might withdraw from European affairs and perhaps not even support Britain against the Soviet Union after the war.[22] But not even that consideration can hide the fact that Eden hoped to cement Anglo-Soviet intimacy by colluding in Stalin's rape of the Baltic states and by offering him concessions whose price would be paid, not by Britain, but by the peoples of eastern Europe. Eden and the senior officials in the Foreign Office anticipated that they might thereby pave the road to joint Anglo-Soviet management of the affairs of postwar Europe. Since a special Anglo-American relationship would also be established, Britain would thus be able to preserve its global status. Diplomatic ingenuity would compensate for economic and military decline. But what Eden did not consider—either then or until almost the end of the war—was the need for Britain, in conjunction with the United States, to embark on a military path capable of halting and containing the influence that the Soviets were expected to exercise in postwar Europe. He failed to appreciate that such a course might have given Britain and the United States a better bargaining position both inside and outside the peace conference, and thereby have enabled them to preclude or minimize their dependence on Russian goodwill. Moreover, he could have adopted that course without prejudicing his basic intention of creating Anglo-Russian understanding.

This line of thought has led some scholars to argue that Eden's policy was nothing but a natural extension of those conceptions held by Britain's ruling elite which had lay behind the policy of "appeasement" toward Germany in the 1930s.[23] Cadogan, an outright anti-Soviet, although he eventually fell in step with Eden and other senior officials in the Foreign Office, also described in his diary his chief's stand vis-à-vis Russia as "appeasement."[24]

Churchill did not accept Eden's prognosis. Mainly, this was because he refused to indulge in political prognoses of any sort at this stage of the war. Another reason was that he was not now convinced of its validity. In practice, however, he implemented—and eventually adopted—Eden's political course. As much became apparent as early as the issue of the Anglo-Soviet alliance.

Once empowered to do so by the Cabinet, Eden during the course of April informed the Russians of Britain's readiness to recognize the annexation of the Baltic states. It was in the light of that information that Molotov prepared to come to London to conclude the details of the alliance. Admittedly, significant objections to Britain's recognition of the Baltic annexations had meanwhile begun to make themselves heard in Parliament where, as Churchill and Eden appreciated, stiff opposition to an Anglo-Soviet alliance on that basis could be expected.[25] (On the other hand, since Rumania and Finland were allied to Germany, Russia's demands concerning those two countries were treated sympathetically; moreover, for the moment, the Russians were prepared to leave the solution of the Soviet-Polish border problem for a later stage.) Nevertheless, when Molotov reached London on May 21 Eden—doubtless with Churchill's sanction—was ready to conclude an Anglo-Soviet alliance on the basis of Britain's recognition of the annexation of the Baltic states. But to the surprise of the British, the Russians raised their price: Molotov categorically insisted that Britain recognize the Curzon line. Even Eden found it difficult to accept that condition—although Cadogan doubted whether the Foreign Secretary's refusal would prove to be long-lasting. The impasse was broken when Eden, at Cadogan's initiative, suggested to Molotov that they conclude an open twenty-year alliance without making any mention of the territorial issue. Surprisingly, and to Churchill's satisfaction, the Russians reversed course and accepted the British proposal.

Why did the Russians retract their demand? Why did they not choose to relinquish their new claim and, instead of expunging the entire territorial issue from the alliance, meanwhile reach a compromise on the basis of Britain's recognition of annexation of the Baltic states?

A hint of the solution to this mystery is contained in the correspondence between Churchill and Eden some eighteen months later, when the subject of the Soviet Union's western borders again arose. The Prime Minister then made mention of "the very strong line I took" early in 1942 against British recognition of Russia's absorption of the Baltic states.[26] But Eden jogged Churchill's memory: as early as the beginning of 1942, he recalled, he (Eden) had believed that Britain had to accept all the Russian demands respecting the Baltic states, Finland, and Rumania. Furthermore,

> His Majesty's Government expressed their willingness to sign a Treaty containing a form of words which, it was agreed, constitute recognition by us of the Soviet claim to the Baltic states. The *draft treaty* then under discussion was not in fact signed, as it was superseded by the twenty years treaty, in which nothing whatever was said about frontiers. *But we are committed to the Soviet Government* on this point in the records of the discussion.[27]

Herein lay the root of the tacit understanding arrived at between the Soviets and the British. It was not a secret agreement, of the sort that Stalin had proposed to Eden in December 1941. Rather, it was a convenient arrangement that—for reasons both alike and dissimilar—in May 1942 suited both parties. British acquiescence is fairly easy to understand. As concluded, the treaty enabled Churchill and Eden effectively to satisfy Russian wishes and attain their own objectives without coming into conflict with the United States.

Russian motives, as is usually the case, are more difficult to penetrate. Feis and Carlton account for the Russian *volte-face* by reference to the fact that Molotov was to travel to Washington after London, and that he and Stalin wished to create an atmosphere of cordiality in advance of that visit. Moreover, cognizant of the impending German attack, the Russians were more interested in obtaining a U.S. promise that a "second front" would be opened in 1942 than in securing recognition of their territorial demands.[28] That explanation is only partial. Stalin and Molotov were aware of both the U.S. attitude and of the impending German assault before Molotov's departure for London and Washington. Their new demand that Britain recognize the Curzon line makes it doubtful whether *at this stage* the Soviets were really interested in an Anglo-Soviet treaty that had any reference to the subject of territories. They knew that the influence exerted by the Polish government in exile and by the U.S. attitude was in any case preventing the British Government, whatever its own wishes might have been, from acquiescing in their demands. Apparently, they sought a middle course. They did not wish to retract their territorial demands and thereby relinquish whatever concessions they had already obtained from the British; neither, however, did they wish to so anger the United States that they might jeopardize the "second front" and U.S.-Soviet relations. By tabling a demand they knew to be unacceptable, the Russians were able to withdraw from their proposition that the alliance was conditional on the territorial issue and thus navigate between this particular Scylla and Charybdis. As a second best, that maneuver would enable them to wriggle out of concluding an Anglo-Soviet alliance before Molotov arrived in Washington.

However much Churchill may have needed Eden's help in refreshing his memory in 1944, it is difficult to imagine that in May 1942 he had been unaware of what was going on. In fact, the situation then prevailing bore distinct affinities with one that had occurred during the previous war. Churchill had not objected when, in 1915, the Russians had specified Constantinople as their postwar demand. But he had suggested postponing the solution of territorial questions until after the war; "in the meanwhile we might signify that we were in sympathy with Russian aspirations." On that occasion Churchill had been overruled by the Foreign Secretary, Sir Edward Grey, who had insisted that an immediate agreement with the Russians on this matter was required if they were to be prevented from reaching a separate peace with Germany.[29] But in 1942 Churchill was free to follow his own course. Accordingly, the Soviets were informed of British "sympathy with Russian aspirations." Stalin's renunciation of his demand for recognition of his annexations of 1940-1941 saved Churchill and Eden considerable embarrassment. It also permitted the Prime Minister to avoid later revealing in *The Second World War* that, notwithstanding the U.S. attitude, the British Cabinet had decided to grant official recognition to the annexation of the Baltic states. Instead, his description of the episode could be, and was, selective and devious. It intimated that what had impressed the Russians, and contributed to their retraction, was "the solidarity of view of the British and American Governments with which they were confronted."[30]

In Washington, Molotov managed to extract from President Roosevelt a public declaration that a "second front" would be opened in 1942. This, however, turned out to be the first of several instances in which Stalin received assurances on that issue that were never kept. Indeed, Roosevelt's promise—to which Marshall objected[31]—was rash and quite devoid of any foundation in the Anglo-American strategy agreed upon before. As will be recalled, the British had already specified their reservations about Sledgehammer, which was originally designed as "an emergency operation" to be undertaken in the event of a Russian or German collapse in 1942. Churchill, at any event, was not now prepared to alter that position. When Molotov returned to London from Washington, the Prime Minister made it absolutely clear to his guest that he could not promise the initiation of a "second front" in 1942, but a massive invasion of western Europe would take place in 1943. During the same meeting, Molotov described Roosevelt's proposal for the postwar establishment of an "international police force," to be staffed by the four Great Powers: Britain, the United States, the Soviet Union, and China. The Axis states would be disarmed, and limitations imposed on the armament of France, Poland, and Rumania.

Molotov said that the Soviet Union entirely agreed with the President's outlook (Russia's enthusiasm is hardly surprising—such an arrangement would grant it the status of a Great Power at a time when a weakened Europe lay at its feet.) Churchill cooled Molotov's ardor. His attitude toward Roosevelt's ideas was one of undisguised scorn. These questions, he stated, had to be left until the peace conference; his own opinion was that "the important thing was to win the victory first rather than, before it was won, to dispute how the advantages were ultimately to be shared."[32]

Churchill journeyed to Moscow early in August 1942. This time it was his turn to give Stalin false promises. A "second front," he told the Russian leader, would not be opened in 1942; but he could assure him that the invasion would be carried out during the following year. By the spring of 1943 about one million U.S. troops would be concentrated in Britain for that purpose. When he got down to operational specifics, Churchill stated that "indeed what had been planned for 1943" were operations that would tie down the German forces opposite the Pas-de-Calais, Cherbourg, and Allied landings at the estuaries of the Loire, the Gironde, or the Scheldt. Stalin doubted whether these plans could be implemented.[33] (Actually, they were not "plans" at all, but only Churchill's private thoughts about the nature of the invasion. Marshall's planning in fact envisioned the invasion taking place between Le Havre and Boulogne). Churchill gave Stalin an assurance which he knew had no foundation. The Prime Minister had already been informed by his own military advisers and the U.S. Chiefs of Staff that the implementation of Torch would preclude an invasion of western Europe in 1943. Furthermore, there existed a written agreement to that effect in the joint memorandum summarizing Marshall's visit to London in July 1942. True, Churchill did himself disagree with that opinion, but he had no authority to give Stalin such a far-reaching promise without first consulting his military advisers, not to speak of the Americans. Churchill had not even coordinated his statement with Alan Brooke before their departure for Moscow.[34] To this must be added his address to a group of senior officers in Cairo, on his way to Moscow. The U.S. Chiefs of Staff, he told that audience, believed that Torch would necessitate the cancellation of Round-up in 1943, but he was himself of the opinion that it would only result in its postponement for three or four months[35] until the summer or autumn of 1943. Churchill did not inform Stalin that the invasion would be delayed; the implication of the words he used during their conversation was that it would be carried out in the spring of 1943.

The Prime Minister was well aware of what he had promised Stalin in Moscow. As much is apparent from his reaction to the Chiefs' strategic plan for 1943, which he received in the autumn of 1942. The plan's declarations that Round-up would not be carried out in 1943, Churchill protested, were "most extreme contradiction to my . . . statements to Stalin in Moscow."[36] As we have seen, his assurance to Stalin influenced Churchill's position in the autumn of 1942, when he disputed strategy with his military advisers. In December of that year, Clark-Kerr, the British Amabassador in Moscow, told the Chiefs of Staff that Stalin had never been informed that Torch would delay or defer the planned invasion of western Europe.[37]

Churchill's promise to Stalin was motivated by the same considerations that had earlier led him to give his agreement in principle to Marshall's plan and that, at a later stage, were to make him argue that the invasion of northern Africa would not be carried out at the expense of that of northern France. He gambled on developments that lay in the distant future in order to secure immediate gains in the present—mollifying Stalin, stiffening Soviet resolve to continue the war, and solidifying the "Grand Alliance." Thus seen, it is impossible to accept at face value Churchill's subsequent claim that "my conscience is clear. . . . I did not deceive or mislead Stalin."[38]

Presaging what was to be a recurrent phenomenon, the Prime Minister returned from Moscow very much heartened by his first meeting with the Soviet dictator. His own impression, he informed the War Cabinet, was that the Russians were determined to continue fighting against Germany and that their situation was not all that precarious. He showered praises on Stalin, with whom he claimed to have established good personal relations, commenting on the Russian leader's acute powers of judgment.[39] In Parliament, Churchill reiterated that it was now the Soviet Union that in fact carried the main burden of the struggle against Teutonic might.[40]

In October 1942 Eden presented Churchill with a memorandum discussing the postwar future of Europe and the world. At root, the document constituted an extension of the line of political thought to which Eden had adhered at the beginning of 1942; it also reflected Foreign Office opinion. Eden hoped that his conclusions would serve as guidelines for British foreign policy during the war. Influenced by U.S. thinking—which at this stage of the war had not yet crystallized—Eden believed that the postwar global political order would rest upon the four Great Powers: the United States, Britain, the Soviet Union and China. It was they who would manage and determine the world's affairs after the war. From Britain's point of view, Eden argued, the best scenario was that these four powers would manage to develop modes of sincere cooperation among themselves. Indeed, such a situation would enable Britain to preserve its leading status, because it would ensure the emergence of a free and Anglophile Europe and prevent the revival of German power. He believed that the United States would abandon its previous policy of isolationism and aspire to global influence, and therefore support that idea. The intricacies of the Soviet position, on the other hand, were less amenable to analysis. Eden was sure that, should the Russians be victorious in the war, they would be capable of attaining global influence. Their principal concern was to ensure their security and preclude the possibility of any further European aggression against them. One way they might achieve those ends was by establishing communist governments in Germany and other European states and by adopting a confrontational posture against Britain and the United States. But Eden thought that Stalin seemed to prefer the alternative of cooperation with Britain and the United States in the belief that he might thereby attain, not only his European goals, but also Russia's aims in the Near and Far East.

Stalin, Eden went on to say, was still not prepared to commit himself. He would support the "Four Power" plan if he were convinced that Britain and the United States were sincerely bent on cooperation with him and desirous of preventing the resurgence of German strength. But Stalin also suspected that Britain had an interest in exhausting and weakening Russia. Those suspicions could only be allayed were the British to show "by word and deed our sincerity in desiring their collaboration, as well as the fixity of our purpose to restrain Germany." Consequently, Eden advised, "we must be prepared to make concessions to Russian desires in Eastern Europe and perhaps in the Near East as well." Should the Russian demands prove to be excessive, they could be cut down to size by a British threat to join with the United States in setting up an anti-Soviet front. On the other hand, should the Americans not accept the Four Power plan as interpreted by Britain, the latter could brandish the possibility of an Anglo-Soviet alliance.

Admittedly, the Russians would certainly place a stiff price on that alliance; but if the Americans refused to undertake any commitments in Europe, Britain would in any case possess no other means of preventing Germany's resurgence. Eden's plan was to entrust the effective management of Europe's affairs to Russian and British hands. Each of those two powers would exercise a supervisory role over the policies of the Continent's smaller states: Britain in northwestern Europe and Russia in the east. In the latter region, two federations would be established—one centered on Czechoslovakia and Poland, and the other on Greece and Yugoslavia—which would work in cooperation with Russia.[41] In other words, Eden accepted the proposal Stalin had submitted in December 1941 for Europe's basic division into Soviet and British spheres of influence. He hoped to seduce Stalin into cooperating by offering him attractive concessions—mostly at other peoples' expense. The Russian dictator might consider those inducements to be more advantageous than the Anglo-American hostility he could expect if he were to pursue a policy based on a series of unilateral measures.

Churchill's reaction was typical of his attitude toward political matters dealing with future and postwar arrangements. He repeated his doubts as to whether the conclusions presently proferred would bear any relation to what would in fact happen at the end of the war. He thought it "even dangerous to discuss some aspects of the problem, for instance the position of Russia." The problem might be simple, since even after Hitler's collapse hard campaigns would have to be waged against Japan. Joint Anglo-American action against Japan would serve as an impetus to cooperation with regards to political arrangements in Europe. Anyway, such "speculative studies" should be left to those who had the leisure for them. As for ourselves, "We shall not overlook Mrs. Glass's Cookery Book recipe for Jugged . . . Hare—'First catch your hare.'"[42]

The Prime Minister's reply disappointed Eden. He argued that the basis of Britain's foreign policy had to be ascertained at the present juncture, since policy would be served by those foundations which would carry it over into the postwar peace. "It is from every point of view bad business," he wrote, "to have to live from hand to mouth where we can avoid it." This would result in the United States determining policy and Britain being forced to follow in its wake. He asked Churchill's permission to present his plan to the Cabinet so that he might obtain its approval for that plan in general.[43] Churchill did allow Eden to distribute his memorandum to the Cabinet, but at the same time expressed his own disagreement with the Foreign Secretary's Four Power plan. The Prime Minister maintained that there was no knowing what sort of Russia would appear at the end of the war, nor what its demands would be—only time would tell. Nevertheless, he added that he was inclined to think that Russia was beginning to undergo a process of internal change, since Stalin had been forced to transfer some of his power to the military.

Churchill wrote that his own thoughts were focused on Europe, even though Britain would have to work together with the United States. He wanted to see the revival of Europe, the mother continent of civilization and modern nations. It would, he declared, be a disaster were "Russian barbarism" to undermine the independence of Europe's ancient states. He believed that what had to be established was a sort of "United States of Europe," which would constitute a political and economic union based on regional confederations, such as the Scandinavian, Danubian, and Balkan states. This union would have an international police force that would ensure Prussia's staying disarmed. The idea of the leading Four Powers did not appeal to him. He argued that he did not wish to find himself "shut up with the Russians and the Chinese" at a time when the European peoples, from the Swedes to the Turks, would be confronted with urgent problems after the end of the war. China, he said, was not a global power and would even assist the United States when the latter attempted to dismantle the British Empire. In any event, he concluded, it was easy to speculate on such matters. But we had now to concentrate our attention on the conduct of the war.[44]

These were not fully formulated ideas. They were thoughts that Churchill—who was somewhat irritated by Eden's pestering—virtually pulled out of his back pocket and offhandedly scribbled down. His attitude toward Russia illustrates how little thought he had devoted to it. While his reference to "Russian barbarism" can be shown to have been consonant with his thinking about Soviet Russia, that is not true of his hope that the Soviet Union might be isolated from European affairs. He was realistic enough to appreciate that the latter would be impossible; indeed, he himself proved as much when the question of the Anglo-Soviet alliance arose. During the 1930s Churchill had been one of the few British leaders to believe in the need to incorporate Russia into the European system. As early as the end of World War I he had emphasized

Russia's influence—benign and baneful—on Britain and on the establishment of peace and of Europe's political order.[45]

Although Churchill himself followed his own advice to Eden to "first catch your hare," he nevertheless left his Foreign Secretary considerable freedom of maneuver. The Foreign Office retained its status and influence throughout the war. In part this was due to the fact that the two men enjoyed a special personal relationship. Churchill often remarked to Lord Moran that he and Eden saw eye to eye on the way to conduct the war. Eden, according to one of his biographers, was the only member of the War Cabinet to exert any substantive influence on the formulation of Churchill's positions on political matters. If we are to follow Dilks, Eden ultimately got his way.[46] He sowed the seeds of his political outlook during the discussions preceding the Anglo-Soviet alliance; thereafter, he required only patience to make his mark fully on Churchill's political positions in general and on his attitude toward Soviet Russia in particular.

■

Churchill, then, believed that a distinction had to be made between two issues. One was the military and operational conduct of the war; the other, the political dimension affecting the conclusion of the war and the character of the peace which would ensue. He maintained that consideration of long-term political aspect had to be left until the concluding stages of the war or even be postponed until it was over. This was a basic conception whose roots were apparent as early as World War I.

That approach contradicts a position modern strategic thinkers conventionally consider as fundamental. Even before World War II, Liddell Hart had written that "while the horizon of strategy is bounded by the war, grand strategy looks beyond the war to the subsequent peace. . . . For the role of grand strategy—higher strategy—is to coordinate and direct all the resources of a nation, or band of nations, towards the attainment of the political object of the war—the goal defined by fundamental policy." Grand strategy is " a policy in execution." According to Liddell Hart, the reason most wars had given rise to inadequate peace settlements was that grand strategy, unlike strategy itself, was still "terra incognita."[47] Even so, that particular field had been carefully analyzed by the greatest of all military thinkers, Carl von Clausewitz, whose concept of the essence of war between nations is encapsulated in his well-known (perhaps over-used) statements that "war is merely the continuation of policy by other means," and that "war is the handmaid of policy." Clausewitz could see no reason in a war whose direction did not accord with political considerations, "unless pure hatred made all wars a struggle for life and death."[48] War is a continuation of policy because it is part of the political process, not distinct from it. The goals and political interests that war was supposed to obtain could range from limited objectives to an attempt to build a completely new political settlement and peace. Anyone who intended to make a "critical analysis" of war, Clausewitz advised, should not stop at the study of military operations after judging them through their immediate aims and effects. Rather, "in many cases, particularly those involving great and decisive actions, the analysis must extend to the *ultimate objective*, which is to bring about peace."[49]

For the greater part of World War II, Churchill acted in a manner contradictory to the ideal to which the strategist should thus aspire.[50] What is more, he did so deliberately; his behavior cannot be attributed to chance or to the fact that he might have been carried away by events. At first glance this is surprising; after all, Churchill won a reputation as a decision maker who did attribute supreme importance to political ends in the formulation of wartime operations. But a closer study of the elements in his approach dispels the surprise and uncovers a facet unique to Churchill. He did attach considerable importance to political considerations when determining those military operations *whose object was to achieve victory in the war*. But his view of the wider strategy, and the *principal* military moves of which it is comprised, was not born of a conception that looked beyond the attainment of victory in war and might have been broad enough to encompass political objectives and the attainment of peace. To put matters another way, Churchill created an (artificial) dichotomy between two processes. One was the enlistment of all military and political means in order to bring about the enemy's defeat; the other was the framing of a strategy that—while similarly designed to achieve that goal—was also directed at attaining the war's political objectives, at dealing with expected political developments, and at formulating the political order of a postwar peace. Throughout most of World War II he elected to follow the first course.

Undoubtedly, Churchill always attached supreme importance to the political aspect in constructing a strategy that aimed at the military defeat of the enemy. In this respect, he kept faith with the principles he had himself laid down in *The World Crisis*:

> The distinction between politics and strategy diminishes as the point of view is raised. At the summit true politics and strategy are one. The manoeuvre which brings an ally into the field is as serviceable as that which wins a great battle.[51]

Churchill had acted in accordance with that approach during the previous war; one good example is provided by the motives that underlay his advocating the Gallipoli campaign. On the other hand, it is hard to discover in the strategic positions he adopted during that conflict any illustration of truly long-term thinking that might have taken account of the peace and European political settlement after the war.

Churchill always considered himself a statesman who had mastered the intricacies of military strategy. As such, he thought he enjoyed an advantage over military men who lacked his grasp of higher strategy, which links the military and political dimensions of war management.[52] It will be recalled that, when confronted with the need to take decisions about military moves whose operational viability had been questioned by his military advisers, Churchill did not hesitate to give preference to political considerations. As has also been seen, from Gallipoli to Greece Churchill's problem remained the same: he was unable to harmonize the operational level with higher political goals. He tended to give too much priority to the political dimension of a strategy designed to bring about the defeat of the adversary; at the same time, he was wont to minimize the weight of operational difficulties.

For better and for worse (usually the latter), this facet found expression in a number of important decisions that Churchill had initiated in 1940 and 1941. On the one hand, he was the leading spirit behind the decision taken late in June 1940 to attack the French fleet at Oran. The hesitations initially evinced by the Cabinet and the Admiralty were subordinate to his general wish to demonstrate Britain's determination to continue the war and, more specifically, to advance the United States' entry into the conflict by demonstrating the extent of joint Anglo-American interests.[53] Churchill demonstrated similar resolve at the end of September 1940, when he compelled his military advisers to carry out the amphibious assault on Dakar, saying that the decisive considerations were political.[54] The Dakar operation failed even though—before it was launched, at any rate—it did seem to stand a fair chance of success. (With all due respect to Marder's eminence, the present writer is unconvinced by his arguments that operational factors had doomed Dakar to failure.)

On the other hand, Churchill led Britain to failure in the Balkans in the spring of 1941—primarily because his gaze was fixed on long-term political and military aims and because he ignored the force of operational difficulties. Not even that blow entirely discouraged him. At the end of 1941 he insisted that, despite Admiralty opposition, the battleship *Prince of Wales* and the battle cruiser *Repulse* had to be sent to the Far East. He emphasized the importance of his political consideration, which was to deter Japan from opening war on Britain. Pound, the First Sea Lord, pointed out that one fast modern battleship could not possibly act as a deterrent; the Japanese could send out four vessels of the same kind to meet it.[55] Nevertheless, *Prince of Wales* and the *Repulse* sailed. Churchill was astounded when he heard that they had been sunk off the coast of Malaya. "In all the war I never received a more direct shock," his *Second World War* recalls.[56] He had not heeded Clausewitz's warning that the political aim is not a tyrant. "It must adapt itself to its chosen means."[57]

Subsequent to these events, Churchill began to strike a new chord. He rejected the operations Imperator and Sledgehammer on the grounds that "political considerations need not be taken into account." Their failure, he argued, would later be cited as "*another* [author's emphasis] example of sentimental politics dominating the calm determination and common sense of professional advisers."[58] In November 1942, when he was himself heavily engaged in a dispute with his military advisers about the implementation of the invasion in 1943, he told Parliament: "No amount of pressure by public opinion or from any other quarter would make me, as the person chiefly responsible, consent to an operation which our military advisers had convinced me will lead to a great disaster."[59]

Churchill was so carried away that he overreacted. He began to minimize the importance of political factors and—contrary to his previous practice—gave priority to considerations of a purely operational nature. This was a fairly easy course to adopt with respect to the political dimensions of the invasion of western Europe; after all, the operational difficulties which that enterprise entailed were known to be not inconsiderable. More remarkable is the extent to which the tendency to shunt aside political considerations became apparent at the highest level, which affected the drawing up of the strategic plans necessary for the formation of the postwar political settlement and peace. Indeed, it was during the period covered by the years 1942–1944, until after the invasion of France, that his overreacting was comprehensive and became a definite trait. Characteristic, in this context, was the Prime Minister's response to the warning given by Brigadier Fitzroy Maclean who, on his return from Yugoslavia in December 1943, predicted that Tito was bound to turn to the Soviet Union after the war. (The British were currently unsure which of the two rival guerrilla movements they ought to support: Mihajlovic's or Tito's). Churchill replied that he did not care which government was established in Yugoslavia after the war; what concerned him was which partisan movement was causing the Germans more harm.[60]

Thirty years earlier, Churchill had told Asquith that "a political career was nothing to him in comparison with military glory"; his life's ambition was "to command great victorious armies in battle." During World War II he was determined to take nothing less than full advantage of the opportunity given him—the almost unhampered military management of the great conflict. He was prone to ignore or postpone the treatment of matters likely to detract from that pleasure.[61] (Churchill's delight in direct command is highlighted when compared to the state of mind of Alan Brooke, whose distress and mental tension are apparent from both his behavior and his diaries.) This, then, was another version of the "Antwerp syndrome" that had affected Churchill in 1914. On that occasion, it will be recalled, he had been prepared to relinquish his senior civilian role as First Lord of the Admiralty in return for a field command. He now transmuted himself into a sort of supreme CIGS, a generalissimo. In so doing, he deferred, or even shelved altogether, treatment of the issues that he should have dealt with in his capacity as Prime Minister. He literally discarded one garb and donned another. During most of his public appearances, as well as his meetings with Roosevelt and Stalin, he adopted military dress. From a sartorial viewpoint, he was closer to the Russian dictator than to the U.S. President, who was Commander-in-Chief of the U.S. forces. This was behavior very much out of character with the nature of the English political tradition. That pose had never been struck by either of the Pitts, Asquith, Lloyd George, or Chamberlain. Indeed they would have been mocked had they attempted to do so. But in Churchill's case his dress excited almost no comment. It was as though his true personality had broken through and assumed its appropriate external form.

"Mr. Churchill," Eden wrote, "did not like to give his time to anything not exclusively concerned with the conduct of the war. This seemed to be a deep instinct in him and, even though it was part of his strength as a war leader, it could also be an embarrassment." Eden repeatedly complained about the Prime Minister's refusal to discuss political questions affecting the postwar period, a refusal that impeded the Foreign Secretary's own ability to conduct efficient negotiations on those issues with the Americans and Russians, who did evince considerable interest in them.[62]

Some qualification is therefore necessary if we are to accept the argument posited by E. L. Woodward, the official historian of British foreign policy during World War II, who remarks: "In 1943, and through most of 1944, the Prime Minister was unwilling and indeed unable to give much thought to the post-war settlement of Europe."[63] Technically, at least, it was not beyond Churchill's ability to adopt a unitarian attitude toward the military management of the war and the long-term political issues it raised. The true barrier was his own arbitrary decision not to do so. Moreover, there was no reason why he could not have reduced his involvement in the operational conduct of the war and at the same time retained his control over the formulation of British strategy. Stalin demonstrated how that could be done. From the start, he refused to distinguish between the war's military conduct and its long-term political aims. Stalin kept the latter constantly in view even when the Soviet Union was close to defeat. (Significantly, Churchill and Eden were both amazed and surprised when the Russian leader tabled his political demands and proposals during the winter of 1941–1942.) At the same time, however, Stalin was no less involved than Churchill in the operational conduct of the war. This is all the more remarkable when it is remembered that he labored under the weight of burdens that the British leader had never to carry. Stalin had to preserve his personal status as an omnipotent ruler—not an easy task for a paranoid personality—as well as the standing of the Party.[64] Furthermore, the strategic decisions he had to take were far more fateful than those which Churchill faced. Once the Battle of Britain was over, the United Kingdom was never in mortal danger. Hitler was then fighting for his life on Russian soil, and not in the British Isles or the Middle East. Nevertheless, the more the war progressed, so too did the extent to which Stalin's political thinking—and even his long-term political objectives—influenced the character of Soviet strategy. Stalin, it seems, had imbibed the habit of long-term strategic thinking from the historical character of Marxist-Leninist doctrine. Engels, and Lenin even more so, had been very much influenced by Clausewitz's idea of the connection between politics and strategy. Stalin too was aware of the bases of Clausewitz's approach.[65] The fact that Churchill was barely acquainted with Clausewitz's ideas[66] did not improve the Prime Minister's attitude toward this aspect of strategy.

It was not only the fact that he was Prime Minister that should have impelled Churchill to maintain a more correct balance between his political responsibilities and his position as military leader. The lessons he had himself distilled from European history should also have played a part. As early as the end of 1918, with the conclusion of World War I, he had warned that Britain—even though it had won the war—might lose the peace, as it had done so often during the course of its history.[67] In *The World Crisis* he wrote that not even the unprecedented nature of the total victory recently attained had solved the European problem or removed the dangers that had led to the outbreak of war.[68] Elsewhere, he argued that it was the fact that no one had anticipated victory and the end of the war in 1918 that helped explain why no suitable European peace was made afterward and why bolshevism had not been uprooted from Russia and Europe. That, too, was why no practical or psychological steps had been taken to deal with the political problems the war had bequeathed.[69] Moreover, after World War I Churchill had noted the strength of the connection between the balance and position of forces in the field and the political settlements concluded at the peace conference negotiating table. He argued that one reason for the failure of the Treaty of Versailles was that in 1919 large and important pieces of European territory (by which he meant parts of eastern Europe and Russia) were not under Allied control. That had not been the case at the time of the Congress of Vienna in 1815, which had succeeded.[70]

Other weighty considerations should have made Churchill pause for very careful thought before deciding to defer treatment of the great political questions until after the war and to separate them from the great military decisions to be taken during the conflict. In his 1942 memorandum Eden had indicated one basic problem very likely to arise at the end of the war: the victory of the Allies would generate an increase in Russian influence in Europe, where a vacuum would be created by Germany's defeat and France's enfeeblement. Eden was correct to point out to Churchill that it would be wrong to gamble on the possibility that Germany and Russia would wear each other out and to hope that the latter, even though ultimately victorious, would be so weak as to be dependent on U.S. and British favor. The history of the twentieth century had already shown how hazardous that gamble might be. Notwithstanding Russia's severe losses in World War I and its defeat by Germany in 1918, and despite being weakened by the ensuing civil war, the Soviets had nevertheless still proved capable of reaching the bank of the Vistula in 1920. This was, in part, because there existed no counterweight to their power in Eastern Europe. As has already been noted, and will be so once again, Churchill did not base Anglo-American strategy on a cynical calculation whose purpose was to cause the mutual attrition of the Soviet Union and Germany. Indeed, the possibility that the Soviet Union would be worn down by the war and would need western economic aid was one of the arguments Churchill employed against Eden, but only in order to strengthen his own view that uncertainty made long-term planning and its preliminary steps valueless at that juncture. There can be no doubt that in war, more than in any other field of human activity, decision makers are made to feel the full force of uncertainty. Ironically enough, however, there was every reason to anticipate that the end of the war would witness the emergence of precisely the problem to which Eden referred.

Still more serious is that there were no grounds for Churchill's sense that, once Germany was defeated, he would have the time and ability to defend and promote the political interests of Britain and, thereby, of the West as a whole. He did have some justification for regarding discussions of future international organization and a postwar political settlement as a superfluous nuisance at that stage of the war. But there was one issue whose examination he could not postpone: how to ensure that, when political arrangements would be determined at the end of the war, Britain and the United States would possess a firm enough hold on the European continent to give them strong bargaining chips against the Soviet Union, be the latter friendly or hostile. What made this question particularly important was the uncertainty which Churchill as well as Eden felt about Russia's postwar *intentions*. That should have been one of the critical considerations in Churchill's thinking, even when he was formulating Anglo-American strategy and coming to crucial decisions on the invasion of western Europe and the development of the "Mediterranean strategy." One reason not to postpone consideration of the manner whereby the necessary bargaining position might best be obtained was the logic of the Clausewitzian connection between politics and strategy. Another, and more pressing, reason was that the Soviet Union's strategic jumping-off point was inherently more advantageous than that available to the United States and Britain. Even when in retreat, the Russian armies were still in Europe; by contrast, the Anglo-American armies had not set foot on the Continent until September 1943. Moreover, in order to do so (either from the south or from the northwest) they had to carry out complicated amphibious operations requiring years of preparation and planning. Even then, the Red Army was still better placed. It could advance on a line of march that lay to the west—which was precisely the direction of Stalin's political objectives. The Soviet leader did not have to choose between various axes of approach. Anglo-American decision makers, by contrast, had to confront the dilemma posed by the existence of several lines of invasion and advance into the Continent, whose military advantages and disadvantages did not always overlap their political merits and faults. In short, Stalin was favored by geopolitical circumstances, which were further buttressed by his own political-strategic approach.

It was in the middle of the war—and not at its conclusion—that British and U.S. leaders, through the perspective of "grand strategy," had to take decisions to attain their political objectives in Europe. But in the decisive years during which the cardinal decisions of Anglo-American strategy were made, Churchill, to use his own phrase, concentrated on a policy enunciated by the maxim, "First, catch your hare." His political thinking and behavior in that period was mainly turned to ensuring the integrity and maintenance of the Grand Alliance against Germany. As will be seen, that outlook was to have important consequences for his strategic positions and for the manner and form in which the war came to an end.

9

"This Battle Has Been Forced Upon Us": Overlord, 1943-1944

When the decision was taken to launch the invasion of Italy, Alan Brooke pointed out to Churchill that the operations there would influence the date of the commencement of operation Overlord (the new code name for the grand invasion of France, which replaced Round-up).¹ Thus apprised, Churchill wrote that preparations for operation Overlord had to proceed with all good faith. However, should it prove impossible to implement Overlord in May 1944, that operation would have to be postponed until August; meanwhile, Norway would be invaded. But he added:

> I have no doubt myself that the right strategy for 1944 is a) Maximum post "Husky" certainly to the Po, with an option to attack westwards in the south of France or north-eastwards towards Vienna, and meanwhile to procure the expulsion of the enemy from the Balkans and Greece. b) "Jupiter" prepared under the cover of "Overlord". I do not believe that 27 Anglo-American divisions are sufficient for "Overlord" in view of the extraordinary fighting efficiency of the German Army, and the much larger forces they could so easily bring to bear against our troops even if the landing were successfully accomplished.²

That statement—to which there is no reference in Churchill's *The Second World War*—constitutes the first occasion on which the Prime Minister committed to paper the possibility of an advance on Vienna. At this stage of the War, his thinking was principally military in character, and Vienna was posited as a goal of equal worth to a westward advance into southern France. As will be pointed out, he had still not begun to consider the possibility of preempting the Russians in eastern Europe and the Balkans.³

In the middle of July 1943 the Russians began their counterattack in the region of Kursk. Mussolini's regime fell on July 25. The Kursk campaign ended in a German defeat on August 23.

At the beginning of August Churchill again set sail for North America, this time bound for the first Quebec conference. The U.S. Chiefs of Staff still doubted the sincerity of British support for the invasion of western Europe.

Their aim was to ensure that Overlord would enjoy absolute priority over the Mediterranean theater.[4] By contrast, their British counterparts wanted to alter the decision taken the previous May, which had stated that seven experienced divisions were to be transferred from the Mediterranean to Britain. Nevertheless, the British Chiefs did not attempt—at least not overtly—to withdraw their commitment to Overlord. According to the official British history, their aim was to impose flexibility on the deployment of forces between the two theaters, which they considered interrelated. The result was that the forum of the Combined Chiefs of Staffs repeated the decisions taken at their previous meeting. The Americans refused to give way on the transfer of the seven divisions to Britain, but did back away slightly from their demand that Overlord receive absolute priority in the allocation of resources. It was also decided to effect a diversionary invasion of southern France (Anvil) in support of the main invasion in the north.[5] These decisions were made on August 17. On the same day Sicily fell to the Allies.

Churchill went his own independent way. While the Americans tried to establish a firm commitment to Overlord, he attempted to lay down equally strict conditions for the launching of the operation. To that end, he seized upon the conclusions reached by General Morgan and his staff (COSSAC), who had dealt with the planning for the invasion of France. They had concluded that the implementation of Overlord necessitated three primary requirements: first, the strength of the German fighter planes in France before the attack must be weak; second, the maximum number of first-rate German divisions in France had to be twelve, with an assurance that the Germans would not be able to transfer fifteen first-rate divisions from the east during the first two months after the invasion; third, a solution had to be found to the problems of supplying the invasion forces for an extended period across open beaches.[6]

During the course of the first meeting with Roosevelt and the U.S. Chiefs of Staff, Churchill announced that carrying out Overlord was conditional on these three requirements. Harry Hopkins asked him to be flexible and not be tied down to arithmetical constraints. Churchill accommodated himself, saying that he "wished to emphasize that he strongly favoured 'Overlord' for 1944. He was not in favour of 'Sledgehammer' in 1942 or 'Round-up' in 1943. However, the objections which he had had to those operations have been removed."[7] He was not to retain that mood for very long. At a subsequent meeting, he stressed that British agreement to Overlord was conditional upon the number of German divisions in the west and on clear Anglo-American air superiority. The implementation of the invasion would have to be reconsidered if it transpired that the ratio of forces was worse than anticipated. Churchill also proposed the execution of Jupiter should an invasion of France prove impossible—even though Alan Brooke had explicitly asked him not to raise that possibility in view of American suspicions about the nature of British support for Overlord.[8] Generous as always, the Americans accepted Churchill's proposal.[9]

On September 3, while Churchill was still in Washington after the conclusion of the Quebec Conference, the Allies invaded Italy. On the same day the Italians signed a secret armistice agreement with Britain and the United States.

Dissatisfied with the conclusions reached at recent conferences, Field Marshal Smuts maintained that the Anglo-American armies had to adopt a more aggressive strategy. He feared that the western nations would suffer a loss in prestige and influence in comparison with the Soviet Union, which was bearing the main burden of the war. Arguing that the advance up the leg of Italy would be too dilatory, Smuts advocated the conquest of Sardinia and Corsica, whence a direct invasion would be launched at northern Italy, bypassing the south. Thereafter "a real attack on the Balkans" had to be mounted from the Adriatic coast. That move would bring Turkey into the war and enable a link-up with the Russians by way of the Black Sea.[10] In reply to Smuts, Churchill wrote: "I have always been most anxious to come into the Balkans which are already doing so well. We shall have to see how the fighting in Italy develops before committing ourselves beyond Commandos, agents and supplies."[11] (In his work, Churchill appended the following comment to this last statement: "This sentence appears inconsistent with my general policy as so often expressed in these volumes. I did not mean 'come into the Balkans' with an army."[12]) The invasion of France, he added, required enormous resources that were absorbing all available manpower and shipping facilities; hence it was impossible to develop a more aggressive strategy in the Mediterranean. On the other hand, the conquest of Italy and the withdrawal of Italian forces from the Balkans might force the Germans to retreat to a defensive line on the Sava and the Danube.[13] Smuts was not convinced. He responded that Italy's surrender had entirely changed the strategic situation and that the decisions reached at Quebec therefore stood in need of reassessment. He was, he said, pleased with the possibility that an Italian front of some twenty Anglo-American divisions could be established, but not with the fact that seven divisions were to be transferred back to Britain. He claimed that the high risks involved in the invasion of western Europe made it imperative to reconsider the decision to mount that operation. The Allies had to wait until the Germans had been very much weakened, and then deal them a coup de grace. He again advocated the establishment of a Balkan front of some four divisions and the conquest of the Dodecanese.[14]

Smuts's messages reached Churchill when he was again conferring with Roosevelt at the White House. Still believing that the Germans would prefer to retreat northward, Churchill suggested the establishment of a fortified line in northern Italy after the German retreat to the Po. This would enable the Allies to ward off a counterattack and to divert Anglo-American forces either to the east or the west. He also suggested the conquest of ports on the eastern coast of the Adriatric, with the object of supporting the guerrillas in the Balkans. Roosevelt expressed interest in the fortified line, but objected to Balkan operations.[15] The latter position was shared by the British Chiefs of Staff, who were slightly alarmed by reports from Washington. Writing from London, they warned the Prime Minister against becoming entangled in operations in the Balkans and opposed the idea of conquering a port in that region. Churchill replied that he had never contemplated large-scale operations or "being drawn into a fresh campaign [in the Balkans] with inadequate forces." But he added that he thought it would be foolish "not to exploit the highly favourable possibilities now offered to us without in any way prejudicing the build up in Italy." By the end of the year the Germans might withdraw to the Danube and the Sava and be deserted by their allies, developments that would make it possible to open the Dardanelles and renew the link with the Russians.[16]

In short, without yet completing an analysis of the Balkan issue, Churchill wanted to place modest forces in that region. But the Balkans were not high on his list of priorities; moreover, he was aware that operations there were opposed by the Americans and lacked the support of his own Chiefs of Staff. Consequently, he refrained from fighting for that point or making it, like the Italian campaign, a fundamental pillar of his strategy. He favored the ideas proposed by Smuts, but responded that the preparations for Overlord could not be frozen since Britain was commited to its implementation. And that commitment lay at the heart of Anglo-American cooperation.[17]

At the beginning of September the Red Army broadened its attacks. The Russians regained control of much of the Donets Basin; by the end of September they had taken Smolensk and were approaching Kiev. On the other hand, in mid-September the Germans started their counterattack against the invasion forces in southern Italy.

In the second half of September and early October Churchill attempted to gain U.S. support and landing craft for the conquest of the Dodecanese, especially Rhodes. He failed. The Americans regarded that move as a dangerous diversion from the Italian campaign and a threat to Overlord. At this stage even Brooke objected.[18] Churchill claimed that gaining control over the Aegean would bring Turkey into the war, open the Straits and a supply route to Russia, and create profound changes in Hungary, Rumania, and Bulgaria.[19] Eden and Ismay, whom Churchill had sent to Constantinople, tried to convince the Turks that the Germans could not attack them if they joined the war;[20] this was presented at a time when Brooke maintained that the Germans could easily conquer Thrace (i.e., European Turkey) and thus dominate the Straits.[21] Roosevelt asked Churchill a seemingly innocuous question: "Strategically, if we get the Aegean islands, I ask myself where do we go from there and vice versa where would the Germans go if for some time they retain possession of the islands."[22] Even Professor Michael Howard, the official historian, finds it difficult to discern the utility of the Aegean move. Somewhat contrary to his general interpretation, he admits that—even had Italy fallen without any German opposition—the other operations the British suggested, from the Dodecanese to Sardinia, would have consumed so many forces that the invasion of France would have been "almost impossibly difficult."[23]

The British high command was still hoping for an imminent German collapse. In the middle of September, the Joint Intelligence Committee completed a detailed survey comparing the conditions and stages that had brought about the German collapse in 1918 with the present situation. Its report concluded that there existed a marked similarity between the German positions at the end of 1918 and at the end of 1943. The various differences canceled each other out. Taking a broad view of the situation, the committee argued, the unavoidable conclusion was that Germany's situation was worse now than it had been at a parallel stage in 1918. Were it not for the totalitarian nature of the present regime, the JIC would have no hesitation in stating that Germany would request an armistice during the current year. Even so, there existed a reasonable chance that a group of generals and civilians might manage to overthrow Hitler[24] (an optimistic assessment echoed by the Chiefs of Staff).[24] Churchill even asked for the intelligence memorandum to be circulated to members of the War Cabinet.[25] But the formulation of that assessment seems to have been influenced too much by wishful thinking and preconceptions. Some time before it was compiled, the intelligence chiefs themselves had determined that the strategic bombing of Germany had so far had a negligible effect. As early as the beginning of 1943 they said that it seemed to them that the army would seize power in Germany once the failures in the east had piled up and the certainty of collapse was understood. The German generals would attempt to reach an agreement with Britain and the United States, while still doing their utmost to check the Russian advance. Portal agreed, and added that in his opinion the German generals would prefer to withdraw and establish a line on the Rhine while concentrating their strength to halt the Russians in the east. In that event, the British and Americans would have to land in Holland, establish an air base, and, by hitting Germany hard from the air, bring about its surrender without having to make extensive use of ground forces.[26]

In any case the Germans in Italy had no intention of collapsing. Contrary to the expectations harbored by Churchill and his advisers, at the beginning of October Hitler decided to defend Italy as far south from Rome as possible. The Allied victory march on Rome became bogged down in the Italian winter against a determined enemy that had the benefit of a terrain ideally suited to defense. The stalemate that began during October deeply disappointed Churchill. He was also worried because it would soon be necessary to begin transferring to Britain the seven experienced divisions for Overlord, as agreed with the Americans. For the first time since the summer of 1940, British forces were about to be returned to the British Isles for the sake of a future operation. The British leadership became agitated. Smuts set out for London with the object of changing the direction of Anglo-American strategy. He decried Overlord, believing that the concentration of forces presently under way in Britain constituted a "military blunder." He argued that efforts had principally to be focused on an assault from the south, by way of Italy and Yugoslavia into Rumania, Hungary, Austria, and southeastern Germany, and joining up with the Russians in 1944. Nevertheless, at this stage, neither Smuts nor Churchill had any thoughts about military moves designed to contain Russian expansion in the east.[27]

In the middle of October none other than King George himself approached the Prime Minister. Influenced by a conversation with Smuts, the King suggested canceling Overlord and expanding the scope of operations in the Mediterranean. Churchill replied to the king that he could not now change something agreed upon with Roosevelt and Stalin, who would be very angry should he try to do so.[28] On the same day similar arguments were put to Churchill from a different quarter. Brigadier Hollis, his military secretary, reported on the unease felt among the staffs because of the binding commitment to agreements with the Americans, which was preventing the exploitation of opportunities in the Mediterranean. Hollis suggested that Churchill instruct the Chiefs of Staff to examine plans for additional operations in the Mediterranean and the Balkans.[29] Churchill did indeed order the Chiefs to study various moves, as well as "a forward policy in the Balkans" within the framework of the Mediterranean strategy—but to do so secretly. He added that the commitment to Overlord could be broken should opportunities arise in various theaters; but that there might possibly be no need to abandon Overlord, only to alter the distribution of effort between the two theaters.[30] To Roosevelt he wrote: "Unless there is a German collapse, the campaign of 1944 will be far the most dangerous we have undertaken, and personally I am more anxious about its success than I was about 1941, 1942, or 1943."[31]

The problem of the connection between the Mediterranean theater and the invasion of northern France was aired at an extraordinary meeting that Churchill convened on October 19. Apart from the Chiefs of Staff, also present were Smuts, Attlee (the Deputy Prime Minister), Cadogan (Eden was in Moscow), and Oliver Lyttelton, a member of the War Cabinet. Churchill was the principal speaker, and for a change he was more forthcoming when expressing his views on the invasion of France. He opened by saying that the commitment to Overlord, an operation that at the earliest would take place in seven months' time (in effect later), would by all accounts adversely influence the campaign in the Mediterranean theater, where it would preclude the exploitation of opportunities—the nature of which he did not explain.

> He [Churchill] felt that by tying ourselves to undertake Operation Overlord there was a serious risk that we should undertake two operations, each employing approximately equal forces and neither being strong enough for the purposes for which it was required. We would thus give the enemy an opportunity of concentrating and defeating our forces in detail.

He continued:

> As far as Operation Overlord was concerned he was not afraid of the Channel crossing or of the landing on the enemy coast. He felt that we should probably effect a lodgement and in the first instance we might make progress. It was the

later stages of the operation which worried him. . . . He felt that by landing in Northeast (sic) Europe we might be giving the enemy the opportunity to concentrate, by reason of his excellent road and rail communications, an overwhelming force against us and to inflict on us a military disaster greater than that of Dunkirk. Such disaster would result in the resuscitation of Hitler and the Nazi regime.

The Prime Minister explained that his commitment to carry out Overlord was strictly conditional on certain requirements being fulfilled. The strategy agreed upon with the Americans was mistaken. Unfortunately, he added, the British were not determining strategy by themselves. Were it up to them to lay down the future strategy of the war, they would proceed as follows:

1. To reinforce the Italian theatre to the full. 2. To enter the Balkans. 3. To hold our position in the Aegean Islands. 4. To build up our air forces and intensify our air attacks on Germany. 5. To encourage the steady assembly in this country of United States troops, *which could not be employed in the Pacific owing to the shortage of shipping* (author's emphasis), with a view to taking advantage of the softening in the enemy's resistance due to our operations in other theatres, though this might not occur until after the spring of 1944.

In conclusion, Churchill expressed his readiness to reopen the strategic agreements reached with the Americans.

Charles Portal remarked that, if such were the case, the Americans would prefer to concentrate their own forces in the Pacific; their dilemma was not between the Mediterranean and the western European theaters, but between the Pacific and the European. Churchill replied:

If, as a result, the latter wished to transfer the *bulk* (author's emphasis) of their forces to the Pacific, he would be prepared to accept this providing they would leave the forces already in this country [in October 1943 only six U.S. divisions were stationed in Britain] and would build up their Air Force for operations against Germany as already promised.

Nobody contradicted those statements. Smuts supported Churchill. Alan Brooke pointed out that wars were not conducted on the basis of legal agreements. Portal added that he did not accept the U.S. argument that Allied air superiority would prevent the transfer of massive German forces from the east to the west after the invasion. At the end of the discussion, it was decided that an effort had to be made to hold another meeting with the U.S. Chiefs of Staff; meanwhile, staff studies affecting the relationship between operations in the Mediterranean and Overlord were to be speeded up.[32] There existed no real difference between the strategic ideas of Churchill and his military advisers. After the war, Alan Brooke attempted to drive a wedge of that sort between them,[33] but on the night following the meeting he had noted in his diary:

C.O.S. at which we received a note from the P.M. wishing to swing the strategy back to the Mediterranean at the expense of the Channel. I am in many ways entirely with him, but God knows where this may lead us as regards clashes with the Americans.[34]

Portal was also afraid. At the Chiefs of Staff meeting held on the following day he said that Anglo-American strategy must indeed be reassessed without regard for prior agreements. But Overlord should not be canceled; Britain's approach should be that of a "residuary legatee." That would inevitably bring about its postponement.[35] Thus, the difference between the Prime Minister and the Chiefs of Staff boiled down to the fact that the latter were pessimistic about the possibility of changing the strategy agreed upon with the Americans, and doubted the utility of attempting to do so.[36] Churchill still had confidence in the force of his own personality and in the fact that, during the course of the war, opportunities would arise that would enable him to effect shifts—and perhaps a revolution—in the Anglo-American strategic line.

In *The Second World War* Churchill made no reference to the discussion of October 19, or its content. At the conclusion of the chapter dealing with this period, he wrote: "The reader of the telegrams printed in this chapter must not be misled by a chance phrase here and there into thinking (a) that I wanted to abandon 'Overlord'; (b) that I wanted to deprive 'Overlord' of vital forces; or (c) that I contemplated a campaign by armies operating in the Balkan peninsula. These are legends. Never had such a wish entered my mind."[37] Churchill and Alan Brooke admitted that differences had arisen at the end of 1943 between themselves and the Americans regarding the allocation of resources to the Mediterranean theater. But they argued that those disagreements were not generated by their opposition to an invasion of France, but by their wish to prevent a deterioration and a turn for the worse in the Italian campaign, whose success would prepare the ground for the invasion in the west. The authors of the official British history have sided with that version.[38] They too take no notice of the meeting of October 19, or reduce its importance.[39] According to Professor Howard, the argument began when the unexpected strength of the opposition the Germans put up in Italy was revealed. It was the need for additional resources to overcome that resistance which impelled the Prime Minister and his military advisers to push for an expansion of the military commitment in Italy. But, he says, they applied that pressure without in any way abandoning Overlord—their principal aim.[40]

That version is not supported by the documents examined throughout the previous chapters of this book, or by the record of the debate of October 19. On the contrary, such sources show that Churchill and Alan Brooke tried to change the decision to transfer seven divisions from the region of the Mediterranean to Britain *before* the invasion of the Italian peninsula and *before* German intentions had become clear.[41] In sum: Churchill did indeed seek "to abandon "'Overlord'" and "deprive" that operation of "vital forces." On the other hand, the facts presented so far do not admit of the claim that he wanted a large military campaign in the Balkans.

A few days later Churchill approached President Roosevelt. He asked for another Anglo-American conference to be held as soon as possible, so that the decisions reached at the first Quebec conference could be reviewed. In his letter to the President he wrote that "unless there is a German collapse" Hitler, with his command of the excellent European communications network, could concentrate forty to fifty divisions in either western Europe or Italy while also successfully defending other fronts. Unfolding circumstances and "arbitrary [Anglo-American] compromises," not strictly strategic considerations, had formed the basis for the original distribution of forces between the Italian and western European theaters (these phrases were deleted from the version of the letter reproduced in Churchill's work). It would be a mistake to transfer forces from Italy for an operation to be carried out seven months' hence, and even then only under "hypothetical" conditions that would probably not be met. "My dear friend," he continued with reference to Overlord, "I feel very much in the dark at the present, and unable to think or act in the forward manner which is needed."[42]

Sensing the way the wind was blowing in London, the President and his Chiefs of Staff tried to avoid further discussions with the British on the decisions reached at Quebec. From his own point of view, Churchill's request to convene another conference was badly timed. For some time contacts had been under way in preparation for the convention of a tripartite meeting with Stalin in Teheran. Roosevelt argued that the Russians would suspect a plot were a separate Anglo-American conference to be held prior to the Teheran meeting. He suggested that the meetings held by the Combined Chiefs be attended by a Russian military representative, who—together with Molotov—would also be present when the British and the Americans met in Cairo on their way to Teheran. He added that, in Cairo, the Chiefs would discuss only operational aspects.[43] Churchill, of course, opposed the participation of a Russian representative at the Cairo talks: "He would simply bay for an earlier Second Front and block all other discussions." Instead, Churchill pressed Roosevelt to set aside additional time for strategic discussions before they were joined by the Russians and the Chinese.[44] In *The Second World War* he wrote that "there was emerging a strong current of opinion in American Government circles, which seemed to wish to win Russian confidence even at the expense of co-ordinating the Anglo-American war effort."[45]

On November 6 the Russians took Kiev, the capital of the Ukraine, and cut off the German land link to the Crimean peninsula.

In late October and early November Churchill and Alan Brooke even began to fear a disaster in Italy. Admittedly, the British planners did believe that Germany was entirely incapable of carrying out an effective counterattack on that front. Together with George Marshall they pointed out that the Allies enjoyed marked air superiority. Portal claimed that the advantage in the air, then about eight to one, meant that the Germans would require a 50 percent superiority on land for their counterattack to reap any successes.[46] Churchill's fears of a disaster in Italy abated during the course of November, not so his considerable disappointment with the results of the Italian campaign. On the eve of the Cairo meeting, he wrote to the Chiefs of Staff that the results of the Italian move were unsatisfactory.

> We shall certainly be rightly accused of short-sightedness or even worse.... The Germans have been able to withdraw several divisions from Italy, including one from the south of Rome in order to meet needs on the Russian front. We have therefore failed to take the weight of the attack off the Soviets.

Apart from airmen, some two million Allied troops were stationed in the Mediterranean region, but only about 170,000 of them were in actual contact with the enemy on the Italian front. (According to General Alfred Jodl, there were then some 412,000 German soldiers in Italy.)[47] Churchill deleted these statements from the memorandum printed in his book.[48] There, his lament is transformed into a paean for the "Mediterranean strategy." He argued that the Italian campaign more than lived up to its expectations, claiming that in October 1943 nineteen German divisions confronted eleven Allied divisions on that front.[49] He did not compare manpower strengths, which, it will be recalled, were the decisive figures. The true situation on the entire Mediterranean front in October 1943 was as follows: Anglo-American land forces numbered 41 divisions, of which 34 were attached to the British Army. Against them, the Germans fielded 31 divisions in southeastern Europe and Italy; about another 10 divisions in the Balkans comprised troops of Germany's allies.[50] A simple numerical count permits a depiction of the true balance of forces in southern Europe. Even if it is assumed that the German "division slice" was complete—and such was far from being the case—Germany and her allies possessed some 820,000 men in the region as opposed to 1.6 million Allied ground forces. Moreover, to the latter figure must be added the large number of Allied air personnel. The Luftwaffe was virtually nonexistent in southern Europe. (Jodl stated that there were 612,000 German troops in the Balkans, a figure which seems too high and is not substantiated by records that came to light after the war.) True, Hitler did transfer some forces from the Russian front to the Balkans to fill the gap created by the disbandment of the Italian divisions that had been stationed there. But, in the final analysis, the price the Allies paid in order to tie down German troops in southern Europe was too high.

To return to Churchill's memorandum: that document stated that the support for guerrilla forces in the Balkans had also failed. The weather apart, there were two reasons for the tardiness of progress in Italy; first, the Allies were too slow to concentrate their forces on Italian soil; second, they were committed to Overlord and its target date. For the latter purpose, two excellent divisions had already been transferred from the Mediterranean to Britain; so had some landing craft. (On November 6 the Americans agreed that the large tank-landing craft to be transported to Britain might be temporarily retained in the Mediterranean.) Churchill suggested halting the planned transfer of troops and landing craft to Britain and investing all energies in the conquest of Rome, in bringing Turkey into the war, and in taking Rhodes.[51] The opinion of the Chiefs of Staff was not very much different. In a memorandum intended for presentation to the Americans in Cairo, they declared their continued support for the implementation of the invasion of France; but they argued against basing joint strategy on a fixed date for the commencement of Overlord. Subservience to any such timing might preclude the exploitation of opportunities in the Mediterranean region. The surest formula for bringing about the defeat of the Germans was to attack them consistently everywhere possible in order to wear them out. They stated that the Allies had to develop their strength in Italy; advance to the Pisa-Rimini line (located far north of Rome); support the Balkan guerrillas and subvert Germany's Balkan allies; bring Turkey into the war; and open the Straits (the latter despite the fact that, only two days previously, the Chiefs of Staff had been surprised to learn that the Russians were not enthusiastic about opening the Dardanelles.)[52] By their calculations the continuation of the assault in Italy would delay Overlord until July 1, at the very least. However, "if we pursue the above policy we finally believe that 'Overlord' (*perhaps in the form of 'Rankin'*) will take place next summer."[53]

"Rankin" was the code name for the plan to launch a swift invasion of the Continent in the event of Germany's collapse, a sort of advanced version of Sledgehammer. One of the bases for that plan was British intelligence assessments of early August, which stated that Germany's collapse was imminent and that in the final stages of the war its leaders would choose to concentrate their forces in the east and abandon their country's defenses in the west, thereby ensuring that Germany would be conquered by Anglo-Saxon forces.[54]

Churchill concurred with the opinion of his Chiefs of Staff. So too did Smuts. Nevertheless, the latter argued that the Balkan and Aegean operations had to be extended to a scale beyond that requested by Alan Brooke and colleagues—on the grounds that the Mediterranean campaign was not secondary to Overlord but of supreme importance in its own right. Overlord was akin to a coup de grace.[55] Churchill replied that there could be no better depiction of "our convictions."[56]

Confronted with a decidedly cool U.S. reception to their proposals on the eve of the Cairo meetings, the Chiefs of Staff abandoned their hopes of altering the strategic decisions taken after the Casablanca conference. Churchill, as we have seen, still retained a degree of optimism—which was to an extent justified by the fact that he had in the past managed to persuade the Americans to accept his positions, partly by exploiting his own force of personality and skill of maneuver. But the postponement of the date of the invasion of western Europe was now clearly emerging as the final British fall-back position. In justifying their case, the British argued the need to exert pressure on the German forces in

Italy and thereby continue to tie them down before the invasion. Why the German divisions had to be pinned down north (rather than south) of Rome is not clear. What was self-evident was that the advance north on Rome, together with the other operations in the Balkans and Aegean, would defer the execution of Overlord. The British hoped that were Overlord indeed to be launched two or three months later than originally planned, it would coincide with a German collapse; thus, in their own words, Overlord would conform to Rankin. Kennedy, the Director of Military Operations and a man whose talents were highly valued by Brooke,[57] articulated a view common amongst members of the Army's General Staff when, on November 22, he confided to his diary that he still believed that a German collapse would precede the invasion.[58]

In Cairo, the U.S. Chiefs of Staff evinced no enthusiasm for the proposals tabled by their British colleagues. The latter were put out—and Churchill openly annoyed—by the manner in which Roosevelt had so arranged matters that the Anglo-American meeting in Cairo lasted only four days, most of which were devoted to questions affecting the Far East and spent on Chiang Kai-Shek and his beautiful wife.[59] European strategic issues were thus left to the Teheran conference of "the big three" held at the end of November 1943. There, Churchill found himself with his back to the wall. The Prime Minister persisted in his efforts to bolster the Mediterranean campaign; specifically, he wanted additional forces allocated to Italy (in order to renew the advance and take Rome) and landing craft for the conquest of Rhodes. But on this occasion Roosevelt stood firm. Moreover, the President was supported by Stalin, one of the few persons to inspire in Churchill any feelings of awe. Roosevelt opposed any operation likely to cause the postponement of Overlord from May 1 to June or July. Stalin argued that the only result of the conquest of Rome and the other Mediterranean operations would be the diversion of effort from the main move, which was the invasion of western Europe. He openly asked Churchill: "Did the Prime Minister and the British Staffs really believe in 'Overlord?'"[60] Not even Churchill was capable of overcoming the combined resistance of both Stalin and Roosevelt and thus could not retreat from his earlier commitment to Overlord. In a last supreme effort, Churchill and Brooke did manage to persuade the Americans to help speed up the advance to the Pisa-Rimini line by deferring until mid-January the transfer from the Mediterranean of the large tank-landing craft (LSTs) designated for Overlord. The *quid pro quo* was the postponement of Overlord until the end of May 1944.

After the Teheran conference, Churchill reconciled himself to the idea that the invasion of France would have to be carried out. But his concurrence with that notion was the result of being compelled rather than acquiescence. Several weeks after the conference, he still depicted his own attitude to Overlord, and that of his military advisers, as that of a "residuary legatee."[61]

During the winter of 1943–1944 Russia made impressive advances. On January 27 the siege of Leningrad was finally lifted; on February 3 Soviet forces penetrated the Estonian frontier. These successes revived Churchill's hopes in an imminent German collapse. In mid-January 1944 he asked the intelligence chiefs to examine the possibility that conditions for the implementation of Rankin might soon be ripe. Having learned from their own previous experience, the intelligence chiefs replied that they could discern no signs that such would be the case.⁶² Thereafter Churchill's hopes for a German collapse in 1944 began to dissolve; he was influenced by the fact that the intelligence estimates that had optimistically and consistently prophesied a German collapse in 1943 had not been fulfilled; he was also impressed by Germany's obstinate resistance in Italy. He now adopted an extremely cautious tone. He believed that Hitler would still rule Germany on September 3, 1944, and complained about the unjustified sense of victory pervading Britain. His own view was that "there is, after all, a risk that we may suffer serious defeats this year, since the Hun is still very tough and his morale has not seriously deteriorated."⁶³

Three days earlier, an outflanking amphibious landing had been carried out at Anzio, an operation on which Churchill pinned great hopes because he regarded the lack of progress in Italy as "nothing short of a tragedy. . . . It was unthinkable that we should admit failure in the Mediterranean."⁶⁴ But the Anzio landing did not attain its objective. Although a bridgehead was established, the advance of the Anglo-American forces was thereafter halted. The German flank was not rolled up and the Allied frontal assault on Cassino was checked on February 12. Churchill was deeply disappointed.⁶⁵ These failures exacerbated his pessimism about the future of the campaign in western Europe. Within a few days he was writing that the most that could be expected from Overlord was the advance of the invasion forces to the Meuse or the Rhine. Hitler would be able to fend off the Russians from the Baltic to the Danube as well as the Allied armies in the west. Overlord would turn out to be nothing but "an important diversionary operation" which would help the Russians advance.⁶⁶ Having so long been optimistic about an imminent German collapse, the Prime Minister now tended to pessimism when assessing Germany's staying power and the influence of the future campaign in western Europe on the war. As we shall see, this frame of mind was to have important consequences.

As the date of the invasion approached, Churchill's fears became more apparent; he did not bother to hide them from his associates. However, once he had spoken of them openly, he did tell Colville, his private secretary, that he was "hardening to [the invasion]."⁶⁷ No less were the fears of his army chiefs. Indeed, it was once he had heard their hesitations that Churchill—the scion of Marlborough—wrote to Alexander Cadogan—the descendant of Earl Cadogan, Marlborough's right-hand man in all of his great continental battles—that "it [was] all wrong for the generals to start shivering." However, he did add that "this battle has been *forced upon us* [my emphasis] by the Russians and by the United States military authorities. We have gone in wholeheartedly, and I would not raise a timorous cry before a decision in the field has been taken."⁶⁸

Thus presented, the facts adduced and laid out above permit one clear and major conclusion: *had the issue been left entirely to the discretion of Churchill*

and the British Chiefs of Staff, they would not have invaded western Europe before Germany's strength had collapsed or been drastically weakened. Neither eventuality occurred during 1944. It therefore follows that they would not have crossed the Channel in that year.[69]

The full meaning and implications of that conclusion will be explored below. What has to be stressed now are the difficulties inherent in arriving at it. These derive from the thick smoke screen with which Churchill and his army chiefs enveloped this subject during and after the war. As we have seen, in *The Second World War* Churchill denied the allegations made by both Americans and Russians that he had opposed the invasion, arguing that such had never been the case. On the contrary, he claimed paternity of concept behind a massive invasion of western Europe. His dispute with the Americans (he reported) did not concern the invasion itself, but its timing. It was to have been mounted in 1944, and not earlier, because only then did the conditions necessary for its success seem ripe. That account was reinforced during the mid-1950s, when Alan Brooke brought out his version of events, and other less senior British military commanders published their memoirs. More important was the fact that Churchill's claim was considerably buttressed by the authors of the series of official British histories of World War II, whose principal volumes appeared during the 1950s and 1960s. It was they who managed to embed the Churchillian-British version of events in historical consciousness and to persuade even respectable U.S. scholars of its veracity. The latter had accepted it even before the relevant documents were opened to public inspection. And recently Churchill's official biographer, Martin Gilbert, has also echoed his subject's record of the "second front."[70]

■

Why did Churchill prefer a peripheral strategy of attrition and oppose an invasion of western Europe before a German collapse had occurred? This is the primary question that has to be addressed. Put another way: why, during the war, did he abandon his old concept at whose center lay the idea that western Europe constituted the principal theater of war on the Continent which was vital for the defeat of Germany? The answer to that question is complicated. As in previous cases, the essential cause must be distilled from various other causes and reasons that are interwoven. There exist three basic explanations. The first is that Churchill feared the heavy losses expected during the Channel crossing and the subsequent campaign to conquer Germany. The second posits that strategic-political considerations lay behind Churchill's desire to postpone the invasion for as long as possible. He wanted the Soviet Union to be very much weakened by the time that the war came to an end. The third explanation argues that Churchill was convinced of the German army's qualitative advantage in fighting capability over Anglo-American forces. This led him to fear that confrontation with the Wehrmacht on the plains of Europe would result in an Allied defeat or—at best—no decision.

Once France had fallen, strategic realities were in one essential basically different from those prevailing when Churchill had supported the dispatch of a large British army to western Europe. Prior to France's defeat, the British Army's forces had only to be sent to, and to join up with, the French army. After the summer of 1940, if Britain and the United States were to establish a land front in the west they had first to launch a seaborne invasion of France against strong German opposition. Admittedly, the fall of France did not lead Churchill immediately to conclude that the idea of a future land front of that sort had to be abandoned. He was prepared to run considerable risks when—without the armed support of any other Great Power—he initiated a British military front in the Balkans at the end of 1940 and the beginning of 1941. Only gradually did he abandon his old idea. Nevertheless, the change in the war situation was sufficiently radical to undermine the strategic concept Churchill had held for many years and to justify its reassessment. The question, of course, is why he should have rejected that concept even though still aware of its advantages.

The operational and tactical difficulties impeding the successful implementation of the invasion were not inconsequential. The possibility of overcoming them became the subject of various arguments and counterarguments. Whether or not those obstacles were to be considered insurmountable hurdles or relatively minor impediments, and whether or not the suggested solutions would suffice, depended—initially as well as ultimately—on the strategic conception of the decision maker. That was the prism through which he viewed the invasion of western Europe. There is, therefore, no point in analyzing all the operational problems here. Nevertheless, two central operational issues, to which Churchill and others attached considerable importance, do warrant discussion. Indeed, their examination promises both to clarify the matters raised and to facilitate further analysis of the deeper reasons for Churchill's behavior.

Several of the obstacles came from the need to execute a large-scale amphibious invasion against a defended hostile coast. In his work, Churchill emphasized the difficulties involved in the cross-Channel amphibious assaults. These, he argued, were underestimated by the Americans—and even more so by the Russians.[71] A study of the documents, however, reveals that Churchill did not consider the amphibious attack and entrenchment on French soil to be the principal impediment to an effort to invade western Europe. On several occasions, Churchill explicitly stated that he was not afraid of failure during the first stage of the invasion, the landings, and the establishment of beachheads. Rather, what he feared was subsequent developments. That was his argument during the important meeting of October 19, 1943. When he met privately with Stalin in Teheran he reiterated that he was not troubled by the landing stage itself, but by developments which would occur in the campaign some thirty to fifty days thereafter.[72] On his own evidence, he was enthusiastic about amphibious operations.[73] From that point of view, the failure at Gallipoli had not left a traumatic imprint. On the contrary, during the course of World War II he initiated amphibious operations in each of the various war theaters, starting with Norway and culminating in Burma. Most had not met with the approval of his military advisers because of the risks involved.

Churchill and his military advisers repeatedly claimed that the Germans were capable of swiftly transferring large forces to the west to repel the invasion. At the end of 1943 he expressed his fear that the Germans would speedily be able to concentrate a large force that even after successful landing and entrenchment could "inflict on us a military disaster greater than that of Dunkirk."[74] But Churchill's attitude on this subject changed several times during the course of the war. A similar issue had already been raised during World War I, specifically at the beginning of 1915, when Churchill and Kitchener had clashed over the transfer of land forces from Britain to the Dardanelles region. Kitchener had then feared a Russian collapse, which would enable the Germans to transfer swiftly numerous forces for an attack in the west. Churchill, on the other hand, had argued that the Russians would hold out and that logistic considerations precluded the possibility of the Germans transferring sizable forces from eastern Europe to France in under two or three months. In *The World Crisis*, Churchill wrote that Kitchener employed his arguments as excuses for positions he had already adopted.[75] At times Churchill himself seems to have been guilty of the same "sin" during World War II. He then first addressed this issue when composing his grand plan at the end of 1941, in which he claimed that the Germans *would not be able* to transfer considerable forces swiftly from one end of Europe to the other. That prediction was one of the foundation stones of his plan. It was expressed when Churchill was in a highly optimistic mood: the Germans had been stopped at the gates of Moscow; the United States had entered the war; Auchinleck was advancing nicely on the North African front. But once Auchinleck had been thrown back, and Singapore and Tobruk had both fallen, Churchill—when dispute arose over Sledgehammer—claimed that the Germans *would be able* to transfer massive forces to the west swiftly. He again reversed himself in late November and early December 1942—after a decision had been won at El Alamein and the Allies had landed in northwestern Africa, and at a time when Churchill was attempting to persuade his Chiefs of Staff of the need to attack in western Europe during 1943. He now argued that the Germans *would not be able* to quickly move large forces to western Europe. Shortly thereafter, however, there was another change of course. At Casablanca, Churchill and Alan Brooke argued that the Germans *would be able* speedily to switch sizable forces to the west. (A month later, British intelligence estimated that the Germans would not be able to do so.) But the Prime Minister held to his position throughout 1943. In October 1943, when the slow pace of the advance up Italy became apparent, he even feared that the Germans would be capable of striking at Allied forces in western Europe and Italy *sequentially*.

In the light of the importance thus attached to Germany's transport facilities, it is surprising that in the months before the invasion Churchill, together with Portal and Brooke, objected to mass air strikes designed to paralyze the communications networks in Belgium and northern France and to quarantine the invasion zone in Normandy. After all, these strikes—which were fundamental to Marshall's planning—were specifically aimed at preventing the swift movement of German forces to western Europe. The Americans insisted that they be carried out. Churchill argued that deep penetration raids against the German interior had to be continued so that the German air force would itself be ground to dust. The ostensible reason for that preference was Churchill's fear that the strikes the Americans proposed would cause severe harm to the French and Belgian populations and to future Anglo-French relations. But that cannot have been the only motive, since he continued to object to them even when it became apparent that civilian casualties were very light.[76] It is highly likely that the British wanted to continue direct pressure on Germany in hopeful anticipation of the collapse that would render the invasion itself superfluous. After the war, Churchill and Brooke admitted that the air strikes had indeed quarantined the Normandy battle zone, and that Allied air superiority had paralyzed enemy movements after the invasion.[77] That approach was not consonant with a belief that Germany's ability to transfer forces to the west would decide the future of the western European campaign one way or the other. Clearly, it was Churchill's general attitude toward the invasion that influenced his assessment of the Germans' logistic capabilities. Ironically, it was precisely during the early years of the war, when Allied fortunes were at their lowest ebb, that Churchill was optimistic; he then maintained that Germany's logistic capabilities were limited and could be made even more so. His capricious prevarications on this issue throughout the war demonstrate that it was not the principal cause behind his decision to avoid an invasion of western Europe.

British caution about the invasion is commonly explained by the fear of heavy loss of life, itself rooted in the memory of the previous world war. In defense of the British attitude, numerous senior British personages advanced and expanded on that argument during and after the war. A typical example is found in the words of the historian Arthur Bryant, who relied upon Alan Brooke's diary and evidence. He claimed that Churchill's fears stemmed from the memory of the failures and horrendous losses sustained during World War I. But Alan Brooke himself, despite his own recollections and fears, recognized the vital necessity for Overlord.[78] In his own work, Churchill explicitly cited the memory of the failure of the frontal assaults at the Somme and Passchendaele, together with the enormous loss of life in those battles, as his reason for adopting a cautious approach; his object was to ensure the most suitable timing for the invasion's success.[79] Nevertheless, it is of interest that Churchill does not grant that claim more prominence than any other arguments he uses to explain his attitude toward the "second front." Unquestionably, the problem posed by the losses and the memory of the previous world war did influence British decision makers. But there are good grounds for maintaining that this was not the *dominant* influence on Churchill's strategic thinking.

It will be recalled that in several discussions devoted to the invasion of western Europe Churchill emphasized that he was not afraid of the frontal assault stages and the establishment of the beachheads on the northern coast of France. It follows that he was not deterred by the fact of frontal attack, as exemplified during the previous war. There remains, then, the question of losses. However, the positions adopted by Churchill during and after World War I do not indicate that in his case (unlike that of other British statesmen) the experience had been so traumatic that it shaped his strategic conception. As we have already pointed out, where outlook on World War I strategy was concerned, discrepancies between Churchill and the British generals of the time were narrower than is commonly thought. True, he had been critical of the frontal attacks on the western front, but the foremost points in Churchill's critiques had been his belief that the attacks had been launched prematurely. He maintained that they were preventing the accumulation of the quantitative supremacy necessary to sustain the grand and decisive assault in the west. The fact that most British generals had been insensitive to loss of life does not make Churchill into a vegetarian.

When the lines in Gallipoli became locked, he pressed for continuing the land attacks (which by their nature were frontal), explicitly stating that they had to be pressed home without regard for losses. It will be recalled that he had objected to the evacuation of forces from the peninsula, believing that a determined assault would succeed and thereafter produce far-reaching consequences.[80] After World War I, in his biography of Marlborough, he was fiercely critical of military strategy commonly pursued in the seventeenth and eighteenth centuries because it was based on maneuver and avoiding decisive battle. Conversely, he lavished praise on the approach adopted by Marlborough, who had sought the decisive battle—even at considerable cost in blood—in order to bring the war to a swift and clear-cut conclusion. As we have also seen, the losses during the Great War and the fear of their repetition in a future conflict did not influence Churchill's outlook on the problem of "the continental commitment," as was the case with the men who actually formulated British strategy during the 1930s. He believed that a large British army had to be sent to France.[81]

After reading the complete correspondence between Churchill and Roosevelt, John Kenneth Galbraith wrote: "It has long been assumed that in resisting Overlord, Churchill was moved by his terrible memories of the Western Front, but this he nowhere makes explicit."[82] That impression is correct, and in no way negated by the claim that the British did raise that argument in their meetings with the Americans. If anything, it is strengthened by the records of Churchill's *internal* correspondence and discussions with his own military advisers, which provide no evidence that the memory of the losses of World War I had made a particular impression, if any at all, on his calculations. The fear of heavy losses was not one of the arguments brought by Churchill to the discussions of October 19, 1943, when he was fairly frank in presenting his reservations about Overlord. On the contrary, throughout the war Churchill grumbled over and over again that his commanders were not prepared to bear what he considered to be a tolerable rate of losses. In April 1941, when he ordered that Egypt had to be defended at all costs, he wrote that the units had to continue fighting until they had sustained losses of 50 percent.[83] When Singapore was surrounded and it became clear to the Prime Minister that its fate was sealed, he instructed Wavell to fight to the very end.

> There must at this stage be no thought of saving the troops or sparing the population. The battle must be fought to the bitter end and at all costs. . . . Commanders and senior officers should die with their troops. The honour of the British Empire and of the British Army is at stake. I rely on you to show no mercy to weakness in any form. With the Russians fighting as they are and the Americans so stubborn at Luzon, the whole reputation of our country and our race is involved.[84]

Equally revealing is Churchill's reaction to the Chiefs' objections to invading northern Norway on the grounds, among others, that the attacking force was likely to sustain heavy losses. "It seems unlikely," he wrote, "that more than one-fifth or one-sixth of the transports and covering craft would be sunk. A military attack is not ruled out simply because a fifth of the soldiers may be shot on the way, provided the others get there and do the job."[85] At the end of the war, in the spring of 1945, he tried to impress Eisenhower with the political importance of taking Berlin before the Russians did so. But generals Eisenhower and Bradley opposed an advance beyond the Elbe, citing as one of their reasons the fear of heavy casualties (Bradley estimated that an advance on Berlin would cost 100,000 casualties; in fact, the price the Russians ultimately paid was 300,000).[86] The significance of that exchange is highlighted by the fact that the Americans—who provided the greatest number of the troops designated for fighting in western Europe—repeatedly assured the British that they were prepared to sustain a high casualty rate to invade France.[87] That background, too, negates the possibility that Churchill's own attitude toward Overlord was predicated on its possible cost. He can hardly have been more concerned about the fate of U.S. soldiers than were their President and senior commander.

In sum, Churchill was not so influenced by memories of World War I that the need to minimize losses would become the primary base of his strategic concept in the second global conflict. His understanding of the nature of war was sufficiently deep for him to recognize that a strategy founded on the avoidance of casualties is ineffective. His line of thinking was that a course had to be selected which aimed at a decision but also—among other considerations—at reducing losses. He was prepared to sustain heavy losses when he considered the objective very worthwhile from a military or political viewpoint. When he thought it possible to attain a swift *decision* in the war by taking a particular move, even at heavy human cost, he was not deterred from attempting it. The facts demonstrate that the fear of heavy losses was not the primary reason in making him oppose a massive invasion of western Europe. *Ex hypothesi*, had he been convinced that there existed a high probability that the invasion would bring the war to a swift conclusion, he would have supported it notwithstanding heavy casualties.

Neither did political considerations move Churchill to oppose the invasion of western Europe or to advocate its postponement for as long as possible. Our preceding chapter has already portrayed his basic position on the connection between military moves and political objectives. Decisions affecting the shaping of the postwar period in general and the treatment of the Soviet problem in particular he deferred to the end of the war. The next chapter will prove that Churchill did not change his attitude until *after* the invasion. Only then did he begin to initiate military moves, or to look upon those that had begun already, in part with an eye to their possible effectiveness in curbing Soviet influence in postwar Europe.

The British intelligence community and he Chiefs of Staff consistently fed Churchill with assessments optimistically forecasting Germany's imminent collapse. These influenced his outlook on the expediency of a massive invasion of western Europe, indicating that it was preferable to bide one's time rather than run the risks such an assault entailed. Those estimates also strengthened the natural inclination to take no action on the matter. Occasionally, albeit infrequently, Churchill questioned the overoptimistic tone pervading the intelligence estimates. Thus, in the opening paragraphs of the Grand Plan written at the end of 1941, he argued against basing British strategy on awaiting a German collapse that, he claimed, was not a precondition for his plan. But, as we have seen, not even in that document did Churchill manage to shake off his dependence on a prior German collapse. His difficulties in doing so reveal the principal reason for his opposition to an invasion of western Europe: he feared the results of a direct and massive clash between the Anglo-American and German forces "in the open field," division against division. His own pessimistic estimate, to which he adhered for a considerable time, was that the campaign would end in the rout of the Allied armies. In his more optimistic moments, he was of the opinion that the fighting in western Europe would not bring about the defeat of the German army—but that result, too, would hardly warrant the risks the invasion would entail. His fear of frontal collision on land was caused by the fact that his confidence in the ability and strength of the British Army had been undermined. He had lost faith in the skills of the field high command and in the fighting spirit of "Tommy Atkins."

Churchill had never had a high opinion of the professional and intellectual abilities of senior British military men and the military establishment. Even at an early stage of his career, his relationships with the Army leaders of the time had been marked by tension. In his first books, he had criticized the military conduct of a number of the late nineteenth-century colonial wars. His opinions were strengthened by the experience of World War I when, so he claimed, "the experts were frequently wrong. The politicians were frequently right." At the

outbreak of World War II, he did not expect his military men to w
But he did anticipate demonstrations of the sort of fierce fighting s
by junior officers and men throughout the long course of British mi
ry and during the previous war. He considered this factor particularly
since he believed that willpower played a very significant role in w
secret Parliament session of 1941 he urged his audience not to forge֡   ..ᴄ
enemy confronted difficulties of his own; all the great struggles of history had
been decided by stronger willpower, which could wrest victory from superior
odds and make the difference between equal forces.⁸⁸ In the memoranda he
wrote during Gallipoli, Churchill maintained that tenacity would ultimately
lead to victory. In *The World Crisis* he claimed that the absence of that resource
had been one of the primary reasons for the failure of the operation.⁸⁹ He considered lack of willpower responsible for the failure of the Germans at the
Marne in 1914 and of the White forces in the Russian civil war.⁹⁰ In April 1941,
at moments of crisis in Greece and North Africa, he launched into a heated lecture to senior officers that went on far into the night; his main point was that
war is at root a contest of wills.⁹¹ He did not shrink from repeatedly drumming
that message into their ears.⁹²

The first stages of World War II gave Churchill no reason to believe that
the British military system might be suffering from a basic flaw. The defeat in
France in 1940 was attributed to French military leadership, the low morale of
the French army, the Germans' innovative fighting doctrine, and that the forces
sent to France had not been large enough. The evacuation from Dunkirk
seemed to provide another vindication of the endurance of the British soldier.
The victories in Africa at the end of 1940 buttressed Churchill's opinion that
the British Army had not been inferior to the German army it had faced in the
battles in the Low Countries.⁹³ Although aware of the weakness of the Italian
army, he was also sensitive to the fact that the British Army had only been partly trained and equipped at a time when, so he believed, its German counterpart
was at the peak of its strength. He thus contemplated the future with confidence. Not even the failure in Greece particularly impressed him. The German
advantage in the air and on land had from the first been too great.⁹⁴ But the
swift German success in the Balkans, together with Rommel's advance in the
western desert, did begin to make their mark on his thinking. At the end of
April 1941 he insisted on retaining Tobruk, which had been invested from the
land, notwithstanding his advisers' desire for its evacuation. As he wrote to
Dill: "Twenty-five thousand men with one hundred guns and ample supplies
are expected to be able to hold a highly fortified zone against forty-five hundred men at the end of seven hundred miles of communications, *even though
those men be Germans; in this case some of them are not.*"⁹⁵

When Crete fell shortly thereafter, something broke in Churchill. On his
advice, General Bernard Freyberg (who had been decorated with the Victoria
Cross) had been appointed to command the forces on the island, which included some of the Empire's best troops. Churchill admired Freyberg's rare brand

of courage, and believed that he would "impart his own invincible firmness of mind to all around him."[96] Through Ultra Freyberg had acquired sound intelligence of German intentions. His assessment was that the German invasion of Crete would be defeated. That view was shared by the commands in Cairo and London. Nevertheless, Crete fell after what seemed to be a classic battle of wills. Within a short time, the counterattack in North Africa ("Battleaxe"), on which Churchill had pinned high hopes, suffered a crushing defeat. Thereafter, he removed Wavell from the Middle East command and sent him to India.[97] Other politicians, too, began to doubt the quality of British military leadership. Eden and Cadogan agreed that the recent failures were the result of weaknesses in the British high command. Henceforth, Cadogan would commit to his diary incessantly scornful remarks about military men.[98] Churchill was far less discreet. At the end of 1941 he informed Colville that the reason it would be unfair to carry out large diversionary operations on the French coast was that the War Office possessed "neither the means nor the intelligence" to operate against the organizational ability and experience of the Germans.[99] Field Marshal Dill, whom Churchill nicknamed "Dilly-Dally," resigned after he and the Prime Minister suffered a mutual crisis of confidence at the end of 1941.[100] Although Wavell was very highly regarded by his senior brother officers, Churchill was from the start unimpressed by him. He was unable to discern in Wavell the power, drive, and determination so vital for victory in battle.[101] Auchinleck, Wavell's replacement, enjoyed no better fate. Senior army commanders were frequently and persistently scolded by Churchill. Alan Brooke's diaries are replete with descriptions of the Prime Minister's attacks on his generals, including those who—like Montgomery and Alexander—were more successful, even during those stages of the war when the Allies were already winning. Churchill informed them, so Dill recalled, that "we had no ideas of our own and, whenever he produced ideas, we produced nothing but objections." Moreover, they were not prepared to take risks, but to attack only when victory was already assured.[102]

With the approach of the opening of operation Crusader at the end of 1941, Churchill harbored higher hopes. The success of Crusader's opening stages also generated optimism in the plan for the conduct of the war he composed en route to Washington. But that mood very soon passed. The fall of Singapore, together with Rommel's counterattack in the western desert, raised his doubts with even greater force. The Prime Minister was deeply influenced by the fact that the British had in Malaya and Singapore surrendered to a far smaller Japanese force. In his own words, that was "the worst disaster and largest capitulation in British history."[103] Especially was this so when Wavell verified his feeling that the troops on the spot had not displayed sufficient fighting spirit.[104] He was so upset that he frankly informed the members of the U.S. delegation visiting London that "there is no explanation of the lack of resistance on the [British] part."[105]

At about the same time, in February 1942, the Defence Committee pondered how German forces had managed to defeat two British armored brigades in Libya, suffering only light losses against patently superior numerical odds. Churchill was not convinced that the reason lay in technical inferiority and in flaws in the British tanks (the explanation advanced by O. Lyttelton, the Government's representative in Cairo).[106] Instead, he began to search for the causes in the superior level of command the Germans had displayed in North Africa. General Auchinleck conceded that the standard of British divisional commanders and brigadiers was not good. Auchinleck also agreed with Lieutenant General Nye, Alan Brooke's Vice-Chief of the General Staff, that the source of the British weakness lay in the prewar period, when their own officers had been only partly and inadequately trained, while their enemies had been well prepared for the coming conflict. Nye, who considered that British inferiority found its expression in command of armored forces but not infantry divisions, hastened to reassure his Prime Minister, pointing out that "there is nothing inherently superior in the German leader or soldier."[107]

At the beginning of June 1942, when the future of Sledgehammer was being discussed, Churchill argued against carrying out a large-scale assault on the French coast; failure, he cautioned, would give rise to "a whole set of inhibitions" against a large operation in that region in 1943.[108] In fact, no failure on the French coast was required to inhibit him. That same month, he suffered a heavy blow when Tobruk fell. Churchill did not conceal his astonishment. His book categorizes as "a disgrace" the surrender of the Tobruk garrison, numbering 33,000 experienced troops, to a force half its size (as had been the case at Singapore). He described the string of defeats suffered by the British Army in the years 1941–1942 as "galling links in a chain of misfortune and frustration to which no parallel could be found in our history."[109] That sentence tells us more about the depth of his feelings than his expertise in British military history. He had begun to lose faith, not just in the military command, but also in the fighting spirit of the British soldier. He was not heartened when, at the beginning of June, Dill advised that the supreme command over the operation to invade western Europe be entrusted to an American—to avoid U.S. accusations in the event of failure and because "the fresh mind of an American would have many advantages over that of some Britons whose cares of the past three years have been so largely centered on defending England."[110] It was a matter of additional concern that the commanders of the British Army in North Africa enjoyed clear advantages. During the course of 1941, and especially in 1942, they possessed considerable numerical superiority over Rommel in the air and on land; by means of Ultra they had also acquired important intelligence about the enemy. Nevertheless, Rommel remained a very hard nut to crack. These facts moved Churchill to conclude at the end of July 1942 that the Germans possessed a mighty military machine. Contemplating the strength of the British Army and the ability of the Anglo-American armies to defeat the Wehrmacht, even in the distant future, his thoughts were dismal.[111]

Churchill was not the only person gnawed by doubts concerning the quality of British military leadership. At the beginning of July, Attlee (the Deputy Prime Minister) and Stafford Cripps (also a member of the War Cabinet) pointed out to him the Army's patent inferiority to Rommel's Afrika Korps. They considered the principal reason for the defeats lay in the British high command's incompetence and old-fashioned approach. Attlee proposed that this subject be discussed without military persons being present.[112] Churchill replied to Attlee that he had never claimed to argue that the British were as adept at ground warfare as the Germans. It was at sea and in the air that the British military system excelled. The Germans had for almost a decade made intensive preparations for war, while in Britain conscription had been introduced only a few months before its outbreak. Prior to the war, few men had chosen to pursue a military career since the attractions of the civilian market were so much greater. "Most of the rewards of British public life went to the politicians." The pacificism rife in British society had exerted an adverse influence on the fighting spirit of the British Army.

> *Continuous reflection* leaves me with the conclusion that upon the whole, our best chance of winning the war is with the big Bombers. It certainly will be several years before British and American land forces will be capable of beating the Germans on even terms in the open field.[113]

Sound or not, Churchill certainly had his reasons for fearing that it would take some years before British ground forces would be able to confront the Germans as equals. But the only basis for his corollary assessment of the U.S. Army was the preconceptions common among the British elite, one of which was the supposition that the U.S. Army could not be better than was the British. When Churchill wrote his letter to Attlee, U.S. troops had not yet fought against Germans—but they had faced the Japanese. The record of those exchanges was significant. The Americans had grimly held on to the Philippines until early May; in doing so, moreover, they had displayed precisely the sort of tenacity Churchill had expected of his own army when defending Malaya (which, together with almost all of Burma, the Japanese had conquered during the same period). At the beginning of June, the Americans—notwithstanding their numerical inferiority—had defeated the Japanese fleet off Midway, thus turning the tables in the Pacific. About a week after Churchill answered Attlee, the Americans landed at Guadalcanal in the Solomon Islands, thereby initiating an assault that was to conclude with Japan's surrender. The British were to need about another year before they could launch Wingate's deep Chindit raid into Burma and thereby shatter their own myth about the undefeated Japanese "jungle fighter." Marshall had good reason to be proud during the Casablanca meeting, when he called attention to the enormous and swift improvement that had taken place in the fighting ability of the U.S. units. They were restoring a faith already grounded in the experience of World War I.[114]

But the roots of the British denigration of the Americans ran too deep.

Alan Brooke's diaries are full of disparaging references to his partners. His comment on Eisenhower was that "he learnt a lot during the war, but tactics, strategy, and command were never his strong points."[115] His opinion of Marshall was better, but not very much so. Pouncing on their prey, the British inflated out of all proportion the failure of the U.S. forces to check Rommel's counterattack at the Kasserine Pass in Tunisia. Moreover, they did so despite the fact that within a few days the Americans had regained the ground lost.[116] The blows the Americans suffered in Tunis constituted one of the arguments Churchill appended to the draft of his letter to Stalin in February 1943 (it was deleted from the final version) where he attempted to explain to the Russian leader the problems of an invasion in 1943.[117] Churchill knew more about the nature of the United States and the Americans than did his colleagues in the military. Unlike them, he had initially anticipated much from the U.S. army as soon as its expansion was complete. As time went on, but before the U.S. army had fully expressed itself, his anticipations withered. But that was mostly because the British Prime Minister had lost faith in his own army.

As has already been pointed out, Churchill's military advisers did not behave as though they were trying to allay his fears. On the contrary, when forthcoming moves were discussed in the autumn of 1942, it was the Planners and Chiefs of Staff who pointed out that accumulated experience indicated the impossibility of invading western Europe before Germany had been very much weakened.[118] They thus reinforced an opinion Churchill had committed to paper as early as July. Nevertheless, the victory at Alamein and the opening moves in Torch did inspire him with some sense of confidence. That factor, together with others (which were more important) led him in the autumn of 1942 to press his military advisers to reexamine the possibility of implementing the invasion in 1943. But as soon as the unforseen delays in the conquest of North Africa became apparent, optimism vanished and pessimism returned. The Italian campaign very much exacerbated the latter feeling. The evaporation of the great strategic hopes they had placed on this campaign came as a considerable disappointment to Churchill and his advisers. They were surprised that they needed to fight a real land war against the Germans (although, commensurate with their own opinion of the fighting capability their adversary had hitherto displayed, they were very much less surprised by the outcome).

The desire of Churchill and his advisors to avoid an intensive land engagement with the Wehrmacht had been one of the principal—albeit, it must be added, less articulated—reasons for their struggle to widen the "Mediterranean strategy" in 1943. Hitler upset their assessments by deciding to defend Tunisia and Italy. All these developments strengthened old tendencies. Churchill subsequently wrote: "I am sure now that . . . the attempt to cross the Channel in 1943 would have led to a bloody defeat of the first magnitude. . . . I became increasingly conscious of this during the whole of 1943."[119] That recollection is not precise. The progress of the war during 1943 merely made stronger his opinion that even an invasion *in 1944* would end in failure or, in the best of cases, that the move was so full of dangers that it had better be abandoned. His appraisal of the check to a German advance up Italy temporarily caused him to draw alarmist conclusions: in October 1943 he feared that in 1944 the Germans would be capable of defeating, sequentially, the Anglo-American forces invading western Europe and those in Italy.[120] His alarm spread to others too. Retroactively, Brooke justified the British position at the end of 1943 by reporting his fears that, unless enough German forces were tied down in Italy, there was a danger that the Germans might defeat the invading forces in the West and then turn to defeat Russia.[121] Whether Brooke did indeed fear that outcome must be considered doubtful. His claim is inconsistent with British intelligence assessments, which ever since the end of 1942 had categorically stated that Germany had lost all chance of victory in the east.

Mention must be made of two further causes—although it is not clear whether these contributed to the creation of that incorrect assessment or merely supported it. One is the slow realization that the thesis of Germany's impending collapse was unfounded; the second, initially somewhat paradoxical, is the enormous success in the sphere of intelligence. Although (as will be recalled) Churchill had indeed doubted the efficacy of the "collapse" thesis early in the war, the more his confidence in the ability of his own army was undermined the more that notion became central to his strategic thinking. The great event was hopefully expected to take place in 1943. But instead of watching Germany buckle—a process supposed to have been accelerated by the blow in Italy—Churchill watched it put up obstinate resistance there. Ironically enough, the collapse that did not happen even strengthened the considerations that had led him initially, albeit somewhat reluctantly, to rely on it. He considered Germany stronger than he had anticipated and the disparity between its army and his own to be even larger. This was a vicious circle. It did not occur to Churchill that perhaps the "German house" had not collapsed simply because it had not been struck at its essential props.

Ultra, the achievement in breaking the German codes, helped the Allied war effort considerably. But its principal contribution was at the operational level of the conduct of the war's campaigns. Project Ultra possessed several clear advantages, but the very nature of the information it supplied also ensured that it suffered from inherent limitations as a source for assessments at the highest strategic level. As has already been demonstrated, one nice example of the way that was so is supplied by the period from the end of 1940 until mid-1941 (during the eve and aftermath of the Greek "fiasco"), when British intelligence in Cairo and London, together with Wavell and the Chiefs of Staff and of course Churchill, attempted to estimate Hitler's intentions in the Balkans and the Middle East, and against the Soviet Union. These were not found out; indeed, so late did British intelligence reach the conclusion that Hitler intended to attack the Soviet Union that its analysis can be described as a statement of fact rather than a prediction. It can reasonably be assumed that it would have reached the same conclusion in equal time on the basis of information derived from more conventional sources. A corollation of the items received through Ultra did indeed help Churchill to anticipate his intelligence advisers and thereby estimate that a German attack on the Soviet Union was imminent; but he could not convince them that such was the case. In any event, it was too late to prevent him from becoming entangled in the Balkans. Ultra did not prevent the mistaken thesis of Germany's collapse. It was not clear-cut information from Ultra that was responsible for the decisions to cancel Sledgehammer in 1942 and to replace it with the invasion of western North Africa, cancel Round-up in 1943, and eventually carry out the invasion in 1944. Hitler's decision, made at the end of 1942, to continue defending North Africa by heavy reinforcements was unforseen. The British committed serious errors of judgment when forecasting his reactions to the invasion of Italy. Information based on Ultra was not even immune to crass errors at the operational level. For instance, no note was taken of German troop movements and concentrations on the eve of the surprise German attack in the Ardennes in the winter of 1944–1945. In sum, the intelligence gained through Ultra was not of decisive weight when the *central* decisions on the high strategic level with regard to the invasion of western Europe were considered and taken.[122]

It would not be too farfetched to suggest that the achievement in the sphere of intelligence undermined rather than strengthened Churchill's confidence in the ability of the Allied armies to launch a successful invasion of western Europe. Supporting that hypothesis is that—notwithstanding the important information received via Ultra, occasionally complemented by a material advantage—British commanders time and again failed in their battles or had experienced great difficulty in defeating their adversaries. Ultra information was considered a great and rare asset. Because of its nature and extremely limited circulation, it was also a personal advantage entrusted to senior field commanders. That was why their failures sometimes seemed to be the result of their own shortcomings and incompetence rather than of circumstances that not even good intelligence can overcome. (Therein lies a partial explanation for the frequency with which Churchill instigated changes in the Middle East high command, which harmed rather than helped.) This did not inspire the Prime Minister with more confidence in his commanders, and exacerbated the way, in any case faulty, in which he assessed the state of the military balance.

As we have seen, it was difficult to determine where principal responsibility lay for Churchill and his military advisers being opposed to the implementation of Sledgehammer in 1942: was it because they had lost their confidence in their army or because the obstacles confronting that operation were too daunting? But it is now possible to discern that Churchill's assessments were born of a misunderstanding of realities. Ironically, his lack of confidence in the Anglo-American armies, together with his overestimate of the capabilities of the German land forces, peaked at the end of 1943. That was precisely when the Wehrmacht had become a defeated army on all fronts. The fate of the war in Russia had been decided, and the Germans were in a state of perpetual retreat in the east. Numerous intelligence items indicated that the German divisions were becoming thinner and weaker in both manpower and equipment. By contrast, the translation of Anglo-American resources into military power was reaching a peak; the Allies now resembled a tight spring that had yet to be released. At the end of 1943, they enjoyed numerical and intelligence superiority, as well as command of the air over northern France, the Mediterranean, and Italy (they were also asserting command of the air over Germany too). Churchill's mistake did not lie in the fact that he was impressed with "the extraordinary fighting efficiency of the German Army," but in that he very much exaggerated the extent of the qualitative disparity between that force and the Anglo-American armies. He did not believe that the advantages enumerated above would overcome that qualitative difference during an invasion of western Europe in 1944.

The foregoing comments assume that the qualitative difference between the armies of the two sides was not large and only sporadic. That assumption does not accord with recent works on the subject, whose authors have praised the German army's fighting capability on the battlefield in comparison with that of its adversaries in World War II.[123] If accepted, their view might justify Churchill's impression, but not its *depth*. After all, the Anglo-American force did effect a successful Channel crossing in 1944 and smite the Germans notwithstanding Churchill's own pessimistic assessment of the extent of its qualitative inferiority. Although the views of those authors have gained wide acceptance, there are in fact good reasons for treating their conclusions with caution. There is something fashionable about the appearance of those studies and the swift concurrence with their results. They reflect a degree of self-denigration (together with the wish of some parties to denigrate others) and even a tendency to fall under the spell of what one author has termed the German "genius for war." Interest in them was at its height at a time when the crisis in the U.S. military system peaked in the wake of the Vietnam War. The Pentagon, together with the U.S. man in the street, was seeking an explanation for the army's failure, a recipe for success, and a model to emulate. The German army in World War II attracted attention because many observers experienced a sense of spontaneous admiration for the Germans having conquered almost all of Europe in a series of lightning blows and thereafter (in the words of one renowned military historian) standing alone "against the entire world" for three- and-a-half years. Researchers set to work to discover the magic secret. But in fact none existed.

Matters are more banal: for one thing, the German achievements were not so impressive and unprecedented; for another, specific circumstances contributed to their efficiency and to the fact that they appeared to be more efficient than they were.

1. For most of World War II the Germans did not fight simultaneously against "the entire world" nor even against all the states of Europe. Germany fought its foes sequentially. Moreover, without a land front in the west, until

June 1944 it conducted a real war only against the Soviet Union. That was an enemy which had in 1941 been considered inferior to Germany (bearing in mind British intelligence estimates of that year, and the opinions of the Germans and of the Russians themselves). Hitler had the benefit of three years, or three "rounds," during which he attempted to defeat his principal rival—having opened the fight under optimal conditions and with the resources of Europe at his disposal. "The rest of the world," meanwhile, had in effect stood on the sidelines, not knowing how to utilize most of its strength against him. The naval blockade was ineffectual, and the strategic bombing raids did not become formidable until the end of 1943. Nevertheless, with its defeat at Kursk in the summer of 1943 Germany had already lost the war on the eastern front, and thus World War II in its entirety—even before the invasion of Italy! Is that record illustrative of military excellence?

It took the Germans three years of war to reach their most extensive lines of conquest; its enemies required two-and-a-half years to regain their losses and physically conquer Germany itself. Moreover, they accomplished that feat even though the western powers carried a heavy amphibious burden, despite the fact that the United States deployed only part of its strength on the European front, and even though Allied land power only exercised itself fully during the last eleven months of the war, after June 1944. (That time span might possibly have been considerably contracted had advantage been taken of the golden opportunity that presented itself on the western front in the summer of 1944. See below.) The root of the Allies' problem in the west, and one explanation for Germany's resilience, lay in their difficulty in translating their quantitative superiority (expressed in the charts replete with tanks, guns, and divisions) from the stores and camps to the battlefield. It will be recalled that no one had better articulated that dilemma than Churchill himself who, in November 1943, had bemoaned the fact that of the 2 million Allied troops in the Mediterranean region, only 170,000 were stationed in the front lines and actually fighting the 412,000 Germans in Italy. At the same time, the Germans themselves estimated that in Russia, where the war had already been decided, about 4 million of their men were confronting 5.5 million soldiers of the Red Army.[124] Where no natural barriers existed, the numerical superiority of the Allies was soon realized. Victory in the war at sea was achieved in 1943 and command of the air over Germany attained months before the invasion.

2. Germany was the first to introduce modern tank warfare and to establish independent armored formations. Together with other factors, this military doctrine gave the offensive an advantage over the defense at the operational-tactical level. During the first stages of the war, Germany's enemies possessed no such forces nor efficient antitank measures. These were the advantages that enabled it to harvest those celebrated successes. But they were offset some time around 1942, by when all the parties had learned the nature of the job—establishing independent armored formations and developing effective antitank measures. Another circumstance then also evolved: the ratio between the offensive

and the defense altogether changed, and reverted to its traditional state, which favored the defense.[125] Thus it was that the German army enjoyed the advantages of the offensive when attacking and of the defense when, in the latter stages of the conflict, it was on the defensive. Its adversaries experienced precisely the opposite: they were on the defensive during the period when the advantage lay with the offense and attacking when it resided with the defense. This was an important tactical consideration, especially for so good and experienced an army as the Germans possessed. Notwithstanding the upheavals of the war, it remained relevant throughout its course. That is why the impression of German fighting excellence persisted throughout the war and after its conclusion.

Some authors argue that an invasion of western Europe would have succeeded in 1943.[126] Their studies are not convincing. By its nature, that hypothesis is not amenable to decisive proof. The present writer does not claim to argue that an invasion was possible in 1943; rather, it will be recalled, our position is that—had the decision been up to the British—no invasion would have taken place in *1944*. But the above-mentioned studies indicate the existence of a contrary argument, for their authors clearly doubt whether the qualitative difference between the armies was very significant—if at all.

Churchill bears more than a little of the responsibility for the development of the very impediments he experienced. Moves that he himself originated lay at the root of the British defeats in North Africa by which he was so deeply impressed. After all, it was he who initiated the establishment of a Balkan front and the dispatch of the best of the Middle East army into a hopeless military campaign in Greece. That venture threw into disarray the process of the Army's buildup—precisely at the time when its success in North Africa was beginning to inspire it with confidence in its own strength. Aware of their Army's brittle ability at that phase of the war (and, equally so, of their own limitations), its commanders showed caution and a wish to concentrate on its preparation. By contrast, Churchill's ambition during the initial stages of the war was to suit the Army to himself, rather than vice versa. It was this situation which generated a dissonance between Churchill and his Army that the war's events didn't repair, but merely exacerbated. Initially, he attributed to his forces a degree of power they did not possess; later, he attributed to them much less strength than they were capable of deploying.

And what of the Chiefs of Staff? The evidence presented here so far indicates that their opinion on the "second front" more or less coincided with that of their Prime Minister. But that is not to say that they shared the same motives. A fundamental analysis of those motives lies beyond the scope of this book; nevertheless, several remarks are in order. First, note must be taken of the extent to which they disagreed with Churchill both as to the importance they attributed to certain factors and about their priorities. The differences, although slight, were significant. More important, the Prime Minister's motives did not encompass all of those of his Chiefs of Staff. As military men, their outlook on the conduct of the war was influenced by the relevant spheres of activity of the different arms they commanded (particularly since those arms competed for the same resources). Moreover, in concert, they represented the bureaucratic interests of a mighty military organization. Their personalities naturally also influenced their calculations. Dudley Pound was too sick and apathetic to insist on his independent opinion on any matter beyond that affecting the conduct of the war at sea and the defense of the fleet's interests. Charles Portal, together with such senior RAF officers as Arthur Harris, believed in the ability of strategic bombing raids to win the war. The latter's faith led to a struggle (ultimately successful) for the allocation of more resources for overwhelming air power—and thus also for reliance on the "collapse thesis." Alan Brooke was himself. On the strength of the prominence already accorded to Brooke's views, readers will surely be able to form their own judgment of his character and motives. Suffice it to say that he was certainly not made of the stuff of Marlborough and Wellington.

Churchill, of course, found it hard to inform the Americans during the war and the readers of *The Second World War* thereafter, that the principal source of his opposition to a grand invasion of western Europe lay in the fact that he had lost confidence in the ability of Anglo-American ground forces to confront the Wehrmacht on the plains of western Europe. Instead, what were presented were secondary reasons and operational and strategic excuses. In order to generate understanding for British caution about an invasion, he dragged up the memory of the massive losses sustained during the previous war. Another explanation invented was strategic opportunism. The following is the manner in which Churchill described the difference between "the American mind" and "the "British mind":

> In the military as in the commercial or production spheres the American mind runs naturally to broad, sweeping, logical conclusions on the largest scale. It is on these that they build their practical thought and action. They feel that once the foundation has been planned on true and comprehensive lines all other stages will follow naturally and almost inevitably. The British mind does not work quite in this way. We do not think that logic and clear-cut principles are necessarily the sole keys to what ought to be done in swiftly changing and indefinable situations. In war particularly we assign a larger importance to opportunism and improvisation, seeking rather to live and conquer in accordance with the unfolding event than to aspire to dominate it often by fundamental decisions.[127]

Thus did Churchill explain away those of his suggestions and steps that clearly seemed to deviate from, or be contrary to, the invasion of western Europe, which he declared to be his principal objective. Undoubtedly, opportunism was a foundation of his strategic thinking and moves during both world wars, but it was never at the core of his nature as a strategist. One of the primary claims offered in this book is that Churchill held certain firm strategic beliefs; those he preserved over a long period of time, and sometimes tried to implement in spite of changes in the general situation. As far as the basics of British grand strategy were concerned, only once did Churchill change his concept after the turn of the century—and thereafter held fast to it. His opportunism was anchored in his strategic beliefs, not a substitute for them. Some maintain that he was an opportunistic statesman and strategist because that is the nature of politicians. But as was argued at the beginning of this book, Churchill was a strategist and statesman (initially only in thought) who became a politician, not the other way around. He did not barter his strategic and diplomatic opinions for a mess of political pottage.

A comparison of his public statements on matters strategic and diplomatic with those he expressed in his private papers reveals hardly any discrepancies at all. He aimed to lead men, and was not led by others. When that was impossible, he preferred to remain on the sidelines. There was some truth to his claim that he switched his political parties but not his opinions. He was not very much inclined to bend before the dictates of domestic and party politics, which he detested. There is surely no need to remind the reader that his standing in his own party and in British public life was not improved by his decision to weaken the force of the Mediterranean fleet in 1912, by his position in favor of "intervention" in Russia in 1919, his support for the uncompromising breaking of the "general strike" in 1926, his opposition to reforms in British rule in India, his attitude toward the "German problem" and support for the conclusion of an alliance with the Soviet Union in the 1930s, or by his support for King Edward VIII's marriage to an American divorcée. To cite such instances is not to suggest that, in the long course of his political career, Churchill never took an opportunistic step. But they do indicate that he cannot be depicted as an opportunistic politician, still less as an opportunistic statesman and strategist.

As far as our specific subject is concerned, the extent to which the last sentence in the above passage is false can be proved by reference to the Greek episode that has here been discussed at so much length. Churchill cleaved to an idea—establishment of a Balkan front—which he had formed some time before the outbreak of war; he took a "fundamental decision" to dispatch an expeditionary force to Greece; finally, and despite the need "to live and conquer in accordance with the unfolding event," he thereafter refused to change that decision in order to exploit the golden opportunity of advancing on Tripoli, which presented itself in the course of the great success in North Africa. The clear and consistent thread running through his positions and moves after the beginning of 1942 is opposition to a massive invasion of western Europe in the face of stiff German resistance. His other ideas—invasion of Norway, invasion of western North Africa, invasion of Sicily and Italy, assault on southern France, reconquest of the Dodecanese, bringing Turkey into the war—appeared and disappeared again and again in what seemed to be an opportunistic manner. But, always, each was given priority and precedence over the invasion of western Europe.

10

Grand Strategy: The Soviet Menace and the End of the War, 1943-1945

Early in 1943, immediately after the Casablanca conference, Churchill met with the leaders of Turkey in an attempt to induce them to enter the war. During the discussions, the Turks gave vent to their deep concern about what might happen in Europe were a victorious and powerful Russia to refuse to cooperate with Great Britain and the United States after the war. Not only were they anxious about Turkey's security; they also feared that communist regimes might be established in the defeated states, and elsewhere. Churchill tried to set their minds at rest. In his opinion, he informed President Inönü that Russia would want to cooperate with the West; besides, it had committed itself for the next twenty years to a treaty of alliance concluded with Britain. Russia would have to devote about ten years, at least, to its own economic rehabilitation and would require Anglo-American assistance. Turkey would attain security within the framework of the international organization to be established after the war.[1] The Turks remained unconvinced. Their Prime Minister explained that Turkey would like its security guaranteed by something more substantive than an international organization. Churchill had difficulty in understanding their concern.[2]

These criticisms moved Churchill to write a memorandum, which he entitled "Morning Thoughts, Note on Post War Security."[3] Howard to the contrary, he did not jot down those notes in preparation for his meeting with the Turks; rather they were written as a consequence of those conversations.[4] At this stage of the war, only pressures from an external source could have prompted him to write on subjects affecting the postwar period. Notwithstanding its promising title, more than half of "Morning Thoughts" was devoted to Turkey and the ways in which its entry into the war might be speeded up. Churchill's ideas about the problem of postwar security constituted an extension of his reaction in late 1942 to Eden's Four Power plan. At the peace conference the victorious powers would ensure that the defeated powers were entirely disarmed. For many years, they would have to devote their energies to the rehabilitation of Europe.

Russia, which had suffered particularly extensive damage, would enjoy all possible assistance. The principles of the Atlantic Charter precluded Russia and Britain from making any territorial gains. However, the Russians maintained that they were entitled to return to the borders of June 1941. Nevertheless, they also recognized that the alignment of their border with Poland was dependent upon Polish acquiescence. An international organization, of which a "European government" would form a part, would be established to preserve peace. This would not suffer from the weaknesses that had plagued the League of Nations (although how such weaknesses were to be avoided was not made explicit). The European government would itself comprise the larger nations of Europe as well as Turkey; the smaller nations would be affiliated within confederations of the Scandinavian, Danubian, and Balkan states. Churchill added that there was no guarantee that the victorious powers would not fall out among themselves; but the experience of the war would teach them that another conflict would result in the extermination of all humanity. This would impose upon them policies of restraint and cooperation. Britain would establish a coalition of states against any aggressive power; it could be assumed that it would be joined by the United States, whose strength and size would make it the world's leader.[5]

These "Morning Thoughts," which Churchill also sent to President Roosevelt, show that Churchill underplayed the extent of the Soviet menace to Europe. As before, he pinned his hopes on the Soviets' moderation—which would itself be the consequence of their dependence on western economic aid after the war. That seems an oversanguine assessment: two weeks later, the intelligence chiefs were to report that Germany's collapse would soon be followed by communist control over Bulgaria, which might even be annexed to the Soviet Union. They also considered it highly probable that the Soviets would also be in control of Rumania, while the fate of Hungary, Albania, and Yugoslavia was not clear.[6]

After the Casablanca conference, Churchill and Roosevelt had the embarrassing task of informing Stalin that a large-scale invasion of western Europe would not take place in 1943, notwithstanding the personal assurances the Soviet leader had received from the British Prime Minister. In an uncharacteristic display of cooperation against Stalin, Roosevelt and Churchill attempted to wriggle out of their duty. After meeting in Casablanca, they told Stalin that they were concentrating forces in Britain "to re-enter the continent of Europe as soon as practicable," and nothing more.[7] In February, Churchill composed a letter to Stalin that adopted a more positive tone about the opening of the "second front." In his draft, Churchill wrote that Britain and the United States intended to invade in August with a force of some twenty divisions; however, the timing of the assault depended on the strength of the German defense and on the weather. It will surely be recalled that, in fact, during the Casablanca conference no agreement had been reached about the implementation of even a limited invasion (such as Sledgehammer) in 1943. Marshall did not believe that one could be carried out. Alan Brooke himself doubted whether it would be possible to transfer from the Mediterranean to Britain sufficient forces and landing craft in time to exploit the eventuality of a German collapse at the end of 1943.[8] In any event, during the weeks following the conference, and in tandem with Churchill's contacts with Stalin, the Joint Planners examined (without much enthusiasm) the possibility of carrying out an invasion on the lines of Sledgehammer that year, after the conquest of Sicily.

When the Chiefs of Staff read the draft of Churchill's letter to Stalin, they protested that he had made what seemed to them an explict commitment. Churchill hastened to reassure them.[9] The reference to the size of the invasion force was deleted from the final version. Once approved by Roosevelt, the letter was dispatched to Stalin on February 12. It implied that a large-scale invasion was still planned for the spring of 1943, but that for various reasons it would be deferred until the end of the summer of 1943. Stalin's immediate response was to demand that the opening of the "second front" be brought forward from August-September to the spring of 1943.[10] After further consideration, he began to grasp what was afoot. On February 17 Maisky, the Soviet ambassador in London, urgently requested a meeting with Churchill. Because Churchill was ill, and in any case unwilling to see the Ambassador, Maisky's request was turned down; he could only meet with Eden, who then relayed his message to Churchill. Maisky, he reported, had been agitated and clearly repeating a direct message from Stalin. Its thrust was the Russian opinion that Germany could be defeated during the current year if simultaneously attacked from the east and the west. It was therefore preferable to transfer the Anglo-American forces from North Africa to Britain and in June to invade France, rather than Sicily and southern Italy. According to Eden's reconstruction of the conversation, Maisky had warned that

> if it were true that the German armies had suffered major disasters in Russia and that as a result the war could end in 1943, it was of the first importance that the German collapse should come about as a result of simultaneous pressure from east and west. In such conditions, the prospects for future collaboration between our two countries would be the best possible. If on the other hand almost the whole military burden had been borne by Russia and Germany was defeated by Russian blows alone, obviously the political position would be less satisfactory not only for ourselves, but, he believed, for Russia also.[11]

Eden rejected the Maisky-Stalin request. Even though Maisky insisted on meeting Churchill, his wish was not granted. Instead, he discussed this subject with Eden on three further occasions during the course of the next ten days.[12] Churchill informed the members of the Defence Committee that there would be no alterations in Anglo-American strategic plans, and that he would explain this point of view to Stalin in a letter to be sent within the next few days.[13] In the first draft he wrote explicitly that an invasion of western Europe would only be carried out should a German collapse first take place.[14] That draft underwent several transmutations, which caused a delay of almost an entire month. (Roosevelt, who read one of the versions, left Churchill to answer Stalin in whatever way he thought fit, which was tantamount to telling him to fry in his own fat.) The lengthy letter that eventually went out on March 11 obfuscated the previously precise reference to the condition of the enemy's weakness. Churchill wrote that the forces in Britain intended to cross the Channel in August; however, "the Channel situation can only be judged nearer the time, and in making this declaration of our intentions there for your own personal information I must not be understood to limit our freedom of decision."[15] One notes that this was written after the Prime Minister had in mid-February given instructions to examine an invasion of Norway instead of Sledgehammer in 1943; after he had also ordered a reduction in the special staff charged with planning the invasion of France; after final confirmation had been received, at the beginning of March, that an operation like Sledgehammer could not be carried out in 1943 (something in fact known earlier); and long after Churchill had himself decided that the Italian peninsula had to be invaded once Sicily was taken—a decision for which he had gained the approval of his military advisers early in April.[16]

The wording of Churchill's letter was apparently designed to give Stalin some reason to hope that an invasion might still be launched in 1943; its object was thus to ensure that the Russian leader would keep on fighting and not develop heretical notions of a separate peace. Besides, should Germany indeed collapse during the course of the current year, Churchill's scenario would not be altogether inexact. Stalin was not persuaded and wrote an irate letter complaining about Churchill's ambiguous response. But he immediately thereafter sent Churchill a telegram congratulating him on the recent successes in the air raids on German cities. Churchill was surprised by this extreme change of tone. He suggested to the members of the Defence Committee that the first Russian message had been inspired by an official Soviet body, while the second had been written by Stalin himself; obviously its tenor was the result of the fact that Churchill had managed to achieve so good a personal rapport with him.[17] Attempting to unravel the intricacies of decision making in Moscow, Churchill began to conjure up the image of a benign "Uncle Joe." Stalin himself remained quiescent until his next outburst. During the uproar, it appears that insufficient attention was paid in London to his warning about the future of Anglo-Soviet cooperation after the war should the Russians eventually defeat the Germans virtually single-handedly.

At the beginning of March 1943, Eden sketched out the future of Germany after the war. He believed that an attempt should be made to encourage the natural process of decentralization that would emerge in postwar Germany; that country should be formed around a federal framework which accorded with its historical and political development. Eastern Prussia and Silesia would be transferred to Poland; the provinces of Alsace and Lorraine would be returned to France; Austria and Czechoslovakia would be reestablished as independent states. German industry, especially in the Rhine region, would be subject to international supervision, and encouragement be given to democratic processes within Germany.[18] That same month, Eden also visited the United States. Roosevelt—who had been influenced by the fears of William Bullitt, the former U.S. ambassador in Moscow—wondered whether the Russians did not intend to impose communism on the Continent after the war. Eden replied that he did not consider that to be a Russian aim; but "even if these fears were to prove correct, we should make the position no worse by trying to work with Russia and assuming that Stalin meant what he said in the Anglo-Soviet Treaty." Reporting to London, Eden confided his feeling that the President was inclined to reconcile himself to the idea that the Baltic states would be annexed to Russia. Nevertheless, he noted that the public feeling in the United States was less favorably inclined toward the Soviet Union than it was in Britain.[19]

Early in April, the Germans announced their discovery in Katyn Forest of a mass grave of about 10,000 Polish officers whom, they claimed, had been murdered by the Russians when the region was under Soviet occupation between 1940 and 1941. This news broke at a time when relations between the Polish government in exile in London and the Soviet Union had begun to deteriorate, because the Poles refused to relinquish their claims to their prewar eastern border. Once they learned of the discovery in Katyn, the Poles demanded the establishment of an international committee of inquiry. Churchill suspected Russian foul play, but nevertheless adopted Eden's advice to follow a policy of restraint and feign unawareness. Both men feared that the tensions generated by the Polish-Russian discord might reach a pitch that could compromise Britain's relations with Russia. The Prime Minister's primary objective was to ensure the smooth continuation of the Grand Alliance. He and Eden in any case favored the Soviets' demand that the Curzon line be recognized as Russia's western border. Accordingly, he advised the Poles to drop the subject of Katyn.[20]

During his visit to Washington in May 1943, Churchill was asked by Henry Stimson (the U.S. Secretary of War) and Sumner Welles (the Under-Secretary of State) what he thought ought to be the nature of the postwar global political order. Churchill replied that the first objective was to prevent renewed aggression by Germany. That could be achieved by cooperation between the United States, Russia, Britain, and China. Those powers would lead a "world council," which would also contain subsidiary regional councils of Europe, the American continent, and the Pacific. He claimed that the failure of the League of Nations could not be attributed to its underlying conception but to the actions of a number of individual states. Under the new arrangement, each state would be entitled to maintain an armed force of a certain size, part of which would be subject to the authority of the regional council. The world council, like a regional council, would be able to employ force against an aggressor state. Europe would be made up of confederations; France had once again to become a strong power, since it was advisable that a powerful state be interposed between Britain and Russia. Bavaria would join the Danubian confederation; Prussia would be detached from Germany; Poland and Czechoslovakia would be affiliated in a confederation friendly to the Soviet Union. He concluded by expressing the hope that some form of union could be forged between Britain and the United States. Stimson and Welles reacted with sympathy and enthusiasm. Churchill's sentiments accorded with their own liberal, Wilsonian vision of the nature of international relations. They stressed that a political settlement on those lines had to be reached while the war was still in progress. Churchill agreed.[21]

When Eden read the record of that conversation he was surprised: the Prime Minister had expressed an outlook similar to that advocated in his own Four Power plan, even though he had again rejected it as recently as the previous February.[22] Eden waxed enthusiastic about the degree of concurrence in their views, but disagreed with Churchill's old assumption that the roots of German aggression lay in Prussia. It was in southern Germany, he pointed out, that Nazism had sprouted forth; accordingly, the German problem would not be solved simply by detaching Prussia.[23]

Churchill had a sound reason for assuaging the Americans with this messianic vision. As will be recalled, it was during that visit that he requested their consent to the invasion of Italy after the conquest of Sicily. At other venues and on other occasions he spoke in cynical terms about similar projects. Roosevelt had long since articulated ideas that approximated those Churchill had put to Stimson and Welles. But in March 1941 Churchill had written to Halifax, the ambassador in Washington, that such notions were unrealistic: policy could not possibly be based on the goodwill and cooperation of the nations of the world; they would act in accordance with their own interests. "It is a pretty tough job to reshape human society in an after-dinner speech," he remarked.[24] In August 1944, the Prime Minister adopted a "cynically jocular" attitude toward the plan for the establishment of a world organization that Eden and Cadogan submitted for Cabinet discussion. According to the sad note in Cadogan's diary "neither he—nor anyone else—would take it seriously."[25]

Fundamentally Churchill was not dissembling. His attitude to this subject was ambivalent. For decades he had believed in the classic balance-of-power system. Nevertheless, he did not regard that as the ideal path to the *final* solution of severe and chronic international problems (as much was seen in our earlier discussion of his opposition to the formation of an alliance with France in 1925). His interest in the League of Nations—that still-born product of the liberal-radical outlook preached by Wilson, Roosevelt's mentor—became apparent only when he required the services of the League in order to ensure the political and military encirclement of Germany. Once World War II had broken out, Churchill sensed the need to work toward a world order of a new kind. Many people had needed only one world war to be convinced of the need to strive for an entirely different matrix of international relations; in Churchill's case, two such conflicts were required. But he did not entirely exchange his old concept for an alternative and universal perspective, which rejected the classic balance of power and policy based on power politics. He veered between both concepts, neither deciding between them nor attempting (which was perhaps impossible) to harmonize them. The realist in him struggled with his idealistic ambitions. Moreover, to a certain extent he was drawn along by his desire to keep pace with what he judged to be the spirit of the age, fearful lest he be stranded as an anachronistic figure desirous of reestablishing the "old order."

The result was paradoxical. Although Churchill believed in the need for an international organization, "he was also one of the main obstacles to adequate British planning and to the actual establishment of the United Nations Organization."[26] But the lack of a more clearly defined outlook was to have effects that extended beyond the problem of the establishment of the United Nations. The absence of a sharply defined basic political concept intensified the distinction Churchill was, in any case, prone to make between long-term policy and the military conduct of the war. This was no help whatsoever when he had to define his attitude toward the Soviet Union, to identify the latter's future intentions, and to formulate an appropriate and timely response of his own.

As has been seen, the Trident conference of May 1943 decided that the invasion of western Europe would take place in May 1944. This removed any last glimmer of hope Stalin might have had that the operation would be carried out in 1943. Once he learned of the decision, Stalin launched into an unprecedentedly sharp attack on Churchill, whom he accused of violating the assurances he had given on the opening of the "second front."[27] Departing from the conciliatory tone he had hitherto adopted in his correspondence with Stalin, Churchill's response was on this occasion decidedly acerbic. He instructed his ambassador in Moscow, Clark-Kerr, to give Stalin "a friendly hint of the danger of offending the two Western powers whose war-making strength is growing with every month that passes and who may play a helpful part in the Russian future."[28] Writing to Roosevelt, Churchill said that, notwithstanding this exchange, he did not forsee a real crisis in the West's relations with Russia. This was because a Soviet-German agreement was improbable and because of "what would appear to be the Russian interest in the future world."[29] Clark-Kerr replied to his Prime Minister that some understanding should be shown of Stalin's attitude toward the "second front." He emphasized the importance of cooperation with Russia after the war, which, he claimed, would to a large extent determine the future of the world. "It seems to me essential therefore," wrote the ambassador, "that we should hold his confidence even at considered cost to ourselves." He remarked that certain signs truly encouraged him to believe in the possibility of establishing good relations with Russia after the war.[30]

Stalin was right to be annoyed. As far as the opening of the "second front" was concerned, Churchill and Roosevelt had not kept their word. Roosevelt had promised that a "second front" would be opened in 1942; Churchill had specified the spring of 1943; even after the Casablanca conference, Churchill (and, to a lesser extent, Roosevelt) had still led Stalin to believe that the invasion would be launched in the summer of 1943. Stalin must surely have drawn unfavorable inferences from such false assurances, believing that the considerations which had led Churchill and Roosevelt to postpone the invasion of western Europe ran deeper than factors of an operational nature. Stalin was himself chronically suspicious, and in the 1939–1940 period had based his own strategic plans on the assumption that an extended war between France and Germany in the west would exhaust both powers, thereby—he hoped—benefiting Russia. He must therefore have found it difficult to believe that the unfulfilled promises were not the product of a British (or Anglo-American) plot, designed to exhaust and weaken Russia. This was a long-standing suspicion, of which London was aware. When, in mid-December 1942, Clark-Kerr tried to pressure Churchill and his military advisers into invading western Europe in 1943, he warned them that Stalin would react fiercely once he learned that it was not to be carried out that year. He might even sign a separate peace with Germany. The Russians, Clark-Kerr noted, maintained that there were enough forces in Britain to invade; they considered that the western Allies deliberately preferred Russia to carry the main burden of the fighting. They even suspected that the Anglo-American army formed in Britain would one day be directed against Russia, in conjunction with the Germans. Those suspicions, the ambassador warned, would only be reinforced by failure to carry out the invasion in 1943.[31] In October 1943 Stalin, "with a gust of laughter," remarked to Eden that "Mr. Churchill had a tendency to take the easy road for himself and leave the difficult jobs to the Russians."[32]

As we have seen, that suspicion was unfounded: no such Anglo-American coordination existed; as for Churchill—whom Stalin mistrusted more than anyone else—his reasons for deferring the opening of the "second front" were entirely different. In the autumn of 1942, the British Chiefs of Staff had indeed stated that Russia would carry the main burden of defeating Germany on land, but they had reached that conclusion from a purely military standpoint and not one of a long-term political nature. Churchill had difficulty in accepting that opinion, and questioned the strategy the chiefs proposed; one of his objections was rooted in his promise to Stalin that a Channel crossing would be carried out in 1943.[33] That "there is little printed evidence relating to the political decision" is admitted even by one of the last remaining Western researchers, who still believes that such an Anglo-American plot was hatched.[34] Unfortunately, however, there does exist sufficient circumstantial evidence to convince those searching for the existence of a policy of that type, particularly if they are as suspicious as was Stalin.

Because the "second front" was deferred, the Soviet Union did shoulder the major burden of the war. By the end of 1943 it had effectively defeated the German army; its forces had reached lines approximating Russia's old borders before the outbreak of World War II. Moreover, it had accomplished such gains at a time when the Anglo-American forces had made only a modest contribution to Germany's defeat on land. It will be recalled that Stalin, through Maisky, had warned that an inequitable distribution of the burdens involved in defeating Germany would severely influence future Anglo-Soviet cooperation after the war. It would not be surprising were Stalin to have concluded that Russia was entitled to a greater share of the European spoils, even should his partners disagree. Were he to have lived up to the expectations of inter-Power cooperation held by Eden, Churchill, and Roosevelt, Stalin would probably have considered himself to be submitting to the strategic and political line they had adopted toward him during the course of the conflict.

Smuts transmitted a further warning to Churchill while the latter was in Quebec and Washington in late August and September 1943. Russia, he cautioned, might conclude that it did indeed have good grounds for suspecting British and U.S. purposes if, by the end of 1944, the Anglo-American forces had "done no better than merely nibbling at the enemy's main positions" while Russia itself had borne the principal brunt of the fighting. The peoples of Europe would regard Russia as the true victor in the war and as a liberator. Should that indeed be the case, a massive shift would take place in the international situation. Russia would be transformed into the "diplomatic master" of the world; "The Bolshevisation of a broken and ruined Europe"—itself "a definite possibility"—could only "be guarded against by supply of food and work and interim Allied control." Smuts called for an intensification of the Anglo-American war effort, so that at the end of the war the Western allies might be seen to be on a par with the Soviet Union.[35] As we have already pointed out, what Smuts had in mind was the development of a Balkan strategy and an advance into southeastern Europe, and the postponement, or even cancellation, of Overlord. At this stage, Smuts was not speaking of a military move designed to preempt the Russians in that region. On the contrary, he wanted to make it easier for the Russians to advance in a westerly and southwesterly direction.[36]

During the final session of the Quebec conference, Roosevelt asked whether studies had been made of "an emergency entrance" into the Continent in the event of a sudden German collapse. His inquiry was prompted by the fact "that he desired the United Nations to be ready to get to Berlin as soon as did the Russians."[37] Other than that, no further discussion of this subject took place during the conference.[38] Churchill's own response to Smuts was somewhat indifferent:

> I think it inevitable that Russia will be the greatest land power in the world after this war which will have rid her of the two military powers, Japan and Germany, who in our lifetime have inflicted upon her heavy defeats. I hope, however, that the "fraternal association" of the British Commonwealth and the United States together with sea and air power, may put us on good terms and in a friendly balance with Russia at least for the period of re-building. Further than that I cannot see with mortal eye, and I am not yet fully informed about the celestial telescopes.[39]

Clearly, Churchill had not yet fully grasped the diminuition in the importance of sea power in relation to land power. As much is apparent from his statement that U.S. and British sea and air power might constitute a counterweight to Soviet land power after the war. It is also surprising that he should have placed his faith in Anglo-American air power; after all, the effectiveness of wartime strategic bombing had so far been limited (and it must be remembered that, at that stage of the war, no one could say whether the atomic bomb would work or what its effect might be). Above all, his reply to Smuts shows that, at that point in time, Churchill still sensed no need for large Anglo-American land forces to advance deep into the Continent, and thereby create a military and political balance of forces in Europe against the Soviet Union at the end of the war and afterward. This was despite the fact that he already understood, as he put it, that Russia would emerge from the war as "the greatest land power in the world."

In October, on the eve of his departure for the Foreign Ministers' conference in Moscow, Eden requested that the Cabinet discuss and determine Britain's attitude on the postwar future of Germany. Churchill refused to retreat from his old position that no commitments were to be made during the course of the war. He argued that the journey to Moscow ought to be devoted to an examination of the Russian positions since "it would be a mistake to try to define too clearly, at this stage, our own attitude on the future of Germany."[40] During the Cabinet discussion that ensued, and which Cadogan described as flippant, Churchill stated that Britain had to avoid weakening Germany too much. Britain might need it against Russia.[41] Eden did not give up; he claimed that deadlock in the Moscow talks could only be avoided were Britain at least to make clear to the Russians that it did not intend to oppose Russia's territorial claims after the war. He asked Churchill for a precise definition of Britain's attitude toward Russia's western frontiers. Following further entreaties, Churchill gave in. His own sketch of the limits of his agreement to Russia's claims undoubtedly exceeded Eden's expectations. Britain, wrote Churchill, had to do "everything in [its] power" to persuade the Poles to accept Russia's territorial demands with respect to the eastern border; in return, the Poles would themselves receive portions of eastern Prussia and Silesia. An independent and strong Poland, capable of defending its western frontier, had to be established. As for Russia:

> We reaffirm the principles of the Atlantic Charter, noting that Russia's accession thereto is based upon the frontiers of the 22nd June 1941. We also take note of the historic frontiers of Russia before the two wars of aggression waged by Germany in 1914 and 1939.

The postwar world order would be based upon the establishment of a global organization, on the lines of the League of Nations, with a military force of its own.[42] He was willing to go so far since the borders of pre-1914 tsarist Russia had extended farther westward than the frontier of June 22, 1941.[43]

October 1943 saw a peak in the Anglo-American dispute over the link between Overlord and the future of the campaign in Italy and the Mediterranean. At this stage, Churchill's complex attitude on this was not influenced by political considerations of an anti-Soviet nature. No mention was made of any such considerations during the course of the extended Chiefs of Staff meeting held on October 19, when Churchill specified his preference for a "Mediterranean strategy" to the invasion of western Europe.[44] The official British historians have ascertained that not until the second half of 1944 and after the Channel crossing did Churchill first begin to consider preempting the Russians in southeastern Europe by military means. As we shall see, that assessment is correct—even though the official history, of course, also adduced that argument in order to buttress its authors' views of British support for Overlord.[45]

When Churchill arrived in Teheran for the meeting of the "Big Three," one of his aims was to reach an agreement in principle with the Russians on the future of Poland before the Soviet forces had crossed the frontiers of June 1941.[46] Stalin, who was now poised on the threshold of Poland, eastern Prussia, and other east European states, refrained from committing himself to any specific plans affecting Germany's postwar future. But the Big Three did agree on the principle of the dismemberment of Germany. The Soviet leader argued that France had to be prevented from once again becoming a great power, and thereby punished for having collaborated with Germany. (Charles Bohlen, the head of the Russian section in the U.S. State Department, immediately twigged that Stalin's aim was to leave a weak Europe prostrate before a strong Russia.)[47] Churchill suggested that the leaders of the three powers reach basic agreement on Poland's frontiers. The arrangement would be put to the Poles, and in effect imposed on them (Roosevelt had himself put the same idea to Eden when the two had met in March 1943).[48] Poland would be shifted westward; the Curzon line would constitute its eastern frontier, with its western border lying along the Oder. Roosevelt agreed; so too, in principle, did Stalin—albeit only after he had made a vain attempt to avoid any discussion of the Polish problem. Notwithstanding Eden's coaching, the Prime Minister forgot to ask Stalin for guarantees that would enable the Polish people to preserve their political freedom after the war.[49] Thus at Teheran basic (although not formal) agreement was reached—behind Poland's back—on a formula that would determine that country's territorial future. Lord Moran heard Churchill say that, were this formula to be ratified by the postwar peace treaty Poland would emerge stronger than it had been prior to the war.[50]

Churchill and his entourage returned from Teheran in an optimistic frame of mind about the future of relations with the Soviet Union. The conference had reinforced the favorable impression Eden and Ismay had of the Russians, and especially of Stalin, whom they had met in October during the Foreign Ministers' conference.[51] Churchill waxed particularly enthusiastic. In January 1944 he reminded Eden that, at the beginning of 1942, he had not been prepared to concede the Russian demand that Britain recognize the annexation of the Baltic states. (In fact, that was far from being an accurate depiction of what had then been his final position). But:

undoubtedly my own feelings have changed in the two years that have passed since the topic was first raised during your visit to Moscow. The tremendous victories of the Russian armies, the deep-seated changes which have taken place in the character of the Russian State and Government, the new confidence which has grown in our hearts towards Stalin—these have all had their effect.

He noted that at Teheran, when Stalin had expressed his wish to annex part of eastern Prussia up to Königsberg, the British had said nothing about the Baltic states that would undoubtedly form part of the great area of "Russian dominions." Russia's recent conquests had in effect solved the question of the annexations of Bukovina, Bessarabia, and the Baltic states. Those were territories that Britain would never ask the Russians to vacate. All that remained, then, was the question of the Soviet-Polish frontier. Churchill wanted to hear Eden's opinion on Russia's western borders, saying that "as far as I can make out the Russian claim in no way exceeds the former Tsarist boundaries, in fact in some parts it falls notably short of them." He concluded with a warning to Eden to avoid any public discussion of these issues, which might adversely affect the postwar election and expose them to Parliamentary criticism. He still maintained that "it would be far better to shelve it all until we reach the discussions, which we shall have to have after the defeat of Hitler."[52]

Eden replied that the British Government was in effect committed to recognizing the annexation of the Baltic states, pursuant to the conversations that had taken place early in 1942.[53] Most Russian territorial claims were justified. Nobody cared about Russian demands on Rumania and Finland. But he agreed with the Prime Minister that publication of Britain's concurrence in the annexation of the Baltic states had to be deferred until the signing of the peace treaty. Prior publication would create a tremendous stir in Britain and generate difficulties with the Americans. On the other hand, Stalin had to be informed that the British Government would not dispute his claims when such problems would be raised toward the end of the war, although pressures of the sort referred to would cause the governments's public position to be different. Matters would be solved at the postwar peace conference.[54] Although both men agreed to keep silent about the subject, the Prime Minister made no secret of his trend of thinking. He informed Parliament that Britain had never recognized Poland's prewar eastern frontier. In return for making concessions in the east, Poland would receive territories in the west at Germany's expense. He referred to Stalin's assurances on Poland's integrity and independence. "I cannot feel that [Russia] for a reassurance about her western frontiers goes beyond the limits of what is reasonable or just," he declared.[55] It is not clear how those remarks squared with the assessment of his ambassador in Moscow that, although the Russians were indeed interested in an independent Poland, they expected the Poles to conduct themselves with "complete subservience."[56]

Thus at the beginning of 1944 Churchill's outlook approximated that which Eden had held ever since early 1942. It is difficult to know whence Churchill had derived concrete evidence to support his claim that "deep-seated changes . . . [had] taken place in the character of the Russian State and Government." However, in a speech he delivered to Parliament in May 1944, he argued that the more the war had gone on and the Red Army's victories had multiplied, so too had Russia divested itself of its ideological hue; it was "the Russian state" that was gaining in strength. As much was indicated by the fact that religion was enjoying a revival; the Soviet national anthem had been changed; the Comintern had been disbanded; the regime was emphasizing the existence of the Russian—not the Soviet—state; English representatives had been received with cordiality; the terms of submission submitted to the Rumanians were "remarkably generous," and did not intimate an intention to alter the character of Rumanian society. The same was true of Russia's relations with Finland. Altogether, Churchill announced, "The Trotskyite form of Communism has been completely wiped out."[57]

All of the indications to which Churchill referred certainly contributed to the formulation of his opinions. But apparently the deep impression left on him by Stalin was also of considerable weight. Simply put, he was enchanted with "Uncle Joe"'s personality.[58] Moreover, in January 1944, Benes, the President of the Czechoslovak Government in exile, cast Stalin in a new light when attempting to convince Churchill of the Soviet leader's moderation. The Russians, he claimed, would have come to Czechoslovakia's aid during the Munich crisis; moreover, the "great purges" in the Red Army during the late 1930s had been justified. Tukhachevsky and Kamenev, who were avowed Trotskyites, had hatched a plot with the Germans that the Czechs had discovered and revealed to Stalin.[59] Churchill was so impressed with this story that he repeated it in July 1945 in the hearing of, among others, Lord Moran. "Stalin was thoroughly justified," he said, "these officers were acting against their country."[60]

Churchill attempted to grapple with the following problem: was Soviet Russia bent on a policy of expansion influenced by Communist ideology? or was its policy in effect an extension of tsarist foreign policy, which he considered to be moderate? At the end of the 1930s and early in the war, he maintained that the Soviet Union's foreign policy actually followed the dictates of traditional geopolitical principles and interests, not ideological imperatives.[61] (During the course of the war, that opinion was to take root in the British Foreign Office.)[62] It was not, apparently, out of sheer force of habit that he continued to designate the Soviet Union as "Russia." He tended to interpret the wartime revival of old Russian national elements—a revival deliberately promoted by the Soviet regime during those years for reasons of morale—as evidence of that sort of historical continuity. He was pleasantly surprised to discover that Soviet territorial gains did not extend to Russia's tsarist frontiers. In 1920, at the peak of his anti-Bolshevik frame of mind, Churchill had believed that Russia would not rest until it had returned to its 1914 borders. Interestingly, and not without relevance to his wartime attitude, he had then looked with some equanimity on the prospect that Poland and the Baltic states might lose their independence—provided that the regime in Russia would be friendly toward Britain and France.[63]

Only his failure to conduct a fundamental study of the issue (for reasons already mentioned), together with wishful thinking, can explain Churchill's adherence to the flimsy evidence he himself drew on to buttress his hypothesis that Soviet foreign policy followed a traditional—and moderate—pattern. Clark-Kerr and Eden (especially the latter) also played their part in dulling his senses and suspicions. But even if he did insist on maintaining that the Soviet Union adhered to a policy of realpolitik decked out in ideological garb, further consideration might have led Churchill to conclude that the threat was nevertheless substantive. If tsarist Russia had acted with moderation in the west, that was to a large extent because it had been bordered there by two great powers, Germany and Austria-Hungary, who had thwarted Russian ambitions in Europe. But—as Churchill had himself written to Smuts a few months earlier—the likelihood was that, at the end of the current war, no central European power would be capable of checking the ascendancy of Russia's strength.

During the first half of 1944, Churchill's optimism about future relations with Russia scaled new heights; even then, however, it was diluted by doubts.[64] In February 1944 Churchill insisted that long-range bombers should be assigned to carry supplies to the Polish underground, despite RAF opposition. He explained that it was in Britain's interest to ensure that Poland would be strong: "Were she weak and overrun by the advancing Soviet armies, the result might hold great dangers in the future for the English speaking peoples." Moreover, during the course of a conversation held at the end of a long day early in March, he had expressed his fears of the Russians' intentions and emphasized the importance of fostering British air power after the war.[65]

These smoldering fears were ignited early in May when the Prime Minister was angered by "Communist intrigues" in Italy, Yugoslavia, and, especially, in Greece. "Are we going to acquiesce in the communization of the Balkans and perhaps of Italy?" he asked Eden. "We ought to come to a definite conclusion about it and if our conclusion is that we resist the Communist infusion and invasion, we should put it to them pretty plainly at the best moment that military events permit."[66] In reply, Eden wrote that it was difficult to prove that the Russians aimed at imposing Communist regimes on the Balkans and Italy. They were indeed lending their support to Tito's movement and to the Communist guerrilla movement in Greece (EAM); but since those were the most effective anti-German movements, so was Britain. There was no indication that the Russians were doing anything amiss in Bulgaria and Rumania. Nevertheless, Eden added, the consequences of recent developments on the postwar situation had to be scrutinized. That was better than limiting themselves to a short-range view, wherein (and here Eden inserted an accurate description of the character of British strategy hitherto!) the only criterion for our steps would be their effectiveness and influence on the progress of the war."[67] Churchill noted on Eden's letter: "You are right."[68] Whether or not he thereby intended to signal his agreement with Eden's reassuring assessment of the Russian intentions or with his masked criticism of the nature of British strategy hitherto is not clear. Whichever the case, May 1944 was far from being "the best moment that military events permit" for adopting a tough line against the Russians. In that month they crossed the old Russo-Polish border and advanced deep into Rumania. Meanwhile, the only foothold the Anglo-American armies possessed on the Continent was south of Rome.

Even at the time that Eden wrote his new assessment of the Soviets' intentions in the Balkans, the British had arrived at an understanding with them on a portion of that region: the British would have a free hand in Greece while the Russians would have a free hand in Rumania. Churchill tried to elicit Roosevelt's support for the arrangement, which he described as one of convenience and not a permanent settlement or a division into spheres of influence. The Russians were in any case in Rumania where they could do as they wished. Roosevelt protested, because he feared that what was being set in motion was a process for the division of Europe into spheres of influence; but Churchill did not retreat.[69]

At the beginning of June Eden presented Churchill with a memorandum containing his evaluation of the Russians' aims in the Balkans. Stressing that his views were shared by the entire Foreign Office, Eden claimed that the Russians did indeed aim to carve out a position of dominance in southeastern Europe for themselves. But there were no indications that they wished to communize the regimes in the Balkans. The Russians were working toward the attainment of their historical regional goals—a degree of influence and status that would preclude any other power controlling the area and thereby preventing what they considered to be a threat to themselves. In the past, Austria-Hungary had served as a bulwark against Russian expansion in the region; no power could presently help Britain do so. Britain could only blame itself for the fact that the most powerful guerrilla movements in Yugoslavia and Greece were Communist. The Russians had merely looked on while the British did their work for them.[70]

Eden went on to examine the Soviet goals in the various Balkan states: From Rumania, he said, the Russians desired territory and a government subservient to the Soviet Union. Since the Communist movement in that country was exceedingly weak, the chances of a Communist regime being established there were very slim. In Yugoslavia, the Russians would attempt to ensure Tito's position; his movement in any case stood a good chance of ruling the country. Their attitude with regard to Bulgaria, in Eden's opinion, was uncertain. They would aim at "a dominant moral position," but desired no more than air bases on Bulgarian soil. They considered Albania important as a point of contact between Tito and the Communist guerrilla movement in Greece. But although they had begun to show an interest in events in Greece, the Russians had recently agreed to leave Britain in control of that country. It would be wrong to jump to the conclusion, argued Eden, that there existed within the region a clash of British and Russian interests that might inexorably lead to conflict. Britain must make its interests in the Balkans clear to the Russians without presenting them with a challenge. Otherwise, they might take a harsh view—and act accordingly—while all the cards were in their hands. Should Britain decide that it had to prevent Soviet expansion in the Balkans, the best way to do so would be to establish an alliance between Greece and Turkey and exploit opportunities for strengthening Britain's position in the region; but it should not enter into direct conflict with the Russians.[71] In this memorandum, together with the temporary agreement reached with the Russians over Rumania and Greece, can be discerned the kernel of the well-known "percentage agreement" of October 1944. Churchill concurred with the spirit of Eden's conclusions and was very annoyed by Roosevelt's attempts to undermine the temporary agreement. Without it, he thought, there was a danger of a clash with the Russians.[72]

On June 7, 1944, just days after the fall of Rome and the landing in Normandy, General Alexander, Commander in Chief of Allied forces in Italy, advocated opening an energetic drive northward. Alexander suggested two alternative lines of advance: one in the direction of Turin and Genoa, aimed at entering France; the other in the direction of Padua and Venice, with the goal of advancing into Austria.[73] During the course of the month, Alexander and General Wilson, Supreme Allied Commander Mediterranean, concluded that an advance toward Vienna was to be preferred to one to the west. When they first raised that suggestion, their perspective was entirely military. At this stage, they had not conceived of the idea of using military means in order to check Soviet expansion in southeastern Europe.[74] What they, and especially Churchill, did have in mind was the frustration of operation Anvil-Dragoon—the invasion of southern France, which had earlier been agreed upon with the Americans. Churchill invested much energy in a struggle to cancel that operation. One reason was because it would demand the transfer of forces from the Italian theater and would slow the advance there; in addition, he doubted whether that move could make any contribution to the campaign in France. Whichever the case, even without the dispute over the invasion of the Riviera, the idea of advancing from Italy either westward or eastward into the heart of Europe was an old one, which was devoid of political objectives. Churchill had floated it during those moments of optimism when he had thought that the advance up Italy would be swift and easy.[75] Now that the Allies' forces had landed in northern France, the advance westward seemed less attractive than the possibility of moving into southeastern Europe.

At the beginning of July, Churchill wrote to Roosevelt:

> On a long-term political view, he [Stalin] might prefer that the British and Americans should do their share in France in the very hard fighting that is to come, and that east, middle and southern Europe shall fall naturally into his control.[76]

These words constitute one of the few weak items of evidence indicating that, in late June and July, Churchill also had political reasons for trying to persuade the Americans to concentrate the effort on an advance northward, and land in the "armpit" of the Adriatic rather than invade southern France. Neither the U.S. Chiefs of Staff nor Roosevelt were impressed by his arguments. They considered those ideas dangerous: they might cause a dispersal of effort and the diversion of forces from the principal theater in western Europe. His elementary geometry lessons, Roosevelt wrote, had taught him that "a straight line is the shortest distance between two points."[77] Besides, and for almost identical reasons, Brooke and Kennedy had opposed the idea of a northern advance as soon as it had been first mooted by Alexander and Wilson.[78]

When he arrived in London early in July, Alexander presented his case to the members of the War Cabinet. Once the Allies had broken into the Po valley, he said, he would prefer to move toward the Danube by way of the Ljubljana valley. He could thus join up with the Russians who would advance from Lemberg. Should the Anglo-American forces reach the Danube valley, the Germans would be forced to abandon the Balkans and the road to Vienna would be open. If the Germans chose to check the Allied advance northward, they would have to transfer fifteen divisions from other theaters in order to do so. That eventuality, said Alexander, might prevent him from reaching Vienna; but it would considerably facilitate advances on the eastern and western fronts. Churchill expressed his enthusiastic support for Alexander's proposed move. Nevertheless, whether he believed that Vienna could be reached must be considered doubtful. This is because, when justifying the move to his ministers, Churchill remarked: "Our advance northeastwards would be a magnet which would draw German forces from other fronts.... Others would reap where General Alexander had ploughed."[79] The record of the discussion contains no mention of the idea of reaching Vienna before the Russians for political reasons. On the contrary, it was they who were expected to be the beneficiaries of the proposed move. Should the Germans elect to transfer additional forces to halt Alexander, they would naturally (for logistic reasons) have to do so from the Balkans and the eastern front.

Early in August, just as the great Polish uprising in Warsaw was beginning, Eden put the finishing touches to another evaluation of the Soviets' intentions in Europe. He still held fast to the attitude he had adopted in 1942. After the war, he argued, the Russians would be able to choose between two political paths: they could either cooperate with the West, or they could break off relations with the West and unilaterally take over most of the states of Europe. A domestic struggle, wrote Eden, might possibly be taking place within the Soviet government between the advocates of these schools of thought; but Stalin favored the first, and he seemed to have the upper hand. Eden believed that the Soviet Union intended to cooperate with the West. Britain had therefore to adopt a frank policy toward it, and preclude the creation of the mistaken impression that the West had an interest in establishing a *cordon sanitaire* around Russia and in strengthening Germany. "I am convinced," wrote Eden, "that the foundation of our post-war European policy must be the Anglo-Soviet Alliance, aimed at preventing any recurrence of German aggression."

After the war, Britain had to prevent any one power dominating Europe and guard against the possibility that the British Isles might be attacked by long-range bombers. Britain would exert an influence over events in western Europe, the Iberian Peninsula, Scandinavia, Turkey, Greece, and Italy. On the other hand, it would not attempt to harm Russian interests in the states of central Europe, Poland, Czechoslovakia, Yugoslavia, Hungary, and Rumania. These states were vital to the defense of the Soviet Union's security against Germany. Notwithstanding Russian enmity toward the regimes in those countries prior to the war, "there have been no signs of any Soviet desire to impose Communist regimes in any of the Central European countries." True, Russian demands from Poland would be stiff; but there were good reasons to believe that should a democratic regime be established in Poland, it would attain true independence and be free of too much intervention in its domestic affairs. In their current confrontations with the Russians, the Poles relied on receiving British and U.S. support. But it would be disastrous for the chances of peace in Europe, and for Poland itself, were Britain to encourage them to rely on its support "instead of staking everything upon achieving good relations with Russia."[80]

The refusal of the Russians to lend support to the uprising in Warsaw did not change the attitude and policy Eden and Churchill adopted toward the Soviet Union. Both the Chiefs of Staff and the members of the War Cabinet believed that the Russians had indeed run out of operational steam in front of Warsaw and that the outbreak of the Polish uprising had been precipitate.[81] Nevertheless Churchill's and Eden's fears and suspicions were aroused. "As the European war entered on its last phase, the shadow of Warsaw lay over British strategic thought."[82] Influenced by the uprising, Duff Cooper, the British ambassador in France, argued at the end of August that Britain ought not to conclude an alliance with Russia, but establish against it a Western European confederation under British leadership. This would follow the lines of the union with France which Churchill had initiated in 1940. Churchill—correctly—remarked that it was not he who had fathered the idea of the union; it had been born of "Cabinet emotion." Eden, on the other hand, hastened to defend his own attitude: a Western European union would provoke Russian hostility and the establishment of a counterallinace in Eastern Europe. "Frank cooperation and friendship with Russia is the proper course," he maintained. Despite everything, throughout the second half of 1944 the Foreign Office remained optimistic and hopeful about the future of relations with the Soviet Union.[83]

At the beginning of August, Churchill reconciled himself to the fact that, since the Americans had not budged from their position, the invasion of southern Europe would be carried out as planned. On August 11 he departed for a tour of the Mediterranean basin and the Italian front, which lasted until August 29. Meeting with his senior officers in Rome, he made clear his determination to prevent any weakening of Alexander's strength in Italy. His object, he said, was to break out toward Vienna through the Ljubljana valley. He added that "the Army in Italy was the most representative Army of the British Empire now in the field." He was prepared to go to "extreme measure to ensure that the operations of this great Army should not be hamstrung." In employing the term "extreme measure," Churchill was referring to his readiness to split the command over the western and Mediterranean theaters between the Americans and the British. Specifically, the Combined Staff of the U.S. and British Chiefs of Staff (CCS) would no longer constitute the supreme body in command of all the European theaters of operation. But neither Brooke nor Portal were enthusiastic about the idea of advancing on Vienna. Brooke argued that the purpose of the Italian campaign was to tie German forces down in that area in order to lend support to the western theater, which was the principal one. He pointed out the difficulties in advancing into the interior of Austria because the mountainous topography hindered movement and worked for the defense. Besides, he added, no advance—if any—into the Ljubljana valley could be carried out before the following spring (Alexander's forces had not yet managed to break into the Po valley). But contrary to the Chiefs of Staff, the commanders on the spot, Wilson and Alexander (especially the latter), stuck to their position. What is even more interesting about this meeting is what it left unsaid: Churchill made no mention of any wish to preempt the Russians in southeastern Europe.[84] The conversation indicates that what he found most difficult to stomach was the thought that the "Army of the British Empire" might constitute no more than an auxiliary for forces in the western theater.[85] He still refused to acknowledge that the Italian theater was to be a secondary one, and that the Anglo-American military effort had to be concentrated in the western one. His readiness to split the command between the two theaters indicates the importance he then attached to the Mediterranean. As will be seen, it indicates that, at that stage, he did not give due importance to the military and political value of the western theater.

At the end of August Smuts reminded Churchill of the enormous political significance of an advance on Vienna to preempt the Russians.[86] Churchill needed no encouragement. From the end of August and the beginning of September, he himself tried to persuade Roosevelt of the importance of the move and of the need to strengthen the Italian theater for that purpose. Roosevelt did not turn him down flat. But he did remark that Alexander had first to break out into the Po valley; the matter could then be discussed at the next Anglo-American conference.[87] Indeed, it was not the Americans who presented the biggest stumbling block to that move; they had been preceded by the British Chiefs of Staff, whose own objections were no less substantial. At the beginning of September, they poured cold water on the wish Churchill and Wilson had expressed to attack the Istrian Peninsula and Trieste and thereby effect a shortcut that would ease the advance of Alexander's forces, who were still bogged down in front of the Po. They could discern no strategic or operational logic in that move.[88] Churchill replied, this time with some asperity, that from a political point of view it was very important that strong Anglo-American forces be present in Austria at the end of the war and that Russia be prevented from completely dominating central and southern Europe. "This is a matter of high political consequences, but also has serious military potentialities."[89] The Chiefs of Staff replied that even were Vienna to be posited as an objective of the highest priority and an amphibious operation in Istria successfully carried out, the advance on Vienna could not take place before the following spring.[90] Here again, and virtually as matter of course, what became apparent was the absence of harmony between Churchill's political and military goals and the operational possibility of their attainment.

At the second Quebec conference held in September, Churchill was surprised to find that the Americans were "without any hesitation" prepared to advance on Vienna should the war last long enough.[91] His patience had worn thin, especially since Alexander was far from breaking out into the Po valley (in fact, the Allies did not reach the Po River until April 1945). He hoped to persuade the Americans to dispatch another two or three divisions to Italy. In October, when he again visited Italy on his way to Moscow, he explained his tactics to his generals: the Americans would be told that the reinforcements were to be assigned to an assault to destroy the German army in Italy and to prevent the transfer of German forces to France; no mention whatsoever was to be made of the advance into Austria.[92] The only novelty in this characteristic tactic was that it was openly stated. But Marshall and Roosevelt had learned a thing or two since they had first begun to work in harness with Churchill. They turned down his request with the remark that the impending winter and the terrain made it altogether impossible to defeat the German forces in Italy. The principal campaign was taking place in the west; its objective was to bring the war in Europe to a swift end.[93] Another blow to Churchill's idea came from Portal and Cunningham, who had stayed in London. Although aware of the political significance of an advance on Vienna, both men were strongly opposed to the transfer of three U.S. divisions to Italy. Like the Americans, they emphasized that the west constituted the main theater; the Italian campaign was designed to support it. Alexander could not open an assault before March 1945, by which time a decision might have been attained in the west.[94]

In January 1945 the British Chiefs of Staff put the lid on the idea of an advance on Vienna. Their calculations led them to the conclusion that the best move was to tie the German forces down in Italy and at the same time transfer six divisions from that front to strengthen the western front in April 1945. If it were decided to open a massive assault in Italy, those same divisions would not be able to take part in the campaign in the west until September 1945; alternatively, should the Germans be pushed back, or elect an orderly retreat from Italy, ten to fifteen German divisions could more speedily be transferred from there to other theaters.[95] Churchill replied that he agreed with the argument that, from a military point of view, it was preferable to transfer divisions from Italy to the western front. Nevertheless, he refused to reconcile himself to that fact altogether and wondered whether—considering the considerable length of time it would take for the divisions to reach France—it would not after all be better to open an offensive in Italy. Brooke responded that even if the six divisions remained in Italy, the German army there could not be destroyed. In any case, the Russians would not allow British forces to take Vienna, but would place them on their own left flank, somewhere south of the city.[96]

The calculations made by the Chiefs of Staff did not only apply to the position appertaining in January 1945. They were also true of the entire campaign in Italy and its connection with the western front. Churchill and Brooke claimed that they had always regarded the Italian campaign as a move designed to do no more than facilitate the success of the invasion of western Europe. As will be remembered, the extent of the contribution which the Italian front might make to the western campaign had been dependent on whether—and how—Hitler might decide to defend Italy. And the credibility of their arguments was to be undermined by their assumption that Hitler would elect to withdraw from Italy.[97] Even when Hitler decided to defend every inch of Italian soil—and thereby served the needs of Anglo-American strategy—the utility of the Italian front might have been immediately obviated had he changed his mind by deciding on a swift withdrawal to the Alps and transferring his divisions to the eastern or western fronts. Churchill had himself pointed out that danger in September 1944, when remarking that a decision on Hitler's part to retreat from Italy would "greatly strengthen" the defense of Germany.[98] Of course, by 1945 action of that sort could not have had very much effect. It could only have produced some hardening of German resistance (apparently in the east) and have left a large Anglo-American army in Italy virtually idle.

When the question of an advance into southeastern Europe arose, the British Chiefs of Staff reversed the attitude that they had adopted during the period preceding the final decision to invade western Europe. They now repeatedly informed Churchill that the principal front was situated in the west and not the Mediterranean. At the present juncture, one did not have to be a strategic genius to reach their new conclusion, especially in view of the considerable progress made during August. Intentionally, and thanks to a convenient lapse of memory, Alan Brooke attributed to the years 1942–1943 his postinvasion opinion about the relationship between the western and Mediterranean theaters. The same is true of Churchill. Nevertheless, Churchill did not adapt himself as quickly as did Brooke to the thought that the best chances of swiftly defeating Germany were to be found on the western front.

■

In *The Second World War* Churchill severely criticized the Americans for refusing to support his plan to advance on Vienna. He also castigated them for their insistence on invading southern France instead of strengthening Alexander's forces in Italy. "For this a heavy price was paid. The army of Italy was deprived of its opportunity to strike a most formidable blow at the

Germans, and very possibly to reach Vienna before the Russians, with all that might have followed therefrom." He claimed that an opportunity had thereby been lost to exert an influence on the political future of southeastern Europe.[99] Chester Wilmot similarly—and still more forcefully—criticized the Americans in his own best-selling book on the war (one of the first to appear after its conclusion),[100] the publication of which met with Churchill's satisfaction.[101] Alexander repeated that version of events in his own memoirs.[102] Thus was born what the official British historians termed the "myth";[103] namely the claim—adduced by both his critics and admirers—that Churchill had possessed a Balkan strategy.

Like all myths, that one too possesses no more than a grain of truth. Wilmot even allowed his imagination to run riot, claiming that Churchill had begun to formulate a comprehensive Balkan strategy aimed at stopping the Russians as early as the end of 1943. As we have seen, that claim is not supported by the documents (which Wilmot never saw);[104] it is also contradicted by Churchill's own correct claim that he did not have a Balkan strategy and that he had never wanted to enter the Balkans with large armed forces.[105] When his adulators praised him for possessing a long-term strategic vision that compared favorably with the naivete of the Americans, Churchill did not fuss over the details in their remarks. The idea of an advance on Vienna was not raised until June 1944. Superseding his wish to preempt the Russians in southeastern Europe in June and July was Churchill's desire to prevent the stagnation of the Italian front and to bring glory to the Imperial Army of the Empire. Only in August, after a decision had been taken about Anvil and under the influence of events in Warsaw, did his political goal begin to become apparent.[106] The British Chiefs of Staff, led by Alan Brooke, had from the first objected to the idea of reinforcing the Italian front and advancing on Vienna, simultaneously maintaining that the invasion of southern France was superfluous. Their opposition was no less than that expressed by the Americans, and in fact grew out of the same strategic considerations. They also ruled out the move on operational grounds. Their evaluations clearly indicated that, even if operation Anvil were cancelled, Alexander could not break out into the Ljubljana Gap and reach Vienna before the spring of 1945. Even should he receive high priority in July-August and descend into the Po valley, the onset of winter would thereafter hold him up in the Alps, where roads can be blocked by small forces. In short, this move was operationally feasible only against an enemy already deprived of all powers of resistance.[107]

Attention must now be focused on the principal question: even if successfully carried out, what would have been the move's military and political value? The first fact to note is that, even under optimum conditions, the Anglo-American forces in Italy could never have matched the Russians' speed of advance into southeastern Europe. On August 25, 1944, Rumania surrendered and declared war on Germany; on September 6 the Russians reached the Yugoslav frontier; on September 9 Bulgaria surrendered; on October 18 the

Russians entered Slovakia; on October 20 Russian troops and partisan forces entered Belgrade; large portions of Yugoslavia were liberated by Tito's partisans; and at the beginning of November Russian forces were in the vicinity of Budapest. At the end of 1944, the Russian advance in this region was broader and swifter than was the case on their front in northeastern Europe (ultimately, Russian forces entered Vienna on April 7, 1945, while Alexander did not cross the Po until April 22). That being the case, the balance of power prevailing in southeastern Europe would not have been very much altered even had Anglo-American forces reached Vienna.[108] Stalin was well aware of that fact. On three occasions (in October and December 1944 and in January 1945) he suggested to the British and Americans that they advance toward Vienna.[109] (These requests remain an enigma to those who attribute unimpeachable importance to Churchill's version of the political value of an advance on Vienna.)[110] Stalin hoped that such a move would draw German forces south and ease his own advance westward, which was held up by particularly stiff resistance around Budapest at the end of 1944. It will be recalled that Alexander and Churchill had at the beginning of July specified precisely that sort of contribution as a justification for their own idea of an advance on Vienna.

■

In any case, from August 1944 Churchill began to formulate his strategic positions with regard to the conduct of the war against Germany from the long-range perspective of "grand strategy." His aim was to half the dangers inherent in Soviet expansion and, with the approach of the end of the war, to improve the western Allies' military and political position. Unfortunately, his gaze and attention were riveted on the wrong war theater. This is because in July and August the most dramatic developments were taking place on the western front. At the end of July, the Americans broke out of the Cherbourg peninsula at Avranches into open terrain, and with this gave the signal for the start of the great advance in the west. The period between August 13 and 20 witnessed the campaign for Normandy, into which Hitler threw his best forces in the west. Most were destroyed. The Wehrmacht was forced into a disorganized retreat. On August 21 the Allies began to cross the Seine. From that stage onward, between the end of August and the end of the first week in September, no organized German resistance existed in the west. The road to the Ruhr, Germany's industrial center, lay open.[111] If it were to be deprived of that region, Germany would be incapable of carrying on the war for more than a few weeks.

It was at that stage that a dispute broke out between Montgomery and Eisenhower, Supreme Commander, Allied Forces Europe. The subject of their controversy was how best to exploit the situation after the victory in Normandy. The original Allied plan called for the Anglo-American forces to advance toward the Rhine on a "broad front"; there would be two main thrusts, toward the Ruhr and the Saar, north and south of the Ardennes. The planners had assumed that German opposition in the west would be stiff and that the logistic capabilities would therefore be able to match the speed of advance of these large forces. When events developed in a manner other than that originally envisaged, Montgomery (on August 17) suggested concentrating the advance on a single thrust by forty divisions into the Ruhr; the southern advance toward the Ardennes was to be held back. Such a plan would overcome the logistics problem that was preventing a simultaneous advance along two axes. He saw it as the best way of increasing pressure on the Germans, whom he estimated to be near to collapse, and thus of bringing the war to a swift end. After discussing the matter throughout the period between August 17 and 26, Eisenhower rejected Montgomery's proposal. He doubted whether the Germans were indeed very close to collapse; he was not sure whether the advance along one axis could be supplied as well as Montgomery wished; he was also afraid that he might generate internal dissension among the Allied armies if he halted the forces of Patton's Third U.S. Army, who during the month of August had raced across France while Montgomery's Army Group was still moving sluggishly.[112]

Notwithstanding Eisenhower's decision, the Allied advance was remarkably swift. Paris was liberated between August 19 and 25; on August 31 the Third U.S. Army crossed the Meuse near Verdun and on the following day penetrated deeply into the Moselle valley by way of Metz. On September 3 the British liberated Brussels and the First U.S. Army reached Namur on the river Meuse; Antwerp fell on September 4. But after the middle of September the advance was checked. One reason was the difficulties of supply, another that the Germans had managed to reorganize their defenses in the west.

To this day Eisenhower's decision remains a matter of controversy. There are some who agree with Montgomery that a great opportunity had been missed. Had his plan been adopted (runs their case) the war could have been ended earlier and under political conditions more favorable to the western Allies.[113] Liddell Hart, for instance, wrote that "the war could easily have been ended in September 1944."[114] Considering the fact that the road to the Ruhr was indeed open between the end of August and the middle of September, the principal obstacle confronting the Allied forces was logistic in nature. Martin van Creveld, who has made a study of this issue, is of the opinion that—as long as the port of Antwerp remained closed—it was only possible to supply the advance of eighteen divisions; but that they would have managed to take the Ruhr. However, while the matter was being disputed—during which period Montgomery was still moving slowly and Patton tearing along in the south—it would have demanded virtually superhuman powers of discernment for Eisenhower to have decided to change the basic strategy. Besides, there is no certainty that the logistic apparatus would have adapted itself to the new situation or have displayed the decisiveness the operation required.[115] In other words, the inherent ability did exist but the principal problem lay in the minds of the decision makers. Historically speaking, commanders have exhibited greater discernment, in more obscure circumstances, when sitting astride a horse and not in a comfortable command caravan.

Uncharacteristically Churchill took no part whatsoever in this episode. Without adopting a stand one way or the other, he devotes to it only about one page in *The Second World War*.[116] The official historian has also noted the Prime Minister's nonintervention. This he explains by saying that—in spite of the issue's importance—Churchill, together with the British and U.S. Chiefs of Staff, refrained from intervening because the disagreement concerned an independent operational theater and affected forces already in place there.[117] That clarification may indeed be sufficient to account for the behavior of the Chiefs of Staffs, but it cannot provide a good explanation for Churchill's conduct. He never attributed importance to such formalities whenever they involved a strategic aspect he considered important. Indeed, where this very theater was concerned, niceties of that sort were not later (in the spring of 1945) to prevent him from attempting to influence Eisenhower to change his plans. If the Prime Minister did not intervene in the debate, it was because he did not appreciate the full significance of this critical and transient phase. There were a number of reasons why that was so. First, he was absent in Italy and the Mediterranean region between August 11 and 29, the very period when the relevant events were taking place and the Montgomery-Eisenhower dispute was raging. Overly preoccupied with maintaining the status of the Italian theater, and with misplaced thoughts about how to reach Vienna, Churchill remained in that region of Europe, far from the western theater, for much of the last quarter of 1944. He spent most of August in Italy, returning sick to Britain on August 30. A few days later, on September 5, he set sail for the second Quebec conference, and returned to Britain on September 25. A few days afterward he departed for Moscow, stopping off en route in Italy (on October 5). He arrived in Moscow on October 9, where he remained until October 20. On his way back to Britain, he again visited Italy (October 21). He ended the year with a Christmas visit to Athens between December 25 and 28.

Another reason for Churchill's nonintervention in the dispute between Montgomery and Eisenhower lies in the ideas he had held before the invasion about the expected course of events on the western front. It will be recalled that his expectations had varied. Sometimes he had made the direst predictions about the consequences of the campaign in France. On other occasions he had voiced less pessimistic assessment that Overlord would, at best, constitute a large-scale diversionary campaign, since Hitler would halt the Allied forces on the Meuse or the Rhine and construct a solid wall in the west.[118] To this was added his growing skepticism about his own intelligence community's repeatedly unfulfilled forecasts about a German collapse. Ironically enough, the heads of intelligence did make a correct evaluation of the situation on the western front in August and early September. As early as mid-July they had maintained that the elements required to bring about a German collapse were now in place. They estimated that, should the Germans continue to be subjected to pressure on all three fronts, they could not hold out beyond December. At the end of August they reaffirmed that evaluation. On September 5 they stated that organized German resistance in the west had ceased, and that whatever steps Hitler might take would come into effect too late to influence events there. Hitler would not transfer forces to the west from his eastern front, which was still organized, lest the latter disintegrate too. The German forces in the west were doomed to crumble before the advance of the Anglo-American forces. Germany's collapse, and the end of the war, were very near.[119] The last evaluation was a fairly accurate depiction of the situation prevailing at the end of August and the beginning of September, but within a few days it had lost its value as a forecast of the future. The British Chiefs of Staff agreed with its spirit. So did their U.S. colleagues, who garnered their information from their own intelligence community.[120]

But Churchill was far from ready to accept it. When in Rome at the end of August he repeated the stand he had taken on the eve of the invasion; he argued that the Germans would hold up the Allies on the Rhine throughout 1944.[121] Three days after reading the evaluation presented by the intelligence chiefs on September 5, he responded with skepticism. He argued that, as far as he could see, it contained nothing new; its conclusions tended to be exaggeratedly optimistic. He pointed out the slow progress of the Anglo-American armies and the supply difficulties caused by the small number of large ports in their possession. In his opinion, Hitler would manage to withdraw and base his defense on the Siegfried line (i.e., the Rhine), exploiting the slowing pace of his enemies' advance. Besides, he could also substantially augment Germany's defense were he to decide to retreat from Italy and be able to transfer the German divisions holed up in the Baltic states. The chances that Germany would remain in the war after January 1 were as even as those that it would collapse before that date. "If he does collapse before then the reason will be political rather than purely military," he concluded.[122] This assessment which Churchill quotes with pride in his memoirs, turned out to be true only at the end of September, by which time the great opportunity of August and early September had been missed. His skepticism about the intelligence analyses cannot be attributed entirely to the fact that (as he put it) he "remembered the German onslaught in March 1918."[123] More revealing were his remarks to Colville on the day that he rebuffed the advice tendered by his intelligence advisers. They were, he said, "being too optimistic about an early victory."[124] Undoubtedly, the fact that he had an exaggerated degree of respect for the ability of the German army also affected his judgment.

Thus it was at the very time that the German army in the west was being dismantled that Churchill was prepared "to go to extreme measure" to further the campaign in Italy. He went (in both senses of that word) to check the Russians in the wrong theater and at the wrong time. It is difficult to be certain that he did so for the reasons stated above only; very possibly, at that stage of the war he had still not appreciated the full political significance inherent in a swift Anglo-American advance in the west to the German interior and beyond as far as possible, which might match the Russian advance from the east.

Hitherto, Churchill had been deeply involved in the operational conduct of both world wars. For the most part his involvement had not been beneficial. But it seems that had he correctly assessed the military and political importance of the opportunity that arose in August, his intervention would on this occasion have been justified. Churchill's own energy and persistence, which had contributed to his failure at Gallipoli, might this time have helped to bring the war to an earlier end. It was he who had always emphasized the importance of operational "willpower" and who had belittled the debilitating weight of logistic factors. Willpower was what the leadership of the Allied armies in western Europe lacked at that time.[125] Also still lacking was a long-term political perspective guiding the operational conduct of the war. There is some irony in the fact that it was Churchill himself who paid so much attention to logistics and other difficulties. Moreover, he did so at a time when—in the circumstances prevailing in August and September—not even the dislocation of Montgomery's plan would have seriously affected the status of the Anglo-American forces in the west. The damage that might have been caused by failure on Montgomery's part was small and in no measure proportionate to the gains that might have accrued. Thus it transpired that a great opportunity escaped the eyes of a man who argued that opportunism was a firm foundation of his strategic concept. With it disappeared the great military success, born of a dramatic move, for which as a strategist he so longed.

■

Churchill's initial consideration of the dangers inherent in the Soviet menace to Europe, and the attempt to avert that threat by a military move in the autumn of 1944, did not cause him to change his attitudes about the political future of Europe. He did not replace them with a new and firm strategic and political concept. Like Eden, he did not yet abandon his basic political course vis-à-vis the Soviet Union, nor his hopes for a different world order based on an international organization. The evaluation that Eden had presented in August still served as a guideline for Churchill's forthcoming moves.

At the end of June, the Soviet government demanded that London return all the Soviet prisoners of war in German hands who had been, or who would be, liberated by Anglo-American armies. This placed Eden and Churchill in a quandary, because they were aware of the dangers that lay in wait for those prisoners on their return home. They advised the War Cabinet to ratify the return of the captives. Their considerations were varied, but principal among them was their wish to retain good relations with the Soviet Union and to reach an agreement with Stalin about the future of the states of central and eastern Europe. On September 4 the Cabinet accepted their recommendation.[126]

At the beginning of August, Churchill was "cynically jocular" about the idea of establishing an international organization. A month later when Cunningham, the First Sea Lord, expressed doubts about the efficiency of such an organization, Churchill responded: "I don't know why you say that, it is the only hope of the world."[127] He had also not yet crystallized his attitude about Germany's future. At the Quebec conference in September 1944, he had agreed to the plan put forward by U.S. Secretary of the Treasury Henry Morgenthau, who had suggested turning Germany into an agrarian state and destroying its industrial base in the Ruhr. This was despite the fact that the notion angered Eden and was queried in the Cabinet.[128] Thus, in October 1943, the Prime Minister had pondered the possibility that Britain might require a powerful Germany against Russia; but a year later, when the war was about to end, he was prepared to crumble Germany to an extent that would leave a vacuum in central Europe, possibly to be filled by Soviet might. Moreover, he was giving serious consideration to that possibility during the very same month that the British Chiefs of Staff were pointing out the need for the west to control the northwestern and industrial sector of Germany, which they considered a security measure lest the Soviet Union turn hostile to Britain. When Eden heard that particular argument, he responded that all such thoughts had to be avoided like a plague whenever the German problem was being discussed.[129] Morgenthau's plan was soon shelved; it was simply unrealistic.

Immediately after the Quebec conference, Churchill hastened to confer with Stalin in Moscow. He informed Colville that his purpose was to prevent Stalin concluding that Britain and the United States intended to join forces against the Soviet Union. He also wanted to inform him of Britain's interest in retaining close relations with Russia.[130] This was an expression of his own idea, and of Eden's wish, that Britain become a power that derived its strength from its status as an intermediary between the United States and the Soviet Union and linked the old world with the new. At the same time, his principal purpose was to refute or confirm his fears about the Soviet Union's intentions; this he would accomplish by attempting to reach a temporary agreement with Stalin on the future of eastern Europe. He thus hoped to find out whether it was possible to continue with the basic line of British policy toward Russia that Eden had formulated as early as 1942. But if he now adhered to the lines of the Foreign Office's policy it was perforce; he perceived that to be a policy of salvation and hope, and not one of choice. This was because the Soviet Union was already firmly planted in eastern Europe. Contrary to the attitude he had adopted in the years 1942–1943, Churchill now wanted to reach a basic agreement on the extent of Soviet influence in southeastern Europe, and on the Polish-Soviet border, before the war had ended and a peace conference had been convened.

In Moscow, Churchill exerted virtually brutal pressure on the Premier of the Polish government in exile in London to agree to recognize the Curzon line. Stanislaw Mihajlovik and his colleagues, who were hastily summoned to Moscow, discovered to their surprise that, as early as the Teheran conference, and hence behind their backs, Churchill and Stalin had framed an understanding with respect to the Curzon line. This they refused to accept. Although unable to solve the Polish problem, Churchill did easily manage to reach an agreement with Stalin on the division of influence between the Soviet Union and Britain in the states of southeastern Europe. This, the well-known "percentage agreement," stated that Russia was to have 90 percent of the influence in Rumania, where other powers would have 10 percent; in Greece, Britain was to have 90 percent (provided the United States agreed) and the Soviet Union 10 percent; Yugoslavia and Hungary were each to be shared fifty-fifty; while in Bulgaria the Soviet Union was to have 75 percent and other powers 25 percent. This marked the finalization of the agreement that had begun to take shape in June between the Soviet Union and Britain, much to Roosevelt's displeasure. Churchill was magnanimous toward the Russians. Although it had been agreed to divide influence in Hungary equally, he said that since the Red Army was presently in control of most of that country "it would be natural that a major share of influence should rest with them." The Prime Minister explained that this agreement provided guidelines for what would be concluded at the peace conference.[131]

The importance of this agreement exceeded its practical aspects. The very fact that it had proved possible to reach almost immediate agreement with Russia inspired Churchill with renewed hope about the future of relations after the war. The political line followed by Eden and the Foreign Office had been affirmed. It was as though the fog of suspicions had been conjured away. Churchill blamed the Polish government in exile in London for the failure to solve the Polish problem in Moscow. He informed his Ministers that the Polish "Lublin government," which the Russians had established, "were neither Quislings nor Communists."[132] Addressing Parliament on his return to London, he attacked the government in exile in London for being stubborn. He argued that its members would have done better to have agreed to the Curzon line becoming Poland's eastern boundary before the Russians advanced into Poland and established a rival government.[133] On his departure from Moscow, he showered Stalin with exaggerated compliments; and in Parliament announced that relations with Soviet Russia were better than ever.[134] His private assessments were no different. At a meeting of the War Cabinet early in November, Churchill was brim-full with optimism about the future of relations with Russia. He was ready to guarantee the independence of Poland within its new borders after the war.

Beaverbrook objected to that idea, reminding Churchill of the lesson of the guarantee extended to Poland in 1939, which Britain had been unable to fulfill. Churchill replied that the postwar situation would be different—the guarantee would be given jointly with the Soviet Union and embodied in the peace treaties; the United States might also accede; on top of all that, it would have the backing of the world organization of nations. Lord Cranborne, the Secretary of State for the Dominions, doubted the Soviet Union's intentions and its readiness to cooperate within the framework of a global organization but Churchill responded that "our whole position had to proceed on the assumption that Russia would in fact rank as a partner."[135] At the end of the month he informed members of the Cabinet that there was no call to establish "a western block" that France would be invited to join. "In his judgement the only real safeguard was an agreement between the three great powers within the framework of a world organization.... Russia was ready and anxious to work in with us." No war was anticipated in the foreseeable future, and the establishment of "a western block" would therefore only impose on Britain a heavy military burden.[136] Nevertheless, by the end of 1944, when the effect of the impression left by his personal meeting with Stalin had begun to wear off, Churchill's suspicions about the Soviet Union's intentions began to surface once again.[137]

In the middle of December, while the Allies were still marking time west of the Rhine, the Germans opened their counterattack in the Ardennes. One of the reasons that they managed to surprise their foes lay in the continued opinion of the heads of British intelligence who believed that the German leadership, as it approached defeat, would prefer to concentrate its forces in the east (a subject discussed below). The Ardennes assault did indeed exhaust Germany's remaining military strength. But it did not improve the position of the Anglo-American armies, vis-à-vis those of Russia, with respect to the final assault on Germany. This was because events in the east were again on the move. On January 20 Hungary signed an armistice. Late in January and early in February 1945, on the eve of the Yalta conference, the Russians established bridgeheads over the Oder, forty miles from Berlin; at that time, the Anglo-American armies were still located some 300 miles from the German capital, and had yet to cross the Rhine. Stalin apparently preferred to halt on the Oder in order to deepen the advance on the southern flank, south of the Carpathians, and to secure his position there. As long as the Allies had not yet crossed the Rhine, he could afford to do so—especially when they told him that they did not intend to cross the river until the beginning of March.[138]

As a result of all this, Stalin's bargaining position at Yalta was much better than that of his partners. Especially was this so since Poland, which constituted the burning issue at the conference, lay within his grasp. Churchill never managed to shake off his sense of inferiority during his wartime meetings with Stalin. Prior to the invasion of western Europe, the problem of the "second front" had been responsible for those feelings; subsequently the cause lay in the fact that the Russians were already in control of most of eastern Europe. In their efforts to ensure Poland's independence, Churchill and Roosevelt could only conjure up their diplomatic charm and appeal to Stalin's goodwill.

Churchill returned from Yalta, as from all his meetings with Stalin, in an optimistic frame of mind and with confidence in the Soviet dictator. Reporting to the War Cabinet on February 19, he announced that "he was quite sure that he [Stalin] meant good to the world and to Poland." Moreover, "he had a great feeling that the Russians were anxious to work harmoniously with the two English-speaking democracies," and would honor the agreements reached with respect to holding free elections in Poland. "Stalin was a person of great power in whom he had every confidence," although very much depended on his staying alive.[139] But during the month of March Churchill realized that Stalin was in no hurry to carry out his promises with respect to Poland. Moreover, the Russian also resorted to unprecedented language when accusing him (and Roosevelt) of conducting negotiations behind his back with the German high command. Now Churchill's pendulum of views on the Soviet Union's intentions swung back—this time for good.

At the end of March and the beginning of April Churchill appreciated that the western Allies had to conquer Berlin and Prague before the Russians and to advance as far east as possible.[140] As he explained after the war, those moves were necessary in order to fill the gap left by the disappearance of German power and to exert an influence on the fate of Poland. One did not have to be a prophet to anticipate those developments. Unfortunately, Churchill only became aware of the full extent of the Soviet menace to Europe when the German threat—the only factor uniting the three powers—was disintegrating before his very eyes. But, wrote Churchill, the U.S. State Department

> did not comprehend the issues involved. The indispensable political direction was lacking at the moment when it was most needed. The United States stood on the scene of victory, master of world fortunes, but without a true and coherent design. Britain . . . could not act decisively alone. I could at this stage only warn and plead. Thus this climax of apparently measureless success was to me a most unhappy time. I . . . sat at a table . . . with an aching heart and a mind oppressed by forebodings.[141]

If his mind was indeed "oppressed by forebodings" it was not only because of the Americans. Another reason was his sudden realization that he had himself long been blind to the true facts, and that Britain's long-standing policy, which had been based on future cooperation with Russia, was collapsing.

Churchill (and in his wake several other authors) have made much of the Americans' refusal to advance and conquer Berlin before the Russians. He cites that instance to demonstrate their insensitivity to the growing Soviet menace and their strategic naivete: they refused to recognize that in war the character of military moves has to accord with political objectives.[142] That is not a truthful reconstruction. The root of the Allies' failure to conquer Berlin before the Russians and to advance as far eastward as possible lay in the demand for Germany's "unconditional surrender" and in the agreement to divide that country into occupation zones. Those moves had been set in motion long before the dispute about the advance on Berlin arose at the end of March and the beginning of April.

President Roosevelt had announced the policy of "unconditional surrender," the terms demanded of Germany, Japan, and Italy, early in 1943, at the concluding press conference of the Casablanca conference. Prior to the conference, Roosevelt had established a special committee to discuss this problem, and it was on the basis of its recommendations that he advised Churchill to adopt that policy. Churchill agreed to the proposal in principle. After the Casablanca conference, Roosevelt told Harry Hopkins that his announcement at the press conference had been a slip of the tongue; Churchill wrote that he had been surprised by the President's announcement. However, it was he who had suggested that the President announce this policy at the concluding press conference, although he did ask that Italy be excluded from the demand.[143] Such strange arguments cannot disguise the basic fact that during the war Churchill and Roosevelt were in agreement, consistent, and convinced that their policy was just. Moreover, their versions of what transpired (supposedly in defiance of their intentions) are true, and together with the evidence which exists, support and complement each other. In principle they did agree on this policy; whether or not Italy was to be included in its terms became the controversial issue that impelled them to postpone its announcement until a later date. But, as Roosevelt said, an unexpected mishap occurred during the press conference. Churchill could do nothing but accede and give the President's announcement his unreserved support. The policy of unconditional surrender was thus born after an incomplete pregnancy.[144]

There were two basic reasons why Roosevelt and Churchill adhered to that policy until the end of the war (after the war, Churchill resorted to both in its defense.) First, they wanted to make the Germans realize that their country had been utterly defeated and thus avoid any sort of commitment to the losers. They wanted a free hand to carry out radical territorial and social changes in Germany. The memory of the misunderstandings supposedly produced by Wilson's Fourteen Points was always in their minds. After World War I, the Germans claimed that they had laid down their arms on the understanding that the peace treaty would be based on Wilson's points, but those who had dictated the terms of the Versailles Treaty had broken the promises they had contained. Germany had been deceived and tricked into laying down its arms without having been defeated. Second, the policy of unconditional surrender constituted a sort of lowest, and most convenient, common denominator, serving to tighten the bonds between the three major parties to the alliance. Any attempt to achieve a joint definition of war aims and methods of surrender, quite apart from being very time consuming, would probably also have had an adverse effect on their mutual relations. And, as we have seen, that was something Churchill wished to avoid for as long as the war was raging. Besides, by adopting this policy, Churchill and Roosevelt hoped to allay Stalin's fears that Britain and the United States might be intending a separate peace with Germany. This was particularly important since they realized that their decision not to invade western Europe in 1943, as had originally been planned, would augment Stalin's suspicions of their intentions. To a lesser extent, they hoped that the policy of "unconditional surrender" would help to prevent a separate Soviet-German peace.[145]

Admittedly, it was Roosevelt who had taken the initiative by translating those views into a formal formula for strategic action. But Churchill did not have to be inspired by the President to act in accordance with the policy of "unconditional surrender." As we have seen, the defeat of the enemy and the attainment of total victory had been basic components of Churchill's strategic concept ever since the Boer War. During World War I, he had been a staunch opponent of a compromise peace with Germany; he had aimed at a decisive military outcome, in the belief that only a result of that magnitude would prevent a renewed European war after no more than a brief interlude. He also believed that a decisive victory would enable the Allies to effect substantive changes in the German regime—and in particular facilitate the destruction of Prussian militarism.[146] From his point of view those arguments were particularly valid during the present conflict, especially in view of his belief that the roots of German aggression still lay in Prussian militarism. At the beginning of August 1940, after the Germans had put out peace feelers, he informed his Ministers that the British would "prosecute the war against Germany by every means in their power until Hitlerism is finally broken." His speeches also left no doubt that Britain would not rest until Germany had been totally and unconditionally defeated.[147] At the beginning of 1941 he insisted that the Duke of Aosta and his Italian forces in Ethiopia should surrender "unconditionally"; moreover, he forced that position on Wavell and General Alan Cunningham, who were conducting negotiations with the Duke on the terms of his surrender.[148]

Churchill and Eden did of course appreciate that the public demand for unconditional surrender, which was virtually without precedent in modern history, might boomerang; deprived of any alternative, the Germans might feel compelled to intensify their struggle. In July 1943 Liddell Hart submitted a memorandum to the British government in which he argued that such a policy would stiffen German resistance and harm efforts to encourage domestic circles within Germany who aimed at deposing the Nazi regime. Hitler's potential opponents would not act against him without clear assurance about Germany's postwar future.[149] It is not clear whether Churchill saw this memorandum, but during the course of the following months he received reports of a similar nature from the British ambassador in Ankara, Knatchbull-Hugessen, and from the naval attaché in the same city. They were based on conversations with the Turkish foreign minister and his deputy. The British ambassador rejected German feelers and informed the Turks that the Allies were insistent on Germany's unconditional surrender. Churchill praised the ambassador's action. He added that recent information indicated that the Nazi machine was disintegrating; hence there was no need to slow down that process by frequent references to the slogan of unconditional surrender. Hundreds of thousands of British and American lives could be saved were the internal rifts within Germany to be widened. The main thing was to avoid entering into any commitment to new factors or personalities in Germany.[150] Churchill's only reservations about Roosevelt's announcement, other than the fact that it was extended to include Italy, concerned the publicity given to that demand.

The Russians did not accede to the demand for unconditional surrender until the end of October 1943, during the foreign ministers' conference in Moscow. But at the Teheran conference, held a month later, Stalin argued that this policy was mistaken from a tactical point of view; he suggested determining joint terms of surrender that would be submitted to Germany. Churchill agreed with him, and put the same idea to Roosevelt after the conference, in January 1944.[151] The President rejected Stalin's proposal and Churchill's approaches.[152] The Russians themselves did not bother to reply to the draft headings of surrender terms submitted by the British Foreign Office.

At about the same time, the heads of British intelligence expressed their own views. They criticized the fact that the nature of the demand for unconditional surrender had not been defined, nor made clear to the enemy. This, they claimed, was leading them to fear the worst and thus strengthening the resolve to fight.[153] During the period between February and April 1944 the Chiefs of Staff, as well as Eden and Cadogan, approached Churchill with the suggestion that he initiate a more moderate surrender formula; they hoped that a document of that sort might weaken German resistance during the invasion of western Europe.[154] (That was apparently the reason for Churchill's earlier approach to Roosevelt.) Churchill's own fears about the invasion were quite as substantial as theirs. But he replied that, although the "unconditional" policy had been Roosevelt's initiative, he supported it in principle. True, the arguments against that policy were weighty. But were the Germans to be presented with detailed terms of surrender—such as the fragmentation of their country into several separate states and the transfer of millions of their countrymen to forced labor in Russia—they would consider them far more severe than the obscure demand for their unconditional surrender. It was therefore better to persist in that policy.[155] That remained his attitude until the end of the war.

The policy of unconditional surrender was popular with the British and U.S. public, and thus attained one of its ancillary goals. Most members of Parliament supported the government's line, even though some did argue that the failure to discuss and provide clear definitions of war and peace aims might result in a situation in which Britain would emerge as a victor in the war but a loser from a political point of view. Critics of this policy during the war were very few. Even they voiced their opinions only after western Europe had been invaded and the Russians had made considerable advances into eastern Europe. Their most vociferous spokesmen, Maurice Hankey and Aneurin Bevan, argued that this policy was bolstering German resistance and protracting the war.[156] But even after the war, critics of the "unconditional" policy were unable to present convincing proof that it had been responsible for lengthening the war; it is doubtful whether that case is at all amenable to verification.[157]

There existed another aspect of the issue. In November 1944 an M. P. named Ryce-Davies pointed out that the unconditional surrender policy was helping the Russians to conquer eastern Europe and advance beyond that region.[158] Indeed, that policy did possess a clear operational meaning that could have been forseen when it was initiated: the war would end when the Russian and U.S. forces had effected a physical junction at some point along the breadth of Europe; after all, it was highly unlikely that the Germans would lay down their arms and agree to unconditional surrender while their forces were still beyond their own borders (providing, of course, that no internal German collapse occurred earlier). Moreover, that was precisely the eventuality that Roosevelt and Churchill attempted to avoid when formulating the demand for unconditional surrender. As has already been noted, they remembered the events of 1918, at the end of which an armistice had been declared without Allied forces present on German soil—a situation that had provided a pretext for all the later German complaints and claims.

Stalin recognized the link between this policy, his own political objectives, and his military moves. That was why his attitude toward unconditional surrender was flexible. He avoided committing himself to that policy until a final decision of the war in the east had been attained. But once that was so, and the Soviet Union had at the end of 1943 reached the old Russo-Polish boundary, Stalin changed his tone. He became an ardent supporter of that policy, and took extreme care to ensure that his allies adhered to it. The closer the war's end came, the more careful he became. In March 1945, he poured heaps of scorn on President Roosevelt because he suspected that Britain and the United States were about to sign a separate agreement that would provide for the surrender of German forces in Italy.[159] His behavior is attributable to his fear that the Germans might reach an agreement for their surrender in the west that would enable them to continue fighting in the east. The demand for Germany's unconditional surrender, in general and on all fronts, helped Stalin to ensure that such an eventuality would not transpire. As long as the Germans continued to resist in the west, the Red Army could more easily advance westward.[160]

There were some grounds for Stalin's suspicions of his allies. Ever since the beginning of 1943 the heads of British intelligence had been saying that they thought the Army would seize power in Germany when its collapse appeared inevitable. The German generals would then try to reach an agreement with Britain and the United States. They would prefer to abandon the western front and concentrate all their efforts on the eastern front in order to "postpone the hour of final defeat and ensure the ultimate occupation of Germany by Anglo-American rather than by Russian forces." They would adopt this course even though Britain and the United States would reject their overtures, and even if they themselves refused to surrender unconditionally because of the severe consequences those terms would have on Germany and because they demanded a cessation of the fighting *on all fronts*.[161] Eden was of the same opinion. But he warned of the possibility that the German generals might try to drive a wedge between Britain and the United States, on the one hand, and the Soviet Union, on the other, by requesting assistance and political assurances before they acted. Hitherto, Britain had rejected their feelers, and would continue to do so in the future. His position was that "the generals must act before we talk." At the same time, however, steps must be taken to ensure that Germany's postwar orientation would favor the west rather than Russia, whom the Germans might veer toward in view of their admiration of power.[162]

Eden had no intention of exploiting what appeared to be an Anglo-American advantage over the Russians where domestic German preferences were concerned. In accordance with his plan, he considered it more important to foster Anglo-Russian relations during and after the war. Churchill likewise gave no encouragement to contacts with anti-Nazi groups in Germany, and forbade that any assurances be given.

After the war Montgomery told Churchill that the foundations for the division of Europe and Russian control of its eastern half had been laid at the Casablanca conference. That was because the demand for unconditional surrender in effect meant that Russian forces would invade the heart of the Continent. Britain and the United States should even at that stage have taken steps to ensure that they would be the first to reach Berlin, Vienna, and Prague.[163] That of course is an exaggeration, but it does contain a kernel of truth. The policy of unconditional surrender involved disadvantages and dangers, just as it also promised certain rewards. The latter were undoubtedly weighty, and possibly justified its adoption. But that was no reason to avoid giving consideration to action that might have minimized its possible damage. Churchill, however, took no considerate steps to obviate the advantages unconditional surrender conferred on the Russians. It is even hard to defend his action by claiming that his complacency was the product of the assessment that, notwithstanding the policy of unconditional surrender, the Germans—when collapsing—would abandon their defenses in the west. There are no signs that he placed any faith in evaluations of that nature. Moreover, as was shown on the eve of the Normandy invasion, when his hopes for an imminent German collapse were undermined, he thought that Overlord would be nothing more than a large-scale diversionary campaign, which would make it easier for the Red Army to advance.[164]

Possibly some people in London did indulge themselves in the hope that, at the end of the war, the Germans might open their gates in the west and allow the Anglo-American forces to advance as far east as possible. But if that was the case, then the British Foreign Office ensured that such hopes would never be realized. In January 1944 the European Advisory Committee (EAC), Eden's brainchild, held its second meeting in London. There William Strang, the Foreign Office's representative, presented the U.S. and Soviet delegates (respectively, ambassadors Winant and Gousev) with a plan for the division of Germany into areas of conquest after its surrender. This proposed that Germany be divided into two principal occupation zones, eastern and western. The former would be under the Soviet Union's control; the latter would be parceled out between Britain and the United States. The northern section of the western border of the Soviet zone lie on the Elbe, while its southern section extended a considerable distance west of the river; thus Berlin would lay in the heart of the Soviet zone. Control within the city itself would be divided between the three Great Powers. After some minor changes had been made, this plan was finally ratified at the Yalta conference held about a year later.

On February 18 the Russians gave their assent in principle to the British proposal. Although they did raise some minor objections, the map of the division into occupation zones they tabled was very similar to that which the British had presented. The Americans delayed their response for various reasons, chief among which was their lack of enthusiasm for receiving the southern area of the western zone. On May 31 Winant officially informed the EAC that the United States accepted the western boundary of the Russian zone, but that it was not prepared to commit itself on the division of the western zone between Britain and the United States. The dispute between the two western powers continued throughout the summer, and was not settled until Roosevelt and Churchill reached agreement at the Quebec conference in September 1944. At that juncture, the Russians hastened to withdraw their objections, and on September 12 the three sides signed the protocol of the division into zones of conquest. A few months later, that document was ratified at the Yalta conference.

It is not difficult to imagine what the Russians' motives might have been. The reason they agreed—with what amounted to haste—to the plan of division proposed to them early in 1944 was that Stalin considered it important to establish the principle of the joint occupation of Germany. For one thing, he recognized the territorial implications of that principle; for another, he saw it as a means of reducing still further the possible realization of something he very much feared: the conclusion of a separate peace or surrender agreement between the western powers and Germany.[165] By raising minor objections at the beginning of 1944, the Russians hoped to play for time during a period when their own advance was in full flood and the western Allies had yet to set foot on the Continent. They thereby reserved the option of attaining a better agreement than that which was proposed to them (although it must be assumed that they were very surprised by the extent of British generosity revealed in the proposed division). In September 1944, when it seemed that Germany was about to collapse and that Anglo-American forces were on the point of crossing the Rhine, the Russians hastened to withdraw their objections and signed the protocol.[166]

T. Sharp has written that Churchill's account of how the agreements on Germany's division into occupation zones were drawn up "betrays a great ignorance of the events which took place, and is very unreliable."[167] In some part that ignorance was the consequence of the Prime Minister's being something of a nonparticipating observer of this issue; the division into occupation zones was one of those "speculative" matters he preferred to leave to Eden. When the plan was first presented to the European Advisory Committee at the beginning of 1944, he considered it to be "purely theoretical." This was because of the prevailing opinion that Russia would not continue fighting once it had reached its borders (i.e., those of June 1941) and that considerable effort would have to be invested in persuading it to do so. "The question of the Russian zone of occupation in Germany therefore did not bulk in our thoughts."[168] That is true; but during the same period of late 1943 and early 1944 Churchill did foresee that the Russians would advance beyond the borders of June 1941.[169] In short, that was not the prevailing opinion when the British put forth their plan. Churchill's explanation contradicts that presented as an extenuating excuse by the senior Foreign Office officials, Strang and G. Webb, who were two of the plan's authors. After the war, they claimed that the proposal to divide Germany was impelled by their wish to ensure that Britain and the United States would have the western portion of that country. They feared that their armies would not manage to invade Germany before the Russians had penetrated deep into its interior.[170] There is an element of truth in that claim; the British and Americans wanted to ensure that their forces would control at least a part of Germany should it collapse before the western Allies had launched their invasion of France.[171] But it is very doubtful whether that was the main motive impelling the British to initiate the proposal for division as sketched on the maps. The enthusiasm they had shown when first proposing the agreement was matched by that they evinced when signing the protocol in September 1944—even though the Russians were then still on the Vistula and Anglo-American forces seemed poised to break into Germany.

The British initiative of early 1944 was but another step in the general policy Eden and the Foreign Office pursued with respect to Russia. Eden hoped to use this generous proposal as a means of showing the Soviet Union that Britain intended to cooperate with that country in the management of European affairs and that he regarded the Russians, together with the Americans, as full political partners. He and his officials thus hoped to add another block to the building of the Anglo-Russian postwar alliance. Believing that the Russians would regard Britain's attitude toward Germany's future as a litmus test, they wanted to use this proposal as a signal that Britain had no intention of resuscitating Germany as a counterweight to the Soviet Union.[172] They preferred the division into separate conquest zones, within the framework of a joint conquest, to the notion that the victorious armies would be stationed throughout Germany. The British committee that discussed those two alternatives came down in favor of the first because it promised to ease the problems of control and supervision (that, it claimed, was the lesson of the conquest of France in 1814 and of Germany in 1918). The committee made that recommendation even though its members were sensitive to the danger that a division into zones of conquest might set in motion a dynamic process that would lead to the creation of national spheres of influence.[173]

In 1944 Churchill did not pay much attention to the question of the division into occupation zones. He was not aware of the political and strategic meaning of the subject until the Yalta conference. There he devoted his efforts to persuading the Americans and the Soviets to grant France a portion of the western zone of occupation. He thereby wanted to aquire a helpmate who would aid Britain in imposing order on the Continent and serve as a counterweight that might improve the standing of western Europe vis-à-vis the giant in the east when the Americans took their "boys" home. He was successful, but he made no attempt to call the borders of the occupation zones into question. He only recognized their implications when Anglo-American forces penetrated deep into the German interior and he was shaken out of his illusion of future cooperation with the Soviet Union. Norman Brook, one of Churchill's private secretaries, told Lord Moran that: "Winston was very cross [sic] when he discovered the boundaries of the agreed zones, and found we had already crossed our limit and had to go back. But though he tries to get away from it, he must have agreed to the zones."[174]

The unconditional surrender policy and the agreement on occupation zones—both moves to which Churchill gave his blessing—worked together, and reinforced each other, in narrowing the room for maneuver available to Britain and the United States during the last phase of the war. The policy of unconditional surrender ensured the creation of a line of contact down the breadth of Europe between the Russian and Anglo-American armies; it considerably reduced the chances that the Germans might surrender in stages, initially in the west and then in the east, and enable the western forces to advance eastward as deeply as possible. Meanwhile, the plan to divide Germany into occupation zones guaranteed the Soviet Union military control over the eastern and central portions of Germany (including Berlin) and Europe, even had its forces not reached the Elbe. That would also have been the case even had the Germans indeed abandoned their western front—despite the demand that they surrender unconditionally and without a prior agreement with the western Allies—and even had Anglo-American forces crossed the partition borders.

That result must almost inevitably occur when one becomes too bogged down in an attitude expressed by the phrase "first catch your hare," meaning, in the present context, in the military conduct of the war. The western Allies took their principal strategic decisions in 1942 and 1943. But neither then nor well into 1944 did Churchill realize, and act on the assumption, that the Anglo-American armies had to advance as far eastward as possible in order to fill the void that would be created in central Europe once Germany had fallen; and that this strategic line had to be adopted without reference to the results of the diplomatic agreements with the Russians over the independence of Poland, Czechoslovakia, and other states in eastern Europe.[175]

In *The Second World War* Churchill claimed that it was understood at Yalta that the agreement on the division into occupation zones would not restrict the movement of the armies: "Berlin, Prague, and Vienna could be taken by whoever got there first." But the protocols of the conference contain no evidence to support his claim.[176] On the contrary, it was Eden and his U.S. colleagues who pressed the Russians to ratify the agreement; they did so because they feared that were the Red Army to advance deeply into Germany—beyond Berlin—the Russians might change their minds about its terms.[177] Besides, it must be considered doubtful whether Churchill was himself prepared to come to an understanding of that sort at the beginning of February, which is when the Yalta conference took place. At that juncture, it was the Russians who were the better placed to take all three of those cities.

On top of all that, the conquest of Berlin before the Russians got there was not operationally possible when, late in March 1945, Churchill brought up that objective. Once again, operational reality was at variance with his wartime political goals. It was simply too late. The opportunity to take Berlin before the Russians was apparently lost in August 1944.[178] At the beginning of April 1945 Eisenhower could see no chance of preempting them. True, some small U.S. forward units did reach the Elbe as early as April 12; but the U.S. armies' center of gravity was situated far to the west. By this time the Russians, who had for long been situated some fifty kilometers from Berlin, had completed their preparations for an assault on the city. Churchill was himself apparently convinced by Eisenhower's arguments. On April 19, after meeting with him, he wrote to Eden: "It would seem that the Western Allies are not immediately in a position to force their way into Berlin. The Russians have two-and-a-half million troops on the section of the front opposite that city."[179] In addition, Eisenhower and Bradley, who commanded the Twelfth U.S. Army Group that had advanced into central Germany, were deterred by the heavy level of losses they expected to incur by crossing the Elbe and taking Berlin. Eisenhower also feared clashes between Russian and Anglo-American forces, each advancing toward the other in obscure and unclear territory. He considered the Elbe to constitute a natural meeting point.[180]

Eisenhower was not naive—he understood the essence of strategy. On April 7 he wrote to Marshall: "I am the first to admit that a war is waged in pursuance of political aims." He made it clear that he was prepared to act in accordance with that gauge, were the Combined Chiefs of Staff to order him to do so.[181] But, in the current circumstances, the U.S. Chiefs of Staff could see no reason to change the basic line of thought that had so far guided them—the war had to be conducted in accordance with one decisive principle, which was to take the most efficient military steps possible to speed its conclusion. Like Eisenhower, they maintained that it would be foolish to try to conquer extensive territory and a fortified city such as Berlin, only ultimately to hand them over to the Russians—which is what would have been required by the agreement on occupation zones that Britain and the United States had signed.[182]

The Russians opened their attack on the central front on April 17; after a week of fighting they had surrounded Berlin and swept westward. On April 25 Russian and U.S. forces met at Torgau, west of the Elbe.

At the beginning of May Churchill perceived the nature of the nightmare that was to prevail in Europe after the war. With horror, he described the Soviet Union's conquest of eastern Europe and the creation of Soviet borders stretching from the northern Cape to Greece; an area that contained the great capitals of eastern and central Europe: Berlin, Vienna, Budapest, Belgrade, Bucharest, and Sofia. He was not mistaken when writing to Eden that that conquest "constitutes an event in the history of Europe to which there has been no parallel, and which has not been faced by the [western] Allies in their long and hazardous struggle."[183] The lines of division into zones of occupation became the borders that divided the two great political camps in their struggle against each other after World War II.

11

Conclusions: Churchill in War and Peace

Churchill initiated the "Mediterranean strategy" at the end of 1940. That move, also the product of natural strategic selection, would have been prudent had it been carried out with circumspection. But Churchill deepened Britain's involvement in the Middle East to a degree greater than that desired by his military advisers. Moreover, he did so without according priority to laying the foundations for future Anglo-American military cooperation, which circumstances dictated would have to find expression in western Europe. This was despite his conviction that the key to victory lay in U.S. entry into the war, which he believed would soon occur. It is he who must bear the principal blame for the decision to send an army to Greece with the purpose of establishing a Balkan front, instead of exploiting a golden opportunity that presented itself at the beginning of 1941 to seize Tripoli and with it, eventually, all of North Africa. That error led to the British debacle in Greece and the Balkans in the spring of 1941 and was responsible for the protracted and unnecessary entanglement in the Middle East and North Africa. Once the United States had entered the war, it was also dragged into this whirlpool. That embroilment exerted a profound influence on both the formulation of Churchill's own strategic concept and on the ability to carry out an invasion of western Europe, and its timing.

The strategy persistently advocated by the British Chiefs of Staff was based on the assumption that no Allied entry into western Europe would be possible unless preceded by a German collapse. Despite some initial reluctance, Churchill adopted the Chiefs' position and thereby disregarded his own long-standing appreciation (predating even World War I) of the importance of fighting in the western European theater. The main reason lay in the large extent to which he had been impressed by the British Army's failures in the period 1941–1942, especially in North Africa, despite its possession of both numerical superiority over the German forces and superior intelligence. This led him to believe, unjustifiably, that the fighting capabilities of the Allied armies were significantly inferior to those of the Germans. The conclusion he drew was that, unless the German army had previously been brought to a state of collapse, the land campaign to take place in western Europe after the invasion would end in a rout of the Allied forces or—at best—in indecision. The longer the war dragged on, the firmer that conviction became. Contrary to his later claim, neither before nor after the U.S. entry into the war did Churchill consider the implementation of a massive invasion of western Europe to be the supreme strategic objective. Fundamentally, the strategy he adopted was one of large-scale attrition: its object was to hasten the German collapse while at the same time cautiously narrowing the zone of land confrontation between Anglo-American and German forces by exerting pressure with ground forces on the periphery of Europe—particularly its southern flank. Unlike his military advisers, Churchill was keen to act on the northern flank too, in Norway. As for the actual invasion of western Europe, that was to take place only after the German collapse and thus constitute a coup de grace that would not require the employment of huge ground forces.

To revert to the old terminology, Churchill had no choice but to abandon the "continental school" and to adhere to the "maritime school." During World War I, the limitations inherent in the "peripheral-maritime" strategy, together with his own shortcomings, had prevented him from then fulfilling his wish to effect the combination of the two schools. He was equally unsuccessful in World War II. This time, the reason lay in the fact that the foundations of the "continental strategy" collapsed when France fell at a very early stage of the conflict. Subsequently Churchill's belief that those foundations might be rebuilt was also undermined.

The Americans prevented Churchill from fully implementing his strategic line. From the moment they entered the war, they believed that the only way to defeat Germany—and quickly—was to launch a massive invasion of western Europe with the purpose of beating the German army on the Continent. It was they who instigated the plan to invade western Europe without making that operation conditional on a German collapse, and they who made the invasion the crux of Anglo-American strategy. As soon as the Americans established that goal, Churchill began a series of maneuvers designed to delay the planned invasion of western Europe for as long as possible. Basing himself on optimistic intelligence evaluations, he hoped that the German collapse would take place before the enterprise was launched. Although he did occasionally harbor doubts about the efficacy of an attritional strategy, his skepticism was not sufficiently strong. His own course may not have inspired him with conviction; but he did know what he did not want. Incessantly, he strove to realize his own positions and to impose them upon the Americans, even after his own military advisers had begun to despair. To that end, he resorted to dexterity, dissembling, and double-dealing with his American partners; where the Russians were concerned, he also deceived.

Churchill's task was light in 1942 when the Americans hoped to carry out an invasion of France on a limited scale, since the conditions for that operation were very unfavorable. Matters were more difficult for him in 1943, the year in which it had been agreed that the invasion of Europe would take place. The entanglement in North Africa, which had implanted in Churchill his pessimism about the fate of the invasion, also provided him with the powerful leverage needed to convince his U.S. allies to widen the campaign in the Mediterranean at the expense of a cross-Channel operation in 1943. He managed to drag the Americans into fighting in Italy. Notwithstanding his claims, he did not regard the invasion of Italy and that country's exit from the war as a prepatory and secondary move, designed to provide support for the planned invasion of western Europe. As far as he was concerned, the invasion of Italy was meant to be an additional step in the peripheral strategy of attrition. Churchill assumed that Italy could be taken easily, because the Germans would choose to evacuate once that country had been invaded and had left the war. That circumstance would accelerate the process of Germany's collapse and at the same time afford opportunities to expand the land campaign in southern Europe. In fact, had Churchill's hypothesis been validated, Hitler would have been in a better, not worse, position to defend western Europe. As it was, Hitler's decision to fight for every inch of Italian soil foiled Churchill's plans. On the other hand, however, it also provided him with grounds for the retrospective claim that he had, from the very first, regarded the fighting in Italy as a prepatory move vital to the success of the invasion in the west.

Once the difficulties in the war for Italy became apparent, and the expectations that Germay would collapse in 1943 proved to be unfounded, Churchill discovered that he had burned his bridges. On the one hand, his position vis-à-vis the Americans had become very much weaker now that his assumptions about the Italian campaign had been shown to be misguided and the attritional strategy had achieved only limited results. On the other hand, he was now bound by his commitment to the Americans and his promise to the Russians that the invasion would be carried out in May 1944, even if a German collapse had not by then taken place. However, at the end of 1943 he again tried to wriggle out of it. But his efforts came to nought. Caught in the vise of U.S. and Russian pressure, he could not escape.

Churchill's attritional-peripheral strategy was not illogical or impracticable. During World War II his strategic concept did not reach the dead end into which it had been driven in World War I. Then, he had (after 1916) called for an attrition strategy that would bring about Germany's final defeat, but had opposed massive offensives in the west. He had not explained how it might prove possible to erode German manpower, which he considered to be vital, without attacking the Germans while the latter themselves refrained from attacking in the west and Russia was crumbling under their pressure. Admittedly, in World War II the attritional strategy initiated by Churchill and his military advisers before the Soviet Union's entry into the war had been ineffectual. They took that course because Britain's determination to continue fighting had left them with no alternative. But once the Russians had joined the conflict, attrition became a viable strategy. Provided the Soviet Union held on and repulsed the German assault, it could have brought Germany to its knees. Besides, thanks to changes in the conditions of warfare, and in particular the return of maneuver to the battlefield, it was possible to bring the war in the east to a decision even before the enemy had been entirely worn down. To this must be added the new dimension provided by strategic air bombardment, on which great hopes were pinned.

Nevertheless, the attritional-peripheral strategy suffered from two defects: one patent, the other latent. First, it was by nature a strategy slow to attain its ends. Saving the lives of British as well as U.S. soldiers and reducing military risks was possible at the cost of a longer war and with it more sufferings borne by the peoples of occupied Europe and the citizens of the Soviet Union. This strategy could not take optimum advantage of the enormous potential of the United States' military manpower and industrial might. Moreover, as a result of their enmeshment in the eastern Mediterranean, it was the British who were for long periods being worn down and tied down, instead of the other way round. The attrition of German ground forces on Europe's southern periphery did not commence until Hitler's dispatch of sizable reinforcements to North Africa at the end of 1942 and his decision to defend southern Italy in October 1943. Even then, the process proved to be of limited effect, and was too late to influence the fate of the decisive campaigns on the eastern front at Stalingrad and at Kursk. The second, latent, defect of the attritional strategy was in some respects derivative of its first drawback. As far as Britain and the United States were concerned, it was an inherently weak method of attaining and defending their long-term political goals in Europe in relation to the Soviet Union. To a large extent, this strategy left the protection of those interests to chance or to Soviet goodwill, or to both.

Of the alternative courses to bring about Germany's defeat, a mass invasion of western Europe was the most efficient path to the attainment of the military and political war aims of Britain and the United States. However, the timing of that enterprise (the summer of 1944) meant that its principal military contribution lay in considerably shortening the war, not in bringing about its decision. During the course of 1943 the Russians had already determined the fate of the campaign on the eastern front, and thereby decided the outcome of the entire war. From the viewpoint of the western Allies, the invasion was thus of greater political than military value. This was because the West possessed but one way of defending at least a portion of its interests with respect to Europe's postwar political future. Only an invasion of western Europe, together with an advance into the German interior and eastward as far as possible to match the Russian advance could have provided an integrated answer to the requirements of "grand strategy" with a minimum of disharmony between its various levels.

However, in the years 1942–1943, when the decisions concerning the opening of the "second front" were taken, Churchill did not endow that move with a complementary measure of military and political significance. For one thing, he did not form a correct estimate of its military value and chances of success. For another, in both concept and practice he distinguished the political from the military dimension. During the period when the principal decisions were taken, he engrossed himself in the military conduct of the war. The result was to delay his recognition of the future Soviet threat to Europe and to prevent the inclusion of that consideration in his assessment of the utility of the invasion of France.

Had Churchill carried the day at the end of 1943, and had the strategic line of his choice been implemented, no invasion of western Europe would have taken place in 1944. He would not have invaded western Europe without a German collapse having first taken place, and it did not happen in 1944. (The short-lived collapse of the German front in the west in August-September 1944 was brought about as *a result* of the invasion and the fighting in western Europe.) Another conclusion can also be drawn. If the lines Churchill had sketched with such clarity in October 1943 had actually been put into effect, he would have been forced to admit bankruptcy if he suddenly changed his mind and decided that political considerations dictated an invasion of western Europe without awaiting a German collapse. In the second half of 1944—when he did begin to integrate military and political actions—the forces stationed in Britain would not have been large enough to carry out a massive and decisive invasion of western Europe in that year against a German army still intact.

As we have seen, in 1942 and 1943, when the principal decisions affecting Anglo-American strategy were taken, Churchill almost entirely compartmentalized the political dimension, with its focus on a postwar peace, from the military dimension. When he did bother to apply himself to the problem of the Soviet Union's future intentions, Churchill was indeed troubled. During the crucial years of strategic decision, his positions on that issue seesawed. In 1943 and at the beginning of 1944 he tended to be optimistic about the future of relations with Russia and its political intentions in Europe. In the last year of the war, when the Russian problem became increasingly acute, his view oscillated with increasing rapidity and extremism between optimism and pessimism, until it finally sagged into despondency in March 1945. Churchill's tendency to temporize on the nature of the future international order added a further element of complication and obscurity. He could not make up his mind whether to adopt a political approach based on a strong global organization and on postwar cooperation among the powers (which would have accorded the Soviet Union an important role) or whether to act in accordance with his long-standing adherence to realpolitik and the doctrine of the balance of power.

It was after the invasion of western Europe that Churchill first integrated the war's military and political dimensions in thought and deed. The change was principally the result of events in the east. By July and August 1944 the Russians had crossed the old borders of the Soviet Union into Poland and other central European states, in the process generating political friction. Assessing that to be a threat that warranted a military response, Churchill began to consider checking the Russians in southeastern Europe by advancing on Vienna. His reaction was not born of foresight. Rather, it constituted a correct, albeit not a definite and swift, reading of circumstances at the moment of their occurrence. Nevertheless, Churchill did not immediately abandon the optimistic foundations of British policy toward Russia that Eden had laid down at the beginning of 1942. Besides, when in August Churchill wanted to forestall the Soviet threat, he did not consider doing so from the western European theater. Had his hands not been tied, it was from Italy that he would have accelerated the Anglo-American advance into southeastern Europe. In fact, however, the presence of western forces in that region could have exerted no more than a limited effect on its political future. An advance along that way could not have influenced the fate of Poland and Germany, the key states of eastern and central Europe.

Churchill accused the Americans of being slow to appreciate the Soviet menace and of refusing to cooperate with him, either militarily or diplomatically, in an effort to avert it. Many students of the topic have echoed that charge, which is not very different from saying that the U.S. leadership was principally responsible for the failure to prevent the sovietization of Europe and the division of the Continent. True, the Americans' attitude toward the Soviets was hardly sophisticated: for far too long they retained their belief in the possibility of Soviet-U.S. cooperation after the war and were slow to appreciate the growing Soviet threat to Europe. Moreover, Roosevelt was averse to close Anglo-American cooperation against the Soviet Union at the end of the war. But, during the war itself, there existed no substantive difference between the ideas of the U.S. and British decision makers as far as the Russian issue was concerned. This was despite the fact that the British decision makers spoke for a richly experienced European and global power, whereas their U.S. counterparts had only just begun to feel their way back to Europe as a permanent global power.

The British as well as the Americans were uniformally optimistic about Russia's intentions. Eden, the Foreign Office, and Churchill all aspired to endow Britain with a special political status by virtue of its position as a global power able to forge a link between the Soviet Union, Europe, and the United States; they also believed—albeit some more devoutly than others—that the affairs of Europe might be placed under joint Anglo-Soviet management. They expected to attain that aim by buying the Soviets' confidence. The Americans pinned high hopes on the establishment of a world organization, built on close cooperation with the Soviet Union. Roosevelt was not enthusiastic about retaining the British Empire, and intended establishing good relations with the Russians, also at Britain's expense. That was precisely what Churchill and Eden were afraid of, and their own pro-Russian policy was in part designed to avert that development. As early as the beginning of 1942, Eden (in whose wake Churchill followed) had initiated a British policy based on concessions to Russia at the expense of the peoples of eastern Europe. At the end of the war, Churchill was compelled to transmute it. What had hitherto been a semiactive policy toward Russia—in part because he had tried to restrain it in view of his antipathy to discussing future political problems while the war was still in progress—now became a policy of salvation. One reason for Churchill's behavior, although not its principal cause, was the United States' unwillingness to cooperate too closely against Russia. Nevertheless, once the war in Europe was over, Churchill was quicker than the Americans to appreciate the Soviet Union's intentions and to realize the need for a sharp shift in the western powers' policy toward it.

But during the war Churchill had been late to recognize the Soviet danger. It is that which accounts for the makeshift nature of the military moves he proposed to check the menace, once he had woken up to its existence. At the end of 1944 he suggested advancing on Vienna and in March-April 1945 advocated taking Berlin before the Russians did so. Neither was a feasible proposal; in both instances, Churchill was foiled by the operational problems involved. His own Chiefs of Staff rejected the proposed advance on Vienna on operational grounds and because they doubted its logic from the point of view of military strategy. The only improvisation that was feasible, albeit only for a short period, and which might also have furthered Anglo-American political aims, was a concentrated thrust north of the Ardennes into and beyond the Ruhr during August-September 1944 when the German front in the west temporarily crumbled. But Churchill failed to perceive that opportunity, which was lost. (The Americans made the same mistake, although for different reasons.) All these moves were subordinated to the constricting and converging implications of the demand for unconditional surrender and the agreement to divide Germany into zones of occupation. The former had been initiated by Roosevelt and supported by Churchill; the latter had been concluded at British instigation without Churchill realizing its political ramifications. Both policies—and especially the latter—would have devalued or negated the advantages that might have been gained had, by some miracle, Churchill's proposed moves in fact succeeded.

In sum: Churchill's charges are without foundation where the military aspects are concerned. Moreover, close Anglo-American diplomatic cooperation against the Soviet Union could have had little influence on the fate of the Continent, which was in fact determined by the conquering armies.

As has been seen, had Churchill's strategic course been adopted, no invasion of western Europe would have taken place in 1944. What also has to be noted is the political corollary to that argument. Had the western Allies entered western Europe only in 1945, their political position vis-à-vis the Soviet Union would most probably have been much worse than it was when World War II actually ended. A postponement of the invasion until 1945 would have prolonged the war; by the time it was over, Soviet forces would have advanced to points beyond those they in any case attained in central Europe, and would probably even have reached the Rhine. Most of Europe would have been clay in Stalin's hands. He could have imposed Communist regimes on additional states, as he did in the east. Had he preferred to reach a political settlement with his wartime partners, his powerful status would have enabled him to dictate a "Russian peace" to Europe.

This possibility was avoided by narrow margins. Western Europe remained under the influence of the western democracies because the Americans—even though they were principally guided by military considerations—insisted on carrying out the invasion of France in 1944 without making its implementation conditional on a prior German collapse.

The political results of war must be judged against the yardstick of the objectives the decision makers set at its outbreak and during its course; and also by judging the significance of a war's outcome independently, without reference to the decision makers' aims. The direct reason for Britain's declaration of war on Germany was its obligation to defend the independence of Poland. Britain's wider and deeper war aims were to prevent Germany from attaining mastery over Europe and to avert the domination of the Continent by an antidemocratic ideology. When the war ended and Germany had been defeated, Poland was occupied by another power, and half of Europe placed under the direct and indirect control of a despotic system of government. Churchill himself did not deny the implications of that situation. To his mind, the political consequences of the war constituted a "great catastrophe," the term he used in his own work on the war to describe the Soviet hegemony over half of Europe. It will be recalled that, as early as 1942, he had argued that it would be disastrous were "Russian barbarism" to impair the independence of the ancient states of Europe. At the very beginning of *The Second World War* he wrote that "the human tragedy reaches its climax in the fact that after all the exertions and sacrifices of hundreds of millions of people and of the victories of the Righteous Cause, we have still not found Peace or Security, and that we lie in the grip of even worse perils than those we have surmounted." He entitled the last of his volumes "Triumph and Tragedy" because, as he put it, "the overwhelming victory of the Grand Alliance has failed so far to bring general peace to our anxious world."[1]

Churchill found it hard to evaluate either the Soviet Union's future intentions, the manner in which the war was to be concluded, or the positions of the victorious armies at its close. He also had difficulty in defining a clear attitude toward Germany's future and the postwar European political settlement. Presumably, his predicaments might be excused on the grounds that World War II was a more extensive and complicated conflict than its predecessor had been. But extenuating circumstances for his methods of dealing with those conundrums are less easy to come by. He chose the easy way out, which was to shelve the issues. He engrossed himself in the strategic conduct of the European war that was guided by a sole aim—the defeat of Germany. (The British Chiefs of Staff behaved similarly. But as military men they were not duty-bound to integrate future political considerations with the general strategy they formulated.) In effect, he decided to deal with the German and Russian problems sequentially instead of concurrently. Thus, when formulating his attitudes toward military matters, he did not adopt a complementary political perspective based on a view of the worst possible situation at the end of the war.

Churchill's error might have amounted to no more than a miscalculation had he, after considered reflection, in 1942 and 1943 reached the conclusion that an invasion of western Europe and an advance as far as possible eastward—although politically important as a means of averting future Soviet threats to Europe (a consideration that was not then inconceivable)[2]—could not be carried out before a German collapse. His mistake might then have been attributable to the fog of war. In fact, however, it was far more serious. There exists no evidence that might indicate that his thoughts were moving on those lines prior to the invasion of western Europe in June 1944. Before the invasion of the west, when he pressed for and nurtured the "Mediterranean strategy" and the advance up Italy, his considerations were entirely military. As far as he was concerned, the Italian campaign did not constitute a military course that might also solve the Russian problem.

In his study of Churchill as a politician and statesman between the turn of the century and the outbreak of World War II, R. Rhodes James wrote that "the dispassionate observer can hardly fail to be struck . . . by his preoccupation with the immediate." Churchill's strength, he adds, "lay in diagnosis rather than in prognosis." His long-term vision was impaired, even though his admirers claimed that to be one of his greatest assets.[3] As far as the period before 1939 is concerned, that judgment is too harsh. On the other hand, it might be considered not harsh enough when applied to Churchill's management of World War II.

What makes Churchill's mistake particularly serious is the fact that, as Prime Minister, he also assumed the Defence portfolio, which was especially created for him. Consequently, he enjoyed as much power and authority during the war as it is possible to attain in a democratic system of government. His two offices enabled Churchill to think and act as both a statesman and a military strategist, and thus to attain the ideal unity of command for which he had striven all his life. But his functional realization of that ideal was not matched by its efficient realization from a conceptual and operational point of view. Notwithstanding his new status, Churchill still suffered from a debilitating weakness. As was frequently demonstrated in both world wars, he was incapable of framing a stable concept that managed to harmonize and achieve a balance between the two basic dimensions of strategy in its widest sense: the military dimension (which also incorporates the tactical and operational level) and the political dimension. His tendency was to oscillate between two extremes, overemphasizing the importance of one or the other of the two dimensions. As to the tactical-operational level, for Churchill that almost invariably remained an insurmountable obstacle on his route to creating a harmonious integration of the two.

That trait did not serve him in good stead as a strategic decision maker. His failure at Gallipoli was not an aberration or the result of specific circumstances beyond his control during his long career as a decision maker. As much is clearly exhibited by a comparison of his attitudes and actions during two separate periods of decision making: that which preceded the Gallipoli campaign and that which preceded the decision to dispatch a military expedition to Greece in 1941. These two failures, it then becomes apparent, were the result of precisely the same patterns of behavior and perception and of exactly the same flaws and weaknesses. It made no difference whatsoever that during World War II Churchill enjoyed the benefit of supreme authority and responsibility, the absence of which he regarded as the most important reason for the mishap at Gallipoli. His flaws constituted an inherent part of his personality and of his very being as a strategist. Sometimes obtrusively and at others latently, they exerted an impact that, in greater or lesser degree, influenced his decision making throughout the period from the Norway campaign of 1940 to the final decision on the "second front" issue.

The conclusion to be drawn is that, even though Churchill's position was radically different in World War II, no real changes had taken place in his nature as a strategist and decision maker. Moreover, what is surprising about a comparison of the characteristics, quality, and implications of the general strategic concepts Churchill formulated during the two world wars is the degree to which they were similar, notwithstanding the differences between those two conflicts and the intervening changes that had taken place in his own personal standing and age.

As a strategist he was not an opportunist in the wider sense of that term. Not infrequently, he stuck too rigidly to plans he had conceived before the outbreak of the world wars, or during their course, even though circumstances had altered. During World War I he remained faithful to the foundations of his strategic conception from beginning to end. During World War II Churchill persistently clung to the strategic ideas he formulated after the unexpected fall of France had forced him to abandon the concept with which he had entered the conflict. His opportunism consisted of simply waiting to exploit developments that would arise as a result of the implementation of the attritional strategy; and of supplying current and retrospective explanations for his moves and attitudes, whose object was to postpone the invasion of France. He sought opportunities where none existed, and missed those that did arise. He passed up the two greatest chances of the war—the conquest of Tripoli at the beginning of 1941, and the momentary German collapse in the west in August 1944.

Before and during both world wars Churchill knew how to avoid defeat but not how to win effectively and realize his political aims. In neither war did he commit a single error that might have brought on Britain's direct military defeat. But, in World War I, his efforts to construct a strategic path that might lead to Germany's defeat ended in a logical and practical cul-de-sac. If followed to its culmination, the course on which he embarked during World War II would certainly have resulted in a belated victory over Germany; but it would also have seriously impaired the western Allies in their struggle against the

Soviet Union over the political future of Europe.

There was, then, a specific congruence between Churchill's concepts and actions in both world wars. Consistency and continuity can also be discerned in the strategic positions he adopted before 1914 and during the interwar period. After 1911, Churchill was convinced that the defense of Britain and the maintenance of the Empire were inextricably tied to the preservation of the European balance of power. He must be given his due for the persistent manner in which, especially during the 1930s, he strove to maintain that balance and to prevent Germany from dominating the Continent. Above all, he insisted on the vital need for Britain to undertake a solid "continental commitment" in Europe when at war with Germany.

But the inherently high standard of his ideas during periods of peace was not equalled by the quality of those he arrived at during the course of the conflicts. There exists a sharp and ironic dichotomy between Churchill the strategist in peacetime and Churchill the strategist in wartime. In peacetime, he displayed a superb ability to formulate a realistic strategic-political concept; some of its consequent strategic evaluations were brilliant. In wartime, when concept and action merged, his quality as a strategist suddenly and dramatically plummeted. The assets that had enabled him, as a statesman, to exercise clarity of vision and formulate a correct strategic concept in peacetime then melted away. The most important of them was his ability to frame political attitudes from a military viewpoint. Confronted by the complex reality of war, his intellectual skills and his understanding of the art of war (although high) proved unequal to the heavy double burden: the need to formulate a superior strategy—military and political as one whole—and to take commensurate decisions; and at the same time to overcome the limitations and flaws of his own personality.

The well-known military thinker, Bernard Brodie, expressed a common opinion about Churchill when analyzing the strategic controversy between the British and the Americans at the end of the war. He categorized their dispute as one between "supporters of the Clausewitzian ideal [which Brodie shared] of keeping political aims always at the forefront of strategic considerations" and advocates of the notion that action must principally be determined by military considerations. "Churchill, who in this respect was the follower of Clausewitz, surely by instinct rather than by learned precept, embodied to a degree unique in contemporary times the experience and insight of the profound student of war combined with the experience and qualities of a great politician and statesman."[4] That image of Churchill has struck deep roots. Indeed, Brodie provided a good depiction of this author's view before I began studying the subject and realizing, to my regret, that it amounted to no more than a preconception about one of my boyhood heroes. In fact, and contrary to the claims advanced by his admirers, it cannot be said of Churchill that "as a manager of war he was nonpareil."[5] Rather, he was a strategist who, for much of the war in which he won world renown, teetered on the brink of shattering failure. It was others, the

Americans, who prevented him from falling into that abyss.

But for all that, Churchill possessed the stuff of greatness. He exhibited greatness when standing alone in the 1930s and when naturally transforming himself from an almost forgotten politician into a charismatic war leader who held aloft the torch of the free world. He was a leader who, in moments of dark crisis, managed to project determination and invincible fighting spirit. He was a leader who inspired his own people, as well as the despondent peoples of conquered Europe, with confidence in the certainty of victory. He was a leader who embodied hundreds of years of Britain's history and of its heroic struggle against European despotism, as well as the most enlightened values of Western culture. His qualities as a war leader helped him to prevent defeat in the war—something that as a strategist he in any case well knew how to do. However, inspired leadership may not of itself ensure that wars are won as quickly as possible and yield results both favorable and long-lasting. But it does guarantee the acquisition of eternal glory.

■

Churchill was deeply imbued with a historical consciousness; he was also highly sensitive to the fact that by action and decision he was influencing the course of history at a critical juncture. He saw himself as a historic hero, with the world as his stage. At times of crises, his knowledge of European military history and his awareness of England's glorious wars in the past fortified him with a feeling of confidence and power. Throughout the war, he referred to and recalled lessons of the past—personal reminiscences, historical views, and analogies—albeit not in a systematic or compelling manner. In varying degrees, these also exerted an influence. Nevertheless, as far as limitations of inquiry allow, it can be said that the formulation of his important strategic views and his resolutions were not *decisively* or *principally* influenced by his historical consciousness or by his ruminations on the past and its lessons. Those factors were not chiefly responsible for the initiation of the "Mediterranean strategy" in general and the dispatch of an army to Greece in 1941 in particular, or for his attitudes toward such subjects as the invasion of western Europe and the question of future relations with the Soviet Union. As has been seen, the same was true of the strategic concept that he framed and of the important decisions he took in peacetime and during World War I.

Moreover, the events of World War II caused Churchill to adopt a strategic approach that differed from his long-standing conception. As early as the years preceding World War I, he had worked out the principal points in a concept that attributed enormous importance to massive British land involvement on the Continent, and especially in western Europe, in case of war with Germany. In doing so he went against the strategic position, which he had held until then, and his interpretation of the nature of the strategy that Britain had successfully implemented in the past. Only in the 1930s, as a result of his studies of Marlborough, did Churchill reach the conclusion that the secret of Britain's success in its historic struggles in Europe lay in the successful integration of a continental strategy—based on sending to the Continent what were, by the standards of the times, large British forces—and a peripheral strategy rooted in naval power. However, during the course of World War II, Churchill abandoned the continental strategy and adhered to a strategy of peripheral attrition. He did not do so because he had again changed his view, but because of the force of circumstances, which he wrapped up in various rationalizations. (Although some of his military advisers believed a peripheral strategy to be the character of the British strategy that had succeeded in the past, and that was how the Americans tended to interpret British thoughts and actions.)[6] To his surprise, France had collapsed in the west. Thereafter, the nature of the campaigns in the Mediterranean theater convinced him that an attempt to reestablish a land front in the west would be doomed to failure. The collapse thesis, partly an analogy taken from the German collapse in 1918—whose main originators came from intelligence circles and the military—did not constitute the point of departure for Churchill's strategy. Rather, it provided a hypothesis that he grasped as a justification for a strategy he selected after he had lost his faith in any other strategic alternative.

■

Churchill, then, was not principally influenced by history when framing his ideas and when arriving at his most crucial decisions. But he did manage to leave a deep imprint on the historical interpretation of World War II. Indeed, he won the Nobel Prize for Literature for his historical writings and oratory and is renowned as a "historian of classic proportions."[7]

Churchill always lived in fear of what he called "the verdict of history."[8] *The World Crisis* was a brief for the defense written by a politician with an eye on his future, but it also constituted a treatise designed to protect his place in history. Contrary to expectations, Churchill's concern about history's verdict did not abate after World War II. In the depths of his heart, he had doubts about the degree of his success as a strategist and statesman in that conflict. As he mournfully put it to Lord Boothby:

> Historians are apt to judge war ministers less by the victories achieved under their direction than by the political results which flowed from them. Judged by that standard, I am not sure that I shall be held to have done very well.[9]

Citations of troubled remarks by Churchill in the same vein also recur in Lord Moran's diary. Indeed, Moran himself claimed that Churchill wrote *The Second World War* with the purpose of assuring his place in history and in order to prove that his strategic positions had been justified and his view of the Soviet Union far-sighted.[10] At first glance, it is difficult to account for the strenuous efforts he invested in writing that book at a time when he was unwell and also burdened with Prime Ministerial office. After all, his personal status was entirely different from that which it had been after World War I. If he had then hastened to write *The World Crisis*, it was because he wanted to reinstate his reputation in the wake of a bitter failure for which he had been held responsible. After World War II, however, he was renowned as a great war leader. The honor and admiration heaped upon him knew virtually no bounds. He had won the glory that ever since his youth, he had always craved. Nevertheless, he was himself ill at ease because, in one way or another, he was aware of his strategic and political mistakes. At bottom, and when not deluding himself, he knew what his attitude had been toward the invasion of western Europe and the Soviet problem. In retrospect, he fully appreciated the joint consequences of his positions on those two issues.

Churchill had learned the lessons provided by the Gallipoli episode, by his authorship of *The World Crisis*, and by his writing of Marlborough's biography. He knew that his pen provided him with a means with which he might himself influence and create his future image in history. Indeed, he was aware of that power when World War II began. Despairing of not having his way in one of his controversies with the Americans, he said that the matter had to be left to history, but added that "he intends to be one of the historians."[11] Had Eden not persuaded him otherwise, Churchill would have issued a similar "warning" to Stalin, to whom he drafted a letter containing the phrase, "But remember, if I live long enough I may be one of the historians."[12] Therein lay a hint of the reason for the haste with which Churchill set about writing his book. By then in the eighth decade of his life, time was running out. There is no doubt that Churchill was constantly aware of the fact that his recorded words, his memoranda, and his directives were not simply a medium for conveying opinions and taking decisions during the war itself. Once the conflict was over, the same texts would provide him with the materials he would need for recording its history; ultimately, they would also constitute the raw material of later research.[13] It would be naive to imagine that his awareness of those possibilities did not affect the phraseology of his memoranda, his form of expression during discussions, and even the positions he chose to convey to his partners at certain stages of the war.

Having thus mentally prepared himself to write a history of the war, and having even provided himself with the technical means to do so, Churchill was ready for the task. It proved to be more difficult than he had first imagined. That was because the thrust of his record of World War II was designed to blur the positions he had actually adopted during the war and to conceal his strategic and political errors. The purpose of the book was to demonstrate his massive contribution to the war's "Triumph" and to absolve him of responsibility for the European "Tragedy." He thereby attempted to assume credit for having possessed a consistent and correct strategic-political concept, congruent with both the moves taken during the war and its results.

Churchill could not deny the success of the invasion of western Europe. After all, the strategic idea behind that had proved its worth. The invasion shortened the war and constituted the western Allies' greatest contribution to the defeat of Germany after the Red Army's victories. At the end of the war, and once it was over, Churchill also appreciated its crucial political implications. That was why, in the version he projected in *The Second World War*, he portrayed himself as the person who had not only emphatically supported the invasion but had even initiated it. By his own account, he had wanted to launch the invasion of western Europe as early as possible, even in 1943. What had compelled him to conclude that 1944 was the most suitable date for the invasion was the force of events and circumstances, together with his realistic appraisal of the relative strengths of the various armies and the operational difficulties the invasion posed. Had the invasion been launched in 1943, it would have led to a disaster of far-reaching effect on the war's course. It was because of his efforts that that danger had been averted. The controversy with the Americans was not occasioned by a matter of principle; it concerned the timing of the invasion and the preparatory moves necessary to ensure its success. The "Mediterranean strategy," and the invasion of Italy carried out within its framework, were vital for the success of the invasion of western Europe. The charges the Americans and Russians had laid against him had resulted from their failure to plumb the depths of his strategic concept, which was both complex and shrewd. The Soviet domination of eastern Europe, "the tragedy," had happened even though he had anticipated its occurrence in good time and in spite of his desperate efforts to avert it by military and political means. It was the Americans who were responsible for the failure to check the Soviet domination of eastern Europe, or at least to restrict its territorial scope. They had been too slow to appreciate the Soviet threat and had refused to cooperate with him.

What Churchill would have written in his book and whom he would have blamed had the invasion failed, can easily be imagined. Armed with his captivating literary style and the documents in his possession, and—above all—fortified by the truth, he would have argued that he had opposed the carrying out of the invasion and warned of its failure, but that he had ultimately been forced to agree to it.

Writing in the mid-1960s, the historian A.J.P. Taylor commented that "Churchill's version of the second world war is likely to dominate the writing of its history for many years to come."[14] Despite fluctuations, that version is indeed still predominant.[15] (Taylor himself, a sharply critical historian, depicted Churchill as "the saviour of his country.")[16] Several circumstances contributed to the fact that Churchill so successfully managed to plant his version into both the academic and nonspecialist communities. To begin with, as Plumb pointed out, Churchill's book was "the first in the field, a fact of which he realized the importance" (and another reason for his rush to write it).[17] Consequently, many students, consciously or subliminally, analyzed the events of the war through the prism that Churchill's own book had established.[18] Similarly influential was the fact that his book was the first to publicize many of the government papers concerning the management of the war. Indeed, the inclusion of such documents endowed his book with a semiofficial aura. At a time when the archives were still closed to public inspection, they made up important primary materials, to which recourse was had by several of the scholars who began to compose initial studies of the war. As sources, however, the papers Churchill cited were not unadulterated.

Churchill brought to his book his authority as a great statesman, who had been both one of the primary heroes of the drama he described and its chief witness. It was the earliest important book to be written about the war. To this day, it is the first work read on the subject by the intelligent "general" public; all too often, it is also the last. Its strength lies in the felicity of its author's special style, which is captivating and replete with stirring rhetoric. Indeed, the power of its language occasionally conceals logical and other weaknesses of some of its arguments. What is more, and as was seen to be the case when an analysis was made of the version of events he presented in *The World Crisis*, Churchill was blessed with the ability to carry away and convince himself. At (not infrequent) moments of convenient amnesia, he tended to believe that he had indeed thought and acted in the manner he had described. When rereading his papers, he did not simply attempt to reconstruct his thoughts and actions at the time of their composition. He also often looked for what he ought to have thought and done. Self-delusion of that sort imparted sincerity and persuasiveness to his retrospective record.[19] To this must be added the fact that, in *The Second World War*, Churchill did accept responsibility for several minor errors and admitted to mistakes of comparatively peripheral importance. Such exhibitions of candor created an impression that his discussion of the war's cardinal strategic subjects was equally frank.

The *basic* version of events Churchill presented in *The Second World War* was buttressed and backed up in an important way by the authors of the official British history dealing with the higher management of the war. The appearance of the first volumes of that work, entitled *Grand Strategy*, more or less coincided with the publication of the last of Churchill's own volumes. This was a convenient coincidence, which deepened the imprint made by his own version some considerable time before the official archives were opened to public access.

The strength of *The Second World War* also lies in its arrangement: at appropriate points throughout the work, numerous documents are reproduced in support of the arguments advanced. Churchill favored that manner of presentation, which he had earlier adopted in both *The World Crisis* and in his biography of Marlborough. The reader is virtually crushed by the weight of the documents and the tomes. But, for all their abundance, the documents provide a portrait that is only partial and distorted. Many are taken from memoranda and instructions he had himself written (and of which he preserved private copies). By contrast, there are almost no citations from the protocols of meetings of the Defence Committee, the Cabinet, or the Chiefs of Staff, or from memoranda written by his military advisers. Replies and other reactions to his memoranda and directives are also nearly nonexistent (here, Churchill benefited from the fact that he could not publish such sources, even had he wanted to). What had in actuality been an incessant dialogue between Churchill and his military advisers, and with his political advisers too, was in his book transformed into a monologue only occasionally interrupted by what were no more than distant voices and echoes. Important documents were left out; others were cut to tailor them to his arguments. Several of his own memoranda were masterpieces of obscurity and ambiguity, especially when they concerned the subject of the invasion of western Europe. In some cases, their opaque nature indicated a lack of clarity in Churchill's own thinking; in others, it was designed to improve his position in the strategic bargaining; in yet a third category, it indicated the extent to which their author had his eye on history. Sometimes, all of those factors came into play. It subsequently proved easy to cast them into the mold of the Churchillian version presented in *The Second World War*.

When all was said and done, even Churchill's powers of expression were limited. The people likely to be easily convinced by his version are those who read his book in its entirety (i.e., Churchill's text as well as the documents with which it is studded) or those who—human nature being what it is—skim the documents and restrict their close reading to Churchill's commentary. A completely different result is obtained when a different technique is adopted, and the text and its attendant documents are placed side by side and read consecutively but separately. What is then apparent are the contradictions between the version advanced in the text and that which can be deduced from the documents that Churchill himself chose to place before his readers.

In *The World Crisis*, we have seen, Churchill composed an incorrect and misleading account of the history of the Gallipoli campaign and his involvement in it.[20] In *The Second World War* he again composed a false version of events, albeit this time on a grander scale and with greater success. Both books make compelling reading and the latter, at least, will for long retain its vitality. It is only a slight exaggeration to say that Churchill excelled more as a creator of his own image as historic hero and in justifying his actions and decisions in war than as a strategist and statesman in both world wars.

Appendix: List of Operation Code Names

Anvil	Allied invasion of the south of France in 1944
Bolero	Buildup in United Kingdom of U.S. forces for the invasion of western Europe
Gymnast	Invasion of French North Africa; later *Torch*
Husky	Invasion of Sicily
Jupiter	Projected invasion of northern Norway
Overlord	Allied main invasion of northwest Europe in 1944
Round-Up	Proposed Allied main invasion of northwest Europe in 1943
Sledgehammer	Proposed Allied emergency invasion of northwest Europe in 1942
Torch	Anglo-American invasion of French North Africa
Armpit	Proposed operations in the Adriatic, 1944
Rankin	Proposed operations to exploit a German collapse

Notes

Introduction

1. Winston S. Churchill, (infra WSC), *Painting as a Pastime*, Penguin Books, 1965 (first published in 1932), pp. 23–27.
2. R. Rhodes James, ed., *Winston Churchill, His Complete Speeches 1897–1963*, 8 vols., Chelsea House Publishers, New York, 1974 (infra *SPHS*),15 October 1908, vol. 2, pp. 1109ff.
3. See T. Jones to friend, 5 September 1926, in *Companion Volumes of Documents* to the official biography of Winston S. Churchill by R. S. Churchill and M. Gilbert, Heinemann, London, 1967–1982, 5 vols. in 13 parts, vol. 5, part 1 (infra *CV* 5/1), pp. 776-778.
4. See M. Ashley, *Churchill as Historian*, Secker and Warburg, London, 1968, ch. 14, especially pp. 210-211.
5. WSC to S. Leslie, 17 November 1930, *CV* 5/2, p. 223.
6. WSC to Lord Riddell, 18 October 1932, *CV* 5/2, p. 484.
7. J. H. Plumb, "The Historian," in A. J. P. Taylor, ed., *Churchill: Four Faces and the Man*, Penguin, 1969, p. 127; Ashley, op.cit., p. 211.
8. Lord Moran, *Winston Churchill: The Struggle for Survival, 1940–1965*, taken from the diaries of Lord Moran, Sphere Books, London, 1968, first published in 1966, p. 147.
9. A. Storr, "The Man," in A. J. P. Taylor, op. cit., pp. 212–215; Moran, op. cit., p. 147.
10. W.S. Churchill, *The Second World War*, Houghton Mifflin, Boston, 6 vols., 1948–1953, vol. 5, p. 450.
11. Quoted in M. Gilbert, *Finest Hour, Winston S. Churchill 1939–1941*, vol. 6, Heinemann, London, 1983, p. 1018.
12. See WSC, *Thoughts and Adventures*, Macmillan, 1943, first published in 1932, p. 207; WSC, *The Aftermath, A Sequel to the World Crisis*, Macmillan, 1944, first published in 1929, p. 451; WSC, *Marlborough, His Life and Times*, G. Harrap, London, 4 vols., new edition revised, published between 1934–1938, vol. 3, p. 433.
13. See *SPHS*, 30 October 1912, vol. 2, pp. 2029–2031.
14. Quoted in M. Gilbert, *Finest Hour*, vol. 6, pp. 860–861; (emphasis in original).
15. WSC, *The World Crisis, The Eastern Front*, Thornton Butterworth, London, 1931, p. 115.
16. WSC, *The World Crisis 1911–1918*, 2 vols., Odhams Press, London, 1938, first published between 1923–1926, vol. 1, pp. 4–5.

17. WSC to his wife, 15 September 1909, *CV* 2/2, pp. 910–912; see also WSC to Lord Beaverbrook, 19 October 1925, *CV* 5/1, p. 560.
18. See *CV* 3/1, p. 163.
19. H. H. Asquith to V. Stanley, 7 October 1914, *CV* 3/1, pp. 176–178.
20. WSC, *My Early Life*, Odhams, London, 1965, first published in 1930, p. 196.
21. A. Storr, "The Man," in A. J. P. Taylor, op.cit., p. 235.
22. See M. Rintala, "The Love of Power and the Power of Love: Churchill's Childhood," *Political Psychology*, vol. 5, no. 3, 1984, pp. 375–390; A. Storr, "The Man," op.cit., p. 235.
23. WSC to C. Attlee, 29 July 19, 42, PREM 3/499/9.
24. Sir William F. P. Napier, author of the classis work, *History of the War in the Peninsula and in the South of France*, 1807-1814.
25. I. Hamilton to WSC, 25 April 1898, *CV* 1/2, p. 929.

Chapter 1: From Isolation to "Continental Commitment," 1900–1914

1. WSC, *My Early Life*, pp. 107–109.
2. Ibid., ch. 4, especially p. 44.
3. A. T. Mahan, *The Influence of Sea Power Upon History 1660–1783*, Hill and Wang, New York, 1983, first published in 1890; its sequel was *The Influence of Sea Power upon the French Revolution and Empire, 1793–1812* [1892].
4. See *The Story of the Malakand Field Force*, Longmans,1898; *The River War*, Longmans, 1899; *London to Ladysmith*, Longmans, 1900; *Ian Hamilton's March*, Longmans, 1900.
5. WSC to Lady Randolph, 8 December 1896, *CV* 1/2, pp. 707–709.
6. House of Commons, 13 May 1901, *CV* 2/1, pp. 56–68.
7. *Daily Mail*, 17 June 1901, *CV*, 2/1 pp. 70–73.
8. *SPHS*, 27 April 1901, vol. 1, pp. 74–76; see also *SPHS*, 17 January 1903, vol. 1, pp. 157–160.
9. House of Commons, 13 May 1901, *SPHS*, vol. 1, pp. 76-86; House of Commons, 24 February 1903, *SPHS*, vol. 1, pp. 164-175; House of Commons, 14 May 1903, *SPHS* , vol. 1.
10. *SPHS*, 15 February 1907, vol. 1, pp. 727–731.
11. *SPHS*, 12 February 1903, vol. 1, pp. 162-164; *SPHS*, 29 May 1906, vol. 1, pp. 627–629.
12. J. Gooch, *The Plans of War, The General Staff and British Military Strategy C. 1900–1916*, Routledge and Kegan Paul, London, 1974, ch. 6, especially pp. 190–191.
13. WSC to President of North-West Manchester Liberal Association, 18 April 1904, *CV* 2/1, pp. 336–338.
14. *SPHS*, 4 August 1908, vol. 2, pp. 1078ff; *SPHS*, 4 February 1909, vol. 2, pp. 1158–1159.
15. M. Howard, *War and the Liberal Conscience*, Rutgers University Press, New Jersey, 1978, pp. 41-47; A. J. P. Taylor, "John Bright and the Crimean War," *Essays in English History*, Penguin, 1976, pp. 79–103.
16. A. T. Mahan, op. cit., pp. 6ff., 18, 76–77.
17. Churchill was not pleased with the school essay his son Randolph wrote on the causes of Rome's victory over Carthage. Echoing Mahan, he wrote to Randolph that it was the command of the sea that had brought Rome victory. See WSC to R. Churchill, 11 December 1925, *CV* 5/1, pp. 617–618.
18. See also W. Reitzel, "Mahan on the Use of the Sea," in *War, Strategy and*

Maritime Power, ed., B. Mitchell et al., Rutgers University Press, 1977.

19. Speech in the Royal United Services Institute, *SPHS*, 4 July 1950, vol. 8, p. 8028.

20. *SPHS*, 14 August 1908, vol. 2, pp. 1082–1087; 17 July 1909, *SPHS*, vol. 2, pp. 1286–1289; *SPHS*, 26 July 1909, vol. 2, pp. 1290–1297; *SPHS*, 9 December 1909, vol. 2, pp. 1404–1409; A. J. Marder, *From the Dreadnought to Scapa Flow, The Royal Navy in the Fisher Era, 1904-1919*, 5 vols., 1961–1970, Oxford U.P., London, vol. 1, pp. 142, 151, 159–161; A.J.P. Taylor, "We Want Eight, and We Won't Wait," *Essays in English History*, pp. 199–203.

21. See N. Mansbergh, *South Africa 1906-1961. The Price of Magnanimity*, Allen and Unwin, London, 1962, p. 25; R. S. Churchill,*Winston Churchill*, vol. 2, Heinemann, 1967, p. 147.

22. WSC, memorandum, 3 November 1909, *CV* 2/2, pp. 961–962.

23. Gooch, op. cit., p. 288.

24. House of Commons, 9 March 1910, *SPHS*, vol. 2, pp. 1500 ff.; WSC to the king, 9 March 1910, *CV* 2/2, pp. 991–992.

25. WSC to Lloyd George, 31 August 1911, *CV* 2/2, p. 1119.

26. WSC, memorandum, August 1911, *CV* 2/2, p. 1105; WSC: "Military Aspects of the Continental Problem," 13 August 1911, in WSC, *The World Crisis*, vol. 1, pp. 42–46; WSC to Sir Edward Grey, 30 August 1911, *CV* 2/2, pp. 1116–1117; WSC to Lloyd George, 31 August 1911, *CV* 2/2, pp. 1118–1119; WSC, *The World Crisis*, vol. 1, pp. 36-37.

27. See "Military Aspects of the Continental Problem," op. cit., pp. 45–46.

28. J. Luvaas, *The Education of an Army*, Cassell, London, 1965, pp. 281, 306–307, 323–327.

29. Lord Roberts to WSC, 25 January 1912, *CV* 2/3, pp. 1500–1501.

30. See *SPHS*, 2 August 1904, vol. 1, pp. 347–350; House of Commons, *SPHS*, 3 April 1905, vol. 1, pp. 457–466; House of Commons, *SPHS*, 9 March 1910, vol. 2, pp. 1500ff.

31. Gooch, op. cit., pp. 284, 301; M. Howard, *The Continental Commitment*, Penguin, 1974, pp. 34–36.

32. V. Cazalet: Diary 5 January 1923, *CV* 5/1, p. 14.

33. See Leo Amery: Diary 5 August 1929, *CV* 5/2, pp. 34-35; see also I. Berlin, "Mr. Churchill in 1940," J. Murray, London, first published in *The Alantic Monthly*, 1949, pp. 15-16; R. Rhodes James, *Churchill: A Study in Failure 1900-1939*, Penguin, 1981, first published in 1970, pp. 442–443.

34. A. Marder, op. cit., vol. 1, pp. 244–245, 389–393.

35. Ibid., vol. 1, pp. 246–251.

36. WSC, "Military Aspects of the Continental Problem," 13 August 1911, op. cit., pp. 42–46.

37. Ibid.

38. See Lord Hankey to WSC, 29 January 1936, *CV* 5/3, pp. 26–27; WSC to Lord Hankey, 30 January 1936 (not sent), 31 January 1936, *CV* 5/3, pp. 27–29. As usual, legends become entrenched. In his popular biography of Churchill, R. L. Taylor described how the slow-thinking generals, led by Wilson, rejected Churchill's brilliant memorandum. See R. L. Taylor, *Winston Churchill, The Biography of a Great Man*, Cardinal, New York, 1954, pp. 235–236.

39. Gooch, op. cit., pp. 281–283, 288.

40. See B. H. Liddell Hart, *History of the First World War*, Pan Books, 1970, pp. 43–44.

41. WSC, *The World Crisis*, vol. 1, pp. 214–217; see House of Commons, *SPHS*, 24 February 1903, vol. 1, pp. 164–175; *SPHS*, 15 February 1907, vol, 1, pp. 727–731; House of Commons, *SPHS*, 17 March 1914, vol. 3, pp. 2262–2267.

42. *SPHS*, 13 May 1901, vol, 1, pp. 76-86.
43. WSC, *The World Crisis*, vol. 1, p. 215; *The Aftermath*, Macmillan, 1944, first published in 1929, pp. 275, 445; see also M. van Creveld, *Supplying War, Logistics from Wallenstein to Patton*, Cambridge University Press, Cambridge, 1977, ch. 4, esp.,pp. 138-141.
44. WSC, "Military Aspects..." 13 August 1911, op. cit., p. 44.
45. WSC, memorandum, 28 October 1911, *CV* 2/2, pp. 1303-1312.
46. WSC, memorandum, 28 October 1911, ibid.
47. See Sir A. Wilson, memorandum, 30 October 1911, *CV* 2/2, pp. 1312-1316.
48. See J. S. Corbett, *Some Principles of Maritime Strategy*, Longmans, 1918, first published in 1911. His earlier books were *Drake and the Tudor Navy* (1898); *The Successors of Drake* (1900); *England in the Seven Years' War* (1907); *The Trafalgar Campaign* (1910).
49. Corbett, *Some Principles of Maritime Strategy*, pp. 11-12.
50. Ibid., pp. 54, 65.
51. Corbett, op, cit., p. 56.
52. Ibid., p. 74.
53. Ibid., p. 73.
54. Ibid., pp. 54-60.
55. Ibid., pp. 59-60.
56. On March 15 Lord Esher wrote to M. Hankey: "Why, my dear Hankey, do we worry about history? Julian Corbett writes one of the best books in our language upon political and military strategy. All sorts of lessons, some of inestimable value, may be gleamed from it. No one, except perhaps Winston, who matters just now, has ever read it.... Obviously history is written for school masters and armchair strategists. Statesmen and warriors pick their way through the dusk." (Quoted in Marder, op. cit., vol. 1, p. 404.) Three days later, the attempt at a naval forcing of the Dardanelles failed.
57. See Minutes of the Committee of Imperial Defence, 118th meeting, *SPHS*, 11 July 1912, vol. 2, pp. 1970-1980.
58. Lord Fisher to WSC, 28, 29, 30 October 1911, *CV* 2/2, p. 1303.
59. WSC to Viscount Haldane, 6 May 1912, *CV* 2/3, p. 1549; see also WSC to Lord Roberts, 12 July 1912, *CV* 2/3, pp. 1594-1595.
60. WSC to the King, 17 March 1910, *CV* 2/2, pp. 997-998.
61. House of Commons, 22 July 1912, *SPHS*, vol. 2, p. 1992.
62. See Lord Esher to WSC, no date, *CV* 2/3, p. 1615; Lord Roberts to WSC, 10 July 1912, *CV* 2/3, p. 1593.
63. See Marder, op. cit., vol. 1, pp. 289ff.; Howard, *The Continental Commitment*, pp. 48-50.
64. Marder, op. cit., vol. 1, p. 304.
65. WSC to E. Grey and H. H. Asquith, 23 August 1912, *CV* 2/3, pp. 1638-1639; WSC to E. Grey and H. Asquith, 23 August 1912, op. cit., p. 1639; see also WSC to Sir Edward Grey, 4 November 1911, *CV* 2/2, p. 1370.
66. Quoted in Howard, *The Continental Commitment*, p. 49.
67. Marder, op. cit., vol. 1, pp. 361-368, 377.
68. Since a discussion of amphibious warfare will be a recurring theme in this study, I define an amphibious operation as the landing of ground forces from the sea on coasts under enemy control for either a short period or in order to effect a permanent entrenchment on his territory. See also Admiral H. Richmond, "Amphibious Warfare in British History," The Historical Association, 1941, pp. 3-4.
69. Marder, op. cit., vol. 1, p. 384.
70. Ibid., pp. 384-394; Richmond, op. cit., p. 27.
71. *SPHS*, 15 May 1912, vol. 2, pp. 1962-1965.
72. See Royal Academy, London, *SPHS*, 3 May 1913, vol. 2, pp. 2113-2114; see

also S. Roskill, *Churchill and the Admirals*, Collins, London, 1977, pp. 26-27.
  73. Marder, op. cit., vol. 1, pp. 344-358.
  74. Gooch, op. cit., p. 291.
  75. *SPHS*, 2 August 1904, vol. 1, pp. 347-350; 3 April 1905, House of Commons, *SPHS*, vol. 1, pp. 457-466.
  76. House of Commons, *SPHS*, 28 February 1907, vol. 1, pp. 745-754.
  77. House of Commons, *SPHS*, 9 March 1910, vol. 2, pp. 1500ff.
  78. Marder, op. cit., p. 357.

Chapter 2: From the Baltic to Gallipoli, 1914–1915

  1. WSC, *The World Crisis*, vol. 1, pp. 160-166.
  2. WSC, *The World Crisis*, vol. 1, pp. 187-189; M. Howard, *The Continental Commitment*, pp. 54-55; Gooch, op. cit., pp. 292-295.
  3. WSC, *The World Crisis*, vol. 1, p. 489.
  4. WSC to J. Churchill, 26 August 1914, *CV* 3/1, pp. 55-56; WSC to Admiral J. Jellicoe, 8 October 1914, *CV* 3/1, pp. 180-182.
  5. See Marder, op. cit., vol. 2, p. 48; Captain Richmond, diary, 24 October 1914, *CV* 3/1, p. 216.
  6. Marder, op. cit., vol. 5, pp. 304-307, 318-321.
  7. WSC, memorandum, undated 1913, *CV* 2/3, p. 1737.
  8. See Corbett, *Some Principles of Maritime Strategy*, pp. 77-78, 90–91.
  9. Ibid., pp. 150-164, 188-189.
  10. Mahan, op. cit, pp. 5-6, 69-70.
  11. Lord Fisher, memorandum, 25 January 1915, *CV* 3/1, pp. 452-454.
  12. WSC, *The World Crisis*, vol. 1, p. 198.
  13. Marder, op. cit., vol. 5, p. 306.
  14. Ibid., vol. 2, p. 43, vol. 5, pp. 334-335.
  15. A. Marder, op. cit., vol. 2, p. 176.
  16. WSC, memorandum, 19 August 1914, *CV* 3/1, pp. 45-46; WSC to Admiral Jellicoe, 8 October 1914, *CV* 3/1, pp. 180-182; WSC to H. Asquith, 29 December 1914, *CV* 3/1, pp. 343-345.
  17. WSC, memorandum, 19 August 1914, *CV* 3/1, pp. 45-46; Grand Duke Nicholas to WSC, 24 August 1914, *CV* 3/1, p. 53.
  18. Marder, op. cit., vol. 2, pp. 178-179.
  19. WSC, *The World Crisis*, vol. 1, p. 53.
  20. Admiral Jellicoe to WSC, 8 January 1915, *CV* 3/1, pp. 397-398.
  21. See Marder, op. cit., vol. 2, p. 192.
  22. Lord Fisher memorandum, November 1914, *CV* 3/1, pp. 284-287.
  23. WSC to Lord Fisher, 22 December 1914, *CV* 3/1, pp. 325-326.
  24. See Marder, op. cit., vol. 2, pp. 194-197; Howard, *The Continental Commitment*, p. 55.
  25. Marder, op. cit., vol. 2, pp. 195-196.
  26. See Sir Edward Grey to Sir F. Villiers, 3 October 1914, *CV* 3/1, p. 156; H. Asquith to V. Stanley, 3 October 1914, *CV* 3/1, pp. 158-159; R. Prior, *Churchill's "World Crisis" as History*, Croom Helm, London, 1983, p. 31.
  27. WSC to H. Asquith, 5 October 1914, *CV* 3/1, p. 163.
  28. H. Asquith to V. Stanley, 5 October 1914, *CV* 3/1, pp. 165-166.
  29. Marder, op. cit., vol. 2, pp. 84-85.
  30. WSC, *The World Crisis*, vol. 1, pp. 326-327.
  31. WSC to Sir Edward Grey, 30 August 1911, *CV* 2/2, pp. 1116-1117; WSC to

Lloyd George, 31 August 1911, *CV* 2/2, pp. 1118-1119.

32. WSC to Sir G. Aston, 25 August 1914, *CV* 3/1, pp. 54-55; WSC to Lord Kitchener, 28 August 1914, *CV* 3/1, p. 64; WSC to H. Asquith, E. Grey, Lord Kitchener, 7 September 1914, *CV* 3/1, pp. 97-99.

33. See *CV* 3/1, p. 163.

34. H. Asquith to V. Stanley, 17 August 1914, *CV* 3/1, p. 40.

35. WSC to Vice-Admiral Troubridge, 18 August 1914, *CV* 3/1, p. 41.

36. Rear-Admiral Limpus to WSC, 26 August 1914, *CV* 3/1, pp. 56-60.

37. Major Cunliffe-Owen to the Foreign Office, 27 August 1914, *CV* 3/1, pp. 61-62.

38. WSC to Noel Baxton, 31 August 1914, *CV* 3/1, pp. 72-73.

39. WSC to C. Douglas (CIGS), 1 September 1914, *CV* 3/1, p. 75; WSC to Rear-Admiral Kerr (commander in chief of the Greek Navy), 4 September 1914, *CV* 3/1, pp. 83-84.

40. Major-General Calwell, memorandum, 3 September 1914, *CV* 3/1, pp. 81-83; Colonel Talbot, minute 5 September 1914, *CV* 3/1, pp. 91-92.

41. Sir Edward Grey to WSC, 6 September 1914, *CV* 3/1, pp. 94-95.

42. WSC to Grey, 6 September 1914, *CV* 3/1, p. 95.

43. WSC to Vice-Admiral Carden, 1 November 1914, *CV* 3/1, p. 243.

44. Marder, op. cit., vol. 2, p. 201.

45. Admiral Slade to WSC, *CV* 3/1, pp. 236-237; Prior, op. cit., p. 45.

46. WSC to Lord Fisher, 30 October 1914, *CV* 3/1, p. 236.

47. Meeting of the War Council, 25 November 1914, *CV* 3/1, pp. 276-280.

48. Meeting of the War Council, 1 December 1914, *CV* 3/1 pp. 290-291.

49. A. J. Balfour to M. Hankey, 5 December 1914, *CV* 3/1, p. 297; H. Asquith to V. Stanley, 5 December 1914, *CV* 3/1, p. 297.

50. WSC, memorandum, 2 December 1914, *CV* 3/1, pp. 291-294.

51. Hankey, memorandum, 28 December 1914, *CV* 3/1, pp. 337-343.

52. Lloyd George, memorandum, 31 December 1914, *CV* 3/1, pp. 350-356.

53. See Hankey, *The Supreme Command 1914–1918*, 2 vols., Allen and Unwin, London, 1961, vol. 1, p. 250.

54. WSC to H. Asquith, 29 December 1914, *CV* 3/1, pp. 343-345; WSC, memorandum, 31 December 1914, *CV* 3/1, pp. 347-349.

55. WSC to Asquith, 31 December 1914, *CV* 3/1, p. 346.

56. Hankey, op. cit., vol. 1, p. 251.

57. Sir G. Buchanan to Sir Edward Grey, 1 January 1915, *CV* 3/1, pp. 359-360.

58. Kitchener to WSC, 2 January 1915, *CV* 3/1, pp. 360-361.

59. Lord Fisher to WSC, 3 January 1915, *CV* 3/1, pp. 367-368.

60. WSC to Vice-Admiral Carden, 3 January 1915, *CV* 3/1, p. 367.

61. WSC to Lord Fisher, 4 January 1915, *CV* 3/1 pp. 370-371.

62. Vice-Admiral Carden to WSC, 5 January 1915, *CV* 3/1, p. 380.

63. WSC to Vice-Admiral Carden, 6 January 1915, *CV* 3/1, p. 381.

64. Marder, op. cit., vol. 2, p. 205.

65. Sir Henry Jackson, memorandum, 5 January 1915, *CV* 3/1, pp. 376-377.

66. Meeting of the War Council, 7 January 1915, *CV* 3/1, pp. 384-390.

67. Marder, op. cit., vol. 2, pp. 188-189.

68. Meeting of the War Council, 8 January 1915, *CV* 3/1, pp. 391-396.

69. WSC to Sir John French, 11 January 1915, *CV* 3/1, pp. 401-402; WSC to Admiral Jellicoe, 11 January 1915, *CV* 3/1, pp. 402-404.

70. Marder, op. cit., vol. 2, p. 206; Prior, op. cit., p. 56.

71. Lord Fisher to Vice-Admiral Oliver, 12 January 1915, *CV* 3/1, pp. 406-407.

72. Marder, op. cit., p. 207.

73. Lord Fisher to Sir William Tyrell, 12 January 1915, *CV* 3/1, note 1, p. 407.

74. Meeting of the War Council, 13 January 1915, *CV* 3/1, pp. 407-411.
75. Quoted in R. Prior, op. cit., p. 47.
76. Marder, op. cit., vol. 2, p. 200; R. Rhodes James, *Gallipoli*, Macmillan, New York, 1965, p. 31.
77. WSC, *The World Crisis*, vol. 1, pp. 552-553.
78. WSC, *My Early Life*, p. 153.
79. Quoted in R. Rhodes James, *Gallipoli*, p. 4.
80. Richmond's diary, 24 October 1914, *CV* 3/1, p. 216.
81. See R. Rhodes James, *Gallipoli*, pp. 28-29.
82. See Marder, op. cit., vol. 2, pp. 206-207, 218-225; R. Rhodes James, *Gallipoli*, pp. 30-31; R. Prior, op. cit., pp. 57-60.
83. H. Asquith to V. Stanley, 15 January 1915, *CV* 3/1, p. 419.
84. Lord Fisher to Admiral Jellicoe, 19 January 1915, 21 January 1915, *CV* 3/1, pp. 429-430, 436.
85. Lord Fisher, memorandum, 25 January 1915, *CV* 3/1, pp. 452-454.
86. WSC to Lord Fisher, 26 January 1915, *CV* 3/1, p. 458.
87. Lord Fisher to WSC, 28 January 1915, *CV* 3/1, p. 460.
88. H. Asquith to V. Stanley, 28 January 1915, *CV* 3/1, pp. 462-463.
89. Meeting of the War Council, 28 January 1915, *CV* 3/1, pp. 463-465.
90. Meeting of the War Council, 28 January 1915, *CV* 3/1, pp.465-468.
91. WSC, *The World Crisis*, vol. 1, p. 591.
92. Prior, op. cit., pp. 76-77.
93. See Prior, op. cit., pp. 63-64.
94. See Lloyd George to WSC, 29 January 1915, *CV* 3/1, p. 472; Grey to WSC, 2 February 1915, *CV* 3/1, pp. 480-481; Prior, op. cit., p. 64.
95. Gooch, op. cit., ch. 10, pp. 299-330.
96. Hankey to Balfour, 10 February 1915, *CV* 3/1, p. 500.
97. Sir Henry Jackson, memorandum, 13 February 1915, *CV* 3/1, pp. 506-512.
98. Meeting of the War Council: Conclusions, 16 February 1915, *CV* 3/1, p. 516.
99. Lord Esher, diary, 16 February 1915, *CV* 3/1, p. 516.
100. WSC to Lord Kitchener, 18 February 1915, *CV* 3/1, pp. 518-519.
101. Meeting of the War Council, 19 February 1915, *CV* 3/1, pp. 527-534.
102. Lloyd George, memorandum, 22 February 1915, *CV* 3/1, pp. 544-547.
103. WSC, memorandum, 23 February 1915, *CV* 3/1, pp. 547-548.
104. Meeting of the War Council, 24 February 1915, *CV* 3/1, pp. 555-561.
105. Meeting of the War Council, 26 February 1915, *CV* 3/1, pp. 567-577.
106. WSC to H. Asquith, D. Lloyd George, and A. J. Balfour, 25 February 1915, *CV* 3/1, pp. 563-564.
107. Meeting of the War Council, 26 February 1915, op. cit.
108. WSC, note, 27 February 1915, *CV* 3/1, p. 587.
109. Meeting of the War Council, 3 March 1915, *CV* 3/1, pp. 610-618.
110. Lieutenant-General Birdwood to Lord Kitchener, 4 March 1915, *CV* 3/1, pp. 625-627; Birdwood to Kitchener, 5 March 1915, *CV* 3/1, pp. 637-638.
111. Kitchener to Birdwood, 4 March 1915, *CV* 3/1, pp. 632-633.
112. WSC to Lord Kitchener, 4 March 1915, *CV* 3/1, pp. 628-629.
113. Lord Fisher to WSC, 4 March 1915, *CV* 3/1, pp. 635-636.
114. WSC, *The World Crisis*, vol. 1, pp. 621-622; Prior, op. cit., pp. 108-110.
115. WSC to Sir John Jellicoe, 9 March 1915, *CV* 3/1, pp. 656-658.
116. Meeting of the War Council, 10 March 1915, *CV* 3/1, pp. 663-673.
117. Vice Admiral Carden to Admiralty, 10 March 1915, *CV* 3/1, pp. 661-662.
118. Sir Henry Jackson to Vice-Admiral Oliver, 11 March 1915, *CV* 3/1, pp. 676-677.
119. WSC to Vice-Admiral Carden, 11 March 1915, *CV* 3/1, pp. 677-678;

WSC to Carden, 13 March 1915, *CV* 3/1, pp. 687-688.
   120. Vice-Admiral Carden to Admiralty, 14 March 1915, *CV* 3/1, p. 693.
   121. Lord Fisher to WSC, 15 March 1915, *CV* 3/1, pp. 698-699.
   122. WSC to Lord Fisher, 15 March 1915, *CV* 3/1, p. 699.
   123. Sir Ian Hamilton to Lord Kitchener, 19 March 1915, *CV* 3/1, p. 710.
   124. Marder, op. cit., vol. 2, pp. 237-238.
   125. Meeting of the War Council, 19 March 1915, *CV* 3/1, pp. 710-716.
   126. Vice-Admiral de Robeck to Admiralty, 23 March 1915, *CV* 3/1, pp. 723-724.
   127. See Marder, op. cit., vol.2, pp. 251-253; Prior, op. cit., pp. 95-96.
   128. WSC to Vice-Admiral de Robeck, 23 March 1915, *CV* 3/1, pp. 724-726.
   129. H. Asquith to V. Stanley, 23 March 1915, *CV* 3/1, p. 726; Lord Kitchener to Sir Ian Hamilton, 23 March 1915, *CV* 3/1, pp. 726-727.
   130. Sir Ian Hamilton to Lord Kitchener, 23 March 1915, *CV* 3/1, p. 727.
   131. WSC to Vice-Admiral de Robeck, 24 March 1915, *CV* 3/1, pp. 728-730.
   132. Vice-Admiral de Robeck to Admiralty, 26 March 1915, *CV* 3/1, p. 747; Vice-Admiral de Robeck to WSC, 27 March 1915, *CV* 3/1, pp. 751-753; Vice-Admiral de Robeck to WSC, 28 March 1915, *CV* 3/1, p. 756.
   133. WSC to Vice-Admiral de Robeck, 27 March 1915, *CV* 3/1, p. 753.
   134. To his brother he wrote what he truly thought. See WSC to J. Churchill, 19 April 1915, *CV* 3/1, pp. 805-806.
   135. WSC, memorandum, 24 March 1915, *CV* 3/1, pp. 732-738.
   136. Fisher, memorandum, 27 March 1915, *CV* 3/1 pp. 754-755; Lord Fisher to WSC, 28 March 1915, *CV* 3/1, pp. 757-758; Fisher, memorandum, 8 April 1915, *CV* 3/1 p. 781.
   137. WSC to Lord Fisher, 28 March 1915, *CV* 3/1, p. 756.
   138. H. Asquith to V. Stanley, 30 March 1915, *CV* 3/1, p. 761.
   139. An informal meeting of the War Council, 6 April 1915, *CV* 3/1, p. 774; H. Asquith to V. Stanley, 7 April 1915, *CV* 3/1, p. 775; A. J. Balfour to WSC, 8 April 1915, *CV* 3/1, p. 779; WSC to Balfour, 8 April 1915, *CV* 3/1, p. 780.
   140. R. Rhodes James, *Gallipoli*, p. 94.
   141. Vice-Admiral de Robeck to WSC, 9 May 1915, *CV* 3/1, pp. 855-856.
   142. Hankey, diary, 11 May 1915, *CV* 3/1, p. 858.
   143. WSC to Lord Fisher, 11 May 1915, *CV* 3/1, p. 862.
   144. Marder, op. cit., vol. 2, p. 276.
   145. Meeting of the War Council, 14 May 1915, *CV* 3/1, pp. 874-883.
   146. WSC, *The World Crisis*, vol.1, pp. 593, 596-597, vol.2, p. 825.
   147. Ibid, vol. 1, pp. 597-599.
   148. WSC, statement to the Dardanelles Commission, 28 September 1916, *CV* 3/1, pp. 1570-1571.
   149. WSC, *The World Crisis*, vol. 1, pp. 630-631.
   150. Marder, op. cit., vol. 2, pp. 236-237.
   151. See also Prior, op. cit., p. 102.
   152. See above pp. 51-53.
   153. WSC, *The World Crisis*, vol. 1, p. 593.
   154. Churchill refrained from injuring his good friend, General Hamilton, even though the latter had been a full party to the decision not to force the straits a second time and to await a ground assault. Partly because of Churchill's pressure, Hamilton was sent to command the land forces at Gallipoli. Even though he did not excel in the post, in *The World Crisis* Churchill directed his shafts only against the commanders who were subordinate to Hamilton.
   155. See Prior, op. cit., p. 80.
   156. Prior, op. cit, pp. 54-55.
   157. WSC, statement to the Dardanelles Commission, 28 September 1916, *CV* 3/2,

p. 1569; WSC, *The World Crisis*, vol.1, pp. 593-594.
    158. WSC, *The Eastern Front*, pp. 255-257.
    159. Marder, op. cit., vol. 2, p. 257; WSC, *The World Crisis*, vol. 1, pp. 631-632.
    160. WSC, *The Eastern Front*, pp. 266-268.
    161. WSC, *The World Crisis*, vol. 1, pp. 630-633, 665.
    162. Ibid., vol. 1, pp. 647-648; WSC, draft statement, 8 September 1916, *CV 3/2*, pp.1553-1557.
    163. See above pp. 52-53, 55.
    164. See above pp. 54-56.
    165. WSC, *The World Crisis*, vol. 1, ch. 13, "The Case for Perseverence and Decision."
    166. Marder, op. cit., vol. 2, pp. 217-218, 248-249.
    167. A. J. Marder, "The Dardanelles Revisited" *From the Dardanelles to Oran*, Oxford University Press, 1974, p. 2.
    168. Ibid., pp. 23, 28-29.
    169. House of Commons, 15 November 1915, *SPHS*, vol. 3, p. 2400; see WSC, draft statement, 8 September 1916, *CV 3/1*, p. 1557.
    170. WSC to J. Churchill, 14 January 1916, *CV 3/2*, p. 1373.
    171. A. Moorehead, *Gallipoli*, Hamish Hamilton, London, 1958, esp. p. 364.
    172. R. Rhodes James, *Gallipoli*, p. 352.
    173. B. E. Schmitt, H. C. Vedler, *The World in the Crucible 1914–1919*, Harper & Row, New York, 1984, pp. 115-117; see also B. Liddell Hart, "The Military Strategist," in A. J. P. Taylor, *Churchill, Four Faces and the Man*, op.cit., pp. 170-171.
    174. Brigadier-General C. F. Aspinall-Oglander, *History of the Great War, Military Operations, Gallipoli*, Heinemann, 1932, vol. 2, pp. 479-486, esp. 479.
    175. For example, see Marder, op. cit., vol. 2, p. 260.
    176. For example, see A. Marder, op. cit., vol. 2, pp. 236-237; Aspinall-Oglander, op. cit., p. 479; E. Wheler Bush, *Gallipoli*, St. Martin Press, New York, 1975, p. 307; and also WSC, *The World Crisis*, vol. 1, pp. 593, 596-597, vol. 2, p. 825.
    177. WSC, *The World Crisis*, vol. 2, p. 879.
    178. Lord Esher, diary, 20 March 1915, *CV 3/1*, p. 719.
    179. R. Rhodes James, *Gallipoli*, p. 353; Prior, op. cit., p. 109.
    180. WSC to J. Churchill, 14 January 1916, *CV 3/2*, p. 1373; see also WSC to Hankey, 2 June 1915, *CV 3/2*, pp. 984-985.

Chapter 3: "How Are We to Win the War?" 1916–1918

    1. See WSC, *My Early Life*, pp. 327-328.
    2. *SPHS*, 18 February 1901, 7 October 1901, vol. 1, pp. 65-66, 105.
    3. House of Commons, *SPHS*, 13 May 1901, 24 February 1903, vol. 1, pp. 76-86, 164-175.
    4. *SPHS*, 3 October 1917, vol. 3, pp. 2573-2575; *SPHS*, 10 December 1917, vol. 3, pp. 2580-2584; *SPHS*, 11 January 1918, vol. 3, pp. 2585-2589. See V. H. Rothwell, *British War Aims and Peace Diplomacy 1914–1918*, Clarendon Press, Oxford, 1971, pp. 36-38, 54-55, 190-197, 284-285, and also chs. 2-5; A. J. P. Taylor, *English History 1914-1945*, Penguin, 1977, first published in 1965, pp. 134-135.
    5. WSC to C. Churchill, 28 January 1916, *CV 3/2*, pp. 1401-1402.
    6. *SPHS*, 5 June 1915, vol. 3, pp. 2378ff.; see also *SPHS*, 23 June 1916, vol. 3, p. 2458.
    7. *SPHS*, 4 July 1918, vol. 3, pp. 2613-2616.
    8. *SPHS*, 5 June 1915, op. cit.

9. See House of Commons, *SPHS*, 2 August 1916, vol. 3, pp. 2476-2478; WSC to the electors of Dundee, 26 July 1917, *CV* 4/1, pp. 115-116.
10. See M. Howard, *War and the Liberal Conscience*, pp. 73-84.
11. WSC to G. Ritchie, unsent letter, 3 August 1918, *CV* 4/1, pp. 362-366. One of the least successful books about Churchill is T. Higgins's, *Churchill and the Dardanelles* (Heinemann, London, 1963). Fundamental to Higgins's book is his argument that Churchill believed in limited war and that he thought strategy had to be managed in such a way as to reap gains that could be used as bargaining counters during the negotiations that would end the war. Basing himself on that claim, which stands in direct contradiction to reality, Higgins dragged Churchill's name through the mud for his part in the Dardanelles campaign.
12. WSC to H. Asquith, 4 October 1915, *CV* 3/2, pp. 1193-1196.
13. House of Commons, *SPHS*, 15 November 1915, vol. 3, pp. 2402-2403; see also Lord Selborne's notion in D. French, "The Meaning of Attrition, 1914–1916," *English Historical Review*, April 1988, p. 398.
14. WSC, memorandum, 1 August 1916, *CV* 3/2, pp. 1534-1539.
15. See WSC, memorandum, 1 June 1915, *CV* 3/2, pp. 977ff.; WSC, memorandum, 18 June 1915, *CV* 3/2, pp. 1034-1041; House of Commons, *SPHS*, 17 May 1916, vol. 3, pp. 2417-2429.
16. See B. E. Schmitt, H. C. Vedler, *The World in the Crucible 1914–1919*, pp. 136-137, 177, 180-182; D. French, "The Meaning of Attrition, 1914-16," op. cit.; Sir James Edmonds and others, *The Official History of the War: Military Operations in France and Belgium, 1914–1918, 1922-1948*, vol. II, 1917, p. 106; Sir E. L. Woodward, *Great Britain and the War of 1914-1918*, Methuen, London, 1967, pp. 148-150, 273-277.
17. House of Commons, 5 March 1917, *SPHS*, vol. 3, p. 2522. Churchill repeated that statement, virtually word for word, in *The World Crisis*, vol. 1, pp. 462-464.
18. WSC, *The World Crisis*, vol.1, p. 464.
19. Ibid.
20. Ibid., vol. 2, pp. 975-977, 990-991.
21. D. French, op. cit., especially pp. 390-399, 404.
22. See above.
23. WSC, *The World Crisis*, vol. 2, p. 971.
24. Ibid., vol. 2, pp. 984-985.
25. Ibid., vol. 1, pp. 474-475.
26. House of Commons, *SPHS*, 5 March 1917, vol. 3, pp. 2515-2524.
27. Marder, op. cit., vol. 4, p. 146.
28. WSC, memorandum, 21 August 1913, *CV* 2/3, pp. 1771-1777.
29. House of Commons, *SPHS*, 15 February 1915, vol. 3, pp. 2363 ff.
30. House of Commons, *SPHS*, 21 February 1917, vol. 3, pp. 2505-2512.
31. WSC, "Naval War Policy 1917," 7 July 1917, *CV* 4/1, pp. 77-99.
32. Sir R. Keyes to WSC, 23 November 1926, *CV* 5/1, pp. 886-887; emphasis in original.
33. A. J. P. Taylor, *English History 1914-1945*, pp. 122-124; Marder, op. cit., vol. 4, pp. 117-119, 135, 160-165.
34. Marder, op. cit., vol. 4, pp. 116-117.
35. WSC, *The World Crisis*, vol. 2, p. 1237.
36. WSC, *Thoughts and Adventures*, pp. 107-108.
37. WSC, *The World Crisis*, vol. 2, p. 915.
38. Hankey, diary, 22 July 1917, *CV* 4/1, p. 108.
39. WSC to Lloyd George, 19 January 1918, *CV* 4/1, pp. 233-234; WSC, *The World Crisis*, vol. 2, pp. 1256-1258.
40. WSC to the War Cabinet, 21 October 1917, in *The World Crisis*, vol. 2, p.

1179.
41. Ibid, pp. 1179-1184; L. Amery, diary, 10 May 1917, *CV* 4/1, p. 60.
42. WSC, "Munition Programme 1919," 5 March 1918, *The World Crisis*, vol. 2, pp. 1265-1274; WSC, memorandum, 22 June 1918, *CV* 4/1, pp. 328-334.
43. WSC, *The World Crisis*, vol. 2, pp. 1210-1211.
44. Ibid., vol. 2, pp. 968-970.
45. See Prior, op. cit., ch. 12.
46. H. A. L. Fisher, diary, 3 March 1920, *CV* 4/2, p. 1044.
47. WSC, *The World Crisis*, vol. 2, p. 1111.
48. Ibid.
49. See WSC, *The World Crisis*, vol. 2, pp. 975-977, 985-991; WSC, *The Eastern Front*, pp. 327-330.
50. WSC, *The World Crisis*, vol. 2, pp. 982, 1396.
51. See C. Barnett, *The Swordbearers: Studies in Supreme Command in the First World War*, Penguin, 1966, first published in 1963, ch. 4, especially pp. 384-391.
52. The "might have beens" and "ifs" are a theme that is repeated tirelessly throughout the book. See, for example, WSC, *The World Crisis*, vol. 1, ch. 13, and pp. 461, 478, 593, 597-599, 632; vol. 2, pp. 876, 879-880.
53. R. Blake in M. Howard, ed., *Soldiers and Governments*, Eyre & Spottiswoode, London, 1957, pp. 49-50; Liddell Hart in A. J. P. Taylor, ed., *Churchill: Four Faces and the Man*, p. 201.

Chapter 4: History and the "Continental Commitment," 1919-1939

1. Howard, *The Continental Commitment*, pp. 74-78; N. H. Gibbs, *Grand Strategy*, HMSO, London, 1976, vol. 1, p. 796.
2. B. Bond, *British Military Policy Between the Two World Wars*, Clarendon Press, Oxford, 1980, p. 34.
3. See *SPHS*, 14 February 1920, vol. 3, pp. 2934-2935.
4. Gibbs, op. cit., p. 38.
5. Ibid, pp. 798-799.
6. Howard, *The Continental Commitment*, p. 80; P. Kennedy, *The Rise and Fall of British Naval Mastery*, Allen Lane, London, 1976, pp. 270-271.
7. See, Gibbs, op. cit., pp. 806-809.
8. Ibid., p. 3.
9. June 1928, *CV* 5/1, p. 1302.
10. See R. Rhodes James, *Churchill: A Study in Failure 1900-1939*, pp. 159-160; C. Barnett, *The Collapse of British Power*, Eyre Methuen, London, 1972, pp. 277-278.
11. See Gibbs, op. cit., pp. 3-6; Bond, op. cit., pp. 23-25.
12. Gibbs, op. cit., pp. 59-60.
13. WSC to A. J. Balfour, 26 February 1921, *CV* 4/2, p. 1379.
14. WSC, Cabinet memoranda, 4 July 1921, 23 July 1921, *CV* 4/3, pp. 1539–1542, 1563-1566.
15. WSC to the Prince of Wales, 2 January 1922, *CV* 4/3, pp. 1709-1710.
16. C. Barnett, *The Collapse of British Power*, p. 272.
17. P. Kennedy, *The Rise and Fall of British Naval Mastery*, pp. 275–280.
18. Barnett, *The Collapse of British Power*, pp. 278-282; Gibbs, op.cit., pp. 4, 62-63.
19. WSC to S. Baldwin, 15 October 1924, *CV* 5/1, pp. 303-307.
20. See A. J. Marder, "The Royal Navy and the Ethiopian Crisis of 1935-6,"

American Historical Review, vol. 75, no. 5, 1969/70, pp. 1327-1356.

21. Churchill, *The Second World War*, vol. 1, pp. 50-51.
22. See below, pp. 93-97.
23. Sir Maurice Hankey, notes for S. Baldwin, 24 July 1936, *CV* 5/3, pp. 261-263.
24. Gibbs, op. cit., p. 60.
25. WSC to W. Bridgeman, 28 November 1927, *CV* 5/1, p. 1115.
26. House of Commons, *SPHS*, 3 March 1919, vol. 3, pp. 2674-2692.
27. WSC, *Marlborough, His Life and Times*, vol. 1, pp. 489-490, 523.
28. See Barnett, *The Collapse of British Power*, pp. 320-326; W. M. Jordan, *Great Britain, France, and the German Problem 1918-1939*, Frank Cass, London, 1971, first published in 1943, ch. 4, pp. 44-56.
29. WSC, Cabinet memorandum (draft), 29 August 1920, *CV* 4/2, pp. 1190-1194.
30. Cabinet, Minutes, 24 March 1922, *CV* 4/3, p. 1822.
31. On Churchill's view toward this issue, see WSC to General Herrington, 18 March 1920, *CV* 4/2, p. 1049; Sir Henry Wilson, diary, 14 April 1920, *CV* 4/2, p. 1072; WSC to Lord Derby, 21 December 1920, *CV* 4/2, p. 1271-1272; H. A. L. Fisher, diary, 30 December 1920; Hankey, diary, *CV* 4/2, pp. 1277-1278; Imperial conference, proceedings, 7 July 1921, *CV* 4/3, pp. 1544-1546; WSC to Lloyd George, 28 January 1921, *CV* 4/3, p. 1677; House of Commons, *SPHS*, 8 Febuary 1922, vol. 3, pp. 3174-3177; Cabinet, Minutes, 24 March 1922, *CV* 4/3, p. 1822; WSC to Lord Curzon (not sent), 26 April 1922, *CV* 4/3, pp. 1875-1877.
32. Quoted in Gibbs, op. cit., p. 41.
33. Ibid., pp. 39, 41; Bond, op. cit., p. 76.
34. Sir E. Crowe to A. Chamberlain, 12 March 1925, *CV* 5/1, pp. 430-432; C. Barnett, *The Collapse of British Power*, p. 330.
35. WSC, "French and Belgian Security," 24 February 1925, *CV* 5/1, pp. 413–417.
36. Committee of Imperial Defence, Minutes, 13 February 1925, *CV* 5/1, pp. 393-397.
37. Ibid.; WSC: A Note of Conversation with the President of the French Republic, 11 January 1925, *CV* 5/1, pp. 338-340; WSC, "French and Belgian Security," op. cit.
38. Committee of Imperial Defence, Minutes, 19 February 1925, *CV* 5/1, p. 406.
39. *CV* 5/1, pp. 417-418, note no. 1.
40. WSC, *The Second World War*, vol. 1, pp. 27-30.
41. Gibbs, op. cit., p. 43.
42. See Howard, *The Continental Commitment*, pp. 94-96; Bond, op. cit., pp. 78-82, 93.
43. A. J. P. Taylor, *The Origins of the Second World War*, Penguin, Harmondsworth, 1973, p. 83.
44. See WSC to Sir W. Fisher and others concerned, 14 September 1928, *CV* 5/1, pp. 1337-1339; WSC to F. Leith-Ross, 23 September 1928, *CV* 5/1, pp. 1348-1349; House of Commons, *SPHS*, 29 June 1931, vol. 5, pp. 5053ff.; and also P. Towle, "Winston Churchill and British Disarmament Policy," *The Journal of Strategic Studies*, vol. 2, no. 3, pp. 336-341.
45. House of Commons, *SPHS*, 2 June 1930, 21 July 1930, 29 June 1931, vol. 5, pp. 4814-4822, 4893-4898, 5053ff.; press interview, 11 December 1931, *SPHS*, vol. 5, pp. 5125-5126.
46. Bond, op. cit., pp. 93-94.
47. Gibbs, op. cit., pp. 70-71.
48. See Prince Bismarck, memorandum, 20 October 1930, *CV* 5/2, pp. 196–199; House of Commons, *SPHS*, 29 June 1931, vol. 5, pp. 5053ff.
49. Prince Bismarck, 20 October 1930, op. cit., p. 197.
50. *SPHS*, 17 February 1933, vol. 5, pp. 5219-5220; *CV* 5/2, 23 February 1934, p.

726.
51. Gibbs, op. cit., pp. 78-84.
52. WSC, *The Second World War*, vol. 1, p. 72.
53. See House of Commons, *SPHS*, 29 June 1931, 13 May 1932, vol. 5, pp. 5053ff., 5170-5175.
54. House of Commons, *SPHS*, 23 November 1932, vol. 5, pp. 5197-5206.
55. House of Commons, *SPHS*, 13 April 1933, vol. 5, pp. 5260-5266.
56. House of Commons, *SPHS*, 23 March 1933, vol. 5, pp. 5234-5241.
57. See, for example, Committee of Imperial Defence, Minutes, 4 December 1924, *CV* 5/1, p. 286.
58. House of Commons, *SPHS*, 7 November 1933, vol. 5, pp. 5296-5299.
59. A record of a conversation between Sir Samuel Hoare, A. Eden, and W. Churchill, 21 August 1935, *CV* 5/2, pp. 1239-1240.
60. Quoted in Bond, op. cit., p. 198.
61. Quoted in Howard, *The Continental Commitment*, p. 108; See also Gibbs, op. cit., p. 111.
62. Gibbs, op. cit., pp. 111-113; Bond, op. cit., p. 204.
63. Howard, *The Continental Commitment*, pp. 108-109; Bond, op. cit., pp. 201-202.
64. Gibbs, op. cit., pp. 97-98.
65. Howard, *The Continental Commitment*, p. 101.
66. Bond, op. cit., pp. 196-197.
67. N. Rose, *Vansittart—A Study of a Diplomat*, Heinemann, London, 1978, pp. 130-131.
68. Howard, *The Continental Commitment*, pp. 110-111; Bond, op. cit., pp. 206-210, 212-213.
69. Howard, *The Continental Commitment*, p. 115.
70. Gibbs, op. cit., pp. 257-258.
71. Ibid., p. 263.
72. See Howard, *The Continental Committment*, p. 116; Bond, pp. 236-238.
73. Howard, *The Continental Commitment*, pp. 117-118; Bond, op. cit., pp. 257-259, 275-277; Gibbs, op. cit., p. 441.
74. See U. Bialer, *The Shadow of the Bomber, the Fear of Air Attack and British Politics 1932-39*, Royal Historical Society, London, 1980, pp. 132-137.
75. Ibid., p. 138; Howard, *The Continental Commitment*, p. 116; Bond, op. cit., pp. 261-265.
76. Howard, *The Continental Commitment*, pp. 118-119.
77. WSC to Major Percy Davies, 5 June 1938, *CV* 5/3, pp. 1054-1055; Bialer, op. cit., pp. 136-137, 157-158.
78. Howard, *The Continental Commitment*, p. 112.
79. See Bond, op. cit., pp. 259-260; Bialer, "The British Chiefs of Staffs and the 'Limited Liability Formula' of 1938," *Military Affairs,* April 1978.
80. Quoted in Bialer, *The Shadow of the Bomber*, p. 140.
81. Bond, op. cit., pp. 259, 272-273.
82. Gibbs, op. cit., p. 454, note 2.
83. Howard, *The Continental Commitment*, p. 122.
84. Gibbs, op. cit., p. 801; see also Bond, op. cit., pp. 280-282; C. Barnett, *The Collapse of British Power*, passim; M. Howard, *War and the Liberal Conscience*, chs. 4-5, esp. pp. 81-107.
85. B. H. Liddell Hart, *The British Way in Warfare*, MacMillan, NewYork, 1933, pp. 7, 17, 37, 41; idem, *Strategy, The Indirect Approach*, Faber, London, 1967 (first published in 1929 under the title *The Decisive Wars of History: A Study in Strategy*), chs. 21, 22.

86. See B. H. Liddell Hart, *Europe in Arms*, Faber and Faber, London, 1937, esp. ch. 10, "The Role of the British Army," pp. 116-141.

87. Bond, op. cit., p. 252.

88. See Bond, *British Military Policy Between the Two World Wars*, p. 252; Bond, *Liddell Hart—A Study of His Military Thought*, London, 1977.

89. J. Luvaas, op. cit., pp. 423-424; Bond, *British Military Policy Between the Two World Wars*, pp. 245-246.

90. See B. H. Liddell Hart, *The Defence of Britain*, Faber and Faber, London, 1939, passim.

91. On the problems in Liddell Hart's strategic theory, see T. Ben-Moshe, "Liddell Hart and the Israel Defence Forces—A Reappraisal," *Journal of Contemporary History*, vol. 16, no. 2, 1981, esp. pp. 369-372; Bond, *Liddell Hart—A Study of His Military Thought*, London, pp. 52-53, 56-57.

92. WSC to B. H. Liddell Hart, 5 May 1932, *CV* 5/2, p. 425.

93. WSC, *Marlborough, His Life and Times*, vol. 1, pp. 3-4, vol. 4, pp. 599-600.

94. Ibid., vol.1, pp. 76-82, 489, 523.

95. WSC, *Marlborough, His Life and Times*, vol. 1, p. 516, vol. 2, pp. 99-101.

96. Ibid., vol. 2, p. 95.

97. Ibid., vol. 3, p. 19.

98. Ibid., vol. 2, pp. 96, 513; Basing himself on Churchill's book, T. Higgins argues that it was because he was himself Tory that Churchill supported a naval-peripheral strategy and opposed the opening of a second front in the west during World War II. Logically and historically that is a strange argument. He had ignored the fact that in the book Churchill praised Marlborough and the Whig's continental strategy. See T. Higgins, *Winston Churchill and the Second Front 1940-3*, Oxford University Press, 1957, pp. 196-197.

99. Ibid., vol. 2, pp. 141, 258-261, 432, 499-500, 594.

100. Ibid., vol. 2, pp. 15, 96-97, vol. 3, p. 6

101. Ibid., vol. 2, pp. 129-140, 591-592.

102. Ibid., vol. 2, pp. 204-208, vol. 3, pp. 67-68, vol. 4, pp. 37-38, 351, 393-396.

103. WSC to Lieutenant-Commander Owen, 6 January 1934, *CV* 5/2, pp. 699-670; see also WSC to Rear-Admiral Dewar, 4 August 1929, 11 September 1929, *CV* 5/2, pp. 33-34, 75.

104. WSC to Rear-Admiral Dewar, 4 August 1929, *CV* 5/2 pp. 33-34; WSC, *Marlborough, His Life and Times*, vol. 2, p. 101, vol. 3, p. 334.

105. Ibid., vol. 3, p. 243; see also vol. 4, p. 108.

106. Ibid., vol. 3, pp. 456-457.

107. Ibid.

108. Ashley, op. cit., p. 157.

109. Ibid., pp. 156-157; cf. WSC to M. Ashley, 13 July 1929, *CV* 5/2, pp. 18-19.

110. WSC, *Marlborough, His Life and Times*, vol. 2, pp. 298-299.

111. Ashley, op. cit., p. 138.

112. WSC, *Marlborough, His Life and Times*, vol. 1, pp. 3-4, 441, vol. 2, p. 44, vol. 4, pp. 599-600, 652; during the 1689–1697 and 1702–1714 conflicts Britain allocated 35 percent of total expenditure to its navy and 40 percent to its army, see P. Kennedy, *The Rise and Fall of the Great Powers*, Unwin Hyman, London, 1988, p. 89.

113. WSC, *A History of the English Speaking Peoples*, Cassell, 1962, vols. 1-4 (first published in 1956), vol. 3, pp. 123-134.

114. Ibid., vol. 3, pp. 204, 231-234.

115. Ibid., vol. 3, pp. 231-234, 238, 251, 268.

116. Ibid., vol. 3, pp. 251-252.

117. Ibid., vol. 3, pp. 258, 264-278, 298-312.

118. C. Barnett, *Britain and Her Army 1509–1970*, W. Morrow, New York, 1970,

pp. XVII-XX, 187-188.
119. Ibid., pp. 161-162.
120. P. Kennedy, *The Rise and Fall of British Naval Mastery*, pp. 84-88, and *The Rise and Fall of the Great Powers*, pp. 95-98.
121. M. Howard, "The British Way in Warfare—A Reappraisal" (J. Cape, 1974), pp. 14-15.
122. WSC to Lady Horner, 5 May 1929, *CV* 5/1, p. 1456; *SPHS*, March 1936, vol. 6, p. 5696.
123. WSC to G. M. Trevelyan, 3 January 1935, *CV* 5/2, pp. 984-985.
124. WSC to Lord Rothermere, 12 May 1935, *CV* 5/2, pp. 1169-1170.
125. *SPHS*, March 1936, vol. 6, pp. 5694-5696; see also WSC to Lord Londonderry, 6 May 1936, *CV* 5/3, pp. 142-143
126. WSC, *The World Crisis*, vol. 1, pp. 161-164.
127. See *SPHS*, 16 October 1936, vol. 6, pp. 5795-5796; meeting of the 1922 Committee, report to the Cabinet, 8 December 1936, *CV* 5/3, pp. 466-472; House of Commons, *SPHS*, 6 April 1936, vol. 6, pp. 5723-5729.
128. House of Commons, *SPHS*, 2 May 1935, vol. 6, pp. 5590-5596.
129. WSC, *The World Crisis*, vol. 1p. 165; House of Commons, *SPHS*, 24 October 1935, vol. 6p. 5681.
130. House of Commons, *SPHS*, 13 July 1934, vol. 5, pp. 5377-5381.
131. A Record of a Discussion Between S. Baldwin and a Deputation from Both Houses of Parliament, 29 July 1936, *CV* 5/3, pp. 277-294.
132. See WSC to A. R. Wise, 9 April 1936, *CV* 5/3 pp. 94-95; M. Hankey to T. Inskip, 19 April 1936, *CV* 5/3, pp. 106-109; WSC to Lady Bonham Carter, 25 May 1936, *CV* 5/3, pp. 171-173; *SPHS*, 19 October 1936, vol. 6, pp. 5797-5798.
133. See House of Commons, *SPHS*, 22 February 1938, 14 March 1938, 24 March 1938, vol. 6, pp. 5911-5917, 5923-5927, 5939-5945.
134. Lord Halifax, Cabinet memorandum, 18 March 1938, *CV* 5/3, pp. 947-948; N. Chamberlain to Ida Chamberlain, 20 March 1938, *CV* 5/3, pp. 952-953.
135. Bialer, *The Shadow of the Bomber*, p. 4.
136. WSC, *The Second World War*, vol. 1, p. 231; R. Macleod, D. Kelly, eds., *The Ironside Diaries 1937-1940*, Constable, London, 1962, 22 September 1938, p. 62.
137. Bialer, op. cit., pp. 146-147.
138. Ibid., ch. 5, pp. 127-150.
139. Bond, *British Military Policy Between the Two World Wars*, pp. 296-302
140. House of Commons, *SPHS*, 21 February 1939, vol. 6, pp. 6069-6071.
141. House of Commons, *SPHS*, 19 May 1939, vol. 6, pp. 6117-6123.
142. Bond, *British Military Policy Between the Two World Wars*, pp. 307-308.
143. House of Commons, *SPHS*, 19 May 1939, vol. 6, p. 6123.
144. See H. Nicolson, diary, 3 April 1939, *CV* 5/3, pp. 1429-1430; V. Cazalet, diary, 25 August 1939, *CV* 5/3, p. 1597.
145. See A. Ulam, *Expansion and Coexistence*, Holt, Rinehart and Winston, New York, 1974, pp. 267ff.
146. Bond, *British Military Policy Between the Two World Wars*, pp. 318-319; Gibbs, op. cit., p. 747; A. J. P. Taylor, *The Origins of the Second World War*, pp. 276-277, 322-323.
147. Gibbs, op. cit., p. 804.
148. WSC, *Marlborough, His Life and Times*, vol. 3, p. 433.
149. See WSC, *The Aftermath*, pp. 450-459; WSC, "Shall We All Commit Suicide?", in *Thoughts and Adventures*.
150. R. Rhodes James, *Churchill: A Study in Failure 1900–1939*, pp. 424-426.
151. WSC to A. Chamberlain, 30 October 1919, *CV* 4/2, pp. 942-943.
152. Lord Moran, op. cit., p. 50.

153. House of Commons, *SPHS*, 3 August 1921, vol. 3, pp. 3121-3127.
154. House of Commons, *SPHS*, 17 March 1930, vol. 5, pp. 4721 ff.; D. Morton to WSC, 4 December 1935, *CV* 5/2, p. 1341.
155. House of Commons, *SPHS*, 16 March 1936, vol. 6, pp. 5705-5713; House of Commons, *SPHS*, 21 May 1936, vol. 6, pp. 5749-5756.
156. Meeting of the 1922 Committee, report to the Cabinet, 8 December 1936, *CV* 5/3, p. 467; Vice-Admiral R. Henderson to WSC, *CV* 5/2, 16 December 1935, p. 1352.
157. Admiral of the Fleet Chatfield to WSC, 5 May 1936, *CV* 5/3, pp. 135-140.
158. See *SPHS*, 18 February 1937, vol. 6, pp. 5827-5829; House of Commons, *SPHS*, vol. 6, 11 March 1937, 22 March 1937, pp. 5836-5847; *SPHS*, 19 October 1937, vol. 6, pp. 5896-5897.
159. See House of Commons, *SPHS*, 17 March 1930, 21 July 1930, 24 February 1936, vol. 5, pp. 4721ff., 4893-4898, vol. 6, pp. 5691-5694.
160. See Vice-Admiral Henderson to WSC, 1 May 1936, *CV* 5/3, p. 127; Admiral of the Fleet Chatfield to WSC, 5 May 1936, *CV* 5/3, pp. 135-140.
161. See A. Marder, "The Influence of History on Sea-Power: The Royal Navy and the Lessons of 1914-1918," *Pacific Historical Review* (November 1972), pp. 421-423, 437-440; WSC: Cabinet memorandum, 20 July 1927, *CV* 5/1, pp. 1030-1035; House of Commons, *SPHS*, 16 March 1939, vol. 6, 6083-6090.
162. See *SPHS*, vol. 6, 19 October 1937, pp. 5896-5897; WSC to Lord Chatfield 18 June 1938, *CV* 5/3, pp. 1064-1065; Lord Chatfield to WSC, 25 June 1938, *CV* 5/3, pp. 1078-1079; *SPHS*, 1 February 1939, vol. 6, pp.6063-6064; House of Commons, SPHS, 16 March 1939, vol 6, p. 6085; Walter Lippmann, notes, 14 June 1939, CV 5/3, pp. 1519-1520.
163. See above pp. 76-77.
164. See WSC to A. Eden, 3 September 1937, *CV* 5/3, pp. 758-759.
165. See P. Kennedy, "Mahan versus Mackinder: Two Interpretations of British Sea Power," in *Strategy and Diplomacy 1870-1945*, Fontana, 1983, pp. 43-85; G. Parker, *Western Geopolitical Thought in the Twentieth Century*, Croom Helm, London, 1985, ch. 3, pp. 32-33, 35-40; and also J. T. Lowe, *Geopolitics and War: Mackinder's Philosophy of Power*, University Press of America, 1981; a good discussion on the decline of British sea power is in P. Kennedy, *The Rise and Fall of British Naval Mastery*.
166. See J. C. Fest, *Hitler*, Penguin, 1977, pp. 323; A. Bullock, *Hitler, A Study in Tyranny*, Penguin, 1975, p. 78; Parker, op. cit., ch. 5; on Hitler's geopolitical program, see also M. Hauner, "Did Hitler Want a World Dominion?" *Journal of Contemporary History*, vol. 13 (1978), pp. 15-32.
167. WSC, *The Second World War*, vol. 2, p. 43.
168. WSC to A. Chamberlain, 30 October 1919, *CV* 4/2, pp. 942-943; WSC to A. Chamberlain, 10 May 1920, *CV* 4/2, pp. 1086-1088.
169. Lord Moran, op. cit., p. 51.
170. *SPHS*, 14 October 1936, vol. 6, pp. 5793-5795; House of Commons, *SPHS*, 12 November 1936, vol. 6, pp. 5805ff.; WSC to Field Marshal Sir C. Deverell, 2 June 1937, *CV* 5/3, pp. 695-696; R. Rhodes James, *Churchill: A Study in Failure 1900–1939*, pp. 306-307.
171. See PREM 3/345/8; A. J. Trythall, *"Bony" Fuller*, Cassell, London,1977, pp. 70, 214, 223, 236-237; J. Colville, *The Fringes of Power: Downing Street Diaries 1939–1955*, Hodder and Stoughton, London, 1985, pp. 304–306.
172. Bond, *British Military Policy Between the Two World Wars*, p. 338.
173. WSC, *The Second World War*, vol. 1, p. 475.
174. House of Commons, *SPHS*, 14 March 1939, vol. 6, pp. 6072-6081.
175. See Liddell Hart, *Europe in Arms*, pp. 83-91.
176. *The Ironside Diaries*, 1 December 1937, p. 38, 6 December 1937, p. 41, 27

August 1939, p. 90; Lord Rothermere to W. S. Churchill, 23 December 1937, *CV* 5/3, pp. 865-866; WSC to Lord Rothermere, 1929 December 1937, *CV* 5/3, p. 869; WSC, recollection, 22 August 1939, *CV* 5/3, pp. 1592-1593; WSC, notes, 23 August 1939, *CV* 5/3, pp. 1593-1596.

177. See chapter 1, pp. 16-19.
178. WSC, *The Second World War*, vol. 1, pp. 473-475, vol. 2, pp. 46-47.
179. See record of a discussion between S. Baldwin and a deputation from both Houses of Parliament, 29 July 1936, *CV* 5/3, pp. 277-294; House of Commons, *SPHS*, 25 May 1938, 21 February 1939, vol. 6, pp. 5967–5975, 6064-6071.
180. WSC to L. Hore-Belisha, 4 June 1938, *CV* 5/3, pp. 1052-1054.
181. *The Ironside Diaries*, 27 August 1939, p. 90.
182. See *SPHS*, 12 April 1939, vol. 6, pp. 6097-6099; House of Commons, *SPHS*, 13 April 1939, vol. 6, pp. 6099-6105; "The Anglo-Turkish Alliance," 18 May 1939, *Daily Telegraph*, *CV* 5/3, p. 1914; *The Ironside Diaries*, 25 July 1939, pp. 83-87.
183. M. Hankey to Inskip, 19 April 1936, *CV* 5/3, pp. 106-109; House of Commons, *SPSH*, 16 March 1939, vol. 6, p. 6088; WSC, "Memorandum on Sea Power, 1939," 27 March 1939, CV 5/3, pp. 1414-1417.
184. Gibbs, op. cit., p. 660.
185. Ibid., P. 668.
186. Ibid., pp. 657-658, 674-675.
187. Ibid., pp. 420-431.
188. Ibid., p. 756.
189. P. Kennedy, *The Rise and Fall of British Naval Mastery*, p. 307; A. Marder, "'Winston is Back'—Churchill at the Admiralty 1939–40," *From the Dardanelles to Oran*, op. cit., p. 148.
190. See P. Salmon, "Churchill, the Admiralty and the Narvik Traffic, September-November 1939" (*Scand. J. History*, 4, 1979), p. 305.
191. Lord Chatfield to WSC, April 1939, *CV* 5/3, p. 1429.
192. A. J. P. Taylor, *The Origins of the Second World War*, p. 336.

Chapter 5: The Genesis of the "Mediterranean Strategy," 1940–1941

1. *The Ironside Diaries*, 8 September 1939, 24 October 1939, op. cit., p. 134; Gilbert, *Finest Hour*, vol. 6, p. 66.
2. Gilbert, *Finest Hour*, vol. 6, p. 5.
3. Ibid., pp. 23, 30.
4. WSC to Prime Minister, 18 September 1939, in WSC, *The Second World War*, vol. 1, pp. 457-459.
5. Gilbert, *Finest Hour*, vol. 6, pp. 10-11.
6. On Churchill as First Lord of the Admiralty and his involvement in the initiation of the Norwegian campaign, see A. Marder, "'Winston is Back'—Churchill at the Admiralty 1939-40," *From the Dardanelles to Oran*, op. cit., pp. 105-178.
7. Gilbert, *Finest Hour*, vol. 6, p. 459.
8. J. Colville, *The Fringes of Power, Downing Street Diaries 1939–1955*, 29 June 1940, 9 August 1940, pp. 177-178, 213.
9. WSC, *The Second World War*, vol. 5, p. 386.
10. See J. Leutze, "The Secret of the Churchill-Roosevelt Correspondence, September 1939–May 1940," *Journal of Contemporary History*, vol. 10, no. 3.
11. Quoted in Gilbert, *Finest Hour*, vol. 6, p. 358.
12. WSC, *The Second World War*, vol. 2, pp. 185-186.

13. See Lord Moran, op. cit., p. 759.
14. J. Kennedy, *The Business of War, The War Narrative of Major-General Sir J. Kennedy*, Hutchinson, London, 1957, p. XII; B. H. Liddell Hart, "The Military Strategist," in A. J. P. Taylor, *Four Faces and the Man*, op. cit., p. 189; B. H. Liddell Hart, *History of the Second World War*, Pan Books, London, 1970, p. 117.
15. Lord Ismay, *Memoirs*, Heinemann, London, 1960, p. 193.
16. J. R .M. Butler, *Grand Strategy*, vol. 2, HMSO, London, 1971, first published in 1957, pp. 308, 554.
17. Gilbert, *Finest Hour*, vol. 6, p. 756.
18. WSC, *The Second World War*, vol. 2, p. 17.
19. See WSC to Wavell, 16, 22 August 1940, PREM 3/296/1.
20. Colville, *The Fringes of Power*, op. cit., 13 July 1940, 9 August 1940, 30 August 1940, pp. 193-194, 214, 233.
21. WSC to General Ismay for C.O.S. Committee, August 1940, PREM 3/266/10A.
22. WSC: "The Munitions Situation," 3 September 1940, *The Second World War*, vol. 2, pp. 458-461.
23. Butler, *Grand Strategy*, vol. 2, pp. 341-345.
24. Defence Committee, 15 October 1940, CAB 69/1 (40) 34.
25. WSC to A. Eden (strictly private), 24 September 1940, PREM 3/296/11; Colville, *The Fringes of Power*, op. cit., 27 September 1940, p. 225.
26. Defence Committee, 31 October 1940, CAB 69/1 (40)39 and Confidential Annex, CAB 69/8.
27. See L. Amery to WSC, 2 July 1940, PREM 3/296/17; Lord Hankey to WSC, 17 July 1940, PREM 3/296/17.
28. Kennedy, op. cit., pp. 62, 112.
29. See WSC to A. Chamberlain, 7 September 1925, *CV* 5/1, pp. 539-540; WSC to S. Baldwin, 7 September 1925, *CV* 5/1; WSC: Notes *CV* 5/1, 19 September 1925, pp. 544-546.
30. H. Nicolson, diary, 24 April 1936, *CV* 5/3, pp. 113-114; WSC, *Marlborough, His Life and Times*, vol. 2, p. 101, vol. 3, p. 334; WSC to Rear-Admiral Dewar, 4 August 1929, *CV* 5/2, pp. 33-34.
31. A Meeting of Ministers, 13 November 1940, PREM 3/296/11.
32. C. Barnett, *The Collapse of British Power*, pp. 586-593.
33. Colville, *The Fringes of Power*, 22 September 1940, p. 248.
34. WSC to Lord Lothian, *The Second World War*, vol. 2, pp. 405-406.
35. Defence Committee, 12 January 1941, Confidential Annex, CAB 69/8 (41)3.
36. Gilbert, *Finest Hour*, vol. 6, pp. 869-875.
37. WSC, *The World Crisis*, vol. 1, p. 462.
38. Ibid., vol. 2, pp. 879-880.
39. However, contrary to the argument advanced by Higgins, it is not true that Churchill considered the war to have been decided on the Salonika front and that the collapse of Bulgaria caused that of Germany. See Higgins, *Winston Churchill and the Second Front 1940-3*, pp. 199ff.
40. See House of Commons, 27 July 1937, *SPHS*, vol. 6, p. 5894.
41. WSC, memorandum, 23 November 1920, *CV* 4/2; WSC to Lord Curzon, 5 September 1922, *CV* 4/3, p. 1977.
42. WSC to N. Chamberlain, 9 April 1939, *CV* 5/3, pp. 1438-1439.
43. *The Ironside Diaries*, op. cit., pp. 105, 170; Gilbert, *Finest Hour*, vol. 6, p. 31.
44. Gilbert, *Finest Hour*, vol. 6, pp. 44-45.
45. WSC to Portal (CAS) and Ismay, 28 August 1940, in WSC, *The Second World War*, vol. 2, p. 434.
46. WSC to Franklin D. Roosevelt, (infra FDR), 27 October 1940, in W. F.

Kimball, ed., *Churchill and Roosevelt The Complete Correspondence*, Princeton University Press, Princeton, 3 vols., 1987, vol. 1, pp. 79-80.

47. WSC to Eden, 2 November 1940, in WSC, *The Second World War*, vol. 2, p. 536.

48. See I. Playfair, *The Mediterranean and Middle East*, HMSO, 1954, London, vol. 1, pp. 230-231.

49. F. Hinsley, et al., *British Intelligence in The Second World War, Its Influence on Strategy and Operations*, HMSO, London, 1979, vol. 1, pp. 254-255.

50. WSC to Eden, 3 November 1940, 4 November 1940, WSC to Dill, 6 November 1940, 7 November 1940, in WSC, *The Second World War*, vol. 2, pp. 538-40.

51. WSC, *The Second World War*, vol. 2, pp. 536-537, 542-543.

52. D. Carlton, *Anthony Eden*, Allen Lane, 1981, pp. 168-169.

53. R. Parkinson, *Blood, Toil, Tears and Sweat, The War History from Dunkirk to Alamein Based on the War Cabinet Papers of 1940–2*, D. Mckay, New York, 1973, pp. 148-150.

54. WSC to Wavell, 26 November 1940, in WSC, *The Second World War*, vol. 2, pp. 546-547.

55. Defence Committee, 13 November 1940, CAB 69/8 (40) 42; WSC to Wavell, 14 November 1940, ibid.

56. Kennedy, op. cit., p. 64.

57. Playfair, *The Mediterranean and the Middle East*, vol. 1, p. 239.

58. M. van Creveld, *Hitler's Strategy 1940–1941: The Balkan Clue*, Cambridge University Press, 1973, pp. 60-61, 177.

59. Ibid., pp. 81-83.

60. M. van Creveld, "Prelude to Disaster: the British Decision to Aid Greece, 1940–41," *Journal of Contemporary History*, vol. 9, no.3, 1974, pp. 68-72, 74-75.

61. Ibid., pp. 74-75.

62. Defence Committee, 2 January 1941, Confidential Annex, CAB 69/8 (41)3; WSC to General Ismay for C.O.S. Committee, 6 January 1941, in WSC, *The Second World War*, vol. 3, pp. 5-11.

63. Defence Committee, 8 January 1941, CAB 69/2 (41)1.

64. Chiefs of Staff, "Assistance to Greece," 9 January 1941, C.O.S. (41)7(0) CAB 80/56.

65. Kennedy, op, cit., pp. 69-76.

66. Ibid., p. 73.

67. Defence Committee, 9 January 1941, CAB 69/2 (41)2.

68. C.O.S. to Wavell, 9 January 1941, Defence Committee, CAB 69/2; 10 January 1941, Wavell to CIGS, in J. Connell, *Wavell, Scholar and Soldier*, Collins, London, 1964, p. 310.

69. WSC to Wavell, 11 January 1941, PREM 3/288/7.

70. Van Creveld, "Prelude to Disaster," op. cit., pp. 76-79.

71. Defence Committee, 16 January 1941, CAB 69/2 (41)5.

72. Wavell to CIGS, 18 January 1941, in Connell, op. cit., pp. 315-316.

73. Defence Committee, 20 January 1941, CAB 69/2 (41)6; WSC to General Ismay for C.O.S. Committee, 21 January 1941, CAB 69/2.

74. Defence Committee, 20 January 1941, CAB 69/2 (41) 6.

75. See, for instance, his words during the Defence Committee meeting of January 8.

76. F. Hinsley, *British Intelligence in The Second World War*, vol. 1, pp. 254-255, 259-261, 437.

77. Ibid., p. 361.

78. Ibid., pp. 429, 440-441.

79. See chapter 2, pp. 75, 79-80 ; WSC, *The Eastern Front*, pp. 259-260, 328-329.

80. WSC to Smuts, 27 June 1940, in WSC, *The Second World War*, vol. 2, pp. 227-228.
81. WSC, *The Second World War*, vol. 3, p. 354.
82. Hinsley, op. cit., p. 447.
83. WSC, *The Second World War*, vol. 3, p. 357.
84. Hinsley, op. cit., vol. 1, pp. 451-452; WSC, *The Second World War*, vol. 3, p. 356-357.
85. WSC to Stafford Cripps (Moscow), 3 April 1941, in WSC, *The Second World War*, vol. 3, p. 358.
86. Hinsley, op. cit., vol. 1, pp. 455-456, 472.
87. Ibid., vol. 1, p. 357.
88. Ibid., p. 251.
89. Defence Committee, 16 January 1941, CAB 69/2 (41)5; Chiefs of Staff to Wavell, 22 January 1941, PREM 3/296/17.
90. Hinsley, op. cit., vol. 1, p. 357.
91. Wavell to C.O.S., 27 January 1941, PREM 3/296/17.
92. WSC to C.O.S. Committee, 31 January 1941, in WSC, *The Second World War*, vol. 3, p. 35.
93. WSC to President Inönü, 31 January 1941, in WSC, *The Second World War*, vol. 3, pp. 33-35.
94. Connell, op. cit., pp. 321-323.
95. L. Amery to WSC, 3 February 41, PREM 3/288/8.
96. C. Barnett, *The Desert Generals*, Pan Books, London, 1983, pp. 59-60, 62-63.
97. Playfair, op. cit., vol. 1, p. 347.
98. Wavell to CIGS, 10 February 1941, in Connell, op. cit., p. 326.
99. Defence Committee, 11 February 1941, CAB 69/2 (41)8 (most members of the committee were already aware of this intelligence evaluation when they convened for their meeting on February 10); van Creveld, "Prelude to Disaster," op. cit., pp. 79-80.
100. According to Eden, Churchill turned discussions of the Defence Committee into a monologue; see J. Harvey, ed., *The War Diaries of Oliver Harvey*, Collins, London, 1978, 3 August 1941, p. 26.
101. Defence Committee, 10 February 1941, CAB 69/2 (41)7.
102. J. Colville, *The Fringes of Power*, 12 February 1941, p. 356.
103. Kennedy, op. cit., p. 75.
104. Ibid., p. 75.
105. Ibid., pp. 75-76.
106. WSC to Wavell, 11 February 1941, CAB 69/2.
107. WSC to Eden, 12 February 1941, in WSC, *The Second World War*, vol. 3, pp. 66-68.
108. Carlton, op. cit., p. 193.
109. D. Dilks, ed., *The Diaries of Sir Alexander Cadogan 1938–1945*, Cassell, London, 1971, 16 March 1940, p. 263, 28 April 1941, p. 374.
110. Kennedy, op. cit., p. 73.
111. Ibid., pp. 81-85.
112. Ibid., pp. 79-80.
113. The Foreign Office's officials were Vansittart, Butler, Seymour, Strange, and Sargent; Cadogan to WSC, 19 February 1941, PREM 3/288/8; *Cadogan Diaries*, 18,19 February 1941, op. cit., pp. 355-357.
114. WSC to Cadogan, 19 February 1941, PREM 3/288/8.
115. Van Creveld, "Prelude to Disaster," op. cit., pp. 80-81.
116. A. Eden, *The Eden Memoirs, The Reckoning*, Cassel, London, 1965, pp. 193-195.
117. Playfair, op. cit., vol. 1, p. 375.

118. Connell, op. cit., p. 336.
119. Quoted in Parkinson, *Blood, Toil, Tears and Sweat*, p. 194 (author's emphasis).
120. Ibid., p. 193.
121. WSC to Eden (Cairo), 20 February 1941, in WSC, *The Second World War*, vol. 3, pp. 69-70.
122. Butler, *Grand Strategy*, vol. 2, p. 447.
123. Quoted in van Creveld, "Prelude to Disaster," op. cit., p. 83.
124. Parkinson, *Blood, Toil, Tears and Sweat*, pp. 195-197.
125. WSC to Eden, 24 February 1941, in WSC, *The Second World War*, vol. 3, p. 76.
126. *Cadogan Diaries*, op. cit., 28 February 1941, 1 March 1941, 3 March 1941, pp. 359-361.
127. WSC to Eden, 1 March 1941, in WSC, *The Second World War*, vol. 3, pp. 97-98.
128. Van Creveld, "Prelude to Disaster," op. cit., pp. 85-86; Connell, op. cit., pp. 346-347.
129. It is also the opinion of Carlton, op. cit., pp. 173-177; C. Cruickshank, *Greece 1940-1941*, Davis-Poynter, London, 1976, pp. 178-180; van Creveld, "Prelude to Disaster," op. cit., pp. 85-86.
130. Eden to Churchill, 24 February 1941, in WSC, *The Second World War*, vol. 3, pp. 74-76.
131. Carlton, op. cit., p. 177.
132. Eden and Dill to Churchill, 5 March 1941, in WSC, *The Second World War*, vol. 3, pp. 99-100.
133. Wavell to the War Office, 2 March 1941, PREM 3/288/8.
134. Defence Committee, 5 March 1941, CAB 69/2 (41) 9.
135. WSC, *The Second World War*, vol. 3, p. 101.
136. WSC to Eden, 5 March 1941, CAB 69/2.
137. Eden, *The Reckoning*, op. cit., p. 214.
138. Quoted in Connell, op. cit., p. 352.
139. Kennedy, op. cit., pp. 92, 100-102.
140. 5, 6 March 1941, *Cadogan Diaries*, pp. 361-362.
141. WSC to Eden, 7 March 1941, in WSC, *The Second World War*, vol. 3, pp. 104-105.
142. *Cadogan Diaries*, op. cit., p. 361.
143. Parkinson, *Blood, Toil, Tears and Sweat*, pp. 206-207.
144. WSC, *The Second World War*, vol. 3, p. 101.
145. WSC to Eden, 14 March 1941, in *The Second World War*, vol. 3, 108-109.
146. See PREM 3/288/7; WSC, *The Second World War*, vol. 3, book one, ch. 11; Gilbert, *Finest Hour*, vol. 6, p. 1055.
147. House of Commons, 7 May 1941, *SPHS*, vol. 6, pp. 6387-6399.
148. J. Colville, *The Fringes of Power*, 28 September 1941, p. 443.
149. PREM 3/288/7.
150. J. Butler, *Grand Strategy*, vol. 2, pp. 457-459.
151. Van Creveld, "Prelude to Disaster," op. cit., p. 92.
152. See D. Carlton, op. cit., pp. 179-182; Cruickshank, op. cit., p. 178; H. Ismay, op. cit., pp. 195-200.
153. Kennedy, op. cit., p. 92.
154. Ibid., p. 38.
155. *Cadogan Diaries*, 1 March 1941, op. cit., p. 360.
156. Lord Moran, op. cit., pp. 35-36.
157. Colville, *The Fringes of Power*, p. 263.
158. Gilbert, *Finest Hour*, vol. 6, pp. 587-588, 631, 685, 1170, 1214-1215.

159. See A. Danchev, " 'Dilly-Dally,' or Having the Last Word: Field Marshal Sir John Dill and Prime Minister Winston Churchill," *Journal of Contemporary History*, vol. 22(1987), pp. 21-44.
160. Kennedy, op. cit., pp. 60, 62-64, 73-74; A. Bryant, *The Turn of the Tide, 1939–1943, A Study Based on the Diaries and Autobiographical Notes of Field Marshall The Viscount Alanbrooke*, The Reprint Society, London, 1958, pp. 210, 216.
161. Bryant, *The Turn of the Tide*, pp. 209-210; Eden, *The Reckoning*, pp. 190-196; Kennedy, op. cit., pp. 60, 74, 90-91.
162. Kennedy, op. cit., p. 92.
163. See WSC to Dill, 13 May 1941, PREM 3/296/17; Dill to WSC, 15 May 1941, PREM 3/296/17.
164. Wavell to Viscount Cranborne, 31 October 1942, PREM 3/288/7.
165. Connell, op. cit., pp. 323-324.
166. Barnett, *The Desert Generals*, pp. 63-64.
167. Quoted in Kennedy, op. cit., p. 87.
168. Ibid., p. 92.
169. WSC, *The Second World War*, vol. 3, p. 94.
170. Cruickshank, op. cit., pp. 182-183.
171. Lord Boothby, *My Yesterday, Your Tomorrow*, Hutchinson, London, 1962, p. 209.
172. Gilbert, *Finest Hour*, pp. 128-129.
173. See WSC to H. Asquith, 31 July 1914, *CV* 3/1; WSC to E. Grey and H. Asquith, 3 August 1914, *CV* 3/1; WSC to E. Grey, 3, 5 August 1914, *CV* 3/1.
174. WSC, *Marlborough, His Life and Times*, vol. 2, pp. 190-191.
175. Playfair, op. cit., vol. 1, p. 335.
176. WSC, *The Second World War*, vol. 3, pp. 61-77.
177. Ibid., vol. 3, pp. 196-202, 344-345.
178. WSC to Eden, 20 April 1941, in *The Second World War*, vol. 3, pp. 228-229; (author's emphasis).
179. Marder's opinion on Churchill at this period of the war was that "he was carried away by his magnificent offensive spirit beyond the bounds of ordinary common sense." See A. Marder, *Operation Menace, The Dakar Expedition and the Dudley North Affair*, Oxford University Press, 1976, pp. 187, 190.
180. J. Colville, *The Fringes of Power*, 29 August 1941, 28 September 1941, pp. 432–433, 443.
181. *The Second World War*, vol. 3, pp. 95, 354.
182. C. von Clausewitz, *On War*, eds. M. Howard, P. Paret, Princeton University Press, 1976, pp. 158-159, 181-182.
183. WSC, *The World Crisis*, vol. 1, p. 462.
184. WSC, *The Eastern Front*, pp. 174, 184-185.
185. After an argument with Churchill on the Far East strategy, Alan Brooke has written Churchill's retort in his diary: "I do not want any of your long-term projects, they cripple our initiative. I told him he must know where he was going, to which he replied that he did not want to know." Bryant, *The Turn of the Tide*, p. 583.
186. J. M. A. Gwyer, *Grand Strategy*, vol. 3, part 1, HMSO, London, 1964, pp. 70-72; J. R. M. Butler, *Grand Strategy*, vol 2, pp. 538-541.
187. See M. van Creveld, "The German Attack on the USSR: The Destruction of a Legend," *European Studies Review*, 2; 1, January 1972; M. van Creveld, *Hitler's Strategy 1940-1*, pp. 170-176, 179-183; idem., *Supplying War*, ch. 5.
188. Van Creveld, *Hitler's Strategy 1940–1*, pp. 81-84, 102-105, 180-181.
189. Conference of Ministers, Minutes, 19 September 1922, *CV* 4/3, p. 1999.
190. Kennedy, op. cit., pp. 110-112.
191. Ibid., pp. 105-107, 109.

192. WSC, Directive, 28 April 1941, PREM 3/296/2.
193. 7 May 1941, PREM 3/296/2.
194. C.O.S, "Brief Survey of Situation in Middle East," 29 April 1941, PREM 3/296/17.
195. WSC to General Ismay for C.O.S Committee, 4 May 1941, PREM 3/296/17.
196. J. Dill, "The Relations of the Middle East to the Security of the United Kingdom," 6 May 1941, PREM 3/296/17.
197. WSC to Sir John Dill, 13 May 1941, PREM 3/296/17.
198. M. Howard, *The Mediterranean Strategy in The Second World War*, F. A. Praeger, New York, 1968, pp. 2, 9-12.
199. Ibid., pp. 34-36.

Chapter 6: The Formation of Anglo-American Strategy, 1941–1942

1. Butler, *Grand Strategy*, vol. 2, p. 425.
2. Gwyer, *Grand Strategy*, vol. 3/1, p. 125.
3. Butler, op. cit., vol. 2, p. 426.
4. Ibid., vol. 2, pp. 478-479.
5. WSC, broadcast, London, *SPHS*, 9 February 1941, vol. 6, p. 6348.
6. Kennedy, op. cit., p. 97.
7. Butler, op. cit., vol. 2, pp. 478-479.
8. Ibid., vol. 2, pp. 547-550; Gwyer, *Grand Strategy*, vol. 3/1, pp. 42-44.
9. Defence Committee, 25 June 1941, CAB 69/2 (41) 44.
10. Defence Committee, 17 June 1941, CAB 69/2 (41) 42.
11. In J. Colville, *The Fringes of Power*, op. cit., 21 June 1941, pp. 403-405.
12. Ibid., 22 June 1941, pp. 405-406.
13. Gilbert, *Finest Hour*, vol. 6, p. 1119.
14. WSC to Smuts, 29 June 1941, PREM 3/296/12; WSC to the Prime Minister of Australia, 29 June 1941, PREM 3/296/12.
15. Hinsley, *British Intelligence in The Second World War*, vol. 2, HMSO, London, 1981, pp. 67-68, 78-79.
16. Defence Committee, 4 July 1941, 7 July 1941, CAB 69/2 (41)46.
17. Barnett, *The Desert Generals*, pp. 71-77; WSC to Auchinleck, 20 July 1941, PREM 3/296/17.
18. Defence Committee, 1 August 1941, CAB 69/2 (41) 53.
19. WSC, *The Second World War*, vol. 3, pp. 423-425.
20. WSC to FDR, 25 July 1941, in W. F. Kimball, ed., *Churchill and Roosevelt, The Complete Correspondence*, vol. 1, p. 224.
21. WSC, *The Second World War*, vol. 2, pp. 243-253.
22. Gwyer, *Grand Strategy*, vol. 3/1, pp. 126-127; see also M. S. Watson, *Chief of Staff: Prewar Plans and Preparations*, Historical Division, United States Army, Washington, 1950, pp. 400-408.
23. Gilbert, *Finest Hour*, vol. 6, pp. 1166-1167.
24. WSC to Smuts, 8 November 1941, PREM 3/476/3; Parkinson, *Blood, Toil, Tears and Sweat*, pp. 282-283, 285.
25. WSC to General Auchinleck, August 1941, PREM 3/296/14; C.O.S, draft, 23 August 1941; WSC to General Ismay 25 August 1941, WSC to R. Menzies, 7 September 41, PREM 3/296/13.
26. WSC, General Directive, Anglo-American-Russian Conference, 22 September 1941, CAB 69/3.

27. WSC to Portal, 7 October 1941, in WSC, *The Second World War*, vol. 3, pp. 508-509.
28. DO(41) 22, CAB 69/2.
29. Defence Committee, 15 October 1941, CAB 69/2(41)64; Defence Committee, 20 October 1941, CAB 69/8(41)67.
30. Defence Committee, 27 October 1941, CAB 69/2(41)69; Defence Committee, 3 December 1941, CAB 69/2(41)71.
31. WSC to FDR, 20 October 1941, in W. F. Kimball, ed., *Churchill and Roosevelt, The Complete Correspondence*, vol. 1, pp. 252-257.
32. Gwyer, *Grand Strategy*, vol. 3/1, pp. 349-352.
33. Joint Planning Staff, "The Basis of Anglo-American Strategy," 16 December 1941, CAB 80/61.
34. British Chiefs of Staff: "American-British Strategy, Grand Strategy," 22 December 1941, CAB 80/61.
35. 18 December 1941, CAB 80/61.
36. WSC, "The Atlantic Front," "The Pacific Front," "The Campaign of 1943," 18–20 December 1941, PREM 3/499/1-2.
37. WSC, *The Second World War*, vol. 3, pp. 655, 659-661.
38. WSC, "The Atlantic Front," op. cit.
39. WSC, "The Pacific Front," op. cit.
40. WSC, "The Campaign of 1943," op. cit.
41. Pound, Dill, Portal to WSC, 20 December 1941, PREM 3/499/2.
42. WSC to Brigadier Hollis for C.O.S. Committee, 21 December 1941, PREM 3/499/2.
43. C.O.S. to WSC, 22 December 1941, PREM 3/499/2.
44. See, Gwyer, *Grand Strategy*, vol. 3/1, pp. 325-348; WSC, *The Second World War*, vol. 3, book two, ch. 14.
45. Gwyer, op. cit., pp. 12-13, 38-41, 342-344.
46. Ibid., p. 13.
47. See Gwyer, op. cit., vol. 3/1, p. 126; C. Barnett, *The Collapse of British Power*, p. 581; J. Colville, op. cit., p. 432.
48. Defence Committee, 31 October 1940, CAB 69/8; House of Commons (secret session), 25 June 1941, *SPHS*, pp. 6431-6444.
49. Broadcast, London, 9 February 1941, SPHS, vol. 6, p. 6348.
50. C.O.S. Meeting, 16 December 1942, CAB 79/58 (42)198(0).
51. Meeting of U.S. and British Chiefs of Staff, 24 December 1941, CAB 80/61.
52. Meeting of U.S. and British Chiefs of Staff, 24 December 1941, CAB 80/61.
53. WSC, *The Second World War*, vol. 2, pp. 288-289, vol. 5, p. 52.
54. Gwyer, op. cit., vol. 3/1, pp. 44-48.
55. Gilbert, *Finest Hour*, vol. 6, p. 1081; Gwyer, op. cit., vol. 3/1, pp. 44-48.
56. See London, *SPHS*, 11 March 1911, vol. 2, pp. 1718-1721; WSC, *The History of the English Speaking Peoples*, vol. 3, pp. 51-52, 256–268; House of Commons, *SPHS*, 11 April 1940, vol. 6, pp. 6201-6211.
57. Gwyer, op. cit., vol. 3/1, pp. 349-352.
58. Ibid., pp. 353-360.
59. See "American-British Strategy," memorandum by the British Chiefs of Staff, 22 December 1941, CAB 80/61; "American and British Strategy," memorandum by the U.S. and British Chiefs of Staff, C.O.S (42)75, CAB 80/33.
60. War Cabinet Discussion (42)8, 17 January 1942, Confidential Annex, CAB 65/29.
61. C.O.S. Meeting, 10 March 1942, Confidential Annex, CAB 79/86 (42)78; C.O.S. Meeting, 17 March 1942, CAB 79/56 (42)9(0); C.O.S. Meeting, 8 April 1942,

CAB 79/56 (42)21(0); J. Butler, *Grand Strategy*, vol. 3/2, HMSO, London, 1964, pp. 568-569.

62. JSM, Washington, to the Chief of Staff, 5 March 1942, London, PREM 3/492/1.

63. Hinsley, op. cit., vol. 2, pp. 88-90.

64. C.O.S. Meeting, 10 March 1942, Confidential Annex, CAB 79/86 (42)78.

65. Pound, "Future Strategy," 21 March 1942, C.O.S. CAB 80/61 (42)71(0).

66. Joint Intelligence Sub-Committee (JIC) (of the C.O.S. Committee), "Enemy Intentions," 6 April 1942, PREM 3/135/2 (this report had already been circulated on March 20). See also Hinsley, op. cit., vol. 2, pp. 92-93.

67. K. Greenfield, *American Strategy in World War II: A Reconsideration*, The Johns Hopkins Press, Baltimore, 1963, pp. 54-55.

68. A. C. Wedemeyer, *Wedemeyer Reports!*, Holt and Company, New York, 1958, p. 49.

69. Ibid., pp. 50-53; see also chapter 4, above pp. 114-115.

70. See ibid., ch. 5, p. 65; M. S. Watson, *Chief of Staff: Prewar Plans and Preparations*, ch. 11, esp. pp. 338-346, 352-357; J. Keegan, *Six Armies in Normandy*, Penguin, Harmondsworth, pp. 31-34.

71. W. S. Dunn, *Second Front Now—1943*, Alabama University Press, 1980, tables 15, 16, pp. 212-214.

72. General Marshall's Plan, *Operation in Western Europe* in J. Butler, *Grand Strategy*, vol. 3/2, appendix III, pp. 675-681; F. Pogue, *George C. Marshall, Ordeal and Hope, 1939-42*, Viking Press, 1966, pp. 304-305; D. Eisenhower, *Crusade in Europe*, Permabooks, New York, 1952, pp. 58-65.

73. Pogue, op. cit., pp. 305-306.

74. FDR to WSC, 3 April 1942, in W. F. Kimball, ed., *Churchill and Roosevelt, The Complete Correspondence*, vol. 1, p. 441 (r-131/1); Dill (Washington) to the Chiefs of Staff, 9 April 1942, PREM 3/492/2.

75. JSM (Washington) to the Chiefs of Staff, 1 April 1942, PREM 3/492/2.

76. Chiefs of Staff for JSM (Washington), 6 April 1942, PREM 3/492/2.

77. Hinsley, op. cit., vol. 2, pp. 92-93.

78. See WSC to General Auchinleck, August 1941, PREM 3/296/14.

79. C.O.S Meeting, 9 April 1942, CAB 79/56 42(23)(0).

80. Pogue, op. cit., p. 317.

81. C.O.S. Meeting, 10 April 1942, CAB 79/56 (42)24(0).

82. C.O.S. 13 April 1942, CAB 80/62 (42)97(0).

83. C.O.S. Meeting, 14 April 1942, CAB 79/56 (42)25(0); Defence Committee, 14 April 1942, PREM 3/333/6 (42)10.

84. J. Butler, *Grand Strategy*, vol. 3/2, pp. 575-581; Ismay, op. cit., p. 249.

85. Lord Moran, op. cit., p. 52.

86. Joint Intelligence Sub-Committee, "Enemy Intentions," 6 April 1942, PREM 3/135/2; JIC "The Possible Course of the Russian Campaign and Its Implications," 6 June 1942, C.O.S.(42)246, CAB 66/25; see also Hinsley, op. cit., vol. 2, pp. 88-96.

87. WSC to General Ismay for C.O.S. Committee, 7 June 1942, PREM 3/395/13.

88. See above p. 181.

89. JSM(Dill) to War Cabinet Office, 31 December 1942, PREM 3/499/7.

90. There are many instances of misunderstandings and misuses of the code names, e.g., Alan Brooke's mistake, War Cabinet Discussion, 27 June 1942, CAB 65/30 (42)82; Dill's mistake, Dill to WSC, 15 July 1942, PREM 3/333/19; Roosevelt's mistake that was noted by Churchill, WSC to C.O.S. Committee, 9 April 1943, CAB 79/60.

91. A. Bryant, *The Turn of the Tide*, p. 284.

92. WSC, "Operation Jupiter," 1 May 1942, in WSC, *The Second World War*, vol. 4, pp. 348-350; C.O.S. Meeting, 27 May 1942, CAB 79/56 (42)46(0); WSC to General

Ismay for C.O.S. Committee, 2 June 1942, CAB 80/63; War Cabinet Discussion, 11 June 1942, Confidential Annex, CAB 65/30 (42)73; WSC, Memorandum-Operation "Jupiter," 13 June 1942, C.O.S. (42) 168 (0), CAB 80/63.

93. C.O.S. Meetings, 27 May 1942, op. cit.; C.O.S. Meeting, 6 July 1942, CAB 79/56 (42)65(0); War Cabinet Discussion, 7 July 1942 (42) 87, Confidential Annex, CAB 65/31.

94. WSC, Memorandum-Operation "Jupiter," 13 June 1942, op. cit. Prime Minister's Notes, 20 July 1942, PREM 3/333/9.

95. WSC, *Operation Round-up*, 15 June 1942, C.O.S. (42)169(0), CAB 80/63; C.O.S. Meeting, 15 June 1942, CAB 79/56 (42)52.

96. Paget, Douglas, Ramsay, comments on the PM's memorandum on Operation Round-up, 15 June 1942, PREM 3/333/2.

97. JSM (Dill) to the Chiefs of Staff, 15 June 1942, PREM 3/492/2.

98. C.O.S. (42)61(0), 30 June 1942, CAB 79/56.

99. C.O.S. to WSC, 8 July 1942, PREM 3/257/5.

100. Dill to WSC, 15 July 1942, PREM 3/333/19; U.S. Chiefs of Staff, memorandum, 21 July 1942, PREM 3/333/9; Pogue, op. cit., vol. 2. pp. 342-346.

101. WSC, Personal Minute, 5 July 1942, PREM 3/257/5; C.O.S. meeting, 6 July 1942, CAB 79/56 (42)65.

102. C.O.S. Meeting, 10 July 1942, (42)70(0), PREM 3/333/19; C.O.S. Meeting, 16 July 1942, CAB 79/56 (42)73(0).

103. C.O.S. Meeting, 15 June 1942, CAB 79/56 (42)52.

104. C.O.S. Meeting, 6 July 1942, CAB 79/56 (42)65(0); War Cabinet Discussion, 7 July 1942, (42)87, Confidential Annex CAB 65/31.

105. WSC to Dill, 12 July 1942, PREM 3/333/19.

106. War Cabinet Discussion, 7 July 1942, (42)87, Confidential Annex, CAB 65/31.

107. WSC to FDR, 14 July 1942, PREM 3/333/19.

108. Dill to WSC, 15 July 1942, PREM 3/333/19; JSM (Washington) to the Chiefs of Staff, 25 July 1942, PREM 3/492/2.

109. Prime Minister Notes for meeting on July 20 1942, 20 July 1942, PREM 3/333/9.

110. WSC: "A Review of the War Position," 21 July 1942, CAB 66/26 W. P. (42)311.

111. WSC to General Ismay for C.O.S. Committee, 23 July 1942, PREM 3/257/5.

112. Ibid.

113. See War Cabinet Discussion, 24 July 1942, (42)95, Confidential Annex, and appendix A, "Proposals for Operations in 1942/3," CAB 65/31.

114. A. Calder, *The People's War, Britain 1939–1945*, Pantheon Books, 1969, pp. 260-264, 297-302.

115. WSC, *The Second World War*, vol. 4, book two, ch. 2, and also p. 659.

116. Pogue, op. cit., vol. 2, p. 345.

117. Roosevelt, memorandum for Hopkins, Marshall, King, 16 July 1942, in WSC, *The Second World War*, vol. 4, pp. 441-444.

118. See WSC, *The Second World War*, vol. 4, book one, ch. 20, book two, ch. 2.

119. 2 July 1942, W.P. (42)278, CAB 66/26.

120. See J. L. Strange, "The British Rejection of Operation Sledgehammer, an Alternative Motive," *Military Affairs*, vol. XLVI, no. 2, Feb. 1982, pp. 6-15.

Chapter 7: The "Mediterranean Strategy" at Its Height, 1942–1943

1. See below pp. 234-235.
2. Lord Moran, op. cit. p. 85.
3. K. Young, *Churchill and Beaverbrook*, Eyre and Spottiswoode, London, 1966, p. 249.
4. WSC, *The Second World War*, vol. 4, p. 509; Butler, *Grand Strategy*, vol. 3/2, p. 639.
5. B. L. Montgomery, *The Memoirs of Field Marshal Montgomery of Alamein*, A Da Capo Paperback, New York, 1982, first published in 1958, pp. 69-70; WSC, *The Second World War*, vol. 4, p. 509.
6. Ibid., vol. 4, p. 510.
7. WSC to General Ismay, 21 December 1942, PREM 3/256.
8. General Ismay to Churchill, 29 December 1942, PREM 3/256.
9. Butler, op. cit., vol. 3/2, pp. 641-642; WSC, *The Second World War*, vol. 4, p. 511.
10. C.O.S. to J.S.M. (Washington), 4 December 1942, PREM 3/492/3; 4 December 1942, PREM 3/256.
11. WSC to General Ismay for C.O.S. Committee, 6 December 1942, PREM 3/256.
12. Butler, op. cit., vol. 3/2, p. 642.
13. Liddell Hart, *History of The Second World War*, pp. 337-341.
14. Montgomery, op. cit., p. 71.
15. Butler, op. cit., vol. 3/2, p. 638.
16. WSC to General Ismay for C.O.S. Committee, 8 June 1942, CAB 66/26.
17. Ibid.
18. M. Howard, *Grand Strategy*, vol. 4, HMSO, London, 1972, p. 219.
19. 20 August 1942, War Cabinet Discussion, (43) 115, Confidential Annex, CAB 65/31.
20. C.O.S. Meeting, 15 September 1942, CAB 79/57 (42) 119 (0); 16 September 1942, WSC to Brigadier Hollis for C.O.S. Committee, CAB 65/31.
21. WSC to FDR, 22 September 1942, PREM 3/333/11.
22. Hinsley, op. cit., vol. 2, pp. 103-107.
23. J. P. (42) 849, 3 October 1942, CAB 79/57; J. P. (42) 880, 18 October 1942, CAB 79/58.
24. C.O.S. Meeting, 22 October 1942, CAB 79/58 (42) 156; C.O.S. Meeting, 23 October 1942, CAB 79/58 (42) 158.
25. WSC, "Policy for the Conduct of the War," 24 October 1942, CAB 66/30.
26. WSC to Lord Cherwell, 24 October 1942, PREM 3/499/10.
27. C.O.S. Committee, "American-British Strategy," 30 October 1942, C.O.S. (42) 345(0), CAB 80/65.
28. WSC to General Ismay for C.O.S. Committee, 9 November 1942, PREM 3/499/6; same to the same, 16 November 1942, PREM 3/499/6.
29. WSC to General Ismay for C.O.S. Committee, 9 November 1942, PREM 3/499/6; WSC, "Note by Minister of Defence," 14 November 1942, C.O.S. (42) 392(0),CAB 80/65.
30. C.O.S. Meeting, 15 November 1942, CAB 79/58(42)181; Defence Committee, 16 November 1942, CAB 69/4(42)17.
31. WSC, "Strategy in 1943," 18 November 1942, C.O.S. (42)399(0), CAB 80/65.
32. 21 August 1942, C.O.S. (42)96(0), CAB 79/57; JSM (Washington) to C.O.S., 10 September 1942, PREM 3/492/3; same to the same, 27 September 1942, PREM 3/492/3; Howard, *Grand Strategy*, vol. 4, pp. 217-218.

33. WSC to FDR, 24 November 1942, PREM 3/333/11.
34. WSC to FDR, 26 November 1942, in WSC, *The Second World War*, vol. 4, p. 653.
35. Ibid., vol. 4, p. 651.
36. C.O.S. Meeting, 20 November 1942, CAB 79/58 (42)186(0).
37. See WSC to General Ismay for C.O.S. Committee, 9 November 1942, PREM 3/499/6; Defence Committee, 16 November 1942, CAB 69/4 (42)17.
38. Kennedy, op. cit., p. 224.
39. WSC, *The Second World War*, vol. 3, pp. 684-685.
40. C.O.S. Meeting, 11 August 1942, CAB 79/56 (42) 85.
41. W. S. Dunn, *Second Front Now—1943*, pp. 212-213.
42. See *The World Crisis*, vol. 2, p. 1209; WSC to Secretary of State for War, CIGS, C.O.S. Committee, 15 April 1943, CAB 80/68.
43. WSC, "The Position of Italy," 25 November 1942, CAB 66/31.
44. Defence Committee, 29 November 1942, CAB 69/4 (42)20; cf. C.O.S.: "American-British Strategy," 30 October 1942, op. cit., C.O.S., "American-British Strategy in 1943," 31 December 1942 (!), C.O.S. (42)466(0), CAB 80/66; Eden to WSC, 2 December 1942, PREM 4/100/8.
45. WSC to General Ismay for C.O.S. Committee, 29 November 1942, CAB 80/66; C.O.S. Meeting, 30 November 1942, CAB 79/58 (42)191; Note by the Minister of Defence, 3 December 1942, C.O.S.(42) 429(0), CAB 80/66.
46. Joint Intelligence Sub-Committee, "German Strategy in 1943," 3 December 1942, PREM 3/190/3.
47. See above pp. 194-195.
48. See W. P. (42)373, CAB 66/28.
49. C.O.S. Meeting, 3 December 1942, CAB 79/58 (42)192(0).
50. C.O.S. (42)432(0), 3 December 1942, CAB 80/66; Joint Planning Staff, "Offensive Strategy in the Mediterranean," 5 December 1942, J. P. (42)990, CAB 79/58; C.O.S., "Future Strategy," 13 December 1942, CAB 80/66; Joint Planning Staff, "Future Strategy," 10 January 1943, CAB 79/59.
51. C.O.S. Meeting, 16 December 1942, CAB 79/58 (42)198(0).
52. Ibid.
53. Dill to the War Cabinet Office, 11 December 1942, PREM 3/492/3; Dill to WSC, 14 December 1942, PREM 3/333/19; U.S. Chiefs of Staff, "Basic Strategic Concept for 1943," 23 December 1942, PREM 3/492/3.
54. See C.O.S. Meeting (42)346, Confidential Annex, 15 December 1942, CAB 79/87; see above p. 207.
55. C.O.S. Meeting, 16 December 1942, CAB 79/58 (42) 198(0).
56. C.O.S. Meeting, 17 December 1942, CAB 79/58 (42)199(0); Bryant, *The Turn of the Tide*, p. 441.
57. WSC, "British Strategy in 1943," 28 December 1942, PREM 3/499/7.
58. See, Bryant, *The Turn of the Tide*, pp. 433-442.
59. WSC to General Ismay, 27 December 1942, PREM 3/499/7.
60. Combined Chiefs of Staff, 55th Meeting, 14 January 1943, Casablanca, CAB 80/67; 58th Meeting, 16 January 1943, CAB 80/67.
61. C.O.S. Meeting, 13 January 1943, Casablanca, CAB 80/67; C.O.S. Meeting, 15 January 1943,Casablanca, CAB 80/67.
62. Minutes of Meeting, Combined Chiefs of Staff, 18 January 1943, CAB 80/67.
63. W. S. Dunn, *Second Front Now—1943*, ch., 5; J. Grigg, *1943—The Victory That Never Was*, Hill and Wang, New York, 1980, pp. 218-219.
64. Combined Chiefs of Staff, "Conduct of the War in 1943," 19 January 1943, CAB 80/67; Minutes of Meeting, Combined Chiefs of Staff, 23 January 1943, CAB 80/67.

65. Bryant, *The Turn of the Tide*, p. 462.
66. "Anglo-American Relations in Washington in the Autumn of 1942," note by the Secretary of State for War, 9 November 1942, W.P. (42) 515, CAB 80/66.
67. Note by the Minister of Defence, 3 December 1942, CAB 80/66; Hinsley, op. cit., vol. 2, p. 113.
68. Ibid.
69. Bryant, *The Turn of the Tide*, p. 437.
70. See above p. 201.
71. Kennedy, op. cit., p. 277.
72. See above p. 186
73. Howard, *Grand Strategy*, vol. 4, p. 208.
74. WSC, *The Second World War*, vol. 3, pp. 659-661, vol. 4, p. 659.
75. See below pp. 277-278.
76. J. I. C., "The German Military Situation," 15 February 1943, W. P. (43)76, CAB 66/34.
77. Brigadier Hollis to WSC, 23 December 1942; Lindemann (Cherwell) to WSC, 23 December 1942; WSC to General Ismay, 27 December 1942; General Ismay to WSC, 30 December 1942; WSC to CIGS (Alan Brooke), 28 February 1943; all in PREM 3/190/3.
78. See W. S. Dunn, *Second Front Now—1943*, chs., 7, 9, 11, 12 esp., pp. 94-97, 133-136, 178-184; F. H. Hinsley, *British Intelligence in The Second World War*, vol. 3/1, HMSO, London, 1984, passim.
79. C.O.S. Meeting, 17 February 1943, CAB 79/59 (43)22(0).
80. WSC to Alan Brooke, 2 March 1943, CAB 79/59.
81. C.O.S. Meeting, 11 March 1943, CAB 79/59 (43)41(0); C.O.S. Meeting, 26 March 1943, CAB 79/59 (43)57(0); Ismay to WSC, 3 April 1943, CAB 79/60; Joint Planning, "European Strategy 1943–44," 7 April 1943, CAB 79/60.
82. WSC to General Ismay for C.O.S. Committee, 2 April 1943, CAB 79/60.
83. Brigadier Hollis to WSC, 12 April 1943, CAB 79/60.
84. C.O.S. Meeting, 13 April 1943, CAB 79/60 (43)75(0).
85. WSC to Secretary of State for War, CIGS, C.O.S. Committee, 15 April 1943, C.O.S. (43)194(0), CAB 80/68; WSC to General Ismay, 18 April 1943, CAB 80/69.
86. Joint Intelligence Sub-Committee, "Operation Subsequent to "'Husky,'" 11 April 1943 (43)160(0), CAB 79/60; J.I.C., "German Plans and Intentions during Summer and Autumn 1943," 20 April 1943, J.I.C. (43)171, CAB 79/60; Alan Brooke, Note, 22 April 1943, CAB 79/60.
87. C.O.S. Meeting, 20 April 1943,CAB 79/60 (43)81(0); C.O.S. Meeting, 22 April 1943, (43)83(0), CAB 79/60.
88. WSC to Dill (for Marshall), 25 April 1943, PREM 3/333/19.
89. C.O.S. Meeting, 10 May 1943, CAB 80/69 (T)10.
90. See W. S. Dunn, *Second Front Now—1943*, ch. 14, esp. pp. 212-213, 220-221; Howard, *Grand Strategy*, vol. 4, p. 419.
91. Dunn, chs. 15-16, esp. pp. 258-259.
92. Minutes of Meeting, Trident, 12 May 1943, 24 May 1943, CAB 80/70.
93. Howard, *Grand Strategy*, vol. 4., p. 425.
94. Minutes of Meeting, Trident, 24 May 1943,CAB 80/70.
95. Minutes of Meeting, Trident, 19 May 1943, CAB 80/70; Combined Chiefs of Staff, memorandum, 25 May 1943, in Howard, *Grand Strategy*, vol. 4, appendix VI(c).
96. WSC, *The Second World War*, vol. 4, pp. 810-811, 816.
97. Ibid., vol. 4, pp. 825-826; Howard, *Grand Strategy*, vol. 4, p. 498.
98. Ibid, pp. 498-499; WSC, *The Second World War*, vol. 4, pp. 825-826.
99. Howard, *Grand Strategy*, vol. 4, pp. 497-507; WSC, *The Second World War*, vol. 4, pp. 810-811, 816-826.

100. See WSC, *The Second World War*, vols. 4-5, passim, e.g., vol. 5, pp. 154, 253-255, 344-346, 426-427.

101. A. Bryant, *The Turn of the Tide*, pp. 510-513, 520-521, 558-561, 580; A. Bryant, *Triumph in the West 1943–1946, A Study Based on the Diaries and Autobiographical Notes of Field Marshall The Viscount Alanbrooke*, Collins, London, 1959, pp. 30-33.

102. Howard, *Grand Strategy*, vol. 4, pp. 421, 565.

103. Joint Planning Staff, "Future Strategy," 10 January 1943, CAB 79/59.

104. See Alan Brooke, Note, 22 April 1943, CAB 79/60.

105. See WSC, "The Position of Italy," 25 November 1942, CAB 66/31; Joint Intelligence Sub-Committee, 3 December 1942, "German Strategy in 1943," PREM 3/190/3; Minutes of Meeting, Trident, 12 May 1943, CAB 80/70; WSC, "Background Notes," 31 May 1943, in WSC, *The SecondWorld War*, vol. 4, pp. 821-825; Joint Planning Staff: "Mediterranean Operations," 28 July 1943, J.P. (43)272, CAB 79/63; Joint Intelligence Sub-Committee: "German Plans and Intentions during second half of 1943," 3 August, 1943, CAB 79/63; Hinsley, *British Intelligence in the Second World War*, vol. 3/1, pp. 100-117; Howard, *Grand Strategy*, vol. 4, pp. 429-431.

In his memoirs, General Ismay put matters the wrong way around. According to his version of events, the British had believed that Hitler would fight over every inch of Italian soil. See Ismay, *Memoirs*, p. 298.

106. WSC, *The Second World War*, vol. 5, p. 52.

107. Ibid., vol. 4, p. 659.

108. Combined Chiefs of Staff Meeting, 14 January 1943, CAB 80/67.

109. F. H. Hinsley, *British Intelligence in The Second World War*, vol. 3/1, p. 173; A. Bullock, op. cit., pp. 710-711; J. Ehrman, *Grand Strategy*, vol. 5, HMSO, London, 1956, pp. 65-69.

110. See below, ch. 9.

Chapter 8: "First Catch Your Hare": The Political Dimension of Strategy

1. Quoted in Howard, *Grand Strategy*, vol. 4, p. 1; Colville, op. cit., 10 August 1940, p. 215.

2. See London, *SPHS*, 27 March 1941, vol. 6, pp. 6363-6366; Eden to WSC, 20 May 1941, PREM 4/100/5; WSC to Eden, 24 May 1941, PREM 4/100/5; House of Commons, SPHS, 9 September 1941, vol. 6, pp. 6480-6481; M. Gilbert, *Finest Hour*, vol. 6, p. 995.

3. See E. J. Hughes, "Winston Churchill and the Formation of the United Nations Organization," *Journal of Contemporary History*, vol. 9, no. 4, 1974, p. 178.

4. Colville, op. cit., 10 August 1940, pp. 215-216.

5. Hughes, op. cit., pp. 178-179; Colville, op. cit., 13 December 1940, pp. 311-314.

6. Gilbert, *Finest Hour*, vol. 6, p. 1237.

7. A. Eden, *The Reckoning*, pp. 289ff.; V. Mastny, *Russia Road to the Cold War*, Columbia University Press, 1979, pp. 41-44.

8. See Parkinson, *Blood, Toil, Tears and Sweat*, pp. 323-324; Carlton, op. cit., pp. 186-187.

9. 3 November 1941, PREM 3/296/17.

10. WSC to Secretary of State for War, 3 December 1941, PREM 3/296/17.

11. Carlton, op.cit., pp. 186-187.

12. WSC to Eden, 8 January 1942, PREM 3/399/6.

13. Quoted in Parkinson, *Blood, Toils, Tears and Sweat*, p. 350.
14. See A. Eden, memorandum, "Policy Towards Russia," 28 January 1942, W. P.(42)69, PREM 3/399/1-2.
15. War Cabinet Discussion, 6 February 1942, W. M.(42)17, Confidential Annex, CAB 65/29.
16. War Cabinet Discussion, 25 February 1942, W.M.(42)24, Confidential Annex), CAB 65/29.
17. WSC to FDR, 7 March 1942, in Kimball, ed., *Churchill and Roosevelt, The Complete Correspondence*, vol. 1, p. 394.
18. See L. Kettenacker, "The Anglo-Soviet Alliance and the Problem of Germany 1941-1945," *Journal of Contemporary History*, vol. 17, 1982, (435-458), 443.
19. War Cabinet Discussion, 25 March 1942, W.M.(42)37, CAB 65/29.
20. Hughes, op.cit., pp. 178-180; see also above pp. 225-226.
21. See above p. 147.
22. Eden to Halifax, 26 March 1942, CAB 65/29; see also G. Ross, "Foreign Office Attitudes to the Soviet Union 1941-1945," in W. Laqueur, ed., *The Second World War*, London, 1982, pp. 255-256; Kettenacker, op.cit.
23. See Mastny, op.cit., pp. 308-310; Kettenacker, op.cit., esp. pp. 435-436.
24. *Cadogan Diaries*, op.cit., 3 May 1942, pp. 448-449.
25. See WSC to Eden, 6 October 1943, PREM 3/399/6; Carlton, op.cit., pp. 195-198.
26. WSC to Eden, 16 January 1944, PREM 3/399/6.
27. Author's emphasis, Eden to WSC, 25 January 1944, PREM 3/399/6.
28. See H. Feis, *Churchill, Roosevelt, Stalin*, Princeton University Press, 1974, first published in 1957, pp. 62-63; Carlton, op.cit., p. 199.
29. Meeting of the War Council, 3 March 1915, *CV* 3/1, pp. 610-612.
30. WSC, *The Second World War*, vol. 4, p. 336.
31. F. Pogue, op.cit., pp. 326-327.
32. Meeting with Molotov, 9 June 1942, PREM 3/333/8.
33. Meeting at the Kremlin, 12 August 1942, W.P.(42)373, CAB 66/28.
34. See above p. 207.
35. Minutes of a conference held at Cairo on August 4 1942, W.P.(42)372, 28 August 42, CAB 66/28.
36. WSC to C.O.S Committee, 16 November 1942, PREM 3/499/6.
37. Record of Meeting with Sir Archibald Clark-Kerr, 15 December 1942, C.O.S meeting (42)346, Confidential Annex, CAB 79/87.
38. WSC, *The Second World War*, vol. 4, p. 659.
39. War Cabinet discussion, 25 August 1942, W.M.(42)118, Confidential Annex, CAB 65/31.
40. House of Commons, 8 September 1942, 11 November 1942, SPHS, vol. 6, pp. 6665-6675, 6696-6709.
41. A. Eden to WSC, October 1942, "Proposals for a Policy," PREM 4/100/7; A. Eden, "The Four Power Plan," 8 November 1942, W. P.(42)516, PREM 4/100/7.
42. WSC to Eden, 18 October 1942, PREM 4/100/7.
43. Eden to WSC, 19 October 1942, PREM 4/100/7.
44. WSC to Eden, 21 October 1942, PREM 4/100/7.
45. See *SPHS*, 17 July 1919, vol. 3, pp. 2820-2822; WSC to Lloyd George (unsent letter), 17 February 1919, *CV* 4/1, pp. 544-546.
46. See Lord Moran, op.cit., p. 587; Carlton, op.cit., pp. 200-201; D. Dilks, *The Diaries of Sir A. Cadogan*, pp. 300-301; E. L. Woodward, *British Foreign Policy in The Second World War*, HMSO, London, 1962, p. XXVI.
47. Liddell Hart, *Strategy, The Indirect Approach*, pp. 335-336.
48. C. von Clausewitz, *On War*, pp. 87, 607.

49. Ibid., pp. 158-159, 605-610.
50. In his book on war and politics, Bernard Brodie examined how this Clausewitzian ideal had been realized during the twentieth century. In his opinion, Churchill was one of the few who had put it into practice (an issue addressed below). B. Brodie, *War and Politics*, Macmillan, New York, 1973.
51. WSC, *The World Crisis*, vol. 1, p. 464.
52. Ibid., vol. 2, pp. 1134-1135.
53. See "Oran, July 1940," in A. J. Marder, *From the Dardanelles to Oran*, esp. pp. 216-217, 220.
54. See A. Marder, *Operation "Menace," The Dakar Expedition and the Dudley North Affair*, pp. 13, 16-17, 25-26, 190.
55. See Defence Committee, 20 October 1941, CAB 69/8 (41)66; A. J. Marder, *Old Friends, New Enemies, The Royal Navy and the Imperial Japanese Navy, Strategic Illusions 1936–1941*, Oxford University Press, 1981, pp. 230-241.
56. WSC, *The Second World War*, vol. 3, p. 620.
57. von Clausewitz, *On War*, p. 87.
58. Author's emphasis, WSC to the C.O.S. Committee, 8 June 1942, CAB 66/26; C.O.S meeting, 8 June 1942, CAB 79/56 (42)51.
59. House of Commons, *SPHS*, 11 November 1942, vol. 6, pp. 6696-6709.
60. Howard, *The Mediterranean Strategy in The Second World War*, p. 63.
61. See above pp. 3, 35-36.
62. Eden, *The Reckoning*, pp. 441-442, see also pp. 272, 282, 350, 517.
63. Woodward, op. cit., pp. XLIII, XLVII, XLIX.
64. Ulam, op.cit., p. 322.
65. See R. Garthoff, *Soviet Military Doctrine*, The Free Press, Illinois, 1953, pp. 9-12, 53-56; J. L. Wallach, *Thorot Zvaiot*, (Hebrew "Military Theories"), Maarachot, Tel-Aviv, 1978, chs. 11, 12, esp. 238, 256-259; A. Rapoport's introduction in C. von Clausewitz, *On War*, Penguin, 1974, pp. 31-40; W. Hahlweg, "Clausewitz, Lenin and Communist Military Attitudes Today," *RUSI*, May 1960, pp. 221-225.
66. See Chapter 1, p. 21.
67. WSC, "The Unfinished Task," 19 November 1918, *CV* 4/1, p. 419.
68. WSC, *The World Crisis*, vol. 1, p. 462.
69. WSC, *The Aftermath*, pp. 22-29.
70. Ibid., pp. 120-121.

Chapter 9: "This Battle Has Been Forced upon Us": Overlord, 1943–1944

1. C.O.S Meeting, 19 July 1943, CAB 79/62 (43)165(0).
2. WSC to General Ismay for C.O.S Committee, 19 July 1943, PREM 3/333/19.
3. See below pp. 292-299.
4. U.S. Chiefs of Staff, "Strategic Concept for the Defeat of the Axis in Europe," 16 August 1943, CAB 80/74.
5. Combined Chiefs of Staff, "Strategic Concept for the Defeat of the Axis in Europe," 17 August 1943, CAB 80/74; Howard, *Grand Strategy*, vol. 4, pp. 559-571.
6. Ibid., p. 565.
7. Quadrant Conference, Minutes, 19 August 1943, CAB 80/74;
8. C.O.S.(Q)17, 19 August 1943, CAB 80/74.
9. Quadrant Conference, Minutes, 23 August 1943, CAB 80/74.
10. Smuts to WSC, 1 September 1943, 3 September 1943, PREM 3/344/1.
11. WSC to Smuts, 4 September 1943, PREM 3/344/1.

12. WSC, *The Second World War*, vol. 5, p. 128.
13. WSC to Smuts, 4 September 1943, PREM 3/344/1.
14. Smuts to WSC, 8 September 1943, 10 September 1943, PREM 3/344/1.
15. Quadrant, White House, Minutes, 9 September 1943, CAB 80/74; WSC, memorandum, 9 September 1943, CAB 80/74.
16. WSC to Chiefs of Staff, 14 September 1943, CAB 79/64.
17. WSC to Smuts, 11 September 1943, PREM 3/344/1.
18. A. Bryant, *Triumph in the West*, p. 50.
19. WSC to FDR, 7 October 1943, in Kimball, ed., *Churchill and Roosevelt, The Complete Correspondence*, vol. 2, pp. 498-499; J. Ehrman, *Grand Strategy*, vol. 5, HMSO, London, 1956, pp. 75-105; WSC, *The Second World War*, vol. 5, pp. 203-204.
20. Ismay, *Memoirs*, pp. 163, 322, 330-331.
21. C.O.S Meeting, 22 October 1943, CAB 79/66 (43)258(0).
22. FDR to WSC, 8 October 1943, in Kimball, ed., *Churchill and Roosvelt, The Complete Correspondence*, vol. 2, pp. 505-506.
23. Howard, *Grand Strategy*, vol. 4, p. 431.
24. J.I.C., "Probabilities of a German Collapse," 9 September 1943, J.I.C.(43) 367, CAB 66/42.
25. C.O.S Meeting, 14 September 1943, CAB 79/64 (43) 215(0); A. Eden, "The Future of Germany," 8 March 1943, CAB 66/34; 25 October 1943, W.P.(43)479, CAB 66/42.
26. J.I.C., "Effects of Bombing Offensive on German War Effort," 22 July 1943, J.I.C.(43)294, CAB 79/63. Joint Intelligence Sub-Committee, "The German Military Situation," 15 February 1943, CAB 66/34; J.I.C., "German Plans and Intentions During Summer and Autumn 1943," 20 April 1943, CAB 79/60; J.I.C., "German Plans and Intentions During Second Half of 1943," 3 August 1943, CAB 79/63; 14 August 1943, PREM 3/333/14; C. Portal, A Note, 24 June 1943, CAB 79/62.
27. Lord Cranborne to WSC, 5 October 1943, PREM 3/344/1.
28. King George to WSC, 14 October 1943, PREM 3/344/1; WSC to King George, 14 October 1943, PREM 3/344/1.
29. Brigadier Hollis to WSC, 14 October 1943, PREM 3/344/1.
30. WSC to Brigadier Hollis for C.O.S. Committee, 19 October 1943, PREM 3/344/2; WSC, "Relations of 'Overlord' to Mediterranean," 19 October 1943, CAB 80/75.
31. WSC to FDR, 17 October 1943, in WSC, *The Second World War*, vol. 5, p. 304.
32. C.O.S Meeting, 19 October 1943, CAB 79/66 (43)254(0).
33. Howard, *Grand Strategy*, vol. 4, pp. 564-565.
34. Bryant, *Triumph in the West*, pp. 55, 59.
35. C.O.S Meeting, 20 October 1943, Secretary Standard File, CAB 79/88 (43)255(0).
36. See Dill to C.O.S, 17 October 1943, in R. Parkinson, *A Day's March Nearer Home, The War History from Alamein to VE Day Based on the War Cabinet Papers of 1942 to 1945*, Hart-Davis, MacGibbon, London, 1974, p. 198.
37. WSC, *The Second World War*, vol. 5, p. 254.
38. WSC, *The Second World War*, vol. 5, book one, ch. 14, esp. pp. 253-255 and 344-346; A. Bryant, *Triumph in the West*, pp. 30–35, 47; M. Howard, *Grand Strategy*, vol. 4, p. 431; J. Ehrman, *Grand Strategy*, vol. 5, pp. 105-121.
39. See J. Ehrman, *Grand Strategy*, vol. 5, pp. 106-107, appendix VI, p. 554; Howard does not mention this meeting in his volume of *Grand Strategy*, or in his other study, *The Mediterranean Strategy in The Second World War*.

In the body of his work, John Ehrman makes only passing reference to some of the statements made at this meeting, which he interprets in accordance with the general thrust of the British interpretation on which I have already remarked. Admittedly, he does quote a short extract from the meeting in an appendix, in order to explain Churchill's attitude on the Balkans. But he does not cite the main discussions of this meeting dealing with the question of the relationship between the Mediterranean theater and the future invasion of western Europe. This discussion has also tended to escape the attention of additional British historians. Parkinson abridged and summarized discussions of the War Cabinet in two narrative works. Although he did not claim to advance a general thesis or interpretation, where the "second front" was concerned Parkinson did not refrain from supporting the claim advanced by Churchill and the official history. Deleted from the protocol, as reproduced in his book, are those inconvenient passages in which Churchill said that the agreed Anglo-American stategy was erroneous, and described what the British would do had they a free hand. (See Parkinson, *A Day's March Nearer Home*, pp. 161, 198-199). This meeting is not mentioned by another researcher, Bruce, who discusses the subject of the "second front" and whose opinion accords with the version put forward by Churchill and the authors of the official history. (See G. Bruce, *Second Front Now, The Road to D-Day*, MacDonald and James, London, 1979.)

40. Howard, *Grand Strategy*, vol. 4, p. 431.

41. See above p. 246.

42. Cf. WSC to FDR, 23 October 1943, PREM 3/344/2, to the same letter in WSC, *The Second World War*, vol. 5, pp. 311-314.

43. FDR to WSC, 26 October 1943, 11 November 1943, in Kimball, ed., *Churchill and Roosevelt, The Complete Correspondence*, vol. 2, pp. 563-564, 597.

44. WSC to FDR, 27 October 1943, in WSC, *The Second World War*, vol. 5, p. 315; WSC to FDR, 12 November 1943, ibid., vol. 5, pp. 319-320.

45. WSC, *The Second World War*, vol. 5, p. 311.

46. WSC to Eden, 26 October 1943, PREM 3/344/2; 27 October 1943, General Marshall to WSC, PREM 3/344/2; 28 October 1943, Joint Planning (43)377, CAB 79/67; C.O.S Meeting, 2 November 1943, CAB 79/67 (43)267(0).

47. WSC: "Future Operations in the European and Mediterranean Theatre," 20 November 1943, C.O.S ("Sextant")1, CAB 80/77; T. Ropp, *War in the Modern World*, Collier, 1985, first published in 1959, pp. 342-343.

48. See WSC, *The Second World War*, vol. 5, pp. 329-333.

49. Ibid., vol. 5, pp. 153-154.

50. See W. S. Dunn, *Second Front Now—1943*, chs. 14-16, esp. pp. 260-262, tables 15, 17, 23.

51. WSC, "Future Operations in the European and Mediterranean Theatre," 20 November 1943, op. cit; WSC, "Future Operations in the Aegean," 21 November 1943, CAB 80/77.

52. C.O.S Meeting, 9 November 1943, CAB 76/67 (43)274(0).

53. C.O.S, "Overlord and Mediterranean Operations," aide–mèmoire, 11 November 1943, PREM 3/344/2; author's emphasis.

54. See 14 August 1943, PREM 3/333/14.

55. Smuts, memorandum for the President and the Prime Minister, 14 November 1943, PREM 3/344/2.

56. WSC to Smuts, 15 November 1943, PREM 3/344/2.

57. Bryant, *Triumph in the West*, p. 41.

58. Kennedy, op. cit., p. 313.

59. See Ehrman, *Grand Strategy*, vol. 5, pp. 155-158, 165-166; Howard, *The Mediterranean Strategy in The Second World War*, p. 54; WSC, *The Second World War*, vol. 5, p. 328.

60. "Record of a Conversation Between the Prime Minister and Marshal Stalin at the Soviet Embassy at Teheran on 30th November, 1943," W. P.(44) 9, 7 January 1944,

CAB 66/45; Ehrman, *Grand Strategy*, vol. 5, pp. 176, 180-181; Bryant, *Triumph in the West*, p. 89.

61. WSC, "Supreme Commander of All Operations Against Germany," 28 December 1943, CAB 66/44.

62. See, 11, 14, 20 January 1944, PREM 3/396/10.

63. See Colville, op. cit., 5, 25 January 1944, pp. 463, 468.

64. See conference held at the Villa Taylor, Marrakech, 7 January 1944, C.O.S (44)35(0), CAB 80/78; Colville, op. cit., p. 468.

65. See Colville, op. cit., 4, 5 February 1944, p. 470; WSC, *The Second World War*, vol. 5, p. 488.

66. WSC, "Operations in South-East Asia and the Pacific," 16 February 1944, CAB 80/80.

67. Colville, op. cit., 4 April 1944, p. 483.

68. WSC to A. Cadogan, 19 April 1944, PREM 3/197/2; author's emphasis.

69. See also Kennedy, op. cit., p. 305.

70. See WSC, *The Second World War*, vol. 2, book one, ch. 13, esp. p. 254; vol. 3, pp. 655, 659-661; vol. 4, pp. 651, 659; vol. 5, pp. 253-255.

Alan Brooke's version is in Arthur Bryant, *The Turn of the Tide 1939–1943*, and in *Triumph in the West 1943–1946*, passim; see also Lord Ismay, *Memoirs*, passim; of all war memoirs published by senior British officers, Major-General J. Kennedy's is an exceptional one, but he was not a member of the first circle; see J. Kennedy, *The Business of War*, passim, esp. p. 305.

E.g., M. Howard, *Grand Strategy*, vol. 4, pp. 208, 421, 431, 565; J. Ehrman, *Grand Strategy*, vol. 5, pp. 105-121; and also M. Howard, *The Mediterranean Strategy in The Second World War*, passim.

For the opinion of U.S. official historians, see, R.M. Leighton, "Overlord versus the Mediterranean at the Cairo-Teheran Conferences," in K. R. Greenfield, ed., *Command Decisions*, Office of the Chief of Military History, Department of the Army, Washington, D.C., 1960, and, "Overlord Revisited: An Interpretation of American Strategy in the European War 1942–1944," *American Historical Review*, LXVIII, 4 July 1963; K. R. Greenfield, *American Strategy in World War II: A Reconsideration*, Baltimore, 1967, first published in 1963; R.W. Coakley, R. M. Leighton, *Global Logistics and Strategy 1943-1945*, Office of Military History, U.S. Army, Washington, D.C., 1968, pp. 25-30, esp. p. 25.

On Churchill's strategy, e.g., R. Lewin, *Churchill as Warlord,* Stein and Day, New York, 1973, passim, esp. p. 247; C. Baxter, "Winston Churchill: Military Strategist?" *Military Affairs*, vol. 47, no. 1, Feb. 1983; M. Gilbert, *Winston Churchill: Road to Victory, 1941–1945*, Houghton Mifflin, Boston, 1986, passim; and also Gilbert, "The Big Two," *New York Review of Books*, vol. 32, no. 2, February 14, 1985.

71. WSC, *The Second World War*, vol. 3, pp. 379-380, vol. 5, book two, ch. 16.

72. See above pp. 250-251; see also "A Record of a Conversation Between the Prime Minister and Marshal Stalin at the Soviet Embassy at Teheran on 30th November 1943," op.cit.

73. WSC, *The Second World War*, vol. 2, pp. 243ff.

74. See above pp. 260-261.

75. WSC, *The World Crisis*, vol. 1, p. 604; vol. 2, p. 840.

76. Defence Committee, 5 April 1944, CAB 69/6 (44)5; Defence Committee, 19 April 1944, CAB 69/6 (44)7; WSC, *The Second World War*, vol. 5, pp. 528-530.

77. WSC, *The Second World War*, vol. 5, p. 530; vol. 6, p. 18; Bryant, *Triumph in the West*, p. 182.

78. E.g., ibid., pp. 53-55; Ismay, op. cit., p. 297; Moran, op. cit., pp. 50-53; H. L. Stimson, *On Active Service in Peace and War*, Harper, New York, 1948, pp. 428-438, esp. p. 436; R. Lewin, *Churchill as Warlord*, pp. 224-225; J. Keegan, *The Face of*

Battle, Penguin, Harmondsworth, 1978, ch. 4; Howard, *Grand Strategy*, vol. 4, p. 561; Bruce, *Second Front Now!*, p. 69.

79. WSC, *The Second World War*, vol. 1, p. 384, vol. 5, pp. 582-583.
80. WSC, memorandum, 1 June 1915, *CV* 3/2, pp. 977ff.; Dundee, *SPHS*, 5 June 1915, vol. 3, pp. 2378ff.; WSC, memorandum, 18 June 1915, *CV* 3/2, pp. 1034-1041; Meeting of the Dardanelles Committee, 23 September 1915, *CV* 3/2, p. 1184; House of Commons, *SPHS*, 15 November 1915, vol. 3, pp. 2390ff.
81. See chapter 4.
82. See J. K. Galbraith's review of W. F. Kimball, ed., *Churchill and Roosevelt, The Complete Correspondence*, in the *Times Literary Supplement*, February 8, 1985.
83. WSC, Directive, 28 April 1941, PREM 3/296/2.
84. WSC to Wavell, 10 February 1942, in WSC, *The Second World War*, vol. 4, p. 100.
85. WSC, Operation Jupiter, 13 June 1942, C.O.S (42)168(0), CAB 80/63.
86. See below pp. 315-316; T. Sharp, *The Wartime Alliance and the Zonal Division of Germany*, Clarendon Press, Oxford, 1975, pp. 133-134.
87. E.g., C.O.S. Meeting, 9 April 1942, CAB 79/56; meeting with Molotov, 9 June 42, PREM 3/333/8.
88. House of Commons (secret session), *SPHS*, 25 June 1941, vol. 6, pp. 6431-6444.
89. See WSC, *The World Crisis*, vol. 2, pp. 900-906, 919.
90. WSC, *The Aftermath*, pp. 275, 445.
91. Kennedy, op. cit., pp. 105-107.
92. E.g., WSC to General Auchinleck, 20 July 1941, PREM 3/296/17.
93. House of Commons, 19 December 1940, *SPHS*, vol. 6, pp. 6316-6322.
94. See above p. 165.
95. WSC to Dill, 22 April 1941, *The Second World War*, vol. 3, p. 249; author's emphasis.
96. WSC, *The Second World War*, vol. 3, pp. 272-273; Lord Moran, op. cit., p. 604.
97. Colville, op. cit., 3 June 1941, 18 June 1941, pp. 394, 400-401; C. Barnett, *The Desert Generals*, pp. 76-77.
98. See *Cadogan Diaries*, op. cit, p. 360; 10 April 1941, pp. 370-371; 3 June 1941, p. 385; 24 April 1942, p. 449, 14 June 1942, p. 458.
99. Colville, op. cit., 28 September 1941, pp. 443-444.
100. See chapter 5; and also A. Danchev, "'Dilly-Dally' or Having the Last Word: Field Marshal Sir John Dill and Prime Minister Winston Churchill," *Journal of Contemporary History*, 22 (1987), pp. 21-44.
101. WSC to Eden, 13 August 1940, PREM 3/296/17; Colville, op. cit., 28 September 1941, p. 443.
102. Bryant, *The Turn of the Tide*, pp. 245, 275, 415; Gilbert, *Finest Hour*, vol. 6, p. 685; *Road to Victory*, pp. 844-845; Colvile, op. cit., 28 September 1941, pp. 443-444.
103. WSC, *The Second World War*, vol. 4, p. 92; Moran, op. cit., pp. 43-44.
104. See Parkinson, *Blood, Toil, Tears and Sweat*, pp. 370-371.
105. R. E. Sherwood, *Roosevelt and Hopkins*, Harper, New York, 1948, p. 523.
106. Defence Committee, 2 March 1942, CAB 69/4 (42)7.
107. Auchinleck to the War Office, 7 March 1942, PREM 3/296/18A; Lieutenant-General Nye to WSC, 22 March 1942, CAB 64/4.
108. WSC, Operation "Imperator," 8 June 1942, CAB 66/26.
109. WSC, *The Second World War*, vol. 4, pp. 383, 549-550.
110. Dill to the Chiefs of Staff, 7 July 1942, PREM 3/492/2.
111. WSC, "Review of the War Position," 21 July 1942, CAB 66/26.
112. Cripps to WSC, 2 July 1942, in WSC, *The Second World War*, vol. 4, pp.

395-396; C. Attlee to WSC, 10 July 1942, PREM 3/499/9.

113. WSC to Dominions Secretary (Attlee), 29 July 1942, PREM 3/499/9; author's emphasis.

114. Combined Chiefs of Staff Meeting (56th), 14 January 1943, CAB 80/67.

115. Bryant, vol. 1., p. 435.

116. See Dunn, *Second Front* Now—*1943*, ch. 13.

117. WSC to Stalin (Draft), 18 February 1943, PREM 3/333/3; the final draft was sent on March 11, 1943.

118. See above pp. 200-201

119. WSC, *The Second World War*, vol. 3, pp. 659-661, vol. 4, p. 659.

120. C.O.S Meeting, 19 October 1943, CAB 79/66 (43)254(0).

121. Bryant, *Triumph in the West*, p. 35.

122. See also R. Bennett, "Ultra and Some Command Decisions," in W. Laqueur, ed., *The Second World War*, pp. 218-235, esp. p. 227.

123. E.g., N. Dupuy, *A Genius for War: The German Army and General Staff, 1807–1945*, Englewood Cliffs, New Jersey, 1977; M. van Creveld, *Fighting Power: German and U.S. Army Performance, 1939–1945*, Westport, Connecticut, 1982; see also P. Kennedy, *The Rise and Fall of the Great Powers*, pp. 352-353.

124. See note 47 above.

125. See Douglas Orgill, *The Tank*, Heinemann, London, 1970, passim, esp. pp. 254-258; John Wheldon, *Machine Age Armies*, Abelard-Schuman, London, 1968, passim, esp. pp. 140-143.

126. E.g., W. S. Dunn, *Second Front* Now—*1943*; J. Grigg, *1943, The Victory That Never Was*, Hill and Wang, New York, 1980.

127. WSC, *The Second World War*, vol. 3, p. 673.

Chapter 10: Grand Strategy: The Soviet Menace and the End of the War, 1943–1945

1. WSC, *The Second World War*, vol. 4, pp. 709-711; Howard, *Grand Strategy*, vol. 4, pp. 376ff.

2. Lord Moran, op. cit., 30 January 1943, p. 105.

3. WSC, "Morning Thoughts, Note on Post-War Security," 1 February 1943, in Howard, *Grand Strategy*, vol. 4, appendix V, pp. 637-639.

4. Ibid., p. 376; Churchill's meetings with the Turks took place on January 30 and 31, while the memorandum was written on February 1. See also WSC, *The Second World War*, vol.4, pp. 711-712.

5. WSC, "Morning Thoughts," op. cit.

6. See Joint Intelligence Sub-Committee, 15 February 1942, op. cit.

7. President Roosevelt and Prime Minister Churchill to Premier Stalin, 26 January 1943, in WSC, *The Second World War*, vol. 4, pp. 742-743.

8. See above pp. 210-212.

9. 9 February 1943, PREM 3/333/3.

10. See PREM 3/333/3; Stalin to Churchill, 16 February 1943, in WSC, *The Second World War*, vol. 4, pp. 745-746.

11. Eden to WSC, 17 February 1943, PREM 3/333/3.

12. See 22 February 1943, CAB 69/5; Eden to WSC, 26 February 1943, PREM 3/333/3.

13. See 24 February 1943, PREM 3/333/3.

14. WSC to Stalin (draft), 18 February 1943, PREM 3/333/3.

15. WSC to Stalin, 11 March 1943, PREM 3/333/3; see also WSC, *The Second*

World War, vol. 4, pp. 747-750.

16. See above pp. 216-218.

17. War Cabinet Discussion, 18 March 1943, W. M. (43)42, Confidential Annex, CAB 65/37.

18. A. Eden, "The Future of Germany," 8 March 1943, CAB 66/34.

19. See Eden, *The Reckoning*, p. 373; Kettenacker, op. cit., p. 448; Parkinson, *A Day's March Nearer Home*, pp. 92-93.

20. Carlton, op. cit., pp. 214-215; Parkinson, *A Day's March Nearer Home*, pp. 92-95.

21. *Record of a conversation at the British Embassy*, Washington, 22 May 1943, CAB 66/37; Halifax to Foreign Office, 11 June 1943, CAB 66/37.

22. See *Cadogan Diaries*, 7 February 1943, p. 513.

23. Eden, "Post-War Settlement," 1 July 1943, CAB 66/38.

24. WSC to Halifax, 1 March 1941, PREM 4/100/8.

25. See *Cadogan Diaries*, 7 July 1944, p. 465; 4 August 1944, pp. 653-654.

26. Hughes, "Winston Churchill and the Formation of the United Nations Organization," op. cit., p. 194.

27. Stalin to WSC, 24 June 1943, PREM 3/333/5.

28. WSC to Clark-Kerr (Moscow), 16 June 1943, PREM 3/333/5; WSC to Stalin, 26 June 1943, PREM 3/333/5.

29. WSC to FDR, 29 June 1943, PREM 3/333/5.

30. Clark-Kerr to WSC, 22 June 1943, 1 July 1943, PREM 3/333/5.

31. C.O.S. Meeting, 15 December 1943, Confidential Annex, CAB 79/87 (42)346.

32. Eden (Moscow) to WSC, 29 October 1943, PREM 3/344/2.

33. See above pp. 200-201, 206-209.

34. The U.S. researcher Walter Scott Dunn reached the conclusion that France could have been invaded in 1943. In his opinion, Churchill and Roosevelt were aware of the fact, but at Casablanca preferred to postpone opening the "second front" because they wanted to weaken the Soviet Union. (W. S. Dunn, op. cit., pp. 1-3, 267-268). It is only right to recall that in his own book Churchill emphasizes his insistence that the decision-making process be conducted in writing (see above p. 126). Had such an important decision been discussed and taken, it would surely have left visible traces in the documents.

35. Smuts to WSC, 20 August 1943, in WSC, *The Second World War*, vol. 5, p. 537; Smuts to WSC, 1 September 1943, PREM 3/344/1; Smuts to WSC, 3 September 1943, PREM 3/344/1; Lord Harlech to WSC, 3 September 1943, PREM 3/344/1.

36. See 3 September 1943, Smuts to WSC, op. cit.; see above pp. 246-247, 249-250, 256.

37. See Quadrant conference, 23 August 1943, Minutes, CAB 80/74; Sharp, op. cit., pp. 29-32.

38. Ibid, p. 32.

39. WSC to Smuts, 4 September 1943, PREM 3/344/1.

40. Quoted in Parkinson, *A Day's March Nearer Home*, pp. 194-195.

41. *Cadogan Diaries*, 5 October 1943, p. 564; J. Harvey, *The Diaries of Oliver Harvey*, Collins, 1978, 6 October 1943, p. 304.

42. WSC to Eden, 6 October 1943, 3/399/6; notes by the Prime Minister for Foreign Secretary at the forthcoming meeting, 11 October 1943, CAB 66/41; Woodward, op. cit., pp. 250-251.

43. Mastny, op. cit., pp. 109-110.

44. See above pp. 250-252.

45. M. Howard, *The Mediterranean Strategy in The Second World War*, pp. 52-53, and his introduction in C. Wilmot's book, *The Struggle for Europe*, Collins, London, 1965 (first published in 1952); J. Ehrman, *Grand Strategy*, vol. 5, pp. 111-112, 393.

46. WSC to Eden, 20 December 1943, in WSC, *The Second World War*, vol. 5, pp. 450-451.
47. F. King, "Allied Negotiations and the Dismemberment of Germany," in W. Laqueur, ed., *The Second World War*, p. 362; Mastny, op. cit., pp. 127-129, 132.
48. Parkinson, *A Day's March Nearer Home*, p. 93.
49. See Woodward, op. cit., pp. 253-255; Mastny, op. cit., pp. 129-132.
50. Lord Moran, op. cit., pp. 160-161.
51. See Eden (Moscow) to WSC, 29 October 1943, PREM 3/344/2; Ismay, *Memoirs*, p. 328.
52. WSC to Eden, 16 January 1944, PREM 3/399/6.
53. See Chapter 8 above.
54. Eden to WSC, 25 January 1944, PREM 3/399/6.
55. See House of Commons, 22 February 1944, 24 May 1944, *SPHS* vol. 7, pp. 6881-6894.
56. Mastny, op.cit., p. 170.
57. House of Commons, 24 May 1944, *SPHS* vol. 7, pp. 6930-6945.
58. See Lord Moran, op. cit., pp. 326-327.
59. See Colville, op. cit., 4 January 1944, p. 462.
60. Lord Moran, op. cit., p. 281; see also WSC to FDR, 6 January 1944, in WSC, *The Second World War*, vol. 5, p. 452.
61. See above pp. 110, 117-118, 133.; WSC, *The Second World War*, vol. 1, pp. 448-449.
62. Kettenacker, op. cit., p. 439.
63. See WSC, Cabinet Memorandum, draft, 29 August 1920, *CV* 4/2, pp. 1190-1199.
64. See Colville, op. cit., 29 February 1944, p. 475; 14 April 1944, p. 484.
65. Defence Committee, 3 February 1944, CAB 69/6 (44)4; Colville, op.cit., 4 March 1944, p. 476.
66. WSC to Eden, 4 May 1944, PREM 3/66/7; see also War Cabinet Discussion, 11 May 1944, CAB 65/46 W.M.(44)63.
67. Eden to WSC, 9 May 1944, PREM 3/66/7.
68. Ibid.
69. See WSC to FDR, 31 May 1944, pp. 502-503, 11 June 1944, pp. 527-529, 23 June 1944, pp.539-541; FDR to WSC, 10 June 1944, 22 June 1944, in Kimball, ed., *Churchill and Roosevelt, The Complete Correspondence*, vol. 3, pp. 177, 201.
70. In his memoirs, Eden mixed truth with untruth when recording that Churchill preferred to support those movements rather than their rivals—because of their military effectiveness. In so doing, he ignored the clash between the short-term goal, i.e., victory over Germany, and the long-term aim, which was the prevention of the ascendancy of the Communists, about which the Foreign Office warned. See Eden, *The Reckoning*, pp. 470-471.
71. Eden, "Memorandum on Soviet policy in the Balkans," 7 June 1944, CAB 66/51.
72. WSC to Eden, 9 July 1944, PREM 3/66/7.
73. Ehrman, *Grand Strategy*, vol. 5, pp. 266-267.
74. Ibid., p. 393.
75. See above p. 245.
76. WSC to FDR, 1 July 1944, in Kimball, ed., *Churchill and Roosevelt, The Complete Correspondence*, vol. 3, pp. 227-229.
77. FDR to WSC, 28 June 1944, 1 July 1944, ibid., vol. 3, pp. 213-214, 232.
78. Bryant, *Triumph in the West*, p. 223; Kennedy, op. cit., pp. 333-334.
79. War Cabinet Discussion, 7 July 1944, Confidential Annex, CAB 65/47 (44)88.
80. Eden, "Soviet policy in Europe," 9 August 1944, CAB 66/53.

81. See Parkinson, *A Day's March Nearer Home*, pp. 352-359.
82. Ehrman, *Grand Strategy*, vol. 5, p. 376.
83. Colville, op. cit., 21 August 1944, p. 504; G. Ross, "Foreign Office Attitudes to the Soviet Union 1941-45," op. cit.
84. See Minutes of a meeting in the British Embassy, Rome, 21 August 1944, Confidential Annex, PREM 3/275/1.
85. WSC, *The Second World War*, vol. 6, pp. 105-107.
86. Smuts to WSC, 30 August 1944, PREM 3/275/8.
87. WSC to FDR, 28 August 1944, 31 August 1944, PREM 3/275/1; FDR to WSC, 31 August 1944, 4 September 1944, PREM 3/275/1.
88. Brooke, Portal, Cunningham to WSC, 7 September 1944, PREM 3/275/2.
89. WSC to General Ismay for C.O.S Committee, 9 September 1944, PREM 3/275/2.
90. C.O.S Committee to WSC, 9 September 1944, PREM 3/275/2.
91. WSC to General Wilson, 13 September 1944, PREM 3/275/2; WSC to War Cabinet, 13 September 1944, PREM 3/275/2.
92. See Alan Brooke to C.O.S Committee, 8 October 1944, PREM 3/275/3; Minutes of a Meeting held in Sachmed's Villa, 8 October 1944, Naples, PREM 3/275/4; WSC to FDR, 10 October 1944, PREM 3/275/3.
93. FDR to WSC, 16 October 1944, PREM 3/275/3.
94. C.O.S Committee to Alan Brooke and WSC (Cairo), 17 October 1944, PREM 3/275/3.
95. Brooke, Portal, Cunningham, "Mediterranean Strategy,"18 January 1945, PREM 3/275/5.
96. C.O.S Meeting, 23 January 1945, PREM 3/275/5 (45)25.
97. See chapter 7, esp. pp. 222-224.
98. Ehrman, *Grand Strategy*, vol. 5, pp. 401-402.
99. WSC, *The Second World War*, vol. 6, pp. 57-66, 100, 126, and also book one, chs. 4-8.
100. C. Wilmot, *The Struggle for Europe*, op. cit., pp. 713-717; see also W. G. F. Jackson, *Overlord, Normandy 1944*, Davis-Poynter, London, 1978, pp. 219-224.
101. Lord Moran, op.cit., p. 554.
102. Howard, *The Mediterranean Strategy in The Second World War*, pp. 61-62.
103. See chapter 10, note 45.
104. See also Howard's introduction in Wilmot's book of the 1965 edition.
105. See above pp. 247-248.
106. See also, Ehrman, *Grand Strategy*, vol. 5, p. 393; M. Howard, *The Mediterranean Strategy*, pp. 65-67.
107. See also Howard, *The Mediterranean Strategy in The Second World War*, pp. 66-67.
108. Ibid., p. 67.
109. See Mastny, op. cit., pp. 236-238, 240; WSC, *The Second World War*, vol. 6, pp. 348-349.
110. Barker, *Churchill and Eden at War*, St. Martin's Press, New York, 1978, p. 282.
111. Liddell Hart, *History of The Second World War*, pp. 583-586; van Creveld, *Supplying War*, pp. 222-223, 225.
112. See Ehrman, *Grand Strategy*, vol. 5, pp. 379-381; Liddell Hart, *History of The Second World War*, pp. 587-588.
113. Montgomery, op.cit., pp. 255-256.
114. Liddell Hart, *History of The Second World War*, pp. 583, 593-594.
115. Van Creveld, *Supplying War*, pp. 227-230.
116. WSC, *The Second World War*, vol. 6, pp. 190-192.

117. Ehrman, *Grand Strategy*, vol. 5, p. 381.
118. See above p. 257.
119. Ehrman, *Grand Strategy*, vol. 5, pp. 395-401.
120. Ibid., p. 401.
121. Minutes of a meeting in the British Embassy, 21 August 1944, Rome, op. cit.
122. Ehrman, *Grand Strategy*, vol. 5, pp. 401-402.
123. WSC, *The Second World War*, vol. 6, p. 148.
124. Colville, op. cit., 8 September 1944, p. 511.
125. See van Creveld, *Supplying War*, ch. 7.
126. See Carlton, op. cit., pp. 239-242.
127. Lord Moran, op. cit., 22 September 1944, p. 208.
128. Parkinson, *A Day's March Nearer Home*, pp. 374-375.
129. Lord Moran, op.cit., pp. 198-201; Kettenacker, op.cit., p. 452; G. Ross, "Foreign Office Attitudes to the Soviet Union 1941–45," op. cit., pp. 262-266; Bryant, *Triumph in the West*, 27 July 1944, p. 242; Parkinson, *A Day's March Nearer Home*, pp. 385-386.
130. Colville, op. cit., 8 October 1944, p. 523.
131. WSC, memorandum, 12 October 1944, PREM 3/66/7.
132. War Cabinet discussion, 24 July 1944, Confidential Annex, CAB 65/47.
133. House of Commons, 27 October 1944, 15 December 1944, *SPHS*, vol. 7, pp. 7013–7018, 7064-7072.
134. Airfield, Moscow, *SPHS*, vol. 7, 19 October 1944, pp. 7012-7013; House of Commons, 27 October 1944, *SPHS*, vol. 7, pp. 7013-7018.
135. See Parkinson, *A Day's March Nearer Home*, pp. 402-403.
136. Ibid., p. 404.
137. WSC to FDR, 6 December 1944, 8 January 1945, in Kimball, ed., *Churchill and Roosevelt, The Complete Correspondence*, vol. 3, pp. 434-436, 501-502.
138. Mastny, op. cit., pp. 238-244.
139. See Parkinson, *A Day's March Nearer Home*, pp. 452-453.
140. Ibid., pp. 464ff.
141. WSC, *The Second World War*, vol. 6, book two, ch. 8, esp. pp. 455-456.
142. Ibid., vol. 6, book two, ch. 17; B. Brodie, *War and Politics*, passim.; Montgomery, op. cit., pp. 296-298.
143. See Minutes of Meeting, 18 January 1943, Casablanca, CAB 80/67.
144. See T. Ben-Moshe, "The Origins of the Declaration of the Policy of Unconditional Surrender—A New Interpretation," unpublished study, The Hebrew University, 1981.
145. See WSC, "Unconditional Surrender," 10 January 1944, PREM 3/197/2; House of Commons, 24 May 1944, *SPHS* vol. 7, pp. 6930-6945; WSC, *The Second World War*, vol. 4, pp. 688-691; A. Armstrong, *Unconditional Surrender*, Greenwood Press, Westport, Connecticut, 1974, pp. 20ff., 34.
146. See Chapter 3 above.
147. WSC, *The Second World War*, vol. 2, pp. 261-262; A. J. P. Taylor, *English History 1914–1945*, pp. 595-596.
148. Defence Committee, 3 April 1941, CAB 69/2 (41)11.
149. Armstrong, op. cit., pp. 155-157.
150. See Knatchbull-Hugessen to Foreign Office, 9 August 1943, PREM 4/100/8; WSC's Notes, 14 August 1943, 4/100/8; telegram from Admiral Kelly, naval attaché, 27 November 1943, Ankara, PREM 3/193/5.
151. Eden to Foreign Office, 30 November 1943, PREM 3/197/2; WSC to Eden, 23 December 1943, PREM 3/197/2.
152. WSC to FDR, 1 January 1944, PREM 3/197/2; FDR to WSC, 6 January 1944,

PREM 3/193/5.
153. J.I.C., "Unconditional Surrender," 7 January 1944, CAB 66/45.
154. See C.O.S., "Unconditional Surrender," 5 February 1944, CAB 80/78; A. Eden, "Unconditional Surrender," 19 February 1944, CAB 66/47; A. Cadogan to WSC, April 1944, PREM 3/197/2.
155. WSC, "Unconditional Surrender," 10 January 1944, PREM 3/197/2; WSC to Eden, 9 February 1944, PREM 3/197/2; WSC to Cadogan, 19 April 1944, PREM 3/197/2.
156. See *Parliamentary Debates (Hansard)*, 18 July 1944, vol. 402, pp. 54ff., 24 October 1944, vol. 404, pp. 55-56, 18 January 1945, vol. 407, p. 451.
157. See M. Balfour, "Another Look at Unconditional Surrender," *International Affairs*, 1970, no. 4.
158. *Hansard*, 30 November 1944, vol. 406, p. 165.
159. See Armstrong, op. cit., pp. 94-96.
160. See Mastny, op. cit., pp. 73-84, 145-156; Lord Hankey, *Politics, Trials and Errors*, Pen-in-Hand, Oxford, 1950, p. 32
161. See Joint Intelligence Sub-Committee: "The German Military Situation," 15 February 1943, CAB 66/34; J.I.C., "German Plans and Intentions During Summer and Autumn 1943," 20 April 1943, CAB 79/60; J.I.C.,"German Plans and Intentions During Second Half of 1943," 3 August 1943, CAB 79/63; 14 August 1943, PREM 3/333/14.
162. Eden, "The Future of Germany," 8 March 1943, CAB 66/34.
163. Lord Moran, op. cit., 5 July 1953, pp. 445-446.
164. See above p. 257.
165. See Mastny, op. cit., p. 150.
166. See Sharp, *The Wartime Alliance and the Zonal Division of Germany*, pp. 12-16.
167. Ibid., p. 7.
168. WSC, *The Second World War*, vol. 6, pp. 507-508.
169. WSC to Eden, 20 December 1943, in WSC, *The Second World War*, vol. 5, pp. 450-451; see above p. 228. Defence Committee, 3 February 1944, CAB 69/6 (44)4; Carlton, op. cit., p. 193.
170. See Sharp, op. cit., p. 4; Kettenacker, op. cit., p. 451.
171. See Sharp, op. cit., pp. 29-33.
172. See also G. Ross, "Foreign Office Attitudes to the Soviet Union 1941–45," op. cit., esp. pp. 255-256, 264; Kettenacker, op. cit., pp. 450-452.
173. Post-Hostilities Planning Sub-Committee, "Military Occupation of Germany: System of Occupation," 6 September 1943, CAB 79/64.
174. Lord Moran, op. cit., p. 733.
175. See also Sharp, op. cit., p. 7.
176. WSC, *The Second World War*, vol. 6, p. 510; Sharp, op. cit., p. 28.
177. Ibid., pp. 110-113.
178. Montgomery, op. cit., pp. 296-297.
179. WSC to Eden, 19 April 1945, in WSC, *The Second World War*, vol. 6, pp. 515-516.
180. Sharp, op. cit., pp. 120-125, 134; F. Pogue, *The Supreme Command, United States Army in World War II, The European Theater of Operation*, Office of the Chief of Military History, Washington D.C., 1954, pp. 441-447; Eisenhower, op. cit., pp. 437-438.
181. Pogue, *The Supreme Command*, p. 446.
182. Sharp, op. cit., pp. 122-125; Pogue, *The Supreme Command*, p. 445.
183. WSC to Eden, 4 May 1945, in WSC, *The Second World War*, vol. 6, pp. 502-503.

Conclusions: Churchill in War and Peace

1. WSC, *The Second World War*, vol. 1, p. IV-V; vol. 6, pp. V, 503.
2. Kettenacker, op. cit., p. 449.
3. Rhodes James, *Churchill: A Study in Failure 1900-1939*, p. 441.
4. Brodie, *War and Politics*, p. 37.
5. For example, Roskill, *Churchill and the Admirals*, p. 282; Lewin, *Churchill as Warlord*, ch. 11.
6. See, for example, M. A. Stoler, "From Continentalism to Globalism: General Stanley D. Embick, the Joint Strategic Survey Committee, and the Military View of American National Policy during The Second World War," *Diplomatic History*, vol. 6, no. 3, 1982.
7. *The New Encyclopaedia Britannica*, 15th Edition, 1988, vol. 16, p. 376.
8. M. Ashley, *Churchill as Historian*, p. 231.
9. Lord Boothby, *Recollection of a Rebel*, London, 1978, pp. 183-184.
10. Lord Moran, op. cit., 28 November 1954, p. 641, 8 June 1959 pp. 790-791.
11. Colville, op. cit., 6 September 1944, p. 509.
12. Quoted in E. L. Woodward, *British Foreign Policy in The Second World War*, HMSO, London, 1971, vol. 3, p. 109.
13. See also, J. H. Plumb, "The Historian," in A. J. P. Taylor, ed., *Churchill: Four Faces and the Man*, op. cit., p. 147.
14. A. J. P. Taylor, *English History 1914-1945*, p. 771.
15. See above, ch. 9, note 70; and also P. Calvocoressi, G. Wint, *Total War*, Penguin, Harmondsworth, 1982, pp. 336-347, esp. p. 337.
16. A. J. P. Taylor, *English History 1914-1945*, p. 29.
17. Plumb, "The Historian," op. cit., p. 148.
18. Ibid, pp. 148-149.
19. The force of this self-delusion can be discerned through an anecdote about Edward VIII's abdication. In *The Second World War*, when he dealt with the affair, Churchill quoted what he had said, according to him, on the spur of the moment in his speech at the opening assembly of the movement "Arms and the Covenant," on December 3, 1936. According to the record of his speech and the testimony of people who were there, however, it emerges that he was earnestly begged by the heads of the movement not to refer to the affair and, with obvious dissatifaction, he agreed to their request. He did not mention the affair on the evening in question (Rhodes James, *Churchill: A Study in Failure 1900-1939*, pp. 346-348). Many years later, his urge to say what he had to say about the affair, the urge repressed that evening, found an outlet in his memory and in his book. Whence it follows that Churchill's memory was not absolutely trustworthy when there was a conflict between what he had wanted and what the actual results were. Churchill himself admitted—where he had discussed the unconditional surrender policy—that "as my own memory has proved defective on some points, it will be well to state the facts as my records reveal them. . . . Memoirs of the war may be vivid and true, but should never be trusted without verification, especially where the sequence of events is concerned." (WSC, *The Second World War*, vol. 4, pp. 685, 686-687).
20. See Chapters 2 and 3 above; and also R. Prior, *Churchill's "World Crisis" as History*, p. 279.

Bibliography

Primary Sources

1. R. Rhodes James, ed., *Winston Churchill, His Complete Speeches 1897-1963*, 8 vols., Chelsea House Publishers, New York, 1974.
2. *Companion Volumes* of Documents to the official biography of Winston S. Churchill by R. S. Churchill and M. Gilbert, 5 vols., Heinemann, London, 1967–1982
    vol. 1, parts 1, 2, 1874–1900
    vol. 2, parts 1, 2, 3, 1900–1914
    vol. 3, parts 1, 2, 1914–1916
    vol. 4, parts 1, 2, 3, 1917–1922
    vol. 5, parts 1, 2, 3, 1922–1939
3. Documents 1940–1945, Public Record Office, London
    PREM 3, Operational Papers, Files of the Prime Minister's office dealing with defence and operational subjects.
    PREM 4, Confidential Papers, Files of the Prime Minister's office dealing for the most part with civil and political matters.
    CAB 65, War Cabinet Minutes.
    CAB 66, 67, War Cabinet Memoranda.
    CAB 69, War Cabinet Defence Committee (Operations), Minutes and Papers.
    CAB 79, Chiefs of Staff Committee, Minutes of Meetings and Papers.
    CAB 80, Chiefs of Staff Committee, Memoranda.
4. W. S. Churchill's books:
    The Story of the Malakand Field Force, Longmans, 1898.
    The River War, 2 vols., Longmans, 1899.
    Savrola, Longmans, 1900.
    London to Ladysmith, Longmans, 1900.
    Ian Hamilton's March, Longmans, 1900.
    The World Crisis 1911-1918, 2 vols., Odhams Press, London, 1938, first published between 1923-1926.
    The Aftermath, a Sequel to *The World Crisis*, Macmillan, 1944 (first published in 1929).
    My Early Life, Odhams, London, 1965 (first published in 1930.)
    The World Crisis, The Eastern Front, Thornton Butterworth, London, 1931.
    Painting as a Pastime, Penguin, 1965 (first published in 1932).
    Thoughts and Adventures, Macmillan, 1943 (first published in 1932.)

Marlborough, His Life and Times, 4 vols., G. Harrap, London, new edition revised, published between 1934-1938.
The Second World War, Houghton Mifflin, Boston, 6 vols., 1948-1953. *A History of the English Speaking Peoples*, 4 vols., Cassell 1962 (first published in 1956).

Selected Secondary Sources

Armstrong, A., *Unconditional Surrender*, Greenwood Press, Westport, CT, 1974.
Ashley, M., *Churchill as Historian*, Secker and Warburg, London, 1968.
Aspinall-Oglander, Brigadier General C. F., History of the Great War, Military Operations, *Gallipoly*, 2 vols., Heinemann, 1932.
Balfour, M., "Another Look at Unconditional Surrender," *International Affairs*, 1970, no.4.
Barker, E., *Churchill and Eden at War*, St. Martin's Press, New York, 1978.
Barnett, C., *The Swordbearers: Studies in Supreme Command in the First World War*, Penguin, 1966.
——*Britain and Her Army 1509–1970*, W. Morrow, N.Y., 1970.
——*The Collapse of British Power*, Eyre Methuen, London, 1972.
——*The Desert Generals*, Pan Books, London, 1983.
Baxter, C., "'Winston Churchill: Military Strategist?'" *Military Affairs* (February 1983).
Ben-Moshe, T., "Liddell Hart and the Israel Defence Forces—A Reappraisal," *Journal of Contemporary History*, vol. 16, no. 2, 1981.
Berlin, I., "Mr. Churchill in 1940," J. Murray, London, first published in *The Alantic Monthly*, 1949.
Bialer, U., *The Shadow of the Bomber, the Fear of Air Attack and British Politics 1932–39*, Royal Historical Society, London, 1980.
——"The British Chiefs of Staffs and the 'Limited Liability Formula' of 1938," *Military Affairs* (April 1978).
Bond, B., *British Military Policy Between the Two World Wars*, Clarendon Press, Oxford, 1980.
——Liddell Hart —*A Study of His Military Thought*, London, 1977.
Boothby, Lord, *My Yesterday, Your Tomorrow*, Hutchinson, London, 1962.
——*Recollection of a Rebel*, London, 1978.
Brodie, B., *War and Politics*, Macmillan, New York, 1973.
Bruce, G., *Second Front Now, The Road to D-Day*, MacDonald and James, London, 1979.
Bryant, A., *The Turn of the Tide, 1939–1943, A Study Based on the Diaries and Autobiographical Notes of Field Marshal The Viscount Alanbrooke*, The Reprint Society, London, 1958.
——*Triumph in the West 1943–1946, A Study Based on the Diaries and Autobiographical Notes of Field Marshal The Viscount Alanbrooke*, Collins, London, 1959.
Bullock, A., *Hitler, A Study in Tyranny*, Penguin, 1975.
Carlton, D., *Anthony Eden*, Allen Lane, 1981.
Coakley, R. W., and Leighton, R. M., *Global Logistics and Strategy 1943–1945*, Office of Military History, U. S. Army, Washington, D.C., 1968.
Colville, J., *The Fringes of Power: Downing Street Diaries 1939–1955*, Hodder and Stoughton, London, 1985.
Connell, J., *Wavell, Scholar and Soldier*, Collins, London, 1964.

Corbett, J. S. *Some Principles of Maritime Strategy*, Longmans, 1918, first published in 1911.
Cruickshank, C., *Greece 1940–1941*, Davis-Poynter, London, 1976.
Danchev, A., "'Dilly-Dally,' or Having the Last Word: Field Marshal Sir John Dill and Prime Minister Winston Churchill," *Journal of Contemporary History*, vol. 22(1987), pp. 21-44.
Dilks, D., ed., *The Diaries of Sir Alexander Cadogan 1938–1945*, Cassell, London, 1971.
Dunn, W. S., *Second Front Now—1943*, Alabama University Press, University, 1980.
Dupuy, N., *A Genius for War: The German Army and General Staff, 1807–1945*, Englewood Cliffs, N.J., 1977.
Eden, A., *The Eden Memoirs, The Reckoning*, Cassel, London, 1965.
Eisenhower, D., *Crusade in Europe*, Permabooks, New York, 1952.
Feis, H., *Churchill, Roosevelt, Stalin*, Princeton University Press, 1974, first published in 1957.
French, D., "The Meaning of Attrition, 1914–1916," *English Historical Review*, April 1988.
Gilbert, M., *Finest Hour, Winston S. Churchill 1939–1941*, vol. 6, Heinemann, London, 1983.
———*Winston Churchill: Road to Victory 1941–1945*, vol. 7, Houghton Mifflin, Boston, 1986.
Gooch, J., *The Plans of War, The General Staff and British Military Strategy C. 1900–1916*, Routledge and Kegan Paul, London.
Grand Strategy, HMSO, London, 6 vols., 1956–1976:
    Gibbs, N. H., vol. 1 (to September 1939), 1976;
    Butler, J., vol. 2 (September 1939-June 1941), 1957;
    Gwyer, J. M., vol. 3, part 1, J. Butler, vol. 3, part 2, (June 1941–August 1942), 1964;
    Howard, M., vol. 4 (August 1942–September 1943), 1972;
    Ehrman, J., vol. 5 (August 1943–September 1944), 1956;
    Ehrman, J., vol. 6 (October 1944–August 1945), 1956.
Greenfield, K., *American Strategy in World War II: A Reconsideration*, The John Hopkins Press, Baltimore, 1963.
Grigg, J., *1943—The Victory That Never Was*, Hill and Wang, New York, 1980.
Hankey, M., *The Supreme Command*, 2 vols., Allen and Unwin, London, 1961.
———*Politics, Trials, and Errors*, Pen-in-Hand, Oxford, 1950.
Harvey, J., ed., *The War Diaries of Oliver Harvey*, Collins, London, 1978.
Higgins, T., *Winston Churchill and the Second Front 1940-3*, Oxford University Press, 1957.
———*Churchill and the Dardanelles*, Heinemann, London, 1963
Hinsley, F., et al., *British Intelligence in the Second World War, Its Influence on Strategy and Operations*, 4 vols., HMSO, London, 1979-1990.
Howard, M., ed., *Soldiers and Governments*, Eyre & Spottiswoode, London, 1957.
———*The Mediterranean Strategy in The Second World War*, F. A. Praeger, New York, 1968.
———*The Continental Commitment*, Penguin, 1974.
———"The British Way in Warfare - A Reappraisal," J. Cape, 1974.
———*War and the Liberal Conscience*, Rutgers University Press, New Jersey, 1978.
Hughes, E. J., "Winston Churchill and the Formation of the United Nations Organization," *Journal of Contemporary History*, vol. 9, no. 4, 1974.
Ismay, H., *Memoirs*, Heinemann, London, 1960.
Keegan, J., *Six Armies in Normandy*, Penguin, 1983.
Kennedy, J., *The Business of War, The War Narrative of Major-General Sir John*

Kennedy, Hutchinson, London, 1957.
Kennedy, P., *The Rise and Fall of British Naval Mastery*, Allen Lane, London, 1976.
———*Strategy and Diplomacy 1870–1945*, Fontana, 1983.
———*The Rise and Fall of the Great Powers*, Unwin Hyman, London, 1988.
Kettenacker, L., "The Anglo-Soviet Alliance and the Problem of Germany 1941–1945," *Journal of Contemporary History*, vol. 17, 1982, 435-458.
Kimball, W. F., ed., *Churchill and Roosevelt, The Complete Correspondence*, Princeton University Press, Princeton, 3 vols., 1987.
Laqueur, W., ed., *The Second World War*, London, 1982.
Leighton, R. M., "'Overlord Revisited: An Interpretation of American Strategy in the European War 1942-1944,'" *American Historical Review*, LXVIII, 4, July 1963.
Leutze, J., "The Secret of the Churchill-Roosevelt Correspondence, September 1939–May 1940," *Journal of Contemporary History*, vol. 10, no. 3.
Lewin, R., *Churchill as Warlord*, Stein and Day, New York, 1973.
Liddell Hart, B., *Strategy, The Indirect Approach*, Faber, London, 1967 (first published in 1929).
———*The British Way in Warfare*, MacMillan, New York, 1933.
———*Europe in Arms*, Faber and Faber, London, 1937.
———*The Defence of Britain*, Faber and Faber, London, 1939.
———*History of the First World War*, Pan Books, London, 1970, (first published in 1930).
———*History of the Second World War*, Pan Books, London, 1970.
Luvaas, J., *The Education of an Army*, Cassell, London, 1965.
Macleod, R., Kelly, D., eds., *The Ironside Diaries 1937–40*, Constable, London, 1962.
Mahan, A. T., *The Influence of Sea Power Upon History, 1660–1783*, Hill and Wang, New York, 1983 (first published in 1890).
Marder, A. J., *From the Dreadnought to Scapa Flow, The Royal Navy in the Fisher Era 1904–1919*, 5 vols., Oxford University Press, London, 1961–1970.
———"The Royal Navy and the Ethiopian Crisis of 1935–6," *American Historical Review*, vol. 75, #5, 1969/70, pp. 1327-1356.
———"The Influence of History on Sea Power: The Royal Navy and the Lessons of 1914-1918," *Pacific Historical Review*, November 1972.
———*From the Dardanelles to Oran*, Oxford University Press, London, 1974.
———*Operation Menace, The Dakar Expedition and the Dudley North Affair*, Oxford University Press, London, 1976.
———*Old Friends, New Enemies, The Royal Navy and the Imperial Japanese Navy, Strategic Illusions 1936–1941*, Oxford University Press, London, 1981.
Mastny, V., *Russia Road to the Cold War*, Columbia University Press, 1979.
Montgomery, B. L., *The Memoirs of Field Marshal Montgomery of Alamein*, Da Capo Paperback, New York, 1982, first published in 1958.
Moorehead, A., *Gallipoli*, Hamish Hamilton, London, 1958.
Lord Moran, *Winston Churchill: The Struggle for Survival, 1940–1965*, taken from the diaries of Lord Moran, Sphere Books, London, 1968.
Parker, G., *Western Geopolitical Thought in the Twentieth Century*, Croom Helm, London, 1985.
Parkinson, R., *Blood, Toil, Tears and Sweat, The War History from Dunkirk to Alamein Based on the War Cabinet Papers of 1940–2*, D. Mckay, New York, 1973.
———*A Day's March Nearer Home, The War History from Alamein to VE Day Based on the War Cabinet Papers of 1942 to 1945*, Hart-Davis, Mac Gibbon, London, 1974.
Playfair, I., *The Mediterranean and Middle East*, vol. 1, HMSO, London, 1954.
Pogue, F., *George C. Marshall, Ordeal and Hope, 1939–42*, Viking Press, 1966.

———The Supreme Command, United States Army in World War II, The European Theatre of Operation, Office of the Chief of Military History, Washington D.C., 1954.
Prior, R., Churchill's "World Crisis" as History, Croom Helm, London, 1983.
Rhodes, James R., Gallipoli, Macmillan, New York, 1965.
———Churchill: A Study in Failure 1900—1939, Penguin, Harmondsworth, 1981.
Richmond, H., "Amphibious Warfare in British History," The Historical Association, 1941.
Rintala, M., "The Love of Power and the Power of Love: Churchill's Childhood," Political Psychology, vol. 5, no. 3, 1984.
Rose, N., Vansittart—A Study of a Diplomat, Heinemann, London, 1978.
Roskill, S., The Strategy of Sea Power, Collins, London, 1962.
———Churchill and the Admirals, Collins, London, 1977.
Rothwell, V. H., British War Aims and Peace Diplomacy 1914–1918, Clarendon Press, Oxford, 1971.
Salmon, P., "Churchill, the Admiralty and the Narvik Traffic, September–November 1939," Scand. J. History, 4, 1979.
Schmitt, B. E., Vedler, H.C., The World in the Cruicible 1914–1919, Harper & Row, New York, 1984.
Sharp, T., The Wartime Alliance and the Zonal Division of Germany, Clarendon Press, Oxford, 1975.
Sherwood, R. E., Roosevelt and Hopkins, Harper, New York, 1948.
Strange, J. L., "The British Rejection of Operation Sledgehammer, An Alternative Motive," Military Affairs, vol. XLVI, no. 2, February 1982.
Taylor, A. J. P., ed., Churchill: Four Faces and the Man, Penguin, Harmondsworth, 1969.
———The Origins of the Second World War, Penguin, Harmondsworth,1973.
———Essays in English History, Penguin, Harmondsworth, 1976.
———English History 1914-1945, Penguin, Harmondsworth, 1977.
Towle, P., "Winston Churchill and British Disarmament Policy," The Journal of Strategic Studies, vol. 2, no. 3.
Van Creveld, M., "The German Attack on the USSR: The Destruction of a Legend," European Studies Review, 2; 1, January 1972.
———Hitler's Strategy 1940–1941: The Balkan Clue, Cambridge University Press, 1973.
———"Prelude to Disaster: the British Decision to Aid Greece, 1940-41," Journal of Contemporary History, vol. 9, no. 3, 1974.
———Supplying War, Cambridge University Press, Cambridge, 1977.
———Fighting Power: German and U.S. Army Performance, 1939-1945, Westport, Connecticut, 1982.
Von Clausewitz, C., On War, eds. M. Howard, P. Paret, Princeton University Press, 1976.
Watson, M. S., Chief of Staff: Prewar Plans and Preparations, Historical Division, United States Army, Washington, 1950.
Wedemeyer, A. C., Wedemeyer Reports!, Holt and Company, New York, 1958.
Wheler Bush, E., Gallipoli, St. Martin's Press, New York, 1975.
Wilmot, C., The Struggle for Europe, Collins, London, 1965, (first published in 1952).
Woodward, E. L., Great Britain and the War of 1914-1918, Methuen, London, 1967.
———British Foreign Policy in the Second World War, HMSO, London, 1962
Young, K., Churchill and Beaverbrook, Eyre and Spottiswoode, London, 1966.

Index

ABC-1, 167
Admiralty, 14–16, 22, 23, 25–27, 30, 32, 33, 44, 45, 47, 48, 50, 52–56, 60, 76, 77, 86, 119, 240; Churchill and, 121, 123; shortsightedness of, 31; sonar and, 113
Afrika Korps, 268
Agadir crisis, 13–16, 23, 27, 29, 35
Aircraft carriers, 113, 174
Air Staff, 98, 99
Air superiority, 183, 187, 210, 246, 251, 253–254, 261, 265, 272, 273, 275, 285–286. *See also* Naval superiority
Alamein, 189, 194, 200, 201, 202, 213, 260, 269
Albania, 145, 291
Alexander, General Harold, 266, 296, 292, 293, 295, 298, 299
Aliakhmon line, 149–153, 157, 158, 160
Allenby, General Edmund, 78
"American-British Strategy," 173
Amery, Leo, 115, 143
Amphibious warfare, 25, 26, 30, 32, 39–41, 55, 56, 60, 66, 67, 106, 107, 119, 170, 173, 175, 187–188, 194, 198, 202, 206, 212, 217, 218, 240, 257, 259–260, 273
Anglo-French Entente, 108
Anglo-Japanese alliance, 85
Anglo-Soviet alliance, 226–233, 236, 280, 281, 294
Anne, Queen, 101
Annexations, 226–228, 231, 232, 281, 287–290
Antisubmarine warfare, 113
Antitank measures, 273
Antwerp: Churchill and, 34–36; defense of, 37

Anvil, 246, 292, 298
ANZAC troops, 49
Aosta, Duke of: surrender of, 309
Appeasement, 88–89, 110, 112; Soviet, 231; support for, 100
Armored warfare, 116. *See also* Tanks
Army General Staff. *See* General Staff
Army reforms, Churchill and, 13
Arnold, General Henry, 181
ASDIC. *See* Sonar
Ashley, Maurice, 104
Aspinall-Oglander, C. F., 66
Asquith, Herbert Henry, 15, 16, 34, 36, 38, 40, 46–51, 54–57, 64, 241
Ataturk, Kemal, 132
Atlantic Charter, 227, 229, 278, 286
Attlee, Clement, 207, 250, 267, 268
Attritional-peripheral strategy, 79, 258, 318–320, 326, 329. *See also* Peripheral strategy
Auchinleck, Claude, 169–170, 172, 174, 260, 266, 267
Autumn Debates, 214, 217

Balance of power, 83, 88, 226, 230, 282, 321; maintaining, 88–100, 327; Marlborough and, 100–112; rejection of, 11
Baldwin, Stanley, 89, 109
Balfour, Arthur, 12, 38, 47, 48, 51, 54–56, 64, 85
Balkan front, 68, 132, 133, 135, 138, 143, 145, 146, 148–151, 154, 155, 158–160, 162, 247, 248, 251, 252, 259, 274, 317. *See also* Greece
Balkan League, 67
Balkans, future of, 291–292, 298
Balkan strategy, myth of, 73, 298–299

Baltic scheme, 15, 32–34, 38, 42, 44, 119, 120, 123
Baltic states, annexation of, 226, 227, 231, 232, 281, 287–290
Barbarossa, 161, 162, 169
Barnett, Correlli, 85, 106
Battleaxe, 169, 266
Battle of Britain, 125, 127, 132, 242
Battle of the Atlantic, 165, 170, 212, 219
Battleships, 42, 46, 54, 112, 113, 114, 118, 123, 240
Beaverbrook, Lord, 169, 171, 172, 179, 193, 197, 229, 305
Beda-Fomm, 144
BEF. *See* British Expeditionary Force
Belgium, neutrality of, 29, 95, 108, 159
Benes, Eduard, 289
Berlin: conquering, 307, 316, 323; dividing, 315
Bessarabia, annexation of, 226, 288
Bevan, Aneurin, 310
Birdwood, General, William, 51–52, 60
Bismarck, Prince, 92
Blake, Robert, 81
Blockade, 15, 32, 33, 76, 81, 119, 127, 128, 168, 170, 171, 173, 273
Blue-water school, 26. *See also* Maritime school
Boer War, 9, 10, 12, 71, 309
Bohlen, Charles, 287
Bolero, 185, 186, 191, 193, 200, 203–206, 210, 212, 218
Bolt-from-the-blue school, 26. *See also* Continental school
Bonaparte, Napoleon, 3, 20, 36, 101, 102, 106, 107, 179
Boothby, Lord, 158, 329
Borkum: attack on, 32–33, 38, 40, 44, 52, 55, 66, 76, 170; Churchill and, 41–42, 77
Bradley, Omar, 263, 316
Breslau (cruiser), 36
British Army, 194, 212, 213, 265, 267, 298; Churchill and, 8–10, 13, 15, 17–18, 269; expansion of, 26, 97; fighting capabilities of, 264, 268, 317; in Mediterranean, 254, 295; reduction of, 91; reforms for, 10; ten years' rule and, 87. *See also* General Staff
British Expeditionary Force (BEF), 16, 17, 34, 91, 95, 97–99; dispatching, 18, 29, 35; establishment of, 96, 110
Broderick, St. John, 10; opposition to, 8–9, 13
Brodie, Bernard, 327
Brook, Norman, 315
Brooke, Alan, 175, 181, 184, 185, 187, 188, 190, 192, 194, 197, 200, 201, 203, 205, 207–211, 214, 215, 216, 218, 220, 222–224, 234, 241, 245, 246, 248, 251–253, 255, 256, 258, 260–261, 266–268, 270, 275, 278, 293, 295, 297, 298
Bryant, Arthur, 261
Bukovina, annexation of, 226, 288
Bulgaria, 290, 291, 298; influence in, 305
Bullitt, William, 281

Cadogan, Alexander, 147, 148, 150, 153, 155, 231, 250, 257, 266, 282, 286, 310
Cadogan, Earl, 257
Cairo Conference, 255, 256
Callwell, Major-General Charles, 37
Carden, Vice-Admiral Sackville, 37, 41–43, 45, 46, 50–53, 59, 60, 62, 64, 164
Casablanca Conference, 200, 209–212, 214–218, 223, 255, 260, 268, 277, 278, 283, 307, 312
Catherine plan, 123
Chamberlain, Austen, 84, 89–90
Chamberlain, Joseph, 115
Chamberlain, Neville, 95, 97, 99, 100, 109–112, 121, 125, 133, 241
Chatfield, Ernle, 96, 113, 119, 120
Chatham (elder Pitt), 4, 105
Cherwell, Lord, 201, 216
Chiang Kai-shek, 256
Chiefs of Staff, British, 87, 89, 91–100, 108–111, 118–119, 124–130, 134–136, 138, 142, 143, 145, 150, 168–171, 173, 175–179, 184, 185, 187–192, 197, 198, 200, 202–204, 206, 208–223, 235, 246–250, 252–255,

260, 263, 264, 269, 270, 274, 279, 284, 287, 294–298, 301, 302, 304, 310, 317, 323, 324, 332
Chiefs of Staff, Combined, 221, 246, 253, 295, 316
Chiefs of Staff, U.S., 180, 192, 210, 212, 222, 234, 245–246, 251, 293, 295, 301, 302, 316
Chiefs of Staff Committee, 124
Churchill, John. *See* Marlborough, Duke of
Churchill, Lady Randolph (mother), 3
Churchill, Lord Randolph (father), 9
Churchill, Randolph (son), 125, 227
Churchill, Winston: admiration for, 327–328, 330; ambitions of, 3–4, 274; criticism of, 325–327; historical consciousness of, 328–330; Mahan and, 12; military education of, 8; opportunism and, 276; resignation of, 71, 73; as strategist, 4–5, 13, 15–19, 27, 31–32, 57–58, 69, 71, 79–81, 111–113, 118, 127, 131, 157–159, 161–163, 165–166, 225, 239, 239–241, 243, 258–259, 263–264, 270, 275–276, 299, 301, 303, 308, 317–319, 321, 323–328, 330, 333; writing of, 330–333
CID. *See* Committee of Imperial Defence
Clark-Kerr, Archibald, 209, 235, 283, 284, 290
Clausewitz, Carl von, 1, 8, 20, 100, 161, 238, 240, 242, 327
Colville, John, 2, 126, 153, 155, 168, 225, 226, 257, 266, 302, 304
Commission of Inquiry into the Operations at the Dardanelles. *See* Dardanelles Commission
Committee of Imperial Defence (CID), 13, 17, 37, 90, 93, 94
Compromise peace, 71–72, 79, 81, 309
Concert of Europe, 89, 94. *See also* League of Nations
Congress of Vienna, 243
Continental school, 7–8, 10, 14–15, 25, 26, 83, 89, 96–99, 101, 104, 110, 262, 318, 329; Churchill and, 213, 318; synthesis with, 27, 30, 35, 71, 81, 106, 121. *See also*

Maritime school
Convoy system, 75–77, 113
Cooper, Duff, 294
Cooperation, 248, 280, 282, 294, 317, 331; Anglo-Soviet, 284–285; Four Power, 281, 285; postwar, 228–230, 233, 235, 236, 321–323
Corbett, Julian, 19, 20, 31, 77, 105, 106–107
Corsica, 221, 247
Cranborne, Lord, 305
Crete, 266
Crimean War, 11
Cripps, Stafford, 169, 193, 229, 268
Crowe, Eyre, 90
Crusader, 172, 174, 180, 266
Cunliffe-Owen, Major, 36
Cunningham, First Sea Lord Andrew, 296, 303
Cunningham, Alan, 309
Curzon, Lord, 226
Curzon line, 226, 231, 232, 281, 287, 304, 305
Czechoslovakia, 289, 315

Dakar, 240
Dardanelles, 17, 36–38, 41, 55, 58–60, 65; attack at, 40, 43, 46, 47, 49, 51, 52, 56–57, 62, 64; Churchill and, 42, 44, 66, 67; opening of, 255
Dardanelles Commission, 37, 46, 58, 60–62
Davidson, F. H. N., 227
Decisive theatre, 29–30, 78, 102, 213. *See also* Main theatre
Defence Committee, 124–125, 127, 130, 131, 136–138, 144, 146, 152, 168, 206, 266, 279, 280, 332
Defence Requirements Committee (DRC), 94–98
De Robeck, John, 53–56, 61, 64–66, 164
Dieppe, raid on, 197, 198, 199
Dill, John, 126, 128, 134, 137, 138, 140, 143–157, 163–166, 175, 177, 186, 188, 190, 191, 211, 214, 265–267
Disarmament, 87–88, 92, 93, 94
Divisions, strength of, 216, 219
Dodecanese, 248
DRC. *See* Defence Requirements Committee

Dunkirk, 260, 265

EAC. *See* European Advisory Committee
EAM, 290
Eastern Europe, fate of, 278, 280, 290–298, 304, 331
Eastern Front, The (Churchill), 62–63
Eastern school, 40, 73, 80, 83. *See also* Western school
Eden, Anthony, 125, 126, 133, 134, 136, 140, 145–154, 156, 157, 164, 221, 225–233, 235–238, 242–244, 250, 266, 277, 279–282, 284–288, 290–294, 303–305, 310–311, 313–316, 322, 330
Edward VIII, 276
Egypt, 263
Eisenhower, Dwight, 182, 204, 220–222, 263, 269, 299–301, 316
Elgin, Lord, 12
Ellington, Edward, 96
Emergency operation, 183–186, 193, 233
Enigma, 141, 142
Esher, Lord, 23, 24
Ethiopia, 86, 96, 309
Eugene of Savoy, Prince, 103
European Advisory Committee (EAC), 312, 313
Expeditionary force. *See* British Expeditionary Force

Falkenhayn, Erich von, 75
Far East, 86–87, 92–93, 94, 117, 127, 131, 132, 166, 167, 172, 176, 184, 236, 256
Finland, 231, 232, 288, 289
Fisher, John, 15, 19, 22, 25, 31–34, 38, 40–41, 43, 45–48, 50–57, 59, 62, 64, 163, 164
Fisher, Warren, 96
Fleet in being, 32
Foreign Office, 12, 13, 23, 111, 228, 229, 238, 289, 291, 294, 304, 305, 310, 312, 314, 322
Four Powers Plan, 235–237, 277, 281, 282, 312–313
Fourteen Points, 308
France, 259, 262, 265, 281, 282, 284, 287, 292; commitment to, 14, 16–17, 23–24, 29; fall of, 124, 125, 131, 159, 213, 318, 326, 329; invasion of, 183, 197, 219, 220, 248, 250, 252, 255, 256, 263, 279, 280, 293, 297, 298, 314, 318–319, 321, 323, 324, 326
Francophobia, 88–89
Frederick the Great, 102
Free trade, Churchill and, 10–11
French, John, 34, 42, 43, 73
French Revolution, 105
Freyberg, Bernard, 265–266
Frontal assault, 198, 261–262, 264
Fuller, John F. C., 116

Galbraith, John Kenneth, 262
Gallipoli, 36–37, 45, 49, 50, 52, 55, 56, 61, 64, 65, 120, 124, 132, 154, 198, 239, 259, 262, 265, 303; attack on, 38, 41, 43, 46, 51, 54; Churchill and, 57–58, 66, 67, 69, 77, 123, 163–164; impact of, 68–69, 325–326, 330, 333; withdrawal from, 73
General Staff, 10, 13–15, 17, 18, 27, 37, 47, 48, 61, 64, 89, 110, 147, 167, 256. *See also* British Army
Geopolitics, 7–8, 114–116, 182, 244
George VI, King, 250
German Army, 302; fighting capability of, 272–274
German fleet, 12; battle with, 25
German War College, 115
Goeben (cruiser), 36, 37, 43, 54
Gousev, Ambassador M., 312
Grand alliance, 118, 235, 244, 281; Churchill and, 108–109; victory for, 324
Grand Plan, 264
Grand Strategy, 332
Grand strategy, 125, 238, 244, 276, 299, 320
Great Powers. *See* Four Powers
Greece, 137, 138, 140, 146–157, 161–162, 164, 166, 194, 213, 239, 265, 274, 276, 291, 292, 317, 326, 328; attack on, 143, 144; Communist intrigues in, 290; defense of, 134–136, 145, 158; importance of, 133; influence in, 305. *See also* Balkan front
Grey, Edward, 13–15, 23, 34, 36–38, 42, 47, 50, 51, 107, 233
Guerrilla warfare, 179
Gumbinnen, 161

Gymnast, 174, 180, 185, 188–95. *See also* Torch

Haig, Douglas, 73, 74, 80
Haldane, Richard, 15, 16, 22; reforms by, 13
Halifax, Lord Edward, 111, 123, 125, 133, 171, 229, 230, 282
Hamilton, Ian, 4, 53–56, 60, 64, 65, 69
Hankey, Maurice, 38–40, 42, 48, 55, 56, 64, 73, 84, 92, 95, 96, 118, 310
Harris, Arthur, 275
Hartle, Major General, 204
Haushofer, Karl, 115, 182
Heligoland Bight, 32–33; blockade of, 76
Hess, Rudolf, 115
Heywood, General, 151
History of the English Speaking Peoples, A (Churchill), 1, 105, 178
Hitler, Adolf, 92, 94, 96, 101, 109–111, 115, 118, 133–137, 140–142, 161, 163, 175, 177–179, 186, 202, 203, 207, 210, 214, 220, 223–225, 236, 242, 249, 251, 253, 254, 257, 269–273, 288, 297, 299, 301, 302, 309, 319
Hollis, Brigadier, 250
Hopkins, Harry, 170, 173, 183, 184, 190, 246, 307
Hore-Belisha, Leslie, 97, 117, 155; Liddell Hart and, 101
Howard, Michael, 96–97, 98, 99, 106–107, 166, 214, 248, 252, 277
Hungary, 306; influence in, 305
Husky, 217, 218, 245

Imperator, 199, 240
Indirect approach, theory of, 101
Influence of Sea Power Upon History, The (Mahan): influence of, 8, 11–12
Inönü, President Ismet, 143, 277
International police force, 233
Ironside, Edmund, 116, 121, 126, 133, 155
Island hopping, 86
Ismay, Hastings, 126, 185, 198, 209, 287
Isolation, 7, 8, 13, 14, 24, 97, 117, 235

Italy, 219, 252, 253, 256, 257, 260, 269, 270, 273, 286, 295–297, 301, 302, 322, 325, 331; armistice with, 247, 311; collapse of, 218, 220, 249; Communist intrigues in, 290; defense of, 320; eliminating, 203, 208, 209; invasion of, 211, 217, 221, 223, 224, 245, 248, 271, 276, 282, 319; problems in, 254; unconditional surrender for, 307–308

Jackson, Henry, 41, 43, 44, 46, 48, 52, 62
Jellicoe, Admiral John, 19, 33, 52
Joint Intelligence Committee (JIC), 169, 186, 200, 207, 215, 218, 221, 249
Joint Planners, 168, 170, 173, 176, 178, 180, 181, 186, 189, 194, 199–201, 218, 222, 223, 269, 279
Jubilee, 197
Jupiter, 172, 187, 188, 190, 200, 216, 218, 245

Kamenev, Lev, 289
Katyn Forest massacre, 281
Kennedy, John, 126, 128, 137, 146, 147, 164–165, 205, 214, 256, 293
Kennedy, Paul, 86, 106
Keyes, Roger, 53, 54, 76, 169
Keynes, John Maynard, 88, 225
Kiel Canal, blockade of, 32, 33
King, Admiral Ernest, 190, 210, 211
Kitchener, Lord, 23, 27, 34–43, 47–51, 53–61, 63–65, 69, 71, 73, 164, 260
Knatchbull-Hugessen, Ambassador, 309
Korysis, M., 144, 148
Kursk campaign, 245, 320

Land power, importance of, 285–286
Lansdowne, Lord, 8, 12, 72
League of Nations, 89, 225, 278, 281, 282, 286; Churchill and, 94; Soviet Union and, 108. *See also* United Nations
Leningrad, 256
Liberal party, Churchill and, 10
Liddell Hart, B. H., 81, 105, 107, 116, 126, 238, 300, 309; influence of,

100–101
Limited liability, 97, 99
Limpus, Admiral Arthur, 36, 38
Lloyd George, David, 12–14, 38–42, 47, 49, 50, 71, 73, 76–78, 88, 89, 226, 241
Locarno Treaty (1925), 91
Logistics, 18, 34, 68, 138, 177–178, 208, 261, 299, 300, 303
Lothian, Lord, 130
Louis XIV, 101, 102, 107
Ludendorff, Erich, 78, 80, 81
Lyttleton, Oliver, 250, 267

Macaulay, Thomas Babington, 8, 9
MacDonald, Ramsay, 84
McKenna, R., 15
Mackinder, Halford, 114, 115, 182
Maclean, Fitzroy, 241
Maginot line, 108, 116, 119
Mahan, Alfred Thayer, 19, 20, 21, 77, 100, 101, 105, 106, 115; influence of, 8, 11–12; misinterpreting, 31
Main theatre, 29–30, 78, 80, 160, 213; importance of, 68. *See also* Decisive theatre
Maisky, 279, 284
Manchuria, Japanese aggression in, 92–93
Marder, Arthur J., 31, 58, 64–65, 66, 76, 120, 240
Maritime school, 11–13, 25, 26, 39, 95, 96, 100, 101, 103, 105; Churchill and, 7–8, 318; synthesis with, 27, 30, 35, 71, 81, 121. *See also* Continental school
Marlborough, First Duke of, 4, 129, 159, 275; balance of power and, 100–112; biography of, 93, 112, 262, 328–329, 330, 332
Marlborough : His Life and Times (Churchill), 87–88, 112
Marshall, George C., 180–185, 187–194, 199, 204–206, 208–212, 219–223, 233, 235, 253, 261, 268, 269, 278, 296, 316
Mechanized warfare. *See* Armored warfare; Tanks
Mediterranean fleet, 23–25
Mediterranean strategy, 133, 166, 171, 208–212, 214, 222, 244, 247, 250, 252, 254, 256, 269,
287, 317, 325, 328, 329, 331
Menzies, Robert, 2, 150, 153
Metaxas, Ioannis, 135, 137, 138, 144
Middle East, 125–131, 133, 135, 138, 140, 154, 155, 158, 162, 164–165, 167, 168, 170, 171, 176, 180, 181, 183–185, 188–190, 192, 194, 197, 199, 205, 317
Midway, 188, 268
Mihajlovic, Stanislaw, 241, 304
"Military Aspects of the Continental Problem" (Churchill), 16–18
Milne, George, 88
Milner, Alfred, 12, 115
Molotov, Vyacheslav Mikhailovich, 135, 193, 231–234, 253
Molotov-Ribbentrop pact, 110–111, 226, 228
Montgomery, Bernard, 197, 198, 266, 299–301, 303, 312
Montgomery-Massingberd, Archibald, 96
Moore, John, 179
Moran, Lord, 112, 116, 155, 197, 238, 287, 289, 315, 329
Morgan, General Frederick, 246
Morgenthau, Henry: postwar plan of, 304
"Morning Thoughts, Note on Post War Security" (Churchill), 277, 278
Mountbatten, Lord Louis, 184, 194, 199, 204
Munich crisis, 98–101, 109, 289
Mussolini, Benito, 134, 222, 245

Napoleonic Wars, 77, 88, 90, 105, 179. *See also* Bonaparte, Napoleon
Naval staff, establishment of, 19
Naval superiority, 8–9, 11–14, 23, 25, 26, 31, 85. *See also* Air superiority
Nazi-Soviet Pact. *See* Molotov-Ribbentrop pact
Nestos line, 149, 150, 151, 153, 158
Nicholas, Grand Duke, 32, 40, 62
1919 Plan, 78
North Africa, 130, 134–136, 144, 148, 153, 156, 160, 162, 163, 169, 174, 181, 184, 190, 191, 193, 195, 199–202, 205, 208, 210, 211, 213–215, 219, 222,

223, 265–267, 271, 274, 317, 319, 320; invasion of, 197, 198, 269, 276
Norway, 123–124, 190
Nye, Lieutenant-General Archibald, 205, 267

Occupation zones, 312–316, 323
O'Connor, Richard, 135, 138, 143, 144, 155, 156, 164
Offensive à l'outrance, 17
Oliver, Vice-Admiral Harry, 41, 46, 52
Overlord, 245–246, 248–253, 256, 257, 261–263, 285, 286, 301, 312; commitment to, 246, 251, 255, 264, 287. *See also* Round-up

Pacific Front, Churchill on, 173, 174
"Painting as a Pastime" (Churchill), 1
Papagos, General, 148–151, 157, 158
Patton, George, 300
Paul, Prince, 142
Peace negotiations, 80, 288, 305
Peninsular War, 20, 21
Percentage agreement, 305
Peripheral strategy, 135, 318, 319, 329. *See also* Attritional-peripheral strategy
Philip II, 107
Pisa-Rimini line, 255, 256
Plan 17, 17
Poincaré, Raymond, 90
Poland, 286, 289, 294, 315, 321, 322; border alignment for, 278, 280, 288, 304, 305; future of, 287, 290, 306, 307, 324
Polish Corridor, 91, 93
Polish underground, supplying, 290
Political goals, 227, 238–244, 264, 281, 300, 303, 307, 316, 320–322, 324–326
Portal, Charles, 138, 140, 149, 152, 155, 175, 184, 207, 209, 211, 218, 249, 251–254, 261, 275, 295, 296
Pound, Dudley, 120, 123, 149, 152, 155, 175, 181, 187, 240, 275
Prince of Wales (battleship), sinking of, 240
Project Ultra. *See* Ultra
Prussian militarism, uprooting, 72, 309
Public opinion, influence of, 84, 240

Quebec Conference, 245, 247, 253, 285, 296, 301, 304, 313
Queen Elizabeth (battleship), 42, 46, 54

Rankin, 255, 256, 257
Rearmament, 85, 87, 93, 94, 99
Red Army, 88, 182, 244, 248, 273, 289, 305, 311, 315, 331
Repington, Colonel Charles, 14, 15
Repulse (battleship), sinking of, 240
Rhodes James, Robert, 66, 325
Richmond, Captain Herbert, 45
Roberts, Lord, 14, 18, 23, 26
Robertson, General William, 55, 73, 74, 80
Rommel, Erwin, 148, 153, 156, 160, 163, 172, 174, 180, 188, 189, 194, 265, 266, 267–269
Roosevelt, Franklin Delano, 12, 125, 130, 133, 165, 170–172, 180–183, 185, 188, 189, 191, 193, 194, 200, 201, 204, 206, 210, 211, 220, 227, 229, 230, 233, 234, 241, 246–248, 250, 253, 256, 262, 278, 279, 281–285, 287, 291–293, 295, 296, 305–308, 310, 313, 322, 323
Roosevelt, Theodore, 12
Rosebury, Lord, 115
Rothermere, Lord, 107
Round-up, 180, 181, 186, 187, 189–193, 200, 201, 203–211, 213, 214, 234, 245, 246, 271. *See also* Overlord
Royal Air Force, 95–96, 109; DRC and, 97; expansion of, 98; ten years' rule and, 87
Royal Naval College, 19, 20
Royal Navy, 113, 117, 129, 187; DRC and, 97; hegemony of, 85; role of, 26–27, 83
Rumania, 231, 232, 288–292, 298; influence in, 305
Russia. *See* Soviet Union
Rutter, 197

Salonika, 145, 146, 148, 149, 151
Salonika front. *See* Balkan front
Sardinia, 202, 203, 206, 210, 220,

221, 247, 248
Savrola (Churchill), 45
Schlieffen Plan, failure of, 18, 75, 141
Sea power, decline of, 285
Second front, 166, 169, 191, 193, 203, 206, 207, 209, 211, 212, 232–234, 253, 258, 274, 279, 306, 320–321, 326; delaying, 284–285; Stalin and, 283–284
Second World War, The (Churchill), 5, 91, 134, 153, 158, 177, 193, 197–198, 204, 214, 223, 233, 240, 245, 252, 253, 258, 275, 297, 301, 315, 324, 331, 332, 333
Seven Years' War, 21, 31, 33, 105
Shipping, 168, 177, 182, 219
Sicily, 191, 202, 203, 206, 210–212, 217, 218, 220–222, 280; conquest of, 215, 219, 246, 276, 279, 282
Siegfried Line, 302
Singapore, 119, 165, 180, 260, 263, 266, 267; base at, 86, 117; fall of, 229
Slade, Admiral, 38
Sledgehammer, 180, 181, 186–189, 192–194, 199, 208, 211, 212, 214, 217, 218, 233, 240, 246, 255, 260, 267, 278–280; canceling, 190, 197, 215, 271
Smuts, Jan, 141, 152, 169, 203, 247–251, 255, 285, 286, 290, 295
Sonar (ASDIC), 113
Soviet Union, 162, 168, 169, 171, 173, 176, 183, 207, 273; annexations by, 226–228, 231, 232, 281, 287, 288; appeasement of, 231; attritional-peripheral strategy and, 320; influence of, 230, 231, 237–238, 243–244, 247, 264, 281, 289–291, 293, 303, 304, 312, 324, 325, 331; intentions of, 305–307, 314, 323, 324, 329; invasion of, 141–142, 161; land power of, 286; League of Nations and, 108; rehabilitation of, 228, 277–278; relations with, 227, 229–230, 236, 283, 285, 290, 294, 328; strategy of, 242, 244; unconditional surrender and, 310–311; weakening of, 258, 284
Spheres of influence, 236, 291, 314
Stalin, Josef, 169, 171, 172, 197, 203, 207–209, 212, 213, 232, 234–237, 241, 250, 253, 256, 259, 269, 278–281, 285, 287, 293, 299, 308, 309, 323–324, 330; demands of, 226–228, 230, 233, 242; influence of, 244, 288–289, 303–306; occupation and, 313; second front and, 283–284; unconditional surrender and, 310–311; warning to, 142
Stalingrad, 207, 215, 320
State Department, U.S., 307
Stimson, Henry, 205, 281, 282
Strang, William, 312, 313
Strategic bombing, 167, 168, 170–175, 181, 184, 206, 211, 223, 249, 268, 273, 275, 286, 320
Strategic natural selection, 194, 317
Strategic reserve, 116–117, 140, 155, 177, 223
Stresemann, Gustav, 91
Submarines, 75–77, 79, 112, 113, 120, 176, 219
Supplementary Naval Law, 22

Tanks, 112, 116, 189, 273
Tannenberg, battle of, 63, 161
Tatoi agreement, 150–151, 157, 158, 159
Teheran Conference, 253, 256, 259, 287, 288, 309
Ten years' rule, 84–85, 87, 92, 93
Territorial Army, 13, 26, 27
Tito, Josip Broz 241, 290, 291, 299
Tobruk, 137, 138, 143, 160, 172, 189, 260, 265, 267
Torch, 192, 198–201, 203–205, 207, 212–215, 234, 235, 269. *See also* Gymnast
Total victory, 79, 308–309
Total war, 20, 71–72, 74
Trafalgar, 31
Treaty of Aix-la-Chapelle (1668), 101
Treaty of Paris (1763), 88
Treaty of Ryswick (1697), 88
Treaty of Utrecht (1714), 88, 104
Treaty of Versailles (1919), 88, 89, 243, 308
Trident Conference. *See* Washington Conference
Tripartite Pact, 142, 150
Triple Entente, 14, 22, 63
Tripoli, 144–148, 162, 276, 317, 326

Tukhachevsky, Mikhayl, 289
Tunisia, 214, 269
Turkey, 36, 39–40; attacking, 42; Churchill in, 215, 277; eliminating, 67, 68; inducing, 145–147, 149–152, 155, 158, 159, 173–175, 201, 203, 209, 217, 220, 221, 247, 248, 255, 276, 278, 292
Turner, T. K., 177
Twenty-Ninth Division, 49–53, 58–61, 63, 164

Ultra, 140–141, 169, 213, 216, 266, 267, 270–271
Unconditional surrender, 307–312, 315, 323
United Nations, 281–283, 285. *See also* League of Nations
United States: entry of, 130–132, 171, 172, 179, 181–182, 240, 260, 317, 318; resources of, 168, 182
United States Army, 269; fighting spirit of, 268

Vansittart, Under-Secretary Robert, 96
Verdun, 75, 79
Vichy France, 144, 174
Victory Program, 182
Vienna, advancing on, 295–299, 301, 322, 323
von Thoma, General, 213

Walcheren expedition, 21
War aims, definition of, 308
War Cabinet, 124–125, 133, 134, 149, 152, 153, 164, 169, 190, 192, 225, 227–229, 235, 249, 293, 294, 303, 305, 306
War Council, 38–44, 46–57, 59–64
War Department, U.S., 180
War Office, 13, 14, 53, 64, 97, 266

War of the Spanish Succession, 102, 105, 106, 178
War Staff, 43, 46, 54
Washington Conference (Trident), 219, 221, 283
Washington Naval Treaty, 85–86
Wavell, Archibald, 126, 133–135, 137, 138, 140, 144, 146, 148–150, 152–157, 160, 163, 164, 169, 263, 266, 270, 309
Webb, G., 314
Wedemeyer, Albert, 182, 183
Wehrmacht. *See* German Army
Welles, Sumner, 281, 282
Wellington, Duke of, 20, 105, 179, 188, 275
Western Front conception, 214. *See also* Second front
Western school, 40, 73. *See also* Eastern school
Weygand, General, 144, 147
Wilhelm II, 12, 101
William III, 101
Wilson, Arthur, 15, 19, 25, 43, 46
Wilson, General Henry Maitland, 160, 292, 293, 295
Wilson, General Henry, 14, 15, 17
Wilson, Woodrow, 282, 308
Winant, Ambassador J.G., 312, 313
Winter War, 226. *See also* Finland
World council. *See* United Nations
World Crisis, The (Churchill), 17, 29–30, 37–38, 44–45, 47–48, 52, 58, 60–61, 62, 64, 65, 66, 69, 75, 78, 79, 81, 128, 161, 239, 243, 260, 265, 329, 330, 332, 333

Yalta Conference, 306, 312–315
Yugoslavia: Communist intrigues in, 290; inducing, 145, 146, 149–153, 155, 158, 159, 161, 162, 291, 299; influence in, 305

About the Book and the Author

Tuvia Ben-Moshe challenges long-standing assumptions about Churchill's role in war and peace as a strategist and a historian. Four main themes are treated in this revisionist history; how Churchill's strategic conception developed, from the turn of the century through World War II; how he reached his strategic decisions; how his conception and his decisions affected the course of the two world wars; and to what extent his books on the wars are reliable historical studies—or justifications of his own policies.

This unique scrutiny, based on a wealth of primary sources, offers an illuminating three-dimensional image of Churchill. Ben-Moshe's reevaluation reveals a consistent Churchillian line—in no way the outcome of chance—leading directly from the 1915 failure at Gallipoli to the 1941 Greek disaster, the "Mediterranean strategy," the matter of the "second front," and the question of Soviet threat to Europe at the end of World War II. Stretches along this line, asserts Ben-Moshe, were successfully blurred by Churchill in his writings on the two world wars.

This book is likely to call into question some previously firmly held beliefs. At the least, it presents fresh ideas and will stimulate thinking along new lines.

Tuvia Ben-Moshe is an instructor in the Department of International Relations at the Hebrew University, Jerusalem.